The Politics of Literature in Nazi Germany

Books in the Media Dictatorship

JAN-PIETER BARBIAN

**Translated by
KATE STURGE**

D0731543

B L O O M S B U R Y

NEW YORK • LONDON • NEW DELHI • SYDNEY

Bloomsbury Academic
An imprint of Bloomsbury Publishing Plc

1385 Broadway	50 Bedford Square
New York	London
NY 10018	WC1B 3DP
USA	UK

www.bloomsbury.com

Originally published as: "Literaturpolitik im NS-Staat. Von der 'Gleichschaltung' bis zum Ruin"
© 2010 S. Fischer Verlag GmbH, Frankfurt am Main.
All rights reserved by S. Fischer Verlag GmbH, Frankfurt am Main.
This English language translation © Bloomsbury Academic 2013

Library of Congress Cataloging-in-Publication Data
Barbian, Jan-Pieter.
[Literaturpolitik im NS-Staat. English]
The politics of literature in Nazi Germany : books in the media dictatorship / Jan-Pieter Barbian ; translated by Kate Sturge.
pages cm
Includes bibliographical references and index.
ISBN 978-1-4411-0734-3 (pbk. : alk. paper) – ISBN 978-1-4411-2033-5 (hardcover : alk. paper) 1. German literature–20th century–History and criticism. 2. National socialism and literature. 3. Politics and literature–Germany–History–20th century. 4. German literature–20th century–History and criticism. I. Sturge, Kate, translator. II. Title.
PT405.B295 2013
830.9'358–dc23
2013005637

ISBN: HB: 978-1-4411-2033-5
       PB: 978-1-4411-0734-3
       ePub: 978-1-4411-7923-4
       ePDF: 978-1-4411-6814-6

Typeset by Fakenham Prepress Solutions, Fakenham, Norfolk NR21 8NN
Printed and bound in the United States of America

"Our memory is the only help that is left to them [the dead]. They pass away into it, and if every deceased person is like someone who was murdered by the living, so he is also like someone whose life they must save, without knowing whether the effort will succeed."

Theodor W. Adorno, "Marginalia on Mahler"

This book is dedicated to the memory of the writers
Georg Hermann, Franz Hessel, Gertrud Kolmar, and all the others
who were murdered.

Contents

Abbreviations

AA	Auswärtiges Amt (Foreign Office)
ADAP	Akten zur Deutschen Auswärtigen Politik (Foreign Office files)
AdK	Akademie der Künste (Academy of Arts)
AO	Auslandsorganisation der NSDAP (NSDAP organization abroad)
BArch	Bundesarchiv (Federal Archives)
Bbl.	*Börsenblatt für den Deutschen Buchhandel*
BDC	Berlin Document Center
BRB	Bund Reichsdeutscher Buchhändler e.V. (League of Reich German Booksellers)
BV	Börsenverein der Deutschen Buchhändler (German Publishers' and Booksellers' Association)
DAF	Deutsche Arbeitsfront (German Labor Front)
DB	Deutsche Bücherei Leipzig (precursor of German National Library)
DGT	Deutscher Gemeindetag (Assembly of German Municipalities)
DHV	Deutscher Handlungsgehilfen Verband (sales clerks' association)
DLA	Deutsches Literaturarchiv (Archives of German Literature)
DVA	Deutsche Verlags-Anstalt (publisher)
EKH	Einkaufshaus für Büchereien (central purchasing house)

ESV Europäische Schriftstellervereinigung (European Union of Writers)

Gestapa Geheimes Staatspolizeiamt Berlin (Gestapo headquarters)

Gestapo Geheime Staatspolizei

GLA Generallandesarchiv (state archives Karlsruhe)

HStA Hauptstaatsarchiv (central state archives for North Rhine-Westphalia)

HAVA Hanseatische Verlagsanstalt (publisher)

LA Landesarchiv Berlin (Berlin State Archive)

NL Nachlass (literary estate)

NSB *Nationalsozialistische Bibliographie*

NSLB Nationalsozialistischer Lehrerbund (National Socialist Teachers' League)

OKW Oberkommando der Wehrmacht (supreme command)

PPK Parteiamtliche Prüfungskommission zum Schutze des nationalsozialistischen Schrifttums (Party Examination Commission for the Protection of National Socialist Writings)

RADB Reichsarbeitsgemeinschaft für Deutsche Buchwerbung (Reich Working Group for German Book Promotion)

RDS Reichsverband Deutscher Schriftsteller e.V. (Reich Association of German Writers)

REM Reichsministerium für Wissenschaft, Erziehung und Volksbildung (Reich Education Ministry)

RFM Reichsfinanzministerium (Reich Ministry of Finance)

RGBL. *Reichsgesetzblatt* (Imperial Law Gazette)

RKK Reichskulturkammer (Reich Chamber of Culture)

RMVP Reichsministerium für Volksaufklärung und Propaganda (Propaganda Ministry)

RSHA	Reichssicherheitshauptamt (Reich Security Main Office)
RSK	Reichsschrifttumskammer (Reich Chamber of Literature)
SD	Sicherheitsdienst (SS security service)
SDS	Schutzverband deutscher Schriftsteller (League of German Writers)
SPD	Sozialdemokratische Partei Deutschlands (Social Democratic Party)
StA	Stadtarchiv (city archives)
StAL	Staatsarchiv Leipzig (Saxon state archives)
Stapo	Staatspolizei (state police)
Ufa	Universum Film AG
VDB	Verein Deutscher Bibliothekare (research librarians' association)
VDV	Verband Deutscher Volksbibliothekare (public librarians' association)
ZfB	*Zentralblatt für Bibliothekswesen*
ZdF	Zentrale der Frontbuchhandlungen (central office for the frontline book dealerships)

1

Introduction

In an era when television and the internet dominate public discourse and the social status of reading culture is in continual decline, it seems almost anachronistic to look more closely at the role of the book during the Nazi dictatorship. But even today, an irresistible fascination still emanates from the "Goebbels experiment" first analyzed by Arthur Weidenfeld, an émigré journalist from Vienna, and his BBC colleague Derrick Sington in 1942.[1] The Reich Minister of Popular Enlightenment and Propaganda himself made sure of that: alongside the publication of numerous books, editorials, and essays for the press, Goebbels recorded his life and work in diaries kept from 1923 to 1945. "For years," wrote his employee Werner Stephan, "every morning, at a considerable cost in time and effort, he dictated facts and thoughts designed to reflect a maximally favorable image of himself for the future." Goebbels devoted much deliberation to the question of how his wartime notes "could be preserved for posterity."[2] In the end, he decided to deposit a complete version, microfilmed on glass plates, in the safe of the Reichsbank. In the chaos of German history, the diaries moved from Berlin to Moscow in 1945, and it

---

[1] Sington and Weidenfeld, *The Goebbels Experiment*, especially 78–86, 222–32; also the collection edited by Hachmeister and Kloft, *Das Goebbels-Experiment*. Stefan Krings's contribution to that volume, "Das Propagandaministerium," rightly points out that we still lack a contextualized presentation of the complex areas of the Reich Propaganda Ministry's work and its internal structures of personnel and power (p. 30).

[2] Stephan, *Joseph Goebbels*, 12, 13.

was only in 1993 that a scholarly edition of the manuscripts from 1923 to 1941, along with the dictations of July 1941 to April 1945, was made accessible to the public in a twenty-five-volume series.[3] A unique source was now available that, as Bernd Sösemann notes, provides insights into the structure of personnel and institutions, the demands and expectations of the state and Party leadership, the mechanisms of power, and the interaction of the rulers with the ruled.[4] However, Sösemann also alerts us to the risk of overlooking the diaries' palpable apologism and myth-building—myths regarding both the Propaganda Minister himself and the Nazi state as a whole. That danger can only be averted by situating the diaries in the context of other sources, supplementing them, comparing them, and contrasting them so as to approach more closely the reality of the years between 1933 and 1945.

Yet building myths and legends was not a process that began only with Hitler's accession to power on 30 January 1933, and neither was it the sole privilege of the Nazi dictatorship. Hermann Stresau, a librarian dismissed in April 1933 for political reasons and forced to earn his living with freelance writing, wrote of the Weimar era in his diary entry for 14 September 1933:

Literature, the literature business [of the Weimar Republic], had reached dimensions that created a deceptive impression of its true role in life. What seemed, because of its massive scale, to be a florescence was at best a false brilliance or a diseased hypertrophy. To give it due credit, literature by no means sidestepped social problems, if anything the contrary; but it made those problems into literature. Fundamentally, political life remained virtually untouched by the influence of literature, and politics made use of the literati rather than the literati themselves constituting an intellectual force. As for genuine poets, they were not numerous, and even less influential.[5]

---

[3] On the controversial issue of the "scholarly edition" undertaken by the Institut für Zeitgeschichte in Munich, see Sösemann, *Alles nur Goebbels-Propaganda?*
[4] Sösemann, "Ein tieferer geschichtlicher Sinn," 164.
[5] Stresau, *Von Jahr zu Jahr*, 57. *Translator's note*: Here and throughout, all translations of German sources are my own unless otherwise indicated.

Similarly critical conclusions can be found in Theodor W. Adorno's 1962 reflection, which identified two poles in the post–1945 idealization of the 1920s: "The pole of a world that could turn to the better, and the pole of the destruction of that possibility through the establishment of powers that were to fully reveal themselves in fascism, and that also found expression in the ambivalence of art—an ambivalence that is genuinely specific to the twenties and does not partake of the vague, internally contradictory notion of modernist classics." During Weimar, the later catastrophe of the twelve-year dictatorship was "incubated" by the era's "own social conflicts, also in the sphere of what one is accustomed to call 'culture.'"[6] And Helmuth Plessner, writing at the same time as Adorno, restricted the Weimar Republic's cultural blossoming to Berlin. The city's "naive snobbery," he noted, "favored and opened up its specific possibilities as an arena for the highest standards, a market of merciless competition to sell the outrageous, on which a disillusioned postwar generation—conformist in its adherence to the limits of the market economy, conscious of and consciously playing with its marketability—was dependent: dependent due to its need to win over an anonymous reading public and to the need for inherent topicality demanded by the matter itself."[7]

But Berlin also incubated the "serpent's egg" of Nazism. From 1926, Goebbels was at work there as a *Gauleiter* of the National Socialist German Workers' Party (NSDAP), and developed completely new methods for his political "battle for Berlin":

I came from the provinces and was still caught in provincial thinking. For now, the masses seemed just a dark monster, and I myself was not yet obsessed by the will to conquer and master them. Without that will, you don't get by for long in Berlin. In population policy terms, Berlin is a conglomerate of masses; anyone who wants to get ahead here must speak the language that the masses understand, and adapt and justify his actions in such a way that the masses can muster sympathy and submission for them. Inevitably, these harsh impressions led me to develop

---

6 Adorno, "Jene zwanziger Jahre," 501, 502.
7 Plessner, "Die Legende von den zwanziger Jahren," 277.

a completely new style of political speech. ... The same applied to all the agitators of the Movement in Berlin. ... A new and modern language was spoken there, which was far removed from antiquated, so-called *völkisch* forms of expression. The National Socialist agitation was tailored to the masses. The Party's modern view of life here sought and found a modern, rousing style.[8]

Gerhard Paul has examined in detail the "uprising of images" that Hitler, Goebbels, and their fellows waged against the Republic, especially in the Reich capital Berlin, but also from provincial cities such as Munich, Nuremberg, and Weimar.[9] There were individual "screenplays" for each of the electoral campaigns between 1928 and 1933; flexibly deployed propaganda media (assemblies, rallies, visual imagery, symbols, press, film, and radio, as well as orchestrations of different media); and the mise-en-scène of a repertoire of counterrevolutionary images and concepts. However, its successful outcome—that is, the destruction of the Weimar Republic and the achievement of political power for the Nazi Party—concealed the deficits of Nazi propaganda in the "period of struggle." It was unoriginal in substance and inefficient in organization. In particular, the neglect of utopian discourse in favor of the discourses of liberation and redemption had negative implications for the Party after 1933: "Because National Socialism had little concrete to offer in 'positive' terms, it relied on ever more potent emotional and aesthetic drugs and a constant supply of new enemies against which its adherents could be mobilized."[10]

Although some propaganda elements from the days of the Party's anti-Weimar struggle persisted, Hitler's assumption of the Reich chancellorship on 30 January 1933 ushered in a fundamental shift in the Party's identity and methods. The militant propaganda of protest and agitation had to be supplanted by a propaganda of integration and allegiance to the state, albeit one that included terror as its "evil twin."[11] Mature and institutionalized forms of communication

---

[8] Goebbels, *Kampf um Berlin*, 46. See also Wildt, "Goebbels in Berlin."
[9] On the following, see Paul, *Aufstand der Bilder*, 83–252.
[10] Ibid. 260–1.
[11] Bussemer, *Propaganda und Populärkultur*, 20.

were the first to fall victim to this state- and Party-directed transformation: public and private institutions, political parties, professional
associations, and advocacy groupings from the Weimar era were
entirely dissolved or aligned with the regime in a process of totalitarian coordination imposed through laws, violence, or erosion from
within. As democratic structures were enfeebled, the media too
lost their freedom: books were banned and burned, newspapers
and journals closed down or regulated, radio and film taken into
state hands. This meant, argues Thymian Bussemer, that the old
institutions themselves disappeared, while their discursive structures and cultural practices remained in place.[12] On the one hand,
the Nazi state monopolized and dominated public communication
on politics, culture, economics, and society, but on the other it also
identified nonpolitical themes, yearnings, and needs circulating in the
population and invested considerable energy and financial resources
into fulfilling them.

Only in terms of this ambivalence of "integrative propaganda"
can we explain why the modern leisure and entertainment industry
that had burgeoned in the Weimar Republic could continue to
flourish under the Nazi dictatorship. Even during World War II, when
propaganda was focusing on the controlled dissemination of news,
appeals to the German people's willingness for sacrifice, and latterly
rallying calls for "final victory," the regime was concerned to keep
the population cheerful. In his diary entry for 30 December 1941,
Goebbels noted: "There is no doubt that a very strong need for pure
entertainment is currently present in the German people, and not
only at home but also at the front, and for this reason we are right,
while giving the war its due, also to ensure that the nation can find
the necessary relaxation in art, theater, film, and radio. The nation
has a claim to that."[13] The "art of propaganda," Goebbels continued,
was "to adapt to the new state of affairs and not try to lead the
people from the bureaucrat's desk. Propaganda is not a dogma, but
an art of elasticity." This leads Bussemer to conclude that "although
at first sight the recipients of National Socialist propaganda seem to

---

[12] Ibid. 78.
[13] Goebbels, *Tagebücher*, Part II, vol. 2, 607.

have been manipulated, in fact they had actively selected particular elements of the propaganda on offer to pick up and make popular."[14] Seeking to explain the discrepancy between the propagated intentions of the Nazis and the realities of German life in the years between 1933 and 1945, Hans Dieter Schäfer diagnosed a "split consciousness" as the characteristic feature of the period.[15] That split derived essentially from the coexistence of Nazi or *völkisch* ideology with conservative nationalist values and behaviors inherited from Wilhelmine times, elements of social and cultural modernity that survived the collapse of the Weimar Republic, and in writing the attempts, especially of a young generation of authors, to create a literature untouched by National Socialism. Kaspar Maase, considering Nazism in the context of the history of modern mass culture, modifies Schäfer's term, referring to "split reality": "The National Socialist impulse for a *völkisch* new beginning became fatefully entangled with the aspirations of the great majority to live out 'normality' in their immediate personal world. It is important to keep in mind both trajectories at once: the participation in twelve years of racism, murder, and war and the *longue durée* of private leisure orientation with traits of an everyday modernity."[16] Götz Aly coined a trenchant term for this phenomenon: the "accommodating dictatorship," or dictatorship of favors (*Gefälligkeitsdiktatur*), which Hitler was able to offer the German people thanks to gigantic public debt, the brutal expropriation of Jews, and ruthless exploitation of the countries annexed or occupied from 1938 onward.[17]

This outline of recent interpretations of the Nazi state is by no means exhaustive. Erhard Schütz regards the Third Reich as a "media dictatorship," a "radical attempt to build a dictatorship *over* the media and *through* the media, yet at the same time also a move toward the *rule by media* that we nowadays almost take for granted."[18] At the forefront were the mass media of press, cinema, and radio, on which great demands were placed in terms of the quality of content,

---

[14] Bussemer, *Propaganda und Populärkultur*, 147.
[15] Schäfer, *Das gespaltene Bewusstsein*, 114–62. On the following points, see also ibid. 7–54.
[16] Maase, *Grenzenloses Vergnügen*, 205.
[17] Aly, *Hitler's Beneficiaries*, especially Chapter 2.
[18] Schütz, "Das 'Dritte Reich' als Mediendiktatur," 138. Original emphasis.

technology, and design, and which also promoted popular themes and lowbrow entertainment. Schütz also highlights the role of the book—as a victim of indexing, as a vehicle of Nazi ideology, as an emblem of the German "cultural nation," and as the object of state "care."

It is striking that most studies on propaganda, and the overviews of the politics, economics, and society of Germany from 1933 to 1945, make almost no mention of literature and the book market. Yet to reduce Goebbels to a "Minister of Entertainment," who merely instrumentalized the mass media for the purposes of the Nazi dictatorship,[19] is to overlook important aspects of his biography and his activities as, simultaneously, the Reich Minister of Popular Enlightenment and Propaganda and president of the Chamber of Culture (Reichskulturkammer) with its approximately 200,000 members. Werner Stephan mentions Goebbels's doctoral degree in German literature and his ultimately unsuccessful literary ambitions, though he credits Goebbels with "only journalistic instincts, not literary ones."[20] But this reservation does not necessarily mean that the Propaganda Minister lost all interest in literature after 1933. In his ministerial appointment document, his profession is described as "writer," and during his twelve years as Minister he also partici-pated in the literary world as a nonfiction author.[21] His diary entries indicate regular reading of books and contact with writers in private conversations or official contexts. In the Chamber of Literature (Reichsschrifttumskammer, RSK), part of his Chamber of Culture, around 12,000 full-time or part-time writers were registered in the early phase.[22] Furthermore, Germany was Europe's biggest producer of books—in terms both of total annual production and of the number of individual new titles appearing each year.[23] In 1937, the approximately 3,500 German publishing houses were spending an annual average

[19] Bussemer, "Zur Medien- und Propagandapolitik von Joseph Goebbels," 53.

[20] Stephan, *Joseph Goebbels*, 32–3, here 33.

[21] See Härtel, "'Soldat unter Soldaten.'" For the text of the letter of appointment, see *RGBL*/Part I, no. 21, 17 March 1933, 104.

[22] Numbers from the memorandum of the Reichskulturkammer legal advisor, Günther Gentz, to the Reichsverband Deutscher Schriftsteller (n.d., c. August/September 1935), BArch R 56 V/73 fol. 1–6a.

[23] On this and the following, see the overviews for 1937 in *Der deutsche Buchhandel in Zahlen*, 10–11, 17, 22, 27, 29.

of 40 million reichsmarks on author fees, 30 million RM on paper, 80 million RM on printing, 10 million RM on printing plates, and 40 million RM on binding. That meant a total of around 200 million RM flowing from the book sector into the German economy. At 650 million RM, the average sales value of the books produced took third place in the statistics on goods, after coal and wheat. In German bookselling of the period, the roughly 10,000 retail bookstores and the wholesalers (concentrated in Leipzig, where fifty-three companies were located) generated an annual turnover of 483 million RM—the third best result after cigarettes and women's and girls' clothing. The foreign trade balance, too, was positive: book exports accounted for 22.715 million RM, as against imports of 7.698 million RM. The figures indicate a degree of economic potential that could not simply be ignored by the Propaganda Minister, who was responsible for the book trade. There were also around 9,500 municipal and free public libraries run by local administrations, along with the state, provincial, and university research libraries.[24] All in all, the Nazis were presented with a very large field of activity for literary policy when they came to power.

The question immediately arises of how the Nazi state exploited this potential. In search of answers, we must distinguish between different levels in terms of time, themes, and persons. Firstly, in the domain of literature the same occurred as everywhere else in political and social life: professional bodies were forcibly aligned with the regime or themselves bowed to the new rulers. One particularity was the wave of book burnings staged across Germany. They were the prelude to a radical "cleansing" of the German book market, replacing politically "harmful and undesirable" literature with a conformist book production, the participants of which included, alongside the Party publisher Eher, several *völkisch*-National Socialist and nationalist-conservative publishing companies and, as a new player, the German Labor Front (DAF). Looked at from the outside, this process seemed to unfold relatively rapidly and smoothly, yet internally—as we will see—it was by no means completed in 1933.

The phase of destroying or hijacking existing structures was followed by the creation and consolidation of new bureaucracies

---

[24] Figures for 1933/34 from H. Dähnhardt, "Zur Entwicklung des öffentlichen Büchereiwesens," *Die Bücherei* 8 (1941), 305–8.

on the level of state and Party. In principle, the preconditions for a totalitarian literary policy had now been established. But just as in other domains, in literature a "polycracy" of competing authorities arose that, all the way through the Nazi dictatorship, prevented the emergence of a unified doctrine and its realization in rigorous administrative action.[25] On the level of the state, the Reich Ministry of Popular Enlightenment and Propaganda and the Reich Chamber of Literature had to share responsibility for literary policy with the new Reich Ministry of Science, Education, and Public Instruction and the Foreign Office. On the level of the Party, several *Reichsleiter* offices established themselves, each of which staked and tried to realize claims to a role in decision-making. The secret police (Geheime Staatspolizei or Gestapo) and the SS security service (Sicherheitsdienst, SD) considered themselves authorized to act on literary policy both by the Reich President's emergency decrees of 1933 and by the supposed need for continued "combating of adversaries." The army initially played only a peripheral role, but with the outbreak of the war it became one of the covert key players.

Bureaucracies typically like to concern themselves with themselves and to compete for responsibilities and power. That tendency was no different in the Nazi state, although the particular structures of Nazi rule meant it took a potentiated form. At the same time, every bureaucracy also wants to actively influence people and events. It can do so by means of laws, prohibitions, regulations, and informal agreements, through the distribution of subsidies, special rewards, and social benefits, or through staging prestigious and effective publicity events. The full repertoire—which also included the consistent removal of Jews and political opponents—was brought to bear during the twelve years of Nazi rule: on writers and publishers; book wholesaling; the retail, door-to-door, and mail-order book trade; secondhand bookstores and book clubs; commercial lending libraries, public libraries, and research libraries. The state-controlled and managed book trade and book-based propaganda targeted both the domestic market and international networks. Finally, the Nazi

---

[25] Key references on this issue are Broszat, *The Hitler State*; Hüttenberger, "Nationalsozialistische Polykratie"; Rebentisch, *Führerstaat und Verwaltung im Zweiten Weltkrieg*.

literary bureaucracy also took up the task of supplying books to the German frontline soldiers of World War II and the population on the "home front."

In view of the gigantic proportions of this effort, what was actually achieved in practice by the countless "norms" and "measures"? The starting point for answering this question must be, firstly, the perspective of the rulers: literature, the book market, and libraries were to be molded into willing and effective instruments in the service of the Nazi state. Yet, as Bussemer has shown, even in the years from 1933 to 1945 communication and rule did not follow a one-way, vertical route. It is for this reason that, secondly, the perspective of the actually or supposedly ruled must also be addressed: the attitudes and behavior of writers, publishers, and booksellers, of librarians and of readers.

Clearly, the histories of people, institutions, and actions can only be told if the necessary data is available, and this applies to the Nazi period as much as any other historical epoch. The material for the stories told in this book is found primarily in archives. The files of the state authorities and Party offices concerned with literary policy are kept in the Federal Archives at Berlin Lichterfelde. The Berlin site now also houses the extensive collections—on the Reich Chamber of Culture and its component chambers, on the employees of the Reich and Party bureaucracy, on the members of the NSDAP and the SS—that were once held in the Berlin Document Center, along with the collections of the former State Archives of the German Democratic Republic and the Reich student leadership files on the 1933 book burnings from the State Archives in Würzburg. The political archives of the Federal Foreign Office in Berlin hold information on the organization, agents, content, and strategies of the cultural foreign policy of the Nazi state.

Other important aspects can be reconstructed using the central archives of Germany's individual federal states. For the State Archives of Saxony in Leipzig, Hans-Christian Herrmann has prepared the material on the Börsenverein der Deutschen Buchhändler, the German publishers' and booksellers' association, which despite severe war damage contains abundant thematic, personnel, and company files. The archive of the Deutsche Bücherei in Leipzig casts light on the political instrumentalization of specialized librarianship for the censorship of "harmful and undesirable" writings and of all literature by Jewish authors. The Berlin State Archive (Landesarchiv Berlin), with its documents on the RSK leadership for the *Gau* of Greater Berlin, offers insights into the mechanisms and effects of central literary policy at local level. The central state archives for North Rhine-Westphalia (Nordrhein-Westfälisches Hauptstaatsarchiv Düsseldorf) have the largest holdings of documents on a regional office of the Gestapo and the SD, with numerous, illuminating records of individual processes. The central Thuringian archives (Thüringisches Hauptstaatsarchiv Weimar) house information on the public library system in Thuringia, which after 1933 became a model for the development of public libraries across the Reich. This makes it possible to retrace the genesis of coordination with the regime, the structure of institutions, and their policies—in other words, the perspective of the rulers—from the sources.

The perspective of the ruled is more difficult to reconstruct. Traces can be found in evidence, scattered through all the archives named, of accommodation, submission, and collaboration, but also of opposition and critique. The archival materials were supplemented by the papers of individual writers and publishers held in the Archives of German Literature in Marbach (Deutsches Literaturarchiv Marbach am Neckar) and the Archives of the Academy of Arts, Berlin.

As well as this extensive archival material, I made use of numerous printed sources and periodicals from 1933 to 1945. Diaries, letters, and memoirs by writers, journalists, publishers, and booksellers, written during or after the Nazi period, round out the perspective of the ruled, even if they include many self-serving interpretations or incorrect factual claims. Also valuable were the descriptions and insights of fellow historians who have studied various aspects of the topic over past years and decades. Some of these have already been mentioned, but I would like to add the name of Volker Dahm, who not only pioneered work on the history of the Jewish book trade and its destruction under the Nazi dictatorship, but also paved the way to understanding the Chamber of Culture as an institution fundamental to cultural life in the years from 1933 to 1945. Siegfried Lokatis's study of the publisher Hanseatische Verlagsanstalt taught me to interpret the structure, profile, and long-term repercussions of the Nazi mass book market. I owe Edelgard and Hans-Eugen Bühler, along with Olaf Simons, a better recognition and knowledge of the German army's extensive activities as a purchaser and producer of books during World War II. Without the studies by Cornelia Caroline Funke, Thomas Garke-Rothbart, Murray G. Hall, Thomas Keiderling, Andreas Meyer, Sabine Röttig, Heinz Sarkowski, Anne M. Wallrath-Janssen, Reinhard Wittmann, and Edda Ziegler, I would not have been able to describe the development of individual publishing houses in such detail. The same applies to the numerous published studies on the public and research libraries. However, despite every care in my research, I have to join Joachim Sartorius in noting: "So much remains unmentioned, first of all those things I didn't see."[26]

It is a special honor that this book, first published by Fischer in 2010, can now appear with Continuum/Bloomsbury, in a translation made possible by the generosity of the Fritz Thyssen Foundation, VG Wort, and Börsenverein des Deutschen Buchhandels. I would like to thank Kate Sturge (Berlin) for her skilled work transforming my book from German into English, and Haaris Naqvi at Continuum for his kind assistance. Finally, without the patience and gentle insistence of Walter H. Pehle, historian and editor of the series in which the German edition appeared, this book would never have been written. It was our shared objective to present a comprehensively updated portrayal of literary policy in the Nazi state, filled out by new sources and new research findings. My personal hope is that in today's society, books will attract as much attention and appreciation as the Nazi dictatorship paid them—but this time in a democratic form, not pathologically and with the intention of abuse.

---

[26] Sartorius, *The Princes' Islands*.

2

Changing Personnel, Changing Agendas: From the Weimar Republic to the Third Reich

The Break with the Pluralism and Internationality of German Literature

The National Socialists glossed their exercise of power with an appearance of legality. On 4 February 1933, President von Hindenburg issued a "Decree for the Protection of the German People"[1] that included a detailed section dedicated to "printed publications." At first sight this was nothing unusual: there had been frequent press bans since the start of the presidential dictatorship in March 1930. But Hindenburg's emergency decree was no longer restricted to periodical publications, covering instead all "publications the content of which is apt to endanger public security or order" (§ 7). If they considered this extremely elastic criterion to be fulfilled, the local police authorities could confiscate and retain a publication, independently or on the instruction of the highest provincial authorities. The "Decree of the Reich President for the Protection of the People and State," issued on 28 February 1933, tightened the regulations further, firstly by suspending Article 118 of the Weimar Constitution, which had guaranteed the right of free expression of opinion through

---

[1] *RGBL*/Part I, no. 8, 6 February 1933, 35–40. On the background, see Strenge, *Machtübernahme 1933*.

"word, writing, imprint, image, or in any other manner,"[2] and secondly by giving the Reich government the right to "temporarily" take over the powers of the highest provincial authority if the province did not itself implement "the necessary measures to restore public safety and order." This provision reinforced, in particular, the position of the Reich Ministry of the Interior vis-à-vis the provincial governments, which had not yet fallen under Nazi control. The state terror that ensued led to numerous arrests and to around 8,600 individuals being expelled from the domains of politics, business, culture, and research.[3] With the Law Regarding the Confiscation of Communist Property of 26 May and the Law Regarding the Confiscation of Assets in the Hands of Enemies of the People and the State of 14 July 1933, the German Communist Party and the Social Democratic Party lost, among many other things, their publishing, printing, and book distribution businesses.[4]

The break with the pluralism and internationality of Weimar literature was marked on the one hand by the "alignment" (*Gleichschaltung*) of writers' advocacy groups or professional associations, on the other by the book burnings of May 1933. Among the first associations to be aligned with the regime was the literature section of the Prussian Academy of Arts. The section had been politically controversial ever since it was founded in 1926—a factor of its high-profile status, for although the section as an institution belonged to the province of Prussia, its members were thought of as representing the entirety of contemporary German literature. However, in 1930 deeper differences of opinion emerged, over fundamental issues regarding the aesthetic positioning of literature and the role of the writer in society; they culminated in the resignation of the president, Walter von Molo, and in January 1931 in the nationalist conservative members Erwin Guido Kolbenheyer, Wilhelm Schäfer, and Emil Strauss stepping down in protest. The split within German literature thus paralleled the political crisis and erosion of the Weimar Republic, and it is hardly surprising that after the Nazi takeover the

---

[2] *RGBL*/Part I, no. 17, 28 February 1933, 83.
[3] Numbers from Möller, *Exodus der Kultur*, 7. Möller estimates the number of émigrés in the domain of culture at more than 4,600 (ibid. 112).
[4] *RGBL*/Part I, no. 55, 27 May 1933, 479–80, and no. 81, 15 July 1933, 479–80. On the context, see Hale, *The Captive Press*, 61–75.

Academy's literature section was the first writers' organization to be subjected to a transformation of personnel.

On 15 February 1933, Heinrich Mann—who had been elected section president two years previously—resigned from his post when the new Prussian Minister of Culture, Bernhard Rust, threatened to disband the section. A declaration of loyalty to the Nazi Reich government, initiated by Gottfried Benn on 13 March, divided the literary camps once and for all. Alfred Döblin, Ricarda Huch (hitherto the vice-president), Thomas Mann, Rudolf Pannwitz, Alfons Paquet, René Schickele, and Jakob Wassermann were all excluded after refusing to put their signature to this unconditional capitulation to the new rulers. Leonhard Frank, Ludwig Fulda, Georg Kaiser, Bernhard Kellermann, Alfred Mombert, Fritz von Unruh, and Franz Werfel, who apparently saw no problem in signing the declaration of loyalty, were nevertheless excluded because, as the Academy's president informed them by registered mail on the basis of "information received from the proper authorities," their membership was no longer sustainable "according to the principles governing the new order of Prussia's state cultural institutions."[5] In the case of von Unruh, Kellermann, and Kaiser, this referred to their political and aesthetic attitudes, while for the other renowned writers the issue was "non-Aryan" descent, both considerations having been interpreted as grounds for exclusion from the Academy membership through a mutatis mutandis application of the Law for the Restoration of the Professional Civil Service of 7 April 1933. Of the previous members, only Benn, Rudolf G. Binding, Theodor Däubler, Max Halbe, Oskar Loerke, Max Mell, Walter von Molo, Josef Ponten, Wilhelm Schmidtbonn, Ina Seidel, and Eduard Stucken now remained in the section.

The places that had been vacated were filled again in early May 1933, as Kolbenheyer, Schäfer, and Strauss returned to the fold and Werner Beumelburg, Hans Friedrich Blunck, Peter Dörfler, Friedrich Griese, Hanns Johst, Agnes Miegel, Börries von Münchhausen, and Will Vesper were newly appointed. More writers followed in October 1933: Hermann Claudius, Gustav Frenssen, Enrica von Handel-Mazzetti, Rudolf Huch, Isolde Kurz, Heinrich Lersch, Jakob Schaffner, Johannes Schlaf, and Josef-Magnus Wehner. The "literati" who had

---

[5] Cited in Jens, *Dichter zwischen rechts und links*, 212.

largely defined public perceptions of the Weimar Republic's literary canon had now been driven out, and the *Dichter*—"poets"—who were, according to the Nazi regime and literary criticism, to define the canon of the Third Reich took up their positions at the most prestigious level.

These nationalist-conservative and *völkisch* authors were backed by publishers such as Langen-Müller, Hanseatische Verlagsanstalt, and Eugen Diederichs, which had already achieved considerable success in book publishing during the Weimar period but now, with the support of the Nazi state, hoped to conquer the German book market once and for all. Yet time confirmed the judgment of Hans Carossa, who declined an appointment to the Academy offered him in May 1933: "A body that stands under such strict state tutelage as this restructured Academy has no true sovereignty and therefore no real dignity."[6] Apart from panegyrics to the new rulers and public appeals to support Nazi foreign policy, in the years that followed the "poets" were chiefly occupied with their own affairs and with their Academy's progressive loss of significance.

In the German PEN Club, the leadership was dealt a severe blow by the emigration of its president, Alfred Kerr, to Czechoslovakia on 15 February 1933 and the resignation of board members Theodor Däubler, Herwarth Walden, and Hanns Martin Elster on 7 March. Kerr had taken on the presidency in December 1931 when the previous officeholder, Walter Bloem, stepped down in protest at the Club's declaration of solidarity with the politically persecuted writer Carl von Ossietzky. In an article for the *Deutsche Allgemeine Zeitung* on 17 March 1933, Carl Haensel, a PEN member and for many years the legal advisor of the Schutzverband deutscher Schriftsteller (League of German Writers), launched a public attack on the German PEN Club's "internationalism." This lawyer with literary pretensions was convinced that "a nation can only be represented to the outside world by someone who is rooted to the very depths in his own *Volk*'s character, and is suffused to the last pore by its sap." In view of the imminent international PEN congress in Dubrovnik, the aim was to restaff the board as soon as possible. In the process, the nationalist-conservative representatives of the German PEN Club—who

---

[6] Carossa to Katharina Kippenberg, 17 May 1933, in Carossa, *Briefe II*, 284.

included Walter Bloem, Hanns Heinz Ewers, Hans Richter, Edgar von Schmidt-Pauli, and Fedor von Zobeltitz—coordinated their actions closely with the Nazi Kampfbund für deutsche Kultur (Combat League for German Culture). Bloem suggested that "members of the Kampfbund might enter the PEN Club so as to be able to carry out the cleansing campaign as rapidly as possible."[7] The goal of the Kampfbund strategists in Berlin, in turn, was "to take over the PEN Club completely and to send clearly National Socialist members to Ragusa [i.e., Dubrovnik]."

The provisional board, including Werner Bergengruen, Hans Richter, Edgar von Schmidt-Pauli, and Fedor von Zobeltitz, prepared a General Meeting for 9 April 1933. This was the occasion to readmit nationalist-conservative and National Socialist authors and journalists—among them Max Barthel, Werner Beumelburg, Paul Fechter, Hans Grimm, Hans Hinkel, Hanns Johst, Erwin Guido Kolbenheyer, Hans Heinz Mantau-Sadila, Börries von Münchhausen, Rudolf Pechel, Ernst Wiechert, and Will Vesper—along with Alfred Rosenberg and Hans Hinkel representing the Kampfbund.[8] The debate on the election of a new board and appointments to the committees saw "some sharp clashes," as Haensel's minutes record. As the oldest member and interim president, Fedor von Zobeltitz was tasked with appointing "a commission of ten gentlemen" who were to draw up a new list—"after conferring with the government authorities." Although the commission did present the required lists of suggestions, the continuation of the General Meeting on 23 April first elected some further new members, including Rainer Schlösser of the Nazi daily *Völkischer Beobachter*, and immediately declared them eligible to vote, in contravention of the Club statutes.[9] The enhanced position of the National Socialists made itself felt during the subsequent debate on the election of the new board. The Kampfbund representatives vigorously protested the supervision of the National Socialist board members that they claimed the "national group" was planning.

---

[7] BArch R 56 I/102, fol. 232, Walter Bloem's visit to Dr. Kochanowski, 27 March 1933. The following quotation ibid.

[8] On this and the following points, see the minutes of the General Meeting on 9 April 1933, Berlin, BArch R 56 I/102, fol. 20.

[9] Minutes of the continuation of the Annual General Meeting on 23 April 1933, ibid. fol. 17–19.

Erich Kochanowski, part of the Kampfbund's Prussian provincial leadership, informed the assembly "at the request of Hinkel and Johst" that the two absentees "would not tolerate anyone advising them." The PEN Club was, he added, "an important instrument in the structure of the state as a whole. And if a new board is elected, it goes without saying that the members will make it their duty to administer the PEN Club very particularly in the interests of the state." To the dismay of his "national" colleagues, Schmidt-Pauli then presented a counter-proposal: that Hinkel, Johst, and Schlösser be elected co-presidents, Johannes von Leers and himself secretaries, and Elster and Kochanowski treasurers. "If this proposal is not accepted, neither the presidents to be elected nor any of the Kampfbund members will take any interest in the proceedings in the PEN Club until the next General Meeting." Continuing Schmidt-Pauli's coercive tone, Kochanowski declared that "we will only agree to a board of this composition," and Wulf Bley added that if the new list were not accepted, the German PEN group would "no longer have the support of the state's leadership." Kochanowski refused to hear any further discussion, on the grounds that all objections had already "been considered by Messrs Hinkel, Johst, and Rosenberg" and that he had every confidence in the new presidents, under whose aegis "the new board will work fully in accordance with the wishes of our new Reich leadership." Upon this, Bloem and other members of the "national group" left the room, allowing the board and committee of the German PEN Club to be appointed unanimously in line with Nazi policy.[10]

Will Vesper, editor of the literary journal *Die Neue Literatur*, remained hesitant. Hoping to win him over, von Leers informed him complacently on 27 April 1933 that everything in the German PEN Club had now been successfully "switched on, off, and over" to a full alignment with "the reshaping" of Germany.[11] However, Vesper still found some members suspect, and was prepared only to wish the German board "the determination and experience to carry out the thorough cleansing of the Club that is so urgently required."[12]

---

[10] New list of board and committee members, ibid. fol. 267.
[11] Ibid. fol. 207.
[12] *Die Neue Literatur* 34 (1933), 365. The following quotation ibid. 366.

He also advised against attending the world PEN congress, since "appearing before an international and, for the greatest part, hostile body of writers" did not promise "the slightest benefit for Germany." Indeed, at the congress in Dubrovnik from 25 to 28 May, Vesper's prediction proved more or less accurate: "nothing but embarrassing confrontations, for which the German delegates were no match."[13] There were condemnations of the German PEN Club's exclusion of politically dissident and Jewish writers, which contradicted the principles of the international body's charter.[14]

Alongside the British and French delegations, it was primarily Schalom Asch, Emil Ludwig, and Ernst Toller, all authors driven out of Germany, who joined forces to attack Nazi cultural policy. The German delegation used Toller's intervention as an excuse to leave the assembly in protest, so that the planned speech by the former lieutenant commander and war-novel author Fritz Otto Busch on "The Freelance Writer and the Press" had to be canceled.[15] However, Busch, Elster, and Schmidt-Pauli succeeded in blocking an anti-German resolution backed by the PEN president H. G. Wells. Instead, the majority of the congress accepted a compromise closing communiqué formulated by the US delegation.[16] In addition, the German club retained its seat on the executive committee, and large parts of the Austrian PEN Club expressed their solidarity with their German colleagues.[17] It was these propaganda successes that were put forward as arguments for remaining part of the international association at a committee meeting of the German PEN Club on 7 July 1933.[18]

If the regime ultimately failed in its attempt to instrumentalize the German PEN section for its foreign-policy objectives, this was due to the specific organizational structure of the international club and the resolute political stance of its British leadership. In early

---

[13] Thus Vesper's self-satisfied conclusion, *Die Neue Literatur* 34 (1933), 422.
[14] For details, see the French and British press reports on the congress reproduced in Wulf, *Literatur und Dichtung im Dritten Reich*, 67–9.
[15] Busch to Kochanowski, telegram, 26 May 1933, BArch R 56 I/102, fol. 104.
[16] See the two reports by Busch and Schmidt-Pauli on 27 and 28 May 1933 on the proceedings of the PEN congress, BArch R 56 I/102, fol. 88–96 and 97–102.
[17] Renner, "Österreichische Schriftsteller und der Nationalsozialismus," 205–17.
[18] Minutes of the committee meeting on 7 July 1933, BArch R 56 I/102, fol. 266.

November 1933, the executive committee in London passed another resolution condemning the oppression of politically dissident writers in Germany. The German delegate at the meeting, Schmidt-Pauli, thereupon announced the German group's resignation from the International PEN Club.[19] Once the withdrawal was confirmed by the German PEN committee, a new Union Nationaler Schriftsteller (Union of Nationalist Writers) was founded on 8 January 1933.[20] The Union absorbed the German PEN group's funds and most of its members. Johst was elected its president; the new member Benn was vice-president, while secretary Schmidt-Pauli and treasurers Elster and Kochanowski were carried over from the previous PEN board. In an appeal "To the writers of all lands!" that was published in the *Völkischer Beobachter* on 1 March 1934, the newly founded writers' association warned of the international danger of communism, pitting "national German literature" against "emigrant literature," the label given to writing by authors driven into exile from Germany.[21] The PEN Club's goal of international reconciliation was replaced by the "cultural personality of the fatherland," defined using the categories of nation and race. Unsurprisingly in view of its pontificating style, the Union of National Writers met with little resonance either at home or abroad, and soon sank into obscurity.

The SDS or League of German Writers—the largest and most politically influential advocacy association of authors, with more than 2,400 members in 1932—was also deeply riven at the end of the Weimar Republic. Since 1931 there had been struggles in the Reich capital between a communist-dominated "Berlin Local Group" and

---

[19] See the report by Schmidt-Pauli, included in the minutes of the committee meeting on 18 November 1933, on the PEN executive committee session, and Schmidt-Pauli's report of early January 1934 on the re-formation of the German PEN group as the Union Nationaler Schriftsteller; p. 2 of BArch BDC/RSK/Schmidt-Pauli, E. von.

[20] On this and the following points, see documents in the above file: the minutes of the committee meeting of 18 November 1933, the record of the General Meeting of the PEN Club on 8 January 1934, the record of the inaugural meeting of the Union Nationaler Schriftsteller on the same day, and the circular of the Union Nationaler Schriftsteller of 25 January 1934, which called upon the existing members of the German PEN Club to join. However, because the General Meeting of 8 January did not reach a quorum of half the members, the PEN Club could not be officially dissolved.

[21] The text of the appeal is reproduced in Wulf, *Literatur und Dichtung im Dritten Reich*, 86–7.

a new "Berlin-Brandenburg Local Group" founded in December that year, which started out with 287 members. By 1933 this grouping of nationalist-conservative writers, headed by Max Barthel, had a membership of 483, and played a key role in the "realignment" of the SDS.[22] In addition, in late 1931 the SDS executive board elected Walter Bloem, the head of the Working Group of Nationalist Writers formed that October, as its new president. Two further representatives of the nationalist-conservative camp were on the board: Hans Richter, the president of the Verband deutscher Erzähler (Association of German Novelists), and the legal advisor Carl Haensel. In April 1932 Bloem resigned from office when, like the PEN Club, the executive board of the SDS—dominated by social democratic and liberal authors and journalists—joined the campaign of support for the imprisoned Carl von Ossietzky. After the Nazis came to power, the "Berlin Local Group" was dissolved. On 10 March 1933, the Working Group of Nationalist Writers mounted a coup at a meeting of the executive board, and succeeded in ousting eighteen colleagues whom they had classified as representatives of republican politics and culture.[23] The remaining board members then elected ten new nationalist-conservative and National Socialist writers to office.[24] The interim presidency devolved to Hans Richter as president and Carl Haensel as his deputy.

On 15 March, the new board resolved that SDS membership was irreconcilable with membership of the Communist Party or any associated organization. In the two weeks that followed, a commission was formed by the board to inspect the SDS membership files and exclude all politically "undesirable" members. With the election of Götz Otto Stoffregen at the General Meeting of 4 May, a National

---

[22] Max Barthel, "Sechzehn Monate Arbeit und Kampf," *Der Schriftsteller* 1933, no. 1/2, 55–6.

[23] "Die Umstellung des Schutzverbandes Deutscher Schriftsteller," *Der Schriftsteller* 1933, no. 3/5, 33–4; H. H. Mantau-Sadila, "Warum wir den SDS gleichgeschaltet haben," *Der Schriftsteller* 1933, no. 6/7, 76–9.

[24] See Rühle, *Das Dritte Reich* 1933, 84. The following remained in the executive board: W. Bloem, W. Goetz (as deputy treasurer), C. Haensel (as vice-president), H. Richter, W. Schendell (the former executive secretary), and H. Spiero. The new board members were the authors Barthel, Bergengruen, von Conring, von Grote, Jahnn, Mantau-Sadila, Meckel, Seitz, Wienand, and Werner.

Socialist took up the leadership of the association.[25] Richter became vice-president, the Nazi authors Hans Heinz Mantau-Sadila and Hans Henning von Grote secretaries. Haensel remained the legal advisor. Werner Bergengruen and Eberhard Meckel, among others, were involved as board members. The Austrian SDS was informed that the fusion the two groups had long been planning would not be further pursued, on the grounds that the Austrian board did "not understand the development that has occurred in Germany, or at least does not intend to join it." The new statutes, accepted unanimously, required of each member "as a precondition for admission" a written declaration "clearly avowing allegiance to the German cultural community in word and deed."[26]

During a lecture at Berlin's Kaiserhof Hotel, organized by the SDS for writers and publishers, Goebbels announced on 19 May that "National Socialism, as the bearer of the revolution, ... strives to draw to itself in a planned and organic way all the circles of the intellect, of scholarship, and of art, bringing them into a direct and indissoluble relationship with the state."[27] Shortly afterwards, on 9 June, the registered association Reichsverband Deutscher Schriftsteller (RDS, Reich Association of German Writers) was formed "at the instigation" of the Ministry of Popular Enlightenment and Propaganda.[28] In late July the SDS, along with the Association of German Novelists, the German Writers' Association, and the Cartel of Poets, was absorbed into this new professional association. From being president of the SDS, Stoffregen now advanced to the status of a "Reich leader"; Hans Richter remained his deputy. There was a degree of continuity with the old SDS in personnel, organizational, and financial terms, and to some extent even in terms of objectives. But the introduction of the "Führer principle"—the principle of the absolute power of the leader—and the requirement of "pure German

---

[25] On this and the following points, see "Hauptversammlung des SDS," *Der Schrift-steller* 1933, no. 3/5, 34.

[26] "Satzung des SDS. 1933. Angenommen in der Generalversammlung vom 4.5.1933," *Der Schriftsteller* 1933, no. 3/5, 35–40, here 35 (§ 3).

[27] Thus the report on the lecture in Mantau-Sadila, "Warum wir den SDS gleichge-schaltet haben," 79.

[28] "Reichsverband Deutscher Schriftsteller e.V. Reichsleitung," *Der Schriftsteller* 1933, no. 8, 93–7. The following points ibid.

descent" and "politically irreproachable" behavior "in line with the new state" as preconditions for admission meant a sharp break with the association's previous practice. The intention was to make the RDS "a compulsory organization, the author's membership of which will in future decide whether a written work can be published in Germany or not." This definition foreshadows a key principle of the later Chamber of Culture legislation—and it was an officer of the Propaganda Ministry, Heinz Wismann, already a member of the RDS board, who would later manage the RDS's transfer into the Chamber of Literature (Reichsschrifttumskammer, RSK).

In parallel with these events, spring 1933 saw preparations for an "Action Against the Un-German Spirit." Reviewing the campaign in a 1934 article entitled "Writers on the Bonfire," the then RSK advisor Werner Schlegel wrote: "The book burning was the symbol of the revolution, the symbol that intellectual decay had been overcome once and for all, the sign of the victory of a new doctrine of values. ... Prerevolutionary Germany had no visible institution of power, no institution that could be grasped and thus confronted. ... The only, and well-known, power in Germany was the literature-generating corporation that ruled public opinion."[29] This interpretation vividly encapsulates the logic of the "cleansing" of the German book market that was inaugurated in early April 1933 by the Deutsche Studentenschaft (the umbrella organization of all student bodies at German universities, based in Würzburg) and that rapidly found broad-based support, both from national and provincial public authorities and NSDAP divisions and from librarians, university professors, schoolteachers, and journalists.

The original agenda of the "Action Against the Un-German Spirit," namely the "public burning of corrosive Jewish writing by the student bodies of the universities in response to World Jewry's shameless smear campaign against Germany,"[30] was considerably

---

[29] Schlegel, "Dichter auf dem Scheiterhaufen," 50–2. Julius Friedrich Werner Schlegel (1900–?) was a preliminary reader in the Reichsstelle zur Förderung des deutschen Schrifttums (Reich Office for the Promotion of German Literature) from 1 September 1933 and in charge of "observation of the German book abroad" for the RSK, 1 December 1933–1 December 1934. BArch BDC/RSK/Schlegel, W.

[30] Thus the circular P No. 2 of the Deutsche Studentenschaft's office for press and propaganda to the individual student bodies, 8 April 1933, here p. 1. BArch NS 38/2416.

expanded in the course of the four-week preparation phase. The "blacklists" that the Committee for Reordering the Berlin Municipal and Public Libraries provided for the student bodies as a basis for the book burnings of 10 May 1933 no longer named only Jewish authors, but now almost every figure of literary modernism who had achieved national and international success during the Weimar Republic. Thus, the "Fiction Blacklist," a first version of which was sent to the Deutsche Studentenschaft by the Berlin librarian Wolfgang Herrmann in late April and an expanded version on 1 May,[31] included works by Bertolt Brecht, Alfred Döblin, Erich Ebermayer, Kasimir Edschmid, Lion Feuchtwanger, Leonhard Frank, Ernst Glaeser, Oskar Maria Graf, Walter Hasenclever, Arthur Holitscher, Erich Kästner, Hermann Kesten, Egon-Erwin Kisch, Irmgard Keun, Alexander Lernet-Holenia, Emil Ludwig, Heinrich and Klaus Mann, Kurt Pinthus, Theodor Plivier, Gustav Regler, Erich Maria Remarque, Ludwig Renn, Joachim Ringelnatz, Joseph Roth, Arthur Schnitzler, Anna Seghers, Ernst Toller, Benjamin Traven, Kurt Tucholsky, Fritz von Unruh, Jakob Wassermann, Franz Carl Weiskopf, Armin T. Wegner, Franz Werfel, Arnold Zweig, and Stefan Zweig. Using the blacklists, in late April and early May the "combat committees" formed in the individual university cities under the guidance of the Studentenschaft searched private bookstores and commercial libraries, and confiscated thousands of books for the planned bonfires.

The lasting impact of the book burnings that took place in the late evening of 10 May on both contemporaries and later generations can be explained by their expert staging, calculated to achieve the maximum media effect. Blacklisted volumes tied to whipping posts, cattle trucks transporting the books, incendiary speeches and slogans, the blaze as a public spectacle at highly visible locations in the cities involved—all this continued Nazi propaganda's "uprising of images"[32] against the Weimar Republic. Particular attention was commanded by the bonfire in front of the Berlin Opera, which was accompanied by literature Ph.D. and Reich Minister Joseph Goebbels as the main speaker; the event was reported live on radio by the Deutschlandsender station and again, via the weekly

---

[31] See ibid. for the list and covering letter.
[32] See Paul, *Aufstand der Bilder*.

newsreels, in movie theaters across the whole Reich.[33] However, book burnings are documented not only in the Reich capital, but in a total of ninety-three locations throughout Germany, each performance attracting large audiences and intense media interest.[34] It was an alliance of younger and older academics (among them several respected German literature scholars), together with teachers, journalists, authors, Party activists of the old and new generation, whose speeches hailed the departure from the liberalism, pacifism, and internationalism of Weimar democracy and the elimination of the "corrosive" literature, "alien to the species and *Volk*," that had formed the canon of the Republic.[35]

The Börsenverein der Deutschen Buchhändler (German Publishers' and Booksellers' Association) might have been expected to criticize the campaigns as damaging the business interests of the sector it represented, but in fact it demonstratively adopted the students' own scale of values. On the title page of the association's daily bulletin, the *Börsenblatt für den Deutschen Buchhandel*, of 13 May 1933, the executive board published a declaration that had been approved in advance by the Nazi Kampfbund and the Berlin central office for German libraries. Readers were informed that the authors Lion Feuchtwanger, Ernst Glaeser, Arthur Holitscher, Alfred Kerr, Egon Erwin Kisch, Emil Ludwig, Heinrich Mann, Ernst Ottwalt, Theodor Plivier, Erich Maria Remarque, Kurt Tucholsky, and Arnold Zweig were "to be regarded as damaging for Germany's reputation. The board expects the book trade to cease disseminating the works of these writers."[36] Paul Fechter, writing in the May issue of the *Deutsche Rundschau*, also welcomed "the substitution of the literatures."[37] The "literature of the bourgeois Left in all its nuances" and literature "of a more or less communist variety" could now be replaced by "poetry [*Dichtung*] in the old German sense," which during the Weimar era had been "a literature under the surface," a literature "of the depths, that was and was not present, because the

---

[33] For detail on the staging of the book burnings in Berlin, see Tress, "Berlin."
[34] Tress, "Phasen und Akteure der Bücherverbrennungen," 13.
[35] Gerhard Sauder, "Akademischer 'Frühlingssturm'" and "Der Germanist Goebbels."
[36] *Bbl.* no. 110, 13 May 1933, 1.
[37] Fechter, "Die Auswechslung der Literaturen," *Deutsche Rundschau* 1933, no. 235, May, 120–2. The following quotations ibid. 120.

generality was not aware of it and only a few people knew it; because it always had to be gathered up by someone knowledgeable, only when it was asked for, and set against that other literature, the literature that was so carefully assembled in academies and literary journals." Fechter was affirming a legend invented by the political opponents of Weimar: the notion that genuinely "national-German" literature had been suppressed between 1918 and 1933. In fact, however, nationalist-conservative and *völkisch* or National Socialist publishers already held a far from minor share of the German book market—a share that the political changeover would enable them to increase significantly.

New Formations in the Book Market

The board of the Börsenverein der Deutschen Buchhändler in Leipzig did not pursue any rapprochement with the Nazis until after the Reichstag election of 5 March 1933. But when the association's "Immediate program for the German book trade" was resolved on 12 April 1933, as the basis for negotiations with the Reich Ministries of Economics and of the Interior, it left no doubt as to what mattered to the profession's representatives.[38] Raising the Börsenverein's status by making membership compulsory for all booksellers; state concessions for commercial book trading; pushing back the bookselling operations of state institutions, trade unions, associations, and political parties; dismantling the book clubs; "immediately and completely eliminating the publishing and bookselling activities of department stores"; and legislative measures "against the unhealthy and *Volk*-damaging expansion of the so-called modern commercial lending libraries [*Leihbüchereien*]"—all these objectives were directed at adjusting the market and strengthening the position of businesses in the traditional book trade. In return for this economic wish list, the Börsenverein board made the following offer to the new rulers: "With respect to the Jewish question, the board places its trust in the leadership of the Reich government. It will carry

---

[38] *Bbl.* no. 101, 3 May 1933, 321–2. The following points ibid.

out government instructions for its own area of influence without reservations."

The extent of accommodation by the Börsenverein is also evidenced by the traditional Cantate Sunday assembly in the Leipzig "Booksellers' House" on 14 May 1933, at which the new Reich Minister of Popular Enlightenment and Propaganda appeared. In his speech, Goebbels adroitly combined an emphasis on the role of the "government of the national uprising" in preserving and renewing the state with a clear rejection of internationalism, pacifism, and the democratic rule of law.[39] If the assembly greeted this authoritarian message "with tumultuous applause," as the minutes note, that should by no means be interpreted merely as an act of courtesy or of naked opportunism. Rather, Goebbels was giving voice to all the values that had been modeled during the Weimar Republic by power elites in politics, public administration, business, and intellectual life. Admittedly, the Börsenverein board could not yet demonstrate the presence of any Nazis in its ranks. At the Cantate assembly, an "action committee" was therefore appointed to lead and monitor the "adaptation of the Börsenverein and its affiliated associations to the economic constitution as it applies to our profession." The members of the committee were well suited to the task of building connections with Party and state: Karl Baur, director of the Callwey house in Munich, who had taken part in Hitler's Munich coup attempt on 9 November 1923 and joined the NSDAP in August 1930; the Hamburg bookseller Martin Riegel; the Leipzig publisher of antisemitic books Theodor Fritsch, Jr.; and Heinz Wismann from the Propaganda Ministry. A further personnel decision enabled the Börsenverein to strengthen its links with Rosenberg's Kampfbund für deutsche Kultur: Hellmuth Langenbucher was appointed chief editor of the *Börsenblatt* with effect from 15 June. Langenbucher, a Party member since 1929, had previously headed the press office of the Munich publisher Langen-Müller, and entertained close contacts with the Nazi press. In June 1933, as a member of the Kampfbund, he played an important part in the establishment of the Reichsstelle zur Förderung des deutschen Schrifttums. This "Reich Office for the Promotion of German Literature," the first National Socialist

---

[39] *Bbl.* no. 112, 16 May 1933, 355.

literature commission, set itself the goal of eradicating the literature of the "System period," as Weimar was contemptuously called, and of propagating *völkisch*-nationalist literature in the Nazi state. Langen-Müller and the Börsenverein both participated in funding the Reichsstelle.

The impression that the Börsenverein wanted Langenbucher as a Nazi calling card is confirmed by a letter from Gustav Pezold, the influential managing director of Langen-Müller. On 12 December 1933, Pezold confided in the Langen-Müller author Hans Grimm that the Börsenverein, which in spring 1933 "found itself in difficulties because it was utterly failing in the field of cultural policy and therefore had every reason to fear for its future position," had tempted Langenbucher away from Langen-Müller with a generous salary offer and guarantees of "the greatest possible independence in managing the Börsenverein's cultural policy affairs."[40] For his part, Pezold accepted the loss of Langenbucher's services with an eye to his own interests. Of the fourteen new members that Bernhard Rust had appointed to the literature section of the Prussian Academy of Arts, no less than nine were Langen-Müller authors. Langenbucher could now promote his former employer in two capacities at once: as chief editor of the *Börsenblatt* and as chief reader at the Reichsstelle zur Förderung des deutschen Schrifttums. As well as Hellmuth Langenbucher, his younger brother Erich was also taken on as a *Börsenblatt* editor. Erich too came with experience of the Langen-Müller house, where he had worked as a secretary in 1932. This cliquism bore especially heavily on the publishers currently suffering most acutely from the political changes. Thus Ernst Rowohlt, in a letter to Hans Fallada on 21 June 1934, understandably deplored the fact that his Börsenverein membership dues were helping to pay the editor of the *Börsenblatt*, who had just published a damning review of Fallada's *The World Outside* in the Nazi daily *Stuttgarter N.S. Kurier*.[41] In the same context, Rowohlt—as ever, excellently informed—reminded Fallada that not only Hellmuth Langenbucher but also Gunther Haupt, Karl Thulke, and Karl Rauch, all prominent

---

[40] DLA NL Hans Grimm/Korrespondenz mit dem Langen-Müller Verlag.
[41] In Fallada, *Ewig auf der Rutschbahn*, 149–50. See also Meyer, "Die Verlagsfusion Langen-Müller," especially 63–75, 141–4.

names in literary policy, belonged to the "Langen-Müller clique" that envied the author his success, as did Will Vesper. Vesper, one of Langen-Müller's hitherto rather unsuccessful authors, used his journal *Die Neue Literatur* (published by Avenarius, closely associated with Langen-Müller) to launch diatribes against all the "asphalt literati" of the Weimar Republic.[42]

In the wake of the book burnings, a "working committee" was formed in May 1933 to gather representatives of the Börsenverein, the Propaganda Ministry, the RDS, the publishing sector, book retailing, and the commercial lending libraries under the aegis of the Kampfbund. In mid-July this committee presented a compilation of works of "belles lettres" that were to be removed from the book market. Further lists of bans were drawn up for the areas of "law, politics, public policy," "history," "education and the youth movement," "world view," and "sexual literature." When sending the belles-lettres list to the Propaganda Ministry, the Kampfbund had suggested that the indexed works be banned for the whole of the Reich. The Kampfbund's executive secretary had even drafted the text of a "notification" by means of which the Börsenverein's "action committee" might impose the ban and the confiscation of "works prohibited for sale and lending."

Because questions of property law and constitutional law had not yet been conclusively clarified, the implementation of the prohibition procedure was delayed until the fall. Then, in early November 1933 through January 1934, circulars were sent out from the Leipzig office in which the Börsenverein, "in agreement with the Kampfbund für deutsche Kultur," informed the publishers affected that "supplying and distributing the works named is undesirable for national and cultural reasons and must therefore cease."[43] If these works nevertheless continued to be traded, added the circular, the publishers would have to expect exclusion from the Börsenverein, because the association had "taken on the task of enforcing the wishes of the proper authorities using the instruments at its disposal." To close, the Börsenverein called "particular" attention to the need to

---

[42] See Vesper's harsh review of *Wer einmal aus dem Blechnapf frißt, Die Neue Literatur* 35 (1934), 444.
[43] Carbon copies of these letters are held in BArch R 55/684.

"treat this communication as *strictly confidential*." The "authorities responsible" would "proceed against any indiscretion in the most rigorous manner." The book bans were, then, to be kept secret—with a particular view to avoiding negative political reactions from abroad, where critical attention had been following Nazi cultural policy since the book burnings of May 1933.

Especially hard-hit by the sales bans were the publishers Deutsche Verlags-Anstalt, S. Fischer Verlag, Gustav Kiepenheuer Verlags-AG, Rowohlt, Ullstein Verlags-AG, and Kurt Wolff Verlags-AG—in other words, the companies that had published the fiction of naturalism, expressionism, Dadaism, and New Objectivity; modern translated literature; and critical nonfiction. Propyläen Verlags-GmbH had to give up works by Brecht, Hasenclever, Heinrich Mann, and, most alarmingly, Remarque's best-seller *All Quiet on the Western Front*. The publisher Sieben-Stäbe-Verlags- und Druckereigesellschaft was forced to cease distributing no less than twenty-one titles by Hanns Heinz Ewers, even though Ewers had propounded the interests of the National Socialists well before 1933. For all these publishers, the bans involved enormous economic losses, while for some they threatened the company's very existence.

Yet publishers appear to have already been so thoroughly intimidated that almost no protests ensued. Only the politics department of Ullstein complained to the Börsenverein offices, on 18 December 1933.[44] As its submission pointed out, State Commissioner Hinkel had asserted during a discussion with Ullstein's legal advisor in the Prussian ministry of education and culture that "the agreement with the Kampfbund für deutsche Kultur which you mention does not exist." Hinkel, at the time still part of the Kampfbund's national leadership, confirmed that "the responsibility for such interventions into a publisher's sales and distribution is currently not clarified." A legal basis for the procedure, at least, "was not given." Since the sale of the indexed books had previously been permitted by the Börsenverein without objections and there had been no change in the legal situation, the Börsenverein could "not at this stage describe the continuation of sales as a violation of membership obligations."

---

[44] Text in Hinkel's general correspondence, vol. 8, BArch R 56 I/89.

Ullstein hoped for support from the recently established Chamber of Culture—a false hope, as would very soon become clear.

As the first year of Nazi rule came to a close, all seemed well with the world for the Börsenverein: its institutional continuity had been maintained intact, as had its top-level personnel. This was to change fundamentally in the course of 1934. First, considerable unease was generated in publishing circles when a Parteiamtliche Prüfungskommission zum Schutze des nationalsozialistischen Schrifttums (PPK), a "Party examination commission for the protection of National Socialist writings," was established on the orders of Hitler's deputy Rudolf Hess on 16 April. The cause for concern was the instruction that "manuscripts dealing with National Socialist problems and topics" must "in the first instance be offered for publication to the central Party publisher [i.e., Eher], which is the property of the NSDAP." In a letter to Hess (addressing him as the Reich Minister, not as the Führer's Deputy) on 17 April, publisher and Börsenverein president Friedrich Oldenbourg submitted that "based on the claim to totality, a literal implementation of the announcement would mean that for the main part Franz Eher Nachf. would now be the only possible publication venue for political writings, as a kind of central state publisher."[45] Due to the "harm this would cause to the sector as a whole," Oldenbourg asked for an "amendment to the decree such that the choice of publisher be left to authors."

While Oldenbourg's petition was perfectly well founded in substantive terms, it rested on an ill-fated misjudgment of the political power balance. Thus, Oldenbourg had signed the letter to Hess in the name of the "action committee" without consulting his colleagues—earning him the immediate censure of Wismann. Angered by the over-hasty publication of the letter in the Börsenblatt of 21 April, which also carried the decree on the establishment of the PPK and the initial provisions for its implementation, Hess refused to enter into any further discussion of Oldenbourg's suggested amendments. In addition, Oldenbourg received a strongly worded message "By registered mail!" from Wilhelm Baur, the protégé of Eher's Max Amann and director of the Eher books division in Berlin. Baur described Oldenbourg's behavior as "consciously oppositional

---

[45] On this and the following, see StAL BV/F 6884 Friedrich Oldenbourg Verlag.

to our National Socialist central Party publisher," and threatened to propose at the imminent General Meeting of the Börsenverein in Leipzig that "the new statutes, which provide for you to remain the leader or head of the Börsenverein for a further three years, be rejected. We strongly object to the Börsenverein being headed by a man who specifically defies us. In the National Socialist state, the Börsenverein should be headed by a real National Socialist, not a Dr. Friedrich Oldenbourg."

It proved possible to avert the dismissal of the contentious head of the association thanks to interventions from Hans-Friedrich Blunck in his capacity as RSK president, RSK vice-president Wismann, and the publisher Karl Baur. But when Oldenbourg also set his face against plans initiated by Wismann and Blunck for the state promotion of German book exports, in late May 1934 he lost his office after all. As his successor, Kurt Vowinckel was proposed as someone the state literary bureaucracy considered easier to manage, with the aims of breaking German booksellers' resistance to the Chamber's export plans, committing the Börsenverein to the Nazi line, and clearing the path for a thorough restructuring of the book trade's professional representation.

However, Vowinckel, a rather insignificant publisher of geopolitical works, remained an interim figure. On 21 September 1934, at a meeting of the Börsenverein board in its Berlin offices, a fanatical Nazi was elected to head the association: the 29-year-old Wilhelm Baur. The enthronement of Baur by the board had been settled by Herbert Hoffmann and Ernst Reinhardt with Wismann and Blunck in advance of the meeting. In fact, that agreement was little more than a formality, for Baur told the board at the meeting in no uncertain terms "that I do not ask for your vote, but that we [i.e. Eher Publishing] have already requested the post on repeated occasions."[46] The Extraordinary General Meeting of the Börsenverein in Leipzig on 11 November 1934, where Baur's presidency was confirmed, marks the end point of the transition from initial accommodation to full "alignment." Even so, the new head of the Börsenverein still felt obliged to dispel the worries of the German booksellers and publishers that, "as the representative of the National Socialist Party

---

46 *Bbl.* no. 224, 25 September 1934, 835.

publisher," he might "not pursue the interests of the book trade as a whole."[47] There was, he stated, no intention "to establish a state publishing company along Russian lines." Rather, Eher would continue to take an interest "in competing as a German publisher alongside the other publishers with the best of German literature." Eher must, though, reserve the right "to publish Party works alone. And no one will be able to contest that right."

It was not legal questions but issues of power that determined the ensuing events. To mark New Year 1934, Hitler thanked his loyal comrade Max Amann for having, through his expansion of the central Party publisher, created the conditions for the "implementation of a literary propaganda that attained critical importance not only in the period of our Movement's attack, but also today, now that we have gained victory."[48] Indeed, Amann had succeeded in building the Franz Eher publishing company, acquired by the NSDAP in Munich in 1920, from very modest beginnings into one of the German Reich's most politically and economically important enterprises. In 1932 the publisher's total production ran to almost 14.8 million copies, with profits of around 4 million RM.[49] Its greatest successes were the *Völkischer Beobachter* (a daily paper with regional editions for Munich, Bavaria, southern Germany, and Berlin), *Der Angriff* (the mouthpiece of Berlin's *Gauleiter* Joseph Goebbels), Adolf Hitler's *Mein Kampf* (with 287,000 copies printed by 1933), and Alfred Rosenberg's *Mythus des zwanzigsten Jahrhunderts* (published by Hoheneichen, which was acquired by Eher in 1928). These were flanked by numerous other high-circulation newspapers and period-icals, political pamphlets, and "belletristic" books by means of which Eher promoted the objectives of the NSDAP.[50]

Hitler's decree on the competences of the "Reich Leader [*Reichsleiter*] for the NSDAP Press," issued on 19 January 1934, gave Amann discretionary control over all the Party's periodical publications.[51] Amann had the right to "pass general instructions

---

[47] *Bbl.* no. 265, 13 November 1934, 990.
[48] Hitler to Amann, 30 December 1933 (copy), BArch NS 11/9.
[49] Hoser, "Franz Eher Nachf. Verlag (Zentralverlag der NSDAP)."
[50] For further detail, see Tavernaro, *Der Verlag Hitlers und der NSDAP*, 31–45.
[51] *Verordnungsblatt der Reichsleitung der NSDAP* 2, no. 64, 31 January 1934, 140. BArch NSD 13/1.

regarding the whole publishing industry to the whole of the press published by Party comrades," as well as decision-making powers "on all publishing questions of fundamental significance beyond the individual publisher concerned." In addition, Amann was to have access at any time "to all Party publishers and their entire commercial organization and management, and the right and authority to exert any influence." All publishers and publishing directors of official Party printed materials were answerable to him. A publishing director could now only be appointed "with the agreement" of Amann, and an application to dismiss a publishing director was "to be granted, if relevant, in the form of an immediate suspension." Going beyond the Nazi press, Amann could also intervene in the remaining press organs of civil society. On 24 April 1935, in his function as president of the Reich Press Chamber, he issued three decrees that inaugurated "a wave of closures, consolidations, and distress sales of large and small [newspaper] publishing houses."[52]

On the book market, too, by 1945 Amann had constructed a monopoly unprecedented in German publishing history. In 1934 Ullstein passed into Eher's hands at a ludicrously low price. Ullstein was the Weimar Republic's most important and economically successful publishing concern, holding a network of daily papers and periodicals, Ullstein books, Propyläen, and the maps publisher BZ-Karten-Verlag, as well as one of Germany's biggest printing plants.[53] In 1933/34 the corporation's value was approximately 50–60 million RM.[54] Yet the Jewish owners were offered only 12 million RM, 25 percent of which was then deducted as capital export tax—having failed to eliminate the publisher through political pressure, in March 1934 Goebbels and Amann had agreed instead to turn the lucrative media concern to good use for the Nazi state. Max Winkler was charged with making the purchase. This versatile manager, the sole shareholder of the holding company Cautio Treuhand GmbH, had previously acted as trustee for the Reich Ministry of Finance and the General Audit Office and as Alfred Hugenberg's financial advisor.

---

[52] Hale, *The Captive Press*, 148–63, here 151.
[53] See the overview of the publications and companies belonging to the Deutscher Verlag (previously Ullstein Verlag) as at 1938, StAL BV/F 9426 Ullstein AG.
[54] Hale, *The Captive Press*, 133. On the following points, see ibid. 131–7.

Walther Funk had made him known to Nazi Party and government circles. Following the purchase agreement signed by Winkler on 30 June 1934, the Ullstein shares were deposited with the Deutsche Bank under the name of Cautio Treuhand GmbH. Eher Publishing then used a loan from the Bank der Deutschen Arbeit to buy the equity stake from Cautio. Amann had managed to persuade Hitler beforehand that Ullstein must not be taken over by the Propaganda Ministry, but must remain in existence as a commercial company in the hands of the Party. There was no outward sign of the change in proprietorship: the name Ullstein initially remained in place, and Ferdinand Bausback was still head of the supervisory board, Max Wiessner the publishing director. Only in the course of 1937 was the company's name changed to "Deutscher Verlag."[55] In 1938, the company's incorporated (*Aktiengesellschaft*) status was altered to a limited commercial partnership (*Kommanditgesellschaft*) with the two partners, Winkler and Bausback, bearing personal liability.[56] In 1940 Wilhelm Baur joined the seven-seat board of directors.[57]

Ullstein, with its roughly 8,000 employees and a turnover many times than that of Eher,[58] was only the beginning of a spectacular series of acquisitions for the Party publishing house. The process was advanced firstly by Rolf Rienhardt, who played a crucial role in the trust and was embedded in Amann's *Reichsleiter* office as the staff manager and in the Reich Press Chamber as the vice-president of the German newspaper publishers' association. Secondly, Wilhelm Baur—who had access to all important internal information as head of the Börsenverein, head of the Book Trade Group in the RSK, and RSK vice-president—was also in a position to nudge the development of the German book trade into line with the interests of the Eher concern. When Rienhardt was ousted in November 1943, Baur took on his responsibilities as well. Eher had its headquarters

---

[55] *Verlagsveränderungen im deutschen Buchhandel 1937–1943*, 26.

[56] Deutscher Verlag to Börsenverein, January 1938, informing it of the change, StAL BV/F 9426.

[57] Zentralverlag der NSDAP [Eher] books department to Börsenverein directories editor, 7 October 1940, ibid.

[58] Questionnaire for the RSK, 15 March 1937, StAL BV/F 9426. At this time, Ullstein AG had sixty-five branches in Berlin and eight outside Berlin, as well as a dispatch center in Leipzig. On turnover, see Hale, *The Captive Press*, 136.

in Munich with a publishing company (headed by Joseph Pickl) and bookstore (headed by Josef Berg), a books division established in Berlin in January 1933 (headed by Wilhelm Baur), and a Vienna branch that opened in 1938 (headed by Heinrich Korth). During World War II it opened branch offices in further locations, including Brünn (Brno), Graz, Klagenfurt, Linz, and Znaim (Znojmo).[59] In addition to this, an official Party document of April 1943 lists thirty-seven publishers that now belonged "to the domain of the *Reichsleiter* for the NSDAP Press."[60] The list includes not only numerous Nazi *Gau* publishing companies, but also respected names such as Deutsche Verlags-Anstalt, Frankfurter Societätsdruckerei, Knorr & Hirth, Albert Langen-Georg Müller Verlag, and Rowohlt Verlag. In early September 1944, finally, came the purchase of Hugenberg's publisher August Scherl GmbH.[61] In contrast to the case of Ullstein's "Aryanization," the shrewd and powerful businessman Hugenberg had Amann pay him 64,106,500 RM—the real value of his newspaper, magazine, and book publishing company.

In fact, by 1944 Amann's trust probably held around 150 companies in the *Altreich*, Austria, and the occupied areas, with around 35,000 employees.[62] It was made up mainly of four large conglomerates: the two subsidiaries Standarte Verlags- und Druckerei GmbH, which produced and distributed the *Gau* press, and Herold Verlagsanstalt GmbH, an umbrella company for a range of publishers, printers, book wholesalers, and retail booksellers; Europa Verlags GmbH, whose companies Eher used to expand across the occupied countries of Europe; and eight separate companies that reported directly to the parent concern. As early as 1939, Eher had become the largest commercial enterprise in the German Reich.[63] Its annual turnover was higher even than that of the chemicals conglomerate I. G. Farben, rising from around 98.9 million RM in 1940 to an estimated 110 million RM in 1944.

---

[59] Dr. Hess to Wilhelm Baur, 5 October 1942, StAL BV/2309.
[60] The list is attached to a letter, signed by Wilhelm Baur, from the Zentralverlag der NSDAP to Rosenberg, 9 April 1943, BArch NS 8/213 fol. 255–255/verso.
[61] See Hale, *The Captive Press*, 308–12.
[62] Ibid. 15–16. On the following points, see also Tavernaro, *Der Verlag Hitlers und der NSDAP*, 63–92.
[63] Hale, *The Captive Press*, 266.

The profits were immense: speaking after 1945, Amann himself put them at around 500 million RM. It was part and parcel of the corruption of Nazi rule that from 1940 to 1945 the Party publisher paid neither corporation tax, turnover tax, property tax, nor trade tax, and neither did it pay the levy on German business's profit that was introduced to fund the war. The administration of the central Party publisher, overlapping almost completely with that of the *Reichsleiter* for the NSDAP Press, employed around 200 people. In contrast, since 1933 the editorial office had had just one member, Karl Schworm. Only in April 1943 was a central editorial office established, its management entrusted to Bernhard Payr from the literature section of Rosenberg's office.

The German Labor Front (Deutsche Arbeitsfront, DAF), headed by Robert Ley, grew to be the biggest mass organization of the Nazi state, even larger than the NSDAP. In 1942 it had almost 25 million members, and a further 10.7 million working people (including those in the areas covered by the RSK) were affiliated through corporate membership of their occupational organizations.[64] When the entire assets of the free trade unions were confiscated on 2 May 1933, the DAF gained possession of a considerable number of publishers, book distribution outlets, and printers. From July 1933 to August 1935, Horst Stobbe headed the Labor Front's publishing house Verlag der DAF, "on behalf of the Party."[65] The owner of the well-regarded Munich bookstore "Bücherstube am Siegestor," Stobbe had only joined the NSDAP on 1 May 1933, but he had excellent political contacts, being Ley's brother-in-law and the employer of Hess's later wife.[66] The DAF publishing company absorbed the trade-union house, Verlagsgesellschaft des Allgemeinen Deutschen Gewerkschaftsbundes, and Sieben-Stäbe-Verlag, the house that had belonged to the federation of salaried employees' unions; it was

---

[64] For details, see Neumann, *Behemoth*, 413–19; Hachtmann, *Das Wirtschaftsimperium*, 47–92.

[65] Stobbe's curriculum vitae, 14 October 1942, BArch BDC/RSK/Stobbe H.

[66] Information on these personal links in *Deutschland-Berichte der Sozialdemokratischen Partei Deutschlands (Sopade)* 1 (1934), here "Aus der Arbeitsfront," August/September 1934, 451.

also responsible for the print products of the sixteen DAF sectoral divisions formed in late November 1933.[67]

In 1933, *Arbeitertum* ("Labor"), the agitational paper of the National Socialist Workplace Cell Organization, became the official journal for all DAF members, thus boosting its total annual circulation from 44,614,891 in 1935 to 88,099,867 in 1938.[68] In all, Verlag der DAF published around 110 newspapers and periodicals, with an overall annual circulation calculated at more than one quarter of a billion. As regards sales and distribution and the acquisition of subscriptions, this highly lucrative market was handled by professional specialists such as Deutsche Verlags-Expedition of Stuttgart and Berlin, one of whose owners from 1937 was the later publisher Georg von Holtzbrinck.[69] Verlag der DAF also produced nonfiction and thematic almanacs, the almanac *Kalender der Deutschen Arbeit*, the daily calendars *Deutscher Werkkalender* and *Kraft-durch-Freude-Kalender*, and an extensive list of culture-related books. With the gigantic expansion of its production, Verlag der DAF's workforce rose from sixteen in 1933 to 876 in 1938.

The DAF operated the book club Büchergilde Gutenberg, founded in 1924 by the educational association of book printers, Bildungsverband deutscher Buchdrucker, as a section of the Berlin publisher Buchmeister. After the arrest of the Büchergilde's director Bruno Dressler in May 1933, Ernst Heinsdorf and the SA *Sturmführer* Otto Jambrowski took on the management until January 1936.[70] Club membership grew from 25,000 in 1933 to around 330,000 in March 1939.[71] In Austria, too, between 1933 and 1938 the Büchergilde gained around 30,000 new members through a DAF front company

---

[67] On this and the following, see the report of the BRB's Berlin branch office for the Leipzig office, 21 May 1935, BArch BDC/RK/fiche Z 0026 fol. 2172–4, with the internal preliminary report of 23 March, ibid. fol. 2170; *Die wirtschaftlichen Unternehmungen der DAF*, 99–137; Lokatis, "Hanseatische Verlagsanstalt," 143–4; Hachtmann, *Das Wirtschaftsimperium*, 266–98.

[68] On this and the following, *Die wirtschaftlichen Unternehmungen der DAF*, 101–2.

[69] See Garke-Rothbart, *Georg von Holtzbrinck*, 52–74.

[70] Report on Büchergilde Gutenberg by the head of the book club section of the RSK Book Trade Group, 24 June 1938, BArch BDC/RSK/Heffe, E. See also Hachtmann, *Das Wirtschaftsimperium*, 298–304.

[71] On this and the following, see *Die wirtschaftlichen Unternehmungen der DAF*, 104–5, 115–37.

in Vienna, Bücherstube Stadttheater GmbH. The number of books sold rose from 200,000 in 1934 to more than 1 million in 1938, so that the share capital could be increased from 5,000 RM (1933) to 100,000 RM (1938).

When the sales clerks' association Deutscher Handlungsgehilfen-Verband was dissolved, its three fiction-oriented publishers also passed into the hands of the DAF. The first of these—the Munich house Albert Langen Buchverlag, founded in 1893 and merged with Georg Müller Verlag in 1932, along with the Theaterverlag Albert Langen/Georg Müller in Berlin—had been publishing the authors now praised as "state poets" since the Weimar period.[72] From 1933, Langen-Müller followed the example of Insel's successful Insel-Bücherei book series to issue Die Kleine Bücherei, a low-cost series whose 122 volumes had sold more than 2.5 million copies by 1939. The second house, Eduard Avenarius Verlag of Leipzig, was founded in 1855 and taken over by Albert Langen in 1928; since 1923 it had been publishing the literary monthly *Die Neue Literatur* edited by Will Vesper, and since 1925 the annual catalogue *Der Buchberater*, a vehicle for polemical attacks on the literature of the Weimar Republic and praise for *völkisch* and nationalist works. Third was Hanseatische Verlagsanstalt (HAVA) of Hamburg, formed by the fusion of two publishing and printing companies in 1917. Its share capital amounted to 4 million RM in 1933. HAVA turnover increased from 3.7 million RM in 1933 to 8.6 million RM in 1937. In 1938 the company employed a total of 751 people. Affiliated to HAVA was Bücherborn Deutsches Bücherhaus GmbH in Hamburg, which employed a further 166 people in door-to-door distribution and the book club Deutsche Hausbücherei. This club, established in 1916, had sales outlets in Hamburg (the bookstore Heinrich Bandholdt) and across the whole of the Reich, and in 1938 was one of the three largest book clubs in Germany, with almost 150,000 members.

DAF-owned printers were August Pries GmbH in Leipzig, a company steeped in tradition and specialized in printing books, art, and non-European scripts; Buchdruckwerkstätte GmbH in Berlin, which carried out printing work for Party offices and administrative bodies; Bochumer Druckerei GmbH; and Geesthachter Druckerei-GmbH

---

[72] See the list of prizes and awards for Langen-Müller authors, ibid. 131–4.

for the production of Hanseatische Verlagsanstalt.[73] However, the enterprises absorbed, purchased, or—as in the case of the Cologne publisher Aufbau in 1936—newly established by the DAF made up a motley collection that was virtually impossible to marshal in terms either of content or of commercial organization. The driving force behind a comprehensive restructuring was Eberhard Heffe, who by his own account was engaged by Ley in August 1935 as the "representative for the entire publishing business of the DAF," though in fact he initially only headed Verlag der DAF and Buchmeister (with its book club Büchergilde Gutenberg) in Berlin.[74] Heffe, born in Berlin in 1899 and active in the paramilitary Freikorps after World War I, had worked in publishing since 1924: first with the August Scherl and Julius Springer houses, and from 1930 as managing director of what he described as an "important agricultural publisher in Berlin." But within the DAF's publishing empire, Heffe first had to make his mark against the well-established publishing bosses Pezold and Benno Ziegler.

To this end, on 23 November 1936 he presented a memorandum detailing the need to "put matters in the DAF publishing companies and printers in order."[75] The independence of the publishing directors and editorial departments should, he argued, be eliminated—primarily for the sake of a unified political orientation, but also because the centrally managed distribution of tasks in production and distribution could be expected to boost profits. Heffe recommended setting up a "parent" or holding company for all the DAF's publishing and printing enterprises, a "central editorial department," and a "central task distribution office." The editorial department was to have the function of a censorship office, operating, Heffe explained, such that "only works and writings compatible with a National Socialist viewpoint may be published, as opposed to continuing to follow the old liberalistic path." "Particular attention" was to be paid to the

---

[73] *Die wirtschaftlichen Unternehmungen der DAF*, 109–11, 124.
[74] On this and the following, see Heffe's curriculum vitae of 8 August 1938, BArch BDC/RSK/Heffe, E., stating that Heffe was an NSDAP member from 1921–23, then rejoined in 1930.
[75] A transcript of the memorandum is held in DLA NL Hans Grimm/ Korrespondenz mit dem Langen-Müller Verlag, 1 June 1937 – 15 August 1938, folder II 1938. See also Hachtmann, *Das Wirtschaftsimperium*, 297–321.

"particular measures of the government," and production "to be angled accordingly."

Whereas Ziegler managed to resist this centralization and was able to maintain the independence of Hanseatische Verlagsanstalt, Pezold of Langen-Müller fell victim to scheming. He had already made enemies in the DAF concern early in 1934: he was paying for reviews of Langen-Müller books to be put out in the press, and his company was presenting itself to the public as the prime publisher of "German poets," "constantly poaching" other publishers' authors, and allegedly "still circulating books by Jews or half Jews."[76] In October 1936 the SS journal *Das Schwarze Korps* launched a sharp attack on an essay by Rudolf Thiel on the 150th anniversary of Frederick the Great's death, published in Langen-Müller's monthly *Das Innere Reich*.[77]

Although Hess's advocacy made it possible to reverse the Propaganda Ministry ban on *Das Innere Reich* that was imposed on 11 October, the DAF now set about ridding itself of the unacceptably self-willed Pezold. Its first port of call was the RSK, which on 25 January 1937 sent three auditors to Langen-Müller to investigate an allegation of tax evasion, at the behest of Wilhelm Baur.[78] Baur asked the auditors, from Cura Revisions- und Treuhand GmbH, to "apprehend the entire business of the Albert Langen/Georg Müller house and in particular to discover what business tactics are applied in dealing with the publisher's authors and the book trade." The audit was required to "produce precise documentation, in the process of which you will please try to gain access to any audit reports that may have been carried out in the past by other parties." In June 1937, during two meetings at the Chamber, Baur was able to confront Pezold with an

---

[76] These were the complaints of the deputy leader of the German salaried workers in the DAF, August Haid, in a letter to Pezold on 29 March 1934, copy in DLA NL Will Vesper.

[77] "Und das nennt sich das 'Innere Reich'!" *Das Schwarze Korps* 2, no. 41, 8 October 1936, 17. In the SD guide to publishing, March 1937, mention is made of the DAF's attempts to guide its publishing companies "into an irreproachably National Socialist fairway" (*Leitheft Verlagswesen*, BArch R 58/1107, fol. 33); in the SD guide to literature "the *Das Innere Reich* circle" is explicitly mentioned as an object of SD "monitoring of literature" (*Leitheft Schrifttumswesen und Schrifttumspolitik*, BArch R 58/1106, fol. 5).

[78] DLA NL Hans Grimm/ Korrespondenz mit dem Langen-Müller Verlag, 15 February 1935–30 May 1937, folder II. A copy of the auditing request submitted on 15 January 1937 ibid.

extensive list of alleged commercial and political misdemeanors.[79] This tactic of attrition having failed to achieve the desired result, the next step was to install a Nazi hardliner, Walter Fischer, as Pezold's manager. Pezold's employment contract, signed in 1930 for a period of ten years, guaranteed him "complete independence" in the management of the publishing house, and he was not minded to accept a gradual disempowerment of this kind. In December 1937 he not only brought in a member of the Deputy Führer's staff, Ernst Schulte Strathaus, but also mobilized his authors—from Alverdes, Britting, Grimm, Hohlbaum, Kolbenheyer, and Mechow to Schäfer, Strauss, Vesper, Weinheber, and Zillich. They expressed their disapproval in a telegram to the Reichskulturkammer president on 4 January 1938.[80]

Unimpressed by this "troupe of rebels," Heffe informed Pezold on 16 January 1938 that the Langen-Müller supervisory board had recalled him from his role as managing director and that he was dismissed "summarily with immediate effect."[81] As a Langen-Müller author, the RSK's president Hanns Johst had a conflict of interest; he delegated the task of dismissing Pezold to Baur, who brought forward the serious accusation that Pezold did not "have the reliability and aptitude needed to direct a publisher in line with National Socialist requirements."[82] At a meeting in Berlin on 23 February 1938, in Baur's presence, Ley particularly rebuked Pezold for having published the "clerical" poems of Paul Ernst and Josef Weinheber.[83]

---

[79] For the thirty-two-page record of these interviews of 21 and 30 June 1937, see BArch BDC/RK/fiche I 0315, fol. 2726–90.

[80] Schulte Strathaus to RSK president, 23 December 1937, ibid. fol. 2592; file note by Wilhelm Baur on 10 January 1938 on a meeting with Heffe at Kolbenheyer's home in Solln on 6 January, ibid. fol. 2616–26; Johst to Goebbels, 15 January 1938, ibid. fol. 2604–8. Kolbenheyer had helped Pezold obtain the position of managing the Albert Langen Verlag in 1930.

[81] Copy of the letter ibid. fol. 2676. This description of the protesting authors as a "rebellierende Gesellschaft" was given by Wilhelm Baur in his conversation with Kolbenheyer on 6 January 1938; ibid. fol. 2626 (p. 6).

[82] Thus Schulte Strathaus, writing on 23 December 1937 to ask the RSK president to send documentary evidence, BArch BDC/RK/fiche I 0315, fol. 2592. On the transfer of the case to Wilhelm Baur, see Johst to Goebbels, 15 January 1938, ibid. fol. 2604.

[83] See Pezold's twenty-four-page record of the second discussion with Ley, in the presence of Stabsleiter Heinrich Simon and Wilhelm Baur, in Munich on 23 February 1938, DLA NL Hans Grimm/ Korrespondenz mit dem Langen-Müller Verlag, 1 June 1937 – 15 August 1938, folder III.

According to Pezold's report of the meeting, Ley—anyway prone to choleric rages—was particularly incensed by the failure of a DAF-led publisher to mirror the program of educating the new Nazi elite "in the spirit of National Socialism."[84]

But these philosophical differences, which resulted from deeply divergent views of literature, were only the pretext for Pezold's downfall, which could ultimately be averted neither by his appeals to Hess and Goebbels nor by the untiring efforts of Grimm.[85] The decisive factor was economic interest: Pezold stood in the way of Heffe's plans to build up an "enormous, capitalist, tax-relieved publishing concern," as Grimm put it in a letter to the publisher Hugo Bruckmann,[86] but Wilhelm Baur too had an axe to grind. Baur, who had consistently pushed for Pezold's dismissal in his capacity as co-director of the DAF publishing companies and as vice-president of the RSK,[87] was hoping to get his Eher books division access to the profitable Langen-Müller house and its prestigious authors. Finally, Hanns Johst envied his colleagues Grimm and Kolbenheyer their "star contracts" with Pezold, and found Langen-Müller's marketing of his own works less than satisfactory.[88]

The DAF's publishing companies reached an enormous circle of readers and buyers. DAF membership journals, bulletins, and

---

[84] Report by Pezold as above, 16. See also Pezold to Grimm, 23 February 1938, ibid.

[85] See Grimm's seven-page report on the Langen-Müller house, "Bericht über den Langen-Müller Verlag. Sein Aufbau. Seine Leistung. Seine Gefährdung durch die fristlose Entlassung des bisherigen Verlagsleiters Gustav Pezold" [1938], and Schulte Strathaus to Grimm, 25 March 1938, DLA NL Hans Grimm/ Korrespondenz mit dem Langen-Müller Verlag, 1 June 1937 – 15 August 1938, folder II.

[86] Grimm to Bruckmann, 20 February 1937, DLA NL Hans Grimm/Korrespondenz mit Regierungsstellen, NS-Parteistellen und Einzelpersönlichkeiten der NSDAP, folder II.

[87] Pezold to Grimm, 25 January 1937, DLA NL Hans Grimm/ Korrespondenz mit dem Langen-Müller Verlag, 15 February 1935 – 30 May 1937, folder II; Pezold to Grimm, 3 February 1938, ibid. The meeting between Pezold and Ley on 23 February 1938 was also crucially influenced by Wilhelm Baur's various accusations. See Pezold's report of the second meeting with Ley, as note 83.

[88] See Kolbenheyer's observation in conversation with Baur and Heffe on 6 January 1938 "that all these attacks on the Langen/Müller house or on Mr. Pezold come from one corner, namely the Johst corner," file note of 10 January, BArch BDC/RK/fiche I 0315, fol. 2624 (p. 5). Johst used the phrase "Starverträge" regarding Grimm and Kolbenheyer to attack Pezold in a letter to Goebbels of 15 January 1938, ibid. fol. 2606. On Johst's dissatisfaction with Langen-Müller, see Johst to Korfiz Holm, 30 November 1937, ibid. fol. 2954.

training materials alone were circulated in their millions. The "leisure literature department" (Lektorat für Freizeitliteratur), headed by Fritz Irwahn since 1935, enabled Hanseatische Verlagsanstalt to build up a "National Socialist mass book market" that served both the multifarious leisure-related activities of the NSDAP with its various divisions and the collective tourism organized by the DAF organization Kraft durch Freude, "Strength Through Joy."[89] The two book clubs Deutsche Hausbücherei and Büchergilde Gutenberg provided a further stable group of purchasers. Club representatives promoted membership of the Büchergilde and its low-priced books in workplaces, while Heffe harnessed the local NSDAP leaderships to propagate the Büchergilde's offerings within the Party.[90] In the factory libraries, which the adult education organization Deutsches Volksbildungswerk had been working to expand since 1936, books published by DAF companies were given special prominence.[91] The DAF also dominated the field of professional journals and specialized books of all kinds, which attracted increased literary promotion after the introduction of the Four-Year Plan. These channels brought DAF publishing millions of reichsmarks in turnover and profit on the German book market. In 1939 its share capital was increased from 800,000 to 2 million RM, in 1940 to 5 million RM, and in 1941 to 10 million RM.[92] During the war, Verlag der DAF planned to create branches in Amsterdam, Brussels, Budapest, Bucharest, Copenhagen, Oslo, Paris, Prague, Bratislava, Rome, and Riga with the aim of opening up the foreign market for its book production and sales.[93] The frontline book trade, subsidized by state authorities

---

[89] For details, see Lokatis, "Hanseatische Verlagsanstalt," 75–89; *Die wirtschaftlichen Unternehmungen der DAF*, 116–22.

[90] Heffe to *Gauleiter* Robert Wagner in Karlsruhe, 16 June 1937, and to the NSDAP director of training in the Baden *Gau*, Wilhelm Hartlieb, 8 July 1937, GLA Karlsruhe 465 d/143.

[91] W. Kindt, "Die Bucharbeit der 'NS.-Gemeinschaft Kraft durch Freude,'" *Bbl.* no. 275, 26 November 1938, 924–5. Alongside specialized and Party literature, the factory libraries were supposed to offer entertainment literature. The "book and library" section of the Deutsches Volksbildungswerk therefore regularly published reviews of the most important new fiction. See Kalbhenn, "Werkbibliotheken im Dritten Reich."

[92] StAL BV/F 9598.

[93] Heffe to Wilhelm Baur, 8 December 1941, BArch BDC/RSK/Heffe, E. See also the overview of the subsidiaries of DAF GmbH, 23 March 1943, StAL BV/9598; Hachtmann, *Das Wirtschaftsimperium*, 322–56.

and the army, constituted a new and remunerative mass market in which the DAF participated both as a publisher and, thanks to its dominant role in the office responsible for sales, the Zentrale der Frontbuchhandlungen, as a distributor.

It is, however, doubtful whether Ley—known for his lack of organizational talent—ever fully grasped the structure of his own highly ramified publishing empire. As early as 1938, Goebbels complained that Ley was having "everything bought for the DAF that could be bought."[94] In 1942 the DAF owned more than twenty publishing houses, seven printers, two book clubs, and a paper factory.[95] It was almost inevitable that the huge profits circulating in this impenetrable web of companies would lead to financial mismanagement.[96] On 1 June 1943, the man who had hitherto pulled the strings in the supervisory boards of all the DAF publishing companies disappeared from the scene: Heffe was fired following accusations of corruption.[97] He was succeeded by the trained bookseller Ernst Tretow (for Verlag der DAF) and the business administrator Heinz Brüggen (for the Buchmeister house)—two longstanding, but ultimately colorless authorized signatories of the DAF publishing companies. It was under their reign that the DAF withdrew from the belletristic publishers, selling the Wiener Verlagsgesellschaft, founded in 1938; the Adam Kraft Verlag of Karlsbad (Karlovy Vary), integrated into the DAF that same year and specializing in Sudeten German literature; and Langen-Müller. Alfred Salat, of Knorr & Hirth, took over the management of Langen-Müller, which now belonged to Eher.[98] Hanseatische Verlagsanstalt was divided up: its printing operations

---

[94] Goebbels, *Tagebücher*, Part I, vol. 5, 131 (2 February 1938).

[95] Lokatis, "Hanseatische Verlagsanstalt," 143.

[96] As Pezold learned from auditor general Ried of the Reich treasury of the NSDAP, the head of the DAF treasury, Paul A. Brinckmann, who was also the president of Langen-Müller's supervisory board, had to resign in April 1938 due to financial irregularities. See Pezold's notes on a series of discussions in Berlin from 27–29 April 1938, here p. 3, DLA NL Hans Grimm/ Korrespondenz mit dem Langen-Müller Verlag, 1 June 1937–15 August 1938, folder III.

[97] StAL BV/F 9598. On Heffe's supervisory board memberships, see *Die wirtschaftlichen Unternehmungen der DAF*, 101–30.

[98] Salat to Grimm, 23 February 1943, DLA NL Hans Grimm/ Korrespondenz mit dem Langen-Müller Verlag 1941–3, folder III. On the sale of Langen-Müller and Hanseatische Verlagsanstalt, see also Hachtmann, *Das Wirtschaftsimperium*, 356–68.

remained with the DAF, while its book production was sold to its managing director Benno Ziegler and the Deutsche Hausbücherei book club went to Eher.[99] The Büchergilde Gutenberg club was closed down in 1944 in agreement with the Propaganda Ministry. With that, the last remaining large monopoly on the German book market was Amann's trust.

The Restructuring of Public and Research Libraries

In an essay entitled "Authority and Public Instruction," published in the librarianship journal *Bücherei und Bildungspflege* at the beginning of 1933, Johannes Beer noted that the current system of government was "not supported by a majority, in fact not even by a significant minority, of the people."[100] For Beer, deputy director of the municipal public libraries in Frankfurt am Main, this justified his demand: "We must want the state that has true authority; as educators we must emphasize this supreme objective, and then we will have our educational goal." What was previously "free" work in adult education must, Beer continued, be replaced with a "committed" version, its objective being to "help to bring about this authoritarian state which we have not yet achieved."

In April 1933, such calls became the official policy of the public librarians' association Verband Deutscher Volksbibliothekare (VDV). The VDV, formed in 1922, now issued a public declaration parting ways with the "theories of the autonomy of pedagogy and of positive neutrality, formerly the public library's protections from the encroachments of a party rule that would switch within the Reich and in the provinces, from province to province and from town to town."[101]

---

[99] "Hanseatische Verlagsanstalt in drei Teilen," *Deutsche Allgemeine Zeitung*, 2 July 1943, StAL BV/F 3591.

[100] J. Beer, "Autorität und Volksbildung," *Bücherei und Bildungspflege* 13 (1933), 19–27 (also the following quotations). Beer's views were shared by many of his professional colleagues, as is shown by Boese, *Das Öffentliche Bibliothekswesen*, 67–70, and Stieg, *Public Libraries in Nazi Germany*, 32–55.

[101] "Erklärung und Aufruf des Verbandes Deutscher Volksbibliothekare," *Bücherei und Bildungspflege* 13 (1933), 97–8 (also the following quotations).

Today it was the association's duty "to identify a core, made up of that which has grown from the deepest sources of German blood and spirit, and starting from there to advance to the *Volk* community in the new German state."

The VDV first aimed to enhance its cooperation with the Kampfbund für deutsche Kultur.[102] At this time the Kampfbund was cultivating close relations with both the Prussian education and culture ministry and the Thuringian Ministry of Public Instruction, two bodies that were pioneering the process of alignment in the public library system.[103] In addition, a committee appointed by Berlin's mayor in April 1933 to "re-order" all the city's municipal and public libraries included a member of the Kampfbund and NSDAP: Max Wieser, the director of the Spandau municipal library.[104] The committee also had two further Party members, Wolfgang Herrmann and Hans Engelhardt from the municipal library of Köpenick, Berlin. Without losing sight of its links with the Kampfbund, in summer 1933 the VDV's managing board began to negotiate on incorporation into the DAF.[105] Such a move would not only have furthered the VDV leadership's aspirations to gather the whole profession together under one roof, but also suited the plans developing within the DAF for a central association of salaried employees that would cover all the different professional sectors. But at the same time, the Propaganda Ministry was also deliberating on how to take over and instrumentalize the public libraries. A lengthy Ministry memorandum in June 1933 described the public libraries—regionally diversified and accessed by all classes of society—as a "highly valuable, indeed ideal means to influence and reshape the thinking and attitudes of

---

[102] "Zum Umbau des deutschen Volksbüchereiwesens," *Bücherei und Bildungspflege* 13 (1933), 169–70.

[103] On 20 May 1933, the provincial advisory office for popular libraries, attached to the Thuringian Ministry of Public Instruction, informed the local Kampfbund leadership in Erfurt that Thuringia's library directors were to be instructed to "promote the endeavors of the 'Kampfbund' in every way." In practice this was to be implemented "by work in the local groups and especially by the libraries themselves acting as locations for new members to sign up for the 'Kampfbund' and convincing readers of its merits." HStA Weimar Thüring. Min. f. Volksbildung/C 698 fol. 112.

[104] "Säuberung der Berliner Stadtbibliothek," *Deutsche Kultur-Wacht* 1933, no. 9, 15.

[105] "Zum Umbau des deutschen Volksbüchereiwesens," *Bücherei und Bildungspflege* 13 (1933), 169–70, here 169.

the nation as a whole."[106] In order to "carry out and accomplish the national tasks of giving spiritual roots to the revolution," however, it would be necessary for a dedicated Reich office to guide the organizational and intellectual "rebuilding" of the public libraries. All "private educational, vocational, and professional organizations" must therefore be "corporately deactivated," even in cases where "their existing leadership believes itself to be 'gleichgeschaltet' by superficially converting to the NSDAP despite, in most cases, having previously actively opposed the Party."

When the Propaganda Ministry's model of bringing together all the cultural professions in the framework of its Reich Chamber of Culture won the day, a "Notification on the Structure of the Reichsschrifttumskammer," issued on 23 December 1933, made membership of the VDV obligatory for all full-time public library employees and all part-time employees and trainees.[107] But this was not the end of the public library system's reorganization. The Chamber's far-reaching ordinances suddenly encountered resistance within the Prussian Ministry of Science, Art, and Public Instruction, which had agreed to the integration of the VDV into the RSK only reluctantly and after strenuous negotiations in October 1933.[108] Minister Bernhard Rust had already set up an "Advisory Committee for Popular Libraries" in July 1933;[109] alongside a representative of the Prussian Ministry, it included the librarians Wilhelm Schuster, Fritz Heiligenstaedt, and Wolfgang Herrmann, and, from October 1933, also Albert Meyer-Lülmann of the Assembly of German Municipalities (Deutscher Gemeindetag) and the Kampfbund member Gotthard Urban. At the end of 1933, this committee merged with the "Special Committee on Catalogues" in the newly created Prussian Provincial Office for Popular Libraries (Preussische Landesstelle für

---

[106] "Denkschrift betreffend Neubau des deutschen öffentlichen Büchereiwesens im Rahmen des die Neugestaltung des gesamten deutschen Volks- und Kulturlebens umfassenden nationalpädagogischen Programms der Reichsregierung. Dem Reichsministerium für Volksaufklärung und Propaganda überreicht durch Dr. Karl Heinl," BArch R 56 V/137 fol. 102–53.

[107] *Bbl.* no. 298, 23 December 1933, here point V, 996.

[108] Kettel, *Volksbibliothekare und Nationalsozialismus,* 66–7. Kettel cites correspondence from the VDV president Wilhelm Schuster to Karl Taupitz, 21 October 1933, and from Schuster to Walter Hofmann, 28 October 1933.

[109] *Bücherei und Bildungspflege* 13 (1933), 170.

volkstümliches Büchereiwesen).[110] As a "supervisory body" directly answerable to the Prussian Ministry of Science, Art, and Public Instruction, the Office's task was to coordinate the activities of all Prussia's local advisory offices for popular libraries, ensuring in particular that each library was aligned "with the spirit of the National Socialist state." More uniformity was also decreed for specialized journals. The announcement that the new librarians' journal *Die Bücherei* was to serve as the publication organ of the Prussian Office was in practice a notification of the enforced merger between the two former professional journals *Hefte für Büchereiwesen* and *Bücherei und Bildungspflege*.

This was the first step in a centralization and uniformity of the public library system that had long been demanded by large segments of the profession, but Rust's decree of 28 December 1933—headed "Do it today!"—should specifically be understood as a response to the Chamber's raid on the public library system some days before. Whereas the public library employees were now incorporated into the Goebbels-controlled RSK in their professional capacity, Rust managed (initially for Prussia) to secure responsibility for the content aspect of the libraries. This division, the outcome of internal power struggles, resulted in paradoxical situations and took the Nazi "Führer principle" to the point of absurdity, as can be seen in the case of Wilhelm Schuster. As head of the VDV, Schuster was now answerable to the president of the RSK, but as director of the Prussian Provincial Office for Popular Libraries he reported to the Prussian Ministry of Science, Art, and Public Instruction.[111] A conflict with the Propaganda Ministry over competencies was inevitable. It broke out in May 1934, when the Reich Ministry of Science, Education, and Public Instruction (Reich Education Ministry) was established, curbing Goebbels's claim to unified leadership in cultural policy across the Reich.

As part of its negotiations with Hitler "respecting the transfer of all matters of art" from the provinces to the Reich, planned for

[110] *Die Bücherei* 1 (1934), 11–13.
[111] See W. Schuster, "Die Neuordnung des Preußischen Büchereiwesens," *Die Bücherei* 1 (1933), 9–17.

mid-June 1934,[112] the Propaganda Ministry once again emphasized the need to take the public libraries completely into its sphere of responsibility. The public libraries were part of literature as a "means of shaping the human being," argued the Ministry, and as such no longer had "anything to do with schooling, school pedagogy, or public instruction in the old sense."[113] Rather, they were "entirely self-contained, independent factors in the great work of suffusing the *Volk* with the spirit of National Socialism." Because the support and promotion of literature had already been "uniformly gathered together" in the Propaganda Ministry, the integration of the public library system was now the only thing missing "for the whole to be rounded off into a life-shaping institution serving only the state." The Reich Education Ministry's special interest in the libraries, in contrast, arose merely from its hope that they could offer a home to "the many superfluous teachers and probationers who can no longer be absorbed by the school system." The Reich Education Ministry, in turn, was not impressed either by such subtle argumentation or by the Propaganda Ministry's insistence on the minutiae of the Chamber of Culture legislation.[114] In the end the Chamber was only permitted to look after the public librarians "in occupational matters" and from 1 October 1934 to supervise the VDV's finances,[115] while the Reich Education Ministry successfully defended its responsibility for the public library system in terms of content, and until 1945 was authorized to lay down the guiding principles for its development within the Nazi state.

In practice, the centralization of the public library system that had been called for by the public librarians meant losing not only independence regarding library holdings, but also the professional association's right to self-regulation. During the annual meeting

---

[112] Note from the Propaganda Ministry legal department, 9 June 1934, BArch R 56 V/166 fol. 1–7, here fol. 1.

[113] Thus Karl Heinl in his memorandum "Für die zuständige Eingliederung des Volksbüchereiwesens …," Appendix C to the file note from the legal department of 9 June 1934, BArch R 56 V/166 fol. 11–15. The following quotations ibid.

[114] See the statement by Wismann, director of the Propaganda Ministry's literature department, of 6 March 1935: "Stellungnahme zur Frage des Büchereiwesens im Anschluss an die Besprechung mit den Vertretern des Unterrichtsministeriums," BArch R 56 V/166 fol. 17–19.

[115] *Die Bücherei* 1 (1934), 584.

of the German public librarians (Deutscher Volksbüchereitag) held in Leipzig on 24–26 September 1938, the VDV's members (in the absence of their president Wilhelm Schuster, "called away to a military exercise") had to resolve the dissolution of their association on the basis of an RSK directive issued on 21 September.[116] The "occupational concerns" of the membership, then numbering 1,126 people, were henceforth to be handled within the RSK, as the "Library Group."

In order to assure the long-term political reliability of the public libraries by means of suitable personnel, the Law for the Restoration of the Professional Civil Service of 7 April 1933 was first used to dismiss all public library employees who were incriminated on political or "racial" grounds. The remaining librarians were "retrained," and a "new type" of public librarian cultivated. From 1938 on, when making new appointments the public library offices were required to obtain not only the proof of "Aryan" descent—if relevant also for the applicant's spouse—but also a political good-conduct certificate from the relevant NSDAP authority.[117] Since May 1935, in the selection of candidates for training as public librarians, educational qualifications had had to be accompanied by substantiation of a "vigorous connection with the *Volk* and a sense of political duty."[118] If a candidate's evaluation "gave noticeable cause for concern in this respect," that could not be compensated even by "evidence of a completed course of training or special individual knowledge." The curricula of the librarianship schools in Leipzig, Cologne, and Berlin were also remodeled in the course of the 1930s,[119] and in 1942 Stuttgart

---

116 "Deutscher Volksbüchereitag," *Die Bücherei* 5 (1938), 671–85, here 684.

117 "Geschäftsführung der Staatlichen Volksbüchereistellen in Preußen vom 15.7.1938," *Deutsche Wissenschaft, Erziehung und Volksbildung* 4 (1938), 356–7, here 356.

118 "Erlass des Reichs- und Preußischen Ministers für Wissenschaft, Erziehung und Volksbildung an den Vorsitzenden des Staatlichen Prüfungsausschusses für das Bibliothekswesen in Berlin vom 6.5.1935," *Deutsche Wissenschaft, Erziehung und Volksbildung* 1 (1935), 205–6.

119 On the curriculum reform in the Prussian schools of librarianship in Berlin and Cologne, see W. Schuster, "Der Stand des deutschen öffentlichen Büchereiwesens," *Die Bücherei* 2 (1935), 242–51, here 248; also W. Schuster, "Die Berliner Bibliotheksschule," *Die Bücherei* 5 (1938), 511–22; E. Thier, "Die Deutsche Volksbüchereischule zu Leipzig," ibid. 522–6; M. Steinhoff, "Die Westdeutsche Volksbüchereischule [Köln] 1928–1938," ibid. 526–9.

received a new training institution for public librarians. On the one hand the state intervention resulted in politicization along Nazi lines; on the other, it meant increased standardization of the different teaching methods and syllabi.[120] As one important step in the standardization process, in September 1939 responsibility for training, and for the deployment of the new generation of public librarians all across the Reich, was transferred to a single state examination office for public libraries, based within the Prussian State Library.[121]

However, most public libraries in small towns and village communities were directed not by graduates of the schools of librarianship, but by people without a formal professional training. To address this deficiency, in June 1938 the Reich Education Ministry offered the employees in question the option to sit a special supplementary examination in librarianship.[122] The first condition was that on 1 July 1938 aspiring candidates had to have "been an employee at a public library for at least four years without significant interruption and have held responsibility for carrying out independent tasks of specialist librarianship." In addition, a "statement of NSDAP membership" was required, as was a "sworn statement on whether the applicant has ever been a member of a political party, a Masonic lodge, a lodge-like organization, or the organizational substitute for a lodge."

But despite these new examinations, the training of new librarians could not keep pace with the growth in public libraries demanded and promoted by the Education Ministry. The results were recruitment worries and a staff shortage that was dramatically exacerbated by the outbreak of war.[123] The "Guidelines for the Public Libraries" of October 1937 gave directors of the State Public Libraries Offices the task not only of attending to public librarians' occupational concerns, but also of providing political training for full- and part-time heads of

---

[120] This ambivalence in the politicization process of public librarians' training is noted by Boese, *Das Öffentliche Bibliothekswesen*, 210–14.

[121] "Erlass des Reichserziehungsministeriums an das Staatliche Prüfungsamt für das Volksbüchereiwesen vom 28.9.1939," *Deutsche Wissenschaft, Erziehung und Volksbildung* 5 (1939), 525.

[122] "Prüfung für den Dienst an volkstümlichen Büchereien," *Deutsche Wissenschaft, Erziehung und Volksbildung* 4 (1938), 332. The following points ibid.

[123] E. Thier, "Lenkung des Berufsnachwuchses," *Die Bücherei* 8 (1941), 273–6; H. Dähnhardt, "Der Arbeitseinsatz der Volksbibliothekare im Jahre 1942," *Die Bücherei* 9 (1942), 121–2.

public libraries in their locality.[124] Thus, for example, the directors of village libraries were to be invited to a training course once a year. For directors of the libraries in small towns, a series of several weekend meetings was recommended, while full-time employees of libraries in larger cities were to receive their continuation training and political instruction via study groups. Like the restructuring of the qualification system, these training measures helped bring the public librarians into harmony with the requirements of the Nazi rulers.

Turning now to research librarians, the profession's association Verein Deutscher Bibliothekare (VDB) did not initially experience the Nazi takeover as a great caesura, any more than did the public librarians' organization. As the VDB's president Adolf Hilsenbeck reminded delegates in Darmstadt at its twenty-ninth General Meeting on 8 June 1933, the association had been arguing since 1920 that, "in contrast to the plague of the parties, professional bodies are a better basis for politics and life."[125] For this reason, the president continued, it had not been necessary to undertake any major adjustment, but "only to line up within the new labor front." Accordingly, the "alignment" demanded by the Reich Minister of the Interior in a memorandum of 27 April 1933 was limited to the promotion of Friedrich Smend—senior librarian at the Prussian State Library and, since 6 May, chairman of the newly formed Union of National Socialist Librarians—to be VDB vice-president under the reelected Hilsenbeck.[126] As well as Hilsenbeck, the secretary and treasurer were also confirmed in their positions.

The eleven-seat executive committee now included six NSDAP members. One of them, Joachim Kirchner, the director of the Frankfurt municipal library for modern languages and music, called

---

[124] "Richtlinien für das Volksbüchereiwesen," *Deutsche Wissenschaft, Erziehung und Volksbildung* 3 (1937), insert 1, p. 478. Schriewer, "Warum staatliche Stellen für das Volksbüchereiwesen," *Die Bücherei* 3 (1936), 13, states that seventy-eight training meetings with 3,200 participants were held in the period from 1 October 1934 to 30 September 1935 alone.
[125] Thus the report of Hilsenbeck's comments by Georg Leyh, "29. Versammlung des Vereins Deutscher Bibliothekare in Darmstadt am 8. und 9. Juni 1933," *ZfB* 50 (1933), 500–4. The following quotations ibid. On the following points, see also Labach, "Der VDB während des Nationalsozialismus"; Haase, "Die Bibliothekartage."
[126] "Bericht über die Mitgliederversammlung des VDB in Darmstadt am 8.6.1933," *ZfB* 50 (1933), 505–7.

on the assembled librarians to commit themselves to their new tasks in the National Socialist state.[127] Wearing a brown SA shirt, Kirchner first praised the "book burnings of Marxist, communist, and Jewish authors, whom we consider corrosive and contrary to our German *Volk* feeling." He stressed that it was now up to the research libraries to "advance the cultural policy goals of the Hitler Movement in an activist manner." Library users should thus be guaranteed access, "if possible with multiple copies," to "scholarly and generally instructive writings that deal with the political goals of the Movement and its leaders, the national-political education of youth, the German cultural values of the past, German history, German law, answers to philosophical and religious questions in a German spirit, homeland and *Volk* studies, racial research and genealogy, racial hygiene, and so on." Like readers, the civil servants and trainees in higher and mid-level librarian posts were also to be "fully permeated by the national idea."

The VDB was integrated into the RSK in late December 1933, but on 5 January 1934 the Prussian Ministry of Science, Art, and Public Instruction decided that "until further notice" no civil servants would be entitled to join the Chamber.[128] On 22 May 1935, the Prussian Ministry's successor, the Reich Education Ministry, informed the VDB conclusively that "for the association and for its members, with reference to § 1 of the Law on the Reich Chamber of Culture, membership of one of the chambers united in the Reich Chamber of Culture (for example the Reich Chamber of Literature) cannot be permitted."[129] The VDB thus left the Chamber on 6 June 1935, and from then on continued its work as an independent "academic specialist association" with voluntary membership.[130] The draft of the new statutes was presented at the General Meeting in Tübingen on 14 June 1935, and submitted to the "potentially relevant

[127] Kirchner, *Das Schrifttum und die wissenschaftlichen Bibliotheken*. The following quotations ibid.

[128] "Bericht über die Mitglieder-Versammlung des Vereins Deutscher Bibliothekare in Danzig am 24. Mai 1934," *ZfB* 51 (1934), 460–1.

[129] Memorandum cited in "Bericht über die Mitglieder-Versammlung des Vereins Deutscher Bibliothekare in Tübingen am 14.6.1935," *ZfB* 52 (1935), 553–5, here 554.

[130] "Bericht über die Mitglieder-Versammlung des VDB am 6.6.1936 in Dresden," *ZfB* 53 (1936), 592–6, here 593.

authorities" for approval.[131] The statutes, now amended to concur with the "Führer principle," finally came into force in October 1935.[132] Hilsenbeck resigned at the Tübingen meeting, drained by behind-the-scenes squabbles between the different factions of Nazi library policy, which had even led to vice-president Smend's exclusion from the Party. The new president was the director of the Tübingen University library, Georg Leyh, who had been pressed to take on the office by Rudolf Kummer, new spokesman for research libraries in the Reich Education Ministry. Leyh's period of office was short, disagreements with the Reich Education Minister having escalated during 1936 with respect to the treatment of Jewish librarians and on fundamental substantive issues of librarianship. Probably as a result of his failure to join the NSDAP, Leyh was not appointed to the new Reich Advisory Board for Library Affairs, and was thus excluded from access to information on current developments in library policy.

At the General Meeting held in Cologne on 21 May 1937, a resolute National Socialist took up the leadership of the now fully "aligned" VDB: Gustav Abb, since May 1935 the director of the Berlin University library and already a member of the Reich Advisory Board.[133] Abb's deputy, Rudolf Buttmann, director general of the Bavarian State Library since October 1935 and co-editor (with Leyh) of the professional organ *Zentralblatt für Bibliothekswesen* since 1936, was even a member of the Party's "Old Guard," the holder of membership card number 4.

In the research libraries just as in other sectors, the Law for the Restoration of the Professional Civil Service triggered a wave of dismissals on "racial" and political grounds.[134] By the end of 1935, a total of 100 Jewish librarians had been driven from their posts. Most severely affected were the Prussian State Library in Berlin,

---

[131] "Bericht über die Mitglieder-Versammlung," *ZfB* 52 (1935), 553–5.

[132] See the reference to the resolution of the Extraordinary General Meeting in Berlin on 19 October 1935, in "Bericht über die Mitglieder-Versammlung am 6.6.1936 in Dresden," *ZfB* 53 (1936), 592–6, here 593.

[133] "Bericht über die Mitgliederversammlung in Köln," *ZfB* 54 (1937), 533–5.

[134] For details, see Happel, *Das wissenschaftliche Bibliothekswesen*, 31–42; Komorowski, "Die wissenschaftlichen Bibliotheken"; Stieg, "The impact of National Socialism"; Müller-Jerina, "Zwischen Ausgrenzung und Vernichtung"; Schochow, "Die Preußische Staatsbibliothek," 30–1; Toussaint, *Die Universitätsbibliothek Freiburg*, 54–68.

which lost ten experienced Jewish academics and librarians, and the Frankfurt Municipal and University Library, from which seven Jewish librarians were dismissed. After 1935 the Nuremberg race laws forced additional specialists out of the library service as *jüdisch versippt*: "Jewish by marriage." Aiming "to ensure a planned procedure following uniform guidelines according with the National Socialist understanding of the state," on 11 October 1934 the Reich Education Ministry instructed the provincial administrations responsible to obtain its approval "for any appointment to directorships or senior librarian positions in all research libraries of the Reich, state, university, and provincial libraries."[135] The Ministry was also to be notified of every vacant or newly vacated director or senior librarian post. For appointments to management roles, libraries were to submit "the evaluations, statements, and wishes of Party offices" regarding the envisaged applicants.

The new training and assessment regulations for the research library service, issued on 18 August 1938 by the Reich Education Ministry, made the politicization of the profession clear.[136] Right from the start, for "admission to preparatory service," applicants had to prove not only professional and physical aptitude but also membership of the NSDAP or one of its divisions. "Whether this requirement can be waived in an individual case" was a question at the discretion of the Reich Minister, "in agreement with the Führer's Deputy." In addition, applicants should have "fulfilled their official duty in the Labor Service and the army." Evidence that the applicant and, if relevant, his or her spouse were of "German or racially kindred blood" had to be attached to the application for admission. The Reich Advisory Board for Library Affairs in Berlin selected candidates, but the Minister of Education made the final decision on admission. The appointment of a trainee librarian in preparation for civil servant status was expressly tied to the requirement that, "on the basis of the political evaluation issued by the Party authorities," the applicant "can assure that he will stand up for the National Socialist state unreservedly at any time."

During their two-year course of studies, the trainees were repeatedly familiarized with the principles of National Socialism: in

---

135 BArch R 21/10 628.
136 BArch R 21/10 634.

the first year of training through a course at the Party civil service training camp in Bad Tölz, which every trainee had to attend "by specific instruction" of the Reich Minister; in the second year as part of their theoretical tuition, which was to include lectures and tutorials on, among other things, "National Socialist Literature." Upon registration for the final examinations, the candidate's file had to include not only the formal and professional documentation but also an "overall assessment" of his "political attitude." The written and oral examinations then offered sufficient further opportunities to test a candidate's political reliability, especially as the Ministry was represented in the examining commission. "Important though it may be to address historical developments," the oral examination was required to "discuss primarily issues relating to the present and to practice."

3

The Institutional Structure of the Media Dictatorship and Its Power over Books

The State Authorities

The Reich Ministry of Popular Enlightenment and Propaganda

When state functions were distributed after Hitler came to power, Goebbels—*Gauleiter* of Berlin and the NSDAP's propaganda chief—was initially left empty-handed. His disappointed diary entry of 3 February 1933 reads: "I am surrounded by an icy boycott. Now Rust is getting education and culture. I'm left out in the cold. It's so humiliating."[1] This was to change after the Party's success in the Reichstag elections of 5 March 1933. Whereas the new Reich Chancellor "immediately," on 7 March, advocated the creation of a ministry that would draw together press, radio, film, and propaganda, Goebbels claimed to be "still doubtful." The establishment of a Reich Ministry of Popular Enlightenment and Propaganda was negotiated at the ministerial discussions of 11 March 1933 "outside the official agenda."[2] Hitler explained the urgency of a decision in terms of the need for "enlightenment efforts" not only in the current situation,

---

[1] Goebbels, *Tagebücher*, Part I, vol. 2/III, 122. The following quotation ibid. 141.
[2] Excerpts from the records of the ministerial discussions on 11 March 1933, BArch R 43 II /1149 fol. 5.

during "preparations for important government actions," but also "in the case of war." The meeting's brief minutes show that the media mogul Alfred Hugenberg tried to have the decision postponed, for the planned resourcing of the new Reich body through a monopoly on press advertising directly affected his business interests. The Reich Minister of Postal Services, too, was reluctant to accept the loss of radio advertising revenue. Despite these concerns, Hitler got his way with the support of Minister of the Interior Wilhelm Frick. Just two days later, President von Hindenburg signed the documents appointing Goebbels as minister and Walther Funk as state secretary.

The "Decree on the Establishment of the Reich Ministry of Popular Enlightenment and Propaganda" at first only set down the new body's general objectives, while the specific tasks were still to be determined by Hitler "in agreement with the Reich ministries involved."[3] On 8 April, Goebbels announced his Ministry's organizational structure via the press. Seven departments were planned: budgeting and economics (I), propaganda (II), radio (III), press (IV), film (V), theater (VI), and public instruction (VII).[4] However, in the weeks that followed Goebbels had to negotiate hard for his Ministry's responsibilities and budget. Only on 30 June was Hitler ready to issue an ordinance making the Propaganda Ministry responsible "for all tasks relating to influence on the intellectual life of the nation; public relations for the state, culture, and the economy; instructing the public at home and abroad about these matters; and administering all the institutions serving these purposes."[5]

For the Propaganda Ministry to carry out these tasks, several other institutions had to cede parts of their previous responsibilities: the Foreign Office, the Reich Ministry of the Interior, the Reich Ministry of Economics, the Reich Ministry of Food and Agriculture, the Reich Ministry of Postal Services, and the Reich Ministry of Transportation. In terms of literature, the Propaganda Ministry took over from the Ministry of the Interior the task of supervising the Deutsche Bücherei in Leipzig[6]

---

[3] *RGBL*/Part I, no. 21, 17 March 1933, 104.

[4] *Das Archiv*, supplementary volume I, 289.

[5] *RGBL*/Part I, no. 75, 5 July 1933, 449.

[6] The Deutsche Bücherei, the precursor of today's German National Library, was founded in Leipzig in 1912 by the kingdom of Saxony and the Börsenverein der Deutschen Buchhändler. It began its systematic collection of publications in German on 1 January 1913, but only became a nationally funded body in 1940.

and combating "trash and obscenity" ("Schund und Schmutz"). But these arrangements by no means concluded the Ministry's construction phase. The members of the cabinet and the provincial governments—especially Göring, as Minister President of Prussia—were unwilling to accept encroachments onto their spheres of interest.

Accordingly, it was Hitler, keen to curb the particularism of the provinces, who provided the greatest support for the Propaganda Minister in this power struggle. On 15 July, he instructed the provincial governors to refrain from establishing "offices for popular enlightenment, propaganda, or any kind of influence on the German or foreign public, however these may be described."[7] In addition, the Propaganda Ministry's legislative and administrative authority was to be observed for "festivities and demonstrations of a national and political nature" and in the field of the press, cinema, theater, and radio.

The Ministry presented a first detailed schedule of responsibilities on 1 October 1933, now including the areas of "music and art" along with theater as Department VI and "defense (defense against lies at home and abroad)" as Department VII; the foundation stones had been laid for the building of a powerful Reich agency. Despite the Reich Minister of Labor's demand, voiced at the ministerial discussions of 11 March, that "a Reich Ministry of this kind be divested of all profit-making character," Goebbels subsequently managed to access the enormous revenues of the state monopoly broadcasting service.[8] This income gave the Propaganda Ministry "large secret accounts" additional to its regular, public budget. The Ministry had ten departments by 1936, and in 1943 reached its peak with seventeen, along with a number of subordinated offices. Initially it had around 350 employees, but by 1942 their number had grown to approximately 1,500.[9] Many of these were National Socialists born around 1900—civil servants or white-collar employees who

---

[7] Reich Chancellor to the provincial governors regarding the division of responsibilities between Reich and provinces in the area of popular enlightenment and propaganda, 15 July 1933, BArch R 43 II /1149 fol. 88.

[8] On this and the following, see the reference to an internal discussion on budgeting between Goebbels, Funk, Erich Greiner, and Karl Ott on 20 January 1937, Goebbels, *Tagebücher*, Part I, vol. 3/II, 335.

[9] Krings, "Das Propagandaministerium," 35. On the following, see ibid.

were now able to rise to the intermediate, higher, and most senior ranks of the civil service. Alongside this "young guard," whose merit lay chiefly in their commitment to the Party during its early days, there were numerous experienced administrative officials who had been taken over from other ministries and upon whose expertise Goebbels had to rely, especially in the early phases.

It is striking that the sphere of literature was not addressed during the negotiations on the new Ministry's structure. In fact, even in the Party's central propaganda leadership there was no dedicated department for writing, and in the Ministry it appeared only as a small section within the propaganda department. However, the head of that section, Heinz Wismann—who, like Goebbels, held a Heidelberg University doctorate in German literature—was responsible for a very widely defined field: "promotion of national literature; the publishing business; authors; book clubs; public libraries; commercial lending libraries; periodicals; Deutsche Bücherei in Leipzig; Reichsstelle zur Förderung des deutschen Schrifttums." This "Reich Office for the Promotion of German Literature," a private association dominated by representatives of Rosenberg's Kampfbund, was a first—and still only semi-official—literature authority. Wismann's involvement in it really only derived from the fact that the Propaganda Ministry provided financial support for the office's activities, as did the Börsenverein and the Langen-Müller publishing house.

Relations between the Propaganda Ministry and the Reichsstelle were thus quite cooperative in the early days. However, the agile Wismann, who was also vice-president of the Chamber of Literature from November 1933, found his ambitious plans to centralize literary policy hampered by the Reichsstelle's independence. At the 16 January 1934 session of the Chamber's council, he made his first announcement of his vision for a "fundamental reform of the Reichsstelle."[10] Reichsstelle head Hans Hagemeyer, an acolyte of Rosenberg's, was not prepared to obey this call from the Goebbels Ministry, and was accordingly dismissed on 30 January 1934 by the head of the Ministry's propaganda department, Wilhelm Haegert.

The result was one of the innumerable battles for competence that were to become the hallmark of Nazi literary policy. Over several

---

[10] Minutes of the council session on 16 January 1934, p. 5, DLA NL Hans Grimm/Konv. Reichsschrifttumskammer, folder III.

weeks, lengthy communications circulated between Rosenberg, Goebbels, Haegert, and Rudolf Hess.[11] Although the Propaganda Ministry took considerable pains to get Wismann made head of the Reichsstelle, in the end Rosenberg succeeded in rescuing the office by taking it with him to his new role as "The Führer's Representative for the Supervision of the Entire Intellectual and Ideological Instruction of the NSDAP." In response, in March 1934 the Ministry started work to set up its own "Reichsschrifttumsstelle," or Reich Literature Office. To legitimate this body, which was to be subordinate to the Ministry, reference was made to the Law to Protect Youth From Trashy and Obscene Literature, which the Propaganda Ministry was responsible for enforcing. Nevertheless, outwardly the Ministry took pains to avoid the Reich Literature Office seeming to be a censorship body. Writing in the *Börsenblatt* of 9 June 1934, Wismann defined its area of activity as "propaganda measures to nurture and promote German literature," an almost word-for-word copy of the title and remit of Rosenberg's Reichsstelle. As well as the works of "young, as yet unknown poets and writers," special emphasis was to be given to "valuable literature from earlier times that was suppressed and silenced during the Jewish-Marxist era."[12]

Working under Wismann's direction in the Reich Literature Office were Curt Reinhard Dietz as manager and Edgar Diehl as advisor. Both men came with knowledge of the literary scene and of bookselling.[13] Erich Langenbucher, appointed in September 1935 as the press expert, maintained good relations with nationalist-conservative publishers. This small staff of employees was supported in its reading tasks by freelancers recruited from universities, journalism, and librarianship. Dietz and Wismann left the Reich Literature Office in 1937, and the office was restructured in 1938. As a result of Goebbels's redistribution of responsibilities between the Reich Chamber of Culture and the Propaganda Ministry, on 1 April 1938 Alfons Brugger (responsible for book promotion), Otto Henning (lectures), and Ludwig Warmuth (specialist publications) moved from

---

[11] For details, see NS 8/171 fol. 227–49, NS 8/177 fol. 225–9.
[12] *Das Archiv* 1 (1934/35), 384.
[13] See BArch BDC/RSK/Dietz, Curt Reinhard (1896–1946); BArch BDC/RMVP/Diehl, Edgar (1906–?).

the Chamber of Literature to the Literature Office. Karl Thielke filled a new post in charge of "scholarly and scientific literature." However, efforts to expand and reorganize the office more systematically were impeded by the fact that the Propaganda Ministry's short-staffed literature department constantly requisitioned Literature Office employees to help it with its work.

As a result, in 1939 an attempt was made to draw a clear dividing line between the two bodies in terms of responsibilities and personnel. The Reich Literature Office was now required to pass all "tasks in the field of cultural policy leadership" to the literature department, and in turn took on all "tasks of advertising and promotion."[14] On this basis, on 1 April 1939 it received the new title "Promotion and Advisory Office for German Literature" (Werbe- und Beratungsamt fur das deutsche Schrifttum). It was led, as before, by the head of the Propaganda Ministry literature department, while the management was carried out by the advertising expert Alfons Brugger, who had been managing the Literature Office since 1 July 1938.

Within the Propaganda Ministry, a separate literature department was only created on 1 October 1934. This simply involved taking the existing section on literature and publishing out of the propaganda department and raising its status to that of an independent department, Department VIII, led by Wismann. Wismann also headed the section within the literature department entitled "German Literature: General," which was responsible for "fundamental issues of nurturing and promoting German literature, the Reich Chamber of Literature, the Reich Literature Office, the Reich working group on German book promotion, the Deutsche Bücherei in Leipzig, the Emergency Association of German Literature." Apart from Wismann, the department consisted of just two further advisors, each with one assistant. The deputy director, Rudolf Erckmann, was responsible for "German Literature: Domestic," with "writers, publishing, bookselling, book exhibitions, book weeks, book prices, charitable foundations, support, book bans, undesirable literature." Paul Hövel took on "German Literature: Abroad," covering writers, publishing,

---

[14] *Nachrichtenblatt des Reichsministeriums für Volksaufklärung und Propaganda* 7, no. 6, 28 March 1939, 37, BArch R 55/436.

bookselling, book exports, promotion of German books abroad, and book bans. A third section, "Libraries," had to be shared by Erckmann (for "lending libraries, factory libraries, the libraries of other private companies such as shipping lines, etc., club libraries") and Hövel (for "libraries abroad, cooperation with international library organizations").

The department's personnel and areas of responsibility remained unchanged until 1937, when Wismann was ousted. Until then, he had successfully molded the Propaganda Ministry's literary policy by means of a large and diverse network of personal contacts and subordinate offices. The circumstances that forced this first head of Department VIII to quit in late October 1937 were dramatic. While the Economic Office for the German Book Trade (Wirtschaftsstelle des deutschen Buchhandels) was being established in 1935, Wismann had fallen out with Wilhelm Baur, the powerful director of Eher books in Berlin and president of the Börsenverein. Determined inquiries by Baur revealed that his rival had been married to a "half Jew" until 1934, and had concealed this fact both when joining the Party in 1932 and when taking up employment in the Propaganda Ministry.

At first, this "unpleasant business"[15] did not induce Goebbels to drop Wismann. His diary entry of 30 June 1937 notes: "Must stay! I can't do without him." But further investigations brought more "offensive" details to Goebbels's attention.[16] The exposure of these faux pas gave Hanns Johst, too, a welcome opportunity to rid himself of his formidable deputy.[17] As late as February 1937, Chamber of Literature advisor Herbert Menz, in a letter to his superior, had reported Wilhelm Baur's opinion that it was pointless to "divest Wismann of his office as vice-president if he was not simultaneously discharged from his post as the head of Department VIII in the Ministry. Wismann had nothing but enemies in the Ministry; but in the view of a very important gentleman there, he was still the best of all the department heads and would therefore be retained, especially as nobody else was available."[18]

---

[15] Goebbels, *Tagebücher*, Part I, vol. 4, 193 (24 June 1937). The following quotation ibid. 202.
[16] See Ihde to Hinkel, 12 July 1937, BArch BDC/RMVP/Wismann, H., vol. 1.
[17] Johst to Goebbels, 30 June 1937, BArch BDC/RMVP/Wismann, H., vol. 2.
[18] Menz to Johst, 8 February 1937, BArch R 56 V/27 fol. 196.

On 23 July, Goebbels himself came to the conclusion that it was "no longer possible to keep" Wismann.[19] He annotated the dismissal with a worried question: "But who will succeed him?" Funk suggested offering the job to the vice-president of the Party commission PPK, Karl Heinz Hederich,[20] and by 28 July Goebbels had agreed as much with the PPK president Philipp Bouhler. Reassured, the Propaganda Minister noted in his diary: "Unity of Party and state. That will stop the troublemaking, too."[21] Certainly, in the initial phase Hederich brought new dynamism to the Ministry's literature department. In November 1937, he submitted a lengthy report setting out restructuring measures. To add suitable emphasis to his proposals, Hederich pointed out the "danger" that "if the work of literary policy continues to be neglected, other offices will take up and carry out these tasks without our being able to present a serious objection."[22] He therefore called for not only a significant increase in personnel and budget, but a completely new structure for the various areas of work. The Chambers should be "depoliticized," he argued, cooperation with the PPK should be enhanced, and the Reich Literature Office's responsibilities should be transferred entirely to the literature department. Hederich envisioned that "all the areas of public life relevant to literary policy should be integrated into the Ministry's literary policy work and the leadership of the Ministry be secured."[23] Ultimately only one central "Reich office" was to remain, absorbing all the other state and Party literature bodies.

By 1 April 1938, the constituent chambers of the Reich Chamber of Culture were required to cede their policy tasks to the respective departments of the Propaganda Ministry. The Ministry's acquisition of Chamber personnel was supplemented by a series of new appointments. The 1938/39 schedule of responsibilities for the literature department took

---

[19] Goebbels, *Tagebücher*, Part I, vol. 4, 228.

[20] Goebbels, *Tagebücher*, Part I, vol. 4, 230 (24 July 1937).

[21] Ibid. 237 (28 July 1937). See also ibid. 239 (30 July 1937): "Hederich has now been decided as Wismann's successor. Bouhler still has a few objections, but we'll soon deal with those"; also ibid. 254 (7 August 1937): "Wismann definitively replaced by Hederich. He has already begun work."

[22] Proposals 1938/39, section "Reordering work and organization," BArch R 55/166 fol. 317–37, here 325.

[23] Budgetary observations on the Reichsschrifttumsstelle, 22 November 1937, ibid. fol. 340.

account of Hederich's suggested structure, as follows. Main Section I, headed by Johannes Schlecht, covered: Section 1 (Schlecht) for the Reich Literature Office, the "board of trustees for German literature," literary work in the Reich propaganda offices, large-scale propaganda campaigns, NSDAP literature, "mobilization" panel; Section 2 (Koch) for book bans, the Index of Harmful and Undesirable Literature, monitoring the book market, communication with all offices involved in book prohibition; Section 3 (Henning) for literary societies, local promotion communities, communication with the Reich propaganda offices (all supervised by the Reich Literature Office); Section 4 (Losch) for the Deutsche Bücherei, public libraries, lending libraries, factory libraries, youth and border-country libraries, club libraries, communication with library sections in other ministries and provinces, Catholic libraries. Main Section II, headed by Rudolf Erckmann, covered: Section 1 (Erckmann) for orientation and promotion of German literature, literary prizes, book exhibitions within Germany, authors; Section 2 (Gruber) for monitoring and promotion of the publishing sector, publishers' readers, editors, publishers' conferences; Section 3 (Benatzky) for sports literature, SA literature, entertainment literature; Section 4 (Langenbucher) for youth literature, annual list of recommended German writing, office for the cultivation of the German language, typographical questions, dialect literature (all supervised by the Reich Literature Office). Finally, Main Section III, led by Paul Hövel, covered: Section 1 (Hövel) for German literature abroad, cultural agreements, literary policy campaigns abroad, writers' exchange programs, book exports, Economic Office of the German Book Trade; Section 2 (E. Kühne) for literature of ethnic Germans outside the Reich, care of ethnic German writers and writing groups, ethnic German literary associations, ethnic German libraries, minority literature, border-country literature, maps and atlases; Section 3 (Ruoff) for book exhibitions abroad, foreign trips by German writers, book reviewing abroad, book propaganda abroad (all supervised by the Reich Literature Office); Section 4 (Schirmer) for translations, monitoring translations of foreign works in Germany and German works abroad, investigation of foreign publishers and authors, national file of authors and publishers.[24]

---

[24] Schedule of responsibilities for the financial year 1939/40, BArch R 55/407 fol. 287–91. See also the personnel list for the literature department, BArch R 55/14 fol. 352.

Despite Goebbels's instructions to his new head of department to avoid antagonizing Rosenberg, at the rally closing the "Week of the German Book" Hederich staked the PPK's claim to a key leadership role in National Socialist literary policy.[25] This nettled Rosenberg, but Hederich went on to discredit himself with Amann and Wilhelm Baur as well, by making dismissive remarks about the Party newspaper *Völkischer Beobachter*. December 1937 saw the beginning of a series of personnel policy altercations that caused Goebbels considerable trouble: while Rosenberg and Amann attacked Hederich, "who has gotten far too big for his boots,"[26] Göring demanded the dismissal of Hinkel due to his attacks on Gustaf Gründgens and on the homosexuality that Hinkel alleged was prevalent in the Prussian State Theater, and Minister of War von Blomberg demanded the removal of Alfred von Wrochem from the ministerial office. "If I give in to this," complained Goebbels in his diary, "I will start to lose all my employees. That's unacceptable. In the end, there will be no one left to stand up for me. I reject that. All three of them have made mistakes. But that's no reason to throw them out."[27]

Although—with the express agreement of Hitler[28]—Goebbels managed to retain Hederich in December 1937, in October 1938 he had to give him up after all. Hederich had embroiled himself in "another hell of a feud" with Amann after banning two Eher brochures "in a particularly insolent way."[29] The hoped-for unification of state and Party jurisdictions turned out to be unrealistic in practice. In the Ministry's personnel and literature departments, there had already been several complaints about Hederich's attempts to pack the department with PPK employees and to carry out certain tasks

---

[25] See Goebbels, *Tagebücher*, Part I, vol. 4, 324 (23 September 1937). Hederich's speech appeared in *Bbl.* no. 260, 9 November 1937, 889–97.

[26] Thus Rosenberg on Hederich in a letter to Rudolf Hess, 2 December 1937, BArch NS 8/178 fol. 35. On the following points, see Goebbels, *Tagebücher*, Part I, vol. 5, 108 (21 January 1938).

[27] Ibid. 50 (14 December 1937).

[28] In a letter of 23 December 1937, Goebbels had informed Rosenberg of his discussion of the "Hederich matter" with Hitler, BArch NS 8/171 fol. 58.

[29] Goebbels, *Tagebücher*, Part I, vol. 6, 45 (17 August 1938); ibid. 49 (19 August 1938). See also the report on Hederich's banning of two Eher publications, drawn up for Goebbels by Berndt on 22 November 1938, and Goebbels to Bouhler, 24 November 1938, BArch BDC/RMVP/Hederich, K.H.

in an undefined zone somewhere between the two literary policy bodies.[30]

Hederich was succeeded by the 34-year-old Alfred-Ingemar Berndt.[31] Berndt had previously worked in the Ministry's press department as the deputy press officer for the Reich government. In early 1939 he, just like his predecessor, submitted comprehensive proposals for reorganizing the literature department.[32] Aiming to prevent further "hollowing out" of the department's responsibilities by the Party-based agencies, he demanded increased staffing for what he called "probably the Ministry's most neglected department." The department's jurisdiction was to be extended by adding new sections for writing related to the press, church, youth, business, administration, law, and science and the social support of authors, and by setting up a nationwide file of authors and a "general section" for archives and historical documents.

Soon after the outbreak of war, Berndt moved to the top level of the Ministry's radio department, taking some of his section heads with him. Because the literature department's deputy head, Schlecht, was clearly unequal to the task of replacing him, on 4 November 1939 Goebbels awarded acting leadership of the department to the highly experienced Hinkel.[33] Hinkel was charged with "bringing some order to the tangles in Literature. Bouhler, Rosenberg, and who knows who else are squabbling there."[34] However, in late November Hinkel had to pass his role back to Haegert. Despite Goebbels's low opinion—he considered Haegert, only thirty-two years old, an "insipid theoretician" and a "man of confusion"[35]—it

---

[30] See Propaganda Ministry personnel department to the state secretary, 23 December 1937, on disputes over responsibilities between Department VIII and the press and propaganda department, BArch R55/886; Schlecht's memorandum of 3 October 1938, BArch R 55/2 fol. 270; Erckmann's notes taken 14 October 1938, ibid. fol. 481.

[31] *Nachrichtenblatt des Reichsministeriums für Volksaufklärung und Propaganda* 7, no. 1, 11 January 1939, 2, BArch R 55/436.

[32] BArch R 55/407 fol. 279–86. The following quotation ibid. fol. 279.

[33] Goebbels, *Tagebücher*, Part I, vol. 7, 181; internal communication from the Propaganda Ministry personnel department, 9 November 1939, BArch R 55/14 fol. 194.

[34] Goebbels, *Tagebücher*, Part I, vol. 7, 197 (16 November 1939). Reference to Hinkel's conversations with Bouhler and Rosenberg ibid. 204 (22 November 1939).

[35] Goebbels, *Tagebücher*, Part I, vol. 5, 108 (21 January 1938), ibid. 114 (25 January 1938).

was this new head who would consolidate the literature department at last. Nevertheless, writing to the Minister in May 1942, Haegert lamented that the department "strangely still has a reputation within our organization of not being one of the political departments, even though it has important political tasks to fulfill."[36]

At this time, every year just two section heads were examining up to 4,000 manuscripts for which an application for paper had been made or whose publication was to be prohibited on political grounds. The Propaganda Minister approved two further head-of-section posts to carry out the work of censorship, along with five reader posts for the Promotion and Advisory Office for German Literature—but in December 1942 the literature department still had to ask the Reich propaganda offices to appoint "reviewers" from the regional press who "have demonstrated particular reliability and sureness of judgment."[37] In future, their reviews were to be used as "book evaluations for the tasks of literary policy, especially for paper allocation": war-related staff shortages ruled out the continued production of evaluations within the Ministry itself.

During the war, the various threads of state literary policy were gathered together within the Propaganda Ministry. In the period from 1933 to 1938, a total of 2,602,537.81 RM (including 1,237,150 RM of subsidies for the Deutsche Bücherei in Leipzig) had been spent on literary policy,[38] but in wartime the budgets were substantially increased, so that by 1942 a further 7,973,201.68 RM had been invested. Added to this sum were the funds available to the Promotion and Advisory Office. In the financial year 1942/43 alone, when the funding of the Office was listed separately for the first time, a budget of 629,000 RM was allocated.[39] Even if literature absorbed only a relatively minor share of the Propaganda Ministry's total expenditure—and the Ministry's regular budget can

---

[36] Haegert to Goebbels, 11 May 1942, BArch R 55/13 fol. 104–6.
[37] See communication from the literature department, 4 December 1942, in LA Berlin Rep. 243, Acc. 1814/3.
[38] See the expenditure data collected for the Propaganda Ministry's tenth anniversary, here "Development of spending in the area of literature (1933–1942)," 6 January 1943, BArch R 55/862 fol. 16. The following figures ibid.
[39] See the figures presented by Dr. Lucerna (budget dept.), 6 January 1943, BArch R 55/862 fol. 16. The first budget of the Reichsschrifttumsstelle (1 June 1934 – 31 March 1935) had come to a modest 53,485.15 RM, BArch R 55/322 fol. 61.

be estimated at more than 880 million RM for the years between 1933 and 1943[40]—such substantial public funding had never before been dedicated to the purposes of literature.

To be sure, the Propaganda Ministry's leadership role was never uncontroversial; nor was its literary policy ever implemented across the board. This becomes clear in a fall 1939 memorandum from the deputy head of the literature department, Schlecht.[41] At that time, Goebbels was talking to him about a "more popular orientation" for the department, which had become "too ivory-tower and too vegetarian" for his taste.[42] Schlecht's memorandum complained not only of the constant skirmishes with Bouhler's and Rosenberg's Party literature offices over jurisdiction—his Minister too had long been "heartily sick" of these "ridiculous trivialities."[43] For Schlecht, an equally serious problem was the independent and unauthorized activity of the Reich Chamber of Literature. He portrayed the Chamber as a "completely disunified structure" wavering between two poles: whereas the policy of the Writers Group within the Chamber was essentially steered by the Chamber's managing director, Wilhelm Ihde, with the full approval of the head of the Ministry legal department, Hans Schmidt-Leonhardt, the Book Trade Group headed by Wilhelm Baur now consulted with the superordinate Ministry literature department "only on formal and operational grounds and *post festum*." Baur, continued the memorandum, primarily represented the interests of Amann's Party publisher, the German Labor Front, and Rosenberg's office, and had come to consider himself "the superior of the head of Department VIII," who was finding it almost impossible to counter Baur's "dictatorial measures." But Wilhelm Baur acted on behalf of Amann, and Amann's position in Party and state was too strong for Goebbels to consider taking targeted action against the policy of special treatment for the Eher house. Until the end of the war the literary policy pursued in Goebbels's name therefore often moved along different paths.

---

[40] Figures from Krings, "Das Propagandaministerium," 35. The total expenditure will have been higher, because the spending from the extraordinary budget is not recorded.
[41] Unfortunately, only pages 5 to 8 of the report, with the handwritten date 1939, are preserved, BArch R 56 V/17 fol. 34–7.
[42] Goebbels, *Tagebücher*, Part I, vol. 7, 146 (10 October 1939).
[43] Ibid. 22 (15 December 1939).

Divergent personal loyalties and interests played an important role in the power complex around Himmler and the SS as well. In the course of the 1930s, the SS had succeeded in gaining the services of several Chamber employees for its security service (SD) activities. In the Propaganda Ministry's literature department, in contrast, the proportion of SS members was small. Of the section heads, only Erich Langenbucher and Günther Lutz belonged to the SS,[44] and of the four men who led the literature department, Berndt is the only one known to have maintained close contact with the SD.[45] Berndt's successor Haegert was a longtime member of the SA with close ties to its chief of staff, Viktor Lutze.[46] When, in mid-January 1945, Haegert was "approved for military service again," Wilfrid Bade became acting head of the department.[47] He had begun working in the press department of the Propaganda Ministry in 1933, was a confidant of Otto Dietrich, and since July 1941 had been heading the newly established periodical press department. Bade realized early on that SS membership could be beneficial to his career, and from 1937 he worked part-time as a reader for the SS publisher Volk und Reich. But in the last months before the regime's collapse and his suicide in May 1945, his priority was to preserve his extensive literary and journalistic oeuvre for posterity.

As well as the literature department, the Ministry had one other department working on important tasks in the field of literary policy: Department II A, led by Hans Hinkel. After moving from the Prussian ministry of education, where he had worked for Prussian Minister President Göring since 1933 on the political reform of theater in Prussia and especially on the expulsion of Jewish artists, in spring 1935 Hinkel was appointed by Goebbels as one of three managing directors of the Chamber of Culture.[48] In this connection, he received the "special ministerial commission" to "monitor and supervise the

---

[44] See the SS personnel files, BArch BDC/SS.
[45] See the personnel report (n.d., 1939) of the SD main office, where Berndt is listed as an employee from 1936 on, BArch BDC/SS/Berndt, A.-I.
[46] BArch Berlin Lichterfelde BDC/SA/Haegert, W.
[47] *Nachrichtenblatt des Reichsministeriums für Volksaufklärung und Propaganda* 13, no. 2, 24 January 1945, 5, BArch R 55/1347. On the following, see Härtel, *Stromlinien.*
[48] On the following, see Dahm, *Das jüdische Buch*, 54–9.

artistic and intellectual activities of all non-Aryan citizens resident in German Reich territory." The specific tasks involved in this can be inferred from a schedule of responsibilities that came into force officially with the transformation of the previous "special section" (*Sonderreferat*) into Department II A of the Propaganda Ministry on 1 April 1938: (1) surveillance of intellectually and culturally active Jews in Germany; (2) surveillance of other intellectually and culturally active non-Aryans in Germany; (3) scrutinizing the ownership of all cultural enterprises in Reich territory for Jewish influence and eliminating such influence; (4) membership of Jews and *Mischlinge* ("mixed-breeds") in the individual chambers.[49] As director of the new department, Hinkel left his position as a managing director of the Chamber of Culture, but he remained, with his existing staff, based in the Chamber of Culture headquarters at no. 10, Am Karlsbad, Berlin.[50] Erich Kochanowski, Helmuth von Loebell, Gerhard Noatzke, and Walter Owens had been working in the *Sonderreferat* at the Chamber of Culture since 1 April 1936 and moved to the Propaganda Ministry at the beginning of 1939;[51] they were Hinkel's longtime political companions and personal confidants. All of them had been NSDAP members before 1933, and after 1933 all joined the SS.

Hinkel's new Department II A was, like his former *Sonderreferat*, responsible for the exclusion of all Chamber of Culture members who were "non-Aryan" or married to "non-Aryans," and the issuing of "special permission" in individual cases—always in close liaison with the SD.[52] "Aryanization" of the Reich German and, from March 1938, the Austrian book trade was the task of Noatzke, who held professional qualifications in commerce and bookselling.[53] In cooperation with *Sonderreferat* III Z and the RSK's Book Trade Group, Hinkel's

---

[49] *Nachrichtenblatt des Reichsministeriums für Volksaufklärung und Propaganda* 6, no. 5, 9 April 1938, 23, BArch R 55/435.

[50] Ibid. 6, no. 9, 2 June 1938, 45, BArch R 55/435.

[51] Ibid. 7, no. 4, 27 February 1939, 21, BArch R 55/436.

[52] See the report on SS Senior Leader Hinkel and his staff's visit to the SD Main Office on 28 September 1938, BArch R 58/984 fol. 86–7.

[53] See personnel note of 15 July 1936 and curriculum vitae of 15 June 1937, BArch BDC/RKK/Noatzke, G.

department forced Jewish publishers, bookstores, secondhand bookshops, and lending libraries to sell or liquidate their businesses. Jews now having been eliminated from German cultural life, in May 1939 Department II A became the "department for personal details of workers in the cultural sector."[54] Still headed by Hinkel, the department was renamed "special cultural tasks" in 1940 and "general section for affairs of the Reich Chamber of Culture" in August 1941,[55] and was the "formally highest authority" on the following matters: checking the "political suitability and reliability" of Chamber of Culture members; "national-political evaluation of all artists working with the troops"; "social support" and old-age provision for German creative artists; the "Aryanization" of the whole of German culture with respect to individuals and cultural enterprises; and the issue of "special permissions" for the few still-tolerated "half and quarter Jews" or those "married to full, half, and quarter Jews."[56] In July 1944, Hinkel became the Reich Film Superintendent and head of the Ministry's film department, and in September the tasks of the "general section for affairs of the Reich Chamber of Culture" were transferred to the new culture department led by Rainer Schlösser.[57] Not only cultural life, but the Propaganda Ministry that was responsible for it, now culminated in "total mobilization."

The Reich Chamber of Literature within the Reich Chamber of Culture

Writing to the Reich provincial governors on 16 July 1933, Hitler announced the establishment of a Reich Chamber of Culture as a "substructure enabling the Reich Ministry of Popular Enlightenment and Propaganda to carry out its tasks." On 11 August, the Propaganda

---

[54] *Nachrichtenblatt des Reichsministeriums für Volksaufklärung und Propaganda* 7, no. 8, 3 May 1939, 49, BArch R 55/436.

[55] Ibid. 8, no. 16, 12 August 1940, 27, BArch R 55/437, and 9, no. 27, 14 October 1941, 74, BArch R 55/438.

[56] Department of Special Cultural Tasks to Ministerial Director Gutterer, 31 May 1940, p. 1, BArch R 56 I/132.

[57] *Nachrichtenblatt des Reichsministeriums für Volksaufklärung und Propaganda* 12, no. 23, 13 September 1944, 77, BArch R 55/441.

Ministry presented the Chancellery with its first draft of a Law on the Reich Chamber of Culture.[58] Members of those professions whose activity fell within the purview of the Propaganda Ministry were to be gathered together in "public corporations." Specifically, seven individual chambers were envisaged, covering literature, the press, radio, theater, music, the visual arts, and film—the latter to be formed from the existing "provisional film chamber," founded on 14 July 1933. An accompanying memorandum explained the "fundamental idea underlying the establishment of a Reich Chamber of Culture."[59] The professional associations, now chambers, were to be charged with fulfilling public tasks "by means of self-administration under state supervision and participation." The new public corporations would handle the "adaptation of the law to the requirements of the National Socialist state," and members of the cultural professions would give up their autonomy. As their professional representation developed, they were to propagate the "fundamental values" of National Socialism within German society. However, this ideological mission was only one of the goals that Goebbels was pursuing by establishing the Chamber of Culture.

Without mentioning the German Labor Front or Robert Ley by name, the memorandum criticized "attempts to push the structure of the professions one-sidedly into the field of social struggle and to make it into a kind of equal community of work by reviving trade-union thinking." The area of culture was "more important to the state," so that, "partly because of the excessive diversity of conditions in this area, which impedes systematic intervention," the relevant office of the Reich government must "supervise it more rigorously than other lines of occupation, however significant these may be." The Propaganda Ministry also, the memorandum continued, required specialized associations representing the individual sectors of culture and media, "not associations of workers and management in which the uniformity of economic interests is stressed as strongly as possible and the differences between conditions in the different lines of occupation are considered secondary." There seem to have been fears in the Propaganda Ministry that Ley, as the heir to the

---

[58] BArch R 43 II/1241 fol. 3. On the following, see ibid.
[59] Ibid. fol. 4–7.

free trade unions and to the sales clerks' association DHV, could now intrude into Goebbels's domain through his Labor Front's book-trade sectoral group. In response to this threatened incursion, on 23 August 1933 Funk wrote Hess to emphasize that the Labor Front had "quite different tasks," in which "we as the Reich Ministry by no means wish to intervene and which will remain untouched notwithstanding our propaganda and cultural work for the social reconstruction of the Reich."[60] It was "therefore quite unnecessary to create artificial oppositions that result only from a harmful and misguided claim by the Labor Front for prestige in the area of culture."

On 25 August 1933, Goebbels received Hitler's approval for the Law on the Reich Chamber of Culture.[61] During cabinet discussions, the Propaganda Minister had to provide assurances that the Reich, provinces, and communes would "not be burdened with costs due to the Law's implementation."[62] State secretary Fritz Reinhardt from the Reich Ministry of Finance and Kurt Schmitt, the Reich Minister of Economics, also contrived to be given a say in all ordinances and general administrative regulations respecting the individual chambers if these touched upon financial or commercial interests.[63] By and large, however, the bill, which had been presented on 11 August, was accepted and the Law on the Reich Chamber of Culture was passed on 22 September.[64]

With the First Directive for the Execution of the Reich Chamber of Culture Law, issued on 1 November 1933, the professional associations that had been founded provisionally under private law were now declared "corporations in public law."[65] The obligation to join one of the seven chambers was applied first to the existing members of the now-redesignated professional associations, then

---

[60] BArch 50.01/162 fol. 3–4.

[61] Goebbels, *Tagebücher*, Part I, vol. 2/III, 253.

[62] Thus Goebbels in a letter of 20 September 1933, informing the Reich Chancellery's state secretary Lammers of the result of ministerial discussions held on 19 September, BArch R 43 II/1241 fol. 8.

[63] Excerpt from the records of the Reich Ministry meeting on 22 September 1933, BArch R 43 II/1241 fol. 13–14.

[64] Goebbels had recommended this to state secretary Lammers in his communication of 20 September 1933, BArch R 43 II/1241 fol. 8. For the text of the law, see *RGBL*/Part I, no. 105, 26 September 1933, 661–2.

[65] *RGBL*/Part I, no. 123, 3 November 1933, 797–800.

to all persons involved in "the creation, reproduction, intellectual or technical processing, distribution, preservation, sale, or facilitation of the sale of cultural goods." The determining factor for obligatory membership of the Chamber of Culture was, thus, the particular activity's presence in the public sphere. It was irrelevant whether that activity was commercial or nonprofit and whether it was carried out by individuals or groups (societies, clubs, private foundations, corporations, or public-law institutions), by citizens of the Reich or foreign nationals in Germany, by freelancers or employees.

Membership of the chambers was gained either indirectly, via the professional associations and groups, or directly if no relevant professional grouping existed. Exemption from the obligation to join a chamber was possible for those engaged in cultural work only as a secondary occupation; decisions on such exemptions, as well as on acceptance or rejection of applicants and on the exclusion of members, were to be taken by the presidents of the individual chambers, based on considerations of "reliability and suitability" (§ 10). The presidents were also entitled to impose fines and bring in the police. However, the final authority was the President of the Chamber of Culture, an office held by the Propaganda Minister. To fulfill their role in monitoring and controlling cultural, economic, and social policy, the chamber presidents could use official notices and rulings setting conditions on the right to establish or run a business and on agreements related to employment and social law. In the case of expropriations, they could even resolve that there was "no right to compensation." It was only over the following years that the momentous implications of these powers would become clear; they were limited solely by the right of the Minister of Economics to share in decisions relating to the book, music, radio, and art business.

The administrative costs of the individual chambers were covered through membership dues. In the Law on Membership Dues of 24 March 1934, the Reich Minister of Finance explicitly acknowledged the tax-like character of the obligatory payments to public corporations.[66] Approval from the Ministry of Finance was in fact required

---

[66] Law to Maintain and Increase Purchasing Power, 24 March 1934, *RGBL*/Part I, no. 33, 26 March 1934, 235–6.

when setting the fees and levies, as well as for the chambers' budget estimates.

The first president of the Chamber of Literature (RSK) was Hans Friedrich Blunck, a writer whose *völkisch*-nationalist epics and ballads were familiar fare in Germany and who had good connections abroad.[67] The RSK council included the writers Hans Grimm and Hanns Johst, publishers Friedrich Oldenbourg and Theodor Fritsch, Jr., and Wismann as the Propaganda Ministry contact. In the initial phase, the formal structure of the RSK was as follows. Department A (Heinz Wismann): president's deputy, supervision of subordinate groups, liaison with other Reich offices, copyright issues; Department B (Gunther Haupt): management office, monitoring of literature, care of young booksellers, lectures, personal assistant to the president; Department C (Werner Schlegel): monitoring of German books abroad; Department D (Karl Heinl): public libraries, cultivation of the German language; Department E (Eberhard Hasper): monitoring of publishing, the book trade and commercial lending libraries; Department F (Wolfgang Reichstein): legal advisor, ordinances.[68] In building up the RSK, the fundamental difficulty was fulfilling the requirement to cover each and every person working in the field of literature, given that only the RDS (Reich Association of German Writers) was available as a nucleus. However, a "notification on the organization of the Reich Chamber of Literature" of 21 December 1933 made membership compulsory for a circle of people reaching far beyond the RDS.[69]

Inclusion into the RSK proceeded on a range of different principles. Existing professional associations might be absorbed in full; this was the case for the booksellers' association Börsenverein der Deutschen Buchhändler, the book trade group in the sales clerks' association DHV, the German association of public librarians, and the German association of research librarians. The members of these bodies thus joined the RSK "indirectly," which in practice meant that although they remained organized in their respective professional

---

[67] On the circumstances of Blunck's appointment, see his memoirs, *Unwegsame Zeiten*, 179–214. Blunck only joined the NSDAP on 1 May 1937.
[68] DLA NL Hans Grimm/Konv. Reichsschrifttumskammer, folder III.
[69] Published in *Bbl.* no. 298, 23 December 1933, 995–7.

associations, they were now also subject to the disciplinary authority of the Chamber and had to pay membership fees to it as well. At the same time, umbrella organizations and newly formed consortia were charged with collecting and incorporating individual societies or occupational sectors: this is what happened to the Society of Bibliophiles, the book clubs, the literary societies, the endowers and awarders of literary prizes, and the publishers' and booksellers' agents. Whereas the public libraries were to be gathered via the Assembly of German Municipalities and from there integrated into the RSK, direct registration with the RSK was required for the factory libraries and the non-commercial adult education libraries of other associations or occupational groups. The same was to apply for the "ministerial, Party, municipal, student, and other book procurement or purchasing offices."

The "Notification on Membership of the Reich Chamber of Literature" of 20 February 1934 attempted to define more precisely which kinds of businesses should be regarded as involved in the distribution of literature.[70] This highly diverse economic sector was to be controlled with the help of a "consortium of small-scale and part-time bookselling operations." On 4 April 1934, chamber presidents Blunck and Amann, in a joint announcement, clarified the distinction between the scope of their respective chambers, Literature and Press.[71] For companies publishing or distributing books, newspapers, and periodicals, the correct chamber membership was determined by the proportion of turnover from these three lines of business; newspaper editors, publishers, publishing employees, retail businesses, wholesalers, and railway bookstores were allocated to the Press Chamber.

An ordinance of 30 July 1934 obliged publishing and bookselling companies to examine the chamber membership of their business partners, authors, employees, and apprentices, and in future, "in order to facilitate reciprocal notification," all RSK members were to "indicate the membership number of their specialist association on their business stationery."[72] The RDS was given the right to request

---

[70] Reproduced in Schrieber, *Das Recht der Reichskulturkammer*, vol. I, 201.
[71] Ibid. 209–11.
[72] Ordinance on proof of membership of the Reich Chamber of Literature, ibid. 222–3.

information from publishers about all the authors and translators whose books had come onto the market since the Chamber was established.

The first watershed in the RSK's development occurred in 1935. It was part of a fundamental change of political course and a personnel shake-up in the Chamber of Culture as a whole. The management of the Chamber of Culture, working under the supervision of Goebbels and Funk, had hitherto consisted of just two officials: Hans Schmidt-Leonhardt for content and legal issues, and Franz Moraller for personnel policy and propaganda. In May 1935, Goebbels made Hinkel a third managing director, responsible for supervising the individual chambers in internal matters. The resulting more exacting style became obvious in the first public statement issued by this new "Reich Administrator of Culture," on 5 June: "National Socialism must repudiate the implementation of National Socialist cultural policy by people who have not yet proved, through their deeds and attitude, that they have truly grasped our idea. Especially in the area of cultural policy, where not simply the evaluation of artistic skill, but decisions on the fundamental orientation of the ideologically conditioned and rooted cultural politics of our era are at stake, National Socialist principles can only ever be understood and realized by National Socialists."[73]

It was Hinkel who orchestrated the subsequent reshuffle in the RSK leadership. By having Johst appointed president, he was reactivating an old comrade from Rosenberg's Kampfbund, who had been sidelined from politics as president of the Prussian Academy of Arts' literature section. Writing to Hinkel in July 1935, Johst explored the RSK's political options for gaining ground among the competing bodies of literary policy at state and Party level: "But I can only eliminate the confusion and conflicts of the current responsibilities if Minister Goebbels puts me in a position to do so. Authority is always primarily a matter of the statesman who delegates it to a trusted man, and only to the extent that he does so. I venture to say that I can integrate literature in the spirit of our movement if I am

---

[73] Speech at the "First meeting on postal and telegraph science for civil servants, employees, and workers of some Reich postal directorates," excerpts published in *Das Archiv* 2 (1935/36), 397.

entrusted with the necessary instruments of power!"[74] Just nine days later, Hinkel informed Johst that Goebbels was "completely in agreement with my own intention as I mentioned it to you before," and had "given me the opportunity to realize it very soon."[75] The new appointment was made official on 3 October. Johst had been an NSDAP member since 1 November 1932 and received the new "NSDAP Prize for Art" at the Reich Party conference on 11 September 1935; on 1 November 1935 he also joined the SS.

Because the new RSK president intended to spend most of his time in his commodious villa on Lake Starnberg, the next urgent staffing problem was finding a manager based in Berlin. The first managing director of the RSK, appointed in November 1933, was Gunther Haupt, who had no party affiliation. As a former employee of the publishers Hanseatische Verlagsanstalt and Langen-Müller, he—like Blunck, Grimm, and Kolbenheyer—was part of the nationalist-conservative network around Pezold. In November 1934, Goebbels appointed the history professor and long-standing NSDAP member Richard Suchenwirth to take up an equal role alongside Haupt, and in October 1935 Haupt left the Chamber along with Blunck, citing personal disagreements.[76]

Suchenwirth was demoted again just a few months later, under circumstances indicating that an orderly distribution of competences between the Propaganda Ministry and the Chamber of Culture had still not been achieved in early 1936. Since being appointed head of the Ministry's literature department, Heinz Wismann had substantially expanded his powers within the RSK as well: working with the RSK president, he was now entitled to make decisions on the "cultural-policy stance and structure of the Chamber," nominate and appoint RSK staff, issue legally binding decrees, hold conclusive negotiations with the Chamber of Culture leadership on matters of principle, exclude members, impose fines, and correspond with the administrative authorities at Reich, provincial, local,

---

[74] Handwritten letters from Johst to Hinkel, 25 July 1935, BArch R 56 V/31 fol. 141–4.
[75] Hinkel to Johst, 29 August 1935, ibid. fol. 140.
[76] On the background, see RSK legal advisor Gentz to the president of the Chamber of Culture, 14 September 1937, regarding the personnel matter of Haupt, BArch BDC/RSK/Haupt, G. On Suchenwirth's appointment, see Goebbels, *Tagebücher*, Part I, vol. 3/I, 137 (16 November 1934).

and Party level and with the presidents of the other chambers.[77] Suchenwirth regarded the "polyarchy" of the triple administrative apex as damaging the efficiency of the RSK's work, especially since, as he acerbically observed in November 1935 during preparations for Goebbels's speech to the Reich Culture Senate, it was anyway far from easy "to fill three typed pages on the future tasks of the Chamber," which meant "racking your brains to think up the material."[78] In February 1936, Suchenwirth abandoned his task, but the appointment of Wismann's confidant Heinl as a successor was only an interim solution. Not until May 1937 did it prove possible to find a managing director who combined party-political reliability with administrative experience: Wilhelm Ihde. Managing director of the Reich Association of the German Press from 1935 to 1937, Ihde had been a member of the NSDAP since 1930 and of the SS since the beginning of 1933.[79]

Nevertheless, for its entire lifespan the RSK remained an unwieldy structure driven by disparate interests. Initially this was a result of the haste in founding the Chamber of Culture, the component chambers of which did not manage to find a binding organizational structure for several years, and even then were hampered by continued structural interventions from the Propaganda Ministry. In addition, the successor to the ineffectual president Blunck, Johst, turned out to be another weak figurehead, so that in February 1938 Goebbels briefly contemplated finding yet another replacement.[80] But the core of the RSK's problem was the need to unify heterogeneous associations and professional groups, with all their differing—not to say conflicting—expectations of the work of the Chamber. As early as March 1934, the best-selling author Hans Grimm complained to Goebbels about the modalities of admission to the RDS, thanks to which, he claimed, the "masters of their craft" were swamped by an army of dilettantes.[81]

---

[77] RSK schedule of responsibilities, December 1935, BArch R 56 V/35 fol. 66.

[78] Wismann's record of Suchenwirth's comments, Wismann to Funk, 3 March 1936, p. 2, BArch R 56 I/137. On the following, see ibid.

[79] BArch BDC/RSK/SS/Ihde, Wilhelm (1899–?).

[80] Goebbels, *Tagebücher*, Part I, vol. 5, 172 (3 February 1938).

[81] Grimm to Goebbels, 21 March 1934, DLA NL Hans Grimm/ Korrespondenz mit Regierungsstellen, NS-Parteistellen und Einzelpersönlichkeiten der NSDAP, folder 3 F–G.

Grimm called instead for the creation of a "body of high-quality professionals" that, equipped with special privileges, would form the RSK's
real "heart and head." He also repeatedly approached RSK president
Blunck with critiques of the paralysis of literature by "bureaus."[82]
These, Grimm said, were staffed by incompetents and, funded by
membership dues, undertook administrative efforts that stood in no
reasonable proportion to the resulting benefits for writers.[83] Grimm
therefore called for the RDS in future to function only as an "initial
reservoir and 'settling tank' led by a writer working full-time at the
task," whereas the "poets," called to their task "by God," should be
organized in a special, autonomous association within the RSK.

Although Grimm's elitist notions completely misconstrued the
intentions of the Nazis, whose objective was to register and control
all those working in the literature business, his attack touched a
sore point. The RDS had been disempowered de jure, but de facto
its administrative apparatus continued to exist within the Chamber.
Götz Otto Stoffregen, head of the RDS, had distinguished himself
during the Weimar Republic only as a political journalist for *völkisch*
groupings and joined the NSDAP in 1932,[84] but his deputy, Hans
Richter, was forced to resign in March 1935 due to his failure to
produce a Party card.[85] The pre-1933 career of Richter's successor,
Hugo Linhard, included work as a purchasing agent for the Rotafix
works and the Stralau glass foundry, as a salesman and broker of
gas stations for Deutsche Gasolin AG, and as the manager of an
engineering office specialized in electric lighting and power plants.[86]
Linhard thus entirely lacked expertise in literature, but he had two
trump cards: membership of the NSDAP (since 1930) and the SS
(since 1931).

The RDS management led by Linhard was organized as follows:
the administrative office; a literature department that shared responsibility for processing decisions on admission, rejection, or exclusion

---

[82] DLA NL Hans Grimm/Konv. Reichsschrifttumskammer, folder I 1933/34 and folder
II 1935/36. See also Grimm's speech to the RSK council on 5 June 1935, BArch R 56
V/187 fol. 8–13.
[83] Grimm to Blunck, 23 April 1935, BArch R 56 V/187 fol. 2–3.
[84] For details, see BArch BDC/RSK/Stoffregen, G.O. (1896–?).
[85] Stoffregen to Richter, 5 March 1935, BArch BDC/RSK/Richter, Hans.
[86] BArch BDC/RSK/Linhard, Hugo (1896–?).

with the "political monitoring office"; a legal department providing advice for members; the editorial office of the association journal *Der Schriftsteller* ("The Writer"); and the offices of the Reich organizations of fiction writers, poets, translators, scholarly and specialized authors, radio authors, librettists, playwrights, and the women's group.[87] The RDS's *Gau*-level branch leaderships also served as the provincial leaderships for the RSK.

A memorandum from the Chamber's legal advisor, sent in summer 1935, pointed out that the RDS management was extraordinarily inefficient.[88] Günther Gentz therefore recommended that its individual administrative sections be merged and taken over by the Chamber administration. On 20 September 1935, the RDS "leadership council" ceded to pressure from the Chamber and the Propaganda Ministry and resolved to wind up the association.[89] As a result, the approximately 12,000 members of the RDS obtained direct membership of the Reich Chamber of Literature with effect from 1 October 1935.

The Chamber's new Department II, "Writers and Cultivation of Writing," had four sections: (1) matters affecting author organization; (2) care and promotion of the German writer and of German literature at home (in this section Rudolf Krieger, taken on from the RDS, was to maintain links with state and Party literary offices and with the foundations and societies affiliated to the Chamber, prepare book exhibitions, run the Emergency Association of German Literature, and attend to the general economic interests of writers); (3) care and promotion of the German writer and German literature abroad, a field in which former president Blunck was to act; (4) legal advice and the specialized advisory offices, to which the offices for screenwriters and book reviewers were now added.[90] In fall 1936, Department II became the Writers Group, now headed by Kurt Metzner.[91]

---

[87] Report by the Berlin auditor Arnold Strehlik, 8 May 1935, on an audit of the RDS administration commissioned by the Chamber of Literature, BArch R 56 V/73 fol. 82–83. The appendix, fol. 106, includes a tabular overview of the organization of the RDS national leadership.

[88] BArch R 56 V/73 fol. 1–6a. The text is not dated, but appears to have been written in August or September 1935 at the latest.

[89] Minutes of the meeting on 26 September 1935, BArch R 56 V/73 fol. 139–45.

[90] RSK schedule of responsibilities, December 1935, BArch R 56 V/35 fol. 68–70.

[91] See BArch BDC/RSK/Masterfile/Metzner, Kurt O. Friedrich (1895–?).

From December 1938 through November 1939, the Writers Group was led by Gerhard Schumann.[92] However, this up-and-coming Nazi author, who had already been awarded the Swabian Literature Prize (1935) and the National Book Prize (1936), did not sufficiently relish his task of supervising the police-controlled bureaucratization of the author's profession.[93] His successor, Metzner again, left the Chamber in April 1941 after a fierce disagreement with Ihde over the handling of a series of politically delicate cases,[94] upon which Alfred Richard Meyer was promoted to lead the department. Meyer was a former publisher and an author associated with literary Expressionism (his pseudonym was "Munkepunke") who had headed the poetry group in the SDS and managed the Emergency Association of German Literature since 1930. In 1935 he had been taken on by the Chamber as a section head.[95]

After the annexation of Austria, the circle of writers covered by the professional organizations expanded once again. With the extension of the Chamber of Culture legislation to cover what was now officially known as the *Ostmark* on 11 June 1938, the coming years saw a total of 1,958 writers submit their membership applications to the provincial Chamber of Literature leadership in Vienna, set up in July 1938.[96] Until that time, Austrian writers principally resident in Austria had not been entitled to join the Chamber. In fact, one side-effect of the dramatically deteriorating relations between Austria and Germany after the National Socialist putsch attempt in July 1934 was that around 450 members who had initially been accepted into the Chamber via the RDS that year were struck off the list again. In 1938 the existing Austrian League of German Writers (Bund der deutschen Schriftsteller Österreichs), founded in December 1936, was made the framework to move members smoothly into the Reich Chamber of Literature and elevate them into the canon of literature promoted by the Nazi state.[97]

---

[92] BArch BDC/RSK/SA/Schumann, Gerhard (1911–1995).
[93] See Schumann to Johst, 15 November 1939, BArch BDC/RSK/Schumann, G.
[94] For details, see BArch R 56 V/186 fol. 26–40.
[95] BArch BDC/Masterfile/Meyer, A.R. (1882–1956): NSDAP member since 1 May 1937.
[96] The number of applications received by 20 July 1938 is given as 887 in Amann, *Zahltag*, 295. The total number is from Renner, *Österreichische Schriftsteller*, 269–73.
[97] See Renner, *Österreichische Schriftsteller*, 252–81, and Amann, *Zahltag*, 191–216.

The RDS was one of the pillars of the Chamber of Literature; the other was the book trade association Börsenverein der Deutschen Buchhändler. However, traditionally the Börsenverein had also organized the foreign associations and publishers working abroad, who were expressly excluded from membership of the Reich Chamber of Culture. As a result, on 19 October 1934 the Börsenverein was removed from the Chamber of Literature and replaced by the new League of Reich German Booksellers (Bund Reichsdeutscher Buchhändler e.V., BRB), established four days earlier. It only remained for the Börsenverein's extraordinary General Meeting in Leipzig on 11 November 1934 to approve a corresponding adjustment of the association's statutes.[98] This was a disenfranchisement, and it weighed all the more heavily due to the considerable impact that the founding of the new professional representation had on the Börsenverein's structure.

The leadership of the new BRB duplicated that of the Börsenverein—the president (Wilhelm Baur), his deputy (Martin Wülfing), and the treasurer (Hellmuth von Hase and from 1935 Anton Hiersemann) all worked for both organizations.[99] In contrast, the specialist and regional groups that made up the Börsenverein were separated off from the regional and sectoral structure of the BRB. The BRB's everyday organizational and substantive work was now delegated to the sector groups (*Fachschaften*) for publishing (led by Karl Baur), retailing (led by Theodor Fritsch, Jr.), wholesalers (led by Felix Gartmann), commercial lending libraries (led by Johannes Mau), and employees (led by Karl Thulke), along with the Consortium of German Book Agents (Arbeitsgemeinschaft, later Fachschaft, Deutscher Buchvertreter, led by Hans Joachim Siber)—some of these bodies further divided into specialized sub-groups.[100] From

---

[98] "Protokoll über die Verhandlungen der außerordentlichen Hauptversammlung des Börsenvereins der Deutschen Buchhändler zu Leipzig am 11.11.1934," *Bbl.* no. 265, 13 November 1934, 989–93.

[99] On this and the following, see the BRB statutes: "Satzung des Bundes Reichsdeutscher Buchhändler e.V.," *Bbl.* no. 257, 3 November 1934, 959–60. Martin Wülfing (1899–1986): NSDAP member since 1926 (BArch BDC/Masterfile).

[100] "Bekanntmachung vom 5.12.1934 über die neue Zusammensetzung der Börsenvereins-Gremien sowie der Fachschafts- und Gaugliederung des BRB," *Bbl.* no. 288, 11 December 1934, 1077–9; "Bekanntmachung über die Gliederung der Fachschaft Verlag," *Bbl.* no. 294, 18 December 1934, 1102–3.

1935 on, the interests of the profession were entrusted to the heads of the BRB's *Gau* branches, units based on those of the NSDAP.[101] The precise procedure for regrouping the members was set down by Wilhelm Baur in a "notification" of 12 November 1934.[102] This required all self-employed publishers and booksellers on German Reich territory to become obligatory members of the BRB "without a separate application"; their membership of the Börsenverein could remain in place if they so desired. Senior employees in the book trade and publishing sector also had to become members of the BRB, but could only remain in the Börsenverein upon express and well-grounded application. The distribution of the members among the six sector groups was coordinated by the BRB's administrative office. The publishing, retailing, and wholesaling groups had a total of 8,353 members, along with 8,600 book sales outlets listed in a "muster book"; the lending library group covered 3,170 members, together with 800 retail bookstores and 1,735 stationery stores that operated lending libraries. The employees' group numbered around 9,200 members, and the book agents' group 3,985.[103]

The Börsenverein was now reduced to a mere economic interest group, in which German and non-German representatives of the book trade regulated legal and economic questions related to production, distribution, and sales. Close links between the two organizations were assured, however, by the presence in the BRB of certain long-standing Börsenverein staff: Max Albert Hess, the managing director (since 1920), Willy Max Schulz as head of the foreign department (since 1925), and Gerhard Menz as the expert on training and general economic issues (since 1920).[104]

---

[101] See "Verzeichnis der Obmänner der Ortsgruppen und örtlichen Arbeitsgemeinschaften im Bund Reichsdeutscher Buchhändler e.V.," *Bbl.* no. 66, 19 March 1935, 226–8; no. 76, 30 March 1935, 257–9; and no. 92, 18 April 1935, 313–14.
[102] *Bbl.* no. 269, 17 November 1934, 1005–6.
[103] Membership numbers from the report on the BRB council meeting at the Berlin office, 20 September 1935, BArch BDC/RK/fiche Z 0025 fol. 1412–68, here fol. 1414 (p. 2), fol. 1418 (p. 4), fol. 1420 (p. 5). For the lending libraries, 2,700 cases had not yet been resolved at this stage.
[104] A. Hess (1885–1948), from 1920 the legal advisor and from 1924 the first managing director (from 1925 the director general) of the Börsenverein: see StAL BV II /3503. W. M. Schulz (1893–?), from 1 July 1925 director of the Börsenverein's German Society for the Foreign Book Trade, from 1926 director of the publicity office, from 1930

Within the Chamber of Literature, the area labeled "book trade/ libraries/monitoring the book market" initially made up Department III.[105] It comprised only two section heads. The first was Karl Heinrich Bischoff, responsible for BRB membership matters, keeping up the register of part-time booksellers, substantive and economic issues affecting the book trade as a whole, training the new generation of booksellers, book advertising, applications for foreign currency, and the approval of calendars;[106] the second was Eberhard Hasper, since 1934 the chair of the "office for the observation of door-to-door book sales," who supervised the work of the six sector groups on behalf of Wilhelm Baur. In other words, for the book trade just as for writers, there were initially two different sets of administration—which were, in addition, geographically split between Berlin and Leipzig.

Uniformity was only achieved after the BRB resolved its own dissolution at a General Meeting in Weimar on 24 October 1936.[107] Department III now took on the title Book Trade Group and was transferred from Berlin to Leipzig.[108] It was headed by Wilhelm Baur, who since 2 April 1935 had also been a member of the RSK council.[109] Karl Thulke became the managing director.[110] As well as administrative activities, Thulke's personal responsibilities

---

head of the foreign department; NSDAP member: see StAL BV II /3503. G. Menz (1885–1954), from 1920 editor-in-chief of the association's paper *Börsenblatt*, member of the Börsenverein's economic and journalistic advisory board; from 1925 professor of business studies in the book trade at the Leipzig School of Commerce: see StAL BV II /3509.

[105] RSK schedule of responsibilities, December 1935, BArch R 56 V/35 fol. 70–1.

[106] BArch BDC/RSK/Masterfile/Bischoff, K.H. (1900–78): from 1919 retailer of foreign-language literature in Vienna, 1923–4 and 1928–35 director of the distribution and advertising department of the publisher and bookstore G.A. v. Halem; NSDAP member since 1 May 1933; pen name Veit Bürkle.

[107] "Bericht über die Hauptversammlung," *Bbl.* no. 253, 29 October 1936, 943–4.

[108] RSK schedule of responsibilities, 1 July 1937, BArch R 56 V/35 fol. 76/verso–77/verso.

[109] *Das Archiv* 2 (1935/36), 140.

[110] BArch BDC/Masterfile/SS/RSK/Thulke, K. (1904–?): from 1925 bookselling assistant in Lübeck; 1929 Freiburg University bookstore; 1931 head of distribution and advertising at Langen-Müller; late 1932 responsible for professional training in the book trade in the DHV; 1933 volunteer director of the RSK group "Book Trade Employees"; 1933–6 publishing director of Brunnen-Verlag/Willi Bischoff in Berlin; from July 1936 Hess's successor as managing director of the BRB; NSDAP member since 1 May 1933; SS member since September 1933.

included supervising the individuals and companies associated with bookselling and publishing who were subject to obligatory Chamber of Culture membership, coordinating the work of the sector groups, and publishing the *Vertrauliche Mitteilungen* ("Confidential notifications") sent to the publishing and retailing groups and to the *Gau* book trade representatives in the Chamber's provincial leaderships.[111] He was also in charge of the "social care" of the members, which consisted in finding employment for book trade employees and book agents, examining applications for financial support, and establishing and managing welfare offices for incapacitated, needy, or elderly booksellers. The section "subject-specific support for members" was made up of the six sector groups of the now dissolved BRB. The section "legal support" was headed by the deputy managing director, Johannes Grewe.

In 1938, the six sector groups were integrated into Section III A, which now covered publishing, book trade and wholesaling, commercial lending libraries, and book agents and employees.[112] The heads of these four component groups were now the contacts for members, and supervised the activities of the sector groups. In 1942, the section responsible for providing legal advice to the sector groups was joined by a section for social issues and improving the book trade's performance. This new section was responsible for training programs and leisure activities, support for the new generation of booksellers, and the deployment of German booksellers abroad.[113]

Until 1941, Bischoff continued to work in his RSK Section III Z, covering "non-Aryan issues"; the Index of Harmful and Undesirable Literature; prohibitions and applications for special exceptions regarding the establishment or expansion of bookselling operations; the training and political instruction of young booksellers, book agents, and commercial lending library operators; and the management of the Reich School for the German Book Trade, founded in 1934.[114] After the annexation of Austria, Bischoff was

---

[111] RSK schedule of responsibilities, 1 July 1937, BArch R 56 V/35 fol. 76/verso. The following points ibid.

[112] RSK schedule of responsibilities, 1 April 1938, BArch R 56 V/35 fol. 83.

[113] RSK schedule of responsibilities, 1941, BArch R 2/4880 fol. 583.

[114] See the RSK schedules of responsibilities for 1935, BArch R 56 V/35 fol. 66–71; 1937, fol. 72–8; 1938, fol. 79–84; 1939, fol. 88–96; and 1940, BArch R 2/4879.

also involved in integrating the Austrian book trade.[115] This involved no fewer than 100 publishers, 800 booksellers, 150 lending library owners, 1,000 owners of subsidiary bookselling operations, 1,200 employees, and 500 publishing and book trade agents.[116] In addition, from 1939 Bischoff headed the Book Editors' Group, which had been separated out from the Book Trade Group in October 1938.[117] When, in fall 1941, Bischoff left the RSK to take on the "Aryanized" publisher Paul Zsolnay in Vienna, his section's responsibilities were distributed between the Chamber management, Department II in Berlin, and Department III in Leipzig.

By 1938, the Book Advertising Group was also being run from Berlin. Department IV had been formed out of the Reich Consortium for German Book Advertising, set up in 1935, the chief task of which was to prepare, carry out, and evaluate the "Week of the German Book."[118] When the change was made on 1 April 1937, three sections were formed: Section A, "advertising the German book at home" (led by Alfons Brugger), took on responsibility for the Book Week and for advertising specialist literature and organizing book exhibitions at Reich and *Gau* level; Section C, "advertising the German book abroad" (led by Rudolf Krieger), was to provide specialist expertise to support the work of the Propaganda Ministry, the Foreign Office, the NSDAP organization abroad (NSDAP/AO), and the foreign department of the Börsenverein; while Section B (led by Gerhard Heidelberger) drew up select bibliographies, coordinated authors' talks, and monitored literary journals and literary competitions.[119] On 1 April 1938, this wide array of responsibilities was transferred to the Propaganda Ministry's Literature Office.[120] The Chamber was left only

---

[115] See the file notes and memoranda on this issue in BArch BDC/RSK/Bischoff, K.H.

[116] Renner, *Österreichische Schriftsteller*, 268.

[117] "Amtliche Bekanntmachung der RSK vom 23.10.1938 über die Eingliederungspflicht der Lektoren und Schriftwalter," reproduced in Ihde, *Handbuch der Reichs- schrifttumskammer*, 263; RSK schedule of responsibilities, 1940, BArch R 2/4879 fol. 455.

[118] E. Langenbucher, "Gemeinschaftliche Buchwerbung. Erste Sitzung der Reichs- arbeitsgemeinschaft für Deutsche Buchwerbung," *Bbl.* no. 78, 2 April 1935, 265.

[119] RSK schedule of responsibilities, 1 July 1937, BArch R 56 V/35 fol. 77/verso.

[120] "Zweite Bekanntmachung über die Gliederung der Reichsschrifttumskammer vom 21.5.1938," reproduced in Ihde, *Handbuch der Reichsschrifttumskammer*, 44–5, here 44.

with oversight of the literary societies, bibliophile clubs, and lecture organizers. These had been combined as a consortium since 1933, from 1938 entitled the Literary Societies and Lecture Organizers Group[121] and from August 1937 the Reich Organization Book and *Volk*.[122]

There was one other important administrative entity based in Berlin and protected from direct intervention by the Leipzig office. Plans to resolve the problem of book exports had been under discussion in the Chamber since winter 1933/34, and they culminated in the founding of a Cooperative of German Publishers in Berlin on 16 March and a Hamburg-Bremen Book Export Cooperative on 20 March 1934.[123] The Börsenverein's resistance to the state centralization of book exports had been broken when its president Friedrich Oldenbourg was ousted, and negotiations on the further detail of the procedure were now continued via the Chamber.

During a meeting at the Reich Finance Ministry on 21 July 1934, RSK section head Schlegel made it clear that the proposed promotion of book exports was a "cultural-policy measure" designed to boost the declining sales of German scientific, literary, and political or philosophical works abroad.[124] At this time, however, neither the Finance Ministry nor the Ministry of Economics was prepared to supply the funding requested,[125] and the talks came to a temporary halt. In summer 1935, Paul Hövel of the Propaganda Ministry literature department came back to the Minister of Finance with two further arguments.[126] Firstly, Hövel wrote, the promotion of book exports was a worthwhile investment because "the German book abroad must

---

[121] "Amtliche Bekanntmachung der RSK vom 5.1.1938," reproduced in Ihde, *Handbuch der Reichsschrifttumskammer*, 265–6.

[122] RSK schedule of responsibilities, 1940, R 2/4879 fol. 503.

[123] Memorandum on the preparation of a law for the central guidance of German cultural policy and for the promotion of German book exports (Reichsschrifttumskammer/ Abteilung C/Werner Schlegel), R 2/4926 fol. 5–35, here fol. 33.

[124] Note by a senior Finance Ministry official on 26 July 1934, BArch R 2/4926 fol. 37. On the following, see ibid.

[125] Ibid. fol. 38–9. Schlegel was recommended to cover the costs by skimming off RSK membership dues and calling in help from the Propaganda Ministry and the Advertising Council.

[126] Hövel to Reich Minister of Finance, 12 June 1935, BArch R 2/4926 fol. 143–6. The following points ibid.

be regarded as paving the way for German exports more generally." Secondly, book exports constituted "the most effective means of foreign propaganda over the long term"—because, he continued, increased exports of books would "conclusively demonstrate" to the world "that the German achievements in the intellectual sphere are indispensable, and that there is no truth to the claims by atrocity propaganda that Germany is a barbarian country and has parted ways with Western civilization."

This new foray found support within the Ministry of Economics, which approached the Finance Ministry using very similar arguments to advocate approval of the requested 15 million RM.[127] Finance Minister Schwerin von Krosigk finally agreed, since 5 million RM of this sum, intended to fund price reductions on each exported book, were to be contributed by the Print and Paper-Processing Economic Group, while the remaining 10 million RM would take the shape of a bridging loan.[128]

On 21 June 1935, Wismann and Vowinckel informed the Börsenverein's president Wilhelm Baur that "the matter of exports is now completely clarified, the relevant legal regulations will be passed in the next few days, and accordingly the book trade must reduce prices by 25 percent."[129] Baur—who had been completely bypassed in the decision-making process—was not minded to accept without protest the implementation of a "book export compensation procedure" agreed without reference to his own authority. He temporarily reactivated the resistance of the Börsenverein, apparently long since overcome, by reporting the objections of the publishers Arthur Georgi, Jr. and Hermann Degener to the state-imposed price cut.[130] For the publishers, the attack on their pricing autonomy remained the crucial grounds for their refusal to approve the carefully negotiated export promotion plans.

[127] Reich and Prussian Minister of Economics to Reich Minister of Finance, 8 June 1935, BArch R 2/4926 fol. 133–7.

[128] Notes taken by Hövel on 13 June 1935 on his meeting at the Ministry of Economics, BArch R 2/4926 fol. 153–4. On the outcome of the later discussions, see Reich Minister of Finance to Reich Minister of Economics, 19 June 1935, ibid. fol. 169–72.

[129] This is how Wilhelm Baur represented the conversation; Baur to Wismann, 17 September 1935, p. 2, BArch BDC/RSK/Baur, W.

[130] See Vowinckel to Wilhelm Baur, 7 August 1935; Wismann to Baur, 2 September 1935; and Baur to Wismann, 17 September 1935, BArch BDC/RSK/Baur, W.

Despite these concerns and opposition, on 1 August 1935 an administrative office was set up to manage the discount procedure, carrying the euphemistic title Economic Office of the German Book Trade. On 27 August, the presidents of the Literature, Press, and Music Chambers issued an ordinance setting out that "in the coming days, all publishers and sellers of books, periodicals, sheet music, and teaching materials based in Germany will receive a memorandum from the Chamber of Literature, Economic Office of the German Book Trade department, on the new regulation of exports to start 9 September 1935. Every exporting publisher and seller of books, periodicals, sheet music, and teaching materials will be obliged to comply with the guidelines set out in that memorandum."[131] From then on the activities of the Economic Office proceeded in secrecy, since other countries were to learn neither of this economic protectionism nor of the Nazi cultural-policy objectives that it pursued.[132]

Hövel was appointed director of the new Economic Office, which was funded by a 0.5 percent deduction from the subsidy paid to exporters. On 1 April 1938, responsibility for the Economic Office moved from the Chamber to the Propaganda Ministry.[133] The "export compensation" system rapidly led to a significant rise in sales of German books abroad,[134] but the Ministry of Finance balked at providing further funding, so that the Ministry of Economics had to contribute millions of reichsmarks in subsidies from its own budget every year.[135] By August 1940, a total of 52,905,951.28 RM had been

---

[131] In Schrieber, Das Recht der Reichskulturkammer, vol. III, 11.

[132] Memorandum on the implementation of the book export compensation procedure, published by the Economic Office of the German Book Trade, Berlin, 27 August 1935/1 September 1939 (3rd edition), BArch R 2/4927 fol. 537–63. Section 1 ("General") noted that: "Apart from the fact of the price reduction itself, nothing regarding the existence of the procedure must be reported to third parties either in Germany or abroad." Violations of this requirement would be punished with fines on the basis of Chamber of Culture or foreign currency legislation.

[133] "Zweite Bekanntmachung über die Gliederung der Reichsschrifttumskammer vom 21.5.1938," in Ihde, Handbuch der Reichsschrifttumskammer, 44–5, here 45.

[134] See the reports from abroad on the impact of the book export compensation procedure, collated by Hövel, 7 July 1936, BArch R 2/4926 fol. 319–57.

[135] Note regarding promotion of book exports, 10 October 1936, BArch R 2/4926 fol. 359–63. For details of the Economic Office's annual budget negotiations, see R 2/4926 and 4927.

paid out in subsidies for book exports.[136] With the outbreak of World War II the procedure's significance declined as the economies of the occupied, annexed, or allied nations were increasingly aligned with German needs. Special export provisions were dropped for several of these countries,[137] and the system was abandoned completely on 1 April 1943.

The continued existence of Hövel's office was nevertheless assured, firstly by the fact that in March 1939 the Propaganda Ministry had given it the additional task of monitoring the importation of books;[138] secondly, in fall 1939 the office also took over the administration of paper allocation.[139] Wilhelm Baur had originally staked a claim to discretionary powers over the allocation of paper and binding materials for the Chamber of Literature, analogous to practices in the Press Chamber.[140] Because of Baur's role within the Party publisher Eher, this would have meant Eher attaining a defining influence on the entire production of book, newspaper, and periodicals publishing. However, during the negotiations with the Propaganda Ministry's literature department and the Ministry of Economics print and paper-processing group, Karl Baur (no relation to Wilhelm; Karl Baur was the owner of the Munich publishing company Callwey and head of the publishing section of the Book Trade Group) made sure that the task of carrying out paper allocation went to the Economic Office of the German Book Trade.

In 1940 the Economic Office, accountable to the Propaganda Ministry, employed ninety-six people.[141] At this time it was structured as follows: direction and management (Department I); accounts

---

[136] RMVP literature department to Reich Minister of Finance, 23 August 1940, R 2/4927 fol. 526.
[137] On this, see Hövel's first set of notes on the continuation of the book export compensation procedure, 23 December 1942, BArch R 2/4927 fol. 571–7.
[138] Confidential circular from the Economic Office of the German Book Trade, 23 May 1939, BArch R 55/828 fol. 6–8, referring to a Propaganda Ministry decree of 6 March 1939.
[139] Record of the audit of the Economic Office carried out by the Propaganda Ministry budget department, BArch R 55/213, fol. 32.
[140] On this and the following, see Wilhelm Baur to Karl Baur, 9 June 1941, pp. 4–5, BArch BDC/RSK/Wülfing, M.; Baur, *Wenn ich so zurückdenke ...*, 356–60.
[141] Observations of principle on the budgeting of the Economic Office of the German Book Trade, 23 July 1940, BArch R 55/405 fol. 69–72.

(Department II); monitoring (Department III, which was responsible for the book export compensation procedure and the surveillance of book imports); records (Department IV); and paper rationing (Department V, which alone accounted for fifteen employees).[142] When the Ministry's Promotion and Advisory Office for German Literature was closed down in August 1944, the Economic Office absorbed its responsibilities as well.[143]

The Reich Ministry of Science, Education, and Public Instruction

By establishing the Propaganda Ministry and the Reich Chamber of Culture, in the course of 1933 Goebbels had tried to attain a unified responsibility for all cultural matters across the country. But when negotiations began on the detail of the Chamber of Culture legislation, the provinces of Bavaria, Thuringia, Baden, Hesse, and Württemberg defied the proposed encroachments into their competencies in the field of culture, which had been guaranteed in the Weimar constitution.[144] The Reich Ministry of the Interior, too, strongly objected to ceding the state's legislative monopoly to the seven component chambers of the Chamber of Culture, arguing that this would mean splitting the state "into a pluralism of conflicting power complexes."[145] The fear of "dualism" in the administration of culture was shared by the Prussian Ministry of Science, Art, and

---

[142] BArch R 55/213 fol. 62–7.

[143] Propaganda Ministry personnel department memorandum, 18 August 1944, ibid. fol. 12.

[144] Bavarian State Minister of Teaching and Culture, Hans Schemm, to RMVP, 14 November 1933, HStA Weimar Thüringisches Ministerium f. Volksbildung/C 957 fol. 1–3; Baden Minister of Culture, Teaching, and Justice, department of culture and teaching, to Thuringian Minister of Public Instruction, 8 December 1933, ibid. fol. 5; Hesse State Ministry, ministerial department of education, culture, art, and folklore to Thuringian Ministry of Public Instruction, 30 December 1933, ibid. fol. 6; Württemberg Ministry of Culture to Thuringian Ministry of Public Instruction, 23 January 1934, ibid. fol. 10.

[145] Interior Ministry official's notes on a meeting with the director of the Propaganda Ministry's legal department on 19 January 1934, BArch 49.01/278 fol. 26.

Public Instruction, at that time responsible for most of the public cultural institutions.[146] While talks on these controversial issues were still under way, the Reich Ministry of Science, Education, and Public Instruction was established on 1 May 1934. Its purview was established in a decree by Hitler on 11 May,[147] which laid down that the Ministry of the Interior was to pass its competencies in the areas of science, education and teaching, youth associations, and adult education to the newly formed Ministry of Education. But Interior Minister Frick was not the only one to lose out through the reorganization. On 8 May, state secretary Funk of the Propaganda Ministry had tried to thwart the emergence of the new Reich agency. At the behest of his minister, and with Göring's approval, Funk put a dual proposal before the Reich Chancellery: that a "Ministry of Culture and Popular Enlightenment" be established in Prussia, and that the Propaganda Ministry be renamed the "Reich Ministry of Culture and Popular Enlightenment."[148] This new title would have helped the Propaganda Minister to assert the Reich's cultural jurisdiction vis-à-vis the provinces and to assert his own primacy in cultural policy vis-à-vis his new ministerial colleague. The scheme foundered, however, on the veto of Hitler, who evidently did not want to allow Goebbels even more power.[149] Rust thus gained ground in the area of cultural policy, becoming a serious rival with whom Goebbels repeatedly had "trouble over competencies."[150]

On his appointment as Reich Minister of Education, Rust retained his post as Prussian Minister of Science, Art, and Public Instruction; the formal division between the two capacities was only dissolved

---

[146] Memorandum on the relationship between the Reich chambers created by the Reich Chamber of Culture Law and the administrative jurisdiction of Reich and provinces, sent by state secretary Wilhelm Stuckart to Education Minister Rust on 18 January 1934 in preparation for a meeting with state secretary Funk, BArch 49.01/278 fol. 249–54.

[147] *RGBL*/Part I, no. 51, 14 May 1934, 375.

[148] Funk to Lammers, 8 May 1934, accompanying the drafts of the "orders discussed on the telephone," BArch R 43 II /1149 fol. 166. On the agreement between Goebbels and Göring of 7 May 1934, see Goebbels, *Tagebücher*, Part I, vol. 3/I, 44.

[149] Lammers's notes on his presentation to Hitler, 9 May 1934, BArch R 43 II /1149 fol. 169.

[150] Goebbels, *Tagebücher*, Part I, vol. 3/I, 250 (21 June 1935). For details, see Nagel, *Hitlers Bildungsreformer*, 138–49.

on 1 January 1935.[151] The Reich Ministry's personnel grew from 282 in 1933 to 672 in June 1944. The career civil servants taken on from the Weimar-era Prussian Ministry of Education were quickly disempowered by newly appointed administrators with close ties to the NSDAP. In the decree of 11 May 1934, Hitler had determined that the new Reich Minister would be responsible for "all tasks, including those of legislation," in the specialist areas assigned to his department. This demoted the education and culture ministries of the provinces other than Prussia into merely intermediate-level authorities, eliminating their previous autonomy.

The Reich Ministry of Education was now also responsible for the whole of the research library system. In the Ministry, which consisted of seven offices, the political monitoring and steering of the research libraries was carried out by the Office for Research. This department's task was to direct the handling of all matters related to the state and university libraries, including the librarians' personnel records, all assistants regardless of their civil-service status, the national exchange center (Reichstauschstelle) and the Central Procurement Office for German Libraries (Beschaffungsamt der Deutschen Bibliotheken), German scientific and scholarly literature abroad, and research libraries both at home and abroad.[152]

In charge of this area was Rudolf Kummer. He had worked as a state librarian since October 1923, in the catalogue and operations department of the Bavarian State Library. In August 1934, Hugo Andres Krüss, the influential director of the Prussian State Library, recommended Kummer to Karl Theodor Vahlen, the head of the Office for Research. For his part, Kummer commended himself to his new superior by outlining a reorganization of the German library system, which he sent to the Ministry on 22 January 1935 using the letterhead of the South Bavarian section of the Reichsstelle zur Förderung des deutschen Schrifttums.[153]

In this memorandum, Kummer first noted that too little value was currently placed on "the German library system's importance

---

[151] See Nagel, *Hitlers Bildungsreformer*, 9–123.
[152] Schedule of responsibilities, Office for Research, 21 January 1937, BArch R 21/1 fol. 14 ff., here fol. 21.
[153] See BArch BDC/Research/Kummer, R.

in the task of influencing our *Volk* along National Socialist lines." Before the libraries could be effectively instrumentalized to this end, "fundamental reforms" to both "the head and the limbs" would be necessary. Kummer suggested establishing a Reich Committee for the German Libraries, with between three and five members headed by "a tried and true National Socialist," who must at the same time "be an outstanding expert in the field." The director general of the Prussian State Library should belong to the Committee as a permanent member, a point of particular importance since Kummer hoped to turn the Prussian library into a "National Library." The special task of the Committee's director would be to supervise the appointment of mid-level and senior civil servants in the libraries, "making it impossible for non-National Socialist directors to take arbitrary decisions." Promotions were to be permitted only after approval by the Reich Ministry of Education, and should be based not merely on professional qualifications, but to "the highest extent" also on the strength of the librarian's ties to the German *Volk*. It was this *Volksverbundenheit* that had "so far been seriously lacking." For Kummer, it was already obvious how the missing sense of the *Volk* could be produced: by "very close cooperation" with the relevant NSDAP cultural organizations. This view won him a place in the Ministry's central administration, as an advisor on "general matters of principle regarding National Socialist writing and the PPK."[154]

Kummer's memorandum became the basis of ministerial policy in the area of research libraries. In 1935, the Prussian union catalogue began to appear as the German Union Catalogue.[155] On 1 December 1936, Rust changed the Prussian Advisory Council into a Reich Advisory Board for Library Affairs (Reichsbeirat für Bibliotheksangelegenheiten).[156] This five-member committee was tasked with writing reports to prepare the Ministry's laws and administrative regulations, directing training and examinations for research librarianship within the Reich, and coordinating the research libraries'

---

[154] Schedule of responsibilities, Reich Ministry of Science, Education, and Public Instruction, 1937: Central Department Z III, BArch R 21/1 fol. 25.
[155] For details, see Komorowski, "Die wissenschaftlichen Bibliotheken," 15–16; Schochow, *Die Preußische Staatsbibliothek*, 46–52 and 135–8.
[156] "Bekanntmachung Rusts vom 7.12.1936," *Deutsche Wissenschaft, Erziehung und Volksbildung* 2 (1936), 532–3, BArch RD 39/1–2.

contacts abroad.[157] It is no surprise that Kummer's patron Krüss was appointed chair of the Reich Advisory Council, for although not a "tried and true National Socialist," as a good civil servant he had placed himself unconditionally at the service of the Nazi state in 1933.[158] The Reich Minister of Education was represented by a "permanent commissioner," a function that was fulfilled by Kummer himself right up to 1945. He was appointed a Ministry section head on 1 February 1935 and rapidly promoted to undersecretary on 1 September 1935—"due to his claim to preferential treatment as a member of the old guard," as the certificate of appointment put it.[159]

Responsibility for public libraries, taken over from the Ministry of the Interior, was held by the public libraries and adult education section of the Office for Public Instruction. The section had existed since October 1934, staffed by a single official: Heinz Dähnhardt.[160] To carry out his operations, Dähnhardt could make use of the Prussian Provincial Office for Public Libraries, which on 1 September 1935 became the Reich Office for Popular Libraries (Reichsstelle für volkstümliches Büchereiwesen), directly accountable to the Ministry of Education. This office was initially headed by Franz Schriewer, the director of the municipal library in Frankfurt an der Oder. In May 1937, he was succeeded by Fritz Heiligenstaedt, who had run the advisory office for public libraries in the province of Hannover since 1919. The Reich Office was intended to steer the work of the State Public Libraries Offices in the provinces, which on paper remained responsible to the provincial administrations of culture and education.[161]

The process of unification thus initiated was continued in October 1937 with the issuing of "guidelines for the public library system."[162] The public librarians had long been expecting

---

[157] On the committee's members and work, see Komorowski, "Die Tagungsprotokolle."
[158] Happel, Das wissenschaftliche Bibliothekswesen, 56–60; Komorowski, "Die wissenschaftlichen Bibliotheken," 4–5; Greguletz, "Die Preußische Staatsbibliothek."
[159] BArch BDC/Research/Kummer, R.
[160] BArch BDC/Partei-Kanzlei-Correspondence/Masterfile/Dähnhardt, H. (1897–?): Ph.D. 1926; 1927–34 history teacher at the school of social work in the Protestant Johannisstift seminary, Spandau, and director of an adult education institute; DNVP member 1919–29; joined NSDAP 1 May 1933. See also Stieg, Public Libraries in Nazi Germany, 43–5, 56–77.
[161] See Schriewer, Die staatlichen Volksbüchereistellen.
[162] Deutsche Wissenschaft, Erziehung und Volksbildung 4 (1937), 473–7.

comprehensive legislation on libraries, but the new guidelines were limited to stipulating the public libraries' political orientation and securing the Ministry of Education's claim to leadership of the public libraries system against the communal authorities, whose competences had been strengthened by the Municipal Code of 30 January 1935.[163] The public libraries were acknowledged as being an "essential component of the communal authorities' cultural and educational responsibilities"—but at the same time the Ministry of Education reserved the right to determine the guiding principles of the structure and development of the libraries in terms of both organization and content. The communal administrations were called upon to ensure that "there is a permanent library in each community having 500 or more inhabitants." That library was to hold at least 200 volumes for communities of 500 inhabitants, 500 volumes for those of 1,000 inhabitants, 1,500 volumes for those of 5,000 inhabitants, and 2,000–4,000 volumes for those of 10–20,000 inhabitants. Larger communities, with 20–100,000 residents, should aspire to establish a reading room and special lending facilities for young people, to expand the permanent library into a study library, and to set up branch libraries. The funding needed to implement these requirements was to come from the communes themselves, while the State Public Libraries Offices would provide the "specialized guidance" for establishing public libraries and prescribe the administrative structure, the arrangement of holdings, the selection of new acquisitions, and the creation of catalogues. The directors of the Public Library Offices were also in charge of the professional and political training of part-time library managers.

All this created the impression of an organizational structure based on sound expertise and clarity of purpose. In fact, however, the reorganization of the public library system was characterized by improvisation and deference to existing responsibilities, as is indicated by the diffuse institutional integration of the State Public Libraries Offices. As local offices, they were first accountable to the provincial teaching administrations, in Prussia to the relevant

---

[163] See H. Dähnhardt, "Richtlinien für das Volksbüchereiwesen," *Die Bücherei* 5 (1938), 1–7 and 130–6, here 1.

district president. Because the Public Library Offices were "if possible to be consolidated with a viable public or municipal library," and the library director was simultaneously to be the director of the Public Library Office, the offices were caught in an ambiguous position between the province and the commune. Prior approval by the Minister of Education was necessary for the establishment of new Public Library Offices, the restructuring of their districts, or the assignation of new tasks. Finally, the Reich Office for Popular Libraries, directly accountable to Rust, was deployed as a centralized advisory and coordination body. As a result, there were four institutions—on the local, provincial, and national level—with a say in the work of the Public Library Offices.

In its commentary on the guidelines, the Education Ministry left no doubt that the "organizational implementation of the measures necessary to fully realize the political and ideological tasks embodied by public library work" must fall under the primacy of the state.[164] However, Dähnhardt was also perfectly aware that the large-scale expansion of the public library system planned by his Ministry depended on cooperation from the communes. This was particularly true with respect to funding, and it was more a call to action than a description of reality when Dähnhardt stated that "the public library system is enjoying increasing consideration within communal budgets." The financial weakness of communities in villages and small and mid-sized towns meant that the majority remained reliant on financial subsidies from the Education Ministry and the State Public Libraries Offices in order to expand their public library provision.[165] Even in the Nazi state, the euphoric claim that the public library was no longer a "welfare facility" forced to "carve out an existence with the help of charity," but now fully acknowledged "as a local cultural institution"[166] was very far from realistic.

---

[164] Ibid. 133; the following quotation ibid. 131.
[165] See, for example, Konrad Heyde, "Die Staatlichen Volksbüchereistellen," 143–4.
[166] H. Dähnhardt, "Richtlinien für das Volksbüchereiwesen," *Die Bücherei* 5 (1938), 1–7, 130–6, here 131. See also Stieg, *Public Libraries in Nazi Germany*, 128–44.

The Foreign Office

In March 1933, during the debates over responsibilities that accompanied the creation of the Reich Ministry of Popular Enlightenment and Propaganda, the Foreign Office's culture department again defended its model of "planned promotional work for German culture abroad" as practiced during the Weimar Republic.[167] This did not, the Foreign Office insisted, involve "'propaganda' in the traditional sense," but a "scrupulous observation of the mood toward Germany abroad, which sometimes prompts us to take a stronger stand and sometimes prescribes a certain temporary reserve, for we must never arouse the impression of wanting to impose our lofty German cultural assets upon another nation." Such was the deep-seated conflict that would continue to beleaguer cooperation both with the Foreign Office's rival, the Propaganda Ministry, and with the Reich Ministry of Education. These two newly founded ministries expressly defined themselves as political instruments of the Nazi state, and to a considerable degree pursued their own initiatives in foreign cultural policy, a sphere previously dominated by the Foreign Office. In these battles for authority, the culture department was weakened by its inadequate personnel and funding and its subordinate status within its own organization; a further handicap was the low esteem in which the Nazi leadership held the elitist and tradition-steeped Foreign Office.

The Foreign Office responded to the new challenges by increasing its personnel from 2,232 in 1932 to 6,458 in 1943,[168] substantially boosting its budget, and introducing a series of restructuring measures that politicized its work, which had previously been based on purely pragmatic considerations. Since 1932, the culture department had been led by Friedrich Stieve, an author and the holder of a humanities doctorate.[169] In 1933/34, when the Foreign Office

---

[167] Memorandum "Cultural Policy," 1 March 1933, Political archive of the German Foreign Office (hereafter PA) PA Kult VI Akten betr. Dienstbetrieb 1927–36, vol. 1.

[168] Sasse, *Zur Geschichte des Auswärtigen Amts*, 44.

[169] Foreign Office personnel files and BArch BDC/RSK/Stieve, Friedrich (1884–1966): 1916 member of press council at the German legation in Stockholm; worked for the FO from 1921; 1928–32 German envoy in Riga; March 1939 on sick leave; from 1942 head of the archives commission; application for NSDAP membership 30 November 1939, joined 1 January 1940.

lost responsibilities to the Propaganda Ministry, the department was reduced and the personnel cut to just six people. In May 1936 it became the "cultural policy department," and in 1937 its tasks were diversified and more sharply profiled with the help of a staffing increase to thirty-five people. In spring 1939, Stieve was replaced by his deputy, Fritz von Twardowski, another experienced diplomat, who did not join the NSDAP until 1940.[170] In turn, von Twardowski was succeeded in late March 1943 by Franz Alfred Six, this time a convinced Nazi who was new to the Foreign Office but whose SD career had been sponsored by Heydrich and Himmler since 1935.[171] On 1 September 1939, there were thirteen civil servants and twenty-nine employees working in the cultural policy department.[172]

This boost in personnel compared to previous years was counteracted by the emergence of new competition within the Foreign Office itself.[173] The information department, newly founded at the start of World War II with a staff rising to 164 by January 1943,[174] immediately took over several tasks including the supervision of cultural writing, book exhibitions, literary readings, authors' associations, translations, and libraries abroad.[175] The Germany department, formed in May 1940 and led by the powerful undersecretary Martin Luther, played a considerable part in the Foreign Office's political radicalization. It launched a fundamental attack on the role of the

---

[170] PA personnel files and BArch BDC/Masterfile Fritz von Twardowski (1890–1970): Ph.D. in political science 1922; worked for the FO from 1923; 1929–32 German Embassy in Moscow; 1932–3 member of the German delegation at the Geneva Disarmament Conference; from November 1935 permanent representative of the head of the culture department; 1943–5 German Consul General in Istanbul.

[171] For detail, see Hachmeister, *Der Gegnerforscher*.

[172] PA Akten betr. Dienstbetrieb der Abteilung VI, Personalien, vol. 4: 26 September 1939–2 October 1940.

[173] See Sasse, *Zur Geschichte des Auswärtigen Amts*, 44–5; memorandum from Dr. Schumburg (section D II) to the culture department, 30 November 1940 (12 pp.), PA Inland II g(eheim), vol. 1; von Twardowski to Luther, 26 January 1942 and Luther to von Twardowski, 9 February 1942, PA Handakten Luther, vol. 15; organizational plan for the 1942 information plan, PA Kult. Geschäftsverteilung, vol. 2 1940–3.

[174] Krümmer section to Luther, 14 January 1943, PA Handakten Luther, Schriftverkehr, vol. 16.

[175] "Umlauf betr. Büro Informationsabteilung Kultur vom 30.9.1942," PA Kult. Akten betr. Dienstbetrieb des Auswärtigen Amts. Geschäftsverteilung, vol. 2 1940–3.

cultural policy department, which it accused of being antiquated and lacking in initiative, and intervened heavily in foreign cultural policy. After Luther's overthrow, the information and Germany departments were dissolved, and on 1 April 1943 the fragmented tasks of foreign cultural policy were brought back together in the cultural policy department,[176] now with a staff of 142.[177] For the first time, there was now also a central literature section, "Kult Lit," responsible for cultural writing, book exhibitions, literary readings, translations, the Mundus holding company, German bookstores abroad, book exports, book advisory offices, information libraries, and libraries for ethnic Germans outside the Reich borders.

By 1941 the cultural fund, which stagnated between 1929 and 1939, had grown from 3.2 to 9 million RM.[178] This enabled the Foreign Office on the one hand to realize its goal of enhanced influence over the cultural and intellectual life of Germany's allies, neutral nations, and German-occupied countries, and on the other to assert the value of its cultural endeavors against the competition of the Propaganda Ministry. A Germany department memorandum of November 1940 compared the Propaganda Ministry's understanding of "cultural propaganda" to the feverish activity of an itinerant preacher or a missionary.[179] Whereas the Propaganda Ministry "always tries to set up large, prestigious events," the Foreign Office put its faith in "tenacious, quiet, and well-camouflaged propaganda and cultural work," aiming to create a positive attitude toward cultural events among the foreign country's population.

For the first time, the Foreign Office now deployed the new instrument of international treaties on intellectual and cultural cooperation. Whereas the cultural agreement with Hungary, signed on 28 May 1936, had come

---

[176] Reich Foreign Minister's ordinance, 25 March 1943, accompanied by schedule of responsibilities for the cultural policy department to begin 1 April 1943, PA Kult. Geschäftsverteilung, vol. 2 1940–3.

[177] PA Akten betr. Dienstbetrieb der Abteilung VI, Personalien, vol. 7: 10 August 1942 – July 1943.

[178] Program of work, "Arbeitsprogramm der Kulturpolitischen Abteilung des Auswärtigen Amts für das Jahr 1942" (19 January 1942), p. 1, PA Kult Pol. Büroleiter, Dienstbetrieb der Abt. Kult, vol. 1. On the budgetary situation in 1929–39, see Stieve's response of 28 February 1939 to a note by the Reich Economics Minister, 15 February, PA Kult H Akten betr. die geheimen Verschlusssachen des Referats Kult H., vol. 2 1938–43.

[179] Memorandum, 30 November 1940, p. 3, PA Inland II g, vol. 1.

about essentially on the initiative of the Ministry of Education, those with Italy (23 November 1938), Japan (25 November 1938), Spain (24 January 1939), Bulgaria (19 June 1940), Slovakia (1 April 1942), and Romania (7 November 1942) were all negotiated under Foreign Office leadership with participation by the Education Ministry and the Propaganda Ministry. All these treaties ascribed an important role to promoting the "German book" and squeezing out anti-Nazi or "emigrant" literature in German.[180]

The lifting of book bans was another crucial item in the negotiations that took place subsequent to a confidential "gentlemen's agreement" of 11 July 1936 on Germany's cultural relations with Austria.[181] In these talks, the German goal was to "free National Socialist literature from being defamed as literature hostile to the state," the better to use it as a propaganda resource in the battle against Austria's attempts to remain autonomous.[182] In the subcommittee of the German-Austrian cultural committee set up to discuss book-related questions, however, the Austrian delegation was reluctant to make concessions.[183] Of a Reich German "wish list" including around 600 titles, only fifty-four books and eight calendars were approved for distribution in Austria.[184] Nevertheless, in July 1937 the ban on Hitler's *Mein Kampf* was successfully lifted.[185] Despite a

[180] See H.U. Granow, "Die Buchfragen in den deutsch-ausländischen Kulturabkommen," *Bbl.* no. 107, 10 May 1941, 13–15.

[181] ADAP 1918–45, series D 1937–45, vol. I, 231–3.

[182] This was the German negotiating strategy as set down in a Foreign Office meeting on 9 March 1937. Records of the meeting in PA Kult Gen Akten betr. Deutsch-Österreichisches Kulturabkommen, here Kult Gen 5 adh. I, vol. 1 1936–7; notes on cultural relations between Germany and Austria and the possibilities of promoting them (December 1936), p. 4, PA Kult Gen Akten betr. Deutsch-Österreichisches Kulturabkommen, here Kult Gen 5 adh. I, vol. 1 1936–7.

[183] Minutes of the negotiations at the meeting of the German-Austrian cultural committee on 23 April 1937 in Berlin, PA Kult Gen Akten betr. Deutsch-Österreichisches Kulturabkommen, here Kult Gen 5 adh. I, vol. 1 1936–7; report of the meeting of the subcommittee for cultural relations between Austria and Germany on 21–24 July 1937 in Vienna, PA Kult Gen Akten betr. Deutsch-Österreichisches Kulturabkommen, here Kult Gen 5 adh. VI, vol. 1 1936–7.

[184] List of bans and list of titles requested for approval, PA Kult Gen Akten betr. Deutsch-Österreichisches Kulturabkommen, here Kult Gen 5 adh. VI, vol. 1 1936–7, and Kult Gen 5 adh. III, vol. 2 1937.

[185] Record of the meeting of the participating government departments and the Party at the Foreign Office on 30 November 1936 to discuss commencing cultural policy negotiations with Austria, p. 3, PA Kult Gen Akten betr. Deutsch-Österreichisches Kulturabkommen, here Kult Gen 5 adh. I, vol. 1 1936–7.

prohibition on advertising it, this Nazi staple was widely circulated in Austria, especially in the cities. In contrast, right up to annexation, the German negotiating team failed in its objective of preventing the Austrian dissemination of "emigrant literature"—which was even used by the Austrian government for its counterpropaganda.[186]

Alongside formal treaties, the Foreign Office also made use of informal influence. A secret "working agreement" concluded between Foreign Minister von Ribbentrop and Goebbels on 22 October 1941 regulated, among other things, the circulation of German writing in and about foreign countries.[187] The Foreign Office and the Propaganda Ministry, with the Party publisher Eher, jointly funded the holding company Mundus AG, an umbrella for "those publishing companies controlled by the two ministries and located in Germany and abroad that produce literature for foreign countries and distribute it into and within foreign countries." A further umbrella company was to bring together the state- and Party-controlled distribution companies abroad. Eher held a majority stake of 51 percent; the Foreign Office and the Propaganda Ministry were each left with 24.5 percent. The company's objective was the dissemination of German literature via publishers and bookstores abroad—whether in German or translated into another language. The Propaganda Ministry was given the right to establish its own "literature advisory offices and information libraries" for the purposes of book propaganda. The cultural advisors deployed in the German missions abroad were already responsible for local book exhibitions, author readings, and lectures,[188] but they were now also charged with influencing foreign publishers, booksellers, and readers. In addition, in early 1942

---

[186] Verbal note from the German legation in Vienna to the Austrian Federal Chancellery, foreign affairs section, 9 December 1937, PA Kult Gen Akten betr. Deutsch-Österreichisches Kulturabkommen, here Kult Gen 5 adh. VI, vol. 2 1937. A "list of anti-German agitational literature" had been handed to the Austrian delegation at the meeting of the books subcommittee in Vienna (21–24 July 1937) with the request that "a ban on circulation in Austria be issued for these works." The report (with the list as appendix 4) is in PA Kult Gen Akten betr. Deutsch-Österreichisches Kulturabkommen, here Kult Gen 5 adh. VI, vol. 1 1936–7.

[187] PA Inland II g Akten betr. Geschäftsgang. The following quotations ibid.

[188] Instructions for cultural advisors in the German missions abroad (n.d., 1940), PA Handakten Luther, Schriftverkehr vol. 2 fol. 39–42. See also ibid. fol. 43–52, with the tasks of the press and culture officials dispatched to the missions.

"experts from the Propaganda Ministry" were integrated into the most important foreign missions, and were to supervise their own areas of cultural work (including exhibitions, speakers, and writing).[189]

These various initiatives could only be successful for as long as the military ascendancy of the Nazi state favored receptivity to German culture in general and the German book in particular. In Vienna in early December 1944, aware of the advancing Allied troops in the West and East, Six urged the cultural advisors of the German missions in southeast Europe to continue their efforts in what was a "psychological factor of prime importance."[190] Although parts of foreign cultural policy must "now be temporarily transferred into the Reich itself," this was, he added, a field that offered "a unique opportunity to acquaint the leading segments of the cultured classes of whole countries with the day-to-day reality of today's fighting Germany and thus to create an experience that may form the foundation of an indissoluble bond with Germany." At stake were the "foundations of a coming European cooperation." Like other institutions, the Foreign Office was now left with little more than rallying cries of this kind, far removed from any objectively grounded or pragmatic political action.

Gestapo and SD

The Reich President's emergency decrees of 4 and 28 February 1933 provided the legal foundations for the Political Police in the provinces to build themselves a powerful role in literary policy. Developments in Prussia were important to this process. A law of 26 April 1933 set up the Geheimes Staatspolizeiamt or Gestapa (Secret State Police Office) to assume political policing tasks that had formerly been held by the provincial criminal police departments. The Gestapa was initially accountable to the Prussian Ministry of the Interior, and was allocated State Police offices as its subordinate executive organs in

---

[189] Secret decree from Luther to the German missions in Rome, Paris, Bucharest, Sofia, and Athens, 7 February 1942, PA Inland II g, vol. 3.
[190] Notes on the fifth meeting (2–4 December 1944), p. 20, PA Kult Pol geheim Akten betr. Balkan.

the Prussian government districts. In the Gestapa's first schedule of responsibilities, of 19 June 1933, Unit II ("Press Police") was responsible for banning and confiscating printed materials and for "utilizing confiscated property."[191] At this stage, however, the Gestapa was not yet a Nazi agency: the new authority's thirty-four employees were recruited mainly from the former "political department" of the Berlin police force. That changed radically after 20 April 1934, when Göring, having separated the Gestapo out from the Prussian Ministry of the Interior using a law of 30 November 1933 and made it subordinate to himself, appointed the Reichsführer SS, Heinrich Himmler, as deputy director of the Prussian Gestapo. Himmler had already had himself appointed commander of the Political Police in all the other provinces of the German Reich. On 22 April 1934, he installed Reinhard Heydrich as head of the Gestapa in Berlin.

The Gestapa schedule of responsibilities dated 25 October 1934 shows new appointments to the press affairs subdepartment, II 2, and a further specification of its tasks. The responsibilities of Press Police II 2 A1 included enforcing the Law on the Reich Chamber of Culture. Section II 2 A2 dealt firstly with "press-police processing and evaluation of the press and printed material within Germany" (in other words, banning and confiscation procedures), and secondly "monitoring journalists, newspaper editors, and publishers within Germany." The schedule of Gestapa responsibilities of 1 October 1935 shows further differentiation within subdepartment II 2. As well as sections for "press and writing within Germany" (II 2 B), for "correspondence, newspaper editors, writers, and reporters within Germany" (II 2 D), and for "foreign press and writing" (II 2 E), there were now dedicated sections for the "church and denominational press" (II 2 C) and for the "emigrant press" (II 2 G). In addition, subdepartment II 2 also ran its own library and a "reading office for books requiring press-police processing" (II 2 J). In April 1935 the subdepartment—directed by the senior civil servant Hermann Gotthardt since 1934 and hitherto dominated by purely administrative and legal experts—was assigned to Fritz Rang, its first SS

---

[191] BArch R 58/840 fol. 4. On the following points, see ibid. fol. 43–4, fol. 69–70.

member from the security service (SD), who had relevant experience in press affairs.[192]

The appointment of Himmler as "Chief of the German Police in the Reich Ministry of the Interior" on 17 June 1936 put an official seal on the de facto unification of the German police. On 1 October 1936, the standardized designation "Secret State Police" (Gestapo) was introduced for the political police forces in the provinces. If in Prussia the Gestapa continued to act as the central agency of the Gestapo, in the other provinces that agency was now termed "state police headquarters" or "state police office." Starting from 1938, these provincial "Stapo" offices adopted the Gestapa's organizational structures, including sections on "press and writing within Germany" analogous to those of the Gestapa.

The processing of press affairs in the Gestapa was subsequently streamlined,[193] and in 1938 the new section "II P" had only three areas of work. The responsibilities of the first of these, Wilhelm Altenloh's II P1, included writing within Germany, the Index of Harmful and Undesirable Literature, and surveillance of writers, publishers, and booksellers.[194] Area II P2, headed by Rang, dealt with foreign and emigrant literature, and II P3 dealt with the church and denominational press along with "literature of sects." In 1939, the department was staffed exclusively by SS members.[195] When the Reich Security Main Office (Reichssicherheitshauptamt, RSHA) was established on 27 September 1939, the whole of the Gestapa's department II was transferred into the RSHA's "Amt IV."[196] Within that office, Rang now headed group IV C. "Matters of the press and

---

[192] BArch BDC/SS/Rang, F. (1899–?): 1933 head of staff and head of the press department of the Oldenburg-Bremen regional farmers' association; from 10 January 1934 head of the press department of the SD office; joined NSDAP 1 October 1932; joined SS 28 April 1933.

[193] Gestapa schedule of responsibilities, 1 January 1938, BArch R 58/840 fol. 163, and 12 January 1939, ibid. fol. 166.

[194] BArch BDC/SS/Altenloh, W. (1908–?): studied law in Heidelberg, Munich, and Bonn; Dr. jur. 1931; probationary judge from 25 November 1934, employed in the Gestapa from 14 February 1935; joined NSDAP 1 May 1933; SA member 1 April 1933–1 March 1935; joined SS 14 September 1935; leader in SD Main Office from 9 November 1938.

[195] Gestapa schedule of responsibilities, 1 July 1939, BArch R 58/840 fol. 186–204, here fol. 196.

[196] RSHA schedule of responsibilities (October 1939/September 1940), BArch R 58/840 fol. 169.

literature" were entrusted to Ernst Hermann Jahr, a Ph.D. in administrative law who had worked for the Gestapa since September 1937.[197]

The Gestapo's supervisory role in literary policy was brought to
bear primarily in the confiscation of books, until 1945 still pursued
on the basis of the President's two emergency decrees of 1933.
On 1 November 1933, the First Directive for the Execution of the
Reich Chamber of Culture Law also made the police the executive
organs of the individual chambers. Upon application by a chamber
administration, the Gestapa and the Stapo offices would supply
general political information on chamber members or police evaluations to help it process applications for membership and exclusion
decisions. The Gestapo was generally requested to comment before
a chamber member undertook a journey abroad. The RSK president's
ordinance on "harmful and undesirable literature," issued on 25 April
1935, charged the Gestapo with seizing and sequestering indexed
books. The police authorities were also responsible for enforcing the
Propaganda Ministry's "informal" book bans and the PPK's prohibitions, and for surveilling the importation of banned literature. The
latter task was not, however, carried out systematically in the initial
phase: only in 1936/37 were special "border police commissariats"
set up, which were informed of the bans on printed matter current
at any one time and had to ensure that such material was stopped
at the border. In addition, the Gestapo was responsible for local
implementation of the closures of Jewish publishers, book stores,
and lending libraries excluded from the Chamber of Literature.

Unlike the Gestapo, the SS security service SD had no legally
sanctioned executive powers at first, but on 9 June 1934 the Führer's
Deputy declared it the sole intelligence service of the NSDAP.[198] In
November 1938, Interior Minister Frick extended this monopoly within
the Party to cover state authorities as well. In January 1935 the SD office
had been promoted to a Main Office of the SS, moving from Munich to
Berlin at no. 102, Wilhelmstrasse. The SD's primary role was to investigate ideas opposed to NSDAP ideology. Great importance was attached
to the evaluation of press and book publishing, and starting in June 1934

---

[197] BArch BDC/SS/Jahr, E. H. (1909–?): Dr. jur. 1937; joined NSDAP 1930; joined SS 1933.
[198] Instruction by the Führer's Deputy cited in Buchheim, "The SS," 170.

a separate SD literature office, headed by Wilhelm Spengler, was set up in the Deutsche Bücherei in Leipzig.[199] Spengler had been examining new church-based publications for the SD's central and southeast Germany region since November 1933, at first as a volunteer. In March 1934 he was taken on by the SD office, and began to put into practice the proposals he had recently drawn up for comprehensive appraisal of the entirety of German-language writing. In the Deutsche Bücherei, the SD had direct access to the catalogues of authors, publishers, subjects, and periodicals, continuously updated by the librarians on the basis of the new publications received for legal deposit.

On 1 April 1936, Spengler and his colleagues were transferred to the press and literature department of the SD Main Office in Berlin; an SD "liaison office" in the Deutsche Bücherei remained in place. The new department, headed by Franz Alfred Six, was renamed "Central Department I 3" in 1936.[200] It had six subdepartments and a large staff of experts and assistants, all recruited from the ranks of the SS. Apart from Spengler, it was mainly Erich Ehrlinger and Walter von Kielpinski who shared responsibility for literary policy within the department. Ehrlinger, the holder of a doctorate in law, had given up his civil service career in Württemberg to work for the SA universities office.[201] When that office was dissolved, he moved to the SD in June 1935. Von Kielpinski had already begun unpaid work for the SD in July 1934, while still a student of German literature and modern languages at Leipzig University.[202] He was taken on full-time by the SD on 15 December 1934 after his graduation.

The organization of the SD's literary policy activities within the RSHA was divided up in late September 1939.[203] Subdepartment II A,

---

[199] Wilhelm Spengler (1907–61) earned his doctorate at the University of Leipzig in 1931 with a study of Schiller's drama. On this and the following, see his CV dated 13 July 1936, BArch BDC/SS, and a 14 October 1943 note from the RSHA/Dept. I A 5 (ibid.).

[200] Security Police Main Office schedule of responsibilities, 31 July 1936, BArch R 58/840 fol. 113–14.

[201] See Ehrlinger's CV dated 1 April 1935 and Six's personnel report dated 30 September 1936, BArch BDC/SS/Ehrlinger, E. (1910–2004). Joined NSDAP 1 June 1931.

[202] Von Kielpinski's response to a "questionnaire for the attainment of permission to become engaged," 15 February 1936, BDC/SS/von Kielpinski, W. (1909–?). Joined NSDAP 1 May 1937.

[203] RSHA schedule of responsibilities, October 1939, BArch R 58/840 fol. 169.

"Investigation of Basic Principles," in Six's Office II, "Investigation of Opponents," was now in charge of the SD liaison office in the Deutsche Bücherei. The main work of evaluating and monitoring literature was carried out in Office III, "Spheres of German Life." Office III's director, Otto Ohlendorf, was actually an economist; he had given up a promising scholarly career to move to the SD Main Office in 1936. He also wrote evaluations for Bouhler's PPK and for the Reich association of the address and advertising register trade. In Ohlendorf's new office, Spengler now headed subdepartment III A on "areas of culture," while von Kielpinski was responsible for "press, literature, and radio"; in 1944 von Kielpinski was made head of the new subdepartment III C4, "propaganda, instruments of government, and central reading office."[204] The literary policy sections were now all based in Markkleeberg-West, near Leipzig. Section III C4b was responsible for "literature, writers, book trade, book printing, libraries, export and import issues, documentation"; III C4d was the central reading office for the press, III C4e for periodicals, and III C4f for books.

In 1936, a "central research library for the entirety of politically undesirable writing" was created in the SD Main Office.[205] The SD sections were requested to examine "holdings of books, brochures, and other printed publications" confiscated by the Stapo offices and the provincial Political Police, and to send the culled material to Berlin. Starting from 1937, publications by persons classified as opponents of Nazi ideology were also included in the reports drawn up by SD Main Office section heads.[206] Guidance was provided by three booklets published in March 1937 for internal use. The *Leitheft Schrifttumswesen und Schrifttumspolitik,* on literature and literary policy, surveyed the political, aesthetic, legal, and economic development of German literature before 1933.[207] According to this guide, the evaluation of literature—drawing on the Deutsche Bücherei as a "source of material"—must be threefold: "politically with respect to

---

[204] Schedule of responsibilities, RSHA office III, 15 September 1944, BArch R 58/792, here fol. 20.
[205] Circular from the Gestapa (unit II 2 J) to all state police offices, 22 January 1936, regarding the gathering of confiscated and undesirable writing in an SD central research library, HStA Düsseldorf RW 36/30 fol. 17.
[206] Internal instructions from Six (n.d., 1937), BArch R 58/544 fol. 63–4.
[207] BArch R 58/1106.

the author," "politically with respect to the publisher," and "substantively with respect to the larger political context." The Main Office depended on input from its sections and external offices when evaluating "the personal lives of the authors and writers," the "internal political circumstances of publishers," and "every organization and company belonging to the German book system in general." Because the existing National Socialist organization of literature was "highly ramified and ultimately inconsistent," the SD saw its opportunity to address "the whole of negative literature in a consistent and unified way."

The *Leitheft Verlagswesen*, on publishing, gave information on the history of publishing legislation before and after 1933, the special fields of publishers, and the growth of the German publishing system from the eighteenth century to the present.[208] Of the country's approximately 5,000 publishers, 300–400 were to be observed by the SD. This surveillance was to focus firstly on the "production of literature," which would be ascertained from the publishers' *Börsenblatt für den Deutschen Buchhandel* with its daily list of new titles, the catalogue of publishers, and the Deutsche Bücherei's bibliographies. Secondly, contacts within the publishing companies, in the NSDAP, the Gestapo, the German Labor Front, and the Chamber of Literature were to observe "internal processes within the publishers." The objective of these investigations was "to reveal and thwart any plans relevant to the SD before they can be put into practice"—the rationale being that retrospective "state intervention against publications or other actions harmful to the *Volk* or state already carried out by the publishers" had proved to be "valuable propaganda rather than disadvantageous" for the publishers concerned.

The guide on the book trade, *Leitheft Buchhandel*, addressed the professional organization of booksellers, the economics of the book trade, the structure of book stocks, the ordering system, bibliographic resources, secondhand bookselling, the organization of the book trade abroad, and the book trade's political significance.[209] In this field, the SD was to search out "undesirable elements" and

[208] BArch R 58/1107.
[209] BArch R 58/1108.

encourage the RSK and Propaganda Ministry to remove them from the organized profession.

When the "functional decree" drew demarcations between the previously overlapping tasks of the Gestapo and the SD on 1 July 1937, the SD's emphasis shifted from monitoring individual political opponents or groups of opponents to obtaining information from all the relevant spheres of social life and analyzing the public mood.[210] Intelligence on current developments in literature became an integral part of the reports that the SD "home affairs" section regularly drew up for the Reichsführer SS, the government, and the NSDAP (*Berichte zur innenpolitischen Lage*, continued from 8 December 1939 as *Meldungen aus dem Reich* and from June 1943 through June 1944 as *SD-Berichte zu Inlandsfragen*).

Reading these reports, it is striking how well-informed the SD was about cultural life in general, and about literary life and the German book trade in particular. SD headquarters obtained its intelligence from an efficient nationwide network of SD sections and approximately 30,000 informants. It had also secured the informal collaboration of several Chamber of Literature employees. RSK president Hanns Johst, for example, was in close personal contact with Himmler.[211] By 1942, this Party writer had attained the rank of *Gruppenführer*, the third highest in the SS hierarchy. In April 1936 Herbert Menz, whom Heydrich had originally intended to manage the Propaganda Ministry's Reich Literature Office, was taken on as Johst's "right hand" in the Chamber after an interview with Himmler.[212] The role enabled Menz to supply the SD with information on the "processing of book ban applications," the "suppression of undesirable literature in the Chamber's sphere," and the "compilation and updating of List 1 of Harmful and Undesirable Literature," until he left the service in fall 1938.[213] Wilhelm Ihde, the Chamber's

---

[210] For details, see Buchheim, "The SS," 166–72.

[211] BArch BDC/SS/Johst, H. See also Düsterberg, *Hanns Johst*, 287–321.

[212] Heydrich (head of the SD Main Office) to Himmler's adjutants office, 11 January 1936, and file note on Menz's meeting with Himmler on 5 February 1936, BArch BDC/SS/Menz, H.

[213] On 1 February 1936, Menz had been transferred to the SD Main Office "for special tasks." Head of Security Police Main Office section I 112 to central department I 4, 13 February 1936, BArch BDC/SS/Menz, H.

managing director from 1937 to 1944, and Günther Gentz, its legal advisor and deputy managing director from 1934 to 1945, were SS members.[214] In the Writers Group, it was Hugo Linhard, an SD Main Office contact, who dealt with membership applications, expulsion proceedings, the "non-Aryan question," and the register of writers.[215] A 1938 internal Main Office personnel report on Karl Thulke, manager of the Book Trade Group in Leipzig, noted that through his position he had "contributed decisively to the cleansing and National Socialist reorientation of the German book trade";[216] his visits to Berlin had "also enabled the discussion and clarification of particular individual cases." The 1940 personnel report noted with satisfaction that "in the course of the past year, it has been possible to implement a series of important ordinances that serve to further combat our opponents in the field of literature." Thulke saw his role as being to "implement National Socialist and SS principles and perspectives uncompromisingly in his area of work." In 1938, his immediate superior, Wilhelm Baur, was also admitted into the SS.[217] Through these contacts in the highest echelons of the Chamber of Literature, the SD could always remain abreast of activities and developments in the German book trade.

The Key Party Offices

Literature Offices in Amt Rosenberg

In June 1933, what was once the "book advisory office" of Rosenberg's Kampfbund became a "Reich Office for the Promotion of German Literature" (Reichsstelle zur Förderung des deutschen Schrifttums), headed by Hans Hagemeyer. The founding members of this private association, based in Leipzig, included some of

---

[214] See their personnel files, BArch BDC/SS.
[215] BArch BDC/SS/Linhard, H.
[216] BArch BDC/SS/Thulke, K.: Joined SS September 1933; transferred to the SD on 21 February 1936.
[217] BArch BDC/SS/Baur, W.: SA member 1922–3 and 1928–30; SS-Standartenführer from 1 June 1938; SS-Oberführer from 30 January 1945.

Rosenberg's longest-standing comrades: Alfred Baeumler, Hans Hagemeyer, Hanns Johst, Hellmuth Langenbucher, Rainer Schlösser, and Gotthard Urban. In August 1933 the Reichsstelle's management office moved to Berlin. Beginning in January 1934, its chief archivist, Bernhard Payr, was responsible for answering bibliographical inquiries and compiling specialized lists; he was also to be the "expert on sensitive literary questions."[218] Elisabeth Waldmann headed a "preliminary reading office," the key task of which for now was to set up a team of specialists able to examine manuscripts and new publications in different fields.[219] The information from their reports was entered into Amt Rosenberg's card index of authors and publishers,[220] and was also the main source for the book advisory periodical *Nimm und lies!* ("Take it and read!"), which from August 1933 appeared under the new title *Buch und Volk* ("Book and nation"), edited by Hellmuth Langenbucher on behalf of the Reichsstelle. Within the Reichsstelle, Langenbucher's role became that of a chief reader, and from November 1933 until 1935 he was also the deputy manager.

Before March 1934, the Reichsstelle was neither registered as an association in private law nor recognized as an agency of the Party or the state. This structural problem became pressing when, in late January 1934, the Propaganda Ministry launched an attempt to swallow up the Reichsstelle. Although Rosenberg was successful in his appeal to the Führer's Deputy opposing the "principle of staging an ambush with the help of the official instruments of power,"[221] by 17 March 1934 the Propaganda Ministry had cut off the Reichsstelle's money supply, and Hagemeyer told his superior that "if I have no clarification of the budget by the end of the month, I will have to request the Reichsstelle's dissolution."[222] In this precarious situation, an avenue of escape was opened by a commission that Rosenberg had received from Hitler on 24 January 1934. A year earlier, in

---

[218] Monthly report (January 1934) on activities of the Reichsstelle's book archives, BArch NS 8/153 fol. 165–6.
[219] Monthly report (January 1934) of the Reichsstelle's preliminary reading office, BArch NS 8/153 fol. 158–64.
[220] Memorandum from Hagemeyer for Rosenberg, 8 January 1934, BArch NS 8/153 fol. 150–4, here fol. 150.
[221] Rosenberg to Hess, 15 March 1934, BArch NS 8/177 fol. 227.
[222] BArch NS 8/153 fol. 138.

December 1933, Ley (the head of the Political Organization of the NSDAP) had complained to Rosenberg of the "severe fragmentation in dealing with questions of worldview" within the Party and asked him, as chief ideologue, to take remedial action.[223] Rosenberg agreed, but only on condition that he receive an "official" mandate to this effect. The decree quickly drawn up by Ley and signed by Hitler gave Rosenberg responsibility for "the entire spiritual and ideological schooling and education of the Party and of all the aligned associations and of the 'Strength Through Joy' organization."

On 6 June 1934, the office of the "Führer's Delegate for the Entire Spiritual and Ideological Education of the NSDAP" was established, and Hagemeyer rose to become head of its new literature section, Hauptstelle "Schrifttumspflege" (the "Cultivation of Literature" unit). This was initially identical with the organization of the old Reichsstelle, which had cut its ties with the Propaganda Ministry on 1 April. Its funding problems remained acute: Ley began to curtail his subsidies to Amt Rosenberg as a whole in 1935, and in 1936 ceased payments altogether.[224] Only in early 1937 did Rosenberg succeed in persuading the NSDAP Treasury to cover the costs of what he himself described as the "Reich Surveillance Office,"[225] while Ley agreed to continue paying for his cultural activities, and thus for the literature unit.[226] From 1 April 1936 the literature unit became an "Office," and finally, in late 1941, the "Main Office for Literature." In 1940 it had four main parts, further divided into twenty-one subsections: "central reading office" with its subsections editing of reports, reading of periodicals, schoolbooks and textbooks, special reading office, the journal *Bücherkunde* ("Book lore"), supervision of readers, and readers' administration office; "evaluation" with its subsections internal library, inquiries, compilation of catalogues, archive of journals and book reviews, and banned literature; "deployment" with

---

[223] Thus Rosenberg's description of the exchange; Rosenberg to Ley, 6 November 1935, BArch NS 8/192 fol. 179.
[224] See Rosenberg's complaints in his letter to Party Treasurer Schwarz, 18 May 1936, BArch NS 8/203 fol. 149–51.
[225] On 25 February 1937, Rosenberg asked Schwarz to absorb the costs of the "Reich Surveillance Office" into the Party Treasury's own budget, BArch NS 8/203 fol. 139–40. On 14 December 1937, he asked him for 77,000 RM in personnel and other funding for 1938, along with a further 10,000 RM for a reserve fund, ibid. fol. 112.
[226] Rosenberg to Schwarz, 8 June 1937, BArch NS 8/203 fol. 135–6.

its subsections supervision of literature, register of employees with evaluation, libraries, promotion of literature, exhibitions and events, mission planning, and statistics and records; and "literary research" with its subsections history of literature and theory of literature.[227] At this time, the office had a total of twenty-seven employees.[228] Most of them had been NSDAP members since 1930 or 1931, had a university education, and were already working actively for the Party before joining Amt Rosenberg from 1938 on. These full-time staff were supported by a whole army of volunteers, and in fall 1934 "*Gau* literature officers" and "district literature officers" were created. Between 1934 and 1941, the number of chief readers rose from twenty to fifty, the number of readers from around 400 to 1,400. From 1936, each *Gau* literature officer had to submit regular reports on his work, which were analyzed in Berlin with summaries circulated to all the *Gau* literature officers.[229] In addition, from 1938 the confidential bulletin *Lektorenbrief*, or "letter to readers," supplied information on the work of the Berlin office, indicated the rejection of individual writers and publishers, and set out the criteria for writing reports.[230]

Although the "Führer's commission" of January 1934 had restricted Rosenberg's activities to the domain of the Party, both the Reichsstelle and its successor offices held fast to the task of "systematically" examining "the entirety of the German literature that has any molding or educative significance for the German *Volk* whatsoever."[231] It was on this basis that, right up to 1945, the large team of chief readers and readers undertook what was probably the most comprehensive review and evaluation of German and foreign literature distributed within Germany. The results were recorded

---

[227] Organizational plan of the Rosenberg office 1940, BArch NS 8/228 fol. 7–74, here fol. 29–40: "Amt Schrifttumspflege."

[228] Ibid. fol. 77.

[229] See the extensive documentation of the *Gau* literature officer for Baden 1936–41, GLA Karlsruhe 465 d/vol. 157; and the list of all *Gau* literature officers (n.d., c. 1935) in BArch NS 15/144.

[230] See the fragmentary documentation in BArch NSD 16/59 1 (1938)–7 (1944). For the years 1934 to 1936, some hectographed Reichsstelle circulars to the local readers survive, BArch NS 12/77.

[231] Queries and regulations of the Reichsstelle zur Förderung des deutschen Schrifttums, circular no. 24, 20 June 1934, p. 1, BArch NS 12/77.

in the journal *Bücherkunde*, which appeared from 1934 and had reached a monthly circulation of 8,000 by the time it ceased publication in 1944.[232] The central organ of Rosenberg's literary apparatus, it published essays on the principles of literary policy regarding authors, publishers, and book-market trends. The Institut für Leser- und Schrifttumskunde, researching reading habits, contributed information on developments in the public libraries; excerpts from the readers' reports were presented; and there were reports on internal events, training courses, and the large-scale public exhibitions organized by the literature office. Beginning in November 1935, *Bücherkunde* included an appendix with the weekly lists of reports produced by the central reading office. This "Gutachtenanzeiger" listed the positively evaluated books and manuscripts on white pages and the negatively evaluated ones on red pages, further distinguishing between "recommended," "recommended with reservations," "not recommended," and "not recommended with restrictions."[233] Because these evaluations were "for internal use only," a special application was required to receive the "B" edition of *Bücherkunde* that included the appendix. The annual compilations of lists were also designated as strictly confidential. The 1936 compilation included 2,914 reports covering forty-two subject areas; for 1937 there were 2,892 reports covering forty-seven areas, for 1938 3,120 reports covering forty-eight areas, for 1939 4,256 reports and for 1940 3,581 reports, in each case covering forty-six areas.[234]

Impressive though these efforts may seem on paper, in practice their relevance remained limited. *Bücherkunde's* recommendations essentially highlighted the very authors whose work was already being promoted by the state, and when it came to implementing its proposed bans, Rosenberg's literature office was forced to rely on the executive authority of the state literary bureaucracy, which was not eager for Party interference into its policy decisions. It would nevertheless be wrong to underestimate Amt Rosenberg's influence. When fundamental political, "racial," or aesthetic principles of the Nazi state were at stake, Party and state literary functionaries

---

[232] Publications of the Rosenberg office (as at c. 1944), BArch NS 8/191 fol. 205–6.
[233] BArch NSD 16/32–5.
[234] BArch NSD 16/27.

acted in concert. Politically negative evaluations by the Reichsstelle, passed on to the Chamber of Literature, the Propaganda Ministry, and the Gestapo, led to book bans in many cases. Starting in 1936, the office's libraries and catalogues section also kept a "register of Jewish authors."[235] Again marked "for internal use only," the index, including around 11,000 names,[236] served as the basis for excluding Jewish or "Jewish-by-marriage" authors, for objections to "special permission" granted by the Propaganda Ministry, and for monitoring the publishing and book retail trade for banned literature or works that were still to be banned.

Rosenberg's literature office also disseminated its aesthetic and political values to a broader public through numerous campaigns and publications. Exhibitions of books—such as "Eternal Germany. Fifteen Centuries of German Literature" (1934), "Germany Defends Itself" (1935), "Political Germany" (1936), or "Nuremberg, the German City. From City of Imperial Diets to City of Reich Party Congresses" (1937)—were skillfully staged propaganda events, oriented on the political events of the day, and met with a very positive response. The 1938 exhibition "Europe's Battle for Destiny in the East" was part of the Nuremberg Party Congress official supporting program; it was followed by the exhibitions "Woman and Mother—Fount of *Volk* Life" (1939) and "German Greatness" (1940).[237]

Every fall from October 1939 on, the literature office also organized an "NSDAP book collection for the German Wehrmacht." Books were collected from private households by neighborhood Party officials and the staff of the Winter Relief campaign, but the donations were

---

[235] *Verzeichnis jüdischer Autoren. Vorläufige Zusammenstellung der Reichsstelle zur Förderung des deutschen Schrifttums* [from part 3 on: *des Amtes Schrifttumspflege bei dem Beauftragten des Führers für die gesamte geistige und weltanschauliche Erziehung der NSDAP und der Reichsstelle zur Förderung des deutschen Schrifttums*], ed. Joachim Menzel, part 1–7 (A–Z), Berlin 1938–9, Deutsche Bücherei classmark 1939 B 2706.

[236] As claimed in the CV of the official responsible for the register, 9 February 1942, BArch BDC/SS/Menzel, J. Menzel was one of the few SS members working for Rosenberg, and had been employed in his literature office since 1936.

[237] For the events organized up to 1937, a total of 686,000 visitors were recorded and 18,000 catalogues sold. "Europe's Battle" attracted 772,000 visitors (58,000 catalogues sold), "Woman and Mother" 594,000 visitors (169,000 catalogues sold), and "German Greatness" 767,000 visitors (133,200 catalogues sold). Rosenberg to Bormann, 31 August 1944, p. 4, BArch NS 15/20.

reviewed by Rosenberg's *Gau* training managers and literature officers, who sorted them into 60–100-volume libraries for the troops. The objective was not only to supply the army with reading matter. As Rosenberg proudly informed his Führer after the first collection in 1939, "the collecting campaign has cleansed private households of undesirable literature that no police or other state authorities have so far been able to access."[238] The Party was also able to "draw conclusions from the donated books as to the spirit and the ideological disposition of the donors." Admittedly, this disposition turned out to be far removed from what Rosenberg had hoped. Party publisher Eher had to "donate" National Socialist works to the value of 100,000 RM when it became clear that there was "little directly National Socialist literature among the books contributed by the public." The official responsible for the campaign tried to explain this deficit by arguing that "naturally enough," the German people was "reluctant to part with its clearly National Socialist books."[239]

Ultimately, the enormous propaganda and organizational effort put into the book donation campaign indicates how hard Rosenberg's literature office was having to work in order to make any substantial contribution to Nazi literary policy. Rosenberg suffered from inadequate or curtailed responsibilities, and now sought a new "Führer commission." On 1 March 1942, Hitler gave him the right, valid in the occupied areas, to "search libraries, archives, lodges, and other ideological and cultural facilities of all kinds for relevant material, and to have this material confiscated for the ideological work of the NSDAP and for future research at the NSDAP University."[240] An Einsatzstab Reichsleiter Rosenberg ("operations staff Reich leader Rosenberg") was created on this basis, and several employees of the literature office were transferred to it.[241] The office itself participated in the activities of the Einsatzstab by inspecting, processing,

---

[238] Report to the Führer on the NSDAP book collection for the Wehrmacht (n.d., 1939), BArch NS 8/176 fol. 95–9, here fol. 98.
[239] G. Utikal, "Die Buchspende für die Deutsche Wehrmacht," *Bücherkunde* 7 (1940), 29–31, here 30.
[240] Hitler's commission is quoted in an overview of the areas of the literature office's work that Rosenberg sent to Bormann on 16 July 1943 as part of consultations on establishing a central literature office for the NSDAP, BArch NS 8/189 fol. 130.
[241] Brenner, *Kunstpolitik des Nationalsozialismus*, 240.

and passing on the confiscated books. As so often during the development of the Nazi state, a particular agency's loss of function was compensated by a criminal mandate conferred by Hitler.

But the relative impotence of Rosenberg's literature office had two further causes. Firstly, the zealous activity of its busy managers was not particularly efficient. On 1 February 1943, Rosenberg's patience with them finally ran out, and he replaced Hagemeyer with Bernhard Payr, who had by then begun to run the central reading office.[242] Secondly, the literature office was constantly embroiled in competency disputes with the PPK, Philipp Bouhler's office for National Socialist writing. Initially, Rosenberg had tried to incorporate the PPK into his self-declared "Reich Surveillance Office" as a kind of preliminary reading bureau.[243] When Bouhler began to steer his own independent course, Rosenberg changed his strategy and tried formal agreements instead. On 8 April 1935 he issued a notification limiting the PPK to examining such writing as "referred to National Socialism in word and image and in content,"[244] whereas Rosenberg's own literature office was to inspect "*all* the German writing that is ideological, political, cultural, or educational in orientation, for the purposes of promotion." Even after this "agreement," Rosenberg was obliged to lament that the PPK, "as can scarcely be avoided," was constantly expanding the boundaries of its authority, "absorbing into its evaluation activities literally everything that is printed in Germany at all."[245] In August 1937, the PPK's deputy president Hederich was made head of the Propaganda Ministry literature department and there publicly declared the PKK to be the central hub of literary policy in the Nazi state, whereupon Rosenberg, supported by Amann, began to inveigh against him, calling him "a subaltern parvenu equipped with executive powers."[246]

Even Hederich's later dismissal from his post in the Ministry literature department did nothing to overcome the "dualism" between

---

[242] Langenbucher having left the Reichsstelle on 1 January 1935 for workload reasons, Payr took on the central reading office on 1 January 1936, BArch NS 8/138 fol. 178. Rosenberg gave the order to replace Hagemeyer on 18 June 1942, but it could only be carried out once Payr had returned from army service, BArch NS 8/128 fol. 115.

[243] Rosenberg to Bouhler, 24 March 1934, BArch NS 8/208 fol. 186.

[244] BArch NS 8/128 fol. 11–13.

[245] Rosenberg to Bouhler, 6 March 1936, BArch NS 8/208 fol. 117–23, here fol. 122.

[246] Rosenberg to Hess, 16 July 1938, BArch NS 8/179 fol. 49.

the two agencies that Rosenberg bemoaned. Evidently, Hess was not prepared to tie Bouhler's hands; a proposed decree to that end drafted by Rosenberg on 30 June 1939 disappeared into the files without comment. But Rosenberg remained obdurate, refusing to accept the role of a "Chinese mandarin" required only to wield the "red pencil."[247] On 28 May 1941, just a few days after Hess's flight to England and the establishment of the NSDAP Party Chancellery, he presented himself at Bormann's office in the Chancellery with the demand that Bouhler's attempts "to completely undermine my commission from the Führer, and to do so now with the authority of the Führer, must cease once and for all after the present clarification."[248]

However, when Bormann, as head of the Party Chancellery, finally began to intervene in this highly contested domain in early 1943, it was due less to Rosenberg's insistence than to the worrying state of the war. He ordered all Party offices to be examined with a view to saving personnel through amalgamations,[249] to which Bouhler responded by suggesting that Rosenberg's long-voiced wishes now finally be considered.[250] On 28 January 1943, Bouhler and Rosenberg signed the "draft of an agreement" that would subordinate the activities of the PPK to Rosenberg's "Reich Surveillance Office."[251] But in early March 1943, Bouhler had second thoughts. In a detailed note to Rosenberg, he set so many conditions and exceptions on the union of the two literature offices that Rosenberg was bound to reject the plan.[252] Just inches from his goal, the Party ideologue now tried to ignore Bouhler's change of heart,[253] and to have Hitler decree a central "NSDAP Literature Office" on the basis of the January 1943

---

[247] Thus Rosenberg's self-portrait, Rosenberg to Hess, 17 September 1940, BArch NS 8/184 fol. 122.
[248] BArch NS 8/185 fol. 46.
[249] Bormann to Rosenberg, 26 January 1943, BArch NS 8/188 fol. 176.
[250] Bouhler to Rosenberg 8 March 1943, BArch NS 8/209 fol. 33.
[251] BArch NS 8/189 fol. 49. See also the "Agreement on general principles of the structure of the 'NSDAP Literature Office,'" BArch NS 8/129 fol. 44, and the "Stipulation on the organizational structure of the amalgamation" of the PPK and the Main Office Literature, ibid. fol. 45–7.
[252] Bouhler to Rosenberg, 8 March 1943, BArch NS 8/209 fol. 33–6.
[253] See Rosenberg to Bormann, 12 April 1943, BArch NS 8/188 fol. 66–70.

agreement.[254] In June 1943, however, Hitler decided that Bouhler should be awarded the new office, with Rosenberg concentrating fully on his "great task in the occupied Eastern territories, which is a life's work on its own account."[255] In fact, no one seems to have attended to carrying out this decision. The amalgamation of the two agencies having initially foundered on Bouhler's refusal to give up Hederich,[256] Rosenberg now refused to subordinate Payr, the head of his literature office, to the PPK.[257] On 1 September 1944 Bormann, who had frequently urged staff cuts in Rosenberg's domain, had to decree the permanent closure of the literature office after Goebbels ordered extensive cutbacks in the area of literature.[258] Even then, Rosenberg—whose powers in the "Eastern Ministry" were under threat from military developments—clung stubbornly to the remnants of his literary policy machine.[259]

The Party Examination Commission for the Protection of National Socialist Writings (PPK)

Philipp Bouhler had become Reich manager of the NSDAP in February 1925, but after the Nazi accession to power his scope to act was considerably restricted by the tight reins of Party Treasurer Franz Xaver Schwarz at NSDAP headquarters in Munich. Bouhler therefore asked the Führer's Deputy for a new task.[260] In January 1934, Hess responded first by mandating him to "handle questions of cultural

---

[254] Draft of a Führer decree on the amalgamation of the NSDAP literature offices, BArch NS 8/188 fol. 89, passed on to Rosenberg's staff manager Stellrecht by Hellmuth Friedrichs, department head in the Party Chancellery, on 25 March 1943, ibid. fol. 88.

[255] Bormann to Rosenberg, 29 June 1943, BArch NS 8/188 fol. 2.

[256] Rosenberg to Bormann, 26 May 1943, BArch NS 8/188 fol. 24–8; Payr's file note of 13 July 1943 "for Rosenberg's consultation with the Führer at headquarters re: Main Office Literature and PPK," BArch NS 8/189 fol. 47.

[257] Rosenberg to Bormann, 31 August 1944, BArch NS 15/20.

[258] Bormann to Rosenberg, 1 September 1944, BArch NS 8/191 fol. 151–2.

[259] Bormann to Rosenberg, 16 September 1944, BArch NS 8/191 fol. 118, in which Bormann complains about Rosenberg's behavior; and Rosenberg's file note of 28 September 1944 on his meeting with *Oberbefehlsleiter* Friedrichs, ibid. fol. 83–4.

[260] This was Rosenberg's portrayal of the events; Rosenberg to Bouhler, 6 March 1936, BArch NS 8/208 fol. 119.

policy" within his own staff,[261] and in March by making him head of the newly established Parteiamtliche Prüfungskommission zum Schutze des NS-Schrifttums, or PPK.[262]

In this matter as so many others, the Führer's Deputy was no more than a stalking horse for someone else's interests. In early 1934, Max Amann of the Party publisher Eher had submitted a "draft law to protect National Socialist literature from unqualified hands," initially to the Propaganda Ministry.[263] His aim was firstly to avoid "opportunistic literature [*Konjunkturliteratur*] being published under a National Socialist banner by presses that, in the days when the Movement was struggling for power, published attacks on our Movement in the most unbelievable way"; Rowohlt was cited as an example. Secondly, the NSDAP's own publisher was to be assured the "right of first refusal on genuinely National Socialist manuscripts." Goebbels voiced reservations on this initiative, and it was passed to Hess for a decision. The decree he issued on 15 March complied with Amann's wishes, not only establishing obligatory examination of literature already in circulation, but also expressing the expectation that "manuscripts dealing with National Socialist problems and topics will in the first instance be offered for publication to the central Party publisher, which is the property of the NSDAP." Amann's plan, then, was to use the PPK as a kind of preliminary reading agency for his Party publisher.

In the early days, the PPK fulfilled Amann's expectations rather well. On 16 April 1934, Bouhler required publishers to present all manuscripts and publications that referred to National Socialism in any way.[264] A fee was charged for the examination process, amounting to "six times the retail price as set by the publisher in

---

[261] *Verordnungsblatt der Reichsleitung der NSDAP* 2, no. 63, 15 January 1934, 137, BArch NSD 13/1.
[262] Signed by Hess on 15 March 1934, dated 16 April 1934, and published on 21 April 1934 in *Bbl.* no. 92, 367. On the dates and the text, see the internal circulars issued to publishers by the PPK, *Verleger-Mitteilungen der Parteiamtlichen Prüfungskommission*, circular 3, Berlin [7 December] 1938, here A 1, pp. 3–4, BArch NSD 2/14. On the following, see ibid.
[263] Amann to Bouhler, 10 December 1938, p. 2, BArch NS 11/9.
[264] On the following, see "Ausführungsbestimmungen des Vorsitzenden der Partei-amtlichen Prüfungskommission zum Schutze des NS.-Schrifttums [...]," *Verleger-Mitteilungen*, pp. 5–6.

the case of published books, and in the case of manuscripts to be calculated and communicated to the Examination Commission along with the submission." The evaluation was supposed to be completed within three weeks,[265] but in fact was usually delayed due to the heavy workload on the readers, most of whom had jobs elsewhere.[266] Once the evaluation was received, the PPK could award an "endorsement of harmlessness": "The NSDAP raises no objections to the publication of this item." In this case, the title was listed in the journal NS-Bibliographie, and thus recommended for purchase by Party libraries and use in training courses.[267] Alternatively, clearance was withheld, with various possible consequences: the text could continue to appear but without official Party promotion; the publication of a manuscript, or the appearance or reprint of a book, could be made conditional on revisions to criticized passages; or publication could be proscribed altogether.[268]

This power of censorship was confirmed by the Reich Chamber of Literature in an ordinance of 16 April 1935, which prohibited the book trade from continuing to distribute any printed item to which the PPK had objected.[269] On 12 October 1934, Bouhler announced that "books treating in a narrative or descriptive form, mostly through loosely strung-together disquisitions and essays, of the National Socialist revolution and the events accompanying it" should, as a general principle, not be promoted by the Party, but only receive the

---

[265] As stated in a PPK circular sent to the Reich Education Ministry on 26 February 1938 along with a book for inspection, BArch 49.01/464 fol. 106.

[266] See author Ernst Grosse's complaint to the Reich Chancellery on 28 October 1937 regarding the delayed evaluation of his manuscript. In its response of 10 November 1937, the Chancellery refused to intervene, saying it was "well known" that the PPK was "extraordinarily busy," BArch 07.01/4102 fol. 122–3.

[267] Summary of the tasks and methods of the PPK, the Rosenberg office, and the Reich Literature Office, drawn up for the head of the Reich Chancellery, BArch R 43 F 4222/ fiche 3, fol. 58–64, here fol. 63. See also Bouhler's 11 April 1935 notification regarding the nature and extent of the PPK's work, Verleger-Mitteilungen, p. 15.

[268] Note to the head of the Reich Chancellery, BArch R 43 F 4222/fiche 3, fol. 63.

[269] "Anordnung betr. Verbreitungsverbot der von der Parteiamtlichen Prüfungskommission beanstandeten Schriften vom 16.4.1935," in Schrieber, Das Recht der Reichskulturkammer, vol. II, 90–1. In his notification of 11 April 1935 (Verleger-Mitteilungen, p. 15), Bouhler pointed out that bans would only be "issued in exceptional cases, when the kind of text and circumstances make such intervention absolutely necessary."

note that "there are no objections to their sale from the Party's point of view."[270] Alongside such restrictions, it was probably the time-consuming and expensive approvals procedure that persuaded many publishers to relinquish their once-profitable business in Nazi-related literature.

At the same time, the PPK was trying, through a series of ordinances, to secure for Eher the exclusive right to publish writings on National Socialism. In October 1934 it was made clear that the Party publisher alone was responsible for "the publication of descriptions and reports of NSDAP events." Any exceptions required prior permission from the PPK president. In July 1935 this restriction was tightened further: the entirety of "Party Congress literature" could now only be published "with the agreement" of the PPK.[271] A pronouncement by Bouhler on 20 October 1934 furthermore obliged Party agencies and their offices "to have all ordinances and publications appear with the Party publisher if they are to be sold through the German book market."[272] On 24 September 1935, Bouhler announced that no German publisher other than Eher had the right "to publish in full or in excerpt" the speeches and writings of Hitler.[273] It was the PPK's task to watch over these extremely lucrative rights. Beginning in July 1936, even works that included quotations from Hitler's speeches had to be submitted for examination.[274] When the NS-Bibliographie began to appear in April 1936, the publication of all lists of Nazi literature was now also restricted to the Party publisher.

If Amann's plan nevertheless failed to bear fruit, that was due to Bouhler's personal ambition to make a name for himself in his new area of work. His goal was furthered when, on 17 November 1934, Hitler appointed him chief of the "Chancellery of the Führer of the NSDAP," a role that gave him—unlike Rosenberg, for example—constant access to Hitler. In the initial phase, the PPK still shared its

---

[270] Bouhler, notification of 12 October 1934, Verleger-Mitteilungen, p. 11. On the following, see ibid. pp. 11–12.

[271] Notification of 11 July 1935, Verleger-Mitteilungen, p. 17.

[272] Notification of 20 October 1935, Verleger-Mitteilungen, p. 13.

[273] Notification of 24 September 1935," Verleger-Mitteilungen, p. 19.

[274] Notification of 20 July 1936, Verleger-Mitteilungen, p. 25. See also the essay by PPK employee K.H. Köpke, "Die Verwendung von Führerworten im Schrifttum," NSB 2, no. 3 (1937), i–viii.

readers with the Eher house.[275] Only after an order from the Führer's Deputy on 6 January 1936 was the PPK able independently to entrust "particular tasks" to "Party offices or individual Party comrades."[276] This allowed Bouhler's commission to make use of staff mainly from the large team of readers based in Rosenberg's literature office, in many cases resulting in identical reports being written on a book for two different literature agencies.[277]

At first the administrative apparatus of the PPK office, which moved from Munich to Berlin in November 1934, was very modest. Its manager, and from 1936 deputy president, was Karl Heinz Hederich. A trained metalworker who had earned his engineering degree at the Technical University of Munich in 1931,[278] Hederich proved to be a skillful organizer, and Bouhler stuck to him through various crises until the very end. In 1936, his office was divided into three departments: administration, examination, and evaluation.[279] Since February 1935, there had also been a PPK "bibliographical information desk" at the Deutsche Bücherei in Leipzig, as the PPK's first external branch.[280] It was this desk, supported by the Library's specialized staff, that collected the material for the *NS-Bibliographie*, published from 1936 to 1944.[281] It also served to monitor German publishing's compliance with censorship requirements.[282]

---

[275] Amann to Rosenberg, 9 July 1934, BArch NS 8/109 fol. 72.

[276] Ordinance from the Führer's Deputy, 6 January 1936, *Verleger-Mitteilungen*, p. 21.

[277] See Ley to Hess, 25 August 1939, p. 4, BArch Slg. Schumacher/212.

[278] Hederich's CV of 1937, BArch BDC/RMVP/Hederich, K.H. (1902–76). Hederich says he joined the NSDAP for the first time in 1922 and participated in Hitler's Munich putsch on 9 November 1923. He was readmitted into the NSDAP on 1 March 1932 (BDC/ Masterfile).

[279] Hederich to Bouhler, 13 October 1936, containing a forty-four-page response to a report by the NSDAP Reich Treasury auditors dated 27 August 1936, here pp. 33–4, BArch NS 11/8.

[280] "Verfügung Bouhlers vom 26.2.1935 über die Errichtung einer Auskunftsstelle der PPK in der Deutschen Bücherei," *Bbl.* no. 50, 28 February 1935, 158–9. From September 1935 to 1 July 1936, this office was headed by Karl Helmut Patutschnik. See BArch BDC/Partei Kanzlei Correspondence.

[281] According to the record of a meeting on 1 April 1936 with Patutschnik and the director-general of the Deutsche Bücherei, Heinrich Uhlendahl, taken down by the deputy director, Werner Rust, on 7 April 1936, p. 1. DB-Archiv no. 611–13.

[282] This point was underlined in the secret instructions for the Leipzig office in the "A-Fall" (outbreak of war) regarding the "organization and tasks of the PPK" (n.d., c. 1937), here point 2a, BArch NS 11/5.

In October 1936, Hederich complained to Bouhler that the PPK had "neither a clear and approved budget" nor a completed organizational structure.[283] As a result, the PPK's income, drawn primarily from inspection fees, did not cover the costs of its administration and personnel.[284] This must have changed radically over the course of 1937 and 1938, because by December 1938 Amann was accusing Bouhler of having let the PPK become completely "bloated."[285] In September 1939, the commission employed no fewer than 127 people, fifty of them as department heads, case officers, or assistant case officers.[286] This immense apparatus seems now to have been funded from the coffers of Party Treasurer Schwarz. The increase in personnel corresponded to the PPK's elevation into a "main office" within the Party leadership.[287] Its central administration dealt with all the agency's personnel and administrative affairs, ran the library, and collected the inspection fees. Individual cases were handled via the departments of registering and requesting publications, reimbursing and inspecting reports, evaluating reports and decisions, NS-Bibliographie (NSB), NSB editorial office, NSB supplements, periodicals (almanacs, journals, newspapers), scholarly works, Führer speeches, and history of the Nazi movement. External PPK branches were established in 1938 in Vienna and in 1940 in Prague (with responsibility for the "Protectorate of Bohemia and Moravia" and for the "General Government").[288]

Bouhler was expected to consider it a special honor for his commission when, in July 1937, Goebbels suggested making Hederich head of the Propaganda Ministry's literature department. Whereas the Propaganda Minister thought he had neatly solved one of his various personnel problems, his new partners were working

---

[283] Hederich to Bouhler, 13 October 1936, p. 1, BArch NS 11/8. On 19 August 1936, Hederich had told Reich Chief Auditor Ried how hard it was "to develop an office practically from the very smallest beginnings starting from a typewriter and a pad of paper" (p. 3).

[284] The accounts for May through October 1936 show an average monthly income of 6,116 RM and expenses of 15,433 RM.

[285] Amann to Bouhler, 10 December 1938, p. 5, NS 11/9.

[286] Tasks and structure of the PPK, BArch R 43 II /585, here fol. 44.

[287] On the following, see the overview of the PPK's personnel (n.d., c. 1937/38), BArch NS 11/5.

[288] Bouhler to Rosenberg, 7 May 1940, BArch NS 8/209 fol. 89–90.

on very different assumptions. In the long term, they hoped not only to amalgamate all the Party literature agencies, but to establish a central literature office covering both state and Party, and Hederich told Goebbels as much in November 1937.[289] What he did not mention to the Minister was his aspiration to place the leadership of Nazi literary policy in the hands of the PPK. This strategic objective becomes apparent in plans drawn up in 1937 and 1938 in connection with the preparation of all NSDAP agencies for war.[290] The plans set out the expansion of the reading office in Berlin, turning it into a "tightly-run censorship office." Whereas compliance with retrospective, "post-"censorship was to be monitored via the Leipzig branch, a new department of "literature and publisher planning" would be established to direct the production of books, newspapers, and journals in both content and technical respects. To that end, the Börsenverein and the Chamber of Literature were to be subordinated to the PPK. This would have given Bouhler's commission authority over preventive, "pre-"censorship as well. A department for the "deployment of literature" would, furthermore, coordinate deliveries to the frontline book trade and supervise the entire library system, including commercial lending libraries and factory libraries. In fact, even the relatively modest project of unifying literary policy within the NSDAP was doomed to fail. Rosenberg and Amann put up fierce resistance and, supported by Ley as Leader of the Party Organization, repeatedly approached Hess with requests to dissolve the PPK.[291]

After the rift with Amann, Bouhler had his responsibility for monitoring the reproduction of "Führer speeches" reconfirmed by Hitler in person on 3 November 1937. On the basis of an "executive directive" dated 1 June 1938, publishers now had to submit all books and articles that contained excerpts from the speeches or

---

[289] Budget notes on the Reich Literature Office, 20 November 1937, BArch R 55/166, here fol. 340.

[290] On the following, see organization and tasks of the PPK (n.d., c. 1937), BArch NS 11/5 fol. 4–5. On the context, see ibid. fol. 12ff., references to discussions and correspondence of the PPK with Fritz Todt (Führer's Deputy staff) from the second half of 1937.

[291] See Rosenberg to Hess and Amann to Bouhler, both 10 December 1938, BArch NS 11/9, and Amann to Bormann, 13 June 1939, BArch NS 8/181 fol. 38–9; also Ley to Hess, 25 August 1939, BArch Slg. Schumacher/212.

from *Mein Kampf* to the PPK in manuscript form.[292] If a reprint was planned, permission from Eher had to be enclosed in the request for examination. In 1939, a first bibliography of all Hitler's speeches from 1933 to 1 April 1939 appeared (including sources and a key sentence for each speech).[293] During World War II, Bouhler published Hitler's speeches on the war and culture with Eher on the basis of phonograph recordings. In December 1937, the PPK was additionally charged with preparing a "history of the Movement."[294]

But the commission had long ceased to restrict itself to its original Party brief. In a short 1937 brochure on the PPK's activities, Hederich justified the expansion of the inspection procedures to cover almost every publication as follows: "After all, in today's Germany there is barely a subject area left that can ignore the reshaping and re-creation of our *völkisch* life without taking a stance on it [i.e., on National Socialism] in one way or another."[295] Accordingly, on 15 May 1934 Hans Frank, head of the NSDAP legal office, authorized the PPK to censor all legal literature that was "presented as National Socialist in title, design, the publishers' advertising, or in the content itself." In 1939 the PPK and the Office for Legal Literature jointly compiled a select bibliography of literature on "the German renewal of justice" published since 1933.[296] Bouhler reached a separate arrangement with Himmler respecting commentaries and treatises on police law and on the literature of the SS. Agreements with the army leadership also allowed the PPK to contribute to evaluating military literature from 1935 until the start of the war. Partly "for reasons of completeness" and partly because of its wide distribution and cultural impact, fiction too was included in the inspection remit—despite the fact that, as Hederich had to admit in 1937, "there are already several offices

[292] Regulations on implementing the Führer's decree of 3 November 1937, *Verleger-Mitteilungen*, p. 37.

[293] *Die Reden des Führers nach der Machtübernahme [1933–1.4.1939]. Eine Bibliographie*, Berlin 1939 (= *NSB*, supplement 2), BArch NSD 2/11.

[294] Führer's decree on compiling the history of the Movement, 3 December 1937, *Verleger-Mitteilungen*, p. 35.

[295] Hederich, *Die Parteiamtliche Prüfungskommission*, 5–6.

[296] *Deutsche Rechtserneuerung. Eine Bibliographie. Erstellt vom Amt für Rechtsschrifttum im Reichsrechtsamt der NSDAP. in Zusammenarbeit mit der Parteiamtlichen Prüfungskommission zum Schutze des NS.-Schrifttums*, Berlin 1939 (= *NSB*, supplement 3), BArch NSD 2/12.

dealing with this form of writing."[297] All manuscripts and publications that "concern or portray questions relating to the Four-Year Plan (Four-Year Plan literature)" had to be submitted for PPK inspection after a February 1937 agreement with Göring.[298] And according to a working agreement with the Reich Education Ministry dated 14 July 1937, the PPK was to handle the entirety of scholarly, pedagogical, and popular educational writing.[299] This expanded in 1939 to cover doctoral and professorial dissertations relating to National Socialism, which were to be evaluated by the PPK readers before going to press,[300] supported from 1942 with an annotated select "register of doctoral and professorial dissertations."[301] On 13 October 1939, Foreign Minister von Ribbentrop pledged to involve the PPK in preparing exhibitions of National Socialist writing abroad.[302]

From 1935, the PPK took on surveillance of the widely distributed genre of calendars, aiming to clamp down on an allegedly increasing "trivialization and greed for profit" along with abuse by "denomi-national-political groups."[303] In 1936 this domain was expanded to include almanacs and annuals of all kinds, along with city address and advertising registers,[304] yielding substantial income for the PPK in the shape of examination fees. In addition, from 1936 publishers were forced to include in their almanacs "an ideological, cultural-political, or generally political contribution," which must describe the "achievements of National Socialism" in the almanac's particular

---

[297] K. H. Hederich, "Zwei Jahre NS-Bibliographie," *NSB* 3, no. 1 (1938), i–xii, here v–vi.

[298] Summary of the PPK's responsibilities, 9 May 1942, BArch R 43 II /585 fol. 58. See also notification by Bouhler, 25 March 1937, *Verleger-Mitteilungen*, p. 49.

[299] Notification of the working agreement between Reich Minister Rust and *Reichsleiter* Bouhler, 14 October [in fact July] 1937, *Verleger-Mitteilungen*, p. 31.

[300] Copy of the decree of 20 October 1939 on the PPK's role in dissertations, BArch NS 11/10 fol. 23–4.

[301] *Hochschulschrifttum. Verzeichnis von Dissertationen und Habilitationsschriften,* Berlin 1942 (= *NSB*, supplement 4), BArch NSD 2/13. See also K.H. Patutschnik, "Über den Wert der in den letzten Jahren erschienenen Doktordissertationen," *NSB* 1, no. 1 (1936), xvii–xxxii.

[302] PA AA Referat Partei, vol. 1 NS-Schrifttum.

[303] See the comments on Bouhler's notification of 11 July 1935, *Verleger-Mitteilungen*, p. 41/n. 1; H. Finke, "Die Kalenderliteratur im Rahmen des deutschen Schrifttums," *NSB* 2, no. 4 (1937), i–iv.

[304] Notification by the PPK on almanacs and address registers, 12 March 1936, *Verleger-Mitteilungen*, pp. 43–4.

field.[305] Despite a drastic drop in numbers with the advent of paper rationing, even during the war up to 700 almanacs a year were arriving on the desk of the PPK reading office.[306]

The PPK also exerted considerable influence on the most important German encyclopedias. The editorial team of the respected Brockhaus Encyclopedia had offered Bouhler the opportunity to "edit a substantial article" while he was still working as the NSDAP manager before the Party's accession to power.[307] Aware of the rapidly spreading repercussions of political and social change, Brockhaus evidently hoped to avoid political problems or expensive amendments in the new edition of the full-length *Grosser Brockhaus*, and asked the PPK to examine and revise more than a hundred articles— even though "by far the greatest part of these articles," Hederich conceded, did "not actually deal with themes covered by the regulations for inspection." The same procedure was applied when preparing the shorter *Allbuch-Brockhaus* and the "pocket" version on contemporary events, the *Taschenbrockhaus zum Zeitgeschehen*.[308] For the eighth edition of *Meyers Konversations-Lexikon*, PPK readers not only examined every heading, but wrote all the politically significant articles themselves.[309] However, the reception of the resulting ideologically saturated encyclopedia abroad was so disastrous that the publisher, Bibliographisches Institut, asked the Propaganda Ministry's literature department to excuse it from working with the PPK on the ninth edition.[310]

Kröner involved the PPK in the revised version of its dictionaries of education, the *Pädagogisches Wörterbuch*, and philosophy, the *Philosophisches Wörterbuch*.[311] Herder, too, suffered from PPK interference in its theological encyclopedia *Lexikon für Theologie und Kirche* (ten volumes, 1930–38), the complete *Der grosse Herder*

[305] Summary of instructions regarding the examination of almanacs, *Verleger-Mitteilungen*, pp. 47–8, here p. 48.

[306] Short progress report 1 September 1939–April 1942, BArch R 43 II /585, fol. 48.

[307] Hederich, ibid. p. 6; the following quotations ibid. See also Keiderling, *F.A. Brockhaus 1905–2005*, 161–5.

[308] Short progress report 1 September 1939–April 1942, BArch R 43 II /585 fol. 51.

[309] Hederich to Bouhler, 13 October 1936, pp. 8, 13, BArch NS 11/8.

[310] See Payr's report on a meeting in the Propaganda Ministry literature department on 5 July 1944 regarding *Meyers Lexikon*, BArch NS 8/249 fol. 58–61.

[311] Short progress report 1 September 1939–April 1942, BArch R 43 II /585 fol. 51.

(twelve volumes + atlas, 1931–5), the *Staatslexikon* published on behalf of the Görres Society (five volumes, 1927–32), and the *Lexikon der Pädagogik der Gegenwart* on contemporary educational theory (two volumes, 1930).[312]

From 1938 the PPK also began to take a greater interest in school-books and teaching materials. With the National Socialist Teachers' League (NSLB) and the NSDAP's race policy office, it published a select bibliography on "writings about family, *Volk*, and race for the use of teachers and pupils."[313] The same year, Bouhler published a class reader entitled *Kampf um Deutschland* ("The struggle for Germany"); a Reich Education Ministry decree made its purchase obligatory for elementary (*Volksschule*) pupils from the eighth grade, middle and higher school pupils from the fifth grade.[314] In October 1940 Bouhler received a mandate from Hitler to remodel school-books in line with National Socialist principles.[315] This enabled him to set up a "Reich Office for Schoolbooks and Teaching Materials" (Reichsstelle für das Schul- und Unterrichtsschrifttum),[316] which mainly depended on the PPK apparatus and on cooperation with the NSLB literature office and its *Gau* sections. This new Reich-level office began to sift through all teachers' handbooks, textbooks and readers for student use, and general educational literature, recording it in a "general catalogue."[317] The textbook publishers were required

---

[312] See the ban on the first six volumes of *Der grosse Herder*, 5 August 1937, BArch R 58/909 fol. 112. Also *Der Katholizismus in Deutschland*, 247–69.

[313] *Schrifttum über Familie, Volk und Rasse für die Hand des Lehrers und Schülers*, zusammengestellt und begutachtet vom NS.-Lehrerbund, Reichsfachgebiet Rassenfrage, und vom Rassenpolitischen Amt der NSDAP, Berlin 1938 (= *NSB*, supplement 1), BArch NSD 2/10.

[314] "Erlass vom 20.6.1938," *Deutsche Wissenschaft, Erziehung und Volksbildung* 4 (1938), 309. The "reader for German Youth" was compiled "at the Führer's request" and published by Eher in 1938. See also "Das Schulbuch ein politisches Erziehungsmittel," *NSB* 3, no. 6 (1938), i–viii.

[315] Reich Minister and head of the Reich Chancellery to the head of Hitler's Chancellery, 2 October 1940 (copy), BArch NS 15/107.

[316] Circular no. 1 from the Reich commissioner for schoolbooks and teaching materials to the members of the Reich committee on schoolbooks and teaching materials, April 1941, BArch NS 8/209 fol. 61.

[317] Short progress report 1 September 1939–April 1942, B. Reichsstelle für das Schul- und Unterrichtsschrifttum, BArch R 43 II /585 fol. 53. See also the notes on demarcating the responsibilities and interests of the Reich office for schoolbooks and teaching materials (n.d., c. 1941/42), BArch NS 11/12.

to rectify any passages queried. The office also worked on creating its own texts: a new atlas; a new book for *Volksschule* lessons in history, biology (now known as *Lebenskunde*, "knowledge of life"), and geography; new textbooks for the lowest-level secondary schools and on "knowledge of the Reich" for vocational schools and colleges; and new schoolbooks for the "Protectorate of Bohemia and Moravia." In 1941 the office, in conjunction with the NSLB, carried out a "cleansing campaign" in all school and teachers' libraries. Based on its findings, in 1942 an index of "Jewish and emigrant authors" claimed to survey the literature that had been "acquired by school and teachers' libraries mainly before the accession to power."

Crucial to the PPK's growing influence on Nazi literary policy was its authorization to censor. This involved, firstly, "post-censorship" or bans on already published items, which the Gestapo was to implement by seizing and impounding the books concerned. In March 1941, at Bouhler's personal request, Hitler expressly reaffirmed that the PPK, just like the Propaganda Ministry, could apply directly to the Gestapo for published books to be confiscated.[318] In the case of books that were in press or had only just appeared, the PPK's applications for confiscation could be considered approved if the Propaganda Ministry had made no objection to them within three weeks. Secondly there was "preventive censorship," carried out in various different ways: publishers were obligated to submit the manuscripts of books and essays touching on National Socialism to the PPK for examination, but from 1941 the commission also had a vote in the Propaganda Ministry committee on distributing paper allocations.[319] This now enabled the PPK to participate in decisions on the projects of every single publisher.

Within the PPK there was much discussion on how to manage censorship in practice. In 1940 the head of the "Führer's Speeches" section, Jürgen Soenke, submitted his Greifswald University doctoral dissertation with the title "Studies on Contemporary Systems of Censorship."[320] It compared "the Catholic Church's censorship,"

---

[318] Bormann to Lammers, 10 March 1941, BArch NS 11/17, and this information passed on to Goebbels, 2 April 1941, ibid.
[319] Summary of the responsibilities of the PPK, 9 May 1942, BArch R 43 II /585, here fol. 59. See also Hövel, "Die Wirtschaftsstelle des deutschen Buchhandels," B14.
[320] Published in book form as *Studien über zeitgenössische Zensursysteme*, Frankfurt/Main: Diesterweg, 1941. BArch BDC/Partei-Kanzlei-Correspondence/Soenke, Jürgen

"censorship in the Soviet Union," and "censorship in Germany before 1933" with the PPK's censorship practices. Soenke argued that the Nazi state's traditional, prohibition-based censorship could become superfluous thanks to the positive "educational work" of National Socialism. However, this theory had little impact on the PPK's actual procedures. Hederich did explicitly reject the Soviet system, favored by Amann, of a central state publisher—"Glavlit"—that evaluated and published all written material; he doubted that the Party publisher Eher had the economic capacity to fill such a role and also feared for Germany's reputation abroad.[321] But the PPK was far from relying solely on positive inducements to change publishers' policies and readers' behavior.[322] Censorship took place subtly, under the surface, and the PPK was willing to turn to the Catholic Church, normally so fiercely denigrated, for lessons in this respect. Writing to Hess in December 1938, Bouhler observed that when it came to the authoritarian management of literature, "several important things can certainly be adopted from the Church's many centuries of experience, even if simply adopting the whole system is out of the question and would contradict the basic principles of National Socialism."[323]

During the war, the PPK apparatus shrank to sixty employees,[324] but it could still draw on more than 500 external readers for the examination process.[325] The fact that the PPK managed to survive as an institution despite its many enemies was due primarily to Hitler's support for Bouhler, the head of his personal office in the Chancellery.

(1907–83): studied German, Russian, history, and church and art history in Vienna, Kiel, and Greifswald; joined NSDAP 1929, joined SA 1931; joined PPK 1 July 1935; 1938 "Führer's Speeches" section; from June 1940 head of the PPK's Prague office. See also J. Soenke, "Zur Geschichte der Zensur," NSB 4, no. 8 (1939), 57–67.

[321] This is Hederich's line of argument in his draft response to the 25 August 1939 communication by Leader of the Party Organization Dr. Ley to the Führer's Deputy, p. 3, BArch NS 11/9. See also J. Soenke, "Glawlit. Marxistische 'Schrifttumspolitik,'" NSB 3, no. 10 (1938), xii–xvi.

[322] See memorandum on aspects to be considered during discussions of the PPK, its sphere of work, and its responsibilities (n.d., 1939), BArch NS 11/6.

[323] Bouhler to Hess, December 1938, BArch NS 11/9, here p. 2.

[324] PPK tasks and structure, BArch R 43 II /585, here fol. 44: 25 male and 35 female employees (May 1942).

[325] Short progress report, BArch R 43 II /585 fol. 47: 692 external readers, of whom 165 were serving in the military in May 1942.

This, in turn, probably arose from the bonus that Bouhler had earned by taking responsibility for implementing Hitler's "euthanasia command" in fall 1939. Finally, in 1943 Hitler also chose Bouhler to head the planned "Main Literature Office of the NSDAP."[326] Although the plan was never realized, blocked by an obstinate Rosenberg, it did enable Bouhler to maintain his commission (incorporated into Hitler's Chancellery as "Office VI" in late May 1941[327]) until the end of the war. He had the backing of Bormann, who—as Rosenberg's office speculated in July 1943, probably correctly—had "the greatest interest" in "paying Bouhler off with literature responsibilities, having siphoned away his authority in the Führer's Chancellery."[328]

The Staff of the Führer's Deputy (from 1941: Party Chancellery of the NSDAP)

Before the PPK was established, Bouhler had already run a literary policy section of his own, in his capacity as the Party's "commissioner for cultural questions (art, literature, music)."[329] From May 1934 this role was taken on by Ernst Schulte Strathaus. An antiquarian book dealer born in 1881, and the son-in-law of writer Ina Seidel, Schulte Strathaus had made his name through Goethe scholarship and bibliophile editions. When the Nazi dictatorship began, he was working as the manager of the respected Munich antiquarian bookstore Julius Halle, the owner of which was Jewish. As a personal acquaintance of Hess's—who ensured that his NSDAP membership application was backdated to 1 January 1934 despite the period of closure for new members—Schulte Strathaus arrived at the Party's "Brown House" in April 1934 as case officer for literature and scholarship.[330] As a result, Führer's Deputy Hess now had two different literature

---

[326] Bormann to Rosenberg, 29 June 1943, BArch NS 8/188 fol. 2.
[327] Bouhler to Ley, 29 May 1941, BArch NS 11/9.
[328] Rosenberg's adjutant Koeppen to Utikal of the literature office, 17 July 1943, BArch NS 8/229 fol. 109.
[329] "Bekanntgabe vom 15.1.1934," *Verordnungsblatt der Reichsleitung der NSDAP* 2, no. 63, 15 January 1934, 137, BArch NSD 13/1.
[330] "Bekanntgabe von Reichsschatzmeister Schwarz vom 23.5.1934," *Verordnungsblatt der Reichsleitung der NSDAP* 2, no. 72, late May 1934, 163, BArch NSD 13/1.

offices at his disposal: the PPK was institutionally incorporated into his staff[331] although the two bodies had been separated geographically since August 1934, while Schulte Strathaus was responsible for "questions of art and culture" at the Munich headquarters.[332]

With many files lost during the war, it is no longer possible to reconstruct the exact commitments of the Führer's Deputy in literary policy. No taxing demands were placed on Hess's employee Schulte Strathaus for the most part, and it seems he only intervened in literary policy when Hess was asked to mediate in a dispute. Initiatives of his own were no longer required when the state and Party established their literature offices—especially since Bouhler and Rosenberg were already waging bitter wars for responsibility in this domain.[333] When Martin Bormann was appointed head of the NSDAP Party Chancellery in May 1941, Schulte Strathaus was scapegoated for Hess's failed mission to England and removed from office, excluded from the NSDAP on Hitler's instructions, and held by the Gestapo until spring 1943.[334] On 29 May 1941, a decree from Hitler transferred all Hess's responsibilities to Bormann,[335] who now integrated the field of art and culture into his Department II, "Internal Party Matters." Headed by Hellmuth Friedrichs since 1934, this department's role went beyond coordinating the "development and expansion of the Party, its divisions, and its affiliated associations" to monitor "developments in the political situation within Germany and their effects on Party and state."[336] Department II's schedule of responsibilities in March 1942 indicates that Office II B3, headed by Fritz Hammerbacher, was responsible for "cultural issues, the

---

[331] See *Nationalsozialistisches Jahrbuch* 11 (1937), 150.

[332] *Nationalsozialistisches Jahrbuch* 10 (1936), 134.

[333] Thus the summary, classified as a "Secret Reich Matter" ("Geheime Reichssache"), of the scope of the "tasks that may be appropriate for the PPK on the basis of the currently applicable working basis and guidelines," p. 2, 15 September 1939, BArch NS 11/6.

[334] *Oberbereichsleiter* Schneider to the leader of the Brown House local group, 28 April 1943, BArch BDC/ Partei-Kanzlei-Correspondence/Schulte Strathaus, E.

[335] See the collection of decrees, ordinances, and notifications issued by the Party Chancellery, Munich 1942–4, BArch NSD 3/12–18, here NSD 3/12: vol. I, 4–5.

[336] Department II schedule of responsibilities, 28 February 1938, BArch NS 6/451.

organization of celebrations, folk culture associations, and questions of literature."[337]

In literature as in other policy fields, the "Führer's Office"[338] now became an influential and radicalizing factor both within the NSDAP itself and vis-à-vis the state's ministries and authorities. With the directive "executing the Führer's decree on the status of the Head of the Party Chancellery" on 16 January 1942, Bormann underpinned his right to intervene in "questions of principle and policy, especially those that contribute to the preparation, amendment, or implementation of laws, decrees, and ordinances."[339] A February 1942 agreement with the Chamber of Culture management laid down that all "ordinances significant in any way" be forwarded to the Party Chancellery for a response, and all "ordinances purely technical and formal in nature" sent for information at the draft stage.[340] This gave the Party Chancellery direct insight into the work of the Chamber of Literature, and Bormann's staff also took an interest in the Chamber's members. In the frequent disputes, the Party Chancellery backed any *Gau* or district NSDAP leadership wanting to bar an author from participating in the Chamber of Literature—as a "National Socialist institution"[341]—due to his or her "political unreliability." References to the author's literary qualities by the Chamber or the Propaganda Ministry literature department went unheard.

The Party Chancellery's encroachments were especially obvious in the field of religious ("confessional") literature. In a circular dated 2 August 1942, Bormann informed state and Party agencies that in future "political-confessional matters" were to be handled

---

[337] Ibid. p. 2.

[338] This was Bormann's definition of the Party Chancellery in a file note for Friedrichs on 4 June 1941, BArch NS 6/126 fol. 7. See also Goebbels's criticism, noted in his diary entry of 26 September 1941, of the Party Chancellery's intention to "place itself above the various Reich Leaders as a superior office," Goebbels, *Tagebücher*, Part II, vol. 1, 499.

[339] In the collection issued by the Party Chancellery, vol. I (NSD 3/12), 5–6.

[340] Party Chancellery to Propaganda Ministry, Chamber of Culture department, 5 February 1942, p. 1, BArch R 56 I/16.

[341] This was the Party Chancellery's interpretation in a 29 September 1942 response to Tiessler re: author Johann Zangerle's complaint against the refusal of his RSK membership application, BArch NS 18/3017.

centrally via the Party Chancellery.[342] In charge of this area was Department III, "Party Law, Economy, Church," headed by state secretary Gerhard Klopfer.[343] Here, Office III D5, under Hermann Landwehr, was to curb "confessional propaganda" and pursue the "de-confessionalization of the tools of political and cultural leadership (literature, press, music, film, visual arts)."[344] To this end, the Party Chancellery cooperated closely with the RSHA, which was already dealing with religious publishing and libraries.[345] Bormann also received information from Rosenberg on the literature that had been set aside from the Borromäus Society's Catholic libraries by district literature officers during the NSDAP book donation campaign.[346]

At first, Bormann interfered in Goebbels's sphere of literary policy only on isolated occasions. For example, the Party Chancellery protested the publication of a new, eighteen-volume collected works of Gerhart Hauptmann, planned by publisher S. Fischer for 1942 to commemorate the dramatist's eightieth birthday and already approved by the Propaganda Ministry.[347] Conversely, in 1943 Bormann personally championed the allocation of paper to a new edition of *Ich kämpfe* ("I fight"), which had been rejected by the Propaganda Ministry's literature department; he wanted the book presented to each youngster joining the Hitler Youth or the League of German Girls. Writing on 21 February, Bormann told Goebbels that in the production of books, "regrettably, and despite the concerns expressed by the Party, equally strict criteria of importance to the war [*Kriegswichtigkeit*]" had "not always been applied."[348] Besides, added Bormann, the Ministry literature department was "hardly in the unpleasant situation of having to deny the Party itself the paper

---

[342] Circular 119/42, 2 August 1942, in the Party Chancellery collection, vol. I, 9–10 (NSD 3/12).

[343] Department III's schedule of responsibilities (1 May 1944), BArch BDC/Partei-Kanzlei-Correspondence/Klopfer, G.

[344] Department III's schedule of responsibilities, I May 1944, p. 12.

[345] Thus, in October 1942 Hammerbacher asked von Kielpinski of the RSHA to draw up a "register of the confessional retail bookstores." File note from Wilhelm Baur on a discussion with von Kielpinski, 20 November 1942, BArch BDC/SS/von Kielpinski, W.

[346] Bormann to Rosenberg, 6 May 1944, on the libraries of the Borromäus Society, BArch NS 8/190 fol. 74.

[347] Note from Hammerbacher for Tiessler, 23 September 1942, BArch NS 18/3005.

[348] Bormann to Goebbels, 21 February 1943, p. 1, BArch NS 18/452.

required for a book that is of indisputable military importance." In December 1941, Bormann had already tried to get Goebbels's approval for paper to print 60,000 copies of Kurt Eggers's anti-Christian collection *Der Scheiterhaufen* ("The stake"). Although the book had just received a very positive evaluation from Hitler, Goebbels rejected the application, citing the lack of interest for such books among the population.[349]

Probably as a result of these differences of opinion, Bormann began to make his own recommendations of books that he considered important to the war, via circulars sent out to NSDAP offices.[350] *Völkisch* literature was also specifically promoted through Deutsche Verlags- und Kunstanstalt, a publishing company funded by the Party Chancellery and managed by the owners of the publisher Volkschaftsverlag.[351]

It was not only the state's literary policy activities that failed to satisfy the head of the Party Chancellery. Always in search of the greatest possible administrative efficiency, he also objected to the duplication of literary tasks by different Reich Leaders, who harassed his Chancellery with their constant squabbles over competencies. However, Bormann's chance to resolve this thorn in his flesh came only with the onset of "total war." On 18 February 1943, the literature department of the Party Main Office for Educators, led by Fritz Wächtler, was the first to be shut down.[352] Bormann then set about unifying the literary policy domains of Bouhler and Rosenberg, though it was only after Hitler's decree of 20 July 1944—giving him

---

[349] See Tiessler's submission on behalf of Bormann, 8 December 1941, with Bormann's handwritten annotations, and the submission of 14 December 1941, BArch NS 18/30.
[350] Circular no. 61/43, 7 April 1943 on A. E. Johann's *Das Land ohne Herz, eine Reise ins unbekannte Amerika* ("Land with no heart: Journey into unknown America"), which Bormann recommended because it unmasked "Americanism as a deadly enemy of genuine humanity and true culture"; circular no. 46/43, 11 March 1943 on Karl Götz's *Brüder über dem Meer, Schicksale und Begegnungen* ("Brothers across the sea: Destinies and encounters"), whose portrayal of the lives of German emigrants and their descendants overseas could, in Bormann's opinion, explain "the meaning of our struggle." Both circulars in BArch NS 18/54.
[351] Payr indicates this ownership structure in his file note for *Bereichsleiter* Koeppen dated 16 October 1944, summarizing a meeting with members of Party Chancellery Department III on 12 October, BArch NS 8/249 fol. 87.
[352] "Anordnung A 10/43 vom 18.2.1943," *Reichsverfügungsblatt der NSDAP* edition A, 1943, BArch NSD 3/3.

the right, as head of the Party Chancellery, to make any arrangement necessary for the waging of total war[353]—that he managed to close Rosenberg's literature office completely. Even then, the officially dissolved office was still not quite silent. In early October 1944 it noted pointedly that on 30 September 1944 the Berlin office of the Party Chancellery had organized an event with *völkisch* authors,[354] some of whom had harshly criticized the Propaganda Ministry's literature department and its one-sided privileging of entertainment literature. Amt Rosenberg's notes observe that "these comments, if made in different circles, would have sent one to the concentration camp." Payr's impression was that "the literary policy work of the Party Chancellery's representatives is completely dominated by a single idea: which poets or writers directly advocate the *völkisch* worldview and an approach to matters of faith that accords with our own."[355] Authors "who cannot be brought into line one hundred percent, yet have made a significant literary contribution" were of "only marginal" interest. As a result, "the Party Chancellery's perspective on literature inevitably becomes very narrow." If neither this functionalization of literature nor the "founding of a new literature office in the Party Chancellery"[356] (as feared by Payr) actually materialized, that was ultimately due only to the collapse of the Nazi regime.

The Literary Apparatus of the Wehrmacht

Because of the loss of so many documents and the myth-making processes after 1945, the supreme command of the German armed forces (Oberkommando der Wehrmacht, OKW) remains a largely unknown factor among the literary policy agencies of the Nazi state. Only rudiments of an independent literary policy can be discerned in

---

[353] "Führer-Verfügung 10/44 vom 20.7.1944," *Reichsverfügungsblatt der NSDAP* edition A, 1944, BArch NSD 3/4–5.

[354] Confidential file note for *Oberbereichsleiter* Dr. Payr, 4 October 1944, BArch NS 8/249 fol. 85.

[355] File note for *Bereichsleiter* Koeppen, 16 October 1944, BArch NS 8/249, here fol. 87/ verso.

[356] Payr, file note for Koeppen, 5 October 1944, BArch NS 8/249 fol. 84.

the Wehrmacht up to the beginning of World War II. From 1936, its propaganda office published the illustrated weekly *Die Wehrmacht* with a circulation of 750,000,[357] but a decision by Hitler later forced the journal's publisher, Verlag Die Wehrmacht, to give up its most important print product; during the war, publication was taken over by Deutscher Verlag, now in the hands of Amann's Eher house. Deutscher Verlag also published the periodicals *Deutsche Infanterie*, *Die Sirene*, and other papers read by Wehrmacht soldiers, giving Amann control over a very lucrative market segment.

The German Army Library in Berlin, founded in 1919, initially supervised seven military district libraries.[358] But from 1935 the Wehrmacht's library network burgeoned along with rearmament, and by 1942 it included seventeen district libraries. In addition to the central library in Berlin, branches in Vienna and Prague were established in 1940. The Army Library and military district libraries possessed not only large holdings and considerable funding for new acquisitions, but also qualified staff—the Berlin headquarters alone had twenty-four trained librarians in 1942.

Until 1940, the director of the German Army Library was also the Reichswehr Ministry's specialist on army libraries. From 1941 the Ministry had a separate office for the "Chief of the Army Libraries," accounting at first to the Army General Staff and from July 1942 to the "Führer's commissioner for the writing of military history." The office was headed by a member of the military, but its substantive work was carried out by a research librarian, Friedrich Bräuninger, right up to 1945. Among its tasks were overseeing the establishment and expansion of the army libraries, supervising their personnel, purchasing books and periodicals centrally for all the army libraries, and examining and evaluating new publications. After top-level competencies within the OKW were redistributed on 1 March 1939, two departments were relevant for literary policy. Major General Hasso von Wedel led the "Department for Wehrmacht Propaganda," which reported to the head of the Wehrmacht Operations Office. It was responsible for the "intellectual supervision" of Wehrmacht members and the journal *Die Wehrmacht* (Group II/Section IId);

---

[357] Bühler and Bühler, *Der Frontbuchhandel*, 67.
[358] On this and the following, see Genge, "Militärbibliotheken."

defense and Wehrmacht propaganda in literature and the "field libraries" (Group II/Section IIe); and providing information on literary questions within Germany (Group III/Section IIIa).[359] The "Home Department," headed by Major Werner Ziegler and reporting to the chief of the Wehrmacht General Office, had the following tasks: cooperation with the Wehrmacht section of the DAF (Group I); "evaluating ideological writing for the Wehrmacht" (Group II); issuing permission for manuscripts written by officers, "monitoring literature on defense policy and the spirit of defense," publishing lists of recommended books for the Wehrmacht, and writing prefaces for books (Reading Office).[360]

The monthly lists of recommended reading, *Bücher für die Wehrmacht*, appeared from February 1939 until 1942. They had two evaluation categories, A for "especially valuable," and B for "no cause for concern." An analysis of the selected titles—up to 600 of them a year—shows that political propaganda, works glorifying war, and practical military techniques were prioritized, with poetry and fiction completely absent.[361] In 1940 the range was extended to cover "history," "German art," and "dictionaries." Nazi and pro-Nazi companies predominated among the publishers featured. Separate selections were printed to guide acquisitions by the Army Library, the military district libraries, and the troop libraries, in the bulletin *Mitteilungen der Deutschen Heeresbücherei* (amalgamated with *Wehrwissenschaftliche Quellenkunde* from 1938). Cumulative lists of recommendations covering six years each were published in 1934 and 1939 by E. S. Mittler & Sohn, under the title *Heer und Wehr im Buche der Gegenwart. Verzeichnis der Neuerwerbungen der Deutschen Heeresbücherei* ("Army and defense in the contemporary book. Register of the German Army Library's new acquisitions"). The lists show a wide spectrum of specialist literature in military science and the art of warfare, military history, National Socialist nonfiction, and local studies, but also some quality fiction and entertainment literature.

---

[359] Schramm, *Kriegstagebuch des Oberkommandos der Wehrmacht*, vol. I, part 2, 887–98 (here 883), 914.

[360] Ibid. 889.

[361] On this and the following, see Bühler and Bühler, *Der Frontbuchhandel*, 32–5; Genge, "Militärbibliotheken," 172–81.

The OKW's transition from an unobtrusive participant to an influential factor in the regime's literary policy is marked by the establishment of a central office for the frontline book dealerships, Zentrale der Frontbuchhandlungen, on 4 September 1939.[362] It was the industrious director of the DAF's publishing activities, Eberhard Heffe, who recognized the enormous potential of the book market now emerging at the front; the OKW was his powerful partner in developing the sector. On the one hand, the Wehrmacht provided the personnel (generally recruited from the book trade) for the approximately 300 stationary frontline dealerships and the buses equipped as mobile bookstores that were deployed in Poland, France, Belgium, Norway, and on the Eastern Front. On the other hand, this new market segment stimulated publishers' production of books for the Wehrmacht. At first, normal editions were sold through the frontline stores, but from 1940 on there was continuous growth in the special "field post" editions, frontline editions, and books produced exclusively to supply the military with reading material. This triggered a radical shift in publishing production, to the detriment of all those publishers left outside the new market and also of retail bookselling, which for the most part was barred from selling the frontline editions with their enormous print runs.

When the Reich Minister of Armaments and Production ordered a restructuring of paper management from 1 June 1942, the split in the market was deepened: the Economic Office of the German Book Trade was now allowed to issue only "permits to cover paper requirements," whereas the OKW, the Army High Command, the German Navy, and the Luftwaffe were able to distribute their paper stocks autonomously by issuing "paper permission checks."[363] Wehrmacht commissions were given preferential treatment as "measures important to the war," and right up to the turn of 1945 both the OKW and the individual forces had huge stores of paper, amassed by pillaging the occupied areas, so that this market attracted more and

---

[362] "Mitteilung von Wilhelm Baur an den deutschen Buchhandel betr. die Gründung von Frontbuchhandlungen," *Bbl.* no. 242, 17 October 1939, 689.
[363] Bühler and Bühler, *Der Frontbuchhandel*, 14–15; Friedländer et al., *Bertelsmann im Dritten Reich*, 466–72.

more publishers. No fewer than seventy-one of them were involved in the "field post" editions alone.[364]

Increasingly, the Wehrmacht also acted as a direct commissioner of publishers or as a publisher in its own right.[365] The process began with the series "Die Tornisterschriften des OKW" ("The OKW haversack books") including 110 titles (1939–42/43) and "Die Soldatenbücherei" ("The soldiers' library") with more than 120 titles (1940–4) and around ten million copies printed. For a long time, their content and design was the responsibility of Benno Mascher, formerly the editor of the well-known Langen-Müller journal *Das Innere Reich* ("The inner realm"). From 1941 to 1943 the series "Soldatenbriefe zur Berufsförderung" ("Soldiers' letters for career improvement") appeared in editions A–D. The Luftwaffe, the Navy, and even individual divisions also published both magazine-format series and individual books. In France, 1942 and 1943 saw special editions of Ernst Jünger's *Gärten und Strassen* ("Gardens and streets"), *Auf den Marmorklippen* (*On the Marble Cliffs*), and *Myrdun*, along with several city guides to Paris, books on the French regions and French cultural history, dictionaries, pocket calendars, and a tome on medieval illuminations magnificently illustrated with reproductions from the Bibliothèque Nationale. For Belgium and Norway, comparable works gave guidance on the country, history, economy, culture, and language; these were flanked by more entertaining works by Felix Timmermans, Wilhelm Busch, or Erwin Guido Kolbenheyer with his novel *Meister Joachim Pausewang* (*A Winter Chronicle*). In Finland and on the Eastern Front, the focus was on portrayals of combat by war reporters and soldiers.

The introduction of the Wehrmacht "paper check" brought a further, time-consuming procedure for accessing paper. First of all, the sections responsible for paper allocation within the OKW, the Army High Command, the German Navy, and the Luftwaffe decided whether—and if so, in what quantity—paper should be made available for a project in principle.[366] Then both the OKW and the Propaganda

[364] For details, see Bühler and Bühler, *Der Frontbuchhandel*, 119–24.
[365] On the following, see especially Bühler and Kirbach, "Die Wehrmachtsausgaben"; Bühler and Bühler, "Die Wehrmacht als Verleger"; Bühler and Bühler, *Der Frontbuchhandel*, 184–231.
[366] On the practical implementation of this rule, see Bühler and Simons, *Die blendenden Geschäfte*, 44–51.

Ministry had to supply a report on the specific content and authorize each individual application. Within this complex process, the OKW's Jürgen Eggebrecht became a key figure for publishers and authors. Born in 1898 to a pastor's family in Saxony, Eggebrecht had fought as a private on the Western Front from 1916 to 1918.[367] During the Weimar Republic he worked as an editor for Deutsche Verlags-Anstalt in Stuttgart (1928–33) and published his own poems in the anthology *Junge deutsche Lyrik* (Reclam, 1928). In 1933 Eggebrecht reworked Werner Beumelburg's popular war novel *Sperrfeuer um Deutschland* ("Barrage around Germany," 1929) for young readers with the Gerhard Stalling house. Stalling, where Eggebrecht became reader-in-chief in 1935, published all Beumelburg's works and, in 1937, also Eggebrecht's biography of him.

From February 1940 up to the end of the war, Eggebrecht held the rank of a major in the war administration, with responsibility for the preliminary censorship of all book publications by the OKW. In this role, he sometimes managed to enable the publication of authors critical of the regime as Wehrmacht editions despite disapproval from the Propaganda Ministry or the Chamber of Literature.[368] In 1944, supported by the OKW, Eggebrecht founded his own publishing company, which was intended to take over the book production previously in the hands of the Zentrale der Frontbuchhandlungen.[369] Publication of around ten million copies was planned for the first year alone. In spring 1945, as the borders of the Reich contracted, the civilian book trade's Economic Office was finally refused all paper—"in future, publishers must generally expect only Wehrmacht supplies."[370] In the 9 April file note to this effect, the president of the Börsenverein added a handwritten comment on 30 April, twelve days after the US Army had occupied Leipzig: "filed as irrelevant."

---

[367] On this and the following, see BArch BDC/RSK/Eggebrecht, Jürgen.
[368] Lange, *Tagebücher aus dem Zweiten Weltkrieg*, 22; Schaefer, *Auch wenn Du träumst*, 286–7; Wallrath-Janssen, *Der Verlag H. Goverts*, 343–7, 377–8; Denk, *Die Zensur der Nachgeborenen*, 382–8.
[369] Goverts's report of a discussion with Eggebrecht in Weimar, 4 March 1944, cited in Wallrath-Janssen, *Der Verlag H. Goverts*, 346.
[370] Meeting with Wülfing on 4 April 1945 regarding Wehrmacht book acquisitions, StAL BV/792 fol. 105.

4

Books in the Media Dictatorship: The Perspective of the Rulers

Person-related Control of Writers

The Chamber of Culture legislation obliged all writers to apply for membership of the Reich Chamber of Literature. According to a legal commentary published in 1934, anyone failing to fulfill this obligation "places himself outside his professional representation, thereby relinquishing the prerequisites for continuing to exercise his profession."[1] A writer's "right to exercise his profession" was also lost if his or her application was rejected or membership terminated. However, decisions to refuse admittance or to exclude an existing member due to insufficient "reliability and suitability" could only be made case by case, "with due consideration of any special circumstances."[2]

For reasons of both economics and Germany's reputation abroad, the drafters of the Chamber of Culture Law had not given it an exclusionary "Aryan paragraph,"[3] so that the Chamber of Literature was initially somewhat doubtful about how to handle the sensitive topic of Jewish writers.[4] Chamber vice-president Wismann was inclined to

---

[1] In Schrieber, *Die Reichskulturkammer*, 24. The following quotations ibid.
[2] Ibid. 28.
[3] On the background, see Dahm, "Kulturelles und geistiges Leben," 79–82.
[4] Grimm to Blunck, 18 November 1933, DLA NL Hans Grimm/Konv. Reichsschrifttumskammer, folder I 1933/1934. The following quotations ibid.

take a hard line, but while Hans Grimm, as he told president Blunck in November 1933, shared the view that "the Jew who now tries to push his way in must be completely prevented from doing so in future, at least for a while," he argued that those "Jews who have written and been decent" should be accepted into the Chamber or permitted to remain members. Blunck wanted "at all costs to avoid treating unfairly those Jewish citizens who distinguished themselves in the war, stood up firmly for our state, and did not participate in the propaganda of decadence; instead we should try ... to eliminate the new generation that is now pushing to enter the Chamber in dispro-portionate numbers."[5]

In early December 1933, the writers' association RDS presented the Chamber with a first relatively comprehensive list of authors whose applications for admission were to be turned down.[6] These applicants were writers who had been rejected by the RDS "on the grounds of previous nihilist or purely destructive activity, yet who did not follow the procession of emigrants in March this year but remained in the Reich and are currently willing to pledge their commitment to the new state as required by the membership declaration." Blunck conceded these "grounds for lenience," but set them against the Chamber's "responsibility to preserve the purity of our repute and to educate toward the highest duty to the common good." He was well aware of the consequences of non-admission: "Rejection means being forced to emigrate or else economic and moral ostracism, in most cases the destruction of civil existence."

Decisions on the fifty-seven "cases" were made at the Chamber council meeting on 16 January 1934. Grimm suggested that those authors who "in the past have taken an attitude that is not nationally minded and is less than gratifying for the reputation of German literature" should only be "put on a provisional list, with definitive admission to the RDS made contingent on their further behavior over the course of one year."[7] This arrangement was immediately applied to thirty-two writers. Even the pacifist Erich Kästner was given the

---

[5] Blunck to Grimm, 20 November 1933, DLA NL Hans Grimm/Konv. Reichs-schrifttumskammer, folder I 1933/1934.

[6] On the following, see Blunck to Grimm, 6 December 1933, ibid.

[7] Minutes of the Chamber council meeting on 16 January 1934, here p. 15, DLA NL Hans Grimm/Konv. Reichsschrifttumskammer, folder III. The following quotations ibid.

opportunity to "prove himself." He was to be allowed to write for one year, "on a trial basis," under his pseudonym Berthold Bürger. The same was settled for the Rowohlt author Mascha Kaléko and several other "non-Aryan" writers. In contrast, the council unanimously rejected the application of Alfred Döblin, who had refused to sign the promise, included in the admission documents, "to take a stand at any time for German literature in the spirit of the national movement."

During a Chamber of Culture conference at the Propaganda Ministry in February 1934, Goebbels—as president of the Chamber of Culture—gave the individual chamber presidents and councils their basic instructions on how to deal with the "non-Aryan question."[8] He had been "disconcerted" to find that "in the absence of an Aryan paragraph, Jews gradually forced out of other professions are seeking a new field of opportunity in the cultural sphere." Although there was "no immediate legal possibility of introducing an Aryan paragraph to the Reich Chamber of Culture and its affiliated associations," he recommended that the chambers apply § 10 of the First Directive for the Execution of the Reich Chamber of Culture Law as strictly as possible: "It is possible to refuse somebody membership of the associations if he must, for particular reasons, be regarded as unreliable or unsuited, and in my view and experience, a Jew is generally unsuited to stewarding Germany's cultural assets!"[9]

This new interpretation contradicted previous readings, and clashed with the request by the Chamber of Culture management in late 1933 for the "racial affiliation" question to be completely deleted from the sector associations' application forms.[10] It heralded

---

[8] Goebbels's speech on the organizational structure of the cultural professions, reproduced in *Erste Früh-Ausgabe des Deutschen Nachrichtenbüros* 1, no. 288, 8 February 1934, BArch R 43 II /1241 fol. 18–19.

[9] See Schrieber, *Die Reichskulturkammer*, 29: "Like foreigners, non-Aryans are thus not excluded on principle from membership of the Reich Chamber of Culture. However, in the case of people of alien descent it is in the spirit of the law to set particularly strict requirements of reliability and suitability, because in general they cannot be considered suitable bearers and stewards of German cultural assets. The non-Aryan will therefore have to provide special evidence of his reliability and suitability. The rules on exceptions included in the civil service legislation (exception for former frontline soldiers) may also be applied here mutatis mutandis."

[10] See Wismann's report for Goebbels, 27 May 1935, BArch R 56 V/194 fol. 1.

a tightening of the selection process. At a meeting of the Chamber of Literature's administrative board on 7 March 1934, Blunck suddenly claimed that he had always "feared a Jewish swamping [*Überfremdung*] of the RDS," and therefore planned to "accept Jews up to a rate of, at most, 5 percent of the RDS's total membership."[11] After the Chamber of Culture president's speech, he added, it was now necessary "to take rigorous care, at least with regard to the writers themselves, to prevent a greater incursion of non-Aryans into the chambers, and only to accept as necessary active war veterans or men with an outstanding record." The Chamber's new guidelines therefore laid down that only those Jews must be admitted to the RDS who could demonstrate that they had been frontline soldiers or, "in the case of female persons, war widows."[12] Exceptions should also be made for older people who would not be able to learn a new trade.

In 1934, 428 Jewish writers were still members of the Chamber of Literature,[13] but pressure to exclude them increased in the second half of that year. Frontline service in World War I now had to be proved with "officially accredited certifications,"[14] and by 1935 exclusions were being imposed without any regard for service to the nation, literary quality, or social hardship. Author Paul Landau, for example, whose membership Grimm had advocated due to "his good German past,"[15] received the notification on 7 March 1935: "In view of the great significance of intellectual and culturally creative work for the life and future development of the German *Volk*, there is no doubt that only those individuals are suited to this work in Germany who belong to the German *Volk* not merely through nationality, but through a deep connection of kind and blood. Only a person who feels connected and committed to his *Volk* through racial

---

[11] Minutes of the meeting of the administrative board on 7 March 1934, DLA NL Hans Grimm/Konv. Reichsschrifttumskammer, folder III.

[12] Interim report by the Reich Chamber of Literature on its work from 1 April – 30 June 1934, ibid.

[13] Wismann to Goebbels, 27 May 1935, BArch R 56 V/194 fol. 2.

[14] Writer Alfred Mombert received a demand to this effect on 16 October 1934, BArch BDC/RSK/Mombert, A.

[15] Grimm to Vesper, 9 January 1935, DLA NL Hans Grimm/Korrespondenz mit Will Vesper, and Grimm to Blunck, 24 January 1935, DLA NL Hans Grimm/Konv. Reichsschrifttumskammer, folder II 1935/1936.

community must undertake a task so profound and far-reaching as that of intellectual and cultural work and thus influence the inner life of the nation. Due to your being a non-Aryan, you are incapable of feeling or acknowledging a commitment of this kind."[16]

Exclusions followed in the same month for Julius Bab, Ludwig Fulda, Heinrich Galeen, Martin Gumpert, Willy Haas, Franz Hessel, Georg Hirschfeld, Mascha Kaléko, Rudolf Kayser, Hans Keilson, Max Mohr, Hans Natonek, Max Osborn, Jakob Picard, Kurt Pinthus, Eugen Rosenstock-Huessy, Alice Salomon, Heinrich Spiero, Max Tau, and numerous other Jewish writers.[17] Alfred Mombert, who had named Chamber president Blunck as a "sponsor" on his RDS application form,[18] was one of the last to be excluded, on 18 October 1935. In other cases, new applications for membership were refused. This was the experience of Hans Baron, Oscar Bie, Ernst Blass, Martin Buber, Erich Eyck, Ludwig Feuchtwanger, Arthur Goldschmidt, Kurt Hiller, Ferdinand Lion, Rudolph Lothar, Felix Salten, Hans Joachim Schoeps, Edgar Stern-Rubarth, Theodor Wiesengrund Adorno, Karl Wolfskehl, and others.

At the end of May 1935, Wismann could report to Goebbels that the number of Jewish writers in the Chamber had been reduced to just five.[19] However, the Reich Citizenship Law of 15 September 1935 reopened the question of "non-Aryan" membership. In a circular of 29 April 1936, the Chamber of Culture's manager, Hans Hinkel, informed the chamber administrations that "all full Jews, three-quarter Jews, half Jews, quarter Jews, spouses of full and three-quarter Jews, and spouses of half and quarter Jews" must be excluded from all the seven chambers by 15 May.[20] The Chamber of Literature could not fulfill this ambitious deadline, if only because staff shortages made it impossible to inspect all the members'

---

[16] Copy of the notification in DLA NL Hans Grimm/Konv. Reichsschrifttumskammer, folder II 1935/1936.

[17] On this and the following, see the list of "non-Aryan" members excluded and applicants rejected for membership on the basis of § 10, 15 March 1937, BArch R 55/21 300. The exact date of the exclusions and rejected applications can be found in a further, 45-page list, ibid.

[18] RDS questionnaire, 29 December 1933, BArch BDC/RSK/Mombert, A.

[19] Wismann to Goebbels, 27 May 1935, BArch R 56 V/194 fol. 3.

[20] Circular in BArch R 56 V/102 fol. 154–6.

"certificates of Aryan descent" in time.[21] The problem was exacerbated by the need to incorporate 1,958 Austrian writers who had applied for Chamber membership after the annexation of Austria. In the end, Goebbels himself modified the requirements in his 1939 "guidelines for the work of the Reich Chamber of Culture."[22] Whereas "Jews as defined by the Nuremberg Laws" continued to be excluded across the board, "half Jews" or the spouses of "full Jews" might, in individual cases, retain their membership with "special permission" by Goebbels. "Quarter Jews" or the spouses of "half Jews" only had to be excluded if they had "committed an offense against the state or against National Socialism or otherwise demonstrated that they incline toward Judaism."

By March 1937, a total of 1,232 "non-Aryan" writers had been excluded from the Chamber or had their applications for membership refused.[23] So had seventeen "Jewish-German *Mischlinge*," among them Elisabeth Langgässer, and twenty-one writers married to Jews. At this time, six "fully Jewish" writers were still members of the Chamber: as Upper Silesians, they were shielded until July 1937 by the minority protection stipulations of the 1922 German–Polish Treaty, guaranteed by the League of Nations. A further seventeen writers who had been classified as "*Mischlinge* of the first or second degree" or were married to Jews were able to remain in the Chamber after receiving "special permission," although this was "revocable at any time." By September 1938, the number of these exceptional permits had risen to thirty-four.[24] The list included such well-known names as Stefan Andres, who was married to a "half Jew," Werner Bergengruen, married to a "three-quarter Jew," Elisabeth Dauthendey, a "quarter Jew," Karl Rosner, a "half Jew," and Josef Winckler, married to a "full Jew." Another writer married to a "full Jew," Jochen Klepper, was protected from a ban

---

[21] See RSK president to RKK president, 22 March 1937, remarking on the length of time required to process the certificates, and RSK manager Ihde to the Propaganda Ministry, 7 September 1938, BArch R 55/21 300.

[22] Directions for the work of the RKK, 3 January 1939, here point II, "Removal of Jews from the chambers," BArch R 56 V/54 fol. 344.

[23] On this and the following, see the RSK lists dated 15 March 1937, BArch R 55/21 300.

[24] List of special permissions ("Sondergenehmigungs-Liste") passed to the Propaganda Ministry by the RSK on 20 September 1938, ibid.

on exercising his profession only by the success of his novel *Der Vater* ("The father").[25] Klepper had been excluded on 25 March 1937, but appealed and was reinstated on 16 August with "special permission."[26] From this point on, however, he had to submit all his manuscripts for approval by the Chamber (from April 1938 by the Propaganda Ministry literature department).

Wilhelm Hausenstein was excluded from the Chamber of Literature on 24 November 1936, but a ministerial decision enabled him to remain a member of the Press Chamber despite being married to a "full Jew."[27] Hausenstein continued to edit the women's and literary supplement of the *Frankfurter Zeitung* and to publish his own books with Societäts Verlag. The "special permission" for Otto Suhr was initially valid only through 31 December 1939, but in early 1940 it was extended "until further notice" because Suhr's wife, a "full Jew," planned to emigrate in the summer of that year.[28] The popular works of Clara Viebig, who was married to the Jewish publisher Friedrich Theodor Cohn, could still be published by Deutsche Verlags-Anstalt and Paul Franke Verlag on tolerance by the Chamber and the Propaganda Ministry. However, Viebig was not granted regular membership of the Chamber until her husband died in June 1936.[29]

The occasional issuing of "special permission" did not detract from the Chamber's fundamentally antisemitic deployment of the mechanisms of professional gatekeeping. Between August 1940 and April 1941, twenty-four authors were excluded from Chamber membership, and therefore from their profession, after being classified as "three-quarter, half, and quarter Jews" or as married to "full and half Jews."[30] This was Rudolf Brunngraber's fate in May 1941, when he refused to abandon his "half-Jewish" wife and their children. In response to Hans Fallada's surprised query about

---

[25] Details at BArch BDC/RSK/Klepper, J.
[26] For the notification of exclusion on 25 March 1937, Klepper's objection on 24 April, and the award of special permission, see ibid.
[27] For details, see Hausenstein's membership file, BArch BDC/RK/fiche B 0066 fol. 2138–312.
[28] Index card in the department for "special cultural matters," BArch BDC/RSK/Suhr, O.
[29] BArch BDC/RK/RSK I fiche B 222 fol. 1240–302. Also the membership card signed by Johst and still bearing the name Clara Cohn, 15 June 1936.
[30] See the list in BArch R 55/21 300.

Brunngraber's exclusion, Heinrich Maria Ledig of Rowohlt said that "grotesquely," at the very same time Brunngraber's best-selling novel *Opiumkrieg* ("Opium war"), published by Rowohlt in 1939, had been added to the Deutsche Tauchnitz series intended for circulation abroad—"at the instigation of the Propaganda Ministry."[31] The suicide of Jochen Klepper and his family in December 1941 further demonstrates the oppressive living and working conditions of the people affected by the Nazis' anti-Jewish policies.

In the case of "full Jews" under the Nuremberg Laws, the limits of tactical concessions were even more narrowly drawn. Egon Friedell took his own life for that reason on 16 March 1938, after the annexation of Austria. His three-volume *Kulturgeschichte der Neuzeit* (*A Cultural History of the Modern Age*), which had appeared between 1927 and 1931 with C. H. Beck (in English with Knopf, 1930–2), was banned in 1937; 2,000 copies were "permanently destroyed" in spring 1938 at the request of the Gestapo.[32] Ludwig Fulda was excluded from the literature section of the Academy of Arts in 1933 and from the Chamber of Literature in 1935. In September 1938, his passport was confiscated; he was forced to make "reparation" payments (*Judenbuße*) after the "Kristallnacht" pogrom of November 1938 and to adopt the name Israel on 1 January 1939.[33] When his plans to join his son in the United States failed, the now desperate author—once highly esteemed both nationally and internationally—committed suicide on 30 March 1939.

In October 1941, a letter to Johst from the publisher Peter Suhrkamp noted the "impossible situation" that "on the one hand there is a Dehmel Archive belonging to the city of Hamburg, a Richard Dehmel Street in Blankenese, and the Dehmel House," while on the other Richard Dehmel's 72-year-old widow "now has to wear the yellow star" because of the race laws.[34] Suhrkamp asked Johst,

---

[31] On this and the following, see Ledig to Fallada, 28 May 1941, in Fallada, *Ewig auf der Rutschbahn*, 332.

[32] See communications from the RSK, the Gestapo, and the publisher from 1937 and 1938, BArch BDC/RK 2110 0007/13.

[33] See Fulda, *Briefwechsel*, vol. I, xxxvii–xxxviii; report for Reichsfreiin A. von der Recke, 3 February 1939, ibid. vol. II, 1037–41; farewell letter to his wife Helene, 29 March 1939, ibid. vol. II, 1042–5.

[34] Suhrkamp to Johst, 4 October 1941, and other correspondence regarding Ida Dehmel in BArch BDC/RK/fiche 0029 fol. 266–368.

as president of the Chamber and an admirer of Dehmel's works, to intercede with his friend Himmler for "exceptional permission," but the request seems to have gone unheard. Ida Dehmel was a writer herself, but since 1935 had been restricted to managing the literary estate of her late husband (d. 1920), a task from which she was then also barred in March 1941. She died on 29 September 1942 from an overdose of sleeping tablets.

When Rudolf Pannwitz petitioned Johst and Blunck in February 1941 on behalf of the 69-year-old poet Alfred Mombert, detained in the French internment camp Gurs since October 1940, Wilhelm Ihde noted receipt of the letter and added in the margin: "We do nothing for Jews, as a general principle. The second phase of this war (see England + USA) is a war against the Jews!"[35] Hans Carossa did remain loyal to his valued colleague Mombert. He asked first Schulte Strathaus, then Goebbels in a personal letter, "as forcefully as is possible nowadays,"[36] for a way of enabling Mombert to emigrate to Switzerland. But Mombert only succeeded in emigrating when Hans Reinhart, a friend in Switzerland, contributed 30,000 francs.

In contrast to Jewish authors, the cases of writers rejected on political grounds were decided individually. In fact, in early 1934 the RDS even had to amend its application forms, on the instructions of the Chamber of Culture management, to remove the question on the applicant's previous political allegiances. The aim was "to avoid the impression arising abroad that the political stance of dissidents in the Third Reich is punished, so to speak, by refusing them admittance to the Chamber."[37] Nevertheless, each admission to the Chamber was preceded by an examination of the applicant's political convictions, the *Gesinnungsprüfung*. From April 1938, requests to the relevant NSDAP *Gau* administration for certification of the writer's "political good conduct" became an integral part of the application

---

[35] Pannwitz to Johst and Blunck, 15 February 1941, and file note with Ihde's handwritten annotations in BArch BDC/RSK/Mombert, A.
[36] As recounted by Carossa writing to Lo Schoenberner on 3 December 1940, in Carossa, *Briefe III*, 135–6.
[37] Wismann in a report to Hinkel, 22 June 1935, re: the composition of the RDS membership, BArch R 56 V/194 fol. 11.

formalities.[38] Previously, *Gau* offices had only become involved when "doubts as to political reliability" had been raised by the applicant's admission questionnaire. Gestapo assessments were generally solicited when an NSDAP evaluation was negative, when "special permission" was to be granted, or when an exclusion was planned. The Chamber asked these external bodies to detail the precise "grounds (facts with times and evidence)" in the case of negative findings, so that it could "present the grounds to the accused person and prove them if he denies it, and enumerate the grounds in any exclusion decision that ensues."

This guideline was intended to prevent frivolous evaluations and to secure the RSK's judgment against any appeal to the president of the Chamber of Culture. In practice, the requirement for detailed "facts" enabled and encouraged the Gestapo and SD to absorb the whole category of writers into their sphere of surveillance, and the *Gau*, district, and local levels of the NSDAP to gather information on writers resident in their area. At the same time, the Chamber of Culture Law, by making exclusions and rejections of admission dependent on credible evidence of inadequate "reliability and suitability" and allowing those affected to contest the decision, proved an effective safeguard for the bureaucrats. The state literary apparatus did not necessarily regard even a negative political report by the police authorities and Party offices as sufficient reason to refuse admission to the Chamber. It also took account of literary quality, propaganda potential, use for the Wehrmacht, political patronage, and the social consequences that exclusion from the profession would have for the author concerned. In fact, in October 1940 the Propaganda Ministry expressly called on the presidents of the individual chambers to exercise restraint in imposing occupational bans, "due to wartime circumstances." They were to scrutinize "whether severity may be avoided in individual cases, in the interest of keeping up general morale."[39]

However, all this depended on a disputed author showing commitment to the principles of the Nazi state, or at least remaining

---

[38] RSK to Reich Minister of Popular Enlightenment and Propaganda re: Party participation in examining the reliability of members, 4 June 1938, BArch R 56 V/51 fol. 110.
[39] RMVP instruction to the chamber presidents, 4 October 1940, BArch R 56 V/12 fol. 30.

politically inconspicuous. Even then, it did not apply to everyone. Erich Kästner, for example, was refused admission to the Chamber after his one-year probationary period, due to his political views and his aesthetic stance during the Weimar Republic. In 1935 all his writings were banned, and in 1936 the German distribution of his works published abroad was also suppressed. A fresh application to the Chamber in January 1939 was rejected once again, on the grounds of insufficient political "reliability." That did not prevent the Propaganda Minister from granting Kästner temporary "special permission" in July 1942 so that he could write the screenplay for *Münchhausen*, the film which was to celebrate the twenty-fifth anniversary of the Ufa studios. In December 1942, on Hitler's personal instructions, Goebbels barred him from any further activity in the field of culture.[40]

Bans on working ordered by Hitler in person also affected the "former defeatist literati" Ernst Glaeser and Arnolt Bronnen.[41] Glaeser had earned opprobrium from the Right during the Weimar Republic with his pacifist autobiography *Jahrgang 1902 (Class of 1902)* and his Communist Party allegiances.[42] After 1933 all his works were banned. On his return from Swiss exile in May 1939, the Propaganda Ministry literature department nevertheless granted him permission to publish literary texts in the press.[43] This concession came with two conditions: the work had to be published under the pseudonym "Ernst Töpfer," and it had to be submitted to the literature department for approval before publication. Goebbels's decision was motivated by the plan that Glaeser would write a trilogy entitled "Homecoming," which "could become an avowal of faith in the German *Volk* and an attack on emigration."[44] Although Glaeser's Heidelberg publisher told the Chamber in February 1941 that the author "had not yet written a line" of this novel of exile,[45] in early

---

[40] The RMVP literature department informed the RSK of Hitler's decision on 21 December 1942, BArch BDC/RSK/Glaeser, E.

[41] Goebbels, *Tagebücher*, Part II, vol. 6, 416 (9 December 1942).

[42] See the political evaluation issued by the Chief of the Security Police and SD (III A 5) for the RSK, 17 May 1940, BArch BDC/RSK/Glaeser, E.

[43] RMVP literature department to Glaeser, 16 May 1939, ibid.

[44] RMVP literature department to RSK president, 23 August 1939, ibid.

[45] File note on the publisher's visit to the Book Trade Group in Leipzig on 11 February 1941, here p. 2, ibid.

1942 a definitive decision on the case was "deferred" until the end of the war.[46] However, on 27 January 1943 the Chamber informed the author, after a "Führer decision," that it would have to withdraw the interim notification "for particular reasons." After this, Glaeser was not permitted to publish either in Germany or abroad.[47]

Arnolt Bronnen, formerly a friend of Brecht's, had worked actively for the Nazi cause since the early 1930s. Even so, his entire literary oeuvre was banned by the Bavarian Political Police in 1934.[48] Bronnen also met with disapproval from the Reich literary bureaucracy. In 1939 he was excluded from the Chamber of Literature due to his classification as "half Jewish."[49] After a legal battle, Bronnen succeeded in proving his "Aryan descent" before the Berlin district court, and in June 1941 his exclusion from the Chamber was rescinded. Backed by Goebbels, the author was now even commissioned by the Propaganda Ministry's foreign affairs department to "create succinct portraits of German writers highlighting their importance for the future Europe, to be used only in promotional work abroad."[50] But when Hitler intervened, a "tacit ban on working" was imposed upon Bronnen, although he was able to remain in the Chamber.

In Albert Daudistel's case, Goetz Otto Stoffregen, the RDS president and a former Freikorps member, refused to contemplate the admission into the RDS of a writer who had fought for the Bavarian Soviet Republic under Kurt Eisner in 1918/19.[51] Blunck, in contrast, wanted to give Daudistel a second chance. His standpoint was "that within the professional front, we should not emphasize political convictions previous to the [National Socialist] revolution if an honest commitment to the new state is made." Since this particular

---

[46] Literature department to RSK president, 2 January 1941, ibid.

[47] The RSK informed Glaeser of this literature department instruction (dated 21 December 1942) in a letter of 27 January 1943. The day before, the RSK told the Ministry that it had asked the Chief of the Security Police and SD "to instigate measures for the surveillance of [Glaeser's] connections abroad." Ibid.

[48] *Verzeichnis der polizeilich beschlagnahmten und eingezogenen sowie der für Leihbüchereien verbotenen Druckschriften*, 33.

[49] Index card in the department for "special cultural matters," BArch BDC/RSK/Bronnen, A.

[50] Bronnen to RSK president Johst, 14 April 1942, ibid.

[51] The RDS rejection note is quoted in a personal letter from Blunck to Hinkel, 3 February 1934, BArch BDC/RSK/Daudistel, A. See also the following.

case was "admittedly more difficult," he advocated a one-year probationary period. Again, Blunck was not prepared to take this decision on his own account, especially since "the representatives of literature" were insisting that Daudistel "until recently attacked the right-wing writers with great virulence."[52] Blunck sought the backing of state commissioner Hinkel, who received Daudistel for a personal audience at the Prussian ministry of education and culture on 9 April 1934.[53] It is unclear whether Daudistel's laments over his unemployment and impoverishment were what tipped the balance, or his willingness to support the Nazi state, signaled by joining the new Union of Nationalist Writers (Union Nationaler Schriftsteller); in any case, Hinkel allowed him to continue working. On 19 June 1935, the writer expressed his thanks by sending Hinkel his novel *Der Bananenkreuzer* ("The banana boat") fresh off the press, pointing out that the manuscript of his new novel *Der Kanonenkönig* ("The cannon king") had been passed by the Chamber and the Reichswehr Ministry, and announcing a trip to the Nahe valley at the invitation of the DAF's Strength Through Joy organization, on which he had been asked, and was eager, to report in the DAF press.[54] Daudistel never made the trip; he emigrated to Czechoslovakia that year.

Other authors of the Left continued working under the Nazi regime. Karl Bröger, an SPD member since 1921, was imprisoned in Dachau from the end of June to early September 1933,[55] but his application to the Chamber went through without difficulty. Until his death in 1944, the state and Party literature offices frequently gave him a prominent role in official events,[56] their aim being to exploit his reputation as a "workers' poet" and to demonstrate the state's "magnanimous" treatment of its former political opponents.[57]

---

[52] Blunck to Hinkel, 23 March 1934, ibid.

[53] Hinkel, file note, ibid. Daudistel preceded the visit with a letter of petition on 29 March 1934, outlining his difficult material circumstances.

[54] Daudistel to Hinkel and response from Hinkel's office, 19 June 1935, ibid.

[55] See Chief of the Security Main Office (II A2, Ohlendorf) to the Gestapa, 25 October 1937, BArch R 58/896 fol. 66.

[56] See head of the NSDAP/AO to Reichsführer SS and Chief of the German Police, 21 December 1937, BArch R 58/896 fol. 71, noting the Propaganda Ministry's promotion of Bröger and the author's deployment in Auslands-Organisation cultural events abroad.

[57] See RSK legal advisor Gentz to the Gestapa, 15 September 1937, BArch R 58/896 fol. 55.

Erich Knauf, too, was admitted to the RDS despite having been an SPD member from 1919 to 1928 and having worked for Social Democrat papers and the (then) trade union book club Büchergilde Gutenberg.[58] He remained a member of the Chamber of Literature even when excluded from the Reich Association of the German Press in 1935, and kept writing, alongside his main job in the advertising department of Tobis-Rota Film, until his imprisonment and his suicide on 2 May 1944. Günther Weisenborn's admission to the Chamber in December 1933 was condemned by the Propaganda Ministry's "central office for intellectual activism," which said the dramatist and novelist had gained a reputation in 1931/32 "as one of the worst communist rabble-rousers at German universities."[59] Weisenborn was nonetheless able to work without hindrance for the stage, film, and radio up to his arrest in 1942. Even during his imprisonment, he was initially permitted—with the acquiescence of the Chief of the Security Police and SD—to write outlines for an anti-English drama entitled *Marlborough* and a Berlin-based popular play, *Die Tiedemanns*.[60] Weisenborn was only excluded from the Chamber of Literature on 28 March 1944. And Axel Eggebrecht, interned in the provisional concentration camp Hainewalde in 1933 due to his former Communist Party membership and work for the leftist weekly *Weltbühne*, kept writing film screenplays until 1945.[61]

In the case of Gerhart Pohl, the Chamber sought an exclusion in 1936 on the grounds that all his writings had been banned[62] and that he was "deeply rooted ... in political Marxism and the Marxist-philosophical world of ideas."[63] But although the head of

---

[58] Questionnaire for members, 25 October 1933, BArch BDC/RSK/Knauf, E. On the following, see Knauf to Hinkel, 13 and 14 August 1935; questionnaire for writers, 3 June 1937, with "Report on my life," 2 June; and the political evaluation by the Stapo Berlin for the RSK, 1 May 1938, all ibid.

[59] Note from the Zentralstelle für geistigen Aktivismus, 5 December 1933, BArch BDC/RSK/Weisenborn, G. On the following, see Weisenborn's RSK member questionnaire, 15 August 1936, ibid.

[60] Chief of the Security Police and SD (IV A) to the Reich Minister of Popular Enlightenment and Propaganda, 25 January 1943, BArch 50.01/210 fol. 578. Outlines: ibid. fol. 579–83.

[61] BArch BDC/RSK/Eggebrecht, A.

[62] Section head Pogge to Linhard, 23 June 1936, BArch BDC/RSK/Pohl, G.

[63] RSK manager Ihde, file note, 5 February 1938, p. 3, ibid.

the Ministry literature department ordered Pohl's exclusion on 15 February 1937 and the Chamber had already drawn up the written notification, a preventive appeal by his lawyer halted the procedure.[64] Chamber official Metzner argued in vain that literary policy was "completely pointless" if "persons who have demonstrated their unreliability in their field so clearly can be served up to the German *Volk* community today just the same as people who are tried and tested in the struggle."[65] Ignoring this view, in February 1938 the Chamber manager reexamined the case in detail and pronounced Pohl's exclusion "questionable."[66] The author had, Ihde pointed out, "committed no offense against the state as defined by our Chamber of Culture laws" in the preceding five years. Furthermore, his novel *Die Brüder Wagemann* ("The Wagemann brothers") had enjoyed a success that was acknowledged even by the Nazi press. Ihde concluded that the probationary period granted to Pohl in 1936 had been completed satisfactorily. Because the Ministry literature department remained adamant,[67] Pohl was nevertheless excluded by the Chamber of Literature president on 23 March 1938, on the grounds that he had not demonstrated the reliability required for membership due to his "political and ideological views before 1933." In fact, even this did not close the case: in spring 1939, Pohl exercised his right to submit a new application for Chamber membership.[68] The provincial officer responsible for Pohl supported him "with great advocacy," and this time the Ministry too accepted his readmission to the Chamber.[69]

Otto Bernhard Wendler had been a school principal and SPD city councilor in Brandenburg since 1927, but in 1933 he was dismissed from the teaching profession and his writings were banned with

[64] On 8 June 1937, lawyer Wolfgang Reichstein presented the RMVP literature department with an objection against the decision to exclude Pohl from the Chamber, although the exclusion had not yet been implemented.
[65] Metzner, file note, 17 September 1937, BArch BDC/RSK/Pohl, G.
[66] Ihde, file note, 5 February 1938, p. 4, ibid.
[67] On 7 February 1938, Ihde had passed "the Pohl case" to the Ministry, through Goebbels as RKK president, for a decision, ibid.
[68] See Pohl's letter to the RSK on 19 May 1939, with thanks for sending him the application forms through the RSK Silesian office, ibid.
[69] RSK management to Wilhelm Baur, 23 February 1943, BArch BDC/RSK/Bonsels, W.

only three exceptions.[70] With the support of the RDS, he tried to build himself a new career as an author of juvenile literature.[71] Wendler also began to make a name for himself writing for film. In October 1939 the NSDAP district office called on the Brandenburg *Gau* leadership to "eliminate him from further public work,"[72] but the Propaganda Ministry literature department praised him as a "talent" who should be given the opportunity "to rehabilitate himself through positive work."[73] When Wendler was set to work on Ufa's Hitler Youth film *Jungens* in 1942, the Party Chancellery brought up the *Gau* leadership's rejection again,[74] and Rosenberg's literature office even requested a "review of whether Wendler's continued membership of the Chamber of Literature can be justified."[75] Chamber employee Meyer added a remarkable annotation to this request, commenting that Rosenberg's office apparently wished to "exercise censorship."[76] Because Wendler's children's books and his post–1933 political attitude had been unobjectionable, he recommended "allowing the matter to rest." However, the Propaganda Ministry film department issued instructions to all film producers not to use Wendler "for political films" in future,[77] although he was still to be allowed to write scripts for entertainment films.

As well as left-wing authors, the religiously affiliated also presented problems for the regime. In 1936, the SD Main Office already had substantial "incriminating" material on the church involvement of Peter Dörfler, a Catholic priest and author who had been appointed a member of the Academy of Arts literature section in 1934 by Education Minister Rust.[78] In June 1940 Dörfler was evaluated by

---

[70] On the following, see Wendler's CV dated 4 February 1935, BArch BDC/RSK/Wendler, O.B.

[71] RSK president to RMVP, 29 July 1939, BArch NS 18/307.

[72] NSDAP district leadership Brandenburg-Zauch-Belzig to Mark Brandenburg *Gau* leadership, 6 October 1939 (copy), ibid.

[73] Literature department to head of the film department, 3 August 1939, BArch NS 18/307. A similar view is expressed in RSK to RMVP, 29 July 1939, ibid.

[74] Note to Tiessler, 9 January 1942, ibid.

[75] Note of 18 August 1942, BArch BDC/RSK/Wendler, O.B.

[76] Meyer, file note for Loth, 24 August 1942, ibid.

[77] Von Reichmeister (RMVP, film department) to Tiessler, 18 February 1942, BArch NS 18/307.

[78] Report by the head of the Security Main Office, Central Dept. I 3, for the RSK, 6 October 1936, BArch BDC/RSK/Dörfler, P.

the local NSDAP group in Gern, Bavaria, as being a clear "opponent of the Movement."[79] In the referendums and Reichstag elections, it complained, he had always voted No. The *Gau* leadership for Munich and Upper Bavaria therefore refused to certify him as "politically reliable."[80] As for Werner Bergengruen, in June 1940 the local NSDAP group Munich-Solln granted that on the appropriate occasions "he hangs the swastika flag at his window, and always willingly donates to collections."[81] But neither he nor his family belonged to any section of the NSDAP, the report continued. They did not use the Nazi salute or take a Nazi newspaper, and they moved in Jewish circles. Bergengruen was therefore categorized as "politically unreliable."

Pastor Dietrich Bonhoeffer applied to the Chamber in fall 1940 for a "certificate of exemption." During the resulting checks, it was found that Bonhoeffer was an "open proponent" of the oppositional Confessing Church[82] and had already, on 22 August of that year, been banned from speaking in public by the Reich Church Ministry "due to his corrosive [*volkszersetzend*] activities." On 25 February 1941 the Church Ministry therefore asked the Chamber to reject Bonhoeffer's application "because, as a leading member of an illegal organization not recognized by the state, he cannot be considered to show the necessary reliability." The Chamber complied with this request on 19 March,[83] so that Bonhoeffer was now also banned from publishing.

Even those authors who were nationalist-conservative and to some extent sympathized with Nazism came into conflict with the state literary bureaucracy if they transgressed the political limits imposed upon them. Thus, when the best-selling conservative author Ernst Wiechert spoke up against the political persecution of Martin Niemöller and refused to participate in the plebiscite on Austrian *Anschluss*, Goebbels had him imprisoned in May 1938, then sent to Buchenwald concentration camp for three months. In a diary

---

[79] NSDAP local group Gern to the NSDAP Munich-Upper Bavaria *Gau* leadership, 13 June 1940, ibid.

[80] Response from the NSDAP Munich-Upper Bavaria *Gau* leadership, 25 June 1940, to an inquiry from the Propaganda Ministry literature department of 2 June 1940, ibid.

[81] Detailed judgment by the NSDAP local group for the Munich-Upper Bavaria *Gau* leadership, 14 June 1940, BArch BDC/RSK/Bergengruen, W.

[82] Note by the the department for "special cultural matters," n.d. (c. 1941), BArch BDC/RSK/Bonhoeffer, D.

[83] BArch R 56 V/80 fol. 146.

entry of 4 August 1938, Goebbels commented: "A piece of trash like that wants to take issue with the state."[84] And on 30 August, after a meeting with Wiechert: "I have the writer Wiechert brought to me from the camp and give him a dressing-down he won't forget in a hurry. I will not tolerate a Confessing Front in the domain that I oversee. I am on my best form and punch him down intellectually. A final warning! I leave no doubt about it. In the end, the delinquent looks very small and says that his detention has made him think it all over and understand. That's a very good thing. Any new offense will only lead to physical annihilation. We now both know that."[85] When Wiechert promised not to make any further criticism of National Socialism, his exclusion from the Chamber was "deferred by special pardon,"[86] although he was required to present every new work before publication for checking by the literature department.

Goebbels took a similarly contemptuous attitude in a meeting with Hans Grimm on 2 December 1938. Having previously admired the author, Goebbels now resented his 1935 criticism of the Chamber bureaucracy, his intercession with Interior Minister Frick for a "naysayer" attacked by party functionaries during the Rhineland referendum, and his organization of the "Lippoldsberg Writers' Days" since 1934. Alluding to Wiechert's treatment, the Propaganda Minister presented an unmistakable warning: "Dr. Grimm, I send people to the concentration camp for four months. If I send them there again, they don't come back."[87] He would "snap" Grimm too, "no matter what the hue and cry at home or abroad."

Special scrutiny was also applied to authors whose work was repudiated for ideological or aesthetic reasons. Goebbels described Count Hermann Keyserling's *Das Buch vom persönlichen Leben* (*Problems of Personal Life*), published by Deutsche Verlags-Anstalt in 1936, as "upper-class hogwash, a mixture of impertinence,

---

[84] Goebbels, *Tagebücher*, Part I, vol. 6, 32.

[85] Ibid. 64.

[86] Literature department, Haegert, to state secretary Pfundtner of the Interior Ministry, 13 January 1940, BArch R 18/5645 fol. 99.

[87] Thus the notes on the meeting that Grimm dictated from memory to his Berlin lawyer on the night of 2–3 December 1938, here p. 1, DLA NL Hans Grimm/ Korrespondenz mit NS-Partei- und Regierungsstellen, folder III. The following quotation ibid. p. 7.

arrogance, and hostility to us."[88] The book was not banned, Field Marshal von Blomberg having "put in a good word" for Keyserling with the Propaganda Minister.[89] However, when Jakob Sprenger, the *Gauleiter* of Hesse-Nassau, presented "damning material" against Keyserling, in November 1937 Goebbels decided to "shut this philosophical windbag's mouth."[90] On 10 December 1937 he declared "Count Hermann Keyserling's public appearance in Germany and abroad" to be "undesirable in terms of national policy," and ordered both "an inspection of all his existing works" and "obligatory submission of any new publications planned."[91] Goebbels responded to the author's protests with the instruction to "take a very critical look at this philosophizing buffoon. If he gets uppity one more time, we'll have him."[92]

In November 1942, Erich Ebermayer was described by the Chief of the Security Police and SD as "one of the decadent phenomena of the System period [i.e. the Weimar Republic]."[93] Particular exception was taken to Ebermayer's efforts for the liberalization of the anti-homosexuality law, paragraph 175 of the Criminal Code. Suspected of homosexuality, he was under constant surveillance by the Gestapo and the SD, but still managed to write very successful screenplays and to keep publishing his books—their tenor now adapted to the political climate—with Zsolnay Verlag of Vienna.[94] Best-selling novelist Hans Fallada, similarly, was classified by Rosenberg's literature office in 1938 as "a typical phenomenon of the corrosion in past years," whose oeuvre if anything outdid the disastrous effect of the works of

---

[88] Goebbels, *Tagebücher*, Part I, vol. 3, 397 (28 February 1937). See also Gahlings, "An mir haben die Nazis beinahe ganze Arbeit geleistet."
[89] Goebbels, *Tagebücher*, Part I, vol. 3, 395 (27 February 1937), and Part I, vol. 4, 32 (3 March 1937).
[90] Ibid. 401 (12 November 1937).
[91] Note marked "Confidential!" to the members of the Reich Cabinet, Hess, Rosenberg, Bouhler, *Gauleiter* Bohle of the NSDAP Auslands-Organisation, and *Reichsstatthalter* Sprenger, BArch R 4901/12 877 fol. 9–10. Enclosed (fol. 10–16) was a detailed evaluation of Keyserling's "personality and works." See also Goebbels, *Tagebücher* Part I, vol. 5, 29 (1 December 1937), 42 (9 December 1937).
[92] Ibid. 60 (19 December 1937).
[93] Chief of the Security Police and SD to film department personnel officer, 6 November 1942, BArch BDC/RSK/Ebermayer, E.
[94] See Hall, *Der Paul Zsolnay Verlag*, 597–614.

individual emigrants.[95] Amt Rosenberg therefore found it incompre-
hensible that Fallada "is still being permitted to write books today."
Although the Propaganda Ministry literature department certainly
shared this view, Goebbels allowed Fallada's novels to continue
appearing with Rowohlt, and even personally evaluated his script for
the film *Der weite Weg* (*The Long Way*).[96] When the Ministry planned
to deploy Fallada during the war as part of its entertainment program
for the troops, the SD complained. It conceded that as a general
principle an author should be "given the opportunity to demonstrate
his active commitment to National Socialism," but considered the
intended deployment "inadvisable" due to Fallada's past and his
"questionable attitude to National Socialism."[97]

The radicalization in the treatment of political dissidents during
the war, demanded by Party agencies and the Reich Security Main
Office, had severe consequences. The number of exclusions and
rejected applications grew, and membership of the Writers Group
dropped from 5,795 in 1940 to 3,980 in 1944.[98] Most authors were
anyway unemployed due to the continuous decline in publishing
production from 1941 on, and in early 1943 the Chamber began
to force them to work for the armaments industry or join the
Wehrmacht as their way of serving "Germany's final victory."[99] In
August 1944, the ten remaining exempted writing occupations were
abolished, so that only twenty-five writers were exempted from labor
deployment instead of the previous 234.[100] All male writers born after
1 August 1884 were now conscripted into the Wehrmacht, while all

---

[95] Amt Schrifttumspflege to Alfred Rosenberg's office, 25 August 1938, BArch NS
8/246 fol. 243. The note was prompted by Propaganda Ministry plans to use Fallada as
a scriptwriter.
[96] See Goebbels, *Tagebücher*, Part I, vol. 5, entries on reading Fallada's novel *Wolf
unter Wölfen* (*Wolf Among Wolves*) 106 (19 January 1938) and 126 (31 January 1938); on
the literature department's negative evaluation of Fallada ibid. 132 (3 February); on the
script for *Der weite Weg* by Fallada and Jannings ibid. 378 (13 July) and 381 (15 July).
[97] SD information dated 21 July 1943 on the RKK management's index card for Rudolf
Ditzen (i.e., Hans Fallada), BArch BDC/RSK/Ditzen, R.
[98] RSK budget estimates, chapter I, item 10 (income from membership dues), BArch
R 2/4879 and 4884.
[99] "Zusammenfassende Übersicht über die vom Reichswirtschafts- und vom
Reichspropagandaministerium erlassenen Bestimmungen über die 'Arbeitseinsatz- und
Stillegungsaktion,'" *Die Reichskulturkammer* 1, no. 3 (1943), 58–61.
[100] RSK to RMVP, 7 August 1944, BArch R 56 V/152 fol. 171.

female writers born after 1 August 1894 had to register for labor duty.[101] If in the initial phase of World War II German writers had been able to legitimate their existence by contributing to the population's "spiritual armament," in the conflict's final months around 3,000 of them, men and women, now had to make their contribution at the front or in the weapons factories.

The Regimented Book Market

Control of Publishers and Their Production

Like the RDS, early in the regime the book-trade association Börsenverein and the League of Reich German Booksellers (BRB) were hard pressed to manage the admission of their members to the Chamber. Around 2,500 publishers had to be processed, along with 6,000 dedicated bookstores and 10,000 subsidiary bookselling businesses.[102] Starting in spring 1935, "*Gau* representatives" and "*Gau* specialist advisors" were appointed, and carried out the local groundwork for the decisions of BRB headquarters in Leipzig regarding applications and exclusions.[103] In the *Gau* of Greater Berlin, the Chamber's largest provincial association in membership terms, two staunch Nazis—Martin Wülfing as regional leader and Gustav Langenscheidt as *Gau* representative—had a crucial say on the admission of applicants to the organized profession. They obtained detailed information on publishers through the district representatives and specialist advisors. These advisors sometimes rejected applications on economic grounds, arguing that opening

---

[101] RSK file note, 10 August 1944, BArch R 56 V/152 fol. 158; "Erläuterungen zu den Goebbels-Anordnungen betr. den 'totale[n] Kriegseinsatz der Kulturschaffenden' vom August 1944," *Die Reichskulturkammer* 2, no. 8/9 (1944), 121–7; "Dichter gehen in die Rüstung," *Bbl.* no. 70, 9 September 1944, 169.

[102] Figures in Langenbucher, *Die Welt des Buches*, 156.

[103] See "Geschäftsordnung für die Ortsgruppen und für die örtlichen Arbeitsgemeinschaften im Bund Reichsdeutscher Buchhändler e.V.," *Bbl.* no. 66, 19 March 1935, 225–6; also Gustav Langenscheidt (BRB *Gau* representative for Greater Berlin) to Dr. Hess (BRB managing director), 1 April 1935, LA Berlin Rep. 243, Acc. 1814/28.

new businesses or expanding existing ones might intensify competition and thus further exacerbate the already serious problems of Berlin's book trade, battered by the Great Depression.[104] In spring 1935, the BRB decided to emulate the antisemitic regulations of the Reich Press Chamber, which required all new applicants and registered Chamber members to present "certificates of descent" reaching back to 1800. Although the regulations were not applied across the board at this stage, they already affected a substantial number of publishers.[105]

The long-term objective of this further restriction of admission to the profession was to exclude all Jews from the German book trade. At the constitutive meeting of the BRB *Gau* committee on 18 May 1935, Wilhelm Baur announced that "demands" would shortly be issued "to the non-Aryans to sell or liquidate their business."[106] Whereas the representatives of the Börsenverein and BRB saw no difficulty with this, Chamber manager Haupt did suggest that before a notice of exclusion was sent out, *Gau*-level and local BRB representatives should hold informal discussions with the "non-Aryans" involved, encouraging them to give up their businesses of their own accord. "Abuse by unreliable people" must at all events be avoided, with the support of the Party offices and police. Baur denied intending to proceed "through blackmail," but stressed that it must be made unequivocally clear to "non-Aryans" that they "no longer have any place in the book trade." At this point, the BRB still had 619 Jewish members, 200 of them publishers.[107] Their exclusion was to be carried out in a manner that avoided "any erosion of economic value and any disruption to foreign relations."[108] This dual goal could only, as Heinz Wismann told his Minister on 27 May 1935, be fulfilled by working "step by step," at each stage replacing "non-Aryan capital with Aryan capital."

---

[104] LA Berlin Rep. 243, Acc. 1814/28: reports on the applications for membership by the companies Pflugschar (19 May 1936) and H. Heinecke (2 June 1936) and by publisher Hellmut Reichel (22 May 1936).

[105] Report on the BRB *Gau* committee session on 18 May 1935 in Leipzig, p. 13, LA Berlin Rep. 243, Acc. 1814/27.

[106] Ibid. pp. 11–12.

[107] Numbers in Wismann's statement for Goebbels, 27 May 1935, BArch R 56 V/194 fol. 1–8, here point 2.

[108] Wismann, ibid. fol. 5. The following quotation ibid.

This was the procedure applied in the "Aryanization" of the publisher S. Fischer. In March 1935, Gottfried Bermann Fischer, probably alerted by the Munich publisher Hugo Bruckmann's sudden interest in buying S. Fischer, decided to "enter the lions' den" and negotiate an "Aryanization" of his company himself.[109] At his meeting in the Propaganda Ministry, Bermann Fischer was surprised to find Wismann more than willing to allow Peter Suhrkamp, who led the detailed negotiations, to become S. Fischer's new director.[110] Wismann also agreed to the contracts implementing the change of ownership, and even checked them personally for compliance with Chamber of Culture law. On 15 April 1936, Bermann Fischer left S. Fischer and Suhrkamp took on its management. As the sole shareholder of S. Fischer Verlag AG, Hedwig Fischer had transferred her shares to the chair of its supervisory board, Berlin lawyer Friedrich Carl Sarre, and to Suhrkamp in his capacity as a member of the executive board—"with the express instruction to sell the publishing company for the best possible price, if necessary dissolving the incorporated company and converting it to a sole proprietorship." In preparation for this conversion, on 15 December 1936 a limited partnership was formed, in which Suhrkamp was the full partner and the limited partners were the Bonn lawyer Klemens Abs, Christof Ratjen, the son of a Berlin banker, and the Hamburg manufacturer Philipp F. Reemtsma. The purpose of the new company, endowed with capital of 325,000 RM, was named as the acquisition of S. Fischer Verlag AG; the contract was signed on 18 December 1936 by Sarre, Suhrkamp, and Hedwig Fischer. Probably the most important element of this contract was that the new "Fischer KG" could take on the "rights from the publishing and theatrical distribution contracts of Fischer Verlag AG, including the associated copyrights and the material."

In the second half of 1935, Jewish members of the BRB began to receive notifications of exclusion.[111] The employees' sector group (*Fachschaft*) had not accepted "non-Aryans" in the first place, and

---

[109] Bermann Fischer, *Bedroht—Bewahrt*, 112.
[110] On this and the following, see BArch BDC/RSK/Bermann Fischer, G.
[111] As indicated in Wilhelm Baur to the Book Trade Group office, 5 December 1936, p. 1, LA Berlin Rep. 243, Acc. 1814/32–34.

had rejected around 180 applications (making just one exception, Klaus Cohen-Bouvier); the sales representatives' *Fachschaft* quickly sacrificed its sixty-eight Jewish members with no regard for financial loss.[112] The Chamber's approach to publishing-house proprietors, managing directors, and authorized signatories was less sweeping. In the case of the Frankfurt company Rütten & Loening, Wilhelm Oswalt, who had directed the company since 1901 as the third generation of his family to do so, and Adolf Neumann, its manager since 1913 and later also a partner in the firm, were forced to sell to the Potsdam-based publisher Albert Hachfeld in 1935.[113] On 14 November 1935, the Munich publisher Reinhard Piper was requested to supply precise information on whether "non-Aryan capital" was involved in his company.[114] Piper's Jewish managing director Robert Freund had been a partner in the company since 1926, and his immediate elimination would have meant "a loss of operating capital" for the company. Wismann therefore negotiated a somewhat more lenient solution. Freund had to leave the company in September 1937, but he was compensated for his investment with a share in profits, and was given the rights and stock of some of the authors he had acquired. His attempt to put this to use by setting up his own company in Vienna foundered just a few months later, when Austria was annexed.

The "Aryanization" of Julius Springer Verlag, which had grown during the Weimar Republic to become the world's largest science and technology publisher, was carried out in stages.[115] Two of the founder's grandsons had been partners in the company since 1906. One of them, Julius Springer, already had to leave the company in 1935 on the instructions of Wismann, who was pushing for a covert but speedy "Aryanization." Julius's cousin, Ferdinand Springer, Jr., was able to remain thanks to "special permission" from the Propaganda Ministry. As late as November 1942, he too sold his

---

[112] See report of the BRB council meeting at the Berlin branch office on 20 September 1935, BArch BDC/RK/fiche Z 0025 fol. 1420 (p. 5) and 1422 (p. 6).

[113] *Verlagsveränderungen im deutschen Buchhandel 1933–1937*, 21.

[114] Ziegler, *100 Jahre Piper*, 133–40; also the Chamber list dated 15 March 1937 of all "full, three-quarter, and half Jews and spouses of full and three-quarter Jews still active in the area of the book trade," here p. 8, BArch R 55/21 300.

[115] On the following, see Sarkowski, *Springer Verlag*, 325–84.

shares to Tönjes Lange in a bid to prevent Springer being carved up between various Nazi businesses. Lange had been working with the house since 1934 as its general agent and a family friend, and in 1935 had taken over Julius's shares in trust.

By early 1936, the register of Chamber members who were "non-Aryan" or "non-Aryan by marriage" still included 162 names for the *Gau* of Greater Berlin alone.[116] Even Hinkel's circular of 29 April 1936, instructing the individual chambers to exclude all "full, three-quarter, half, and quarter Jews" and all persons married to "full, three-quarter, half, and quarter Jews" by 15 May,[117] at first remained largely without consequences for the book trade. The reasons for this temporary reprieve can be inferred from a letter to Hitler from the president of the Reichsbank, Hjalmar Schacht, dated 13 February 1936.[118] In it, Schacht—responsible for "managing the business" of the Prussian and Reich Minister of Economics—lodged a complaint against the individual chambers' "increasing" practice of excluding Jewish businesspeople, who were consequently approaching him with petitions for help. While agreeing with the "necessity of eliminating the Jewish influence on the shaping of German culture," he added that "from the standpoint of the concerns for which I am responsible" the closure or "Aryanization" of Jewish businesses in the cultural sector was having a negative impact, due to the loss of jobs and foreign currency. Precisely in publishing, "which depends to a particular degree on individual efforts and relationships," Schacht considered the "switch of ownership" virtually impossible to carry out "without damaging turnover." He also cautioned against preventing Jewish publishers involved in exports, after their emigration, from "selling German-language works printed abroad that are not hostile to the state," because "German book exports are still far more

---

[116] See the twelve-page list dated 16 January 1936 in LA Berlin Rep. 243, Acc. 1814/32–34.

[117] BArch R 56 V/102 fol. 154–6.

[118] On the following, see Schacht to Hitler enclosing a list of the submissions from Jewish publishers and bookstores, BArch R 43 II /1238 C fol. 11–19. Also a letter marked "Strictly confidential!" from Rosenberg's Reichsstelle to the NSLB's Breslau (Wrocław) *Gau* leader, 7 May 1936, BArch NS 12/252. In connection with information about a Jewish company in Breslau publishing scientific works, it notes the "tension between the Reich Chamber of Culture and the Reich Economics Ministry" during the "Aryanization" of the book trade.

significant than book imports." Schacht felt that his views on the whole matter were being ignored by the Propaganda Ministry, and tried to obtain some influence for his department, "necessary for urgent economic reasons," directly through the "Führer and Reich Chancellor." The response on 9 March, from Reich Chancellery head Lammers, left no doubt that Hitler regarded eliminating Jews from the German book trade as part of Goebbels's authority in his capacity as president of the Chamber of Culture.[119] However, exclusions from the individual chambers must only be made on the grounds of insufficient "reliability and suitability" in line with § 10 of the First Directive for the Execution of the Reich Chamber of Culture Law, and not because the owners were "Jewish or Jewish by marriage." The Propaganda Ministry was therefore requested "to rectify the grounds given in the notifications."

The Berlin Olympics had brought another respite, in order to avoid protest from abroad. When this expired, pressure on Jewish businesses in the book trade was stepped up again. After a meeting in the Propaganda Ministry, Wilhelm Baur informed the Book Trade Group office on 5 December 1936 that those companies included in "List A" and in receipt of an exclusion order in late 1935 would now be given "a final deadline of 31 March 1937" to dissolve their business and sell their stock.[120] The letters to this effect were to be written "personally," in other words "not as duplicated copies." In case of objections, Baur had arranged with Hinkel that any complaint would be rejected by Chamber of Culture president Goebbels. Businesses that had not been "Aryanized" or dissolved by 1 April 1937 would be closed by the police. Bookstores selling only Judaica were also excluded from the Chamber, but were permitted to carry on business under supervision.[121] The "non-Aryan" companies in Lists B through D, in contrast, were to be allowed to remain in the Chamber "for the time being."[122] To help the Book Trade Group's *Gau* representatives

[119] BArch R 43 II /1238 C fol. 22.
[120] LA Berlin Rep. 243, Acc. 1814/32–34.
[121] First circular from Hinkel's *Sonderreferat* to the persons and companies of the "Jewish book trade," 30 July 1937, re: regulations for production and distribution of Jewish literature on German Reich territory, DB-Archiv no. 507/5–509/1.
[122] Baur to Book Trade Group office, 5 December 1936, p. 2, LA Berlin Rep. 243, Acc. 1814/32–34.

monitor compliance with the deadlines, in February 1937 they were sent information from the Leipzig office regarding the "non-Aryan" companies that must now be permanently excluded.[123] In a "list of all full, three-quarter, and half Jews and spouses of full and three-quarter Jews still active in the area of the book trade" drawn up by the Chamber in mid-March 1937, different stages of elimination were distinguished: 146 companies had been excluded with "fixed deadlines"; thirty had been excluded but no deadline had yet been set; twenty-eight had lodged objections against exclusion which had not yet been processed; twenty (twelve of them publishers) had "special permission"; and two address and advertising register firms in Cologne and Berlin were to be closed down by 1 April 1937.[124] The Chamber examined each of the seventy-seven publishing companies affected, and in each case reached its decision in consultation with Hinkel's *Sonderreferat*, the anti-Jewish "special section" in the Propaganda Ministry.

Publisher Rolf Bielefeld from Ettlingen received "special permission" because he was championed by the NSDAP technology office, the Ministry of War, the Ministry of Aviation, and the Chamber of Culture due to his "various inventions of military significance and his special contributions in terms of language."[125] Petropolis Verlag of Berlin specialized in producing literature in Russian, which was sold via a wholesaler to Russian emigrants in Germany and abroad; its owner, Jacob Bloch, received "special permission" on condition that he limit himself to book exports, only supply export companies within Germany, and present all new publications to the Chamber of Literature for examination. Sixty-five-year-old Ernst Denys Hofmann defended his eponymous Darmstadt-based publisher by arguing that "even before the political change" it had "published antisemitic works" and that several of its publications had received "recognition in important National Socialist reviews." The Chamber judged these assertions "grotesque!" but gave Hofmann an extension until

---

[123] See Book Trade Group to Book Trade Group *Gau* Berlin, February 1937, marked "confidential," LA Berlin Rep. 243, Acc. 1814/32–34.

[124] List dated 15 March 1937 and overviews using these distinctions in BArch R 55/21 300.

[125] List dated 15 March 1937, p. 2, ibid. On the following, see ibid. pp. 3–28.

30 September 1937 "to deliver his consignments and recover his outstanding debts."

For Philo Verlag, in February 1937 Ernst G. Löwenthal, Hans Reichmann, and the authorized signatory Lucia Jacoby sent the Chamber "extensively reasoned submissions and objections" to the company's exclusion, noting that it had even opened a branch in Amsterdam "to increase exports." The authorized signatory of Prestel Verlag in Frankfurt, Annemarie Loeb-Cetto, was permitted to remain in the Chamber only if she could prove that "her divorce from her Jewish husband living abroad has now been completed." The owner of Verlag Gustav Lyon, Louis Joseph, was granted a deferral on the grounds of the excellent turnover achieved by his fashion magazines. In 1935 alone, the Reichsbank had earned more than 1 million RM in foreign currency from Gustav Lyon's magazine sales abroad. The company employed around 650 people in Germany; it was also vital to the survival of the Leipzig wholesaler Wilhelm Opitz, with forty employees, and the owners of seventy-five sales outlets. In the case of Heinz Karger, proprietor of a publisher specializing in natural sciences and medical journals, coercive measures were avoided "in view of the size and importance of the operation." Karger was able to transfer his internationally respected company from Berlin to Basle on 1 April 1937 with the Chamber's consent.[126] Viktor Goldschmidt, in contrast, missed the favorable moment to sell the profitable Grieben Verlag, known worldwide for its travel guides. In February 1939, under coercion from the state authorities, Grieben was "bought" for a ludicrously low sum by Erich Kupfer, managing director of the already "Aryanized" Albatros Verlag.

Bermann Fischer, too, felt the effects of the radicalized "dejudaization policy." After the annexation of Austria, the Gestapo closed down the company he had founded in Vienna in 1937,[127] and the Propaganda Ministry made sure that Bermann Fischer Verlag could not take either tangibles or rights with it when it moved to Stockholm.[128] By the end of 1939, 18,914 of the 26,263 Jewish-owned

---

[126] On this and the case of Viktor Goldschmidt, see Dahm, *Das jüdische Buch*, 90–9; also list dated 15 March 1937, pp. 9, 15–16, BArch R 55/21 300.

[127] File note from RSK *Sonderreferat* III Z re: Bermann Fischer Verlag, Vienna, n.d. (1938), BArch BDC/RSK/Bermann Fischer, G.

[128] Instructions from the RMVP literature department to the RSK president, 5 December 1938, ibid.

companies in Austria, including publishers and booksellers, had been liquidated.[129] Those book-trade companies spared for purely economic reasons were transferred to "Aryan" proprietorship.[130] In the case of the successful art-book specialist Phaidon Verlag, in spring 1938 the British publisher George Allen & Unwin bought the stock and rights from Béla Horovitz, who had emigrated to London.[131] This put the Nazi authorities in the "painful situation" of having to allow Phaidon's politically "undesirable" production, now in the hands of Allen & Unwin, to continue in the German Reich, since otherwise the Austrian printing and bookbinding industry would lose out on lucrative commissions. Ralph A. Höger's and Herbert Reichner's Viennese companies were both taken over by Carl Schünemann Verlag in October 1938.[132]

The case of Zsolnay Verlag, Vienna, exemplifies how unscrupulously personal interests were pursued through the "Aryanization" process.[133] Publisher Paul von Zsolnay emigrated to London in fall 1938. He initially tried to retain a say in the management of his company by means of a "pseudo-Aryanization," but the managing director he had put in place, Felix Costa, was dismissed in March 1939, as was the figurehead owner Albert von Jantsch-Streerbach. In the ensuing power struggle over the company, Josef Bürckel as Hitler's "Reich Commissioner for the Reunion of Austria with the Reich" (later "Reich Governor of the Ostmark") and his bureaucracy confronted Propaganda Minister Goebbels, with Hinkel's Department II A (responsible for "Aryanizing" the culture industry), the Ministry literature department, and the Chamber of Literature. In April 1939, lawyer Wilhelm Hofmann, then working for the Vienna branch of the Party's Central Propaganda Office (Reichspropagandaamt), was installed as the publisher's "trustee." Two years later Hofmann, under whose management Zsolnay Verlag had made net profits of 650,000 RM, was ordered to sell the publisher. On the recommendation of the Propaganda Ministry, Karl Heinrich Bischoff's bid was

---

[129] Renner, "Österreichische Schriftsteller," 274. The exact number of Austrian publishing and bookselling companies actually in business is unknown.
[130] For details, see Hall, "Jüdische Buchhändler und Verleger."
[131] On this and the following, see StAL BV/F 7163.
[132] StAL BV/F 4126.
[133] On the following see Hall, *Der Paul Zsolnay Verlag*, 644–769.

accepted,[134] and he was able to acquire the company for just 45,120 RM. As a section head in the Chamber of Literature, Bischoff had been advancing the "Aryanization" of the German book trade since 1935 and its Austrian counterpart since 1938. He now made himself one of the "Ostmark's" leading publishers. However, Bischoff was not the only one to profit from this coup. Behind the scenes, Zsolnay's capital was transferred to the account of its Berlin branch, and from there was signed over to the German Reich in December 1941. The 900,000 RM became the nucleus of a Propaganda Ministry fund to purchase and subsidize publishing companies intended to work abroad for the benefit of the Nazi state.

In June 1942, the company's name was changed from Paul Zsolnay to Karl H. Bischoff Verlag of Vienna and Berlin. Thanks to his excellent connections with the state literary bureaucracy, Bischoff succeeded—despite the worsening paper shortages—in overtaking all his competitors in the field of quality fiction. By 1944, Bischoff led the field in terms both of new publications and reissues and of the number of titles overall.

In the course of 1938, the few remaining "non-Aryan" publishers and the "non-Aryan by marriage" were excluded from the Chamber once and for all.[135] The only option now left to them was work in the "ghetto book trade" that Hinkel's *Sonderreferat* had established in July 1937 to absorb a limited number of companies under his surveillance.[136] Thirty book publishers ended up in this sector, including such long-standing and respected names as Verlag J. Kauffmann of Frankfurt (est. 1832), Verlag Siegfried Scholem (1861), Jüdischer Verlag (1902), Verlag der Jüdischen Rundschau (1902), Verlag Leo Alterthum, Brandussche Verlagshandlung, Philo Verlag (all 1919), Joachim Goldstein Verlag, and Salman Schocken Verlag (both 1931), as well as Hans Joachim Schoeps's Vortrupp Verlag and Erwin Löwe, both founded after 1933.[137]

---

[134] See file note from the head of the literature department to the head of the RMVP personnel department, 10 April 1942, BArch R 55/170 fol. 49–50.

[135] See Dahm, *Das jüdische Buch*, 146–51.

[136] First circular from the *Sonderreferat* to the persons and companies of the "Jewish book trade," 30 July 1937, DB-Archiv no. 507/5–509/1.

[137] "Regelung der Frage jüdischer Buchverkäufer und Buchverleger im Reichsgebiet," with a list of all the Jewish book publishers and distributors permitted to operate

eceived commissions from the Wehrmacht and
ontbuchhandlungen, which accounted for almost
rnover and secured the continued existence of
e having withdrawn that year), until it was finally
tember 1944.[150]

too, had to maneuver carefully. On the one hand,
zi-related nonfiction and reoriented his program
litical fiction and travel literature.[151] On the other,
gal requirements by continuing to employ his
Clara Ploschitzki and his Jewish editors Franz
ayer, kept on politically controversial authors such
k Reger, and published translations of contem-
and French literature. As a political safeguard,
NSDAP in 1937.[152] He was nevertheless excluded
er by Goebbels in May 1938, having "become
tainable,"[153] and emigrated to Brazil, his second
The exclusion was carried out as a matter of
or" initiated by the Book Trade Group due to
tion of books by Jewish authors: he had reissued
first book, *Das Lyrische Stenogrammheft* ("The
ok of poetry") of 1933, and her 1934 *Kleines
ße* ("Little reader for grown people"), and in 1936
f Adalbert Stifter by Urban Roedl (i.e., Bruno Adler).
Deutsche Verlags-Anstalt (DVA) in Stuttgart, already
Eher through Vera-Verlagsanstalt GmbH,[154] acquired

, addressed to the provincial representative for the book trade
ibid. Kiepenheuer's annual turnover rose from 101,551.13 RM in
M in 1942.

sily identified, and cut little ice with the NSDAP. See the SD's
, BArch R 58/1107 fol. 28, and Amann to Bouhler, 10 December
11/9.

rfile/Rowohlt, E. Ernst Rowohlt applied for membership on 2
was accepted, with his membership backdated to 1 May. It was
t reinstated on 17 December 1943 when he produced reasons
his dues and made up the outstanding sum. See Rowohlt to
Berlin-Grünheide, 25 August 1943, BArch BDC/Partei-Kanzlei
ohlt, E.

cher, Part I, vol. 5, 326 (31 May 1938). See also "Jahreslagebericht
hauptamtes," *Meldungen aus dem Reich*, vol. 2, 156.

heft *Verlagswesen* (1937), BArch R 58/1107 fol. 32.

Up to their closure in late 1938, "Jewish book publishers"
were permitted to publish solely "Jewish literature" for a "Jewish
audience," as long as this literature was not already banned.[138] The
definition of "Jewish" literature included "books and writings—
regardless whether they are written in German, in Hebrew, Yiddish,
or in another foreign language—whose authors, editors, or contributors are Jews." This meant especially Judaica and Hebraica, but
also translations "if the author of the original work is a Jew." Before
publishing "every single work," publishers had to obtain approval from
the *Sonderreferat*, and to present the manuscript before printing "for
inspection and permission with a carbon copy or two proof copies of
the work." The application also had to include "evidence" that "the
author is a Jew." When a book appeared, a specimen copy was to
be sent to the Deutsche Bücherei, but Hinkel instructed that the
librarians must not list "the works of Jewish literature received"
either in the daily register of new publications or in Series A of the
German National Bibliography.[139] From the beginning of 1939 until
1942, Jewish book production in the German Reich was restricted
to the Verlag des Jüdischen Kulturbundes, the newly established
publishing house of the Cultural League of German Jews.

On 31 March 1939 the Chamber issued an order "for the
protection of the individual responsible in the book trade," explicitly
reaffirming that persons "who cannot produce, for themselves
and for the spouse to whom they are married at the time of the
coming into effect of this ordinance or with whom they later enter
into matrimony, proof of their descent from ancestors of German or
kindred blood back to the year 1800" would no longer receive the

---

in the German Reich territory (except Austria), arranged by location, supplement to
Vertrauliche Mitteilungen der Fachschaft Verlag 37, 13 October 1938. This list was
"intended only for internal use and to be treated confidentially." On the activities of
Jewish publishers after 1933, see Dahm, "Kulturelles und geistiges Leben," 199–212,
and *Das jüdische Buch*, 203–501; Schreuder and Weber, *Der Schocken Verlag/Berlin*;
Schenker, *Der Jüdische Verlag*, 429–509.
[138] On this and the following, see First circular from the *Sonderreferat* to the persons
and companies of the "Jewish book trade," 30 July 1937, DB-Archiv no. 507/5–509/1,
pp. 1–3.
[139] Hinkel to director of the Deutsche Bücherei, 18 September 1937, DB-Archiv no.
507/5–509/1.

Up to their closure in late 1938, "Jewish book publishers" were permitted to publish solely "Jewish literature" for a "Jewish audience," as long as this literature was not already banned.[138] The definition of "Jewish" literature included "books and writings— regardless whether they are written in German, in Hebrew, Yiddish, or in another foreign language—whose authors, editors, or contributors are Jews." This meant especially Judaica and Hebraica, but also translations "if the author of the original work is a Jew." Before publishing "every single work," publishers had to obtain approval from the *Sonderreferat*, and to present the manuscript before printing "for inspection and permission with a carbon copy or two proof copies of the work." The application also had to include "evidence" that "the author is a Jew." When a book appeared, a specimen copy was to be sent to the Deutsche Bücherei, but Hinkel instructed that the librarians must not list "the works of Jewish literature received" either in the daily register of new publications or in Series A of the German National Bibliography.[139] From the beginning of 1939 until 1942, Jewish book production in the German Reich was restricted to the Verlag des Jüdischen Kulturbundes, the newly established publishing house of the Cultural League of German Jews.

On 31 March 1939 the Chamber issued an order "for the protection of the individual responsible in the book trade," explicitly reaffirming that persons "who cannot produce, for themselves and for the spouse to whom they are married at the time of the coming into effect of this ordinance or with whom they later enter into matrimony, proof of their descent from ancestors of German or kindred blood back to the year 1800" would no longer receive the

---

in the German Reich territory (except Austria), arranged by location, supplement to *Vertrauliche Mitteilungen der Fachschaft Verlag* 37, 13 October 1938. This list was "intended only for internal use and to be treated confidentially." On the activities of Jewish publishers after 1933, see Dahm, "Kulturelles und geistiges Leben," 199–212, and *Das jüdische Buch*, 203–501; Schreuder and Weber, *Der Schocken Verlag/Berlin*; Schenker, *Der Jüdische Verlag*, 429–509.

[138] On this and the following, see First circular from the *Sonderreferat* to the persons and companies of the "Jewish book trade," 30 July 1937, DB-Archiv no. 507/5–509/1, pp. 1–3.

[139] Hinkel to director of the Deutsche Bücherei, 18 September 1937, DB-Archiv no. 507/5–509/1.

Chamber's permission to exercise their profession.[140] Exceptions were now only made for "quarter Jews" and those married to "half Jews."[141] Fritz Brockhaus, for example, could not provide complete proof of the "Aryan descent" of his mother Milly Brockhaus, née Weisz.[142] A June 1939 report by the Reich Office for Genealogical Research classified him as a "half Jew" and his two nephews Hans and Wolfgang Brockhaus as "quarter Jews." Based on this, the three owners of F. A. Brockhaus ought to have been excluded from the Chamber of Literature. However, in this case the Nazi state overrode its own regulations. On the one hand, it was not in the interest of the PPK's Karl Heinz Hederich to lose the leverage on reprints and new editions of Brockhaus encyclopedias that he had been building up since 1934. Hederich advised the owners to petition Hitler directly—which they duly did in July 1939. At the same time, F. A. Brockhaus was a well-established company that enjoyed great respect both at home and abroad. Two of its authors, Sven Hedin and Colin Ross, offered propaganda support for Hitler and the Nazi state. This context may help explain why, with Goebbels's backing, Hinkel issued "exceptional permission" for the three Brockhaus owners in spring 1940.

Walter List, director of the Leipzig-based publisher List & von Bressensdorf since 1929, was also classified as a "quarter Jew." In 7 December 1936 he had written to Hinkel personally, asking for support and promising, "in accordance with my conduct and the cultural contributions of the two publishing businesses that I run, to continue as before my participation in the struggle for Adolf Hitler's Reich."[143] In December 1938, List was accepted into the Chamber as a regular member, and on 10 June 1939 (in other words, after the ordinance on proof of descent) his membership was expressly reconfirmed.[144] The publisher received "special permission" and was able to continue working until the end of the war, safeguarding his

---

[140] Ihde, *Handbuch der Reichsschrifttumskammer*, 97–9, here p. 97 (§ 1 d).

[141] See the "List of names of the quarter Jews and those of German blood whose spouses are half Jews" issued by the RSK on 11 December 1942 at the request of the RKK central management, BArch R 56 V/51 fol. 149–59.

[142] On this and the following, see Keiderling, *F.A. Brockhaus*, 166–70.

[143] List to Hinkel, 7 December 1936, BArch BDC/RK/fiche B0119 fol. 1022–4.

[144] RKK management index card, 1941, ibid. fol. 1030.

production primarily by outsourcing printing jobs to the occupied areas.[145]

Around 70,000 Book Trade Group personnel files were lost when Leipzig was bombed in early December 1943, and it is now difficult to reconstruct in detail how the instrument of restricting admission to the profession was deployed against politically "undesirable" publishers. Starting in November 1936, the relevant local NSDAP *Gau* leadership was requested to comment on each membership application received.[146] By this time, however, the majority of the Weimar Republic's left-wing publishing houses and book distribution outlets had already been expropriated and their directors forced into exile.[147] Publishers Ernst Rowohlt and Gustav Kiepenheuer, almost all of whose Weimar production had been banned in 1933, were admitted to the Chamber—but both were highly restricted in their scope to act. Kiepenheuer's firm had gone bankrupt in late April 1933, and he was only able to rejuvenate it in the fall by obtaining financial help from Ernst Rowohlt, removing his politically "undesirable" authors (who moved to Querido of Amsterdam, sent by Fritz Landshoff), and reducing his production substantially.[148] The company faced new difficulties after Rowohlt withdrew in June 1934 and Otto Pankok's *Die Passion in 60 Bildern* ("The passion in 60 pictures") was confiscated in 1937, but it avoided another bankruptcy by taking the wealthy Hans Korte into partnership. The Chamber had considered excluding Kiepenheuer on political grounds, but decided in 1938 to let him stay and give him "a chance to show what he really thinks."[149] The publisher promised "to work hard to prove his suitability and reliability," and adapted his list in consultation with the Chamber. Starting

---

[145] List of "*Mischlinge*" in the RSK (6 February 1943), BArch R 55/21 300. Applications to the RSK to outsource printing jobs for books with print runs of between 3,000 and 10,000 to printers outside Germany, 1941 and 1942, BArch BDC/RK/fiche B0119.

[146] RSK Book Trade Group, Leipzig, to RSK, Berlin, 3 June 1938, BArch R 56 V/51 fol. 116.

[147] See the SD's *Leitheft Verlagswesen* (1937), BArch R 58/1107 fol. 27.

[148] Börsenverein, Berlin branch, to Karl Baur, head of the publishers' *Fachschaft*, 10 March 1938, BArch BDC/RSK/Kiepenheuer, G. On the following, see Funke, "*Im Verleger verkörpert sich das Gesicht seiner Zeit*," 187–230; Röttig, "Der Gustav Kiepenheuer Verlag," 12, 23–85.

[149] Bischoff (Dept. III Z), file note, 14 June 1938, on Kiepenheuer's visit to the Chamber, BArch BDC/RSK/Kiepenheuer, G. The following quotations ibid.

in 1942, he even received commissions from the Wehrmacht and the Zentrale der Frontbuchhandlungen, which accounted for almost half of his total turnover and secured the continued existence of the company (Korte having withdrawn that year), until it was finally closed down in September 1944.[150]

Ernst Rowohlt, too, had to maneuver carefully. On the one hand, he brought out Nazi-related nonfiction and reoriented his program toward largely apolitical fiction and travel literature.[151] On the other, he ignored the legal requirements by continuing to employ his Jewish secretary Clara Ploschitzki and his Jewish editors Franz Hessel and Paul Mayer, kept on politically controversial authors such as Fallada and Erik Reger, and published translations of contemporary American and French literature. As a political safeguard, Rowohlt joined the NSDAP in 1937.[152] He was nevertheless excluded from the Chamber by Goebbels in May 1938, having "become completely unsustainable,"[153] and emigrated to Brazil, his second wife's homeland. The exclusion was carried out as a matter of "professional honor" initiated by the Book Trade Group due to Rowohlt's distribution of books by Jewish authors: he had reissued Mascha Kaléko's first book, *Das Lyrische Stenogrammheft* ("The shorthand notebook of poetry") of 1933, and her 1934 *Kleines Lesebuch für Große* ("Little reader for grown people"), and in 1936 also a biography of Adalbert Stifter by Urban Roedl (i.e., Bruno Adler). In October 1938, Deutsche Verlags-Anstalt (DVA) in Stuttgart, already incorporated into Eher through Vera-Verlagsanstalt GmbH,[154] acquired

---

[150] Confidential note I, addressed to the provincial representative for the book trade (Berlin), 29 May 1943, ibid. Kiepenheuer's annual turnover rose from 101,551.13 RM in 1938 to 273,525.51 RM in 1942.

[151] This tactic was easily identified, and cut little ice with the NSDAP. See the SD's *Leitheft Verlagswesen*, BArch R 58/1107 fol. 28, and Amann to Bouhler, 10 December 1938, p. 2, BArch NS 11/9.

[152] BArch BDC/Masterfile/Rowohlt, E. Ernst Rowohlt applied for membership on 2 December 1937 and was accepted, with his membership backdated to 1 May. It was canceled in 1940, but reinstated on 17 December 1943 when he produced reasons for his failure to pay his dues and made up the outstanding sum. See Rowohlt to NSDAP local group Berlin-Grünheide, 25 August 1943, BArch BDC/Partei-Kanzlei Correspondence/Rowohlt, E.

[153] Goebbels, *Tagebücher*, Part I, vol. 5, 326 (31 May 1938). See also "Jahreslagebericht 1938 des Sicherheitshauptamtes," *Meldungen aus dem Reich*, vol. 2, 156.

[154] See the SD's *Leitheft Verlagswesen* (1937), BArch R 58/1107 fol. 32.

Deutscher Verlag's shares in Rowohlt Verlag GmbH.[155] Heinrich Maria Ledig became Rowohlt's managing director.[156] On 1 November 1943, Rowohlt GmbH was merged with DVA "and thus dissolved."[157]

Publishers of Christian literature were also subjected to considerable political repression. In the course of the 1930s, the Chamber repeatedly ordered police raids on "confessional" publishers, printers, and libraries in search of "harmful and undesirable literature."[158] Around the distribution of Pius XI's encyclical "Mit brennender Sorge" (With burning concern), in 1937 twelve printers were closed by the Gestapo and their owners expropriated.[159]

The SD complemented such individual measures by subjecting this economically strong and politically influential group of publishers to increasingly systematic surveillance. The handbook *Leitheft Verlagswesen* of 1937 gave SD personnel a detailed survey of publishers with a Catholic or Lutheran orientation.[160] From 1938 on, the reports researched by local SD divisions and collated as *Meldungen aus dem Reich* regularly mentioned the production of confessional publishers. Thus, the 1938 Security Main Office annual report noted that confessional literature took up second place among new publications, and that the most highly ranking group in numerical terms, fiction, also contained many religiously influenced books.[161] The SD also reported that "the propaganda literature of political Catholicism (brochures), designed for mass impact, is giving way to the more sophisticated book, intended to serve entertainment, edification, and the deepening of Christian thinking and

---

[155] Rowohlt Verlags GmbH (H.M. Ledig) to the authors, employees, and friends of Rowohlt Verlag, 20 December 1938, StAL BV/F 7815.

[156] Börsenverein to Pudor Verlag, 8 February 1940, ibid.

[157] Clipping from *Bbl.* no. 176, 30 November 1943, ibid.

[158] See, for example, the December 1935/January 1936 processing of Richard Wirtz, *Das Moselland. Ein Heimatbuch* ("The Moselle region. A book of the homeland") (Trier: Paulinusdruckerei), BArch R 58/974 fol. 156–89; internal notification from Gestapa section II 2 C 102 to II 2 B, 29 February 1936, re: writings of the Borromäus Society, BArch R 58/769 fol. 75; the PPK ban on the first six volumes of the encyclopedia *Der grosse Herder*, 5 August 1937, BArch R 58/909 fol. 112; the halt to deliveries ordered by the PPK on 9 August 1937 for Kösel & Pustet's handbook of education *Handbuch der Erziehungswissenschaften*, BArch R 58/907 fol. 50.

[159] See Graf, "Der Trierer Buchdrucker," especially 276–88.

[160] BArch R 58/1107 fol. 25, fol. 30–1.

[161] *Meldungen aus dem Reich*, vol. 2, 155. The following quotations ibid.

belief." In December 1939, *Meldungen aus dem Reich* registered an increase in confessional titles as a proportion of literature as a whole compared to the previous year, from 9.5 percent to 10.5 percent.[162] Paper rationing, introduced by the Propaganda Ministry partly with the objective of containing the flow of confessional literature, was apparently having little practical effect. Although the production of the confessional publishers fell by around 17 percent in the first quarter of 1940,[163] this was actually less dramatic than the drop in the German book trade's total production, which averaged 21 percent. As the SD pointed out in early July 1941, some Catholic publishers even managed to further boost their production significantly during the war.[164] Another irritant for the SD was the flood of around 7,000 booklets onto the market, spreading "confessional propaganda" against Nazi ideology.[165] From the high print runs of some religious works even in mid-1942, the SD inferred that the religious publishers must still have access to large stocks of paper of their own.[166]

Various measures were planned to stifle Christian publishing. The ordinance "for the protection of the individual responsible in the book trade" laid down that "companies placing themselves primarily in the service of a particular worldview not according with that of the German *Volk* as a whole, a religious creed, or an institution serving its purposes, ... must express this objective in their company names in a way that is clear and easily recognized by all."[167] A directive for the execution of this ruling, issued on 3 May 1939, further underlined that a publisher was already "placing himself in the service of a religious creed" if he published just one work of fiction, popular science, or scholarship with religious content. This initiated something that might even be described as a "ghettoization" of Christian publishing:

---

[162] *Meldungen aus dem Reich*, vol. 3, no. 30, 18 December 1939, 582.

[163] *Meldungen aus dem Reich*, vol. 4, no. 84, 3 May 1940, 1092.

[164] See the information on the increased turnover of the publishing houses Ferdinand Schöningh (Paderborn) and Buzon & Bercker (Kevelaer) and the printer Bonifatiusdruckerei (Paderborn) in 1938 through 1940, *Meldungen aus dem Reich*, vol. 7, no. 200, 7 July 1941, 2492.

[165] As indicated ibid. 2491. Quotations from several brochures are included as evidence, ibid. 2493–5.

[166] *Meldungen aus dem Reich*, vol. 10, no. 301, 20 July 1942, 3971.

[167] Ihde, *Handbuch der Reichsschrifttumskammer*, 98–9. On the following, see ibid. n. 6, 100–5.

companies such as Herder, Kösel & Pustet, Ferdinand Schöningh, or Vandenhoeck & Ruprecht that had previously offered a mixed program now had to decide within a year whether to give up the religious elements of their production entirely or to label themselves as exclusively religious publishers.[168]

The Propaganda Ministry and the Chamber often discovered that the publishers and authors of Christian writings were working without having acquired Chamber membership at all.[169] To close this gap in the system of control, on 17 July 1940 the Ministerial Council for the Defense of the Reich (Ministerrat für die Reichsverteidigung) issued a directive on "proving membership of the Reich Chamber of Literature."[170] This set down that the printer of any text destined for public circulation must ascertain, before accepting the job, that "its publisher or, if there is no publisher, its author has fulfilled his obligations toward the Reich Chamber of Literature." The check was to be carried out by asking to see the client's membership card or exemption permit. In addition, Goebbels ordered that admission to the Chamber be refused to all clerics who were rejected by the relevant NSDAP *Gau* leadership or by the Gestapo and SD.[171] Finally, in August 1943 the previous freedom of distribution for works priced at below 0.50 RM was withdrawn, enabling control of the enormously widespread religious brochures and also of magazine-format detective and adventure stories.[172]

In 1941 a "more rigorous combing out or closure of confessional printers" was introduced in the hope of slowing down or completely halting the production of religious publishers.[173] To the same end, paper allocations were refused, preventing the appearance of around 1.6 million copies of Christian publications between June and July

---

[168] This is the tenor of the commentary by G. Gentz, "Neue Bekanntmachungen der Reichsschrifttumskammer," *Bbl.* no. 87, 15 April 1939, 293–5, here 293.

[169] Thus Ihde in a file note of 15 November 1940 re: processing the questionnaires on paper-use statistics, BArch R 56 V/43 fol. 225, and Goebbels to Bormann, 27 July 1941, BArch NS 8/186 fol. 106.

[170] Ihde, *Handbuch der Reichsschrifttumskammer*, 60–1.

[171] Goebbels to Bormann, 27 July 1941, BArch NS 8/186 fol. 105.

[172] Ibid. (point 3). See the RSK's directive on the distribution of literature, 26 October 1940, reproduced in Ihde, *Handbuch der Reichsschrifttumskammer*, 208.

[173] Goebbels to Bormann, 27 July 1941, BArch NS 8/186 fol. 105 (point 6). On the following, see ibid. fol. 105–6.

1941 alone. Goebbels nonetheless had to concede to Bormann in late 1941 that the churches had thwarted a "definitive solution of the problem" through "systematic sabotage using all possible means." The Propaganda Ministry therefore moved to a gradual elimination of the religious publishing houses themselves by a combination of refusing paper allocations, imposing partial bans or prohibiting the entire production of individual publishers, and conscripting their employees away from publishing and printing operations. Yet even the "combing-out campaigns" by the Propaganda Ministry in 1943 did not result in the sector's collapse. Neither large religiously affiliated companies such as Bertelsmann, Herder, Schöningh, Kösel & Pustet, or Josef Bercker in Kevelaer nor medium-sized ones such as Vandenhoeck & Ruprecht or Bachem Verlag in Cologne closed down completely.[174] Apart from Rufer Verlag, which was part of Bertelsmann, these sanctions by the state literary bureaucracy affected primarily small family businesses. Their fate was to serve as a warning to others of what the religious book trade as a whole could expect to experience after the "final victory."

Alongside its control of admission to the profession, the Chamber used a complex array of other formal and informal political measures to steer publishing into Nazi channels. The confidential bulletin of the publishing section, *Vertrauliche Mitteilungen der Fachschaft Verlag*, which appeared between 1935 and 1945, gave publishers both purely technical information and extensive political instructions. "Observation" or "advisory" offices were established to provide information on the production of particular groups of publishers and to push it in the required direction. From April 1934, every work intended for door-to-door distribution had to be reported to the Observation Office (from 1936 Advisory Office) for Door-To-Door Book Sales and submitted for examination.[175] In February 1936 an Advisory Office for

[174] List of the publishers to be maintained (mid-1943), BArch R 56 V/182 fol. 358–67. Bertelsmann, originally on the list of publishers to be closed (ibid. fol. 378–414, here fol. 388), was retrospectively added to this list (fol. 370/verso). Vandenhoeck & Ruprecht was also included on 12 June 1943, on the instructions of the RMVP literature department, ibid. fol. 215, as was Kösel & Pustet. RSK to the provincial economics office Munich 23, 28 June 1943, BArch R 56 V/109 fol. 44.

[175] "Anordnung über die Einrichtung einer Beobachtungsstelle für den Reisebuchhandel vom 15.4.1934," in Schrieber, *Das Recht der Reichskulturkammer*, vol. I, 213, and the rules for implementation issued on 12 June 1934, ibid. 220–1.

Astrological and Related Literature was established.[176] The publishers of "writings with an astrological, graphological, chirological, or occult content" were obligated to present their entire production, "before its appearance," for inspection by the office whenever requested. In late April 1936, an Advisory Office for Specialist Publishers in the Reich Chamber of Literature followed.[177] Its tasks were to intensify the promotion of specialized literature that had been pursued by the state since 1935, to eliminate "undesirable" specialized works from the book market, and to influence publishers' planning for the benefit of the economy as a whole. In October 1936 came an Advisory Office for the Address and Advertising Register Trade,[178] the chief responsibility of which was to "monitor pricing and the mode of distribution"; it was also required to issue "guidelines on customary practice" in the area of address and advertising registers. In spring 1937, the advisory offices were grouped together in the Advisory Office for Publishing, which now also included a section for "folk medicine."[179] In April 1938, responsibility for this Advisory Office moved from the Chamber to the Propaganda Ministry's literature department.[180] Together with the Reich Literature Office and the Economic Office of the German Book Trade, it regulated the production of German publishers to an increasing degree.

The operating principles of the Advisory Office for Entertainment Literature, established in July 1935,[181] to which all relevant new publications had to be presented before going to press, are illustrated by the case of Wilhelm Goldmann Verlag. Goldmann, who had built his company in the 1920s largely on the foundation of high-selling detective fiction, had to present forty-seven books to the Chamber for inspection as early as fall 1934. In July 1935, he asked the Chamber

---

[176] Schrieber, *Das Recht der Reichskulturkammer*, vol. IV, 92.

[177] "Mitteilung der Reichsschrifttumskammer," *Bbl.* no. 98, 28 April 1936, 383.

[178] "Anordnung über die 'Beratungsstelle für das Adress- und Anzeigenbuchverlags-Gewerbe' vom 21.10.1936," in Schrieber, *Das Recht der Reichskulturkammer*, vol. V, 82–3.

[179] "Amtliche Bekanntmachung des Präsidenten der RSK Nr. 118 vom 25.3.1937," in Schrieber, Metten, and Collatz, *Das Recht der Reichskulturkammer*, RSK I, 52, p. 74.

[180] "Zweite Bekanntmachung über die Gliederung der Reichsschrifttumskammer," in Ihde, *Handbuch der Reichsschrifttumskammer*, 44.

[181] "Anordnung zur Förderung guter Unterhaltungsliteratur vom 24.7.1935," in Schrieber, *Das Recht der Reichskulturkammer*, vol. III, 125–6.

for news on "whether there are likely to be any objections at all to these works, so that we are able to take such aspects into account when deciding on future publications."[182] On 12 August, the publisher received his response from the Chamber: a demand that he present proposed reprints of his entertainment fiction to the Advisory Office on a regular basis.[183] Goldmann's requests for permission to acquire the translation rights of British and American detective novels were rejected by the Chamber "on considerations of principle."[184] In March 1937, he was then instructed by the Chamber to join the "Working Group of Publishers of Popular Literature."[185] Goldmann reacted to this attempted regimentation by announcing that he planned to sell out all his existing entertainment fiction and reorient his program toward quality fiction and scholarship.[186] In fact, however, Goldmann initially only divested titles by Jewish authors, from which he could no longer expect to make much profit anyway.[187] In June 1937, the Chamber was able to prove that Goldmann was still bringing out entertainment literature in new editions or reprints.[188] It reiterated its demand that he submit his publications, threatening him with exclusion from the Chamber "in the case of violation."[189] In August, after consulting with the Book Trade Group's legal advisor, Goldmann finally sent the Chamber the required list of all his entertainment titles,[190] and later in the year also submitted his planned reissues of Edgar Wallace novels for approval.[191] Ultimately, Goldmann was only able to escape the political pressure of the state literary bureaucracy—which left its mark on his company's economic viability—by

---

[182] Goldmann to RSK president, 5 July 1935, BArch BDC/RSK/Goldmann, W.

[183] RSK Advisory Office Publishing (Beratungsstelle Verlag), entertainment literature dept., to RSK Dept. III, 21 June 1937, ibid.

[184] Goldmann to RSK, 28 October 1936, ibid.

[185] Statement by the Book Trade Group on Goldmann's obligation to present his publications for inspection, 22 June 1937, ibid.

[186] Goldmann to Book Trade Group, 25 August 1937, ibid.

[187] Stapo office Leipzig to Gestapa, 8 February 1937, Stapo office Dresden to Gestapa, 2 March 1937 (copies), and RSK to Gestapa, 7 April 1937, all ibid.

[188] Statement by RSK Dept. III, 22 June 1937, ibid.

[189] RSK, Advisory Office Publishing, entertainment literature dept., to RSK Dept. III, 21 June 1937, ibid.

[190] Goldmann to RSK Book Trade Group, 25 August 1937, ibid.

[191] Goldmann to Advisory Office Publishing, entertainment literature dept., 15 December 1937, BArch 50.05/fiche 53 436 fol. 19.

shifting his focus to international politics and economics, history, art, and, to a lesser extent, quality fiction.[192]

In October 1941 the Chamber made its first appeal to book publishers to employ only the minimum number of personnel "required for the orderly fulfillment of the production necessary for the war, applying the strictest of criteria."[193] From August 1942, the Propaganda Ministry literature department began systematically withdrawing staff from those publishers "for whose book production no further paper allocations can be granted in wartime."[194] By the end of 1942, raw materials shortages and the war economy's thirst for labor had become so severe that the first plans for extensive closures of publishers were discussed. However, Chamber manager Ihde expressed strong objections to these in a statement of 5 January 1943.[195] Because the intended reduction of publishers from the existing 2,000 to around 500 would affect primarily small and medium-sized, family-owned businesses, whereas the bigger employers would remain untouched because of the war-related nature of their work, Ihde calculated that the closures would free up only 100–200 employees. Furthermore, he argued, the surviving publishers could be expected to approach the Chamber without delay, asking for more personnel in order to assure their production. He also disapproved of the drastic structural changes that he believed would inevitably result from an inefficient campaign of closures: authors would be shackled to the few remaining, large-scale publishers; publishing would be concentrated in big cities such as Berlin, Leipzig, Munich, Stuttgart, or Hamburg, ushering in an "intellectual atrophy of the wider Germany"; ceding highly skilled and younger members of the book trade to more lucrative economic sectors would mean a "suicidal decimation of personnel"; substantial economic capacities would be lost for the long term; and

---

[192] See Goldmann to Johst, 12 December 1942, enclosing a list of the titles available for delivery at Christmas 1942, BArch R 56 V/20 fol. 133–4.
[193] "Bekanntmachung über die Freimachung von Arbeitskräften aus dem Buchverlag vom 10.10.1941," *Bbl.* no. 258, 4 November 1941, 381.
[194] See the strictly confidential note to the Central Propaganda Office Berlin, 26 August 1942, LA Berlin Rep. 243, Acc. 1814/3. Enclosed was a five-page list of publishers who were to fall under this heading.
[195] BArch R 56 V/26 fol. 135–8. On the following, see ibid.

Germany would be deprived of the "cultural and creative" initiative of many publishers. For all these reasons, Ihde recommended that rather than closing around 1,500 publishers as planned, the local-level Party propaganda offices should be asked to gather information on the specific options for releasing personnel and their respective effects. As for the publishers "in whose program we have no cultural-policy interest or whose program must even be rejected by the state leadership," Ihde too now saw both opportunity and obligation to "close them ruthlessly."

Despite these arguments, the Propaganda Ministry insisted on the closure of at least 1,200 publishers,[196] though the measures were to be carried out "only in consultation with the Reich Chamber of Literature (via the relevant provincial leaders)." In April 1943, the Chamber told the publishers affected to draw up a full list of their book stocks and current production, and to sell it off according to Chamber instructions.[197] Production for which paper had already been allocated was to be completed, but no further paper applications were to be submitted. The authors attached to the closed-down publishers were not allowed to sign option agreements or general contracts with the remaining companies. If they did, they could expect paper allocation for their works to be blocked.[198] All that was permitted was to transfer a "limited right of publication without ancillary rights" to a surviving publisher. At a meeting of the Börsenverein and the Book Trade Group in Leipzig on 5 October 1943, however, it was noted that the closure campaign had so far had no "great impact" on book publishers.[199] Although the Ministry literature department had presented an extensive "list of publishers to be closed" in mid–1943,[200] the complex administrative decision-making processes made rapid implementation impossible. And just as Ihde had predicted, appeals from the companies and interventions

---

[196] Ihde to Johst, 25 February 1943, BArch R 56 V/26 fol. 111.

[197] "Anordnung zur Regelung von Fragen, die sich aus der Schließung von Buchverlagen ergeben," *Bbl.* no. 84, 22 April 1943, 73.

[198] "Erste Mitteilung der Reichsschrifttumskammer zur Anordnung Nr. 157," ibid. 55–6. See also the legal interpretation by G. Gentz, "Schließung von Buchverlagen," ibid. 74–6.

[199] Report of the meeting, here p. 2, StAL BV/737. On the implementation of these closures, see BArch R 56 V/182, 108, 109.

[200] BArch R 56 V/182 fol. 378–414.

by the Reich Defense Commissioners, *Gau* economic advisors, and provincial cultural administrators (*Kulturwalter*) resulted in numerous publishers being removed from the closures list and added to the "list of publishers to be maintained."[201]

The closure plans do not appear to have succeeded even as a means of eliminating politically irksome firms. For example, Peter Suhrkamp Verlag—regarded by the RSHA and Rosenberg's literature office as "still having exceptionally strong moments of liberalism"[202]—was placed on the closures listed in early March 1943, but the decision was abandoned when high-profile figures from German cultural life complained to Goebbels. The Wehrmacht supreme command, which had originally agreed to the closure, now backtracked, describing its vote as "an error by our representatives." Even the Party Chancellery was prepared to set aside its "concerns about Suhrkampf [*sic*]" once the Propaganda Ministry gave it assurances that the publisher would "do decent work in future in terms of ideology." At the end of March 1943, the head of the literature department informed the committee working on the closures list that Goebbels had decided to close publishers "not according to cultural policy, but purely based on the needs of the war economy; the Suhrkamp case was presented as a particular example of the unacceptable exploitation of total-war measures."

Large-scale closures only began after Hitler appointed Goebbels as Reich Plenipotentiary for Total War on 20 July 1944. New production of belles lettres was then discontinued completely as of 1 August. Of the approximately 30,000 people still at work in the German book trade as a whole, "at least half" were to be released for military purposes.[203] Writing on 22 August, Goebbels authorized the presidents of the individual chambers to release their members for use by the Wehrmacht or the weapons industry.[204] The "instructions for the total mobilization of the book trade" enclosed in the *Börsenblatt*'s 9

---

[201] See the applications for amendments and the notifications of literature department decisions, and the list of the publishers to be maintained, ibid. fol. 358–67.

[202] File note by von Kielpinski of the RSHA re: Verlag Peter Suhrkamp, BArch NS 8/249 fol. 48. The following quotations ibid.

[203] RSK to RMVP, 7 August 1944, BArch R 56 V/152 fol. 171.

[204] "Der totale Kriegseinsatz der Kulturschaffenden," *Die Reichskulturkammer* 2 (1944), 121–7.

September 1944 edition obligated publishers to deliver to the Party-affiliated wholesaler Lühe & Co. all cloth-bound or half-bound books that had been produced without a special permit from the Economic Office of the German Book Trade. Lists of the binding materials still in stock had to be submitted to the Economic Office. The owners and employees of all companies subject to obligatory Chamber membership had to report to the relevant labor office, "of their own accord," by 15 September for deployment in the arms factories.[205] The only exceptions were now for the holders of exemption certificates from the Chamber of Culture and employees of businesses important to the war. By the end of September 1944, 1,902 publishers had been closed in twenty-nine *Gaue*.[206] In the eleven remaining *Gaue*, further closures were supposed to be carried out by the end of October, even though the released employees were now unlikely to find work in other economic sectors.

This still did not mean the end of publishing activity in the Nazi state. In the case of some publishers, part of their production fell under the authority of other chambers, so that the Chamber of Literature could only issue a partial closure notice.[207] Several publishers were able to prove they were doing work of military importance for the administration, economy, Wehrmacht, or SS.[208] Some used personal contacts in the Propaganda Ministry literature department to get a closure order reversed, so that, as the Chamber manager complained in early January 1945, "in book trade circles" it could easily seem "as if the Chamber's hard-heartedness always had to be corrected by the generously understanding attitude of the

---

[205] The instruction sheet wrongly states that age may exempt a person from the requirement to report. See the correction, stating that all persons irrespective of age must report to the labor offices, in the report of the joint session of the Börsenverein's council and the board of the Book Trade Group on 27 September 1944 in Rathen, near Leipzig, p. 4, StAL BV/583.

[206] Numbers ibid.; they differ from those given in an RSK file note of 13 November 1944, BArch R 56 V/152 fol. 20, namely 1,269 publishers, 1,410 retail bookstores, 555 mail-order bookstores, 139 wholesalers, 4,178 book sales outlets, 1,015 lending libraries, and 101 lending libraries carried out as adjuncts to other businesses. Exemptions from arms industry deployment were still held by 3,477 book-trade employees at this time.

[207] The Berlin provincial leadership of the RSK pointed this out to the local labor office on 9 January 1945, LA Berlin Rep. 243, Acc. 1814/66 fol. 6.

[208] See LA Berlin Rep. 243, Acc. 1814/66, on Adler Verlag (fol. 9), A. W. Hayn's Erben (fol. 253), and F. A. Herbig Verlagsbuchhandlung (fol. 265–72).

Ministry."[209] All this meant that commission and retail bookselling operations had to be sustained, at least on a restricted scale, in order to assure the distribution of continued publishing production, and to absorb and distribute the stock of the publishers that had been closed down.[210] Both the Chamber and the Börsenverein, furthermore, had an interest in maintaining a future for the book trade after the end of the war. From this point of view, the loss of experienced and newly qualified professionals to other areas of the economy was a great cause for concern.[211]

But even if efforts continued until the very end to implement the "combing-out campaigns" in the most accommodating way,[212] the ultimate outcome was a rump book trade, severely distorted not only by political regimentation but also by massive interference in its operational and ownership structure. The list of publishers issued on 4 November 1944 now included only 273 companies, mostly based in the *Gaue* of Berlin (74), Saxony (53), Württemberg-Hohenzollern (29), Munich-Upper Bavaria (19), Vienna (16), and Brandenburg (11). Almost 74 percent of German publishers were concentrated in six *Gaue* with their large towns and cities, whereas in the remaining thirty-five *Gaue* only a few individual houses survived.[213]

Methods and Instruments of Book Censorship

In December 1933, Berlin writer and publisher Wilhelm Jaspert drew the Propaganda Ministry's attention to the fact that "since the Führer came to power," more than a thousand printed publications had

---

[209] Gentz, file note on a discussion with Erich Langenbucher on 8 January 1945, BArch R 56 V/152 fol. 4.

[210] See RSK to RMVP, 7 August 1944, BArch R 56 V/152 fol. 172, and report of the Börsenverein meeting on 27 September 1944 in Rathen, p. 4, StAL BV/583.

[211] See Wülfing's preliminary report preparing the session of the Börsenverein's council on 12 and 13 May 1944 in Rathen, p. 4, StAL BV/737, and the report of the Rathen meeting on 27 September 1944, p. 8, StAL BV/583.

[212] In Berlin, even in early 1945 experts from the RSK provincial leadership, the *Gau* labor office, and the *Gau* chamber of commerce were still meeting weekly to consult on the "combing" and closure measures. See file note by the RSK provincial leadership Berlin, 12 January 1945, LA Berlin Rep. 243, Acc. 1814/66 fol. 278.

[213] As analyzed by Bühler and Bühler, *Der Frontbuchhandel*, 83–4. List of the publishers to be maintained, divided by *Gau*, with three addenda, in StAL BV/881.

been banned and confiscated.[214] No fewer than twenty-one agencies had been involved in this process, causing substantial "unease" among the "book-buying public, but especially in book retailing and publishing." Jaspert therefore found it "high time either to put a general stop to the bans or to create a centralized office that can be approached when printing a manuscript or beforehand, or which is the only official agency authorized to ban books already in print." He concluded by pointing out the negative media coverage abroad— book bans had been made public not only in the internal *Deutsches Kriminalpolizeiblatt* and the *Deutscher Reichsanzeiger*, but also "in the arts sections of almost all newspapers, including the very big, leading popular papers."

More than a year after this submission, Heinz Wismann, head of the Propaganda Ministry literature department, had to admit to Goebbels that the book-banning system was in "a very sorry state."[215] In mid-December 1934 there was still no "unified synopsis, and consequently no unified set of criteria and precepts," according to which a ban could be decided "in each specific case." Wismann proposed that the book bans be issued not by the Ministry, but by the president of the Chamber of Literature, on the basis of § 10 and § 25 of the First Directive for the Execution of the Reich Chamber of Culture Law. They should be done without bringing in the police "to any great extent, or if possible not at all." In January 1935, Wismann also recommended drawing up a single "Reich index of banned and confiscated literature."[216]

This was the path followed when the "ordinance on harmful and undesirable literature" was issued on 25 April 1935.[217] It gave the Chamber responsibility for keeping two lists of bans. The first would include "books and writings" that "endanger the cultural will of National Socialism" and that must therefore be neither lent by public libraries nor sold through the "book trade in any form (publisher, bookstore, mail-order, door-to-door, lending libraries, etc.)." The second

---

[214] BArch R 56 V/158 fol. 4–5. The following quotations ibid.
[215] Wismann's report to Goebbels via the ministerial office, 17 December 1934, re: book banning, BArch R 56 V/158 fol. 23–4, here fol. 23. The following quotations ibid.
[216] Wismann to Goebbels, 23 January 1935, BArch R 56 V/158 fol. 26–9.
[217] "Anordnung über schädliches und unerwünschtes Schrifttum," *Bbl.* no. 99, 30 April 1935, 338.

was to list works considered morally harmful to the young; these had hitherto been suppressed using the Law to Protect Youth from Trashy and Obscene Literature of 1926, which was repealed on 10 April 1935. The books on this second list were not to be displayed in store windows or on bookstalls, distributed by booksellers without fixed salesrooms, or issued to young people under the age of eighteen. Anyone in violation of these rules was threatened with exclusion from the Chamber on the grounds of insufficient "reliability and suitability," or "in less serious cases" with a fine. Applications for works to be added to one of the lists could be submitted to the president of the Chamber, who would make his decision "in agreement" with the Propaganda Minister. In the case of scientific and scholarly literature, inclusion in List 1 was only possible if the Reich Minister of Education had proposed the ban or given it his approval. All the bans pronounced "according to the previous regulations" would continue to apply.

The Reich and Prussian Ministry of the Interior was quick to issue a circular to all police authorities, pointing out that the Chamber's new rules did not affect the duties placed upon them by § 7 of the Decree for the Protection of the German People issued on 4 February 1933.[218] The confiscation and sequestration of printed matter under the emergency decree still remained the responsibility of the Gestapa for all of Prussia and the Stapo offices and external branches, along with the "Berlin chief of police as the provincial police department (with effect for the entire German territory), in cases where a violation of morals and decency endangers public security or order."[219] This Interior Ministry intervention wrecked the intended unification of book banning almost before it was introduced.

Accordingly, in late 1935 the Propaganda Minister learned of "a series of erroneous book bans" made by the Bavarian Political Police and the Bavarian provincial police headquarters.[220] In the view

---

[218] Copy of the circular decree of 16 May 1935, preserved in the files of the Duisburg-Hamborn police headquarters, in HStA Düsseldorf RW 36/30 fol. 11.

[219] Ibid. Bans on periodical publications based on § 9 ff. of the emergency decree of 4 February 1933 were to be carried out "as before" via the provincial governors, the Gestapa, Berlin's chief of police, and the provincial police departments.

[220] Indicated in Schmidt-Leonhardt's report to Goebbels, 2 January 1936, re: book bans by local Bavarian authorities, BArch R 43 II /1150 fol. 9–12, here fol. 9. The following details ibid. fol. 11–12.

of lawyer Hans Schmidt-Leonhardt, the head of the Ministry's legal department, this case was just "one more link in the long chain of local measures which have brought ambiguity and confusion to the Reich government's policy." The root of the problem, he argued, was that the Propaganda Ministry had been compelled from the very beginning to fight "a tenacious battle for the consistent and correct regulation" of matters within its own sphere of responsibility. "Only through disproportionate effort" had the Ministry managed to reach "interim agreements here and there," but these had not proved sustainable in practice. Schmidt-Leonhardt therefore advised Goebbels to have the Ministry's competences reconfirmed and specified by Hitler in person.

After another round of negotiations between the Propaganda Ministry and the Ministry of the Interior over the handling of book and press censorship again failed to bear fruit,[221] this "Führer decision" was finally obtained by state secretary Lammers: on 15 April 1936, Goebbels received the confirmation he wanted, securing his responsibility for all the domains subordinate to the Propaganda Ministry "including the police-related tasks."[222] On 7 May he issued a circular decree setting out the future handling of the book-banning procedure for all the provincial governments, the provincial governors and district presidents, and the chief of police in Berlin.[223] According to these instructions, books could now only be confiscated if they were included in the "list of undesirable writings" compiled by the Chamber of Literature. For a queried work to be added to the list, an application had to be made to the president of the Chamber. Goebbels reserved for himself the final say regarding objections to books published abroad. In urgent cases, the police authorities were permitted to carry out a "provisional confiscation" as long as they immediately informed the Propaganda Minister of their rationale.

In formal terms, the state's literary bureaucracy now possessed the instruments of power it needed to implement its book bans.

---

[221] Report of the meeting between representatives of the RMVP and the Reich Ministry of the Interior on 31 January 1936 in the Reich Chancellery, BArch R 43 II/1150 fol. 19–20, and Reich and Prussian Ministry of the Interior to Reich Chancellery, 26 March 1936, ibid. fol. 22.
[222] Official notification by Hitler, 15 April 1936, BArch R 43 II/1150 fol. 22/verso.
[223] BArch R 2/4750.

In terms of content, though, it was far from having resolved its problems. The publication of List 1 of Harmful and Undesirable Writing had been announced on 25 April 1935, but the list only appeared at the end of the year, with entries going up to October. With its sections for individual titles, collective works, and periodicals, the list was essentially a compilation of existing indexes, above all the "register of publications seized and sequestered by the police and those banned for distribution by commercial lending libraries" that the Bavarian Political Police had issued in fall 1934, covering 6,834 titles by a total of 2,293 authors.[224]

The Chamber's list included 3,601 individual fiction or nonfiction titles and 524 bans on authors' complete works. It affected a large number of Jewish authors, but racism was not the sole criterion for indexing an item. There were also bans on political literature: the publications of the labor movement in Germany and those by leading SPD figures; writings from the milieu of the Soviet revolution and the German Communist Party; the works of certain nationalist-conservative authors; the publications of Otto Strasser's "Black Front"; all titles by or about Ernst Röhm; "opportunistic literature" on National Socialism and race research; books on the political system of the Weimar Republic; and the complete works of several pacifists. Bans on legal literature primarily hit Jewish legal authors.[225] Further "undesirable and harmful" publications were those of the Confessing Church and on anthroposophy, women's emancipation, abortion, nudism and sex education, erotica, and pulp fiction. Of quality fiction, almost the entirety of modernist literature—whether by German authors or in translation—was indexed.

List 1, like the other indexes, bore the note "Strictly confidential! For internal use only!"[226] The original plan had been to publish new

---

[224] Aigner, *Die Indizierung*, col. 955. Writing to Hederich on 2 July 1936, BArch R 56 V/72 fol. 217, RSK manager Heinl noted that "when compiling our List 1, I carefully read through" the Bavarian list, and "adopted only a certain number of the books listed there, in particular those that turned out, upon comparison, also to be banned in other provinces or in the Reich as a whole."

[225] For details, see Jung, "Der literarische Judenstern."

[226] Upon receiving a copy of the index, employees of the Ministry, the Chamber, or its provincial branches had to sign the following affidavit: "The book [i.e., the index] is always to be kept locked up, and must not be left lying around when its owner is outside his office. It may only be used for answering inquiries, and must not be made

entries on a running basis in the *Deutsches Kriminalpolizeiblatt* and the *Börsenblatt*,[227] but secrecy seemed to offer two advantages: it would help prevent further international protests against Nazi cultural policy;[228] and it would force the German book trade to work very closely with its "professional representatives" and the Ministry literature department—since these would be the only sources of information on indexed publications "in cases of doubt."[229] It also required members of the book trade to develop their own "intuitive sense" of which publications were likely to be "undesirable and harmful."

The index was continually expanded, initially by the Chamber. Starting in July 1936, decisions on bans were made at regular censorship meetings, chaired by Wismann of the literature department and attended by representatives of the Chamber, the PPK, the Gestapa, SD Main Office, and the Reich Ministry of Education.[230] The new bans were collated into printed lists at irregular intervals.[231] However, it soon became clear that these addenda, like the basic list itself, were impractical for day-to-day use. For one thing, the documents did not include any information on the publisher or the place and year of publication for the works prohibited. They were also riddled with errors in the spelling and classification of authors and the listing of book titles and series—a result not only of haste in

---

accessible for inspection by anyone except the personal owner. It must not be taken out of the office into any other office or into the owner's private home. In compliance with the orders of Reich Ministry of the Interior Dr. Frick, any use of the book going beyond internal use or any loss of the book will result in the culprit's instant dismissal." A declaration of this kind can be found in BArch BDC/RSK/Langenbucher, E.

[227] Gentz, *Das Recht der Reichsschrifttumskammer*, 68/n. 1.

[228] This justification was given by literature department head Wismann on 19 March 1937 in Leipzig, during a meeting of the wholesalers' *Fachschaft* within the Book Trade Group. See report of the meeting, p. 2, in StAL Koehler & Volckmar/119.

[229] See "Verbotenes und unerwünschtes Schrifttum," *Der Buchhändler im neuen Reich* 2 (1937), 41–2, and Hugo Koch, "Die Bekämpfung des schädlichen und unerwünschten Schrifttums," *Jahrbuch des Großdeutschen Leihbuchhandels* 1941, 138–50, here 146–7.

[230] *Leitheft Schrifttumswesen und Schrifttumspolitik*, March 1937, BArch R 58/1106 fol. 80. Unfortunately no minutes of these censorship meetings (*Verbotskonferenzen*) survive, and it is unknown when they ceased to be held.

[231] These "Addenda I–III to List 1 of Harmful and Undesirable Literature," BArch R 56 V/71 fol. 100–15, contained the book bans ordered by the RSK between October 1935 and 10 June 1936. Hectographed compilations for the period 10 June 1936 through 31 October 1937 in BArch R 56 V/71 fol. 77–99, fol. 128–53, fol. 154–61.

the compilation, but also of inadequate expertise within the offices involved.[232] During the great shake-up of competencies between the Propaganda Ministry and the Chamber of Culture's component chambers on 1 April 1938, therefore, responsibility for processing the applications for bans was passed to the Ministry literature department. From now on, the Chamber could do no more than take cognizance of the entries added to the List by the ministerial bureaucracy.[233] From December 1938, Goebbels gave himself exclusive personal responsibility for decisions on bans relating to the whole domain of his Ministry's operations.[234]

In late 1939 a thoroughly revised and expanded new edition of the List of Harmful and Undesirable Literature was presented,[235] drawn up at the request of the Propaganda Ministry by the Deutsche Bücherei's bibliographical staff. The librarians had corrected and completed the indexes of 1935 through 1937, integrating all the titles newly banned up to 31 December 1938. A preface reminded users that the works listed were prohibited "in all their impressions" and, for works that had appeared with different publishers, also "in all their editions."[236] The ban also applied to "all their translations, irrespective of whether or not these have already been made." The List now included a total of 4,175 individual titles and 565 bans on complete works,[237] as well as bans on series and periodicals and, for the first time, on the entire production of particular publishers.

The new edition of List 1 contained an official reference to the special authority for prohibitions held by Himmler as the Reichsführer SS and Chief of the German Police in the Reich Ministry of the Interior. This explicit authorization was considered necessary

---

[232] See Aigner, *Die Indizierung*, col. 975–7.

[233] "Zweite Bekanntmachung über die Gliederung der Reichsschrifttumskammer," in Ihde, *Handbuch der Reichsschrifttumskammer*, 44.

[234] Notification in *Nachrichtenblatt des Reichsministeriums für Volksaufklärung und Propaganda* 6, no. 18, 7 December 1939, 112.

[235] *Liste des schädlichen und unerwünschten Schrifttums. Stand vom 31. Dezember 1938*, Leipzig n.d. [1939]. On the date of the new edition, see the Deutsche Bücherei's overview of the "dispatch of the main list of harmful and undesirable literature," DB-Archiv no. 580/0–3.

[236] Preface to *Liste des schädlichen und unerwünschten Schrifttums. Stand vom 31. Dezember 1938*.

[237] Aigner, *Die Indizierung*, col. 984.

because the Chamber's ordinance on "harmful and undesirable literature" did not fully exploit the legal options offered by the Reich President's emergency decree of 28 February 1933. The decree allowed the basic right to freedom of expression to be waived, giving the Political Police de facto unrestricted scope to act against political and ideological opponents of the regime.[238] A further deficiency of the Chamber's ordinance was that it obliged only Chamber members to comply with the ban on distribution. If required, this restriction could be revoked by Himmler (on his own initiative or at the request of other state or Party offices) issuing "an additional, complete ban on particular publications."[239] Because the emergency decree made "warrants for house searches, orders for confiscations, and restrictions on property ... permissible beyond the legal limits otherwise prescribed," access now extended to the bookshelves of private households or of private institutions not controlled by the Chamber.

By order of the Propaganda Ministry, from 1 January 1939 the Deutsche Bücherei published a monthly "list of printed materials kept locked away by the Deutsche Bücherei."[240] The lists included two categories of works, "banned" and "secreted." The category "banned" covered firstly all the publications that had been added to the List of Harmful and Undesirable Literature by the Propaganda Ministry since 1939; secondly those publications not included in the List of Harmful and Undesirable Literature but listed as confiscated in the *Deutsches Kriminalpolizeiblatt*; and thirdly all new publications by publishers or authors whose production was banned in its entirety. "Secreted" were firstly all publications not destined for the

---

[238] As pointed out by Dr. Klüber of the Cologne administrative court in "Die Organisation der Schrifttumsüberwachung," *Bbl.* no. 204, 1 September 1934, 769–71, no. 206, 4 September 1934, 778–9, and no. 210, 8 September 1934, 789–90, here 789.

[239] For example, when all publications by Bermann Fischer in Stockholm were to be added to List 1 of Harmful and Undesirable Literature, Goebbels applied to Himmler to additionally "ban its publications within Reich territory on the basis of the Reich President's decree of 28 February 1933." See literature department (signed by Goebbels) to RSK president, 1 February 1939, BArch BDC/RSK/Bermann Fischer, G.

[240] On the following, see Deutsche Bücherei to Dr. Koch, RMVP, 12 June 1939, here p. 1, DB-Archiv no. 580/0–3. The monthly lists were compiled by the Library's bibliographical department, using the censorship decisions passed on by the state literature agencies. The proofs of each list were sent to the literature department for correction and approval.

public in the first place (such as the confidential bulletins of Party or state bodies); secondly publications "to be treated as confidential for specific reasons" (such as guidelines for air-raid protection, military science, or anthroposophical writings); and thirdly works that the SS liaison office in the Deutsche Bücherei had classified as either "harmless in content, but to be secreted due to the person of the author" or else "not completely irreproachable in content, but not worth an application for banning." Four Deutsche Bücherei librarians worked on the indexes, and the library billed the Börsenverein for their services.[241] The last monthly list was presented to the Propaganda Ministry literature department as late as February 1945.[242] For each year from 1939 to 1943, the monthly lists were collated into an annual list.[243]

The "harmful and undesirable literature" ordinance was revised on 15 April 1940, so that publications "contrary to the cultural and political objectives of the National Socialist state" could not only not be published, sold, distributed, lent, rented out, displayed, advertised, or otherwise offered to the public, but must not even be stored.[244] For the first time, the writings of all "full- and half-Jewish" authors, whether living or dead, were now banned across the board, independently of any individual entry in the index. A number of transitional arrangements were permitted for specialized and technical literature—for example, any copies of standard works of German science and intellectual history still in stock could be sold off, and new impressions could even be printed if the Propaganda Ministry gave its "explicit consent." The existing stock of edited collections, handbooks, and scholarly journals in which "full- or half-Jewish" authors had participated could also be sold out; for reprints of these,

---

[241] See Uhlendahl to Dr. Hess, 4 November 1940, with a bill for 260 hours of work, DB-Archiv no. 580/0–3.

[242] Uhlendahl sent Hövel the proofs of the January/February 1945 list on 20 February 1945, ibid.

[243] For the annual lists 1939 through 1941, see the facsimile reprints of the *Liste des schädlichen und unerwünschten Schrifttums* (Topos, 1979). The annual lists for 1942 and 1943 are held in the Deutsche Bücherei archives.

[244] Unusually, the new version of the RSK ordinance appeared not in the editorial section of the *Börsenblatt*, but only in the *Börsenblatt*'s restricted "A edition," no. 117, 23 May 1940, 2453. Reproduced in Ihde, *Handbuch der Reichsschrifttumskammer*, 75–6. On the following, see ibid. 78–9.

the agreement of the Propaganda Ministry had to be sought "in advance." Multi-authored scholarly and scientific works and reference books written or edited "for the most part or exclusively" by "full- or half-Jewish" authors had to be registered by 31 December 1940 with the Propaganda Ministry, which planned to reach individual decisions on their future distribution. Scholarly or scientific literature by "full- or half-Jewish" authors that had appeared before 1850 was exempted from the ban on distribution unless it was indexed individually.

The ordinance also mentioned a further index to be kept by the Chamber, a "list of books and writings not to fall into the hands of young people or to be held in libraries." This index for young people had already been announced in 1935, as "List 2 of Harmful and Undesirable Literature,"[245] but it appeared only in October 1940, as the "List of Publications Unsuitable for Young People and Libraries," compiled by the Deutsche Bücherei and issued by the Propaganda Ministry literature department.[246] Unlike List 1, this index was distributed publicly, by the Börsenverein's own publisher. The first edition included twenty extensive series and several hundred individual titles: crime and detective novels (with 151 titles by Edgar Wallace alone), adventure novels and westerns, science fiction, and romances. Later additions were recorded in the 1942 and 1943 updated versions of the list.

An analysis of the state lists of book bans from 1935 to 1943 shows that being indexed did not necessarily affect a particular author's permission to exercise his or her occupation. In fact, even a "total indexation" of all an author's works did not always result in exclusion from the profession. If a Chamber expert argued in 1936 that it should be impossible for authors whose complete works had been banned to retain membership of the Chamber,[247] this view did not prevail. It was also by no means unknown for an existing ban to be lifted. Thus, the version of List 1 dated 31 October 1935 includes

---

[245] RMVP literature department to head of the DB bibliographic department, Wilhelm Frels, 1 August 1940, DB-Archiv no. 580/0–3.

[246] Uhlendahl to the managing director of the Börsenverein, 4 November 1940, DB-Archiv no. 580/0–3. The literature department informed the DB of new indexations on a running basis. See ibid. for a copy of the first, seventy-seven-page list along with the next two editions.

[247] Pogge to Linhard, 23 June 1936, BArch BDC/RSK/Pohl, G.

six titles by children's author Waldemar Bonsels, but his work is absent from the revised list dated 31 December 1938. The reason was that, "in view of the beneficial effects abroad" of Bonsels's books and because of his willingness to adapt to political circumstances, the Propaganda Ministry literature department had decided not to create "any more difficulties" for him.[248]

Frank Thiess's novels *Frauenraub* of 1927 (*Interlude*, 1929) and *Die Verdammten* ("The damned") of 1930 had been included in the list of "undesirable literature" issued by Rosenberg's Kampfbund für deutsche Kultur in 1933, labeled as "morally confusing and corrosive."[249] When the Rosenberg Reichsstelle proposed a ban on Thiess's entire oeuvre in 1934, the author asked for support from Hans Hinkel as state commissioner in the Prussian ministry of education and culture.[250] Hinkel responded by arguing the author's case with Rudolf Hess and Karl Hanke, the head of Goebbels's ministerial office.[251] Although the two novels banned in 1933 were included in List 1, and the state literary bureaucracy opposed any promotion of Thiess "because his themes, his portrayals, and his diction are so strongly characterized by the individualistic liberal era that he cannot be counted among the forward-looking authors,"[252] in September 1934 Goebbels agreed to Hinkel's proposal "to undertake a full examination of the new publications planned by Thiess and to treat his work case by case according to its results."[253] No further bans on Thiess's books were issued by the regime. On the contrary, he was permitted to write the screenplay of his novel *Der Weg*

---

[248] RSK manager Ihde to Wilhelm Baur, 23 February 1943, BArch BDC/RSK/Bonsels, W. See also the political evaluation of Bonsels by NSDAP-*Kreisleiter* Starnberg, 28 July 1939, ibid.

[249] BArch R 56 V/70 fol. 72.

[250] See Thiess to Hinkel, 26 October 1934, BArch BDC/RSK /Thiess, F. For the reference to the Reichsstelle's efforts to obtain a complete ban on Thiess's works, see RMVP literature department to Hinkel, 5 September 1935, ibid. Literature department official Erckmann remarked that this would "in practice have little effect" because "the Reichsstelle's measures are not officially backed either by the Party or the government."

[251] See Hinkel to Hess, 1 November 1934, and Hinkel to Hanke, 11 December 1934, ibid.

[252] Erckmann to Hinkel, 5 September 1935, ibid.

[253] See the handwritten notes by Hinkel planning his submission to the Minister re: Frank Thiess, 15 August 1935, and Erckmann to Hinkel, 5 September 1935, ibid.

zu Isabelle ("The path to Isabelle") for Tobis, and despite paper shortages his books sold in very high numbers up to 1944.[254]

For other authors, however, the indexation of their books made continued work in Germany impossible. The bans on Irmgard Keun's novels *Gilgi, eine von uns* of 1931 ("Gilgi, one of us") and *Das kunstseidene Mädchen* of 1932 (*The Artificial Silk Girl*, 1933) ended the career of a promising young author.[255] Refused admission to the Chamber in 1936, she went into exile in Belgium and the Netherlands. A negative report by the Reichsstelle led to a 1935 ban on the novel *Bohème ohne Mimi* ("Bohemian life without Mimi") by Joachim Maass, published by S. Fischer in 1930.[256] In 1939 Maass left for the United States before his novel *Ein Testament* ("A testament") appeared, seeing no further opportunities for artistic development within the Nazi state.[257] In the case of Elisabeth Langgässer, a damning Rosenberg office review of her novel *Der Gang durch das Ried* ("Walking through the Ried") combined with her 1936 classification as a "half Jew" to exclude her from the Chamber of Literature.[258] Georg Kaiser's decision to emigrate to Switzerland in 1938 was closely related to the suppression of his work.[259] Three plays written by this Expressionist dramatist in the 1920s were included in the first version of List 1, four in the 1938 version.[260] His post–1933 work was neither printed nor performed.[261] One novel and three plays by Kaiser appeared with publishers in exile in 1940, but their distribution in Germany was banned immediately.[262] As for Herbert Eulenberg, although only two of his works were listed

---

[254] Hall, *Paul Zsolnay Verlag*, 617–27.

[255] *Liste 1* of October 1935, 64. On the ban in 1934/35, see BArch R 58/914 fol. 36–57.

[256] *Liste 1* of October 1935, 78. The Reichsstelle report is in BArch R 58/918 fol. 153, the banning procedure ibid. fol. 148–52. Peter Suhrkamp's letter protesting the book's seizure, submitted to the Gestapo Berlin on 21 November 1935 (ibid. fol. 159), had no effect.

[257] On the background to his emigration, see Maass to Thomas Mann, 20 June 1940, and Mann's response, 24 June 1940, DLA NL J. Maass.

[258] *Bücherkunde* 3 (1936), 282–3. The exclusion is noted in a list of "Jewish-German *Mischlinge*" sent to the RMVP by the RSK on 27 August 1938, BArch R 55/21 300.

[259] See BArch BDC/RSK/Kaiser, G.; Schnell, *Dichtung in finsteren Zeiten*, 148–60.

[260] *Liste 1* of October 1935, 61, and of 31 December 1938, 68.

[261] Gestapa (I/12) to the RSK president, 5 April 1938, here p. 2, BArch BDC/RSK/Kaiser, G.

[262] See annual lists 1940, 10, and 1941, 8–9.

in the state index, the Gestapo blocked his efforts to publish new work, stage his plays, and have his books translated for publication abroad.[263]

On 4 August 1936, the PPK notified the Gestapo that a selection of Gottfried Benn's poems from 1911 to 1936, published by Deutsche Verlags-Anstalt, gave "serious cause for concern" and could "under no circumstances be considered an edifying contribution to creativity in our times."[264] Not only would Benn's poems "do credit to a devotee of Freudian psychoanalysis," but their "cynicism and pathological self-abuse" easily matched that of "works by former leading lights who have now had their citizenship withdrawn and have emigrated." Hederich therefore requested the Gestapo to "consider whether the publisher should be called to account, and whether he should be informed that further distribution of this book in its present form is out of the question." This PPK view echoed the rigorous rejection of the book that had appeared in May in the SS paper *Das Schwarze Korps*, headlined "The Autoeroticist!"[265] The Gestapo alerted the Chamber of Literature, which ignored the matter, as did the Propaganda Ministry. On the instructions of Chamber president Johst, no action was to be taken against Benn and his writings,[266] but in 1937 Benn, working as a doctor at the army recruitment inspectorate in Hannover, found himself under renewed attack after the publication of Wolfgang Willrich's polemic *Säuberung des Kunsttempels* ("Cleansing the temple of art"). This time, Johst called in Himmler personally—having been an Expressionist colleague of Benn's in the past, the Chamber president was all too aware that a campaign against the writer would reflect badly on him as well. Although Himmler was able to prevent an anti-Benn campaign inside the SS, the political pressure continued, and on 18 March 1938 Goebbels required the Chamber to exclude Benn due to his lack of

---

[263] *Liste 1* of 31 December 1938, 34; note from Stapo office Düsseldorf, 26 April 1939, re: state police objections to Eulenberg's publication *Selbstbildnis* ("Self-portrait") (fol. 19). See also the negative response by the Stapo in Berlin re: Eulenberg's application to travel to Prague, 10 May 1940 (fol. 27). HStA Düsseldorf RW 58/34 125.

[264] BArch R 58/893 fol. 28–9.

[265] *Das Schwarze Korps* 2, no. 19, 7 May 1936, 7.

[266] Gestapa note, 21 August 1936, BArch R 58/893 fol. 32.

"suitability" in the terms of § 10 of the First Directive, and thus to prohibit him from working as an author.[267]

Despite his compliant attitude to the regime, Hanns Heinz Ewers featured in List 1 of October 1935 with a ban on "all works" with the exception of the novels *Horst Wessel* and *Reiter in deutscher Nacht* (*Rider of the Night*).[268] As a result, Ewers lost the income from sales of the books he had published between 1900 and 1933, and his work since the Nazi accession to power was also excluded from publication. In June 1940, Ewers complained to the Chamber regarding the "complete idiocy of this general ban," and told the Propaganda Ministry that "every single line I wrote must be released from the ban."[269] In response, the ban was narrowed down slightly, to "all works before 1933" with the further exceptions of *Die toten Augen* (*Immortal Eyes*) and *Die Ameisen* ("The ants"),[270] but when Ewers appealed to the Chamber once again in June 1941 for the release of his books, after detailed consideration the general rejection of his pre–1933 works was upheld, on the grounds that they offended "the healthy sentiment of the *Volk*."[271] The Propaganda Ministry literature department also prevented the planned 1942 reissue of *Reiter in deutscher Nacht* by refusing Cotta Verlag's paper application for the project.[272]

The censorship decisions of the state agencies contributed to a climate of uncertainty that was further exacerbated by censorship

---

[267] Benn sent a copy of the Chamber's exclusion notice to Friedrich Wilhelm Oelze on 26 March 1938: Benn, *Briefe an F.W. Oelze*, 186–7. On 29 March 1938, Johst informed Himmler of the exclusion, which had been personally ordered by Goebbels "at the instigation of Field Marshal Göring," and asked him to support an appeal. On 4 April 1938, Himmler responded that, "regarding Benn, I'll try to do whatever can be done." BArch BDC/SS/Johst, H.

[268] *Liste 1* of October 1935, 35.

[269] See Ewers's complaint to the RSK, 6 June 1941, BArch BDC/RSK/Ewers, H.H., and Ewers to Dr. Koch (RMVP literature department), 10 June 1940, ibid.

[270] Instructions from the RMVP literature department, 6 August 1940, ibid.; see also the corrigenda in the 1940 annual list, 21.

[271] Bischoff (RSK Dept. III Z) to Ewers, 24 July 1941, BArch BDC/RSK/Ewers, H. Nine-page overview evaluation of Ewers's work by a specially commissioned reader, ibid. A further objection by Ewers, this time directed to Hinkel, was also rejected by the Chamber: Dept. III Z to the RKK central management, 24 July 1941, ibid.

[272] See file note by Meyer for RSK manager Ihde, 16 March 1942, and the correspondence between the RSK, J. G. Cotta'sche Buchhandlung, and Ewers between February and April 1942, ibid.

applications from a plethora of Party offices and interest groups. One example is the attack on Kurt Ziesel's novella *Der Vergessene* ("The forgotten man") in 1941. Ziesel, anything but ideologically hostile to the Nazi cause, had described the fate of a crippled man in post-WWI Austria, struggling to survive as an organ-grinder. The stark realism of his portrayal enraged the war victims' welfare association,[273] and Goebbels duly ordered the book to be confiscated—but the first impression had already sold out, and the Reich Ring for National Socialist Propaganda and Popular Enlightenment was only able to request revisions of the objectionable passages for the next printing.[274] In another example, the head of the farmers' organization asked the Chamber president in June 1937 for a ban on further distribution of the brochure *Warum magenkrank?* ("Why dyspepsia?") by Dr. med. Erwin Silber.[275] His reasoning was that the chapter entitled "On the toxins in food" was "untenable" in view of the current situation of food production. The "errors and exaggerations" in the brochure, he argued, "severely hampered" the work of the farmers' leadership, "especially in terms of the Battle for Production, the campaign against food spoilage, and the fulfillment of important Four-Year Plan tasks." Another occupational lobby group, the automotive industry association, applied to the Reich Literature Office on 23 July 1937 for a ban on Walter Allerhand's travel book *Der schwarze Schatten. Ein Auto fährt nach Afrika* ("The black shadow. An automobile goes to Africa").[276] The association, which had become powerful with the rapid development of the German autobahn network, was disgusted that the author "only allows the good condition of Swiss roads, upon which, incidentally, he claims never to have seen a German automobile, even though the German automotive industry supplies the largest proportion of Swiss motor vehicles." It was nothing less than "insolent" that Allerhand denigrated all other European roads as "Augean stables" compared with the Swiss highway system—and this "even though on page 41

---

[273] NS-Kriegsopferversorgung central office, propaganda section, to Party Central Propaganda Office, 17 November 1941, BArch NS 18/107.
[274] Tiessler to Haegert, 19 January 1942, BArch NS 18/107.
[275] Reichsbauernführer to RSK president, 8 June 1937, in BArch BDC/RKK/file "Schädliches und unerwünschtes Schrifttum" VI.
[276] BArch BDC/file "Schädliches und unerwünschtes Schrifttum" I.

the author mentions driving for a short stretch on the German Reich autobahns and at that point describes them as good and broad."

After Theodor Heuss's weighty biography of the liberal politician Friedrich Naumann appeared with Deutsche Verlags-Anstalt in 1937, Eher's Wilhelm Baur wrote Max Winkler, whose company Vera GmbH administered the DVA share capital, to express his indignation.[277] Baur regarded the very publication of the book as "highly unnecessary for political reasons"; the fact that it was written by "one of the best-known members of the Jewish Democratic Party," who had also drawn negative attention to himself in 1932 with *Hitlers Weg* ("Hitler's path"), and published by a National Socialist company amounted "yet again" to "some nerve from Mr. Kilpper," the director of DVA. Baur could only see two possible explanations: either Kilpper was "that politically naive," or he "considers us, who are responsible for the political orientation of the book trade today, so stupid that he thinks he can get away with something like this." On his mettle, Baur continued: "If Mr. Heuss believes that today the time has come when he can erect 740-page memorials to old democrats during the Third Reich, he is very much mistaken." Heuss had to publish his 1939 biography of Hans Poelzig with E. Wasmuth, and his 1940 book on Anton Dohrn, the founder of the German zoological research station in Naples, with Atlantis. The Chamber only realized in 1941 that the books had appeared without their author having obtained RSK membership.[278] As well as writing essays and book reviews for several different journals, in the years that followed Heuss worked on a detailed biography of Robert Bosch, which could not be published until 1946.

When the Franconian NSDAP tried to have a novel by a woman physician suppressed because it allegedly gave an incorrect portrayal of the role of women in German society, even the Chamber's manager, Wilhelm Ihde, found that things had gone somewhat too far. Writing to Johst in April 1943, he complained with surprising perspicacity: "That an objection could be made in the first place is itself one of the disheartening aspects of literature today: anything

---

[277] Baur to Winkler, 21 December 1937, BArch BDC/RSK/Heuss, Th.
[278] See RSK to Heuss, 1 March 1941, imposing a 50 RM fine, and Heuss's response, 11 March 1941, ibid.

that extends beyond the template has to go. In some people's opinion, the capacity simply to read seems to be equated with the capacity to criticize. This kind of criticism acts as if the National Socialist idea were such a quivering straw in the wind of public life that the most trifling literary error could snap it forever. We preach at the volume of an ancient Germanic horn: live dangerously! If someone does, we knock him on the head. Any muse with a scrap of self-respect is bound to veil her face."[279]

Book censorship was not limited to German authors. The indexes drawn up from 1933 onward included many Soviet writers, as well as American, British, and French ones. Even works by Balzac, Boccaccio, Diderot, Maupassant, and Zola were classified as "harmful and undesirable." From July 1935, publishers had to obtain permission from the president of the Chamber before signing contracts on "the printing and publication of foreign works in Germany."[280] In the literary and trade press, members of state and Party literature agencies criticized the large number of translations on the German book market.[281] But only with World War II did the opportunity arise to systematically suppress the literature of entire countries. On 15 December 1939, German publishers and book retailers were informed in their sector groups' confidential bulletins that the further supply and distribution of translations of literary, popular scientific, and biographical works from English and French would remain "undesirable" for the duration of the war against Britain and France, unless they were already out of copyright.[282] The aim was to prevent "the further sale of these translations from accumulating foreign-currency demands to the benefit

---

[279] Ihde to Johst, 14 April 1943, BArch R 56 V/26 fol. 94. See also Ihde to the deputy *Gauleiter* of the NSDAP Franconia *Gau*, 31 January 1943, ibid. fol. 95–7.

[280] "Bekanntmachung betr. Anzeigepflicht bei dem Erwerb ausländischer Verlagsrechte vom 25.7.1935," in Schrieber, *Das Recht der Reichskulturkammer*, vol. III, 126.

[281] See, for example, B. Payr, "Überflüssige oder begrüßenswerte Übersetzungen?" *Bücherkunde* 4 (1937), 87–9; H. Franke, "Unerwünschte Einfuhr," *Die Neue Literatur* 38 (1937), 501–8; M. Hieronimi, "Zur Frage der ausländischen Übersetzungsliteratur," *Der Buchhändler im neuen Reich* 4 (1939), 209–15; P. Hövel, "Das Übersetzungsschrifttum—politisch gesehen," ibid. 286–93. See also Sturge, *"The Alien Within."*

[282] See the "confidential" reference to the treatment of British and French literature reproduced in Ihde, *Handbuch der Reichsschrifttumskammer*, 199. The following quotations ibid. According to the Berne Convention, only works by authors who had died before 1904 were free from copyright.

of countries that are using every method of economic warfare to try and starve the German people." Exceptions were made for "purely scientific works serving research or teaching," along with translations of works by Irish and US authors. Distribution could also be continued in cases where the Propaganda Ministry considered it "particularly desirable."

Starting in October 1940, the same rules applied to translations from Polish.[283] German translations of books by Polish authors were not to be sold, lent, or advertised "until the end of the war," the importation and distribution of Polish literature already having been under surveillance since November 1939 on Goebbels's instructions.[284] Applications to import French-language literature were still being "rejected on principle" in March 1941, "since there is not yet a state of peace with France, and at the same time no necessity to spread such writing within Germany can be recognized."[285] Only official bodies were permitted to have books and periodicals imported from France, which they did via a dedicated company, Auslandszeitungshandel GmbH in Cologne.[286]

In July 1941, the distribution of all works by Russian authors was halted.[287] The ban initially applied to "both contemporary Russian literature and that of earlier epochs," but in early October 1941 it was relaxed slightly so that "classic Russian literature published up to 1914" could be sold if the literature department gave its approval.[288] There were also exceptions for writings whose continued distribution was desirable in line with "propaganda requirements."[289]

---

[283] Instructions in *Vertrauliche Mitteilungen der Fachschaft Verlag* no. 56, 14 October 1940, reproduced in Ihde, *Handbuch der Reichsschrifttumskammer*, 202.

[284] Minutes of the secret ministerial conference of 7 November (here point 2), in Boelcke, *Kriegspropaganda 1939–1941*, 220.

[285] Circular from the Stapo office Düsseldorf, 11 March 1941, HStA Düsseldorf RW 18/31 fol. 23.

[286] Ibid. On the establishment and tasks of Auslandszeitungshandel GmbH, see Boelcke, *Kriegspropaganda 1939–1941*, 220.

[287] Instructions issued on 11 July 1941 by the literature department in *Vertrauliche Mitteilungen der Fachschaft Verlag* nos. 93–7, 15 July 1941, reproduced in Ihde, *Handbuch der Reichsschrifttumskammer*, 202–3.

[288] *Vertrauliche Mitteilungen der Fachschaft Verlag* nos. 116–62, 1 October 1941, in Ihde, *Handbuch der Reichsschrifttumskammer*, 203.

[289] "Anweisung der Schrifttumsabteilung vom 11.7.1941," in Ihde, *Handbuch der Reichsschrifttumskammer*, 202–3.

The Propaganda Ministry ordered a ban on performances of "works by Russian authors including composers, writers, dramatists, etc., without exception,"[290] but the ban on "anti-Bolshevist writing" that had been imposed following the Hitler–Stalin Pact of 23 August 1939 was lifted in 1941.[291]

Shortly after the United States entered the war, on 22 December 1941 Himmler, "in agreement" with the Propaganda Ministry, issued a ban on the distribution of all US newspapers, periodicals, and books.[292] In February 1942 the Stapo offices, local police, and provincial authorities were ordered to search book and newspaper stores, along with commercial lending libraries, for any remaining stocks of such publications.[293] In the same year, the Ministry literature department issued a "register of English and North American authors" to support the "cleansing" of the book market and libraries from Anglo-American literature. The register was compiled with the help of the Deutsche Bücherei on the basis of the "ascertainable translations published in the last forty years."[294] It did not include purely scientific and scholarly works, as these remained "still permitted in general." Authors who had died before 1904 were included in the register, but their work, being out of copyright, was exempt from the ban on distribution. For some of the authors, "special permission" was given for the continued sale and lending of individual titles.

In the initial phase, the surveillance of publications imported from abroad relied largely on chance and specific denunciations. When the banned periodical *World Jewry* was delivered to state secretary

---

[290] RSHA circular decree, 14 August 1941, reproduced in a circular from Stapo office Düsseldorf of 5 September 1941, HStA Düsseldorf RW 18/30 fol. 51.

[291] "Anweisung der Schrifttumsabteilung vom 11.7.1941," in Ihde, *Handbuch der Reichsschrifttumskammer*, 202–3.

[292] Copy of the notification signed by Heydrich in BArch BDC/file "Schädliches und unerwünschtes Schrifttum" VI. See also the instructions on dealing with North American and British translated literature in *Vertrauliche Mitteilungen der Fachschaft Verlag* nos. 187–95, 5 January 1942, reproduced in Ihde, *Handbuch der Reichsschrifttumskammer*, 204.

[293] See circular from Stapo office Cologne to the Bonn office, the provincial authorities, the Cologne chief of police, and the Mayor of Bonn, 5 February 1942, HStA Düsseldorf RW 18/9 fol. 111.

[294] *Verzeichnis englischer und nordamerikanischer Schriftsteller*, Introduction. The two following quotations ibid.

Ludwig Grauert by the post office in Berlin's Schöneberg district, the Reich and Prussian Ministry of the Interior complained to the Reich Postal Minister, Paul von Eltz-Rübenach. In his response on 23 December 1935, von Eltz-Rübenach said it was "out of the question" that his personnel be expected to "carry out the general and local confiscation orders, adding up to thousands every day, that apply for every single post office," especially since they were "also expected to keep a watchful eye on all other politically suspect consignments in the postal service."[295]

A generalized surveillance of imports was only initiated with the Foreign Currency Office decree "on foreign currency applications by the sectors and individuals subject to the Reich Press Chamber, Reich Chamber of Literature, and Reich Film Chamber" issued on 2 July 1936.[296] Companies in the book trade now had to submit their applications for foreign currency to the Chamber for an "opinion." In March 1939, the Propaganda Ministry authorized the Economic Office of the German Book Trade to extend its monitoring activities from book exports to imports.[297] Starting in May, companies had to make a separate application for permission to import each individual foreign book title. Deliveries of an imported book were only permitted once approval had been received from the Economic Office and a "foreign currency use permit" had been issued by the Reich Paper Office. When the war started, book importers received a confidential circular regulating the procurement of books from Britain, France, and the United States.[298] This laid down that a company could only import books from these three countries if it had included in its import application a legally binding, signed declaration that the import was necessary "on the grounds of national policy, military considerations, or the war economy," and that the book to be imported could not

---

[295] BArch R 22/1507 fol. 1–5, here fol. 2/verso.
[296] Schrieber, *Das Recht der Reichskulturkammer*, vol. V, 3–4. The following quotation ibid.
[297] Confidential circular from the Economic Office re: regulation of book imports, 23 May 1939, BArch R 55/828 fol. 6. Excepted from the new arrangements were newspapers, periodicals, sheet music, graphic teaching aids, and other book-trade articles.
[298] Circular of 5 October 1939, BArch R 55/828 fol. 9.

"be obtained within Germany either commercially or through a library loan."

In October 1939, the Economic Office acquired a further instrument of censorship: the management of paper and binding materials for book publishers.[299] The introduction of paper rationing had been rejected at a May 1939 meeting of the publishers' *Fachschaft* in the Chamber, on the grounds that the book trade's use of paper accounted for only 2 percent of total paper use and that rationing would disproportionately affect the publishers of entertainment literature, and thus the less established authors.[300] However, following the outbreak of war, on 25 November 1939 an ordinance on paper-use statistics compelled book and art publishers to report the "precise and complete print run" for every new publication, reprint, or new edition, along with the "quantity and type of paper used," starting from 1940.[301] Although this data was supposed to be analyzed by the Börsenverein and the Chamber for political purposes,[302] paper rationing could not yet be deployed as a form of preventive censorship because the Chamber lacked the necessary personnel to work through the paper-use reports in detail, especially as they were only submitted after the books' publication. This began to change in February 1940, when Goebbels instructed publishers "for reasons of expediency" to "present books and brochures addressing political, especially foreign-policy, economic, and military issues to the relevant offices for inspection in good time."[303] The Ministry literature department further specified the ruling on 1 April: publishers were to report their planned program in the field of military writing, political and literary writing "to the extent that it touches upon the interests of the Wehrmacht or refers to the Wehrmacht in

---

[299] Circular from the Economic Office to members of the publishers' *Fachschaft*, 26 October 1939, BArch R 55/828 fol. 23. This informed publishers of the Economic Office's new responsibility, set out in Goebbels's order of 10 October 1939. Paper rationing was to apply to all publications within the *Fachschaft*'s remit.

[300] File note for the head of RSK Dept. II, 17 May 1939, re: meeting of the publishers' *Fachschaft* on 6 May 1939, BArch R 56 V/43 fol. 126–7.

[301] Ihde, *Handbuch der Reichsschrifttumskammer*, 146–7.

[302] On this and the following, see RSK manager Ihde, file note, 15 November 1940, BArch R 56 V/43 fol. 225.

[303] *Vertrauliche Mitteilungen der Fachschaft Verlag* no. 46, 1 February 1940, in Ihde, *Handbuch der Reichsschrifttumskammer*, 137.

its title," and foreign-policy and historical writing "to the extent that it is connected to the present war."[304] Accepted manuscripts or those already at proof stage had to be presented for inspection in two copies.

In addition to the works subject to the "planning report requirement," publishers had to apply to the Economic Office for an allocation of paper and binding materials for each title. Their applications were evaluated by the Economic Office in close cooperation with the Propaganda Ministry literature department. At the Börsenverein's annual meeting in spring 1941, the department's Rudolf Erckmann prepared publishers of fiction (fiction made up the largest share of book production in 1940, with 72 million of the total 250 million copies printed) for the introduction of a "systematic selection by value, based on considerations of literary policy."[305] In this process, the publishers would have to respect "that law of the primacy of politics over aesthetics" which "has been expressed and applied by us for many years as a principle of National Socialist cultural policy," but from which "tendencies to retreat" had become "clearly evident in several publications" over the preceding two years.

Paper allocation fully evolved into an instrument of preventive censorship with the invasion of the Soviet Union and the start of generalized raw materials rationing.[306] On Goebbels's orders, in the second half of 1941 the Economic Office set up a commission, chaired by Paul Hövel, to make individual decisions on each application for production submitted by publishers.[307] The sessions were attended by members of the Propaganda, Education, and Economics Ministries, the Chamber, the OKW, the PPK, Rosenberg's office, the NSDAP Party Chancellery, and the RSHA.[308]

---

[304] *Vertrauliche Mitteilungen der Fachschaft Verlag* no. 49, 27 March 1940, ibid.

[305] R. Erckmann, "Probleme und Aufgaben unseres Schrifttums. Rede vor der Arbeitsgemeinschaft schöngeistiger Verleger zur Buchhändler-Kantate in Leipzig 1941," *Die Bücherei* (1941), 308–16, here 310. The following quotation ibid. 311.

[306] See Hövel's confidential circular to the members of the publishers' *Fachschaft*, 2 August 1941, BArch R 56 V/43 fol. 53–6.

[307] Hövel, "Die Wirtschaftsstelle des deutschen Buchhandels," B13.

[308] This composition can be deduced from a report by the head of Rosenberg's literature office on a 5 July 1944 meeting at the RMVP literature department about *Meyers Lexikon*, which lists the representatives of the various agencies by name, BArch NS 8/249 fol. 58.

In order to handle the escalating battles over distribution with at least a degree of rationality and to give the procedure some external credibility, in fall 1941 the literature department worked out a grid for the "systematic distribution of paper according to principles of responsibility to the *Volk*."[309] It categorized as areas important to the war effort "contemporary political and defensive writing, research writing in all important scientific fields, the elevated literature of past and present, entertaining and relaxing literature in all domains, the German schoolbook in the key subjects, reference works for the occupations important to the war, children's and young people's writing." Ultimately, however, the granting of a paper allocation depended on the extent to which books to be published within these categories would exert "a beneficial influence on our *Volk*'s struggle for existence." The assessment of quality was now no longer based solely on the manuscript itself, but "on the total quantity of paper available." New titles deemed of military importance were prioritized over reprints, in order to demonstrate the continued productivity of German publishing even under wartime conditions. Likewise, "the internationally unique wealth and diversity of German book production" was to be sustained by imposing a standardized limit on print runs, which could then be repeated if necessary.[310]

Persuasive as these principles may have been in theory, they did not reflect the everyday practice of literary policymakers. In February 1942, Hövel complained openly—and in disagreement with his colleague Erckmann—of the unfortunate situation that "unbelievable quantities of paper are being used up for political propaganda material, and that the men who authorize this paper know from the start that absolutely no one in Germany—at most, abroad—will ever pick up these publications, let alone read them."[311] In contrast, he added, fiction came off badly in the paper allocation process, and was disadvantaged for other reasons as well: "The constant prying

---

[309] R. Erckmann, "Grundsätzliches zur Papierfrage," *Der Buchhändler im neuen Reich* 7 (1942), 171–5. The following quotations ibid.

[310] Erckmann mentioned novels, for which the standard print run was 5,000, and short texts consisting of fewer than six sheets, for which it was to be 10,000.

[311] Hövel's comment is reported in RSK manager Ihde (who attended the meeting) to Johst, 20 February 1942, BArch R 56 V/26 fol. 189/verso. On the following, see ibid.

into the poet's intellectual workshop" robbed "his work of its internal polarity; every element of tension is eliminated at the outset." Further problems arose from the considerable delays in production that were inevitably caused by the complex permissions procedure. From the manuscript's acceptance, to the application for paper and its approval and allocation, to the book's printing and appearance, the process took an average of eighteen months.[312] With the raw materials situation worsening rapidly from 1943, the Economic Office had to impose a freeze on paper applications on several occasions.[313] The use of wood-free and groundwood paper had already been controlled by the Economic Office since 1940; now the office also began to regulate the format of bindings with increasing severity.[314]

Hoping to speed up the production and delivery of approved books, on 1 April 1944 the committee on printing attached to Speer's Armaments Ministry introduced three degrees of priority for print jobs.[315] In parallel, the Propaganda Ministry literature department replaced the previous permissions procedure with a system of approval for "core production."[316] This meant that publishers no longer had to present separate applications for each book title, but were granted paper allocations on the basis of a Propaganda Ministry evaluation of their entire year's program. It was then up

---

[312] Sketch of the situation of the German book trade 1933–45, p. 2, StAL BV/829. See also the report "Zur Lage im Schrifttum," *Meldungen aus dem Reich* vol. 12, no. 349, 11 January 1943, 4652–63.

[313] "Mitteilungen der Wirtschaftsstelle vom 15.2.1943," *Bbl.* no. 43, 20 February 1943, 33; "Mitteilungen der Wirtschaftsstelle vom 29.3.1943," *Bbl.* no. 77, 3 April 1943, 58; "Mitteilungen der Wirtschaftsstelle vom 4.9.1943," *Bbl.* no. 139, 4 September 1943, 156; "Mitteilungen der Wirtschaftsstelle vom 27.12.1943," *Bbl.* no. 3, 12 January 1944, 3.

[314] Economic Office circular to members of the publishers' *Fachschaft*, 6 June 1940, BArch R 55/828 fol. 30–2; "Ergänzung 1 zur Anweisung Nr. 1 der Wirtschaftsstelle des deutschen Buchhandels vom 15. Juni 1942," *Bbl.* no. 163, 25 July 1942, 148; "Ergänzung 4," *Bbl.* no. 98, 1 June 1943, 99–100; instructions from the Economic Office on 13 December 1943 that publications were no longer to be produced with hard covers, *Bbl.* no. 180, 27 December 1943, 212.

[315] See *Bbl.* no. 22, 18 March 1944, 43.

[316] On the following, see the explanations by Erckmann and Haegert during a meeting between literature department staff and representatives of the publishers' *Fachschaft* on 9 March 1944, held at Verlag der DAF in Berlin and reported in a Börsenverein employee's file note dated 10 March 1944, here pp. 2–3, StAL BV/733.

to the publishers themselves to decide how to divide up the paper and binding materials they had been allocated. Certainly, the literature department still kept to its own list of priorities, which gave preference to "standard works (of the type produced by Eher)" and aimed to "curb the flood of so-called 'political' works." Scientific and technical literature remained a high-priority category, as did "quality" entertainment literature, which had been ruled especially important to the war effort by Hitler and Goebbels in fall 1943.[317]

A final attempt to increase efficiency was undertaken in early 1944, when Albert Speer, in his function as Reich Minister of Armaments, appointed the then head of the literature department, Wilhelm Haegert, as special commissioner for "Management of Books, Propaganda, and Printing."[318] This new planning body, funded by the Propaganda Ministry to the tune of half a million RM, was structured both by topic and by region.[319] There were production committees for the fields of "technology and raw materials," "forms," "scientific and scholarly books, textbooks, and maps," "books and brochures," "proof of need," and "publishers' and printers' bookbinding businesses." Haegert was in charge of seven provincial commissioners, eight area commissioners, and twenty-two district production commissioners. The bookbinding committee, which included book-trade representatives, was empowered to regulate production, instruct companies on book manufacture, make decisions on the deployment of labor, and carry out company audits.[320] Its authority extended to all businesses and operating divisions in the industrial and craft bookbinding sector, including public institutions and private ones under state control.

Despite these far-reaching powers, the bottlenecks on the book market became more and more difficult to cope with. On 8 March 1945, at a Book Trade Group meeting in Leipzig, Erckmann tried to rally his colleagues: "Today more than ever before, we must all

[317] Notification by Wilhelm Baur at a joint meeting of the Book Trade Group board and the Börsenverein council on 5 October 1943 in Leipzig, minutes p. 1, StAL BV/737.

[318] RMVP budget department to RMVP personnel department, 15 February 1944, BArch R 55/10 fol. 2.

[319] Budget department plan, 15 February 1944, ibid. fol. 8. On the following, see ibid. fol. 9–10.

[320] "Mitteilung über die Errichtung des gemeinsamen Produktionsausschusses," Bbl. no. 76, 21 October 1944, 190.

improvise."[321] Centralization, "that is, unconditional adherence to rulings received from above," would now no longer be enough to ensure the book trade's survival.

The Regimentation of Book Wholesaling

During the Weimar Republic, Koehler & Volckmar AG & Co. had reached an 80 percent market share of the commission business and book wholesaling. It participated in foreign trade (especially with the Soviet Union) and employed around 1,500 people in its printing and distribution divisions.[322] In the early 1930s, power within the company shifted toward the Volckmar group: Hans Volckmar (and from 1931 his adoptive son Theodor Volckmar-Frentzel) directed the company as a whole and by the mid–1930s held 75 percent of the partnership shares. But Hermann von Hase, the head of the Koehler & Amelang and K. F. Koehler houses, was also on the board. An NSDAP member since 1933, von Hase was eager to push the Volckmar family out of the company and thereby radically change its ownership structure. Koehler & Volckmar's case exemplifies the coincidence of personal interests with those of the state literary bureaucracy.

The F. Volckmar commission business was under surveillance by the Leipzig Gestapo as early as 1934 and 1935, on the orders of Political Police headquarters in Berlin.[323] The suspicion was that banned literature could be entering Germany from abroad via the Leipzig wholesale trade. Felix Gartmann, a director at Koehler & Volckmar and volunteer head of the book wholesalers' *Fachschaft* in the Chamber, refused to name the retailers to whom the relevant books had been delivered, pointing out that he was "not a policeman."[324] He also observed that there were anyway no regular

---

[321] Erckmann's comments at the meeting, called by the Book Trade Group to decide how to supply the book dealers fleeing from the eastern territories, are recorded in a file note of the discussion between Börsenverein representatives and the Leipzig commissioners on 9 March 1945, p. 3. StAL BV/733. The following quotation ibid.

[322] In the following, as well as the cited sources see Keiderling, *Unternehmer im Nationalsozialismus.*

[323] See file note by W. M. Schulz (Börsenverein), 1 April 1935, StAL BV/F 47.

[324] For this and the following quotation, see Schulz's file note of 25 August 1934, ibid.

checks on book shipments entering and leaving the country. This comment only served to confirm the state authorities' misgivings, but the conflict that would unnerve the whole German book trade in 1936 and 1937 did not come to a head until the first state censorship index was created. The secrecy of the list put wholesalers, strategically located between publishers and the retail book trade, in an impossible situation. Koehler & Volckmar's 1935/36 stock catalogue inevitably included numerous indexed book and periodical titles, so that the retail book trade—which took its cue from the catalogue of Germany's largest book distributor—could unwittingly order "harmful and undesirable" works. On the Chamber's instructions, the Gestapo therefore searched the premises of Koehler & Volckmar in Leipzig and Koch, Neff & Oettinger in Stuttgart on 14 March 1936.[325] Sixty-two copies of the 1935/36 stock catalogue were confiscated. Only after lengthy negotiations was the company able to retrieve at least those copies that had already been ordered by bookstores—on condition that in each copy "all the titles of undesirable books be blacked out."[326] The Gestapo destroyed the banned German publications that it confiscated during this raid and a subsequent one on 19 March, though works by foreign publishers could be either exported or returned to the originating publishing house.[327]

Hoping to avoid a repeat of such costly events, on 24 April 1936 Koehler & Volckmar's management sent the Chamber detailed "suggestions to prevent the distribution of undesirable literature."[328] These shifted the burden of responsibility from wholesalers onto publishers: in view of the "enormous number of orders placed with commission agents for publishers and their dispatch departments,

---

[325] Original documents on this procedure from the RSK, Gestapa, or the Stapo office Leipzig have not survived. The events are mentioned in a letter from the management of Koehler & Volckmar AG & Co. to the RSK president, attn. Undersecretary Dr. Heinz Wismann, 24 April 1936, p. 1, StAL Koehler & Volckmar/120.

[326] RSK president to Koehler & Volckmar AG & Co., 1 July 1936, StAL Koehler & Volckmar/120.

[327] See file notes by the company's legal advisor Herbert Schott, 29 April 1936, re: telephone call with Bischoff (RSK); 30 April 1936, re: meeting with Wismann; and 9 May 1936, re: further discussion with Bischoff; also Schott to Leipzig police headquarters, 8 July 1936, StAL Koehler & Volckmar/114.

[328] Koehler & Volckmar to RSK president, attn. Undersecretary Dr. Heinz Wismann, 24 April 1936, StAL Koehler & Volckmar/120.

and in view of the rapidity with which these must be passed on and exchanged in the Leipzig clearing system," it was impossible to check every order form for banned titles. Commission agents and wholesalers, the company suggested, should be informed by the publishers without delay of the titles whose further distribution had been prohibited by the state. If a publisher failed in his obligation to inform the book wholesale trade, or even continued to distribute banned literature through additional deliveries, "contact on the basis of trust between the Reich Chamber of Literature and the whole-salers' *Fachschaft*" was all that would be needed "to quickly detect such cases and take action against the publisher concerned." So that it could verify the publishers' information itself, Koehler & Volckmar suggested that "each of the most important generalist businesses in the book trade, especially book wholesalers, be issued with one copy of the Reich Chamber of Literature's confidential lists regarding undesirable literature, and all the necessary addenda or corrections to those lists." As for the 1936/37 stock catalogue, it was proposed that the Chamber be given access to the page proofs—"as long as the Reich Chamber of Literature is able to inspect each set of proofs within two days and send it back stamped as unobjectionable." In order to avoid delays in compiling the catalogue and ensure it was delivered "in good time for the Christmas rush," the company was even prepared "to bear the expenses that would accrue from enabling a Reich Chamber of Literature officer, with the necessary authorizations, to be present in Leipzig during the most important phases of the catalogue's production."

In the end, the Chamber was willing neither to give publishers sole responsibility for the removal of "undesirable" literature from the book market, nor to give distributors access to List 1 of Harmful and Undesirable Literature.[329] In July 1936, the wholesale division of Koehler & Volckmar therefore had to ask its "business associates in publishing" for help in drawing up the 1936/37 stock catalogue.[330] The publishers were asked to supply information on whether the company's distributors in Leipzig and Stuttgart were still holding "items from your esteemed house" that "a) have been confiscated

---

[329] Schott, file note of 29 April 1936, p. 2, StAL Koehler & Volckmar/114.
[330] Copy of the circular making this request, StAL Koehler & Volckmar/114.

on your premises or elsewhere, or that have been described to you or to a third party as 'undesirable' for distribution in Germany and thus prohibited from further distribution, b) or that you for any reason (e.g., on the grounds of content or of the person of the author, contributor, coeditor, etc.) no longer list in your own publicity or will no longer list in future, or will no longer have delivered yourselves or no longer have delivered within Germany." The purchasing and sales divisions were dependent on such information "due to a lack of detailed knowledge of the content, authors, contributors, etc.," and needed continuous updates on "undesirable literature." But, the company added, cooperation of this kind was also in the interests of publishers, since it would avoid the stock catalogue "accidentally, or due to a failure of notification on your part, including items that might occasion any objections or repercussions, especially given that the publisher bears full responsibility for the works he brings out."

The Chamber took Koehler & Volckmar up on its suggestion to have the proofs of the 1936/37 stock catalogue checked for banned literature. However, in his August 1937 letter to this effect, Chamber vice-president Heinz Wismann insisted that the checks must be done in Berlin. Starting from 7 September 1936, four proof sheets of sixty-four pages each were to be sent per day from Leipzig to a reader in the SD Main Office, who would send the corrected proofs back to Leipzig the following day. Wismann set aside three employees to carry out this work, and Koehler & Volckmar were to pay for their services at 0.50 RM per page corrected.[331] The company's management agreed to bear these costs—"on a trial basis and without prejudicing the arrangements for subsequent years"[332]—but Wismann rigorously rejected its request to have the examination carried out in the presence of a Koehler & Volckmar representative.[333] For the company, this would have had the advantage of providing

---

[331] In his letter of 21 August 1936 (p. 1, StAL Koehler & Volckmar/114), Wismann required the proofs to be sent to Herr Herbert Pfeiffer at "Berlin SW 68, Wilhelmstr. 102," in other words the SD Main Office building. In the Security Police Main Office schedule of responsibilities dated 31 July 1936, *SS-Oberscharführer* Pfeiffer is named as the relevant expert in Six's Central Department I 3, BArch R 58/840 fol. 113.
[332] Wismann to Koehler & Volckmar, 21 August 1936, pp. 1–2. StAL Koehler & Volckmar/114.
[333] Wismann to Koehler & Volckmar, 28 August 1936, ibid.

immediate information on any deletion from the proofs, so that deliveries of the item could be halted or else a reasoned objection to the ban submitted. Wismann considered "instruction and advice" of this kind quite inappropriate, because Koehler & Volckmar had "publicly demonstrated, through the composition of last year's catalogue, for which you bear sole responsibility," that it was "not capable of undertaking the revision according to the only applicable criteria." Refusing any further discussion on the practicability of his proposed procedure, Wismann decreed "that your first consignment of proofs shall arrive at the address named on 1 September."

The Chamber's policy of intimidation showed its first results in the case of Nobel Prize-winner Thomas Mann. Unlike the works of his brother Heinrich Mann and his children Erika and Klaus, at first Thomas Mann's books appeared in Germany without hindrance.[334] The Bavarian Political Police had banned the novels *Der Zauberberg* (*The Magic Mountain*) and *Königliche Hoheit* (*Royal Highness*), along with some of Mann's speeches and essays, in 1934,[335] but it was only after Mann was deprived of his citizenship on 2 December 1936 that the Chamber requested the Gestapa to confiscate all copies of his work "still present on Reich territory."[336] On the morning this order went out, a Koehler & Volckmar employee asked the Chamber for information on how to deal with Thomas Mann and another writer deprived of citizenship, Dietrich von Hildebrand.[337] Thinking ahead, the company had "naturally called an immediate halt to all deliveries for Leipzig and Stuttgart." But the books of the two expatriated authors still appeared in the stock catalogue of 1936/37, and Koehler & Volckmar was instructed to send a circular to all recipients of the catalogue within Germany, telling them that the works of Thomas Mann and von Hildebrand "will no longer be delivered."[338] A notice of this fact was also to be published in the *Börsenblatt*. Purchasers

---

[334] As indicated in RSK to Dresden police headquarters, political department, 23 August 1935, BArch BDC/RSK/Mann, T.

[335] *Verzeichnis der polizeilich beschlagnahmten ... Druckschriften*, 154.

[336] RSK to Gestapa, 4 December 1936, BArch BDC/RSK/Mann, T.

[337] Telephone call from Dr. Sickel (Koehler & Volckmar), recorded in a file note by Chamber section head Menz, 4 December 1936, ibid. The following quotations ibid.

[338] This instruction, issued by Menz after consulting with RSK manager Heinl, picked up on one of the three suggestions that Koehler & Volckmar itself had made for solving the "problem"; ibid. point 2.

abroad were to be informed of the delivery's cancellation "without naming reasons."[339]

But such gestures of subservience by Koehler & Volckmar soon ceased to satisfy the Chamber. On 23 January 1937, Johst excluded its director, Theodor Volckmar-Frentzel, from the Chamber on the grounds of insufficient "political reliability."[340] The decision was backed up with five "facts": in 1933 Volckmar-Frentzel had prevented the publication by Koehler of an anti-religious exposé supported by Rosenberg; the 1935/36 Koehler & Volckmar stock catalogue had included a very large number of books that had "long since" been banned; until 1935 Volckmar-Frentzel had refused to hang Nazi flags from the Koehler building in Leipzig on "the appropriate occasions"; he had stopped his employees from taking up unpaid roles in the German book trade's "professional representation"; and Koehler & Volckmar's contributions to the Adolf Hitler Fund of German Trade and Industry and the Winter Relief campaign had been utterly inadequate in view of the company's capital and profits—a detailed list of the donations was enclosed. The same day, Hans Volckmar was also barred from further activity as the chair of the company's supervisory board, on the basis of his marriage to a "half Jew."[341]

The aim was to attack the company's nerve center by eliminating its top management. When Gartmann asked the Book Trade Group's office for information on the further handling of the Volckmar-Frentzel and Volckmar cases on 27 January 1937, Wilhelm Baur advised him to recommend that the two men make urgent efforts to sell their shares in the company.[342] Gartmann pointed out that there was no legal basis for such a suggestion, to which Baur responded that "a legal foundation can easily be created."[343] As president of the Börsenverein and a close associate of Amann's, Baur wanted "the current legislation of the Press Chamber, according to which capital

---

[339] Handwritten note by Menz, ibid.
[340] Original notification in StAL Koehler & Volckmar/122. The following quotations ibid.
[341] StAL Koehler & Volckmar/121. Hans Volckmar's removal from the company's management had already been urged by Wilhelm Baur at a meeting with Gartmann on 21 December 1936. Gartmann, file note, 22 December 1936, p. 2, StAL Koehler & Volckmar/115.
[342] Gartmann informed the Koehler & Volckmar management of this recommendation the very same day. See file note of 27 January 1937, StAL Koehler & Volckmar/121.
[343] Gartmann's paraphrase of Baur's comments, ibid. The following quotations ibid.

must be in purely Aryan hands, to be adopted by the Chamber of Literature as well, and furthermore that in future book-trade businesses must only be owned by people who fulfill the requirements of the Reich Chamber of Culture Law." If Volckmar-Frentzel and Volckmar did not follow his advice to sell their shares at once, Baur implied, there were always "other instruments" that could be applied: making public their exclusion from the Chamber, which would amount to expulsion from the book trade, or installing a proxy. Baur closed by drawing Gartmann's attention to the fact that Hermann von Hase, the head of Koehler & Amelang and K. F. Koehler and the Chamber's key witness against Volckmar-Frentzel, enjoyed "the protection of the Reichsführer SS."

Despite this browbeating, on 17 February 1937 Volckmar-Frentzel sent the Chamber of Culture a detailed letter of complaint against his exclusion.[344] The subsequent arguments of his lawyer, Karl-Friedrich Schrieber, highlighted not only the incompatibility of the Chamber of Literature's decision with Chamber of Culture legislation,[345] but also the shortcomings in the existing implementation of censorship policy. For example, it was easy for Schrieber to demonstrate that although List 1 of Harmful and Undesirable Literature had been announced by the Chamber of Literature president in April 1935, it had not been published until much later, so that it could not have been taken into account during the compilation of the 1935/36 stock catalogue.[346] In addition, several publishers had continued delivering publications included in the index.[347] At the end of his carefully argued justification, Schrieber—a clever choice by Koehler & Volckmar, since he was also acting as a legal advisor for the Chamber of Culture at the time—observed that the decision against Volckmar-Frentzel had been taken "on the grounds of a very general rejection of his person for political or ideological reasons."[348] These reasons had not been named in the decision of 23 January 1937,

---

[344] BArch BDC/fiche RK Z 0003 fol. 1066–92.

[345] See the supplementary points made by Schrieber regarding Volckmar-Frentzel's complaint to the RKK president, 29 April 1937, StAL Koehler & Volckmar/120.

[346] Schrieber's comments ibid. pp. 7–8.

[347] Examples given ibid. pp. 9–15.

[348] Ibid. p. 17. Schrieber had gained this impression from a 13 April 1937 discussion between Theodor Volckmar-Frentzel and Wismann that he attended. See Schrieber's file note on this meeting, made on 16 April 1937, p. 4, in StAL Koehler & Volckmar/119.

and for as long as this remained the case they must, "according to all the principles of law that apply to every proceeding, be disregarded."[349]

But Wismann (who was, alongside Baur, the driving force behind the attacks on Koehler & Volckmar) refused to retreat from his long-term objective of completely subjugating the wholesale book trade. On 2 March 1937, he informed Gartmann and a Koehler & Volckmar representative of the "Chamber's wish" that "someone who is especially well-informed regarding the Chamber's cultural-policy objectives examine the particular circumstances of the wholesale book trade and determine how far wholesaling may be involved more closely in the fulfillment of the cultural tasks devolving upon the book trade as a whole."[350] When Gartmann had agreed to this plan and held out the prospect of support from businesses in the wholesale trade, on 6 March Wismann gave his trusted colleague Gunther Haupt a "special commission" valid through 31 March (later extended to June that year).[351] Haupt, formerly the Chamber's manager, received the following instructions: "A permanent stop must be put to processes like those that have repeatedly occurred in the compilation of stock catalogues, the import and export of undesirable books, the heedlessly capitalist treatment of persons and companies belonging to German minorities abroad, and the often purely business-oriented advertising by book wholesalers."[352]

The results of Haupt's investigations were presented in monthly reports and, in June 1937, in a lengthy "memorandum on the possible reorganization of the wholesalers Koehler & Volckmar, Leipzig, and Koch, Neff & Oetinger, Stuttgart."[353] This reiterated the political

---

[349] Schrieber's written complaint of 29 April 1937, p. 18, StAL Koehler & Volckmar/120.
[350] Gartmann to Wismann, 3 March 1937, rendering the content of their meeting in Leipzig the previous day, StAL Koehler & Volckmar/119.
[351] Wismann to Haupt, 6 March 1937, BArch BDC/RSK/Haupt, G.
[352] Ibid. In Gartmann's notes on the meeting with Wismann, taken on 3 March 1937, StAL Koehler & Volckmar/119, a different and more sober note is struck: the Chamber president's representative is to inspect commission agents and wholesalers in Leipzig with regard to "questions of the prevention of the distribution of undesirable literature and, in connection with this, questions of deliveries to foreign publishers, the importation of foreign writing, parcel post through the Leipzig hub, and the advertising activities of wholesalers including work on the stock catalogues."
[353] Monthly reports for March and April 1937 in BArch BDC/RSK/Haupt, G.; memorandum, ibid.

unreliability of the two wholesalers when it came to "cleansing" the book market of "harmful and undesirable literature," criticized the "monopoly position" that had resulted from skillful concentration and interpenetration "in the setting of an exclusive interest in capitalist considerations and private interests," and identified in the two firms' business practices a general, even deliberate, endangering of the "thrust and measures of official and semi-official book promotion policy." Haupt concluded that responsibility must be passed immediately "on the one hand to the state, via the Reich Chamber of Literature authorized to carry out its requirements, and on the other to the entirety of the book trade, which depends upon a wholesale sector that is reliable in every way." Book wholesaling must "become a seamlessly functioning, excellent instrument of National Socialist cultural policy and of the German book trade, a sector that, in terms of both its cultural policy and its financial conduct, transparently and irreproachably serves not the interests of an ambitious group of proprietors, but solely the book and thus the nation." Haupt saw the key to realizing his demands in the establishment of a cooperative, which would act as the commercial framework for the Koehler & Volckmar distributors and in which "every German bookseller" should have a share. The manager of this cooperative would, "as manager of all wholesale operations, report to the president of the Reich Chamber of Literature regarding the cultural-policy aspects of the wholesalers' work, and to the cooperative regarding its commercial and organizational aspects."

However, this plan was not carried out, Wismann having fallen from grace in late June 1937. The mission of his "special commissioner" was also terminated on 1 August, not least because Haupt had raised the hackles of wholesaling companies through his unprofessional demeanor.[354] Haupt clearly conflated his public mandate with the pursuit of his own personal interests in the case of the Leipzig-based commission agents Carl Friedrich Fleischer, the other highly regarded and economically powerful German wholesaler in

---

[354] See the six-page "Survey of the activities of Dr. Haupt" drawn up on 21 May 1937 by Koehler & Volckmar's legal advisor Schott, StAL Koehler & Volckmar/119; RSK Dept. III file note of 21 July 1937 re: the activities of Haupt respecting Carl Fr. Fleischer in Leipzig; RSK manager Ihde to RKK president re: the personnel matter of Dr. Gunther Haupt, 14 September 1937, all BArch BDC/RSK/Haupt, G.

the Leipzig book-trade hub alongside Koehler & Volckmar,[355] for when Wismann excluded the long-time director of Carl Friedrich Fleischer, Otto Wilhelm Klemm, from the Chamber due to alleged deficiencies in political "reliability," the "special commissioner" quickly offered his services as Klemm's successor. Even if Haupt's attempt at a shameless exploitation of his powerful position ultimately failed, Klemm still had to wait until October 1939 for readmission into the Chamber. Despite repeated applications, and support from Schulte Strathaus in the Deputy Führer's staff, it was consistently refused by both the Chamber and the Ministry's literature department. The procedure dragged on for more than two years, and was finally resolved by a decision from Hitler, whom Klemm had petitioned directly in an attempt to rescue his rights and reputation.

In the case of Koehler & Volckmar, the Chamber's endeavors to eliminate the powerful group by political means continued after the departure of Wismann and Haupt. On 2 November 1937, Chamber president Johst asked his colleague Amann for support in the matter.[356] Johst had learned from Himmler's personal staff that Volckmar-Frentzel had allegedly "sabotaged" the Press Chamber's order for anonymous capital companies to be transformed into partnerships with personal liability. As a result, the president of the Press Chamber was to exclude Volckmar-Frentzel on the grounds that his fundamentally anti–National Socialist attitude had "also prompted him to neglect an order by the Reich Press Chamber." However, the head of the Propaganda Ministry's legal department, Hans Schmidt-Leonhardt, was not prepared to accept such retrospectively constructed evidence, and reversed Volckmar-Frentzel's exclusion on 6 December 1937.[357] Karl Heinz Hederich, by now head of the literature department, went on to criticize the Chamber of Literature harshly for its careless record-keeping, its unsatisfactory substantive justification for the exclusion, and the "dictatorial" impression that the officials involved had created through the style

---

[355] On the following, see Dahm, "Ein Kampf um Familienerbe und Lebenswerk," which draws on the extensive documentation in BArch BDC/RSK/Klemm, O.W. and the company files BV/F 10 983 in StAL.

[356] Johst to Amann, 2 November 1937, p. 1, StAL Koehler & Volckmar/123. The following quotations ibid.

[357] BArch BDC/fiche RK Z 0003 fol. 1254–5.

and tone of their correspondence with the company.[358] Even so, Hederich too regarded the available evidence as indicating "an overall ideological picture of a group and its management" that made the Chamber "appear justified in demanding that a National Socialist leadership be installed in this most important publishing corporation, or that a solution be found in full accordance with the needs of the Party and the state." An intervention by Himmler, who had been supporting both Johst and von Hase behind the scenes since fall 1936,[359] led to a "settlement" in September 1938. This was to the financial disadvantage of Koehler & Volckmar in that it gave von Hase the capital he needed to create a separate business from his shares. Yet despite the massive political interference, in the end von Hase failed to achieve his personal objectives while remaining within the group; neither did several highly influential functionaries in the Nazi state literary bureaucracy succeed in fully eliminating the most respected—and economically most important—corporation of the German wholesale book trade.

Wilhelm Baur did not accept this outcome without a fight. Starting in fall 1937, he pursued the plan of establishing a "competitor and combat company"[360] intended to eradicate Koehler & Volckmar. Once again Baur turned his position as president of the Börsenverein to good account: on his instructions, the Börsenverein put 55,000 RM into the new limited commercial partnership Lühe & Co. KG, founded on 23 October 1939 in the Berlin offices of the Party publisher Eher with a share capital of 100,000 RM[361]—even though the Börsenverein's statutes expressly ruled out any commercial participation and its members had not been informed of the share purchase. Baur also passed customers to Lühe & Co.'s managing director, Karl Seeliger. Lühe & Co.'s principals were Eher and the Eher subsidiaries.[362] In agreement with Eberhard Heffe of the Labor Front publishing operations, the Zentrale der Frontbuchhandlungen initially

---

[358] Ibid. fol. 1246–50.

[359] See Chamber section head Bischoff to Gestapa, 8 October 1936, ibid. fol. 1388.

[360] A "Konkurrenz- und Kampfunternehmen" is the description given in the instructions for Nieland, the lawyer responsible for liquidating Lühe & Co., on 9 July 1945, p. 1, StAL BV/1192.

[361] See the deeds in StAL BV/861–63.

[362] See overview dated 21 June 1945, StAL BV/1192.

ordered exclusively from Lühe & Co.[363] The Propaganda Ministry, the Foreign Office, the Reichsführer SS, and various NSDAP offices increasingly awarded large contracts to the new Party enterprise.[364] By 1942, its annual turnover had risen to 10 million RM.[365] Yet the "model National Socialist company"[366] that Baur had aimed to create turned out to be incapable of transacting its business in an orderly manner. The auditor found serious fault with Lühe & Co.'s financial conduct. Unable to access reliable information on its assets and earnings at 31 March 1941, in August 1942 he refused to approve the company's accounts.[367]

On 1 July 1941, Langen-Müller Verlag acquired a 5,000 RM share in Lühe & Co.,[368] and in July 1942 the Börsenverein's contribution was boosted to 150,000 RM, while Eher paid in 150,000 RM, bringing the total capital to 450,000 RM.[369] Well aware of the scarcity of books that would shortly arise, in October 1941 Baur gave the managing director of Lühe & Co. an insider tip, advising him to stockpile "as much as you can."[370] The resulting large purchases, along with a high level of receivables, forced Seeliger to ask for the company's bank credit to be increased several times. However, Heffe appears to have been dissatisfied with Lühe & Co.'s services to the Zentrale der Frontbuchhandlungen, and from September 1942 he began to award half of his lucrative contracts to Koehler & Volckmar.[371] With the complete destruction of Lühe & Co.'s book warehouse during the bombing of Leipzig on 4 December 1943, the company entered a desperate financial crisis. Its turnover had fallen drastically and its capital was eaten away, so that suppliers of books on commission,

---

[363] Koehler & Volckmar to the DAF trustee, 11 July 1945, StAL BV/1861.
[364] Seeliger to Baur, 13 October 1941, StAL BV/861–63; certificate from the Book Trade Group for Lühe & Co., 25 January 1945, StAL BV/F 5918.
[365] Volckmar-Frentzel to Dr. Hess, 11 July 1945, StAL BV/1192.
[366] Anton Hiersemann, Börsenverein treasurer, to Wilhelm Baur, 6 May 1944, StAL BV/861–63.
[367] Auditor Gottfried Bürger, Leipzig, to Börsenverein management, 28 August 1942, StAL BV/861–63.
[368] Dr. Hess to Wilhelm Baur, 7 September 1940, ibid.
[369] Deeds dated 6 July 1942, ibid.
[370] As indicated in Wilhelm Baur to Dr. Hess, 7 October 1941, ibid.
[371] See Koehler & Volckmar to Heffe, 15 September 1942, StAL BV/1861.

including the NSDAP's Eher, faced long delays for payment.[372] Baur resolved to top up the capital once more, but this time even he was unable to persuade the Börsenverein manager and treasurer to commit yet more funds to the company.[373] In April 1944 the necessary capital had to be acquired through Herold Verlagsanstalt GmbH, an Eher subsidiary,[374] and even that was not enough. In August Baur had to help the company out yet again, with a 200,000 RM loan channeled through Herold Verlagsanstalt, and in October he had to field Foreign Office complaints about unfulfilled orders from Lühe & Co.[375] In other words, the second attempt to oust Koehler & Volckmar and replace it with a Nazi-controlled monopoly—this time backed by huge financial and political resources—had come to nothing.

The Regimentation of Book Retailing

In contrast to the wholesale book trade, marked by the predominance of one large corporation and a relatively small number of medium-sized businesses, the multitude and diversity of the companies involved in selling books to the public hampered the literary bureaucracy in its attempts to target them efficiently. For these booksellers, admission to the Chamber was carried out through *Gau* representatives and *Gau* sector advisors, who, in turn, based their decisions on evaluations by the Chamber's local representatives and sector advisors. Surviving reports from the *Gau* of Greater Berlin for 1936 cite economic considerations, alleged deficiencies in professional expertise, or the sale of inferior literature as grounds to reject applications.[376] Only one rejection was politi-

---

[372] Wilhelm Baur to Dr. Hess, 4 April 1944, StAL BV/861–63.

[373] See Hiersemann to Dr. Hess, 18 April 1944; Hess to Wilhelm Baur, 20 April; Baur to Hiersemann, 28 April; and Hiersemann to Baur, 6 May, all ibid.

[374] Eher's share in Lühe & Co. was also transferred to Herold Verlagsanstalt. See Wilhelm Baur to Börsenverein, 28 April 1944, ibid.

[375] See Wilhelm Baur (using Herold Verlagsanstalt letterhead) to Börsenverein, 24 August 1944, StAL BV/861–63; and Baur to Six, 16 October 1944, BV/F 5918.

[376] Reports on the Chamber applications of the Schöneberg lending library and bookstore Wolf. G. Liebrecht, 22 May 1936, the W. Schlawitz lending library, 28 May 1936, the Richard Schubert stationery store, 22 May 1936, and the Artur Bonss secondhand bookstore, 20 May 1936, LA Berlin Rep. 243, Acc. 1814/28.

cally motivated in the narrower sense: the owner of a bookstore in the Schöneberg district was sent to a concentration camp "because while selling scientific literature and National Socialist writing, he also sold banned and undesirable writing."[377] An excessive orientation on profit was considered reprehensible as well. The district representative characterized one bookseller in the fashionable west of Berlin as the "prototype of a commercial operator, who is so dangerous for the German book trade because he regards the book only as a commodity, not as a spiritual product."[378] In contrast, the application of a Charlottenburg bookseller was supported despite certain concerns about her professional aptitude, because "thanks to her overall attitude and confidence-inspiring stance, in her small domain she works in harmony with the book policy of the Third Reich."[379] Another applicant from the west of the city was praised as an "assiduous young bookseller" because he had "Aryanized" a once-Jewish business.[380]

From 1935, efforts to eliminate "non-Aryans" working in retail and secondhand bookstores were intensified. Just as in the publishing companies, lower-level employees were successively excluded from the Chamber on rigid deadlines, whereas for the proprietors, managing directors, and authorized signatories of the 133 companies involved, the Chamber examined each case individually and with occasional latitude.[381] Thus, the Leipzig bookstore Josef Saul Ardel was able to continue business until 1938 because it was earning foreign currency through exports and still had "considerable accounts outstanding" from its book sales to Greece and Bulgaria.[382] Wilhelm Salomon, too, benefited from the "dominant role" of his mail-order export operation Francken & Lang in Nuremberg, which earned foreign currency of almost 100,000 RM a year. Artur Arndtheim, managing director of the Erfurt department store Kaufhaus Römischer Kaiser, had been forced

---

[377] Greater Berlin *Gauobmann* to BRB head office in Leipzig, 27 May 1936, ibid.

[378] Report on Hermann Sack, 25 May 1936, ibid.

[379] Report of Greater Berlin *Gau* to the BRB re: the examination of Clara von Flemming's suitability, 27 May 1936, ibid.

[380] Report on Max Perl's application for admission, 25 May 1936, ibid.

[381] On the following, see the Chamber's list dated 15 March 1937, pp. 1–28, BArch R 55/21 300; also Schroeder, "Die 'Arisierung' jüdischer Antiquariate."

[382] Explanatory note in list dated 15 March 1937, p. 1; also StAL BV/F 12 405.

to sell out and banned from buying new books of any kind as early as March 1936. But although in December that year the Book Trade Group *Gau* representative responsible for Arndtheim showed he had been making "impermissible book sales," in March 1937 the Chamber granted him one more extension. Sixty-five-year-old Albert Carlebach of Heidelberg, pointing out that his "secondhand and antiquarian bookstore specialized in books on Baden and the Palatinate," asked for permission to carry on his business until the end of his life. Sixty-three-year-old Albert Cohn also put it to the Chamber—in writing, then in person on 5 March 1937, accompanied by the attorney of his local section of the Central Association of German Citizens of Jewish Faith—that if he sold Janus, his Leipzig bookstore with a specialized secondhand business in science writing, he "would have no means of subsistence."

This outcome threatened several other elderly booksellers as well. Richard Frank, seventy-one, asked to be "allowed to remain active in the sphere of the RSK for a few more years" so that he would be able to draw his pension. On 25 February 1937, 77-year-old Max Harrwitz applied to the Chamber "to be treated with humanity." He planned "to gradually dissolve his old antiquarian business (the literature of past centuries, which has been supplied to libraries and museums, e.g. the British Museum in London)," saying that neither a career change nor emigration was open to him. Sixty-eight-year-old Albert Jolowicz reminded the Chamber that he had sold books for fifty years and was now "very ailing." His bookstore in Berlin specialized in supplying books on Polish themes to German state libraries and authorities. He asked for an extension of the deadline, since liquidating his company, which had celebrated its 75th anniversary in October 1937, "with so many long-standing obligations ... could not possibly be carried out in three months; it would take several years." Franz Seeliger asked for a three- to six-month extension "in consideration of his age (seventy-four years)" and of the difficulties in selling his Berlin bookstore and secondhand dealership. Otto Rothschild, the manager of the Altmann secondhand and antiquarian bookstore in Berlin, emphasized in his February 1937 submission that he was "part of a family that has resided in Germany for more than four generations," and therefore "felt closely connected to German culture and German cultural work." He asked the Chamber to reverse its decision to exclude him.

Otto Landsberg managed a book and art dealership with a secondhand section in Oldenburg, together with his father Moritz and his brother Walter. On 30 October 1935 the League of Reich German Booksellers (BRB) notified him that "in the course of the elimination of non-Aryan persons from bookselling operations ... your resignation from the League ... will be necessary in the near future."[383] The BRB letter added that he would be given "the opportunity to schedule this resignation yourself," and requested information by 15 November "respecting the earliest date by which you can carry out the sale of your company to a suitable Aryan personage or liquidate the business." Raising the pressure, on 31 December Chamber vice-president Wismann declared himself "regrettably obliged" to exclude Moritz Landsberg, since "you are of Jewish descent" and therefore "not suited to activity in a culture-related occupation." The three proprietors appealed against this exclusion on 16 January 1936. They cited their many years of professional experience: Moritz Landsberg had worked in the bookstore (founded by his own father in 1836) since 1877; his sons Otto and Walter since 1920. Nor, they argued, could their "reliability be doubted," especially given that they had been accepted as Chamber of Culture members on 15 July 1934. The exclusion would have "severe economic consequences" for the three families involved, "because the alternative job opportunities are extremely limited due to age, professional training, and the general difficulties of starting a new business." The appeal did achieve a deferral, which lasted for twelve months thanks to the international attention attracted by the 1936 Olympics. On 24 December, Wilhelm Baur set Moritz Landsberg a final deadline of 31 March 1937 to sell or liquidate his company. The proprietors tried to buy further time by submitting another appeal on 1 February 1937, but their negotiating position was weakening fast because buyers were proving hard to find, and Bischoff, the Chamber official responsible for "Aryanizing" the book trade, was pushing for a swift resolution of the "case." In view of their 1936 turnover of 21,000 RM and stock worth 19,500 RM, the Landsbergs set a purchasing price of 25,000 RM. Bischoff

---

[383] On this and the following, see BArch BDC/RK/fiche C 0003 fol. 2138–252.

assumed that "Landsberg is trying to obstruct the sale in advance by making untenably high demands," and in late May 1937 had the three owners summoned to the chief of police in Oldenburg to justify their statements. Moritz, Otto, and Walter Landsberg realized their situation was hopeless, and on 11 July signed a contract with the Bremen art dealer Heinrich F. Jördens at a price far below their original expectations. Of the purchasing price of 7,100 RM, the new "Aryan" owner paid only 500 RM in cash. He took on 5,661.03 RM of the bookstore's liabilities. The outstanding amount was to be paid in monthly installments of 100 RM starting on 1 January 1938.

In the end, the "Aryanization" or liquidation of businesses could be forestalled neither by foreign currency earnings nor by the supply of specialized literature, neither by long-standing tradition, nationalist sentiment, nor social hardship. When the German–Polish Treaty's minority protection ran out in July 1937, Ludwig Freund in Beuthen, Carola Graetzer in Gleiwitz, and Fritz Ring in Berlin also had to sell their bookstores.[384] Ursula Wertheim's "special permission" lapsed upon the Wertheim department store group's "Aryanization" that same year—since its assets were transferred from her husband Georg Wertheim in 1934, she had been the official proprietor of Berlin's biggest department store, with a book department in the prestigious Leipziger Strasse branch.[385]

From July 1937, the "Jewish book distributors" still permitted by Hinkel's *Sonderreferat* were only allowed to serve "a Jewish clientele."[386] This included "all Jews on German Reich territory as defined by the Nuremberg Laws and their executive orders; all companies of the Jewish press and the Jewish book trade permitted by the Special Commissioner; the associations organized within the Jewish Cultural League; synagogue congregations; Jewish schools; Jewish houses of learning; the Jewish associations

---

[384] Chamber's list dated 15 March 1937, pp. 8, 10, 24, BArch R 55/21 300. On the sale of Ring's profitable "Buchhandlung am Zoo," see Dahm, *Das jüdische Buch*, 99–100.

[385] See list of "special permissions" issued by the Book Trade Group, *Fachschaft* 1–3, dated 15 March 1937, p. 2 (no. 16), BArch R 55/21 300. On the "Aryanization" of Wertheim, see Fischer and Ladwig-Winters, *Die Wertheims*, 263–335.

[386] First circular from the *Sonderreferat* to the persons and companies of the "Jewish book trade," 30 July 1937, DB-Archiv no. 507/5–509/1. On the following, see ibid. pp. 2–4.

and organizations on German Reich territory authorized by the Reich Ministry of the Interior; Jews of non-German nationality." This section of the population was now only permitted to buy "Jewish literature." For other "literature of general Jewish interest, but by non-Jewish authors," for "works by Jewish authors published by Aryan companies," and for the "importation of Jewish literature from abroad," a permit from the Special Commissioner had to be presented in each separate case. The forty-eight "Jewish book distributors" that still existed in August 1938 were closed in the wake of the pogrom of 9–10 November, with effect until the end of that year. Only those booksellers classified as "quarter Jews" or "Jewish by marriage" now remained in the Chamber, on the basis of "special permission."

Alongside the Jewish-owned retail bookstores and secondhand or antiquarian dealerships, the Chamber's suspicion fell chiefly on door-to-door and mail-order bookselling, which took place not in fixed sales spaces but through representatives or advertising. Through its Advisory Office for Door-To-Door Book Sales, set up in April 1934, the Chamber was able to access precise information on the business practices of this sector. On 22 October 1936 a freeze on new business start-ups in the door-to-door and mail-order book trade was decreed,[387] in the hope of reducing the companies in this domain to a manageable number. The Chamber also regarded subsidiary and small-scale bookselling operations as problematic. In February 1934, the owners of such businesses, whose turnover from book sales accounted for up to 50 percent of their total annual turnover to a maximum of 10,000 RM, were initially admitted to the Chamber via their membership of the Börsenverein.[388] When the Börsenverein was separated out from the Chamber again, the BRB set up a "muster book of subsidiary and small-scale operations."[389] An application to the BRB for inclusion in this register was obligatory for each bookselling outlet run as an adjunct to a retail company if

---

[387] Schrieber, *Das Recht der Reichskulturkammer*, vol. V, 83.
[388] "Bekanntmachung über die Mitgliedschaft in der Reichsschrifttumskammer vom 20.2.1934," *Bbl.* no. 194, 17 March 1934, 241–2.
[389] See "Anordnung zum Schutze der Bezeichnung 'Buchhandlung' und 'Buchhändler,'" 6 February 1935, in Schrieber, *Das Recht der Reichskulturkammer*, vol. II, 88.

turnover from book sales made up at least 10 percent of its total turnover.[390]

Despite these regulatory efforts, it was by no means certain that book distributors were actually complying with the Chamber's orders in their daily work. In April 1936, *Das Schwarze Korps* complained that "even today, ill will can still be found in large segments of the German book trade, far more among retailers and lending library operators than among publishers."[391] The standard works by Hitler and Rosenberg prominently displayed in bookstore windows were "often only the political fig leaves with which these booksellers try to cover the stark nakedness of their reactionary attitudes." Piled up behind the few tomes by leading figures of the Nazi state, there were allegedly "all too often, unfortunately, the products of a liberalistic or one-sidedly Christian thinking that some German publishers still stoop to publish." The article suggested that the bookstores in the shopping boulevards of western Berlin and the publishing hub of Leipzig, especially their secondhand departments, be inspected to find out how many "harmful and undesirable" books indexed by the Chamber they were still offering for sale. This polemic was quickly followed by a series of raids on Leipzig bookstores and secondhand dealerships in spring 1936.[392] During the searches, the Gestapo "brought to light large amounts of banned literature." In the district of Königsberg, too, the Gestapo confiscated around 3,000 books in sixty-three bookstores during May 1936.

The results of these two campaigns, intended as spot checks, triggered a "thorough overhaul of all bookselling businesses." Between October 1936 and June 1937, across the Reich "swift and unanticipated" raids were made on around 5,000 bookstores, secondhand booksellers, and commercial lending libraries. In the Düsseldorf district, the local Stapo office worked with the SD's western Germany section to carry out thirty-eight search campaigns

---

[390] Schrieber, *Das Recht der Reichskulturkammer*, vol. V, 77–9.

[391] "Reaktionärer Buchhandel," *Das Schwarze Korps* 2 (1936), no. 17, 23 April 1936, 2. The following quotations ibid.

[392] On this and the following, see the general report on the searches of bookselling businesses carried out between October 1936 and June 1937, BArch R 56 V/67 fol. 310–15.

between September and November 1936,[393] raiding 898 businesses and confiscating no fewer than 37,040 volumes. In his closing report, the head of the Düsseldorf Stapo was able to inform the Gestapa that in general the booksellers had been "gratified" to have "this kind of literature removed from their warehouses and sales floors." Admittedly, many traders had "regretted" that they could not "get hold of the List [of Harmful and Undesirable Literature], which would enable them to know, as soon as members of the public place orders, whether the books in question can be procured at all." Lack of access to the List, the report continued, had frequently been given as an excuse for the relatively large quantities of banned literature found in the bookstores.

In the Koblenz district, sixty-one bookstores and lending libraries were searched "systematically and without warning" in October 1936 by representatives of the SD Koblenz and Stapo officers.[394] Here, too, substantial quantities of prohibited literature had to be removed. The Gestapa sent the Chamber its surveys of the literature confiscated in the bookselling businesses of the two districts, "with the request to initiate whatever action you believe these reports necessitate."[395] The Chamber accordingly issued numerous booksellers with warnings and fines.[396]

Given that more than three years had passed since the "internal and external reordering of German literature," the total number of around 300,000 books confiscated struck even Nazi literary functionaries as being "surprisingly high." Reasons for this disappointing outcome were sought first and foremost in the political failure of individual booksellers and their primary focus on economic considerations, the nondisclosure of List 1, and the advertising of "undesirable books, authors, and publishers" in trade journals such as the *Börsenblatt* or in catalogues and bibliographies. However,

---

[393] Stapo office Düsseldorf to Gestapa, 15 February 1937, p. 3, in BArch BDC/RSK/158 B: "Unerwünschtes Schrifttum"—Gestapo/Regierungsbezirke Düsseldorf, Koblenz. On the following, see ibid.

[394] Report by Stapo office Koblenz to Gestapa, 1 December 1936, BArch Berlin Lichterfelde BDC/RSK/158 B: "Unerwünschtes Schrifttum"—Gestapo/Regierungsbezirke Düsseldorf, Koblenz.

[395] Gestapa to RSK president, 12 December 1936, 13 March 1937, and 28 July 1937, ibid. Lists of the companies and the confiscated books, ibid.

[396] RSK notifications sent during March and April 1937, ibid.

the report on the raids also blamed earlier campaigns' deployment of Gestapo officials who were "inadequately trained in literary matters" and who had applied "search techniques ill-adapted to the labyrinth of a bookselling business." There was harsh criticism of the fact that in the businesses of BRB representatives, "particularly numerous confiscations had to be carried out, as these people evidently considered themselves safe from searches due to their official positions." The confiscated books included works by émigré and Jewish authors, Marxist and Christian literature, texts attacking National Socialism, "trash and filth," and pornographic works.

Although the SD Main Office considered that banned literature had now been "removed from the book trade for the most part,"[397] "occasional raids" would still be necessary because the book trade, primarily the secondhand and antiquarian sector, was "recurrently inundated with banned literature from private bookshelves," and because it was not possible to keep the book trade constantly updated on the bans of particular books. The revised Chamber ordinance on "harmful and undesirable literature" of 15 April 1940, which now also banned the storage of indexed literature, gave the Gestapo and the SD further authority to act against the bookselling sector. "In light of recent events," in January 1941 the Chamber reminded its members of their duty "to present to the Gestapo any banned and harmful books, or to make them unreadable by ripping them and then keep them in a separate room until they can be sent for pulping."[398]

When the systematic deportation of Jewish Germans began in 1941, their private libraries, including large numbers of banned books, flowed into the secondhand book trade, especially in big cities. As a result, in spring 1942 the Chamber found it necessary to instruct secondhand book dealers to immediately remove from their stock "all harmful and undesirable, Marxist and Jewish writings," usually acquired at auction, and either to have them pulped or to turn them in to the Deutsche Bücherei in Leipzig.[399] Selling scholarly and scientific literature by Jewish or "half-Jewish" authors, which had been

---

[397] BArch R 58/1108 fol. 31. The following quotation ibid. fol. 31–2.
[398] *Vertrauliche Mitteilungen für die Fachschaft Handel* no. 7, 25 January 1941, 2.
[399] RSK Dept. III in Leipzig to RSK in Berlin, 19 May 1942, BArch R 56 V/67 fol. 205.

possible up to the end of 1942 with "special permission," was banned completely from 1943 for both retailers and publishing houses.[400] However, accurate monitoring of the bookstores' compliance with this regulation was impossible even for the Gestapo, since it too lacked "adequate documentation as to who actually is a Jew or a half Jew."

For all the detailed briefings, "instructive" articles in the book trade press, and political training courses, the distribution of banned literature was never completely prevented. This was due not only to the mass of regulations and special arrangements, but above all to the discrepancy between growing demand and shrinking supply, which had become acute since 1941. In a May 1942 issue of the *Börsenblatt*, the Chamber noted with displeasure that the "shortage of new reading material due to wartime conditions" was tempting booksellers to satisfy their customers' needs by "occasionally resorting to previously unsalable, outdated, and in some cases inferior book stocks."[401] Addressing retail booksellers and secondhand dealers in particular, Johst warned: "Anyone who exploits the wartime economic situation to disseminate worthless dead stock or politically undesirable books is contravening his professional duty and will be called to account." Despite these strictures, the *Vertrauliche Mitteilungen für die Fachschaft Verlag* of 20 June 1944, referring to "numerous reports received," was obliged to criticize once again the unfortunate fact that retail bookstores and especially secondhand dealers "are increasingly offering the public literature that is outmoded, long-since obsolete, and politically and ideologically suspect."[402]

Deutsche Hausbücherei, Büchergilde Gutenberg, and Deutsche Buch-Gemeinschaft were the three largest book clubs in Germany.[403] A report by the Chamber's book clubs working group, commissioned

---

[400] File note of 25 January 1943 on the meeting between the RSK legal department and RMVP literature department (Lutz) on 22 January, BArch R 56 V/67 fol. 179–80. The following quotation ibid. fol. 180.

[401] H. Johst, "Aufruf," *Bbl.* no. 93/94, 5 May 1942, 89.

[402] *Vertrauliche Mitteilungen für die Fachschaft Verlag* nos. 500–11, 20 June 1944, here no. 502. On the following, see ibid.

[403] On the following, see BArch BDC/RK 2110/Deutsche Buch-Gemeinschaft C.A. Koch's Verlag Nachf.

by the Propaganda Ministry in July 1934, estimated the membership of Deutsche Buch-Gemeinschaft (founded in Berlin in 1924) at 156,000–200,000. Its total turnover ran to approximately 4 million RM in 1934. Added to this was income of around 120,000 RM from the club's procurement department through book sales in five businesses in Berlin, Frankfurt am Main, Hamburg, and Dresden, and approximately 50,000 RM from the mail-order department. The company was owned by Paul Leonhard. Although he was Jewish, Deutsche Buch-Gemeinschaft was listed as an "Aryan" business in 1933 because all his shares had gone to his non-Jewish widow Erna upon his death. The same year, two NSDAP members were installed on the supervisory board: Wilhelm Baur (until September 1936) and the author C. M. Köhn as chair. Although this meant Deutsche Buch-Gemeinschaft could be regarded as "fully aligned," in 1936 the Chamber still distrusted the ideological reliability of the long-standing managing directors Heinrich Siemer and Paul Gützlaff. Its doubts were fueled by information passed on by the Economic Office of the German Book Trade, once again acting as an extension of the censorship authorities. The Office several times alerted the Chamber to banned books—such as works by Thomas Mann, Valeriu Marcu, Georg Forster, and a selection of "German novellas" including one by Stefan Zweig—that Deutsche Buch-Gemeinschaft was exporting and that had been invoiced within the book export compensation procedure. However, the Chamber had to agree with the managing directors that in view of the 1.5 million books dispatched by the club every year, these individual titles must be seen merely as "occasional organizational slips." In a letter to the Chamber on 22 April 1937, the management also offered to "show you in detail, on our own premises, the precautions that we have taken with reference to harmful and undesirable literature," and to present the report of a recent Gestapo inspection of the warehouse and catalogues in Berlin. In 1940, Deutsche Buch-Gemeinschaft was merged with C. A. Koch's Verlag under the management of Erich Semrau and Gustav End.[404]

After the reorganization of the book clubs' ownership and programs, during the war the Chamber increasingly intervened

---

[404] *Verlagsveränderungen im deutschen Buchhandel 1937–1943*, 6.

in the structure of their business operations. In an ordinance issued in late September 1940, establishing new book clubs or incorporating them into existing bookselling companies was made subject to approval by the Chamber president.[405] Licensed editions could only be distributed by the book clubs one year after the appearance of the original edition. The simultaneous publication of a work by a publisher and a book club was permissible if the cover design of the book club version differed from that of the original edition. On 1 August 1941, a freeze on new members was imposed for all book clubs.[406] But whereas advertising within Germany was completely prohibited, for propaganda reasons the Book Trade Group advised the operators of book clubs to intensify their advertising abroad.

Starting in 1942, book clubs were only allowed to send out half the number of books that the membership agreements stipulated as standard,[407] with exceptions only for foreign members.[408] The Chamber was primarily responding to the war-related shortages in book manufacture, but the consequence was to buttress the positions of Deutsche Hausbücherei and Büchergilde Gutenberg— the book clubs owned by the NSDAP—against their rivals in the highly competitive book market.

The Regimentation of Lending Libraries

The Nazi literary bureaucracy's relationship with the commercial lending (subscription) libraries was defined partly by the knowledge that they were capable of reaching a much wider readership than was the retail book trade. The competition of the two sectors had intensified during the Depression; the population's dwindling purchasing power prompted a boom in new lending libraries as more and more

---

[405] "Anordnung über den Betrieb von Buchgemeinschaften vom 30.9.1940, in der Fassung vom 27.2.1941," in Ihde, *Handbuch der Reichsschrifttumskammer*, 166–7.
[406] "Direkte Anweisung des Leiters des Deutschen Buchhandels an die Buchgemein-schaften vom 1.8.1941," ibid. 167–8.
[407] "Zur Anordnung über den Betrieb von Buchgemeinschaften vom 1.10.1941," ibid. 168.
[408] "Zweite Mitteilung des Präsidenten der Reichsschrifttumskammer zur Anordnung über den Betrieb von Buchgemeinschaften vom 27. Februar 1941," ibid.

readers turned to the cheaper option of borrowing rather than buying books. The state literary apparatus hoped to turn this situation to its own purposes by harnessing the lending libraries to the task of educating the public in the spirit of National Socialism.[409] At the same time, however, it was fundamentally suspicious of the lending library sector, querying not only the proprietors' specialist expertise and economic future, but also the suitability of their stocks.[410]

At the beginning of 1934, the Chamber ordered a halt to the establishment of new lending libraries, which was extended repeatedly until 1945.[411] The block prevented expansion in the sector and made it easier to keep track of lending library operators. In February 1934, the Chamber issued a set of regulations for working in the lending library business,[412] stipulating that lending libraries could now "as a rule" only be run as sole traderships. All lending library proprietors and their employees must have Chamber membership, and lending libraries must no longer be operated "in building entrances, hallways, on streets, paths, etc., or on open stalls," but only "in stores or in enclosed, appropriate premises." The logistics of book purchasing were also regulated, so that new acquisitions could now only be made through publishers or wholesalers.

In May 1934 the lending librarians' *Fachschaft* in the Chamber announced the creation of a membership register that would list the names and addresses of all those permitted to continue operating a lending library business.[413] Companies not included in this register or in the "address register of the German book trade" could not be supplied with new books by publishers, wholesale distributors, or commission agents. In order to check adherence to this rule, the companies entitled to supply the lending library trade had to send a list of their customers to the *Fachschaft*. These arrangements also

---

[409] Hürter, "Kulturpolitik in und durch die Leihbüchereien," 19.
[410] Mau, "Die Entwicklung und der gegenwärtige Stand"; von Heuduck, "Die Organisation der Fachschaft"; Hasper, "Über die notwendigen Maßnahmen."
[411] "Amtliche Bekanntmachung der RSK vom 4.1.1934," *Bbl.* no. 5, 6 January 1934, 13; Schrieber, *Das Recht der Reichskulturkammer*, vol. I, 215, vol. II, 89, vol. III, 124, vol. IV, 95; Ihde, *Handbuch der Reichsschrifttumskammer*, 224–5; *Die Reichskulturkammer* 2 (1944), 148.
[412] "Rahmenbestimmungen für die Ausübung des Leihbüchereigewerbes," in Schrieber, *Das Recht der Reichskulturkammer*, vol. I, 207–8.
[413] *Bbl.* no. 109, 12 May 1934, 425.

helped the authorities to identify Jewish-operated lending libraries, of which fourteen were closed down by the police on Chamber instructions by 1937.[414] A further ordinance in May 1934 made the minimum lending fees negotiated by the libraries and the *Fachschaft* representatives legally binding for every lending library operator.[415]

In mid-September 1934, Wismann proposed to Goebbels that a comprehensive "purification of the lending library trade" be carried out, covering the following segments of its stock: the "banned and confiscated books still present" in the lending libraries; books that had not been banned and confiscated, but that "can be described as undesirable and have therefore already been eliminated from the book trade without police intervention, on the basis of the list that I respectfully presented to you some time ago"; and the large number of "literary concoctions that are neither banned nor confiscated, nor on the list of undesirable literature, but in terms of their content ... are so shallow and worthless that they too must be eliminated from the lending library trade."[416]

Regarding the first two of these categories, the Chamber vice-president had already charged the lending librarians' *Fachschaft* and its Reich Book Office with carrying out a "cleansing campaign" in early August 1934.[417] Goebbels having given his approval, a new Supervisory Office for Lending Libraries was established and began work. The Supervisory Office first called on each lending library to send in its inventory, confirming the list's completeness with a sworn statement. In October 1934, six readers began working through the inventories. When they had finished, the library owners were notified of the books that must be withdrawn immediately and delivered to offices set up by the *Fachschaft*'s committees on or before a precisely stated date.[418]

---

[414] See the overview drawn up by the Chamber, 15 March 1937, BArch R 55/21 300.

[415] "Anordnung zum Schutz der Mindestleihgebühren im Leihbüchereigewerbe," in Ihde, *Handbuch der Reichsschrifttumskammer*, 225; "Leihgebührenordnung," ibid. 226.

[416] Submission by Wismann for the Minister via the ministerial office and the head of Dept. II, 15 September 1934, BArch R 55/682 fol. 59.

[417] Report by Reichsbuchamt, lending librarians' *Fachschaft*, 29 October 1934, BArch R 55/682 fol. 56–8, here fol. 56. On the following, see ibid. fol. 56–7.

[418] See ibid. fol. 91 for a preprint of the supervisory office's circular ordering lending libraries to withdraw the queried books.

By the beginning of 1935, 3,875 of the approximately 5,000 commercial lending libraries had submitted their lists to the Supervisory Office; 3,290 of these had already been processed.[419] In the district of Berlin alone, where a total of 994 businesses were affected by the campaign, around 28,000 "undesirable" books in 950 companies had now been identified, and 23,170 of them handed in. However, the district representative of the lending librarians' *Fachschaft*, C. von Heuduck, registered serious concerns regarding the "cleansing campaign" in a lengthy memorandum of December 1934.[420] In particular, "all the lending libraries without exception" had failed to understand the indexation of work by Waldemar Bonsels, Bruno Frank, Georg Hermann, Alexander Lernet-Holenia, Jakob Wassermann, Romain Rolland, and others, since these authors' books were "world literature that are quite incapable of harming today's state in their style or content, are not kitsch, and are not banned on German territory." In addition, the books could be found on private bookshelves "in many thousands of copies," and were still being bought new or secondhand in bookstores and borrowed from public libraries. Von Heuduck concluded that the Chamber's actions amounted to a "legally unjustified measure that denigrates the independent lending library trade and forces it into a degrading special status." He also criticized the obligation to hand in the books to which objections had been made. This rule was, he pointed out, regarded unanimously as "an illegal infringement of private property and a breach of law." It hit a sector "whose members are facing extremely severe economic pressure and have managed to organize the book acquisitions necessary for their libraries only at great personal sacrifice."

The literary bureaucrats ignored these criticisms; neither did they respond to von Heuduck's suggestion that compensation, at 30 percent of the retail price of the confiscated books, be offered or vouchers issued for the purchase of new titles. The Supervisory Office's task of purging the lending libraries of "undesirable literature" and its authority to impose binding stipulations on the libraries' proprietors, especially demands to send in queried books, were expressly

---

[419] Update on the lending libraries cleansing campaign, 8 January 1935, ibid. fol. 32.
[420] BArch R 55/682 fol. 85–9. The following quotes ibid.

reiterated by a Chamber ordinance on 6 April 1935.[421] Furthermore, lending library owners were proved right in their fear, reported by von Heuduck, "that it will not stop at this one measure, but that at any moment additional, similar measures may be determined."[422]

The searches carried out by the Stapo offices and SD regional sections in fall 1936 also affected the lending libraries. The Stapo office for the Düsseldorf district noted in its closing report that the raids in these businesses had proceeded "without a hitch."[423] In the Koblenz district, eighteen lending libraries were searched,[424] with even the *Gau* advisor for the *Fachschaft*, who ran the "Neue Moderne Leih-Bücherei" in Koblenz, receiving an official warning from the Chamber for lending "harmful and undesirable literature."[425] In June 1940, the sector bulletin *Vertrauliche Mitteilungen für die Fachschaft Leihbücherei* once again reminded lending library owners of their "duty" to examine their inventories for "banned and undesirable literature."[426] If in doubt, and in cases where the inventory had been examined "some time ago," they were "recommended" to submit a copy to the Promotion and Advisory Office for German Literature for checking. One year later, they were "confidentially" instructed that books indexed on the List of Publications Unsuitable for Young People and Libraries must also be submitted to the Gestapo or pulped directly.[427] The lending libraries on the register of permitted businesses were, at least, still given the option of selling such publications off or storing them outside their business premises.

The Propaganda Ministry literature department issued its "first basic list for German lending libraries" in 1940, under the title *Das Buch ein Schwert des Geistes* ("The book, a sword of the spirit"); by

---

[421] Schrieber, *Das Recht der Reichskulturkammer*, vol. III, 122–3.

[422] BArch R 55/682 fol. 87/verso.

[423] Stapostelle Düsseldorf to Gestapa, 15 February 1937, p. 1, BArch BDC/RSK/158 B: "Unerwünschtes Schrifttum"—Gestapo/Regierungsbezirke Düsseldorf, Koblenz.

[424] Overview enclosed in Gestapa to RSK president, 12 December 1936, ibid.

[425] RSK president to Neue Moderne Leih-Bücherei, J. Willeke, 8 March 1937, ibid.

[426] *Vertrauliche Mitteilungen der Fachschaft Leihbücherei* 1, June 1940, reproduced in Ihde, *Handbuch der Reichsschrifttumskammer*, 232.

[427] "Verkauf der auf die 'Liste der für Jugendliche und Büchereien ungeeigneten Druckschriften' gesetzten Bücher," in Ihde, *Handbuch der Reichsschrifttumskammer*, 233.

1943 two further such lists had been drawn up. These selections were intended as a "model" for expanding holdings and a "touchstone" for the state of the lending libraries. The lending librarians' journal *Großdeutsches Leihbüchereiblatt*, published by the Book Trade Group from 1939, included regular advice on "improving" stock, designing window displays, and advising customers. Efforts were also made to educate the commercial librarians into a more political under-standing of their profession. But commenting in November 1940 on a Thuringian Ministry of Public Instruction report on young people's use of lending libraries, the director of the State Public Libraries Office in Thuringia, Joseph Caspar Witsch, had to concede that state control had "not had the necessary success."[428] "Evidently," he wrote, there had been "no opportunity to tackle the root of the malady by banning the production of inferior literature for youngsters in the first place, that is, the production of the publishers that supply the private lending libraries in great quantities." The legal framework, complained Witsch, permitted the removal and destruction of explicitly banned books, but this only dealt with a small proportion of the "unsuitable holdings." Furthermore, "the owners and staff of the lending libraries are completely devoid of knowledge about good literature, and run their library no differently than they run their ice-cream parlors or tobacconists." And even if a complete elimination of harmful and undesirable literature proved possible, the fundamental precondition for "positive work" would still be missing: "people who can really tell the difference between a good book and a bad one."

Witsch drew the disappointed conclusion that an effective reform of the lending libraries was "possible neither in terms of their stocks nor of their personnel," for, in the end, the very principle of their existence was to distribute "kitsch and trash." In November 1942, Erich Langenbucher lamented that the libraries' inventories could not be examined effectively for "harmful and undesirable literature" because the author catalogues were kept scrappily or not at all.[429]

---

[428] Thuringian State Public Libraries Office, Joseph Caspar Witsch, to Thuringian Minister of Public Instruction, 11 November 1940, HStA Weimar Thüringisches Ministerium f. Volksbildung/C 629 fol. 278.

[429] E. Langenbucher, "Von der inneren und äußeren Sauberkeit unseres Standes," *Großdeutsches Leihbüchereiblatt* 4 (1942), 301–4, here 302. The following quotations ibid.

As a result, it was not unknown for "the works of Jews and the associates of Jews [*Judengenossen*] who have long since emigrated to appear in a store window," or for books to be displayed "that have eulogies to Jewish books and Jewish authors on their covers." Finally, Langenbucher complained that many lending libraries did not even take a trade journal, so that both the *Großdeutsches Leihbüchereiblatt*'s good advice and the Chamber's ordinances might as well have been addressed to a brick wall. He could hardly have painted a clearer picture of the gap between the theory of literary policy and the practices of the book trade on the ground.

Book Propaganda and the Book Industry

The Great Depression hit the German book trade hard.[430] In 1932 the production of new titles and reprints in book form dropped by 10.9 percent compared to the previous year, from 24,074 to 21,452. The average retail price of books also fell, from 6.16 RM to 5.08 RM, and sales abroad had been declining steeply since 1929.[431] The crisis was particularly severe in scientific and scholarly literature, traditionally the German book industry's strong suit; due to high prices, specialist books and journals from Germany were losing their secure position in libraries abroad.[432] Numerous German publishers and book distributors were bankrupted by falling turnover on the domestic and foreign market.[433] The Nazi state reacted to the sector's difficulties with two instruments: propaganda for the German book at home and abroad; and state subsidies for the export of German books. These

---

[430] "Geschäftsbericht des Vorstandes des Börsenvereins der Deutschen Buchhändler zu Leipzig über das Vereinsjahr 1932," *Bbl.* no. 99, 29 April 1933, 297–313, here 302. On the following, see also L. Schönrock, "Der deutsche Büchermarkt im Jahre 1932," *Bbl.* no. 58, 9 March 1933, 168–72.

[431] Memorandum from Hamburg-Bremer Buch-Export-Genossenschaft m.b.H., 11 July 1934, on the threat to German book exports, PA Kult Pol VI W, vol. 10.

[432] See memorandum from the Tübingen publisher Oskar Siebeck on the outlook for scientific and scholarly publishing in Germany, 30 June 1933, HStA Weimar Thüringisches Ministerium f. Volksbildung/C 626 fol. 107–10, and the reports of the German foreign missions 1933 through 1935, PA Kult Pol VI W, vols. 10–13.

[433] L. Schönrock, "Der deutsche Büchermarkt im Jahre 1932," *Bbl.* no. 58, 9 March 1933, 168–72.

strategies benefited the German book industry economically, but at the same time they also increased the regime's political leverage over books and book-buyers.

From 4 to 11 November 1934, the first nationwide "Week of the German Book" was held under the slogan "Stand up for the German book!" It appealed for books to be given as gifts to "relatives, friends, and acquaintances in the Reich" and for books to be sent abroad.[434] Book Week was opened in the Berlin Palace of Sport, where Goebbels told an audience of 15,000 how the book trade's crisis could best be overcome: literature must "seize the problems of the day, so that the *Volk* finds its own being and existence, its life and its cares, its hardships, its joys, its enthusiasm reflected in the book."[435] As soon as a literature "close to the *Volk*" had taken root, the Propaganda Minister optimistically continued, book weeks to win over new groups of buyers and readers would become superfluous, "because then the *Volk* itself will reestablish its relationship with the book." In March 1935 the Reich Working Group for German Book Promotion (Reichsarbeitsgemeinschaft für Deutsche Buchwerbung) was set up to organize future book weeks, bringing together state and Party literature offices along with the Advertising Council, the Reich Committee for Economic Enlightenment, and the Reich *Fachschaft* of advertisers.[436] At the Working Group's constitutive session on 27 March Wismann, in his capacity as its manager, clearly delineated the political rationale of state-organized book advertising: "To the extent that the book is a purely spiritual accomplishment and therefore one that influences the *Volk* in its thinking and feeling, the public—and the offices and organizations responsible to the public—have an interest not only in the book itself, but also in book advertising."[437]

Starting in August 1935, enormous media efforts were devoted to preparing for the second Book Week, which was to run from 27 October to 3 November under the motto "The book—a sword of the spirit." In early September the *Börsenblatt* published a Reich

---

[434] "Auftakt zur Woche des Deutschen Buches 4. bis 11. November 1934," *Bbl.* no. 248, 23 October 1934, 927–30.
[435] Speech reproduced in Goebbels, *Reden*, vol. 1, 168–73.
[436] See *Bbl.* no. 70, 23 March 1935, 237.
[437] E. Langenbucher, "Gemeinschaftliche Buchwerbung," *Bbl.* no. 78, 2 April 1935, 265.

Working Group "plan of work" that informed local advertising groups of the events they were expected to organize.[438] As well as a large-scale opening rally, the groups would arrange lectures, readings, and "book hours" across Germany. A window display competition for bookstores and lending libraries was announced; the winners would have clearly expressed the idea of "the community that exists in book production between the spiritual providers of literature, the technical manufacturers, and businesses."[439] Cultural documentaries on the German book were screened in movie theaters, schools, and the accompanying programs for book exhibitions.[440] The press and radio were urged to cover the events in detail.[441] Goebbels used his opening speech in Weimar on 27 October to lay wreaths on the tombs of Goethe and Schiller.[442] As was to be expected, the official evaluation of the 1935 Book Week was upbeat: responses to the rallies, book shows, readings, and parades within Germany, and to the events now also organized in the German colonies, were judged to have been very positive.[443]

The Düsseldorf district branch of Rosenberg's literature office, however, found itself unable to share this view.[444] The rally in a Düsseldorf factory planned by the DAF's Strength Through Joy section, with a reading by poet Heinrich Lersch, had not actually taken place, and the results of the window display competition were

---

[438] *Bbl.* no. 208, 7 September 1935.

[439] "Richtlinien für die Zusammenarbeit der Dienststellen der Reichsbetriebsgemeinschaft Druck und der örtlichen Beauftragten der Verbände und Organisationen mit den örtlichen Werbegemeinschaften der Reichsarbeitsgemeinschaft für Deutsche Buchwerbung," *Bbl.* no. 216, 17 September 1935, 762.

[440] Reference to screening of the documentary *Die Entwicklung des Buches* ("The development of the book") at the Ufa-Palast, Berlin Zoo, in *Bbl.* no. 232, 5 October 1935, 828; also to the films *Das Buch—ein Freund für's Leben* ("The book—a friend for life") and *Das Buch—wie es wurde* ("The book—how it came about"), both commissioned by the Reich Working Group, in *Bbl.* no. 278, 30 November 1935, 1022.

[441] "Die Sendungen des Rundfunks in der Woche des Buches," *Bbl.* no. 248, 24 October 1935, 890–2.

[442] E. Langenbucher, "Festtage in Weimar," *Bbl.* no. 252, 29 October 1935, 905–9.

[443] W. Baur, "Die Woche des deutschen Buches 1935," *Bbl.* no. 261, 9 November 1935, 945; Reich Working Group for German Book Promotion to the Foreign Office cultural department, 19 December 1935, PA Kult Pol VI W Akten betr. Deutsche Buchpropaganda, vol. 14.

[444] Report on the Book Week in Düsseldorf, 8 November 1935, StA Düsseldorf NL Dr. O. Mücke fol. 502–4. The following quotations ibid.

so meager that the district manager wondered "if some opposition to an order" had been at work. Many bookstores had displayed "a huge number of books that had no connection with the allotted theme" of "man and work," whereas the ten books on the prescribed topic "could hardly be seen." The Düsseldorf official castigated the local BRB group's members as "a group of people who in many cases have not yet risen to the call of the National Socialist revolution, but continue to feel perfectly at home in their old, liberalistic slackness."

From 1936, the Reich Working Group joined forces with the Party's foreign section NSDAP/AO to involve other countries more closely in the Book Week events.[445] Author readings and book exhibitions were planned to promote knowledge and dissemination of "the German book" abroad. Financial support from the Foreign Office's culture department made it possible for the first time to arrange Book Week events in various major cities of Europe, South Africa, South America, and China and in Alexandria, Tokyo, and Bombay.[446]

Goebbels announced the motto for the 1936 Book Week as "The *Volk* lives in the book." In a resolution agreed in Weimar on 23 October, "The German book trade for world peace," the book sector's professional leadership called for a ban on producing and distributing books "that, by maliciously distorting historical truth, insult a country's head of state or a people, or contemn the institutions and traditions that are sacred to a people."[447] Stern tones also prevailed in the Book Week's opening speeches on 25 October.[448] Comparing the pen with the sword and the ploughshare, Goebbels encapsulated his understanding of an authoritarian literature: "Just

---

[445] Order from Foreign Office (AA Kult W) to all German foreign representations, 11 August 1936, PA Kult Pol VI W, vol. 19. A confidential decree of 28 September 1936 from the Foreign Office cultural department ordered the German embassies, missions, and consulates general to intensify their propaganda for books abroad, PA Deutsche Botschaft Rom (Qu.), Propaganda—Verbreitung politischer, wirtschaftlicher und wissenschaftlicher Literatur pp. im Ausland und sonstige politische Propaganda (Pol 19a2, 831b). See also R. Erckmann, "Die Buchausstellung als Mittel nationalsozialistischer Schrifttumspropaganda," *NSB* 2, no. 10 (1937), I–XII.

[446] Statement of utilization, 16 January 1937, re: the 6,000 RM provided by the Foreign Office to the Reich Working Group for events around German Book Week, PA Kult Pol VI W, vol. 19.

[447] *Bbl.* no. 250, 26 October 1936.

[448] E. Langenbucher, "Festliches Weimar," *Bbl.* no. 251, 27 October 1936, 933–6. The following quotations ibid.

as the soldier cannot be permitted to strike and shoot whenever and wherever he pleases, … just as one cannot allow the farmer to sow and harvest whatever and wherever he pleases, so the writing man does not have the right to trample the boundaries of the *Volk*'s welfare in pursuit of his own individual inner life." The "state and Party's profession of faith in the book" must be answered by "the book's profession of faith in National Socialism as the guardian of all culture." Goebbels also called on the book trade to respond to enhanced state promotion of books with a reduction in book prices. The 1936 Book Week program included an "annual showcase of German literature," with a selection of around 350 books on the themes of "politics and worldview," "poetry and story-telling," and "culture and nature."[449] In this and subsequent years, the exhibition could be visited in more than sixty towns and cities.

A propaganda triumph was scored at the 1937 World Exposition in Paris. The Propaganda Ministry had entrusted the task of selecting books for the German pavilion to the Deutsche Bücherei's director of art prints.[450] He arranged the exhibits, mostly of apolitical German book art, in six groups, each adorned with the emblems of Nazi rule: the bookbinder's art; monumental art books and bibliophile or private printings; typographic art; illustrated books; quality nonfiction; and children's books. German publishers received several prestigious awards at the Exposition, including one to Eher for the copy of Hitler's *Mein Kampf* on show at the pavilion.[451]

The Week of the German Book in fall 1937, under the heading "The era comes to life in the book," began to prepare the public for the regime's policy of violent expansionism. "The national policy of a *Volk*," declared Goebbels in his opening speech, "finds its most eloquent expression, its symbol, in the book and the sword."[452] The

---

[449] Reference to the book show in *Bbl*. no. 237, 10 October 1936, 877–88; "Mitteilung für die Gauobmänner und Vertrauensmänner der Reichsarbeitsgemeinschaft für Deutsche Buchwerbung über die Vorbereitung und Durchführung der Ausstellung," *Bbl*. no. 245, 20 October 1936, 912.

[450] H. Cordes, "Das deutsche Buch auf der Weltausstellung in Paris," *Bbl*. no. 144, 26 June 1937, 545–6.

[451] "Internationale Anerkennung der deutschen Buch- und Druckerzeugung auf der Pariser Weltausstellung 1937," *Bbl*. no. 287, 11 December 1937, 993.

[452] Speech printed in *Bbl*. no. 252, 3 November 1937, 867–70, here 867. The following quotations ibid.

book was "the weapon of the peaceful spirit of development," the sword "the weapon safeguarding the very foundations of the nation's life." These were "not opposites; they are mutually conditional." To emphasize this symbiosis, the closing rally on 7 November was held in Essen: while Weimar represented the book "as the city of German poetry, the custodian of a great tradition and protectress of our heritage," the industrial town of Essen, "as the newly emerging arsenal of a proud nation," would stand for the sword.[453]

Outside Germany twelve exhibitions were held, each presenting 3–4,000 books.[454] Important locations were Kovno (Kaunas) in Lithuania, Brussels, Belgrade, Zagreb, and Shanghai; there was also a traveling exhibition for South America. In several Polish cities, too, the "new creativity in German books" and the cultural production of German minorities were promoted.[455]

After Austrian *Anschluss* and the annexation of the Sudetenland, in fall 1938 the first "Greater German Book Week" was staged. At the opening rally, Goebbels pronounced the increased production and sales of scholarly and fiction publishers to be successes "of our warm-hearted nurturing of the German book."[456] Under the slogan "A home library for every home," he made the case for even more book-buying than before. The book show in Vienna aimed to convey "a vivid picture of the breadth and importance of cultural life in the German Southeast." The closing rally, held in Munich, focused on Sudeten German literature.

In parallel to the Week of the German Book, on 27 October 1938 the Propaganda Ministry's literature department organized the first "Weimar Authors' Meeting," which was intended to express "the inner unity between literary artists and the literary leadership."[457] The literature department had taken care to ensure that it was not only loyal Party writers who attended the Weimar event, but

[453] "Weimar und Blücher," *Bbl.* no. 260, 9 November 1937, 889–910, here 889.

[454] Minutes of the first meeting of the Reich Working Group's (RADB) overseas board on 5 July 1937, PA Kult Pol VI W, vol. 19. See also, ibid., the plan of work for events abroad on the occasion of the Week of the German Book in November 1937, signed by the NSDAP/AO culture office and the RADB.

[455] "Buchwoche und deutsche Buchausstellung in Polen," *Bbl.* no. 291, 16 December 1937, 1002–3.

[456] Goebbels's speech published in *Bbl.* no. 255, 2 November 1938, 851–4, here 852.

[457] R. Erckmann, "Der Dichter im Volk," *Weimarer Reden des Großdeutschen Dichtertreffens 1938*, 14.

also high-profile representatives of nationalist-conservative literature, preferably ones with a reputation outside Germany.[458] Thus Ernst Wiechert, recently released from Buchenwald, was among those invited—although he was well aware that his role was only that of a "poster hung in public view to show everyone how magnanimous the Third Reich was."[459] Many of his colleagues set off for Weimar without such scruples, though they too were little more than walking advertisements for the regime. Very few had Hans Grimm's courage and determination in consistently evading his invitations.

The Propaganda Ministry's concerns also permeated the themes chosen for the Authors' Meeting conferences and lectures. When Friedrich Bodenreuth represented the "authors of the Sudetenland *Gau*" under the 1938 motto "The literature and reality of the *Volk*," he called on his colleagues to "earn the lyre by wielding the sword."[460] The second meeting, in 1940, was no less martial in tone: its motto was "Literature in the battle for the Reich," and many of the over one hundred delegates attended in Wehrmacht uniform.[461] At the opening event on 26 October in the NSDAP's Weimar offices, Rudolf Erckmann of the Ministry literature department proclaimed that "during the war, writing and poetry have exerted an effect far beyond that in peacetime. German books serve the German struggle."[462]

Book exhibitions held in Rome and San Sebastian in May 1939 underlined the Nazi state's close bonds with the Italian and Spanish fascist regimes. At Trajan's Market in Rome, 2,500 books were on show, including political literature, German translations of Italian works, and scholarly, scientific, and technical writings.[463] Scientific

---

[458] See, for example, the list of participants in the 1941 Weimar Authors' Meeting given in *Bbl.* no. 251/252, 28 October 1941, 366.

[459] Wiechert, *Jahre und Zeiten*, 528.

[460] Bodenreuth, "Die deutsche Dichtung und die Gegenwart," in *Weimarer Reden des Großdeutschen Dichtertreffens 1938*, 80.

[461] "Buch und Schwert—Sinnbild unserer Zeit. Das 'Großdeutsche Dichtertreffen 1940,'" *Bbl.* no. 253, 29 October 1940, 393.

[462] R. Erckmann, "Sinn und Aufgabe des Großdeutschen Dichtertreffens 1940," *Die Dichtung im Kampf des Reiches*, 7.

[463] Report by German Ambassador von Mackensen to the FO, 31 May 1939, re: preparing, setting up, and carrying out the exhibition; PA Deutsche Botschaft Rom (Qu.), Politik: Deutschland—Propaganda (Pol 19a1), Sonderband: Buchausstellung (831a).

and scholarly literature had been included in the exhibition at the last minute, when the organizers realized that "the absence of precisely this kind of literature at a foreign exhibition might provide ammunition for anti-German propaganda alleging the decline of scholarship in Germany."[464] To accompany the exhibition, the Propaganda Ministry issued a list of Italian translations of contemporary German literature.[465]

The San Sebastian exhibition, organized by the Spanish section of the NSDAP/AO, included 4,000 volumes.[466] The Reich Working Group supplied publications about National Socialism and recent German literature, while the German bookstores in Barcelona and Madrid, familiar with the interests of Spanish readers, contributed large numbers of medical, chemistry, and technical works.

The 1939 Week of the German Book within Germany had to be canceled due to the invasion of Poland that fall, but book propaganda abroad continued unabated. In December 1939, an exhibition in Belgrade—opened "in the presence of the Prince Regent of Yugoslavia and the Yugoslav cabinet"—displayed around 4,000 books in the areas of philosophy, ideology, education, and the history of literature, art, and music.[467] The southeast European region being of particular importance for Nazi foreign policy, exhibitions followed in 1940 in Sofia, Budapest, and Bucharest.[468] They accentuated writing in technology, the natural sciences, and medicine. The exhibition shown in Madrid in December 1940 and Barcelona in February

---

[464] FO decree to the German Embassy in Rome, 15 March 1939, PA Deutsche Botschaft Rom (Qu.), Politik: Deutschland—Propaganda (Pol 19a1), Sonderband: Buchausstellung (831a); and RMVP literature department to German Embassy in Rome, 30 March 1939, re: expansion of the book exhibition in Rome, ibid.

[465] W. Ruoff, "Die deutsche Buchausstellung in Rom," *Bbl.* no. 162, 11 May 1939, 402–3.

[466] Report by German Ambassador von Stohrer to the FO, 22 May 1939, re: German book exhibition in San Sebastian, PA Akten der Deutschen Botschaft Madrid betr. Buchausstellungen—Woche des deutschen Buches (1937–1940).

[467] W. Ruoff, "Prinzregent Paul auf der Belgrader Deutschen Buchausstellung," *Bbl.* no. 294/295, 19 December 1939, 765–6.

[468] W. Ruoff, "Das deutsche Buch im Südosten. Minister Wassileff eröffnete die Buchausstellung in Sofia," *Bbl.* no. 41, 17 February 1940, 55; K. Baur, "Deutsche Buchausstellung in Budapest," *Bbl.* no. 115, 21 May 1940, 193–5; W. Ruoff, "Das deutsche Buch im Südosten. Unterrichtsminister Braileanu eröffnete die Deutsche Buchausstellung in Bukarest," *Bbl.* no. 237, 10 October 1940, 361–2.

1941 presented political and military works, along with fiction and scholarly literature.[469]

To the north, an exhibition in Copenhagen's Charlottenborg Palace aimed to stimulate "interest in the intellectual assets of National Socialist Germany."[470] The focus of a book and graphics exhibition in the Stockholm National Museum, opened by the Swedish Crown Prince, was on quality fiction, German translations of Swedish books, and children's and youth literature, along with scientific and technical books.[471] In spring 1941 a book show was held at the Finnish National Gallery in Helsinki under the heading "Statesmen, thinkers, poets mold the *Volk* (Books make history)."[472]

From 1940 to 1942, within the Reich there were no longer Book Weeks but "Autumn Events for German Writing." The synthesis of "book and sword" recurred as the motto every year. As well as the annual show, many other book exhibitions in Germany and the occupied areas were used for the regime's propaganda purposes.[473] The Propaganda Ministry and the Foreign Office had quickly recognized that Germany's military hegemony in Europe would need to be underpinned by a more far-reaching order. From mid–1940, German government offices therefore began to work on a wide range of bilateral agreements, treaties, declarations, and joint institutions to be established in the field of politics, economics, and culture. In this process, argued Erckmann, the role of contemporary German literature was to "convince Europe of the spiritual power of the new Germany and itself to intervene, on behalf of spiritual orderliness,

---

[469] W. Ruoff, "Das deutsche Buch in Spanien. Madrider deutsche Buchausstellung als Buchstiftung für Spanien," *Bbl.* no. 289, 10 December 1940, 457–8; K. Baur, "Deutsche Buchausstellung in Barcelona vom 7. bis 23. Februar 1941," *Bbl.* no. 51, 1 March 1941, 73–5.

[470] W. Ruoff, "Das deutsche Buch im Norden," *Bbl.* no. 269, 16 November 1940, 429.

[471] W. Ruoff, "Das deutsche Buch im Norden. Kronprinz Gustav Adolf bei der Eröffnung der Deutschen Buch- und Grafikausstellung in Stockholm," *Bbl.* no. 27, 1 February 1941, 34–5; W. Ruoff, "Zur Nachwirkung der deutschen Buchausstellung in Stockholm. Bedeutsame Äußerungen der schwedischen Presse," *Bbl.* no. 71, 25 March 1941, 110.

[472] H. G. Otto, "Buchausstellung in Helsinki," *Bbl.* no. 128, 5 June 1941, 231–2.

[473] E. Langenbucher, "Jahresschau des deutschen Schrifttums 1940," *Bbl.* no. 237, 10 October 1940, 362–3; K. Felchner, "Buch und Schwert. Die Jahresschau des deutschen Schrifttums 1941," *Bbl.* no. 251/252, 28 October 1941, 371–2.

into the events of world history—events that after our victory must proceed on a scale we can now only guess at."[474] Accordingly, the Weimar Authors' Meeting in October 1941 was given the theme "Literature in the Europe to come." For the first time, the German writers were joined by guests from fourteen other European countries, including Felix Timmermans, Robert Brasillach, Pierre Drieu la Rochelle, John Knittel, and Ernesto Giménez Caballero.[475] To open proceedings, participants were shown a "display of anti-Bolshevist writing," with the aim of reminding them "that, particularly during this Weimar Meeting, we must all keep in sight the profound importance of the battle in the East."[476]

This third Weimar Authors' Meeting served as the occasion to found a European Union of Writers (Europäische Schriftstellervereinigung, ESV). The formation of the ESV as an "alliance of German and foreign authors" was supposedly a "spontaneous act" initiated by the writers Knut Hamsun from Norway, Stijn Streuvels from Flanders, and Maila Talvio from Finland.[477] In fact, however, the driving force was the Propaganda Ministry's literature department, which suggested to Goebbels that a European association of writers be founded under his aegis.[478] In the run-up to the ESV's inauguration, the literature department organized and funded a three-week tour of Germany for fifteen foreign and five German writers, who were received by Goebbels at the Propaganda Ministry with "a short address on Europe's new spiritual and organizational order."[479] The delegation then traveled on to Weimar, where Hans Carossa also attended at the express request of the literature department, having failed to participate in either of the

---

[474] R. Erckmann, "Zur europäischen Aufgabe unseres schaffenden Schrifttums," *Bbl.* no. 107, 10 May 1941/Cantate Meeting supplement, 2.

[475] W. Haegert, "Zum Dichtertreffen 1941," *Die Dichtung im kommenden Europa*, 6–7.

[476] "Im Zeichen von Buch und Schwert. Die Veranstaltungen in Weimar zur Kriegsbuchwoche 1941/Das Dritte Deutsche Dichtertreffen," *Bbl.* no. 251/252, 28 October 1941, 365.

[477] W. Ruoff, "Die Stunde des europäischen Geistes," *Bbl.* no. 258, 4 November 1941, 381–2.

[478] Goebbels, *Tagebücher*, Part II, vol. 2, 95 (11 October 1941).

[479] Ibid. 163 (23 October 1941). The costs of the tour and of "souvenir gifts" for the participants totaled 52,695 RM. Record of expenses, BArch R 55/705 fol. 266. On this and the following, see also Dufay, *Le voyage d'automne*, and Hausmann, *Die Europäische Schriftsteller-Vereinigung*, 107–86.

previous authors' meetings.[480] Carossa was taken aback to be offered the presidency of the new association—an offer, as he observed, that "could not be refused without causing great embarrassment to the gentlemen from the Ministry and the Minister himself, given the large numbers of foreign visitors present."[481] Goebbels deliberately remained in the background, not wishing "for the time being to compromise the ESV also [sic] in the eyes of the enemy powers" by taking a public stand.[482] But he kept his goal very firmly in mind: "Every great writer in Europe has a large circle of admirers, and it is these admirers who must be won over through the writer."[483]

The ESV's subsequent activities were not coordinated by its president—who surmised that he was no more than a "decorative piece of furniture" chosen "because some of my books are read abroad"[484]—but by its secretary, the author Carl Rothe.[485] Rothe was appointed to the literature department's general section "Spiritual Europe,"[486] where he was responsible for the "care and guidance of foreign authors: supporting the European Union of Writers, authors' meetings."[487] His colleague Wilhelm Ruoff edited the journal *Europäische Literatur*, launched in 1942 to promote the ESV's goals.[488] Goebbels charged Wilhelm Baur with agitating within the

---

[480] In his memoirs, *Ungleiche Welten*, 117, Carossa recalls that the Chamber had told him in no uncertain terms to attend the Weimar event. In fact, the request came from the ministerial department.

[481] Carossa to Roger de Campagnolle, 22 December 1941, in Carossa, *Briefe III*, 167. This letter also indicates that just seven hours before the vote, Carossa had been "quite unaware of the whole matter."

[482] Goebbels, *Tagebücher*, Part II, vol. 2, 190 (27 October 1941).

[483] Ibid. 186 (26 October 1941).

[484] Carossa to Carl Rothe, 3 February 1943, in Carossa, *Briefe III*, 200.

[485] Carl Rothe (1900–70): 1924–31 head of the DHV's education section; 1933–7 head of department in the league for "Germandom abroad" (Volksbund für das Deutschtum im Ausland); later freelance writer. Curriculum vitae (n.d., 1938), BArch BDC/RSK/Rothe, C.

[486] "Generalreferat Geistiges Europa," literature department schedule of responsibilities, 1 November 1942, BArch R 55/1314 fol. 43/verso.

[487] RMVP schedule of responsibilities, 1 November 1942, amendments 1 November 1943, BArch R 55/893 fol. 118.

[488] Ruoff to Johst, 26 December 1941, BArch BDC/RMVP/Ruoff, W.; record of the subsidies for special campaigns allocated by the Promotion and Advisory Office for the financial year 1942, BArch R 55/688 fol. 32. This mentions subsidies for the journal amounting to 2,563.59 RM.

book trade for those foreign authors who had joined the ESV to be "promoted in every possible way";[489] the sale of works by those who had refused to join, in contrast, was to be prevented through informal instructions in the confidential bulletins of the Chamber's publishing and bookselling sector groups.

But despite the considerable resources that the literature department invested in the project, by 1942 the public profile of the ESV had already dwindled to almost nothing.[490] Although writers from sixteen European countries took part in the Weimar Authors' Meeting of 8–11 October that year,[491] ESV president Carossa did not trouble to interrupt a stay in Ischia to attend in person what he later called the "congress of unfree shadows";[492] he was represented by the vice-president, Finnish writer V. A. Koskenniemi. Several well-known French authors also avoided attending. Once Germany's military ascendancy collapsed, the ESV "quietly petered out," just as Carossa had predicted in December 1941.[493] The meeting planned for October 1943, for which Carossa had agreed to give a "ceremonial address" to make up for missing the previous year's event, was canceled "on account of the war."[494]

The Weimar Authors' Meetings themselves were also coming to an end. At a rally on 10 October 1942 with the slogan "Poets and warriors," Goebbels reminded German authors once more of their duty to the Nazi state.[495] Whereas the state rejected a certain

---

[489] Baur to the RSK management in Berlin and Leipzig and the Börsenverein, 31 October 1941, BArch R 56 I/102 fol. 39–40.

[490] BArch R 55/688 fol. 29, 30, 32, recording the cost of a lecture tour by Rothe to France and Belgium, a "souvenir gift for the participants in the Germany tour of foreign authors," and the "care of the foreign authors during their stay in Germany"; also RMVP budgetary department to Reich Finance Ministry, 10 January 1942, BArch R 2/4927 fol. 429–30, naming the figure of 35,000 RM for ESV personnel and materials.

[491] "Die Herbstveranstaltungen des deutschen Schrifttums in Weimar. Tagung des Europäischen Schriftstellerverbandes—Das Deutsche Dichtertreffen—Der Staatsakt in der Weimarhalle," *Bbl.* no. 235, 17 October 1942, 217.

[492] Carossa, *Ungleiche Welten*, 135.

[493] Carossa to Roger de Campagnolle, 22 December 1941, in Carossa, *Briefe III*, 168.

[494] Carossa to Ernst Bertram, 19 September 1943, in ibid. 213. On his agreement to Erckmann's request, see Carossa to Rothe, 15 February 1943, ibid. 202.

[495] Report and speech in *Bbl.* no. 235, 17 October 1942, 220–3. See also "Stimmen zum Staatsakt anlässlich des Weimarer Dichtertreffens," *Meldungen aus dem Reich*, vol. 11, no. 327, 19 October 1942, 4345–6.

"type of intellectualism" that "knows too much to believe out of instinct and knows too little to believe out of insight," declared the Propaganda Minister, the contribution of the "national intelligentsia to the German *Volk*'s struggle of destiny" must be given its due. Year on year, authors had, "out of their profound closeness to the *Volk* and their sense of artistic responsibility, created many valuable works" in which the *Volk* recognized itself and "to which it returned again and again in moments of reflection and profundity." Nevertheless, Goebbels saw deficits in contemporary narrative fiction, which seemed "hesitant" to address the issues of the day. He noted with regret that the events of the war, urban life, and the world of the working class were neglected. There was also an urgent need for "light, captivating literature that does not demand a great emotional effort but unobtrusively leads the reader away from everyday cares." In such works, the language and content should cater to the "broad mass of our compatriots and our soldiers." The plot should catch hold of the reader "without long-winded hints and ruminations" and "draw him into the spell of the book." This was an overt demand for literature to place itself in the service of the state.

As well as the Week of the German Book, every spring from 1936 the Reich Working Group for German Book Promotion organized three-month promotion programs for professional or specialized literature (*Fachliteratur*).[496] The local promotion groups brought together repre-sentatives of state and Party agencies, local government officials, and delegates of the eighteen sector divisions of the German Labor Front. Their role was to supply the local press with news; involve factories in the promotion of professional literature through posters, circulars, and appeals; and distribute the specialized book lists drawn up by the Reich Working Group.[497] In his 1936 appeal for the promotion of such literature, Wilhelm Baur stressed that "every German must hold his own at his workplace, and for that purpose he will need to have constant recourse to the valuable German

---

[496] E. Langenbucher, "Die Werbung für das deutsche Fachbuch. Arbeitstagung der Reichsarbeitsgemeinschaft für Deutsche Buchwerbung," *Bbl.* no. 299, 28 December 1935, 1115–16.
[497] For details, see "Arbeitsplan für die örtlichen Werbegemeinschaften zur Werbung für das Fachbuch im Frühjahr 1936," *Bbl.* no. 25, 30 January 1936, 93. On the following, see ibid.

professional textbook and reference book, which teaches him new paths and forms, new thoughts and ideas in his occupation." The German nation needed "not only political warriors, but also skilled soldiers of labor."

The spring 1936 promotion events tried to heighten public awareness of the economic importance of professional literature,[498] and this principle received even greater emphasis after the announcement of the second Four-Year Plan in September 1936.[499] As the Reich Working Group's plan for the promotion events in 1937 put it: "The professional book and the enhancement of performance are so inseparable that in order to achieve the great objective set out in the Four-Year Plan, we must succeed in supplying every working man with the technical literature relating to his profession."[500] The professional literature promotion campaign—headed "We can do it, with the professional book!"—was now, like Book Week, opened by a rally broadcast on national radio. Labor Front leader Robert Ley spoke on the theme of "The working man and his book." Book exhibitions were organized for factories, Labor Front training facilities, vocational colleges, training workshops, and short courses.

Large-scale exhibitions of reference books were held in the cities of Saarbrücken and Cologne.[501] Lists of recommended works, drawn up by a "German professional book board" established in 1937 within the Chamber of Literature, were distributed in large numbers via the book trade.[502] In April a window display competition was announced, intended to give practical expression to the following basic principle: "The Führer demands top-quality skilled workers. If you are not one

---

[498] E. Langenbucher, "Der zweite Schritt: Die Grosse Fachbuchwerbung," *Bbl.* no. 25, 30 January 1936, 98.

[499] See the calls by Hanns Johst and Wilhelm Baur, "Die Fachbuchwerbung im Zeichen des Vierjahresplanes," *Bbl.* no. 2, 5 January 1937, 1, and the 1937 calls for promotion of the professional book by Göring, Goebbels, Ley, and Schirach in *Bbl.* no. 36, 13 February 1937, 129–30.

[500] The plan of work was published with explanations by E. Langenbucher, "Die Pflicht jedes Einzelnen: Leistungssteigerung," *Bbl.* no. 2, 5 January 1937, 2–3.

[501] "Die Fachbuchwerbung 1937 auf dem Höhepunkt," *Bbl.* no. 105, 11 May 1937, 413–14.

[502] E. Langenbucher, "Das Fachbuch als Grundlage deutscher Wertarbeit. Das 'Kuratorium für das deutsche Fachbuch' gegründet," *Bbl.* no. 20, 26 January 1937, 74–5; L. Warmuth, "Die Bedeutung des Fachbuches im Rahmen nationalsozialistischer Schrifttumspolitik," *Bbl.* no. 93, Cantate Meeting issue, 24 April 1937, 34–5.

yet, become one! ... National Socialism is no enemy of high wages. Exceptional performance must be rewarded exceptionally. If you are dissatisfied with your income, take a sober look at what your current performance is worth. Enhance it according to your own abilities. The reward will follow. The path: professional books!"[503]

The professional book promotions in 1938 and 1939 were given the motto "The professional book—a path to performance and success." The opening event for 1938 (in Hamburg) and for 1939 (in Frankfurt's IG Farben building) featured the obligatory speeches by literary policy functionaries and the opening of large exhibitions of professional literature.[504] Further public rallies and book shows were staged in several other large cities.[505] Because in previous years the events had erroneously advertised outdated or out-of-print technical books, from 1939 the publishers were required to collaborate in the compilation of recommended book lists, confirming not only the bibliographical details but also the authors' "Aryan descent."[506] They also now had to pay a 4 RM levy for each title included in the list. A "core collection of the most important technical works available through the book trade" was to be provided in every workplace.[507] At the first national meeting of the professional book board, held in Berlin in March 1939, several measures were announced: a reduction in the number of different professional titles, accompanied by increased print runs and lower prices; the publication of cheap paperback editions; a standardization of format; "eradication of all old and therefore often dangerous professional books from all libraries";

---

[503] "'Wir schaffen es mit dem Fachbuch!'. Großer Schaufensterwettbewerb des Reichsdeutschen Buchhandels zur Fachbuchwerbung 1937," *Bbl.* no. 56, 9 March 1937, 210.

[504] G. von Kommerstädt, "Das Fachbuch—ein Weg zu Leistung und Erfolg. Feierliche Eröffnung der Fachbuchwerbung—Großkundgebung in Hamburg," *Bbl.* no. 56, 8 March 1938, 189–91; "Das Fachbuch—ein Weg zu Leistung und Erfolg. Eröffnung der Fachbuchwerbung 1939 im I.G. Hochhaus zu Frankfurt a. Main," *Bbl.* no. 56, 7 March 1939, 185–8.

[505] Plans of work published in *Bbl.* no. 32, 8 February 1938, and *Bbl.* no. 26, 31 January 1939.

[506] Karl Baur, head of the publishers' *Fachschaft*, and K. von Wissel, head of the professional publishing sub-group, "Fachbuch-Auswahllisten 1939," *Bbl.* no. 28, 2 February 1939, 93.

[507] [W.] Baur, "Das buchhändlerische Fachbuch in die Betriebe!" *Bbl.* no. 62, 14 March 1939, 205.

the establishment of dedicated reading rooms for professional literature in the public libraries; and "simplification of content and descriptions in professional books."[508]

However, in late May 1940 the *Börsenblatt* published an unusually self-critical review of the previous four years' promotion of professional literature. "By and large," the summary ran, promotion campaigns had "not yet had the striking success that we expect of them, either among working people or among retailers."[509] Nevertheless, efforts were to be sustained, because professional literature had a preeminent role to play in the "arsenal for the front." The motto would remain "The professional book—a path to performance and success," but the exhibitions and book lists would now focus more specifically on the war economy: "Books for armaments factories and for armaments workers, for issues of wartime administration and raw materials management, books on rapid induction and retraining, the battle for production, household management in wartime, and the health leadership of the German *Volk*."[510] The Börsenblatt recommended that relevant technical books also be sent to the "members of your workforce who are away at war."[511]

The close enmeshment of book propaganda with the book industry is further illustrated by the "book export compensation procedure" administered by the Economic Office of the German Book Trade. The Office had an economic objective—using state subsidies to reinvigorate the limping German export book trade and thus to strengthen the German economy—but this was primarily a springboard for its political objective, of using books to carry out cultural propaganda for Nazi Germany abroad.[512] Purchasers abroad were unaware of the background of the compensation procedure: the 25 percent price cut for German books, graphic teaching aids, periodicals, and sheet

[508] "Erste Reichstagung des Kuratoriums für das deutsche Fachschrifttum," *Bbl.* no. 162, 1 April 1939, 264–5.

[509] A. M. Kreuser, "Fachbuch und Krieg," *Bbl.* no. 121, 28 May 1940, 201–2.

[510] Speech by J. Schlecht at the closing rally on promotion of the professional book 1941 in Litzmannstadt (Łódź): "Zehn Millionen Fachbücher im Dienste der Kriegswirtschaft," *Bbl.* no. 103, 6 May 1941, 178–9.

[511] A. M. Kreuser, "Fachbuch und Krieg," *Bbl.* no. 121, 28 May 1940, 202.

[512] See RMVP literature department to Reich Finance Ministry, 12 June 1935, BArch R 2/4926 fol. 143/verso; RMVP to RFM, 23 August 1940, BArch R 2/4927 fol. 530.

music was to appear as a purely commercial measure undertaken by German publishers in response to appeals that had long been coming from abroad.[513] Thus, book exporters were only permitted to notify customers of the price reduction itself, and under no circumstances to "inform third parties, either at home or abroad, of the existence of the procedure."[514] Booksellers violating this obligation to secrecy were threatened with fines, to be imposed by the relevant chambers and the law courts on the basis of foreign currency legislation. The procedure worked by the Economic Office reimbursing export companies, upon application, for the losses they had incurred due to the price reduction officially decreed on 9 September 1935 and the 25 percent discount for every article exported after that point.[515] In order to qualify for compensation, the items exported had to carry a retail price protected by the Börsenverein and to have been manufactured entirely within the German Reich.[516] To ensure compliance with the regulations, the Economic Office was given the right to inspect exporters' business records. Invoices submitted by the exporters were only approved "provisionally, subject to further scrutiny at a later date." If erroneous or deliberately false statements were discovered, the culprits could be fined or excluded from the Chamber.

In October 1935, Palestine was struck off the list of countries receiving these preferential terms;[517] Switzerland and Liechtenstein were added to the list in October 1936.[518] As Nazi Germany expanded,

[513] Head of the RMVP literature department to Foreign Office informing the FO of this background, 26 August 1935, p. 2, PA Kult Pol VI W, vol. 12.

[514] Third edition of the instructions for implementing the book export compensation procedure, Economic Office of the German Book Trade, Berlin 27 August 1935/1 September 1939, BArch R 2/4927 fol. 537–63, here fol. 539 (point 13). On the following, see ibid. fol. 539–40 (point 16).

[515] Confidential circular from the Börsenverein central office, 4 September 1935, re: compensation for stock loss, BArch NS 12/86; section 5, "Award of compensation," in the Economic Office instructions, BArch R 2/4927 fol. 543.

[516] Economic Office instructions section 4, "Articles covered and excluded," BArch R 2/4927 fol. 542.

[517] Circular 1 on the instructions for carrying out the book export compensation procedure, issued by the RSK, Economic Office of the German Book Trade department, 21 October 1935, p. 3, PA Kult Pol VI W, vol. 13.

[518] "Bekanntmachung der Wirtschaftsstelle vom 15.10.1936 betr. Änderung der Ausfuhrregelung," in Schrieber, *Das Recht der Reichskulturkammer*, vol. V, 81.

special promotion was withdrawn from Austria, the Sudeten German areas, the "Protectorate of Bohemia and Moravia," Poland, Gdańsk, and the Memel area after transitional periods. In contrast, in the early days of the war the export of "book-trade articles" to neutral countries was to be kept up "at all costs."[519] Even for deliveries to enemy countries, there were "no objections" if the opportunity to carry out business via third countries arose.

The book export compensation procedure's importance declined steadily until it was discontinued on 1 April 1943,[520] but taken as a whole it was among the most successful instruments of Nazi literary policy. A confidential Börsenverein survey of the thirty-four largest German publishers at the turn of 1935 to 1936 indicates that these companies' foreign sales had already seen growth—in some cases considerable growth—just three months after the scheme's introduction.[521] The German foreign missions, too, almost unanimously reported that the discount was impacting positively on the dissemination of German books.[522] According to the Propaganda Ministry, in the first year of the procedure around 4,000 companies were involved and sales of German books abroad rose by 40 percent.[523]

The chief beneficiaries of the state subsidies were the publishers of scientific and scholarly literature. Their share of promoted exports grew between 1938 and 1939 from 21 to 27.4 percent for books and

---

[519] Economic Office circular no. 1/39, 21 September 1939, BArch R 2/4927 fol. 565. Countries to which German exports must "at all costs" be maintained were the Netherlands, Hungary, the USSR, Norway, Lithuania, Luxembourg, Sweden, Switzerland, Slovakia, Estonia, Yugoslavia, Finland, Belgium, Romania, Italy, Latvia, Denmark, and Bulgaria.

[520] "Gemeinsame Anordnung über die Aufhebung der Ausfuhrregelung der Präsidenten der RSK, der RPK und der RMK vom 30.3.1943," Bbl. no. 77, 3 April 1943, 57.

[521] Hövel to the Reich and Prussian Minister of Economics, 31 January 1936 (copy), PA Kult Pol VI W, vol. 15.

[522] Reports by the German foreign missions to the FO 1935 through 1937, PA Kult Pol VI W, vol. 13–19. These reports, entitled "Die Auswirkungen des Buchexport-Ausgleichverfahrens," were compiled by the head of the Economic Office as the basis for the annual negotiations with the Ministries of Finance and Economics over the continuation of the compensation procedure. Reports for October 1935 through May 1936, BArch R 2/4926 fol. 319–57; January and February 1938, BArch R 2/4927 fol. 83–107.

[523] State secretary Funk (RMVP) to Reich Minister of Finance Schwerin von Krosigk, 14 November 1936, BArch R 2/4926 fol. 379–81.

from 16.6 to 19.7 percent for periodicals.[524] In the same period, the share of fiction and political literature fell from 24.6 to 18.4 percent, that of professional or technical works from 2.9 to 2.7 percent, and that of children's and picture books from 0.9 to 0.7 percent. The drop in the share of Catholic literature from 3.2 to 2.4 percent had been deliberately engineered by excluding liturgical writings from the procedure in May 1937.[525] The subsidies granted up to August 1940 totaled 52,216,386.41 RM,[526] funded mainly by the Ministry of Economics through an export levy on industrial companies. They paid off in many respects. For one thing, they contributed substantially to consolidating the German book trade, the export turnover of which had risen to an annual average of around 60 million RM by 1940. This was a significant economic and foreign-currency factor, especially taking into account exports of scientific books and journals to the United States and Japan, which rose steadily up to the outbreak of war.[527] The fact that scientific literature from Germany was able to regain its international status in the course of the 1930s was a success not just in economic terms, but also for cultural policy: it undermined the boycott of German goods being practiced in some countries, and helped to combat the hostile attitude of foreign intellectual elites toward the Nazi state.[528] For the sake of this prize, the Nazi literary bureaucracy was prepared to swallow the slight drop in exports of political literature and ideologically approved fiction, for which there was little demand abroad.

---

[524] See survey of the different areas of writing promoted by the export compensation procedure in 1938 and 1939, RMVP to Reich Minister of Finance, 23 August 1940, BArch R 2/4927 fol. 523–35. The following figures ibid.

[525] RMVP literature department to Reich and Prussian Minister of Economics, 31 March 1938, BArch R 2/4927 fol. 109–14, here fol. 113.

[526] RMVP to RFM, 23 August 1940, BArch R 2/4927 fol. 526. The following figures ibid. fol. 527.

[527] As indicated in Hövel, "Die Wirtschaftsstelle des deutschen Buchhandels," B12.

[528] RMVP to Reich Minister of Economics, 28 July 1938, BArch R 2/4927 fol. 131, and to Reich Minister of Finance, 23 August 1940, BArch R 2/4927 fol. 530–2.

Managing Readers' Choices: The Public and Research Libraries

Public and Municipal Libraries

Education Minister Rust's December 1933 decree headed "Do it today!" charged the Prussian provincial office and local advisory offices for "volkstümliches Büchereiwesen"—popular or folk libraries—with "ensuring that all public libraries work in the spirit of the National Socialist state."[529] To this end, each public library was required to present a complete list of its collections to its allotted advisory office by 15 January 1934. "Harmful and undesirable literature" was then screened out using the guidelines of the Prussian Office for Popular Libraries and on the instructions of the advisory office directors.

This left the problem of how to "cleanse" collections on a unified, national level still largely unresolved. The instructions issued at intervals since 1933/34 by the education and culture ministries of the provincial governments and the provincial Offices for Popular Libraries set down what was to be eliminated: political literature, pacifist writings, publications likely to defame Germanness and German culture, "liberalistic and democratic tendentious and ideological literature," writings on sex education, the works of "asphalt and civilizational literature," and books by Jewish authors—but in many individual cases, opinions and practices differed both between the provinces and locally within them. There was also uncertainty regarding the treatment of foreign literature and translations into German, and on the precise definition of "racially alien" or "corrosive" literature. Without a complete and binding list of Jewish authors, not even the racialized purging of the public libraries found itself on a firm footing.

Nor did the Chamber of Literature's circulation of List 1 of Harmful and Undesirable Literature in December 1935 simplify the situation. In terms of the number of titles indexed, this first nationwide register actually lagged behind the lists of bans already issued in Thuringia

---

and Bavaria. Moreover, as the Reich Education Minister told the provincial departments of education and culture in April 1937, the basic list and its addenda generally contained such "quantities of defects and inaccuracies" that they would no longer be circulated.[530] Responsibility for screening out unwanted literature now returned to librarians on the ground, who also had to decide on new acquisitions. The Ministry therefore recommended that a library's director of lending should "have an interest in politics"—since the "library's censorship" must "ultimately extend to the library user, his reliability, and the objectives he is pursuing."

A further challenge in purging the collections was highlighted in spring 1935 by the director of the Hagen public library, Rudolf Angermann.[531] The elimination of politically undesirable work in the widest sense having been at least provisionally completed, Angermann now demanded a "cultural cleansing." He decried the continued presence of "sentimental novels of love or social manners from the old days," "hypocritical peasant stories, drawing-room Tyrolean romances, musty old Red Indian tales for boys; obsolete polemics, anachronistic social problems, unrealized utopias; above all, phony adventure stories and the so-called detective and crime novels that amount to nothing more than mere intellectual suspense," the "foolish 'military humoresques' and guardroom stories of the old sort ... and many of the joke books." But that was not all: "jingoistic books of former days, cruelly illustrated novels idealizing the aristocracy," the "enormous mass" of war reportage, "work smacking of the little tract, of unctuous and officious moralism," "everything that is linguistically sloppy and clichéd," and "everything that is outdated in its content" must also disappear from local libraries. Due to the inadequate funding of public libraries and their neglect by most local administrations, Angermann argued, collections in many towns and villages were antiquated and "cleansing" would deliver a long-overdue modernization of the books on offer to readers. This was

---

[530] REM circular decree, 9 April 1937, HStA Weimar Thüringisches Ministerium f. Volksbildung/C 619 fol. 280. The following quotations ibid.
[531] "Säuberung nach der Säuberung," *Die Bücherei* 2 (1935), 281–3. See also Stieg, *Public Libraries in Nazi Germany*, 78–108.

the only way to satisfy the expectations placed on the contemporary library and the needs of new groups of readers.

Not until 1939 was a reliable instrument for filtering the collections of public libraries created, in the shape of a thoroughly revised edition of the List of Harmful and Undesirable Literature and its monthly updates.[532] However, the lack of standardized criteria for weeding out "undesirable" literature was not the only problem; practical implementation also varied across the country. Whereas in Prussia the task of checking the collections of all public libraries had been completed by September 1935, in Thuringia the Office for Popular Libraries director, Kurd Schulz, had to admit, answering his Minister of Public Instruction's inquiry, that at this point he had only been able to examine a small proportion of the province's more than 500 public libraries, and that the work was unlikely to be finished until "some time in the next few months."[533] As a preliminary finding, Schulz noted that there was "still banned literature here and there," despite the fact that a list of authors and titles to be eliminated had been sent out to every public library in September 1933. He attributed the unsatisfactory state of affairs primarily to substandard cataloguing in the smaller libraries. The head of Baden's office came to similar conclusions at an even later stage, in December 1937.[534]

The question of what should actually be done with the books eliminated from the shelves continued to occupy the state library agencies for a long time. In decrees of 17 September 1934 and 3 April 1935, the Reich Ministry of Education had obligated all libraries to "secrete" the banned literature, keeping it out of general use.[535] In May 1937 the Ministry then ordered the physical removal of "harmful and undesirable literature" from the public libraries: in Prussia, the items were to be handed in to the Prussian State Library by 1 August, in Bavaria to the Bavarian State Library, and in the remaining

---

[532] Reich Education Ministry circular decree, 30 June 1939, HStA Weimar Thüringisches Ministerium f. Volksbildung/C 619 fol. 316.
[533] Thuringian Advisory Office for Popular Libraries to Thuringian Ministry of Public Instruction, 11 September 1935, HStA Weimar Thüringisches Ministerium f. Volksbildung/C 619 fol. 230.
[534] Heyde, "Die Staatlichen Volksbüchereistellen," 137–8.
[535] Reference in REM circular decree, 16 December 1936, HStA Weimar Thüringisches Ministerium f. Volksbildung/C 619 fol. 246.

provinces to libraries designated by the provincial ministries of education and culture.[536]

Even today, it has not proved possible to identify completely and reliably how many individual books and authors were affected by the various purging campaigns in the public libraries. For the Leipzig municipal library, Engelbrecht Boese finds that 12,132 volumes had been withdrawn by the end of 1935—10.7 percent of the library's collection.[537] In Düsseldorf, the total holdings of the district's public libraries fell from 126,387 items in the financial year 1932/33 to 100,869 in 1934/35: around 20 percent of the books in the areas of young people's literature, entertainment, and nonfiction had gone.[538] In Berlin, the number of library books removed from public use in 1936 was somewhere between 10 and 40 percent of the previous total collection.[539] For Cologne, the city's administrative report for 1933/34 notes a reduction in holdings by around 3,500 volumes (3.5 percent) and for 1934/35 by a further 11,000 (around 10 percent).[540] And in Baden, by 1936 only 177,392 books were left of the 283,000 held by the province's libraries in 1934.[541] These figures include natural wastage as worn-out or obsolete items were removed,[542] but they do indicate that the Nazi literary bureaucracy succeeded in eliminating its hated literature from the public libraries on a large scale and relatively fast.

This very success raised the vital question of how to fill the gaps created by "cleansing." Here, the directors of the provincial Offices for Popular Libraries were to play a key role. In Prussia, since December 1933 new acquisitions had, as a general rule, required previous approval from the advisory offices, which in turn based their decisions on the guidelines issued by the Prussian provincial

[536] "Runderlass vom 10.5.1937," *Deutsche Wissenschaft, Erziehung und Volksbildung* 3 (1937), 274.
[537] Boese, "Die Säuberung der Leipziger Bücherhallen," 294–5.
[538] Rischer, *Die nationalsozialistische Kulturpolitik in Düsseldorf*, 22.
[539] Anderhub, "Zwischen Umbruch und Tradition," 244/n. 25.
[540] Robenek, *Geschichte der Stadtbücherei Köln*, 67.
[541] Heyde, "Die Staatlichen Volksbüchereistellen," 139.
[542] See the 1938 report by the head of cultural affairs in the municipality of Düsseldorf on five years of "National Socialist cultural work in Düsseldorf," here p. 29, StA Düsseldorf NL Ebel/142; information on Freiburg and Potsdam in Boese, *Das Öffentliche Bibliothekswesen*, 234–5.

Office for Popular Libraries in Berlin.[543] This principle of steering and surveillance was extended to the Reich as a whole in 1937. The Reich Office for Popular Libraries, in cooperation with the Reich Ministry of Education, set the general parameters from the center, while the mid-level authorities in the provinces were responsible for monitoring the collections policy of their municipal and village libraries.[544]

A further tool for regulating acquisitions policy was created in April 1934 with a central purchasing house based in Leipzig, the Einkaufshaus für Büchereien (EKH). Shares in the EKH were owned by the governments of Prussia and Saxony, the Chamber of Literature, the public librarians' association VDV, and the Börsenverein.[545] In spring 1935 the EKH's stock list included 1,330 titles.[546] The sales statistics dated 1 December show that village and small-town public libraries ordered primarily war books (23 titles and 5,150 volumes delivered); in second place were political nonfiction and political novels (26 titles and 4,812 volumes delivered).[547] These were followed by peasant and countryside novels (17 titles/2,592 volumes), historical novels (12 titles/2,075 volumes), faraway countries, travel, and adventure (14 titles/1,982 volumes), biographical novels (6 titles/736 volumes), and books about pilots (2 titles/218 volumes).

By the close of 1936, the EKH's total turnover had almost trebled,[548] a growth attributable partly to the large number of newly opened public libraries and partly to increasing acceptance of the EKH as a central purchasing agency. By now some striking changes to the pattern of new acquisitions were making themselves felt.

---

[543] Die Bücherei 1 (1934), 12.

[544] R. Kock, "Die Neuordnung der Beratungsstellen," Die Bücherei 1 (1934), 18–28; W. Schuster, "Der Stand des deutschen öffentlichen Büchereiwesens. Vortrag, gehalten auf der Schulungstagung des Reichserziehungsministeriums für die Leiter der Landes- und Beratungsstellen am 10. Mai 1935 in Berlin," Die Bücherei 2 (1935), 242–51; F. Schriewer, "Warum staatliche Stellen für das Volksbüchereiwesen," Die Bücherei 3 (1936), 6–13, and Die staatlichen Volksbüchereistellen, 86–92.

[545] "Bekanntmachung des Aktionsausschusses des Börsenvereins der Deutschen Buchhändler betr. Lieferungen an Volksbüchereien," Bbl. no. 99, 30 April 1934, 394.

[546] F. Schinkel, "Die Aufgaben und Arbeitsgrundsätze des Einkaufshauses für Büchereien G.m.b.H.," Die Bücherei 2 (1935), 348–9.

[547] G. Tschich, "Was die deutsche Volksbücherei im letzten Jahr gefördert hat," Die Bücherei 3 (1936), 49–54. The following figures ibid.

[548] G. Tschich, "Die hundert Bücher des Jahres. Zur Verkaufsstatistik des Einkaufshauses für Büchereien," Die Bücherei 4 (1937), 14–20. The following figures ibid.

Although war books and political writings (fiction and nonfiction) still led the field, with 28.5 percent of purchases (23 titles/8,621 volumes) for the former and 25.8 percent (28 titles/7,813 volumes) for the latter, in the area of general fiction the peasant novel—a genre promoted by the regime—had dropped from 14.8 percent to 9.7 percent (11 titles/2,928 volumes), while historical novels rose from 11.8 percent to 15.6 percent (15 titles/4,726 volumes). Books about foreign countries, travel, and adventure and animal or hunting stories also enjoyed growing popularity (from 11.3 percent to 12.1 percent, 14 titles/3,664 volumes). In other words, the underlying political tone remained constant, but the increase in "apolitical" domains indicates that the public libraries' acquisitions policy was now taking more careful account of the public's desire for entertainment and informative nonfiction.

As well as the EKH, from 1939 the acquisitions lists for village and smaller town libraries issued by the Reich Office for Popular Libraries also helped to guide the structure of collections into Nazi-approved channels.[549] Finally, in collaboration with its provincial branches the Reich Office accelerated the expansion of public library provision in the countryside, using the model introduced in Thuringia in 1937 whereby standardized "blocks" of books were supplied centrally to form the nucleus of each new library.[550] The core holdings of village libraries were now ordered and delivered via the EKH on the basis of the Reich-level acquisition lists. Additional suggestions for the acquisition of regionally specific works could be made by the local state offices.[551] The directors of the libraries themselves had little say in the structure and development of their collections. In small towns, the state library apparatus had a free hand, and—given that thousands of new libraries were established in the countryside and small towns during the Nazi regime using the regime's core lists—it could determine the shape of the collections to a very large extent. The same did not hold for mid-sized and larger cities, where the

---

[549] The "Reich lists" were compiled for the REM, and doubled as the stock lists of the EKH.
[550] See the report by the director of the Thuringian Office for Popular Libraries, Joseph Witsch, n.d. (March 1937), HStA Weimar Thüringisches Ministerium f. Volksbildung/C 707 fol. 11–12.
[551] *Reichsliste für kleinere städtische Büchereien* 1936, Preface, 2.

Reich Education Ministry was confronted with institutions that had evolved over many decades and library directors with considerable self-confidence and expertise. As a result, existing librarians were in many cases replaced by tried-and-tested Party members from 1933 onward.[552] This was the catalyst for a transformation of collections in larger cities.

When the war began, the public libraries were declared "base camps for deploying the book, strengthening the defensive spirit at home, and providing instruction on the intentions of our adversaries."[553] This heightened politicization failed to capture the taste of the reading public. In March 1942, the SD's *Meldungen aus dem Reich* reported that the public libraries' potential for mass impact was impeded not only by the more attractive range of reading on offer in commercial libraries, but also by the public libraries' image as "official institutes."[554] Thus, the religiously affiliated population, especially in the west of Germany, saw public libraries as "clearing houses for National Socialist literature that have ousted their traditional parish libraries." In general, the SD informants reported, the public "did not wish to be 'trained and educated.'"

But even a skillfully mixed collection, combining ideological reading with harmless entertainment, youth fiction, and self-improvement, could not prevent large numbers of readers migrating to the commercial libraries and their lighter fare.[555] Faced with the mass popularity of light entertainment fiction, librarians returned to a debate on literary value and taste that many had believed resolved once and for all by the advent of Nazi rule.[556] As it turned

---

[552] For details, see Boese, *Das Öffentliche Bibliothekswesen* (contract book title), 205–14.
[553] "Gegenwärtige Aufgaben der öffentlichen Volksbüchereien. Ministerialerlass vom 12. September 1939," *Deutsche Wissenschaft, Erziehung und Volksbildung* 5 (1939), 507.
[554] *Meldungen aus dem Reich*, vol. 9, no. 268, 16 March 1942, 3473–5, here 3474. The following two quotations ibid.
[555] Thuringian State Public Libraries Office to Thuringian Minister of Public Instruction, 11 November 1940, HStA Weimar Thüringisches Ministerium f. Volksbildung/C 629 fol. 277–8.
[556] E. Thier, "Zur Entwicklung der Wertfrage in der bibliothekarischen Diskussion," *Die Bücherei* 11 (1944), 12–25; J. Witsch, "Über die Relativität der Begriffe 'Unterhaltung' und 'Entspannung,'" ibid. 25–32; K. Hecker, "Zum Phänomen des 'schlechten Geschmacks,'" ibid. 301–21; E. Thier, "Von der 'reinen Liebe' bei Hedwig Courths-Mahler und bei ihren Schwestern im Geist," ibid. 322–9.

out, managing the structure and development of collections only solved one aspect of the problem; the second, and crucial, task was to change readers' behavior.[557] The accomplishment of that task foundered both on the lack of competent Nazi authors and on the traditional reading preferences of broad segments of the population.

Nonetheless, in the midst of the war, the Reich Education Ministry felt that substantial progress had been made. In 1933/34, the provinces and communities of the German Reich had maintained 9,494 public libraries and a further 5,692 lending locations for 144 mobile libraries, but on 1 April 1933 only 6,231 of these facilities were actually functional, with 3,263 of the permanent libraries existing only on paper.[558] By 30 March 1940, 2,085 libraries had been "rebuilt and newly opened after complete reorganization" and a further 5,592 established from scratch. Austrian *Anschluss* and the annexation of the Sudetenland added 2,840 libraries to the German tally, bringing the total number of public libraries to 16,748 by 1940. By 1943 this had risen yet again, to more than 21,000.[559]

During the war, smaller communities in particular had to cut back their budget allocations, which had been rising consistently since the mid-1930s, and funds for new acquisitions became tight.[560] The process of modernizing the public libraries—initiated by the Reich Education Ministry at great effort and expense—began to falter. Further difficulties arose from the shortage of books on sale, worsening from 1941 on. Because apparently neither the Ministry nor the library offices subordinate to it made any arrangements for a systematic distribution of new publications across the country,

---

[557] E. Thier, "Leserkunde als Aufgabe," *Die Bücherei* 9 (1942), 269–88; H. J. Kuhn, "Leserkundliche Probleme im Lichte der Schichttheorie," *Die Bücherei* 11 (1944), 113–27.

[558] H. Dähnhardt, "Zur Entwicklung des öffentlichen Büchereiwesens," *Die Bücherei* 8 (1941), 305–8. See also G. Menz, "Die deutschen Volksbüchereien," *Bbl.* no. 182, 8 August 1935, 641–3, which gives statistics on expenditure in the various regions and an overview of public libraries in German cities.

[559] Figures in F. Heiligenstaedt, "Zur Buchbeschaffung im Büchereiwesen," *Bbl.* no. 133, 21 August 1943, 146–7.

[560] "Zur Lage im Büchereiwesen," *Meldungen aus dem Reich*, vol. 5, no. 126, 23 September 1940, 1597–8. This note refers to information from Neustettin (now Szczecinek), according to which towns had cut spending on libraries by around one third compared to prewar figures.

the public libraries' uncoordinated orders through publishers and the retail book trade increasingly went unfilled.[561] Quality literature and classics, in particular, were in extremely short supply, while political writings, unpopular with the public, continued to flood the market in high print runs.[562]

Against all the odds, however, the Reich Education Ministry held fast to its intention of maintaining the public library service even during "total war."[563] A decree of 15 May 1943 even required the Reich governors, the provincial teaching administrations, and the provincial and district governors to extend the opening hours of the public libraries into the evening, so as to "account adequately for the needs of those working all day."[564] With the evacuation of many residents from areas badly affected by bombing, the administrative offices of the receiving *Gaue* and communes were instructed to adapt their local libraries' collections to the expanded demand.[565] In the bombed-out larger cities, too, the population was to be assured a steady supply of reading by rebuilding libraries or setting up provisional lending facilities.

All these measures were intended to demonstrate faith in the unbroken viability of the Nazi regime, but the Minister of Education was also responding to genuine needs that found expression in a substantial increase to the number of readers during the war. As the range of books on offer from bookstores and subscription libraries grew more and more impoverished, the public libraries finally had a

---

[561] "Lücken in der Belieferung der öffentlichen Bibliotheken mit Büchern," *Meldungen aus dem Reich*, vol. 12, no. 336, 19 November 1942, 4486–7; Assistant Secretary Dr. Otto Benecke (DGT) to DGT Württemberg provincial office, 22 May 1944, BArch R 36/2355.
[562] Stuttgart city councilor Dr. Känekamp to DGT provincial office in Stuttgart, 11 April 1944, re: meeting of the local cultural association, ibid.
[563] H. Dähnhardt, "Die öffentlichen Büchereien im totalen Kriege der Nation," *Die Bücherei* 10 (1943), 91–8, and "Warum bleiben die Büchereien geöffnet?" *Die Bücherei* 11 (1944), 297–301.
[564] "Öffnungszeiten der öffentlichen (Stadt- und Volks-) Büchereien," *Deutsche Wissenschaft, Erziehung und Volksbildung* 9 (1943), 175.
[565] "Runderlass an die Reichsstatthalter in den Reichsgauen, die Unterrichts- verwaltungen der Länder und die Regierungspräsidenten in Preußen vom 17.9.1943 betr. Verstärkter Einsatz der öffentlichen (Stadt- und Volks-) Büchereien in den Aufnahmegauen für die aus den stark luftgefährdeten Gebieten umquartierte Bevölkerung und deren Einsatz in den luftgefährdeten Gebieten selbst," ibid. 333–4.

chance of tempting a larger segment of the population through their doors. But the growing discrepancy between supply and demand, along with the destruction of many library buildings,[566] would soon put paid to the plan of a comprehensive and attractive network of public libraries—pursued since 1933 with the aim of achieving the ideological saturation of the German population.

State, Provincial, and University Libraries

Sympathetic though they doubtlessly were to the "National Socialist revolution," the majority of state, provincial, and university librarians agreed from the start that the literature rejected as "harmful and undesirable" should not disappear completely from their institutions.[567] In fact, this position was supported officially. The Reich Ministry of the Interior pointed out that § 7 of the Reich President's emergency decree "for the protection of the German people," issued on 4 February 1933, was a "discretionary" provision.[568] It was acceptable not to confiscate a publication whose content endangered public security or order "if the personality of the owner warrants that the communist or Marxist literature in his safekeeping will only be used for permitted purposes, namely for research."[569]

The special treatment for research libraries was driven by political considerations: the Bavarian Ministry of Education and Culture explained on 5 April 1933 that banned literature was not to be physically removed from the research libraries "because scientific combating of the Bolshevist, Marxist, and pacifist poison depends for its success on knowledge of the relevant literature."[570] The

---

[566] See Dähnhardt's 1 October 1943 report on his visit to various western German cities on 25 September 1943, BArch R 36/2355.

[567] See, for example, Prinzhorn, *Die Aufgaben der Bibliotheken*, 6–7; H. P. des Coudres, "Das verbotene Schrifttum und die wissenschaftlichen Bibliotheken," *ZfB* 52 (1935), 459–71; R. Buttmann, "Nationalsozialistische Bibliothekspolitik," *Bbl.* no. 49, 27 February 1936, 181–3; Happel, *Das wissenschaftliche Bibliothekswesen*, 404–5.

[568] Reference to this interpretation in des Coudres, "Das verbotene Schrifttum und die wissenschaftlichen Bibliotheken," 460.

[569] Thus des Coudres's paraphrase of the Reich Interior Ministry statement, ibid.

[570] Bavarian Minister of Teaching and Culture's decision, cited ibid. 461.

research libraries therefore retained their existing archival role and were shielded from arbitrary interference by Nazi activists. This did not, however, resolve the question of how banned literature should be handled in librarians' everyday work.

It was only on 3 April 1935 that a Reich Education Ministry decree obligated every research library on German territory to examine its collections closely and lock away—"secrete"—the "harmful and undesirable literature" it found. To be sure, the detail of what was to count as banned literature had to be worked out painstakingly by the librarians themselves.[571] Initially, their only assistance in this task came from the Börsenverein's journal *Börsenblatt*, which since 1933 had been reproducing bans published in the *Deutscher Reichsanzeiger*, the *Deutsches Kriminalpolizeiblatt*, and the *Bayerisches Polizeiblatt*. This did not offer an effective overview of banning decisions, since the *Börsenblatt* reprinted only a selection. The release of List 1 of Harmful and Undesirable Literature seemed to offer a remedy for the information deficit; the list was sent to research libraries in March 1936 with an order to inspect their collections carefully and place the indexed literature under lock and key.[572] However, after a series of spot checks in university institute and department libraries, in December 1936 the Reich Education Ministry was disappointed to find that "the seriousness" of the need to secrete banned literature had "not yet been grasped."[573] In some of the libraries investigated, even "Marxist and Bolshevist literature" could still be found on open shelves, so that "works by Lenin, Bukharin, Rosa Luxemburg, Karl Liebknecht, Kurt Eisner, Erich Mühsam, etc." were freely accessible.[574] Evidently, at this point library managements still did not have a unified idea of how "secretion" was to be carried out in practice.[575]

---

[571] Reference to this situation ibid. 464.

[572] REM confidential circular to the teaching authorities of the provinces, 23 March 1936, Thüringisches HStA Weimar Thüringisches Ministerium für Volksbildung/C 619 fol. 239.

[573] REM circular decree, 16 December 1936, Thüringisches HStA Weimar Thüringisches Ministerium für Volksbildung/C 619 fol. 246.

[574] Ibid. A case study is provided by Greguletz, "Die Preußische Staatsbibliothek."

[575] See Schochow, *Die Preußische Staatsbibliothek*, 31–3; Toussaint, *Die Universitätsbibliothek Freiburg*, 150–72, and *Die Universitätsbibliotheken Heidelberg, Jena und Köln*, 59–64 (on Heidelberg), 107–14 (on Jena), 305 (on Cologne); Lemberg, *Verboten und nicht verbrannt*, vol. II; Ruppelt, "Die Herzog August Bibliothek," 377– 81.

The Reich Education Ministry now adopted a more strident tone, insisting that all items of "harmful and undesirable literature" must be kept physically separate from the rest of the collection. This still left the problems of cataloguing and granting access to the books. In this respect, too, the Education Ministry's instructions do not appear to have resulted in a uniform practice.[576] For example, the Deutsche Bücherei in Leipzig left the indexed items in its publicly accessible main catalogue, merely adding a note that the books in question were not available for general loan. In other libraries, the titles were removed from the general catalogues and listed in an internal or special catalogue not accessible to the public. Readers wishing to see banned or "undesirable" books and periodicals generally had to present evidence that they needed the item for their research.

The requirement to secrete literature categorized as "harmful and undesirable" was itself a flagrant incursion into research librarians' day-to-day work. In addition, special political tasks were often imposed upon the library directors. In 1940 Volkmar Eichstädt, a Prussian State Library employee since 1934, tried to persuade his fellow librarians to participate more actively in "research into the Jewish question."[577] The state libraries in Berlin and Munich, the National Library in Vienna, the municipal and university library in Frankfurt, the library of the Reich Institute for the History of the New Germany in Munich, and its affiliated Institute for Research into the Jewish Question in Frankfurt were all already in possession of large book and manuscript collections of Judaica and Hebraica. In Eichstädt's opinion, however, it was now necessary to reorganize the subject catalogues in all research libraries along racial lines. The model was to be the catalogues of the NSDAP libraries, in which "the Jewish question" was "mostly classified as a subsection of the race question or else in the category of National Socialism's ideological opponents." Eichstädt also called on his colleagues to help with the registration of all Jewish authors and Jewish writers of doctoral dissertations, and with the scrutiny of all "Jewish-German

---

[576] See des Coudres, "Das verbotene Schrifttum und die wissenschaftlichen Bibliotheken," 466.
[577] Eichstädt, "Das Schrifttum zur Judenfrage in den deutschen Bibliotheken," *ZfB* 57 (1940), 60–73. The following quotations ibid.

mixed marriages as regards their descendants and branches." This point was motivated by the fact that, more than seven years after the Nazis came to power, libraries—like the book trade and all other institutions involved in disseminating literature—lacked a comprehensive and authoritative list of all "Jewish" or "Jewish-by-marriage" authors, whose works were, after all, supposed to be removed without trace from public use and the minds of the German population. In April 1940 a general ban on all writings by "fully and half-Jewish" authors had been imposed.

To address this problem, in June 1941 the Deutsche Bücherei received a new commission from the Propaganda Ministry literature department. Collaboration on the List of Harmful and Undesirable Literature having gone so smoothly, the DB staff in Leipzig were now asked to compile a "general register of Jewish literature in the German language."[578] The librarians were all too aware of the difficulties attending the question of who should be counted as a "Jew"—the distinction between "Jews by religion" and "Jews by race who no longer profess the Jewish faith" had been nullified by the race legislation of the Nazi state.[579] In the absence of statistical material, the proportion of "Jewish authors" among the 2.18 million publications that had appeared in Germany between 1901 and 1940 could only be guessed at. Curt Fleischhack, a librarian in the Deutsche Bücherei's bibliographical division, believed it was "around 5 percent" and thus "approximately 105,000 publications."

The Propaganda Ministry supplied special funds of 27,200 RM, and on 1 August 1941 work began, under the management of librarian Hans Ruppert. Working from the "register of Jewish authors" drawn up by Rosenberg's Reichsstelle, the most important Jewish and antisemitic reference works and many other sources were first consulted.[580] Extensive and detailed reviews followed of disserta-

[578] Head of literature department to Propaganda Minister, 24 June 1941, DB-Archiv no. 612/0 fol. 5–6.

[579] Memorandum from Curt Fleischhack, 5 April 1941, on the "Bibliography of Jewish Literature in the German Language 1901–1940" sent to Dr. Koch (RMVP literature department) by Uhlendahl on 8 April, ibid. fol. 1–3. The following points ibid.

[580] On this and the following, see Uhlendahl to Propaganda Ministry, 30 November 1942, ibid. fol. 25, and the two reports by Ruppert on the March 1944 version of the bibliography, DB-Archiv no. 612/1.

tions, the Deutsche Bücherei's alphabetical catalogue from 1913, Hinrich's catalogues for 1901 through 1912, and both Jewish and antisemitic periodicals. By March 1944, a total of 28,000 index cards had been created, which were used to answer inquiries from state and Party agencies. Once the research was finished, Heinrich Uhlendahl promised in November 1942, the Deutsche Bücherei would "be in a position to provide absolutely accurate information on all questions related to Jewish authors." However, in spring 1944 work on the register was halted by war-related staff shortages.[581]

Wartime brought the research libraries quite other problems as well. In the course of the 1930s, arbitrary political decisions and difficulties in obtaining foreign currency had already torn holes in their collections of foreign literature,[582] and with the tightening of book censorship in fall 1939 restrictions were placed on acquisitions of new scholarly and scientific publications first from France and Britain, later from the Soviet Union, the United States, and other enemy nations.[583] In addition, when aerial bombing began in earnest, the German research libraries were largely unprepared for its intensity.[584] The Baden State Library in Karlsruhe was one of the first to be almost completely destroyed, in a raid on 3 September 1942.[585] In view of the losses, that same month Adolf Jürgens, the director of the national exchange center and the Central Procurement Office for German Libraries based in the Prussian State Library, suggested to the Reich Ministry of Education that "processing the damage" should be coordinated "from a centralized office."[586] That way, Jürgens argued, "competition between damaged libraries to purchase the

---

[581] Ruppert to Dr. Elisabeth Frenzel, 15 September 1944, ibid. Frenzel, who worked for Rosenberg's visual arts office, took a special interest in the role of Jews in German cultural life.

[582] Richards, "German Libraries," 158–63; Happel, *Das wissenschaftliche Bibliothekswesen*, 67–71; Komorowski, "Die wissenschaftlichen Bibliotheken," 19.

[583] Happel, *Das wissenschaftliche Bibliothekswesen*, 70–1; Toussaint, *Die Universitätsbibliothek Freiburg*, 105–7; Richards, "German Libraries," 163–9.

[584] See Leyh, *Die deutschen wissenschaftlichen Bibliotheken*, 8–34; Schochow, *Die Preußische Staatsbibliothek*, 55–67; Friedrich, *The Fire*, 470–9.

[585] Report on the destruction of the Baden provincial library in Karlsruhe by the air raid of 2/3 September 1942, BArch R 21/10 648 fol. 52.

[586] Memorandum, 7 September 1942, BArch R 21/10 651 fol. 20–3. The following quotations ibid.

books that come onto the market" could be eliminated and the costs of rebuilding the system prevented from "rising unnecessarily." The necessary replacement of books was to be achieved in six ways: by "accessing confiscated holdings," some from Gestapo seizures of banned literature within the Reich and others from the plunder of books in Alsace, Lorraine, Luxembourg, and Poznán; by using the collections of dissolved libraries and institutes—here Jürgens was thinking especially of the state institutions that would become redundant in the planned new order of the German Reich, and of the Polish universities that would be dissolved; by purchasing books in Germany and abroad; by dispersing the duplicates held by research libraries and the national exchange center; and by filing claims for German libraries' bombing-related losses of foreign literature when the expected peace treaty was negotiated.

In August 1943, Education Minister Rust stipulated that the reconstruction of libraries destroyed by bombing would be carried out by the national exchange center in cooperation with the Reich Advisory Board for Library Affairs.[587] By the end of the war, the majority of German research libraries had suffered substantial damage: the state libraries in Berlin, Hamburg, and Munich; the provincial libraries in Darmstadt, Dortmund, Dresden, Düsseldorf, Kassel, Kiel, Oldenburg, and Stuttgart; the university libraries in Bonn, Frankfurt, Giessen, Göttingen, Jena, Leipzig, Munich, Münster, Rostock, and Würzburg; the libraries of the technical universities in Aachen, Berlin, Darmstadt, Dresden, Hannover, Karlsruhe, Munich, and Stuttgart; and the public libraries in Aachen, Dortmund, Dresden, Duisburg, Erfurt, Essen, Frankfurt, Leipzig, Mainz, Magdeburg, Mannheim, and Nuremberg.[588] At the end of August 1944, around 7 million volumes of scientific and scholarly literature with a total value of approximately 120 million RM had been lost.[589] The political destruction

---

[587] "Runderlass des Reichsministeriums für Wissenschaft, Erziehung und Volksbildung vom 13.8.1943," *Deutsche Wissenschaft, Erziehung und Volksbildung* 9 (1943), 266.
[588] For details, see Reich Education Ministry's information on the research libraries "damaged by enemy action," BArch R 21/10 648, especially the lists of damage to German university and provincial libraries and the libraries of the technical universities, ibid. fol. 98–9; Leyh, *Die deutschen wissenschaftlichen Bibliotheken*, 35–198.
[589] National exchange center, Dept. III (Reconstruction of libraries) to REM, 31 August 1944, BArch R 21/10 651 fol. 147.

from within the library system had now been followed by physical destruction from without.

Books for the Wehrmacht during World War II

Alfred Rosenberg's appeal for contributions to an "NSDAP book collection for the German Wehrmacht" in mid-October 1939 brought the question of soldiers' reading material to public attention.[590] The first collection, carried out within the Winter Relief campaign in 1939/40, focused on publishers and booksellers; later ones addressed the public at large. The books they donated were intended to go to fighting troops and those in field hospitals, infirmaries, and assembly camps. The campaign's objective was less to collect the greatest number of books than to obtain "especially good literature," as defined by Rosenberg's literature office in the form of a list of suggested titles.[591] After the fourth collection, which brought in almost 10.5 million books, Rosenberg informed Hitler of a historic event: the German people had "given its soldiers the largest library in the world."[592] By winter 1943/44, Rosenberg's book donation campaigns had yielded a total of over 43 million books.[593] Given that the potential donors were themselves suffering from the war-related scarcity of books, it is hardly surprising that in 1942 the OKW complained to the NSDAP Party Chancellery regarding the "often shamefully poor content" of the books donated for its soldiers.[594] As so often, Rosenberg's literature brigades had organized enthusiastically, but ineffectively.

Considerably more successful in supplying the army with reading material was the Zentrale der Frontbuchhandlungen (ZdF), which

---

[590] "Ein Aufruf Alfred Rosenbergs: Spendet Bücher für unsere Soldaten!" *Bbl.* no. 240, 14 October 1939, 685.
[591] Hagemeyer, "An die Verleger und Buchhändler Deutschlands," *Bbl.* no. 255, 2 November 1939, 705.
[592] Rosenberg to Hitler, 3 June 1943, BArch NS 8/176 fol. 23.
[593] Rosenberg to Bormann, 14 August 1944, BArch NS 8/191 fol. 211, citing the figure of 43,471,018.
[594] Party Chancellery to Rosenberg, 2 October 1942, re: Rosenberg book donations, BArch NS 8/187 fol. 39.

coordinated frontline bookselling. Set up on 4 September 1939, it came to dominate the German book market in the years that followed.[595] Leadership of the new company fell to Eberhard Heffe, the head of the German Labor Front (DAF) publishing operations. The managing director was Theodor Leidel. The DAF also gave the ZdF the capital it needed to pay the salaries of the full-time frontline book dealers and carry out its other tasks. The ZdF established ten depots, in Paris, Brussels, Oslo, Rovaniemi, Riga, Warsaw, Lemberg (Lviv), Dnipropetrovsk (Odessa from late fall 1943), Vienna, and Rome (Meran from late fall 1943).[596] The depots were supplied with books directly, bypassing the retail book trade, and in turn delivered considerable quantities to the frontline bookstores in the occupied areas. In 1943, there were more than 300 such "book sales outlets" across all the occupied regions, at the front, in field hospitals, and in the soldiers' lodgings. In France alone, their number grew from sixty to ninety-eight between 1942 and the end of 1943.[597] There were also twelve "bookmobiles" traveling the front lines, and in Norway even several motorboats.[598] On paper, the ZdF cooperated on an equal basis with the OKW, the Propaganda Ministry, the Chamber of Literature, and the Börsenverein; in practice, however, it was with OKW support and Propaganda Ministry toleration that Heffe gradually built up a distinct distribution network and publishing structure, increasingly in competition with the traditional book-trade system inside Germany.

The process began quite innocuously. In 1940, the Promotion and Advisory Office for German Literature initiated a propaganda campaign in which the *Volksgenossen* at home were asked to send books to their friends and relatives at the front. Lists of the most suitable books to send could be obtained free of charge from bookstores. The first two lists, in 1940, included around

---

[595] On the following, see especially Bühler and Bühler, *Der Frontbuchhandel*; Bühler and Kirbach, "Die Wehrmachtsausgaben."

[596] Provisional report on the 1943 financial year by Zentrale der Frontbuchhandlungen, 10 January 1944, StAL BV/792 fol. 185–8, here fol. 185. The following figures ibid. fol. 186.

[597] Hinze, *Frontbuchhandlung Paris*, 8. See also A. Martin, "Nachschub für die Bücher-'Front'. Vom Bücherwagen zur ortsfesten Frontbuchhandlung," *Bbl.* no. 180/181, 15 August 1942, 163.

[598] Provisional report on the 1943 financial year, StAL BV/792 fol. 186.

1,500 titles, mostly books published by Nazi companies. The third list, of spring 1941, proposed 350 titles, a mixture of political or ideological categories (with headings such as "In the force field of politics and economics" or "German blood on foreign soil"), war books ("Enduring soldierliness"), and entertaining and reflective fiction ("For entertainment and contemplation," "Wisdom for the knapsack").[599] When selecting the titles, the Propaganda Ministry and the NSDAP's Central Propaganda Office took great care to reflect the soldiers' own reading interests as accurately as possible. A survey of Wehrmacht soldiers carried out at the turn of 1941 to 1942 by the Reich Ring for National Socialist Propaganda and Popular Enlightenment showed that the troops preferred detective stories, Karl May's Winnetou novels and other adventures, and romantic fiction.[600] In February 1942 the Ring's director, Walter Tiessler, therefore advised Goebbels to arrange for 95 percent of the books sent to the front to be entertainment-based.[601] Only the remaining 5 percent should be ideological in nature, and even here it was important "not to serve up heavy fare, but books that are easy to grasp." Tiessler had already recommended the production of ideological literature of this kind—"in an interesting form, with gripping descriptions or in the style of a novel"—in 1940.[602] Following the model of the Church's stories of the saints, for example, authors should be encouraged to give literary expression to "the lives of Party comrades who are playing an outstanding part in the war or in everyday life."

In 1941 the ZdF issued its own list of recommendations, containing 2,600 titles. Unlike the Promotion and Advisory Office's list, this one emphasized quality fiction and entertainment, drew on

---

[599] K. Felchner, "Sendet Bücher an die Front. Ein Überblick über die Dritte Buch-Feldpostliste und die damit verbundene Werbeaktion," *Bbl.* no. 59, 11 March 1941, 88–90.

[600] Confidential circular from Tiessler to Party comrades in the Wehrmacht, 8 January 1942, with a selection of responses, BArch NS 18/483.

[601] Submission to the Minister via state secretary Gutterer re: literature for the front, 17 February 1942, BArch NS 18/483. See also R. Stoffregen, "Was lesen unsere Soldaten im fünften Kriegsjahr?" *Bbl.* no. 177, 2 December 1943, 207–8; G. E. Ter-Nedden, "Was wünscht der Soldat zu lesen?" *Unseren Kameraden bei der Wehrmacht diese Mitteilungen der Reichsschrifttumskammer*, October 1944, 6–7.

[602] Tiessler to Haegert, 17 April 1940, p. 1, BArch NS 18/89.

a broader spectrum of publishing houses, and included books by writers outside the state or Party literary canon. Among the millions of soldiers in the occupied regions, such book lists and the establishment of more and more frontline bookstores helped to create demand, fulfilling which was, according to Wilhelm Baur's instructions of November 1940, to be treated as a top priority.[603] That posed no problem until increasingly restrictive paper rationing began to limit the manufacture of books from 1941/42 on. A completely new book market then arose, following its own rationale and fostering the corruption that always thrives when resources are scarce.[604] More and more publishers in the Reich were now producing licensed and military editions for the Wehrmacht; they received preferential paper allocations from the Economic Office of the German Book Trade for such editions, although the actual printing, in very high print runs, was frequently carried out in France, the Netherlands, Belgium, Norway, Prague, Brno, or Riga. This lucrative business benefited not only the Nazi publishing companies or those with close links to the regime, but also the great traditional houses with no NSDAP affiliation, which were all able to increase their turnover substantially in this period.[605] In addition, the OKW had enormous paper allocations of its own. They were invested in dedicated series produced by civilian publishers (such as the Sonderaktion Feldpost, "field post campaign") or commissions to branches of the DAF's publishers in the occupied areas, and in the Wehrmacht's own production of premium quality books, printed in the occupied countries.[606]

In total, around 75 million copies of standard or frontline editions were produced in this market segment between 1939 and the end of 1943.[607] Between 1942 and 1943, the proportion of books that were produced for the Zentrale der Frontbuchhandlungen using a

---

[603] W. Baur, "An alle Berufskameraden vom Verlag!" *Bbl.* no. 281, 30 November 1940, 445.
[604] See Bühler and Simons, *Die blendenden Geschäfte.*
[605] Bühler and Bühler, *Der Frontbuchhandel*, 133–83; Bühler and Kirbach, "Die Wehrmachtsausgaben." See also Chapter 5, "Publishers and Booksellers."
[606] See Bühler and Bühler, "Die Wehrmacht als Verleger" and *Der Frontbuchhandel*, 184–231; provisional report on the 1943 financial year, StAL BV/792.
[607] Figures in G. Schönfelder, "Buchhandel in der Entscheidung," *Unseren Kameraden bei der Wehrmacht diese Mitteilungen der Reichsschrifttumskammer*, November 1944, 1–4, here 3.

Wehrmacht paper allocation rose from 7 percent to 55 percent.[608] As a result, in 1943—when the book market was suffering more and more drastic shortages inside Germany—the ZdF was still able to sell 3.5 million copies and more than double its turnover, from 16,740,843 RM in 1942 to 35,000,000 RM in 1943. Even in late 1944, it had stocks of 8.7 million copies worth 20.4 million RM.

In view of this enormous financial and logistical potential, publishers and the largest commission and wholesale book dealers (that is, Lühe & Co. and the Volckmar companies L. Fernau of Leipzig and Hermann Schultze of Stuttgart) increasingly relied on obtaining commissions from the OKW, the Army, Luftwaffe, and Navy High Commands, individual divisions, and the ZdF, and eventually also Organisation Todt and the Waffen-SS.[609] From 1942 onward, commissions of this kind served to safeguard continued production and thus economic viability, but in the context of the negotiations over publishing company closures in 1943/44, they also seemed to promise businesses a chance of survival as producers important to the war effort. On the other hand, the functionaries of the Chamber of Literature and the Börsenverein had to watch in frustration as their new partners—the publishers' new clients—went above their heads, organizing the allocation of paper rations and the printing of the books manufactured using those rations, setting out standards for book design, fixing book prices and purchase discounts, and arranging the distribution of huge quantities of books within the occupied areas. In 1944, retail booksellers in the German Reich no longer had any access at all to this market, and found it ever more difficult to explain to their customers why books still on sale in the

---

[608] Provisional report on the 1943 financial year by the Zentrale der Frontbuchhandlungen, 10 January 1944, StAL BV/792 fol. 185. The following figures ibid.

[609] See the list of book publishers involved in the defense economy, divided by military district (as at spring 1942), BArch R 55/689 fol. 33–49. The skilled employees of these more than a hundred companies were exempted from military service on the basis of an agreement between the RMVP and the OKW. Among the tasks of the wholesaler Lühe & Co. was to supply the Zentrale der Frontbuchhandlungen and establish division libraries for Nazi officers. See attestation by the Book Trade Group, 25 January 1945, StAL BV/F 5918. On the Waffen-SS's entry into this market, see SS Main Office (Office for Ideological Education) to Börsenverein, 22 June 1944 and 25 January 1945, StAL BV/792 fol. 53, 84.

frontline trade could no longer be obtained in local bookstores within Germany.[610]

The Chamber of Literature made some attempts to master the problems arising from the ZdF's unregulated activity. But the draft of an "official notification" that the Chamber circulated in late November 1944 testifies to a general failure to grasp the realities of the situation. Criticizing the draft in a letter to the Börsenverein's manager in December 1944, Johannes Roeseler, the general agent of Deutscher Verlag, pointed out that "with the official authority of the Chamber, the few and small editions still being produced by, especially, fiction publishers are almost entirely commandeered for public purposes."[611] He was referring to the fact that 30 percent of every edition was requisitioned by the OKW and the Propaganda Ministry for the troops, by Lühe & Co. for evacuated and bombed-out Germans, and by the libraries' purchasing house EKH. A further 50 percent usually had to be dispatched straight to the ZdF, so that in all, 80 percent of each printing had to be "given up to the public authorities without the involvement of book retailing." Because research libraries, public agencies, and bombed-out retailers also had a right to "special allocations," the "civilian book-buyer" was left with very little to choose from. Kurt Kretzschmar, the director of the commerce *Fachschaft*, asked Wilhelm Baur "to place your protective hand over the survival of book retailing."[612] Instead of granting monopoly rights to an "apparatus" like the ZdF that was both costly and cumbersome, he argued, more support should be given to the far more efficient retail book trade, which was better tailored to the individual needs of each locality. The Chamber's draft proposal to ameliorate this discrepancy between civilian and army access to paper was picked up by the Propaganda Ministry, since the head of the literature department there was keen to arrange the control of print runs himself "on a case-by-case basis."[613] However, this only masked the fact that, with Propaganda Ministry support, the large-scale demand of the Wehrmacht was actually supplied "exclusively

[610] See, for example, the specialist bookstore Schmorl & von Seefeld Nachf. (Hannover) to Börsenverein, 23 November 1944, StAL BV/792 fol. 126.

[611] Roeseler to Börsenverein, 4 December 1944, StAL BV/792 fol. 133.

[612] Kretzschmar to Baur, 20 December 1944, ibid. fol. 151.

[613] RSK manager Gentz to Dr. Hess and others, 21 December 1944, ibid. fol. 159.

via the ZdF," while the retail book trade had to make do with the few scraps left over.[614]

Book Shortages on the Home Front

On Cantate Sunday 1940, the head of the Propaganda Ministry's literature department used his first appearance at a Börsenverein Annual General Meeting to spell out the role of books in wartime.[615] The book was, Haegert declared, "a light and convenient vehicle for thoughts, and even today—after developments in press, radio, and film—still the most important means of influencing the spiritual and intellectual stance of the German *Volk* in all its profundity." This applied both to the soldier, who could carry books with him "up to the very front line and into battle," and to the civilian population. Because civilians' life in war was necessarily played out "in their own homes far more than was formerly the case," they had "more time than before to devote to books." Book manufacture and sales, as a domain of cultural life, therefore made an essential contribution to "our nation's power of resistance and attack."

In the initial phase of the war, publishers and booksellers had no difficulty in fulfilling this state-imposed mission, but by 1940 it was already proving impossible to complete more than 40 percent of orders in the book trade.[616] From 1941, with permission from the Chamber and the Economic Office of the German Book Trade, print jobs were more and more frequently passed on to printers in Belgium, the Netherlands, France, Sweden, the "Protectorate of Bohemia and Moravia," and to a limited extent Switzerland.[617] Hoping to prevent manufacturing shortages from worsening even further, in April 1941 the Chamber of Literature ordered a freeze on the establishment of new publishers.[618] It remained in force until the

---

[614] Gentz to Dr. Hess, 21 March 1945, ibid. fol. 178.

[615] "Schrifttum und Buchhandel im Kriege," *Bbl.* no. 94, 23 April 1940, 148–52.

[616] *Meldungen aus dem Reich*, vol. 5, no. 117, 22 August 1940, 1492. On the following, see ibid. no. 136, 28 October 1940, 1713.

[617] For the individual procedures, see BArch R 56 V/105.

[618] "Grundungssperre für Verlagsbuchhandlungen," in Ihde, *Handbuch der Reichsschrifttumskammer*, 135. On the background, see RSK Dept. II, Leipzig, to RSK headquarters, Berlin, 22 February 1941, BArch R 56 V/107 fol. 38–9.

end of the war, and covered new publishing divisions within existing companies, new publishing companies, and the incorporation of publishing operations into bookselling companies. Any exceptions required special approval from the Propaganda Minister.[619]

In September 1941, Haegert and Wilhelm Baur appealed to booksellers to offer their scant stock "first and foremost" to soldiers, armaments workers, and "German working women," since these groups, "before others, can today claim a right to the values and power of German culture."[620] Such calls had little basis in commercial reality, for retail booksellers could not in practice turn away the mass of book-buyers that began to besiege them in 1939/40. It brought them booming profits, albeit at the cost of high taxes and rapidly emptying warehouses.[621] Wholesalers and publishers, too, were hard pressed to keep up with the unbridled public demand, and by late 1941 the entire book distribution system within German borders was tottering. In 1942 the total copies of books published in Germany shrank by around 100 million, to 244,208,108, while annual paper consumption fell from 61,432,196 kg to 50,351,034 kg.[622]

To help it cope with the deteriorating supply situation, in May 1942 the book trade was given permission "to ration its stocks by setting aside a limited number of copies for sale, and to refuse further sales once this quota has been exhausted."[623] The idea was to prevent bookstores from becoming completely emptied out; window displays and sales floors were to sustain the illusion of a good range of books still on sale. In December, however, publishers and retailers were once again officially requested "to put their stocks on sale to the very greatest extent possible, disregarding their own personal interests," since Christmas was on the way and "the German book must

---

[619] The authority to grant such exceptions was originally reserved to the RSK president; see the text of the order reproduced in Ihde, § 2. The Ministry literature department informed the RSK of the change on 13 June 1942, BArch R 56 V/107 fol. 13.

[620] "An den deutschen Buchhandel," *Bbl.* no. 226, 27 September 1941, 329.

[621] *Meldungen aus dem Reich*, vol. 8, no. 235, 6 November 1941, 2951.

[622] These figures, from the book production statistics for 1942, can be found in the report on the joint session of the Börsenverein's council and the board of the Book Trade Group on 5 October 1943 in Leipzig, p. 3, StAL/BV 737.

[623] G. von Kommerstädt, "Idealismus und Tatkraft. Dienstbesprechung des Leiters des Deutschen Buchhandels mit den Landesobmännern aus allen Gauen," *Bbl.* no. 104, 16 May 1942, 98–100.

substitute for other gifts to an enhanced degree."[624] The provincial representatives of the book trade were asked to investigate "all complaints by individual *Volksgenossen* regarding books being kept back." As an incentive, booksellers were promised that books would "certainly be available again in greater quantities" in future thanks to the "current large-scale approvals for paper applications."

By spring 1943, the managers of the German book trade had already forgotten this undertaking. "Because the share of book production accounted for by the Wehrmacht, and especially the frontline bookstores, must not be restricted," wrote Baur in the *Börsenblatt*, the continued reduction in the book rations available for distribution was bound to "affect primarily the retail book trade."[625] It would thus be necessary to limit sales to absolutely essential works, such as schoolbooks and technical literature. "All other works, especially ones that serve political orientation and entertainment, must in future be lent out ten times, twenty times, if possible even thirty times." This comment reflected an "official notification" by the Chamber on 8 March 1943 obligating each book retailer to set up a "wartime lending library" within its business.[626] Although the lending requirement had the positive effect of expanding the distribution of sought-after books, it also gave rise to new difficulties. On the one hand, it ratcheted up the competition—both for book rations and for customers and turnover—between retailing and the commercial library sector. On the other, retail booksellers were unfamiliar with the workings of commercial lending, and had little time to acquire the necessary experience and expertise.[627] Furthermore, the new "wartime lending libraries" could offer only a small range of books, so that book retailers still found themselves having to share out crumbs to a book-hungry public.[628]

---

[624] "An den deutschen Buchhandel," *Bbl.* no. 282/283, 12 December 1942, 253. The following quotations ibid.

[625] W. Baur, "Ist das Buch nur für einzelne da?" *Bbl.* no. 60, 12 March 1943, 45.

[626] Published in *Bbl.* no. 64/65, 18 March 1943, 49.

[627] G. Gentz, "Jede Sortimentsbuchhandlung wird Kriegsleihbücherei," *Bbl.* no. 64/65, 18 March 1943, 50–2; K. Kretzschmar, "Einrichtung von Kriegsleihbüchereien," *Bbl.* no. 81, 15 April 1943, 66; W. Franke, "Kriegsleihbüchereien des Sortiments—eine dringende Notwendigkeit," *Bbl.* no. 103, 12 June 1943, 103–4.

[628] *Meldungen aus dem Reich*, vol. 8, no. 235, 6 November 1941, 2953; vol. 12, no. 349, 11 January 1943, 4656–7.

When the Propaganda Ministry ordered a series of bookstore closures in spring 1943, its aim was partly to release labor for the war, but—importantly—also to secure the resulting book stocks for further distribution.[629] Within two weeks of receiving their notification to close, the stores affected had to send the relevant provincial economic office (Landeswirtschaftsamt) a full list of their existing stocks of new and secondhand books or other book-trade articles. As soon as the closure notice came into effect, the sale or removal of any book included on this list was prohibited.

It had been assumed that up to 15 percent of retail bookselling companies across the Reich would be closed,[630] but the situation differed widely by region because decisions on closures had been placed in the hands of the provincial economic offices. When the Börsenverein and the Chamber's Book Trade Group met in Leipzig on 7 May 1943, retailer Albert Diederich pointed out that the *Gau* of Southern Hannover had seen "very extensive closures," whereas in Saxony only around 5 percent of companies had been affected. In Hamburg there had been no closures at all, because the destruction caused by bombing meant there was no other employment available for the labor that would have been released. In the *Gau* of Berlin, the closure of 167 retail bookstores with 533 employees had been planned, leaving only 185 businesses open.[631] But even the provincial leadership of the Chamber advised that "the initiative be carried out slowly" here, because the gains in terms of labor would be "proportionately extremely minor" due to the age structure of Berlin's booksellers and the requirement to protect bomb victims. If the closures in retail bookselling were now expected to be modest in scale, the wholesale trade was to be "maintained as far as possible," since the stocks of closed-down publishers still needed to be sold. [632]

---

[629] "Amtliche Bekanntmachung vom 1.4.1943," *Bbl.* no. 79, 10 April 1943, 61–2.

[630] Estimate by von Kommerstädt at the joint session of the Börsenverein's council and the board of the Book Trade Group on 7 May 1943 in Leipzig, recorded in the report of the session, p. 4, StAL BV/737.

[631] RSK provincial leadership Berlin file note re: closure of retail bookstores, 30 March 1943, LA Berlin Rep. 243, Acc. 1814/5–6.

[632] Wilhelm Baur at the joint session of the Börsenverein's council and the board of the Book Trade Group on 7 May 1943 in Leipzig, p. 1, StAL BV/737.

Only for door-to-door bookselling were "fairly substantial closures" to be undertaken.

A further attempt to solve the crisis in production and distribution was the introduction of very large editions. In a June 1943 article in the *Börsenblatt*, Erckmann rejected the US practice of best-seller publishing, fearing it could be associated with "the one-day wonder, press sensationalism, mass suggestion, and standardized literature."[633] "In the days when it was still ruled by Jews," Erckmann continued, German literature too had "followed such principles, which are alien to its nature." But the systematic deployment of large, 50,000-copy editions was now the only way to guarantee maximally efficient production and thus satisfaction of "the present hunger for books." The procedure, controlled by the ministerial bureaucracy, would only apply to certain types of publications: "great contemporary literature," nineteenth-century classics, entertaining and edifying literature, "outstanding books addressing our era," and children's and youth books. The severity of shortfalls in these areas can be inferred from the fact that in April 1943 the Börsenverein already banned further sales of children's and young adult literature "to guard against the danger of a serious shortage arising at Christmastime."[634]

Starting in fall 1942, new titles and reprints in the field of political and literary works, books for young people, and picture books were no longer to reach book retailers only through the usual ordering system, but also via a central allocation system.[635] Publishers had to choose one of these forms of distribution, and their choice then applied to the entirety of their production in the specified fields. In order to safeguard the book supply to smaller and mid-sized cities, publishers were prohibited from selling the whole print run of a book through sales representatives. On the other hand, they were permitted to set upper limits on orders if they wished.

---

[633] R. Erckmann, "Zum Thema 'Großauflagen,'" *Bbl.* no. 103, 12 June 1943, 102–3. On the following, see ibid.

[634] Wilhelm Baur's announcement of 12 April 1943, reproduced in "Rundschreiben no. 1 der RSK-Abteilung III (Gruppe Buchhandel) an die zum nebenberuflichen Buchverkauf zugelassenen Firmen," p. 7, Deutsche Bücherei classmark ZB 47441/1943 Geheim.

[635] "Bekanntmachung über den buchhändlerischen Bestell-, Liefer- und Zahlungsverkehr vom 9.10.1942," *Bbl.* no. 232/233, 15 October 1942, 209–11.

"Fantasy orders" by bookstores were to be "set aside without being processed and without specifically notifying the orderer." In the allocation procedure, which more than 200 publishers had chosen by the end of November 1942,[636] publishers could make their own decisions on the companies they wished to include in their allocation list. Scientific, scholarly, and technical literature, along with school-books, remained exempt from the new arrangements for the time being. Their publishers were merely required to ensure that the large research libraries received the necessary copies. A specified share of new titles and reprints had to be kept in reserve for this purpose.

The production of school textbooks soon had to be restricted as well, and on 21 April 1943 the Reich Education Ministry decreed a standardized ordering procedure for all nonspecialist schools.[637] Students preparing to move up to the next grade had to fill in an order form, provided to the school by the book trade, listing all the textbooks they would need for the academic year 1943/44. The forms—checked by the class teacher, signed by the parents, and stamped by the principal—were to be handed in "without fail before the start of the summer vacation" to local bookstores or the book sales outlets authorized to sell textbooks. These passed the orders on to publishers and wholesalers, enclosing a signed undertaking that they had deducted from the order those schoolbooks they still had in stock.

In April 1944 the Chamber barred publishers and book retailers from selling schoolbooks to private individuals.[638] Deliveries were now supposed to be made solely to the institution responsible for the school concerned. The dispatch of textbook allocations was handled by special "delivery offices" set up in twenty locations across the country by Eher's schoolbooks subsidiary Deutscher Schulverlag, based in Berlin. In this way, Deutscher Schulverlag functioned as the distribution agency for its own publications—it

[636] See the list in *Bbl.* no. 159, 21 October 1943, 10–12, with addenda in the subsequent issues.

[637] On this and the following, see Baur's ordinance "Vertrieb der Schulbücher für allge-meinbildende Schulen," *Bbl.* no. 96, 27 May 1943, 93.

[638] "Amtliche Bekanntmachung der Reichsschrifttumskammer Nr. 162," *Bbl.* no. 37, 13 May 1944, 73. See also the clarifications by W. Hellmann, "Die neue Regelung des Schulbuch-Vertriebes," *Bbl.* no. 41, 27 May 1944, 86–7.

had been commissioned by the Reich Office for Schoolbooks and Teaching Materials to produce standardized textbooks for each subject and each school type. Every school had to open a "lending library for schoolbooks," from which students could borrow the books they needed "for the duration of one school year upon payment of a lending fee."

In the case of university textbooks, the Börsenverein began regulating distribution in September 1943.[639] The publishers of specialized medical, scientific, and technical literature now had to keep back "the majority of the print run" of new titles and reprints in order to guarantee that the needs of university students would be covered. For textbooks in politics and economics, the level of reserves was left to "the discretion of the publisher." From the winter semester of 1943/44 publishers could still supply university bookstores directly, with allocations based on the student numbers in the city concerned,[640] but students were only allowed to buy one textbook for each subject wherever they were studying; freshmen could only purchase beginners' textbooks and seniors only exam-relevant literature.[641] However, production capacity was far too low for any guarantee that all textbooks could be stocked by the retail book trade. Because war invalids and other military participants were to take priority in advance reservations for reprints, the *Börsenblatt* advised students to "be ready to take any opportunities that arose" to acquire their books.[642]

In August 1944, all publishers were instructed by the Börsenverein to join the allocation scheme.[643] Allocations applied to all new titles and reprints; publishers could now only reserve a maximum of 10 percent of their total print runs for "special cases" (export, supplying businesses affected by bombing, Wehrmacht commissions, etc.).

---

[639] "Bekanntmachung des Börsenvereins-Vorstehers vom 20.9.1943," *Bbl.* no. 147, 23 September 1943, 167.

[640] H. F. Schulz, "Über die Lehrbücherversorgung im Kriege," *Bbl.* no. 71, 16 September 1944, 173.

[641] This system had been trialed at the universities of Freiburg im Breisgau and Strasbourg. See H. F. Schulz, "Erläuterungen zur Bekanntmachung über die Versorgung der Studierenden mit Hochschulbüchern," *Bbl.* no. 147, 23 September 1943, 167–70.

[642] H. F. Schulz, "Über die Lehrbücherversorgung im Kriege," *Bbl.* no. 71, 16 September 1944, 173.

[643] "Anordnung über das Zuteilungsverfahren," *Bbl.* no. 66, 23 August 1944, 153.

For certain types of publications, retailers were no longer permitted to place orders for general purposes. The "instructions for the total mobilization of the book trade" issued on 9 September 1944 directed bookstores to sell all their new cloth-bound or half-bound books in the field of fiction, politics, and popular science to the new lending sections of bookstores in their *Gau*.[644] The commercial lending libraries were to cease new lending immediately and complete their existing business within two weeks. By the end of September 1944, the Chamber had closed down 5,160 book-retailing operations, 955 door-to-door and mail-order booksellers, 113 book wholesalers, and 910 lending libraries.[645] Door-to-door bookselling, mail order, and bookselling in department stores were all discontinued completely. Of the book wholesalers, only one or two companies per economic region (each comprising two to three *Gaue*) were to remain in place.[646] The few purely scientific and scholarly retailers were exempted from the closure campaign, and 50 percent of general bookstores were to be kept open so as to ensure at least that school-books could be supplied and the stocks of closed-down publishers distributed. In view of the dramatic collapse in book production, however, in December 1944 the Chamber predicted that many of the surviving retail bookstores and subsidiary bookselling operations would "succumb of their own accord," without a closure order.[647] Referring to the increasing devastation of German cities in early 1945, a Börsenverein *Gau* representative sarcastically asked his association's Leipzig headquarters: "Why have we been taking such trouble to close down businesses in past weeks? The Americans can do it much faster and more thoroughly."[648]

Since fall 1943, aerial bombing had been compounding the already desperate state of the German book market. In the night of 3/4 December 1943, the attack on a completely unprepared city of Leipzig obliterated 516 publishers, book wholesalers, commission

---

[644] "Merkblatt zur totalen Mobilmachung des Buchhandels," p. 1 (point I.a.). The only exceptions were art books and books of illustrations.

[645] Report of the joint session of the Börsenverein's council and the board of the Book Trade Group on 27 September 1944 in Rathen, p. 4, StAL BV/583.

[646] RSK to RMVP, 7 August 1944, BArch R 56 V/152 fol. 172.

[647] RSK manager to president of the RKK, 14 December 1944, BArch R 56 V/152 fol. 13.

[648] StAL/BV 733.

and retail booksellers, lending libraries, and door-to-door businesses and destroyed an estimated total of 50 million books.[649] The graphics industry, printing workshops, type foundries, and bookbinders were also severely affected.

Faced with this disastrous blow to the hub of the German book trade, and anticipating further attacks, the Propaganda Ministry literature department drew up plans to decentralize the commerce in books, which had previously converged on Leipzig. In a confidential circular of 8 February 1944, the Börsenverein's deputy president informed its members of the planned changes.[650] They included a general ban on the "storage of book-trade items" in Leipzig by publishers and the wholesale book trade. Commission agents based in Leipzig had to carry out their deliveries through emergency warehouses, fifty of which were set up within 300 km of the city. Publishers were to deliver their products directly to these alternative storage facilities, and to dedicate their printing capacity to the immediate production of new publications. Commission agents had to supply retailers "if possible" directly from the emergency warehouses.

One of the reasons for the enormous losses of books in the bombing campaigns was that publishers and the wholesale book trade, driven by the scarcity of resources, had begun to hoard large quantities of books. In response to this trend, in late November 1943 the head of the Propaganda Ministry literature department called on the trade "in future ... to offer the book supplies in storage to the public completely and as fast as possible."[651] This instruction caused considerable perplexity. The Rieping bookstore in Rheine, Westphalia, drew the Börsenverein's attention to the fact that the retail book trade "could easily sell out all its stocks completely within a week, given the daily increase in demand."[652] Although this would comply with the instructions of the literary bureaucracy, the bookstore would then only be able to open "for 1 hr. per day," in order to "pass the books arriving that morning straight on to customers. Is this really

---

[649] Börsenverein to NSDAP Party Chancellery, 12 April 1944, StAL BV/881. An enclosure names 209 of the bomb-damaged publishers and bookstores.
[650] StAL BV/881.
[651] *Vertrauliche Mitteilungen für die Fachschaft Verlag* no. 476, 28 November 1943.
[652] StAL BV/881. The following quotations ibid.

the intended way out of the current adversity? Is the bookseller no longer to continue as before his efforts to ensure that the book, and not only the professional book, fulfills its purpose and finds its most suitable purchaser?"

In spring 1944 the Chamber tried to enable the bomb-damaged retailers and lending libraries to rebuild their businesses fast by ordering publishers to submit 10 percent of their production to the Party-owned wholesaler Lühe & Co. in Leipzig.[653] On behalf of the Chamber, Lühe & Co. now put together "foundation" sets of up to 1,800 volumes each, which could be obtained without charge "immediately after the damage occurs."[654] At the same time, an "old books campaign" initiated by the Chamber appealed to private households to clear their bookshelves of quality fiction, classics, encyclopedias, reference books, and specialized works, "as long as they are not obsolete and undesirable."[655] These items, which would be bought by secondhand booksellers, general and specialized bookstores, and the central lending library agency Leihbüchereihaus GmbH, were intended to benefit first and foremost those bomb victims "who require the books in order to carry on their professional work" and the lending libraries, factory libraries, and public libraries now lying in ruins.

---

[653] Report of the joint session of the Börsenverein's council and the board of the Book Trade Group on 12/13 May 1944 in Rathen, p. 3, StAL BV/737.

[654] "Aufruf an den deutschen Buchhandel," *Die Reichskulturkammer* 1 (1943), 42–3; report of the joint session of the Börsenverein's council and the board of the Book Trade Group on 5 October 1943 in Leipzig, p. 2, StAL BV/737. Overview of the book allocations dispatched by Lühe & Co. in February and March 1945, StAL BV/F 5918.

[655] "Bekanntmachung der Reichsschrifttumskammer vom 26.2.1944," *Bbl.* no. 22, 18 March 1944, 41.

5

Books in the Media Dictatorship: The Perspective of the Ruled

Latitude and Limitations: Writers

The Nazi dictatorship began with a demolition process. With very few exceptions, everything that is now considered part of the literary canon of the Weimar Republic was banned and progressively eliminated from the German book market. The public book burnings of spring 1933, for which the first "blacklists" of undesirable literature were drawn up, were greeted with enthusiasm not only by the mass of the public, but also—or especially—by sections of the educated bourgeoisie. Literary scholar Hans Naumann, for example, used his speech beside the pyre in Bonn on 10 May to vilify the reading material offered by commercial lending libraries, literature

that for the most part only started spilling over us in the last few decades, and was so shamelessly disintegrative and corrosive in its worldview and morals that, leafing through the catalogues, we asked ourselves in horror: where were the authorities, where were the churches, where was the "inner mission"? For the very greatest part this writing, which we will symbolically annihilate today, had its origin in foreign races and foreign countries, but perhaps it was more rampant here than abroad, and in this sense was a veritable continuation of the war against Germany by different, subtler, and more infamous means, attacking yet more vulnerable spots.[1]

Even the apparently reputable Ernst Bertram, professor of German at the University of Cologne and an Insel Verlag author, in 1933 celebrated "the virtues of a German 'rebarbarization.'"[2]

As such alarming comments proliferated, on 27 May a perplexed Thomas Mann in Switzerland asked: "What is going on in these people's minds? Returning to Germany now, one would be a foreigner who did not know how to behave. A strange experience that while one is outside, one's country runs off somewhere and cannot be regained."[3] In the same period Hans Carossa described Nazi activism with desperate irony: "We are cleansed, purified, sifted, disinfected, separated out, toughened up, nordicized .... Not good prospects for writers, who, like nature, bring forth their best work when some mixing is involved."[4]

For authors who could not or did not want to emigrate, what were the possible responses to these new constraints upon their work? It should firstly be said that not all of them accepted the book bans without protest. Frank Thiess, for example, successfully appealed the general ban on his works demanded by Rosenberg's office,[5] making full use of his ministerial contacts in Berlin. In the Prussian ministry of education and culture, he found support for his case from both Minister Rust and theater commissioner Hinkel.[6] Although the Propaganda Ministry literature department remained adamant on banning his novels *Frauenraub* and *Die Verdammten* and excluded him from the list of authors worthy of special promotion,[7]

---

[1] Naumann's speech cited in Sauder, *Die Bücherverbrennung*, 250–4, here 251. See also Bodsch, "Bonn. 10. Mai 1933."

[2] Carossa, *Tagebücher*, 248 (10 June 1933).

[3] Thomas Mann, *Tagebücher 1933–1934*, 93.

[4] Letter to Erika Mitterer, 28 April 1933, in Carossa, *Briefe II*, 281.

[5] See the review of Thiess's *Die Verdammten* in the Rosenberg journal *Bücherkunde* 1 (1934), 7, and of *Johanna und Esther*, *Bücherkunde* 2 (1935), 167–8 (headed "Novels of the kind we do not wish to see").

[6] Wismann (RMVP literature department) referred to Rust's support for Thiess in his reply to an inquiry by Rainer Schlösser (RMVP theater department), 13 September 1935, BArch 50.01/182 fol. 52.

[7] Erckmann (RMVP/dept. VIII) to Hinkel, 5 September 1935, BArch BDC/RSK/Thiess, F.

it permitted him to continue working. Like several of his colleagues, Thiess fell back on writing screenplays for entertainment films.[8] He returned to the book market in 1937 with the novel *Tsushima* (*The Voyage of the Forgotten Men—Tsushima*, 1937), describing the May 1905 naval battle between Japan and Russia from the perspective of Germany's now Axis ally. Not only was his book a best-seller, but his political kowtow restored him to the regime's good graces.

Walter von Molo went a step further. None of his books was blacklisted, despite claims to the contrary in his 1957 memoirs. In August 1935 he informed Gunter d'Alquen, editor-in-chief of the SS paper *Das Schwarze Korps*, that he had switched "from a non-Aryan, foreign publisher to an Aryan one in Germany"—from Paul Zsolnay of Vienna to Holle & Co., Berlin.[9] He applied to Bouhler of the PPK, and to Goebbels himself, seeking protection against attacks "by a few wild dogmatists ... for 'not being a folkish [*volkhaft*] author.'"[10] To counter this slander, von Molo stressed the nationalist stance he had taken in his 1918–21 trilogy *Ein Volk wacht auf* ("A nation awakes") and resumed in the novel *Eugenio von Savoy* of 1936. However, Goebbels found the "material against Molo" assembled by the literature department "rather sensitive after all," especially because the author had "stood up for [the banned writer] Remarque." Rosenberg's literature office, too, adhered to its rejection of von Molo's work.[11]

Those writers who felt no affinity with Hitler and the Nazi government in 1933 quickly withdrew into their own private and literary worlds, or were sent there in no uncertain terms. The answer to the question of where Oskar Loerke lived until his early demise in 1941 would have to be "in literature."[12] Many other authors made similar retreats into protected aesthetic niches. On 17 May 1933, Carossa—whom Rust was trying to win for the restructured

---

[8] On this and the following, see Renner, "Frank Thiess," and Hall, *Der Paul Zsolnay Verlag*, 617–27.

[9] Von Molo to d'Alquen, 7 August 1935, BArch BDC/RSK/von Molo, W.

[10] Goebbels, *Tagebücher*, Part I, vol. 5, 106 (19 January 1938).

[11] Ibid. 130 (2 February 1938); "Walter von Molo über Erich Maria Remarques 'Im Westen nichts Neues,'" *Bücherkunde* 3 (1936), 352; "Walter von Molo schrieb ein neues Buch ... Wir blättern in der Gutachtenmappe," *Lektoren-Brief* 2, no. 1 (1939), 1–3.

[12] See his diaries from 1933 to 1941 in Loerke, *Tagebücher*.

literature section of the Prussian Academy of Arts—wrote to Katharina Kippenberg: "Let the new state establish itself as it wishes; *I* plan to keep my little intellectual empire free and independent, and am firmly convinced that this is how I can best serve the *Volk.*"[13] Writing to the singer Gertrud Full on 28 May 1942, he confessed to a "double life": "one in the external world, which never stops pressing its claims, the other in seclusion and quiet, and many things take shape there that belong to the soul alone."[14] Even the disputatious Hans Fallada, now based in provincial Mecklenburg, told his publisher Ernst Rowohlt on 9 January 1937 that he wanted to "retreat like a snail from everything that is happening in the world."[15] Emil Barth, Wilhelm Lehmann, Rudolf Alexander Schröder, and Heinrich Wolfgang Seidel, and younger writers such as Peter Huchel, Friedo Lampe, Reinhold Schneider, or Eugen Gottlob Winkler, also turned to cultivating their own notions of literary aesthetics, detached from the political circumstances around them.

Authors who were affected by the race laws, politically suspect, or vulnerable due to their Weimar writings behaved and wrote as inconspicuously as possible, trying not to exacerbate an already precarious position. This was the case for Stefan Andres, Werner Bergengruen, Wilhelm Hausenstein, Jochen Klepper, Friedrich Alfred Schmid-Nörr, Otto Suhr, and Josef Winckler, whose marriages to "non-Aryans" meant they could only continue working with "special permission" from the Propaganda Minister; for Alfred Andersch, Friedrich Bischoff, Karl Bröger, Axel Eggebrecht, Ehm Welk, and Ernst Wiechert, who were briefly held in jails or concentration camps; for Walter Bauer, Ernst Glaeser, Theodor Heuss, Erich Kästner, Hermann Keyserling, Gerhart Pohl, and Erik Reger, who had been high-profile opponents of Nazism during the Weimar Republic; for Ernst Barlach, Kasimir Edschmid, Herbert Eulenberg, and Georg Kaiser, whose works were rejected on aesthetic and moral grounds; and for religious writers such as Karl Barth, Dietrich Bonhoeffer, Peter Dörfler, Theodor Haecker, Kurt Ihlenfeld, Jochen Klepper, or Reinhold Schneider, who faced increasing repression and the withholding

---

[13] Carossa, *Briefe II*, 284.
[14] Carossa, *Briefe III*, 178.
[15] Fallada, *Ewig auf der Rutschbahn*, 219.

of paper rations for their books from 1940 on. Gottfried Benn, too, resolved "no longer to speak, write, communicate with anybody or anything" after he was pilloried in *Das Schwarze Korps* in May 1936 for poems he had published with Deutsche Verlags-Anstalt.[16]

Despite the need to compromise on content and form in their books after 1933, these authors remained deaf to the calls for a new "National Socialist literature" that regularly came from Nazi cultural functionaries such as Goebbels, Rosenberg, or Johst, literary critics such as Hellmuth Langenbucher, Paul Fechter, or Will Vesper, and literary scholars such as Heinz Kindermann, Franz Koch, Walter Linden, Arno Mulot, or Hans Naumann. On publishing his first literary works in September 1934, Hermann Stresau observed that "it does seem possible to write without making concessions to NS ideology."[17] Like Stresau, other authors also moved to writing for daily papers and magazines, with feuilleton-style articles that avoided ideology completely or else could be interpreted as criticizing the era through a Swiftian procedure of allegorical or coded satire. Examples include Martin Beheim-Schwarzbach, Otto Flake, Albrecht Goes, Sebastian Haffner, Ernst Heimeran, Gustav René Hocke, Hermann Kasack, Kurt Kusenberg, Oskar Loerke, Ernst Penzoldt, Sigismund von Radecki, Oda Schaefer, Dolf Sternberger, and Wolfgang Weyrauch.[18] In a December 1940 issue of the censors' bulletin *Lektoren-Brief*, the Rosenberg literature office complained that there was a whole "in-between realm" of authors whose "inner stance and attitude, as expressed in their works, we must treat with particular caution."[19] These authors, "without actually displaying a clear-cut physiognomy," were "in most cases closer to the literati's scribblings of the era before 1933 than to the *volkhaft* poetry of our own times." Particularly worrying to the *Lektoren-Brief* was the emergence of a "literary clique" that was "already staking claims to intellectual power and seems to be enjoying more and more popularity among readers." Even in National Socialist papers, ran the lament, book reviewing was not rising to this challenge.

---

[16] Letter to Tilly Wedekind, 21 May 1936, in Benn, *Briefe an Tilly Wedekind*, 189.

[17] Stresau, *Von Jahr zu Jahr*, 92 (14 September 1934).

[18] See Haffner, *Das Leben der Fußgänger*; Orlowski, "Krakauer Zeitung 1939–1945"; Oelze, *Das Feuilleton der Kölnischen Zeitung*, 94–162; Schwarz, *Literarisches Zeitgespräch*, col. 1312–28; Gillessen, *Auf verlorenem Posten*, 329–69.

[19] "Jahresbericht 1940 des Hauptlektorates 'Schöngeistiges Schrifttum,'" *Lektoren-Brief* 3, no. 12 (1940), 4, BArch NSD 16/59.

The censors' perception that segments of contemporary literature were failing to conform with the system is corroborated by a 1940 entry in Horst Lange's diary: "Violence, barbarity, worlds sinking. And I keep on writing my play as if I were sitting in Greece and conversing with philosophers and had goddesses reclining on my couch. Sometimes it seems like a flight from reality. Then again like a counter-offensive."[20] In Lange's case it was *Schwarze Weide* ("Black willow") of 1937 and *Ulanenpatrouille* ("Uhlan patrol") of 1940 that aroused particular disapproval in both aesthetic and ideological terms; for August Scholtis it was the 1938 novel *Das Eisenwerk* ("The ironworks"), set in Upper Silesia.[21] Stefan Andres used historical settings to cloak his critique of Nazi dictatorship in the novella *El Greco malt den Großinquisitor* ("El Greco paints the Grand Inquisitor") of 1936, as did Werner Bergengruen in *Am Himmel wie auf Erden* ("In heaven as on earth") of 1940.[22] A similar strategy was pursued by other writers as well: Albrecht Haushofer with the drama trilogy *Scipio* (1934), *Sulla* (1938), and *Augustus* (1939); Adam Kuckhoff, whose 1937 novel *Der Deutsche von Bayencourt* ("The German of Bayencourt") withdrew into a time before World War I and whose detective story *Strogany und die Vermissten* ("Strogany and the missing persons") of 1941, written with Peter Tarin, took as its theme a series of murders in St Petersburg in 1909/10; or Friedrich Reck-Malleczewen in his 1937 novels *Bockelson. Geschichte eines Massenwahns* (*Bockelson: A Tale of Mass Insanity*, 2008), on the dictatorship of the Anabaptists in sixteenth-century Münster, and *Charlotte Corday. Geschichte eines Attentats* ("Charlotte Corday. Story of an assassination"), portraying the death of the revolutionary despot Jean Paul Marat.[23]

---

[20] Lange, *Tagebücher*, 24 (4 June 1940).

[21] See the review by Eberhard Ter-Nedden, "Zerrbilder aus Schlesien. Horst Lange— August Scholtis: Ein Fall," *Die Weltliteratur* 3 (1941), 80–2, and the author's response with an additional critique by the editors, "Scholtis: Schelt- und andere Briefe," ibid. 118.

[22] See Schäfer, "Horst Langes Tagebücher"; Denk, *Die Zensur der Nachgeborenen*, 303–9, 373–81; Ehrke-Rotermund and Rotermund, *Zwischenreiche und Gegenwelten*, 276–314, 464–84.

[23] See Reck-Malleczewen, *Diary of a Man in Despair*, 19–21; Denk, *Die Zensur der Nachgeborenen*, 275–91, 310–19; Denkler, "Katz und Maus"; Schoeps, *Literatur im Dritten Reich*, 239–57; Ehrke-Rotermund and Rotermund, *Zwischenreiche und Gegen- welten*, 59–102, 527–46.

As early as June 1933, Carossa had mocked the naive expectation that great literary achievements would follow on the heels of political change.[24] Friedo Lampe, whose own innovative ventures into "magic realism" were suppressed, described Karl Benno von Mechow's novel *Vorsommer* ("Early summer"), published in October 1933, as "very pious," "horribly boring. Not authentic in its views and stagnant in its language";[25] the description would have matched the majority of literary production at the time. As was his way, Gottfried Benn passed considerably harsher judgment. When Harald Braun invited him to contribute to a Christmas anthology entitled *Dichter schreiben an ihre Kinder* ("Authors write to their children") and Ina Seidel sent him her memoirs to read, he commented in September 1935: "What existences! How vastly important this trumpery, what pomposities. Really, these days the maddest contradictions coexist unremarked and leave each other undisturbed."[26] The regime's great difficulty in "aligning the domain of literature," noted Hermann Stresau in December the same year, was "that National Socialism yields so little in terms of ideas. Neither has it brought anything of its own to the field apart from Rosenberg's *Myth of the Twentieth Century*, the collected works of Dietrich Eckardt [i.e., Eckart], and Horst Wessel's SA hymn, and none of those is very likely to cause a literary revolution."[27] No formal experiments could be expected: "When the ideal and the order is to write in an easily understood style," Theodor Haecker remarked in his journal, "anyone who is difficult to understand is *eo ipso* suspect."[28]

Alongside idealized nature writing, the most important growth area was heroic portrayals of the frontline experiences of World War I soldiers, but this genre too contained little of literary interest. In April 1939 Reck-Malleczewen sketched its representatives: "Are they not typified by the World War cadet who was never promoted, emerged from the war to write one powerful book based on powerful and unique experience, and then, faced with the fact that he lacked all ability to tell a story, was unable to complete a second book founded

[24] Carossa, *Tagebücher*, 252 (30 June 1933).
[25] Letter to Johannes Pfeiffer, 22 October 1933, in Lampe, *Briefe*, 109.
[26] Letter to Elinor Büller, 17 September 1935, in Benn, *Briefe an Elinor Büller*, 100.
[27] Stresau, *Von Jahr zu Jahr*, 106–7 (12 December 1935).
[28] Haecker, *Journal in the Night*, 101.

on fantasy and imagination?"[29] A year later, Horst Lange described the era as "a completely hopeless literary interregnum."[30] It was "a sign of the most profound cultural abasement that literature (most creators of which are nowadays epigones) lacks all yardsticks and tenets."

If none of the Nazi literary products survived for posterity, this does not mean there was no distinctly Nazi literary arena. On the contrary, its participants included the very highest representatives of the state. By 1945, 9.84 million copies of Hitler's *Mein Kampf* had appeared, published in two volumes in 1925/27 and then in cheap editions from 1930.[31] The book was not only distributed through the usual sales channels and an obligatory item on every public library's shelves, but also a prestigious gift from the state and Party; many town halls even presented it as a wedding gift to newly married couples from 1937.[32] The only writer whose success approached similar heights was the Propaganda Minister himself, whose collection of speeches and essays *Die Zeit ohne Beispiel* ("The time without precedent"), published in 1942, had been printed in 250,000 copies by July that year. His own assessment of his edited diaries *Vom Kaiserhof zur Reichskanzlei*, 1934 (translated in 1935 as *My Part in Germany's Fight*), was "an absolute book sensation."[33] The works of Rosenberg, Bouhler, Darré, Göring, Ley, and Hinkel and the volumes of annotated photos by Hitler's personal photographer Heinrich Hoffmann were disseminated in large numbers—these authors freely used their political influence to pressurize their publishers for especially energetic advertising and excellent sales.[34] Chamber of Literature presidents Blunck and Johst both became best-selling authors and top earners in the period after 1933.[35]

---

[29] Reck-Malleczewen, *Diary of a Man in Despair*, 78.

[30] Lange, *Tagebücher*, 18 (17 April 1940). The following quotation ibid. 19.

[31] Tavernaro, *Der Verlag Hitlers und der NSDAP*, 38.

[32] For details, see Plöckinger, *Geschichte eines Buches*, especially 405–44.

[33] Goebbels, *Tagebücher*, Part II, vol. 5, 94 (10 July 1942).

[34] See, for example, Hinkel's correspondence with Fritz Hasinger of Knorr & Hirth from 1937 through 1940 regarding his book *Einer unter Hunderttausend* ("One among one hundred thousand"), BArch BDC/RK/fiche B 0066 fol. 218–364. On his extensive journalistic activities in the Party's *Kampfzeit*, see his curriculum vitae for 1901–35, BArch R 56 I/107.

[35] Blunck's income statement to the Chamber noted 70,067.85 RM for 1940 and 149,898 RM for 1942, BArch BDC/RSK/Blunck, H. F.; on Johst's income, see Düsterberg, *Hanns Johst*, 253–5.

The close link between writers' political office and their opportunistic placement of their own books on the market is well illustrated by the case of Wilfrid Bade.[36] Bade joined the NSDAP in 1930 and worked in the Propaganda Ministry press department from 1933 to 1945, carefully adapting the themes of his writing to the flows of changing political taste. His literary career began in 1933 with a biography of Joseph Goebbels, the first volume of a history of the Third Reich, and *Die SA erobert Berlin. Ein Tatsachenbericht* ("The SA conquers Berlin. A factual report"), 60,000 copies of which had been printed by 1938. *Deutschland erwacht. Werden, Kampf und Sieg der NSDAP* ("Germany awakes. Emergence, struggle, and victory of the NSDAP") was published in a print run of 600,000 by Cigaretten-Bilderdienst, a company specializing in cigarette cards and funded by the tobacco giant Reemtsma. The book contained spaces for cards that could be collected from cigarette packages and pasted in like a family album. In 1934 *Trommlerbub unterm Hakenkreuz* ("Drummer boy under the swastika") followed, along with volume 1 of *Das Hohelied vom Dritten Reich* ("The song of the Third Reich"), entitled *Arbeit und Brot* ("Work and bread"), which was designed to be read as a "film in book form." In 1935, working with the *Berliner Illustrirte Zeitung*'s picture editor Kurt Zentner, Bade published his first "picture chronicle" of the year's events with Ullstein, Berlin. He responded to the public, literary, and media euphoria over the new German autobahn network with a 1938 "biography of the motor car," *Das Auto erobert die Welt* ("The automobile conquers the world"), which sold 53,000 copies by 1942. In 1939, with Otto Dietrich, Helmut Sündermann, Gunter d'Alquen, and Heinz Lorenz, he published the illustrated volume *Auf den Straßen des Sieges. Erlebnisse mit dem Führer in Polen* ("On the roads of victory. Experiences with the Führer in Poland") with the Eher house. In 1941 and 1943, he edited collections of war-related essays with Zeitgeschichte Verlag, *Das heldische Jahr. Front und Heimat berichten den Krieg* ("The heroic year. Front line and homeland report on the war"). Finally, in 1943 his poems *Tod und Leben* ("Death and life") provided aesthetic glorification for the "heroes' deaths" that were now multiplying in the real world.

Whereas political celebrities entered the literature business in search of publicity and profit, many writers took up their pens for

---

[36] On the following, see Härtel, *Stromlinien*.

the state out of conviction. Among these "bards" were Rudolf Ahlers, Heinrich Anacker, Werner Beumelburg, Friedrich Bodenreuth, Herbert Böhme, Bruno Brehm, Hermann Burte, Edwin Erich Dwinger, Kurt Eggers, Richard Euringer, Gustav Frenssen, Robert Hohlbaum, Mirko Jelusich, Erwin Guido Kolbenheyer, Herybert Menzel, Agnes Miegel, Ernst Moritz Mungenast, Georg Schmückle, Gerhard Schumann, Josef Weinheber, Will Vesper, and Hans Zöberlein. Most of them were showered with literary prizes for their panegyrics. Numerous traditionally minded, nationalist-conservative writers also put themselves at the service of state propaganda, such as Paul Alverdes, Richard Billinger, Hermann Claudius, Friedrich Griese, Enrica von Handel-Mazzetti, Kurt Kluge, Wolf von Niebelschütz, Josef Friedrich Perkonig, Josef Ponten, Wilhelm Schäfer, Friedrich Schreyvogl, Ina Seidel, Hermann Stehr, Georg von der Vring, Karl Heinrich Waggerl, or Josef Magnus Wehner. The Weimar Authors' Meetings of 1938 through 1942 testified to their efforts, as did the author readings organized and funded in Germany and abroad between 1937 and 1942, which the Propaganda Ministry promoted by providing lists of recommended speakers. Author readings were also arranged by Rosenberg's "National Socialist Cultural Community" (NS-Kulturgemeinde), the adult education agency Deutsches Volksbildungswerk, and the Strength Through Joy organization. As divisions of the well-funded DAF, these three agencies were able to trump other Party bodies by tempting authors with high fees even during wartime.[37]

However, so few writers were politically endorsed by the Party that competition for the rare attractive ones among them seems to have been fierce. In July 1939, Bruno Brehm complained that he was frequently scheduled for readings "which have the great misfortune to take place on the same day in different locations."[38] Brehm advised the state and Party literary offices to "talk to each other now and again." If not, he planned to call in sick and stay at home. Carossa, too, felt "worn out" in November 1940 by the constant

---

[37] See the complaint from Reich Propaganda Office Tyrol to RMVP, 19 May 1944, BArch BDC/RK/fiche Y 0027 fol. 2246.
[38] Brehm to Teichmann (organizer of Deutsches Volksbildungswerk's author readings), 26 July 1939, BArch NS 8/197 fol. 101.

stream of invitations: "Now I was supposed to travel to Slovakia, now to Prague, now to Bucharest and Budapest, now (at the wish of a journal editor) to make a public profession of faith in our victory; all things that distract from the essential matters."[39] Even the cultural section of the Party's Central Propaganda Office noted in 1942 that the readings organized by the government and Party had become so numerous as to prevent the authors concerned from carrying out their actual work of writing.[40]

For certain writers, membership of the Chamber of Literature was not a burdensome act of submission but a necessary condition and valorization of their professional existence. On 5 April 1938 Hans Henny Jahnn protested vigorously against his exclusion from the Chamber, which he considered an "unkind act against me, likely to further worsen my difficult situation."[41] In fact, Jahnn's exclusion had only been resolved because he had moved his main residence to Denmark and therefore no longer fell within the Chamber of Culture's remit. In May 1939, 26-year-old Curt Hohoff asked the Chamber to replace his exemption certificate, issued because he was only writing part-time, with "full membership of the Reich Chamber of Culture."[42] The number of his publications had risen considerably since 1937, he argued, and he now intended to become a full-time freelance author. In May 1940 Marie-Luise Kaschnitz applied for her full membership to remain in place despite her now only minor and part-time literary activity, "since I have belonged to the Reich Chamber of Literature for many years, have submitted my Aryan certificate and paid my dues punctually, and myself see no reason to resign."[43] Heinz Günther (better known in postwar Germany as the popular novelist Konsalik) actively sought admission to the Chamber in 1940, aged just seventeen, because he wanted to publish poems and dramas.[44]

There were other Chamber applicants whose careers only took off after the war. The 20-year-old Wolfgang Borchert, who had begun an

---

[39] Letter to Maximilian Brantl, 17 November 1940, in Carossa, *Briefe III*, 108.
[40] Head of the RPL main cultural section to Deutsches Volksbildungswerk, 1 June 1942, BArch NS 18/419.
[41] BArch BDC/RSK/Jahnn, H. H.
[42] Hohoff to RSK, 21 May and 6 June 1939, BArch BDC/RSK/Hohoff, C.
[43] Kaschnitz to RSK, 22 May 1940, BArch BDC/RSK/Kaschnitz, M.-L.
[44] BArch BDC/RSK/Günther, H.

apprenticeship in bookselling in April 1939, applied for membership in early 1941 so that he could publish poems and his play in progress, *Hyperion*.[45] His application named his mother and the professional authors Walter Gättke, Paul Alverdes, and Hermann Claudius as having nurtured his "urge to write." Gerhard (Gerd) Gaiser, a teacher who had been contributing to the literary journal *Das Innere Reich* and the weekly *Das Reich* since 1940, applied for membership of the Chamber in May 1941 upon Langen-Müller's publication of his poems *Reiter am Himmel* ("Rider in the sky").[46] Karl Krolow, based at the Katowice branch of the "Reich Commissioner for the Consolidation of Germandom" (Reichskommissar für die Festigung deutschen Volkstums), told the Chamber on 8 March 1942: "My work for large German newspapers can be expected to expand. Furthermore, I have begun negotiations with a publisher regarding a book. I therefore consider my registration and request for admission to be imperative."[47] Businessman Hans-Erich Nossack applied to the Chamber in early October 1942 because he had, "through a chance acquaintance in the Suhrkamp house," "come closer" to publishing a first volume of poetry.[48] Alfred Andersch had previously been a Chamber member, registered in the Book Trade Group, until he left the Munich publisher J. F. Lehmann in 1937.[49] From 1941 he supplemented his day job in the advertising department of a Frankfurt perfume manufacturer with literary work, "seriously and on a significant scale," and on this basis applied for readmission, this time to the Writers Group, in February 1943.

Nor was the Chamber itself regarded only as an apparatus of irksome control. Far from it—many writers saw the new professional representation as a useful ally in their attempts to improve their position. Otto Flake appealed to the Chamber of Culture in December 1934 for state intervention against the "unified front

---

[45] Membership application, 18 January 1941, and handwritten curriculum vitae, 20 January, BArch BDC/RSK/Borchert, W.

[46] Membership application, 15 May 1941, completed questionnaire, 31 May, and Chamber exemption certificate, 21 June, BArch BDC/RSK/Gaiser, G.

[47] BArch BDC/RSK/Krolow, K.

[48] Application and curriculum vitae, 15 October 1942, BArch BDC/RSK/Nossack, H.-E.

[49] On this and the following, see the curriculum vitae enclosed in Andersch's application of 16 February 1943, BArch BDC/RSK/Andersch, A. On 24 February he received exemption as a part-timer.

of publishers and retailers" that had so far thwarted all efforts to increase authors' share of the profits of their books.[50] And the RDS, as the association representing authors' interests within the Chamber, picked up on a demand voiced by its predecessor, the SDS, during the 1920s: in November 1934, it began negotiations on a "standard publishing contract for fictional works" with the publishing *Fachschaft* in the booksellers' association BRB. Gustav Pezold, at this time still the powerful managing director of Langen-Müller, regarded this as nothing but "the purest class egoism, in other words Marxism, and at the same time a mechanization and depersonalization of inward human relationships, in other words Bolshevism."[51] Bargaining continued all the same, and on 3 June 1935 the skeleton agreement was issued as binding Chamber law, substantially improving the status of fiction authors in all future contracts with publishers.[52] In 1937 the "standard publishing contract" was extended to cover juvenile literature.[53] In December 1943, a standard contract for screen adaptations followed, for the first time regulating the rights of scriptwriters, even if the Chamber made only partial headway against the state movie industry backed by the Propaganda Ministry's film department.[54]

In the negotiations over fundamental amendments to copyright and publishing law, under way at the Academy for German Law in Munich since 1933, the Chamber of Literature was the advocate of authors' interests, albeit an unsuccessful one in the long term.[55] It also acted as a mediator to deal with all sorts of disputes between authors and publishers. Authors approached the Chamber if, like von

---

[50] Flake to RKK, 6 December 1934 in BArch R 56 V/178 fol. 121.

[51] Pezold to Niels Diederich, head of the BRB's fiction and popular science publishers' group, 14 March 1935, p. 1, DLA NL H. Grimm/Korrespondenz mit dem Langen-Müller Verlag, folder II 1935–7.

[52] Schrieber, *Das Recht der Reichskulturkammer*, vol. II, 93–7.

[53] "Anwendung des Normal-Verlagsvertrags auf Jugendschrifttum," *Bbl.* no. 188, 17 August 1937, 657.

[54] *Bbl.* no. 181, 30 December 1943, 213–15. On the movie industry's success in defending its interests within the Propaganda Ministry, see Ihde, file note of 22 January 1943, BArch R 56 V/26 fol. 127, and RSK manager to Johst, 16 September 1943, ibid. fol. 32–3.

[55] See Ihde to RMVP literature department, 3 February 1939, BArch R 56 V/83 fol. 51–2.

Molo, they considered their rights to have been violated by criticism of their work or person in the Nazi press;[56] if they wanted to leave a publisher to which they were bound by an option contract; if, like Hermann Hesse in 1939, they were dissatisfied with their publisher's presentation and distribution of their works;[57] if they felt badly treated by their publisher regarding royalty payments; if their works were prevented from appearing by the refusal of paper rations; if they wanted cancellation fees for manuscripts or proofs destroyed by bombing; and in similar conflicts.[58]

Because writers' material situation was deteriorating in the second half of the 1930s, appeals were also made to the Chamber for better welfare support. The falling incomes of most authors resulted first of all from the cutbacks in culture spending that began with Hitler's announcement of the second Four-Year Plan in September 1936. By early November that year, the Chamber had already received complaints from several Bavarian authors via the NSDAP *Gau* leadership in Munich. They all agreed that their financial situation had "changed for the worse since the National Socialist revolution."[59] In radio and the press, the fees for literary contributions had dropped considerably. Many book publishers had shifted their profile to favor political literature, and paid badly or only after long delays. In addition, professional authors found themselves in competition with "double earners"—for example civil servants, who sometimes even offered their work for free. The foreign market was as good as closed to German writers because publishers abroad refused to take on literary works from Nazi Germany. In spring 1937, the Party author Heinrich Anacker complained to Chamber president Johst that the Four-Year Plan Office's instructions to reduce paper use by 10 percent across the board had forced newspapers to drastically prune down their already meager culture sections, impacting

---

[56] See von Molo to RSK president Blunck, 12 August 1935, regarding an attack in *Das Schwarze Korps*, and to section head Metzner, 3 September 1937, regarding a negative review of his novel *Eugenio von Savoy* in the educators' periodical *Reichszeitung der deutschen Erzieher*, BArch BDC/RSK/von Molo, W.

[57] See Hermann Hesse to RSK, 2 April 1939, BArch BDC/RSK/Bermann Fischer, G.

[58] These examples are based on personnel files in the former BDC, now in the Federal Archives, Bundesarchiv Berlin-Lichterfelde.

[59] BArch R 56 V/81 fol. 53–6, here fol. 53.

on literary articles in particular.[60] When Goebbels ordered radio broadcasting to entertain Germans returning from their working day with animating and gripping programs, cuts were made to authors' lectures, readings, and debates. In late April 1937, the author Günter Eich told the Chamber's broadcasting *Fachschaft* that radio drama had also been affected by the reorientation in radio programming.[61]

Only the booming film industry remained as a lucrative source of income, attracting established authors such as Alfred Braun, Eberhard Frowein, Thea von Harbou, Georg C. Klaren, Felix Lützkendorf, Gerhard Menzel, Ernst von Salomon, Heinrich Spoerl, or Walter Wassermann and newcomers including Hans Bertram, Kurt Heuser, Peter Huchel, Jochen Klepper, Horst Lange, and Wolfgang Koeppen. Even politically controversial writers such as Arnolt Bronnen, Erich Ebermayer, Axel Eggebrecht, Hans Fallada, Ernst Glaeser, Erich Kästner, Alexander Lernet-Holenia, Walter von Molo, Hans Reimann, Robert A. Stemmle, Arnold Ulitz, Günther Weisenborn, and Otto Bernhard Wendler were commissioned to write screenplays. Of the 10,118 writers registered with the Chamber in 1942, 874 worked for the movie industry regularly or occasionally.[62]

The Chamber tried to help the majority of German writers at least keep their heads above water through a range of support measures. To this end, from 1936 the Propaganda Ministry substantially boosted the budget of the German Schiller Foundation in Weimar. Even so, most German authors had to get by with modest incomes, as can be seen in the Chamber of Literature's yearly breakdown of earnings before tax, used to calculate membership dues (Table 1).[63]

During World War II, conditions worsened further for the writing profession. Anyone who could not—or did not wish to—contribute directly to the war effort, whether by offering propagandist affirmation, spiritual edification, or escapist entertainment, gradually disappeared from the book market. This was the result of severe

---

[60] Anacker to Johst, 11 March 1937, BArch R 56 V/81 fol. 12.

[61] Eich to RSK, 25 April 1937, BArch R 56 V/81 fol. 9.

[62] *Schriftsteller-Verzeichnis*, 254.

[63] BArch R 2/4876 (1937) and R 2/4877 (1938), here the information on membership dues from authors, chapter I, section 10, point 2 of the budget estimates. For comparison: the official average annual earnings in the German Reich were 1,856 RM in 1937 and 1,947 RM in 1938.

Table 1: Authors' income 1937–8

Gross annual income	Number of members	Year
Group 1: up to 2,400 RM with reduced-rate dues	2,000	1937
Group 2: up to 2,400 RM without reduction	2,635	
Group 3: up to 4,800 RM	1,100	
Group 4: up to 7,200 RM	200	
Group 5: over 7,200 RM	65	
Group 1: up to 1,200 RM	6,328	1938*
Group 2: up to 3,600 RM	1,424	
Group 3: up to 6,000 RM	467	
Group 4: over 6,000 RM	102	

*Now including Austria

restrictions on the production and sale of books after 1941 due to paper rationing, personnel shortages, company closures, and war damage among publishers, printers, and bookstores. The beneficiaries of shrinking supply were those few best-selling novelists, playwrights, and scriptwriters whose publishers were able either to pass on commissions from the film industry or to use their contacts in the Wehrmacht and the frontline book trade, the NSDAP, and the German Labor Front to obtain approval for large quantities of paper and thus high print runs.[64] Between 1940 and 1943, certain authors—such as Blunck, Hauptmann, Jelusich, Kolbenheyer, or Spoerl—were still making more than 100,000 RM a year, putting them among Germany's highest earners.[65] The wartime income of the profession

---

[64] Bühler and Kirbach, "Die Wehrmachtsausgaben," 265–89.

[65] Amann, *Zahltag*, 298; BArch BDC/RK/fiche B 0066 fol. 1388–96: G. Hauptmann's earnings declared to the RSK, and fiche Z 005 fol. 436–40: H. Spoerl's earnings declared to the RSK.

as a whole, based on authors' declarations for the Chamber, is summarized in Table 2.[66]

The bulk of writers in the period may be counted among the political "fellow travelers" and the ranks of "loyal reluctance,"[67] and only for very few groups or individuals is there any evidence of open protest, let alone actual resistance to the regime. Starting in August 1934, the German Communist Party reactivated the League of Proletarian-Revolutionary Writers and operated it clandestinely.[68] This resistance group of a dozen authors published its own journal and circulated political pamphlets. Hans Schwalm, who headed the group until his emigration to Paris in summer 1935, used the exile press to publish literary texts on life in Germany, under his pseudonym Jan Petersen,[69] but by October 1935 the Gestapo had tracked down the League and arrested its members. The articles on cultural policy in the SPD's periodical *Deutschland-Berichte*, published in exile between 1934 and 1940, indicate that the authors who remained in Nazi Germany included some who were willing to make directly oppositional reports.[70]

How narrowly the limits of acceptable behavior were drawn becomes apparent in the brutal intimidation of writers, with Goebbels's attacks on Hermann Keyserling, Ernst Wiechert, and Hans Grimm in 1937 and 1938; the March 1937 arrest and eight-year imprisonment of Ernst Niekisch; or the arbitrary Gestapo detainment of authors such as Theodor Haecker, Erich Kästner, and Eugen Gottlob Winkler. Although Rudolf Pechel, editor-in-chief of the literary periodical *Deutsche Rundschau* since 1919, published several articles that criticized the regime from behind a veil of faraway historical or geographical settings,[71] when he openly censured Goebbels's news

---

[66] BArch R 2/4880 (1941) fol. 533, R 2/4881 (1942) fol. 264, and R 2/4883 (1943), p. 5. For comparison: the official average annual earnings in the German Reich were 2,297 RM in 1941, 2,310 RM in 1942, and 2,324 RM in 1943.

[67] See Mallmann and Paul, "Resistenz oder loyale Widerwilligkeit?"

[68] On the surveillance and destruction of the Bund Proletarisch-Revolutionärer Schriftsteller, see the documents in BArch R 58/736.

[69] Lämmert, "Beherrschte Prosa," 418–21.

[70] "Die Stimmung unter den Künstlern," *Deutschland-Berichte* 2 (1935), 226–9; "Kunst und Volksbildung im Dritten Reich," ibid. 710–22; "Dichtung und Theater im Dritten Reich," *Deutschland-Berichte* 4 (1937), 1632–52.

[71] See Pechel, *Zwischen den Zeilen*; Mirbt, "Theorie und Technik der Camouflage."

Table 2: Authors' income 1941-3

Gross annual income	Number of members	Year
Group 1: up to 1,200 RM	3,229	1941
Group 2: up to 3,600 RM	1,092	
Group 3: up to 6,000 RM	335	
Group 4: over 6,000 RM	406	
Group 1: up to 1,200 RM	2,100	1942
Group 2: up to 3,600 RM	1,100	
Group 3: up to 6,000 RM	340	
Group 4: over 6,000 RM	400	
Group 1: up to 1,200 RM	1,860	1943
Group 2: up to 3,600 RM	1,050	
Group 3: up to 6,000 RM	390	
Group 4: over 6,000 RM	680	

policy in April 1942 he was arrested and his magazine closed down. Pechel remained imprisoned in various jails and concentration camps without trial until April 1945. Among the few authors who actively worked to overthrow the Nazi dictatorship were Adam Kuckhoff (executed in August 1943) and Günther Weisenborn of the "Rote Kapelle" resistance group, and Dietrich Bonhoeffer and Albrecht Haushofer, both executed in April 1945 for their involvement in preparations for the coup attempt of 20 July 1944. Erich Knauf, Erich Ohser, and Friedrich Reck-Malleczewen, too, paid with their lives for their intellectual resistance to the regime.

The system of institutional management and control of literature was by no means unbroken or complete. Indeed, it was not even uniform in its decision-making structures—the bureaucracies of the state and the Party being run by people with different educational backgrounds, personal histories, motivations, and political objectives. Nevertheless, it was sufficiently effective and brutal to prevent, or immediately curb, any open resistance within the writing profession.

Politics, Profits, and Professional Ethos: Publishers and Booksellers

For a large number of *völkisch*, Nazi, and nationalist-conservative publishers, the NSDAP's rise to power opened up the prospect of being able to dominate the German book market at last. In this sense, the "Aryanization" of Jewish companies and the closure or neutralization of left-wing publishers and book distributors were welcomed by many in the sector not solely as an economic consolidation, but also as a victory in cultural politics. The publishing, retailing, and wholesaling *Fachschaften*, brought together in the book-trade association BRB in 1935, included 1,552 NSDAP members, one third of whom had joined the Party before 1933; there were also 640 Party members in the approximately 9,200-strong *Fachschaft* of book-trade employees.[72]

The prime beneficiaries of the new developments were the NSDAP's central publishing house Franz Eher, Verlag der DAF, Hanseatische Verlagsanstalt, and Langen-Müller Verlag. Aside from these Party-owned concerns, several mid-sized private companies, some of them rich in tradition, also drew profit from the new formation of the book market: Verlag C. Bertelsmann, Verlag Hugo Bruckmann, Eugen Diederichs Verlag, Hammer Verlag (directed by Theodor Fritsch, Jr.), Haude- und Spenersche Verlagsbuchhandlung, Verlag Junker und Dünnhaupt, W. Kohlhammer Verlag, Knorr & Hirth GmbH, Gustav Langenscheidt Verlag, Verlag "Der Eiserne Hammer" Karl Robert Langewiesche, J. F. Lehmanns Verlag, E. A. Seemann Verlagsbuchhandlung, Verlag Gerhard Stalling, Velhagen & Klasing Verlag, Verlagsbuchhandlung Georg Westermann, and Zeitgeschichte Verlag Wilhelm Andermann. All these businesses had already

---

[72] Figures in report on a session of the BRB board at the Berlin office on 20 September 1935, BArch BDC/RK/fiche Z 0025 fol. 1414 (p. 2) and fol. 1420 (p. 5).

published nationalist or Nazi literature during the Weimar Republic, and needed only to expand their program in fiction, nonfiction, professional literature, and schoolbooks in line with the era's requirements. New actors also emerged with their own book production: the SS with Volk und Reich Verlag (headed by Friedrich Heiss since 1925, based in Berlin with branches in Amsterdam, Prague, and Vienna) and Ahnenerbe-Stiftung Verlag led by *Obersturmführer* Dietrich Wolff (from 1938); the Wehrmacht during the war; and the Party Chancellery with Deutsche Verlags- und Kunstanstalt.

A total of 160 publishers emigrated, probably the best-known of them Gottfried Bermann Fischer, Bruno Cassirer, Babett Gross, Jakob Hegner, Wieland Herzfelde, Edith Jacobsohn, Willi Münzenberg, Herbert Reichner, Salman Schocken, Rudolf Ullstein, Kurt Wolff, and Paul von Zsolnay.[73] For those companies that stayed in Germany despite a skeptical view of the Nazi regime, yet wished to maintain high-quality publishing, the twelve years of dictatorship posed a special kind of test. Rowohlt alone had lost books worth around half a million RM by 1936 due to bans and confiscation.[74] Book censorship inflicted significant damage on the wholesale and retail book trade as well, and booksellers began to return items from publishers and authors rejected by the state or Party agencies or to avoid ordering them in the first place. Instead, as Ernst Rowohlt told his frustrated author Erik Reger on 7 December 1933, bookstores now filled their windows "only with National Socialist literature or books from the rubber-stamped right-wing publishers"; as for book reviewing, even "the few remaining independent papers" no longer dared to say much at all.[75] Added to these problems was the impact of the Depression on consumers' purchasing power. The reading public was only prepared to buy books at prices between 2 and 4.80 RM, preferring to borrow more expensive items from the commercial libraries. Furthermore, wrote Rowohlt on 21 December 1935, the book trade was suffering from the absence of "the previous buyers of good books: the Jews." Those who had not emigrated were "no

---

[73] Möller, *Exodus der Kultur*, 59–61. See also the overview of communist publishers in StAL BV/F 13 321.

[74] Gieselbusch et al., *100 Jahre Rowohlt*, 110.

[75] AdK Archiv Reger/367. The following quotations from Rowohlt's letters ibid.

longer, for the most part, in a position to buy books for themselves. We are feeling that loss very badly."

Non-Nazi publishers found themselves under pressure from two sides: they had to respond to political censorship by the state and Party authorities, but also to secure the economic survival of their companies, which meant a program that kept the reading public happy without leaving the company open to attacks from the regime. To square this circle, publishers needed very particular strategies, the everyday success of which determined the fate of their books and authors. It was vital for them to keep constantly updated on political developments, create and cultivate personal contacts within the apparatus of literary policy, remove "undesirable" authors from their lists, compromise on revising new editions, and insist on their authors keeping a low political profile. The criteria for assessing manuscripts had to be adapted: at stake were no longer only literary quality and the promise of commercial success, but also the likelihood or not of political objections. The question was not whether these strategies were applied but how skillfully, and how far a publisher succeeded —despite all the concessions—in preserving intact the core of what he or she saw as professional ethics and values.

The Rowohlt company managed to sustain its "community of destiny" with its politically controversial author Hans Fallada,[76] begun in 1919, throughout the Nazi period by steering him skillfully through the shoals of dictatorship. Thus, the 1933 reissue of Fallada's best-selling 1932 novel *Kleiner Mann—was nun?* (*Little Man, What Now?*, 1933) appeared with numerous revisions to take account of changed political circumstances. On 15 May 1934, when Ernst Rowohlt was planning a *Börsenblatt* advertisement for the cheap edition of *Bauern, Bonzen und Bomben* (*A Small Circus*) along with the remainder of the first edition, he asked Fallada specifically whether the book "contains anything at all against National Socialism." If it did, he warned, "they might be able to turn it against us." On 4 March 1935, Rowohlt wrote to his author about a manuscript entitled "Und wenn der ganze Schnee verbrennt!" ("And if the snow all

---

[76] Letter to Alfred Günther, 26 December 1941, in Fallada, *Ewig auf der Rutschbahn*, 346. On the following points, see Fallada's correspondence between 1933 and 1945, ibid.

burns!"), telling him he would have Peter Suhrkamp read it before it went to press. Suhrkamp advised against the title, and added that "very minor deletions in your previous books could have avoided the wrath of those in power."

As a letter of 10 October 1935 shows, when the Chamber of Literature withdrew permission for Fallada's books to be translated Rowohlt called in Johannes Roeseler (the influential director of Ullstein Verlag, now "Aryanized" by Eher) to persuade vice-president Wismann to reverse the decision. Licensing agreements with foreign companies now became possible again, and supplied income that Fallada was finding it harder and harder to access within Germany. The 1934 books *Wer einmal aus dem Blechnapf frißt* (*Who Once Eats Out Of the Tin Bowl*, 1934) and *Wir hatten mal ein Kind* (*Once We Had a Child*, 1935), *Märchen vom Stadtschreiber, der aufs Land flog* of 1935 (*Sparrow Farm*, 1937), and *Altes Herz geht auf die Reise* of 1936 (*Old Heart Goes on a Journey*, 1936) all sold badly—thanks to negative reviews in Rosenberg's *Bücherkunde* and other Party journals,[77] which further increased booksellers' reluctance to stock the author. Only with *Wolf unter Wölfen* (*Wolf among Wolves*, 1938), published by Rowohlt in fall 1937 despite political qualms and after the author's deletion of potentially objectionable passages, did Fallada's fortunes recover. In November the first printing was already sold out and the second and third were ready for dispatch. Even the Nazi press (with the exception of *Bücherkunde*) praised the novel, and Goebbels was enthusiastic.[78] The cheap edition of *Bauern, Bonzen und Bomben* now began to sell, reaching 50,000 copies by March 1939.

Der Eiserne Gustav of 1938 (*Iron Gustav*, 1940) broke this run of success; the novel was savagely attacked in the press and some *Gauleiter* instructed booksellers in their area not to display it in shop windows. Gustav Kilpper of Deutsche Verlags-Anstalt, which took over Rowohlt in 1939, reassured Fallada on 19 April "that we monitor,

---

[77] *Bücherkunde* discussed Fallada's work several times, always in negative terms. See the reviews of *Bauern, Bonzen, Bomben, Kleiner Mann was nun?, Wer einmal aus dem Blechnapf frißt*, and *Wir hatten mal ein Kind* in *Bücherkunde* 1 (1934), 153–6; "Die Rumpelkammer" (on *Wolf unter Wölfen*), *Bücherkunde* 5 (1938), 47–9; Eberhard Ter-Nedden, "Ein Wort über Fallada," *Bücherkunde* 8 (1941), 326–31.

[78] Goebbels, *Tagebücher*, Part I, vol. 5, 126 (31 January 1938).

nurture, and manage with the greatest care all business matters and everything related to your standing with the public and the book trade. In recent years almost every respected author has come under fire at one point or another." The company tried to restore confidence with the help of the Propaganda Ministry literature department, going through Franz Moraller, the former Chamber of Culture manager who now headed Rowohlt in Stuttgart together with Heinrich Maria Ledig.

Otherwise, the established procedure continued under the company's new management. The author practiced self-censorship—for example by "deleting somewhat objectionable passages especially on the sexual side" in the proofs of *Der ungeliebte Mann* ("The unloved man"), as he noted in a letter of 14 August 1940—or the publisher requested revisions, as in the reprint of *Kleiner Mann— was nun?* Here, Fallada wrote on 22 October 1940, "remarks on the Jewish question and about Jews" were to be deleted. Emotionally drained by the repressions, on 23 January 1941 he complained to Ledig about retrospective deletions of this kind: "They don't improve anything, just forfeit the respect of some readers ..., and the majority doesn't even notice them." In the end, Fallada chose the most common way out, switching to purely entertaining and politically innocuous works: the tale *Das Abenteuer des Werner Quabs* ("Werner Quabs's adventure") in 1941; a love story for the *Berliner Illustrirte Zeitung* in which there were "no wicked people at all" and "at bottom everyone is terribly good and noble," as the author told Rowohlt on 28 June 1941; a book of memoirs in 1942 and a second volume, *Heute bei uns zu Haus* ("Today at our house") in 1943—the only book Rowohlt Verlag published that year before being closed down on 1 November.

As for Insel Verlag, in August 1933 political uncertainties induced the publisher to withdraw from a project it had already advertised, *Deutsche Chronik 1918–1933* ("German chronicle 1918–1933") compiled by Katharina Kippenberg and Otto von Taube.[79] The books of the Jewish authors Martin and Paula Buber, Leonhard Frank, Heinrich Heine, and Alfred Mombert and of the politically "undesirable" Johannes R. Becher, Heinrich Mann, and Albrecht Schaeffer were removed from the Insel list, as—with perhaps exaggerated caution

---

[79] On this and the following, see Sarkowski and Jeske, *Der Insel Verlag*, 297–415.

prompted by its subject matter—was Egon Caesar Conte Corti's two-volume best-seller *Die Rothschilds* (1927/28) (*The Rise of the House of Rothschild* and *The Reign of the House of Rothschild*, 1928). The company's series Insel-Bücherei lost a total of twenty-nine titles by nineteen authors. Director Anton Kippenberg stepped in personally to contest the ban on Stefan Zweig's works, approaching RSK vice-president Wismann in Berlin in early December 1933. He had only limited success: individual titles could be sold until the end of 1934, but the wider ban was sustained. Reluctantly, Kippenberg had to pass Zweig's new works to the Herbert Reichner house in Vienna. At first they could still be sold within Germany, but after List 1 of Harmful and Undesirable Literature indexed all the author's writings in October 1935, the Gestapo confiscated 2,247 copies from Koehler & Volckmar in Leipzig and sent them straight back to Vienna in March 1936.

The finely illustrated map of Germany that Rudolf Koch, a typographic artist from Offenbach, had been working on for Insel since 1925 turned out to be particularly explosive. The map was revised several times after 1933 and not published until February 1935—only for the Propaganda Ministry to impose a ban on its distribution that March because it was being used by anti-German campaigners in Italy, France, and Poland. In this case, Kippenberg called in the cultural affairs officer in the Deputy Führer's staff, Ernst Schulte Strathaus, with whom he shared a passion for bibliophile editions of Goethe's works. After painstaking corrections, on which Jewish illustrators with "special permission" were allowed to work, a new edition of the map was published in November 1937. Just four months later it was rendered hopelessly out of date by the *Anschluss* of Austria.

In its fiction program, Insel Verlag maintained its focus on German classics and the work of Rilke, along with contemporary authors such as Hans Carossa, Gertrud von le Fort, Ricarda Huch, Edzard Schaper, Wilhelm von Scholz, Friedrich Schnack, Reinhold Schneider, Rudolf Alexander Schröder, and Konrad Weiss. The fiction list also included authors closely affiliated with the Nazi regime, notably Ernst Bertram, Rudolf G. Binding, Blunck, Hermann Stehr, Helene Voigt-Diederichs, and Karl-Heinrich Waggerl. The Insel-Bücherei series, the publisher's flagship since 1912 and—with 20 million copies sold by 1937—also its economic backbone, did not falter during the war, accumulating more than forty new titles as well as eighty licensed editions for the frontline book trade. Whereas Insel traditionally attracted the nationalist-conservative middle class, Verlag Philipp Reclam jun. had mainly targeted the liberal bourgeoisie before 1933.[80] However, in response to the political attacks on the book market after the Nazis' rise to power, Reclam jettisoned both classic Jewish authors (Auerbach, Börne, Heine, Lassalle, Saphir) and contemporary ones (Arthur Schnitzler, Jakob Wassermann, Franz Werfel, and Arnold and Stefan Zweig). A planned reissue of Hermann Hesse's 1929 personal canon of world literature, *Eine Bibliothek der Weltliteratur*, stalled in December 1934 when Hesse refused to erase Jewish authors from his list or make other concessions to the new political environment. Stefan Zweig's introduction for a 1927 selection of Goethe's poems was replaced in the 1938 edition with an essay by the Nazi scholar Heinz Kindermann.

After the war, Reclam laid claim to political integrity by citing its publication of authors such as Richard Benz or Edwin Redslob and Rudolf Pechel's literary monthly *Deutsche Rundschau*, which appeared with Reclam from October 1937 through September 1939. However, from 1939 onward the company also participated heavily in the profitable market of frontline bookselling, with the dedicated frontline series Reclams Feldpostdienst, Reclams Feldpostpackung, Reclams Feldkassetten (boxed sets of ten or twenty-five volumes), and Reclams Feldbücherei (mini "libraries" of 100 short volumes each); military or special editions of the renowned low-price series Reclams Universal-Bibliothek (1941–3); and the brochure-format Reclams Reihenbändchen (from 1943).[81] At the same time, for the SD's *Meldungen aus dem Reich* in January 1943 Reclam exemplified the pressures on the German book trade caused by the wretched state of paper management.[82] Of the 90,000 kg of paper requested by Reclam for the first quarter and approved by the Economic Office in January 1942, not even half had been delivered by July: Reich

---

[80] On the following, see the unfortunately brief and incomplete study by Bode, *Reclam*, 101–13.

[81] Bühler and Bühler, *Der Frontbuchhandel*, 163–71.

[82] *Meldungen aus dem Reich*, vol. 12, no. 349, 11 January 1943, 4658–9.

Paper Office cutbacks took 7,500 kg of the allowance out of circulation, 22,500 kg were supposedly on their way, and nobody knew when the remaining 20,000 kg would be delivered.

S. Fischer Verlag was in a special position in many respects. After the book bans of 1933 and the dispersal of Fischer's authors in the course of its "Aryanization," in April 1936 the new director, Peter Suhrkamp, took up a dogged battle to preserve the humanist intellectual heft and internationalism that had set Fischer apart since it was founded in 1886. Of its German authors, the company was able to retain Otto Flake, Gerhart Hauptmann, Manfred Hausmann, Hermann Hesse, Bernhard Kellermann, Alexander Lernet-Holenia, Oskar Loerke, Ernst Penzoldt, and Hans Rehberg. By 1943/44 they had been joined by both established authors (Ernst Barlach, Carl Haensel, Max Kommerell, Felix Lützkendorf, Wolf von Niebelschütz, Rudolf Alexander Schröder) and younger ones (such as Lothar-Günther Buchheim, Albrecht Goes, Hermann Kasack, Clemens Podewils, and Luise Rinser-Schnell). Even so, on 25 November 1936 Annemarie Suhrkamp wrote despondently to her sister Ina Seidel: "Every day, every profession becomes more arduous, more grueling, more hopeless in the intellectual sense. I almost regret that a year ago, when there was a moment of decision, I did not wholeheartedly vote to live on our little remaining money in Kampen, and there to tend a gradually growing flock of sheep."[83] The company survived only with the greatest difficulty. The number of new titles dropped from thirty-two in 1936 to just twelve in 1941, turnover from 642,000 RM in 1936 to 348,000 RM in 1939.[84] The year 1940 was the only one to bring any significant rise in income, with the unexpected success of the two-volume anthology *Deutscher Geist* ("German spirit"), edited by Peter Suhrkamp and Oskar Loerke, and the Pantheon series edition of Goethe's *Kampagne in Frankreich* (*Campaign in France in the Year 1792*).

Fischer Verlag's already difficult situation was exacerbated during the war by the ban on books by French, British, and US authors. Conscription ate away at the company's workforce, and problems in accessing paper supplies meant production had to be partly shifted

---

[83] DLA NL Ina Seidel/Briefe an sie von Annemarie Suhrkamp, folder 2.
[84] Pfäfflin and Kussmaul, *S. Fischer, Verlag*, 572–3. The following points ibid. 588–91.

abroad. Added to this was the financial burden placed on Peter Suhrkamp by the cost of transferring the company ownership, tax arrears, and the additional tax levy through which the state took its slice of the book trade's war-related sales success.[85] At the beginning of 1943 the threat of closure was hanging over the renamed company, Suhrkamp Verlag, but on 17 March Annemarie Suhrkamp was able to report that, "after fourteen turbulent days during which our existence was seriously threatened by some highly personal machinations,"[86] the worst danger seemed to have passed. Even when the Gestapo arrested Peter Suhrkamp on 13 April 1944, the company survived; Hermann Kasack, who had become a Suhrkamp editor after the death of Loerke in February 1941, became its temporary director.[87] He had to make do with one-fourth of the previous staff, and in late September 1944 was forced to halt publication of the literary magazine *Neue Rundschau*. The remnants of Suhrkamp were taken over in the war's final months by Heinrich Gruber, since 1938 responsible for "monitoring and promoting the entire publishing sector" in the Propaganda Ministry's literature department.[88]

Henry Goverts and Eugen Claassen, who founded H. Goverts Verlag on 20 December 1934 in Hamburg, were also proponents of liberalism and cosmopolitanism.[89] Claassen contributed his experience as books director of Societäts Verlag, a publisher associated with the newspaper *Frankfurter Zeitung*, while Goverts brought excellent Weimar-era contacts with academic, political, and literary circles of the liberal left and social democracy. The new company's program was marked by its careful combination of contemporary German literature by non-Nazi authors with translations from Italy, France, Norway, Britain, and the United States and works of cultural history and scholarship. Starting in 1940, it increasingly included literary treatments of the war, some of which reached the frontline book trade as licensed editions. Before each title was published, the two directors discussed in detail whether its content or style could be

---

[85] See Suhrkamp to Seidel, 5 July 1941, DLA NL Ina Seidel/Briefe an sie von Annemarie Suhrkamp, folder 3; Pfäfflin and Kussmaul, *S. Fischer, Verlag*, 588.

[86] DLA NL Ina Seidel/Briefe an sie von Annemarie Suhrkamp, folder 3.

[87] Pfäfflin and Kussmaul, *S. Fischer, Verlag*, 603–6.

[88] BArch BDC/RSK/Gruber, H.

[89] On the following, see Wallrath-Janssen, *Der Verlag H. Goverts*.

expected to cause problems with censorship. Between 1937 and 1939 they decided against the publication of a volume of novellas and the novel *Das unauslöschliche Siegel* ("The indelible seal") by Elisabeth Langgässer, *Das Holzschiff* (*The Ship*) by Hans Henny Jahnn, and the continuation of Robert Musil's *Der Mann ohne Eigenschaften* (*The Man Without Qualities*).

Self-censorship and preemptive revisions to manuscripts were common practice at Goverts. For example, deletions were made before the publication of Dolf Sternberger's *Panorama oder Ansichten vom 19. Jahrhundert* (*Panorama of the Nineteenth Century*), Joachim Maass's *Ein Testament*, Horst Lange's *Ulanenpatrouille* and his short-story collection *Die Leuchtkugeln* ("The flares"), Werner Martin's historical study of German emigration *Die fernen Söhne* ("Faraway sons"), and a work on cultural sociology by Henry Goverts's thesis advisor Alfred Weber, *Das Tragische und die Geschichte* ("History and the tragic"). At times, such interventions were made in agreement with censors like Karl Heinrich Bischoff at the Chamber or Jürgen Eggebrecht in the OKW, with whom Goverts was in personal contact. In the case of Rudolf Krämer's debut novel *Jacobs Jahr* ("Jacob's year"), preprinted from February to April 1943 in the *Kölnische Zeitung* in a censored version, Claassen was so concerned about the book version that he stopped delivery of the whole print run. The 11,000 copies, ready for distribution, went up in flames during the bombing of Leipzig in December 1943. It seems that Claassen and Goverts did not want a politically dubious publication to endanger the existence of their company, already under threat from the closures planned by the Propaganda Ministry.

There is evidence of retrospective censorship in some Goverts reprints. In October 1940, at the request of the Ministry literature department, all works by Martin Beheim-Schwarzbach were banned, including his 1938 Goverts novel *Die Verstoßene* ("The outcast"), because he had emigrated to England and been excluded from the Chamber in June 1940 as an "enemy alien."[90] Goverts thereupon removed his name as the translator of Margaret Mitchell's *Gone With the Wind* (translated as *Vom Winde verweht* in 1937) in the fifteenth and sixteenth printing of the novel, which had been permitted in

---

[90] RSK to RMVP, 18 February 1941, BArch BDC/RSK/Beheim-Schwarzbach, M.

1941 with the approval of Koch and Thielke of the Ministry.[91] Due to its alleged violation of sexual taboos, Maass's novel *Ein Testament* had to undergo further deletions when it was reissued in 1940. Church-affiliated publishers responded to the challenges of the Nazi-dominated book market with a range of different strategies. Herder Verlag tried to fend off individual bans through personal interventions. Defending his record after the war, Theophil Herder-Dorneich, Hermann Herder's son-in-law and the company's managing director and co-owner since 1928, listed twenty-eight Herder publications that were banned during the dictatorship.[92] For one of them, Friedrich Zoepfl's 1937 *Das Reich als Schicksal und Tat. Die deutsche Geschichte dem Volk erzählt* ("The Reich as destiny and deed. German history told to the people"), the Propaganda Ministry's Koblenz-Trier office applied to the Chamber of Literature for a ban in September 1937.[93] On 12 October the Chamber instructed Herder Verlag to submit a statement on the controversial passages and to refrain from further distribution of the book until a final decision was made. In his response of 22 October, Herder-Dorneich defended the book as a "popular, easy-to-understand historical portrayal of the whole of Germany." The new work was permeated by the author's "pain at Germany's tragic fate of division and disunity," and his "concern for the wholeness of Germany, the importance of which for our Reich today he indicates in his introduction and conclusion," was "understood on all sides and has met with much keen approval." Notwithstanding this, both author and publisher were "most willing, in the case of a new edition, to amend the problematic sentences so as to rule out all misunderstanding or misinterpretation." On 28 October the Chamber asked the Koblenz-Trier propaganda office to comment, and on 16 November received the following reply:

The National Socialist state has entrusted the thorough investigation of German history to the newly formed Reich Institute, in

---

[91] Henry Goverts to RSK, 12 February 1941, and RMVP literature department to RSK, 27 February 1941, ibid.

[92] BArch BDC/RK 2110/Herder-Dorneich, T. The list was enclosed with the questionnaire he had to complete for the US Military Government in Germany.

[93] The following is based on records of the banning procedure in BArch BDC/RSK/Zoepfl, F.

order to reveal the life story of the German *Volk* afresh, purifying and clarifying the previously distorted portrayal. It is necessary to eliminate the toxins that have accumulated due to the intellectual features of the liberal era and its historians and to the religious attitude of the Ultramontane tendency and its representatives. In my opinion, the latter group includes the author of the above-mentioned book, as well as its all too well-known "Catholic" publisher, Herder Verlag of Freiburg.

Despite this harsh dismissal, in December 1937 the Chamber's Herbert Menz arranged a personal meeting in Berlin with Josef Knecht, the deputy manager of Herder Verlag. On 9 December, Herder-Dorneich asked for a further meeting with the "gentlemen responsible" at the Propaganda Ministry, to discuss "the reasons for the ban." Not until 4 May 1938 was the book finally banned by the literature department.

Talking personally to officials was, then, one possible strategy; another was accentuating the publisher's importance to the interests of the German Reich. Thus, Herder's annual report for 1936 included a brochure entitled *Der Verlag Herder im Ausland. Pionierarbeit für das deutsche Buch* ("The Herder house abroad. Pioneering work for the German book"). The company could point to a long-term presence in Spain, Italy, Austria, the Netherlands, Czechoslovakia, Britain, the United States, South America, and Japan. Between 1866 and 1936, it had published a total of 1,297 translations into foreign languages. The focus was on Spain, where it published not only translations from German, but also books in the original German, printed in Freiburg. The company's Barcelona bookstore Libreria Herder, established in 1926, became the sole Spanish distributor for several German scientific and scholarly publishers. Among Herder's partners were bookstores, universities, research libraries, schools, missions, and even governments. The booklet went on to praise the publisher's "care for Germandom abroad," dedicating a whole chapter to the encyclopedia *Der grosse Herder*, which it said had been designed "to connect the homeland with the Germans outside the Reich" and was "borne along by the idea of the community of Germans across borders." Several articles were cited as evidence for this claim. Herder also boasted of its collaboration with Sophia University in Tokyo on a five-volume Catholic encyclopedia in Japanese, under preparation since 1935 (it was completed in 1939).[94] To close, the company drew attention to the valuable foreign currency that its growing earnings from exports brought into the German Reich, and noted that book exports actively fostered scholarly and cultural exchange between Germany and the rest of the world.

A different path was taken by the Gütersloh-based Lutheran house Verlag C. Bertelsmann.[95] For this publisher, established in 1835, the Nazi accession to power was not a significant caesura: the nationalist-conservative, antimodern, and antidemocratic values of its publications dovetailed easily with the state's ideology. In both theology and fiction, Bertelsmann had been publishing works suffused with antisemitic prejudice well before 1933; the fact that so little adjustment was required after that date does not cast a good light on the publisher's output. Furthermore, since 1921 Heinrich Mohn had practiced a patriarchal management style—revolving around "social care, commitment, and a sense of duty"—that proved highly compatible with the Nazi regime. Bertelsmann even expressly aspired to be "a miniature model of the *Volk* community."[96] From fall 1934, the company expanded its fiction program, which had been inaugurated in 1928 to complement the previous focus on theological books and periodicals. Bertelsmann's fiction was now dominated by regional, historical, romantic, and entertainment novels and, increasingly, fictionalized or autobiographical accounts of World War I. Bertelsmann was catering to a rapidly growing demand that accompanied the remilitarization of German society and reevaluations of the history of the lost war. The title of Paul Coelestin Ettighoffer's 1932 novel *Feldgrau schafft Dividende* ("Field gray pays dividends") is apt here: Bertelsmann made healthy profits from the new mass business in war writing.

There were, though, more than purely commercial reasons for the shift in the publisher's emphasis in the late 1930s; it must be seen in the context of the battle between the Nazi state and Germany's

---

[94] See section on international contacts in Herder Verlag, *175 Jahre Herder*, 49–53, here 52.
[95] On the following, see Friedländer et al., *Bertelsmann im Dritten Reich*.
[96] Ibid. 335–53.

two main Christian churches for a monopoly on ideology, a struggle that escalated from 1936. Twenty-two incidents of censorship are documented between 1935 and 1944, affecting both Bertelsmann itself and its July 1939 acquisition Rufer Verlag. Individual publications were indexed, and the refusal of paper rations, as an instrument of preventive censorship, impinged on book production to an ever greater extent. It resulted in the discontinuation of most of Bertelsmann's theology list as early as 1941. In other words, the publisher's early reorientation toward light and nationalistic fiction—areas propagated with particular zeal by the Nazi regime and eagerly purchased by the public—assured not only its economic viability but also its political survival.

During the war, Bertelsmann succeeded in acquiring Wehrmacht commissions for enormous print runs. It designed special "field post" series for the frontline troops stationed all across Europe, and had licensed editions printed and distributed via the frontline book trade. But these deals, worth millions of reichsmarks, were not always reached through the lawful channel of nurturing personal contacts in the OKW and the individual forces; downright corruption was also involved, in which a key role was played by one of Bertelsmann's agents, Matthias Lackas. Between 1939 and 1945, Lackas rose from being Deutscher Verlag's general agent for the Rhineland, based in Cologne, to managing the mail-order company Arnold in Berlin, then became probably the Reich's most important paper racketeer.[97] His arrest in late August 1943 and the revelation of his illegal transactions, in which top-level Bertelsmann employees were involved, gave the NSDAP's publisher Eher a welcome chance to subdue its most powerful competitor. Although Bertelsmann initially remained in business—unlike Rufer, which was closed down in 1943—and even managed to secure a large-scale commission for Organisation Todt, a special edition of Hans Grimm's *Volk ohne Raum* ("A people without space"), the Chamber of Literature ordered its closure on 26 August 1944. The decree was an immediate consequence of the discredit brought by the spring 1944 court martial of Lackas and some of his business partners for crimes against the war economy, bribery, and embezzlement. Even the Propaganda Ministry, which had so far

---

[97] Ibid. 466–79. See also Bühler and Simons, *Die blendenden Geschäfte*, 34–148.

shielded Bertelsmann from harm, was neither able nor willing to support the publisher any longer.

The whole of the German book trade was negatively affected by the massive political regimentation that the Nazi state initiated in 1933. The sector's structure was dominated by small and medium-sized businesses, with 86.9 percent of the approximately 10,000 businesses in the retail book trade employing five people or fewer, and 84.5 percent reaching an annual turnover of 50,000 RM or less. Of the remaining retailers, the 7.6 percent employing six to ten people had a turnover of below 100,000 RM, and only the 5.5 percent employing more than ten people had a turnover of over 100,000 RM.[98] Of the approximately 3,500 publishers, 43.1 percent had an annual turnover of less than 20,000 RM, 13.8 percent up to 50,000 RM, and 13.7 percent up to 100,000 RM, while only 9.6 percent reported sales of up to 200,000 RM and 19.8 percent higher than that. More than 80 percent of these businesses were small-scale publishers, bringing out fewer than thirty new titles a year on average; they accounted for 40 percent of the country's total book production. Mid-sized publishers comprised 17.8 percent of companies and 44.4 percent of annual production, while large publishers with more than 200 new titles a year made up only 1.3 percent of businesses and 15.6 percent of annual production.

The pessimistic mood on the German book market becomes very obvious in the economic reports that Gerhard Menz had been compiling for the Börsenverein every quarter since 1928.[99] Menz gathered information from a selection of publishing companies representing different company sizes and specializing in different fields: science and popular science, fiction, schoolbooks, children's and youth books, periodicals, and art prints and sheet music. He collected the quarterly data on sales, the number of new titles, retail

---

[98] On this and the following, see *Der deutsche Buchhandel in Zahlen*, 18–20. The figures on turnover are from 1937, and were probably far lower overall in the preceding years.

[99] On the following, see the documents in StAL BV/643 and 644. On the development, implementation, and objectives of the surveys, see Börsenverein manager Hess to president of the Reich Statistical Office, Berlin, 16 March 1939, BV/643. A list of the publishers can be found in the enclosure to Menz's circular re: questionnaires on business statistics, 12 March 1937, ibid.

prices, employment contracts, and expectations for the coming months. Table 3 compares the fourth quarter of 1933 and the first and second quarter of 1934 in absolute numbers.[100]

The retail price of books stagnated for most of the companies questioned. Some publishers had to reduce prices, and none was able to raise them. Stagnating or declining turnover in some cases resulted in layoffs, short-time work, and pay cuts. Although the trends varied by field—scientific and schoolbook publishers suffered worst from the continuing crisis—the overall sentiment was "still not optimistic,"[101] the situation assessed as "still exceptionally serious,"[102] and the results even of Christmas business "unsatisfactory."[103] Clearly, the book sector was not benefiting from the slight revival in other parts of the domestic economy. Foreign business, too, had been severely dented by the critical foreign reaction to political events in Germany, the difficult foreign-currency situation, and the fact that German books and periodicals were overpriced on the global market.

The book market's predicament did not stem from economic factors alone. Constant political interference by state and Party agencies also played its part, causing considerable economic damage through the banning and confiscation of thousands of publications and the rapid changes in jurisdiction, legal regulations, and school and university curricula. In February 1934, for example, Gottlieb Braun of N. G. Elwert'sche Universitäts- und Verlagsbuchhandlung in Marburg estimated that his company had incurred losses of around 200,000 RM either by having to suspend finalized publications on civil law and the municipal and rural community ordinances due to the unpredictability of legal developments, or because the delays in decreeing new curricula had caused "uncertainty regarding teaching materials."[104]

---

[100] From "Konjunkturberichte" no. 24 (February 1934), no. 25 (May 1934), and no. 26 (August 1934), StAL BV/643.

[101] Response by a science publisher in the report on Q4/1933, p. 3. Similar points were made by a schoolbook publisher and a sheet music specialist, ibid. p. 7.

[102] Response by a popular science publisher, ibid. p. 6.

[103] Response by a fiction publisher, ibid. A publisher specializing in youth literature and picture books also reported a substantial decline in sales during November and December 1933.

[104] Braun to Börsenverein, 14 and 21 February 1934, StAL BV/643.

Table 3: Book market developments 1933–4

Domestic turnover	Foreign turnover	Total turnover	New titles
Q4/1933 (59 companies/110 replies)			
14 higher	6 higher	11 better	12 increased
19 same	14 same	18 same	28 unchanged
63 lower	74 lower	73 worse	67 reduced
			3 none
Q1/1934 (55 companies/115 replies)			
22 higher	13 higher	21 better	8 increased
23 same	24 same	23 same	52 unchanged
58 lower	64 lower	69 worse	49 reduced
			5 none
Q2/1934 (53 companies/103 replies)			
12 higher	5 higher	11 better	7 increased
32 same	27 same	30 same	32 unchanged
51 lower	62 lower	59 worse	56 reduced
			5 none

This gloomy picture was not the one presented to the public. Menz's economic reports were marked "Confidential! Not for press use!" and the monthly commentaries on business trends that he published in the *Börsenblatt*, like the detailed annual statistics on the German book market compiled and annotated by Ludwig Schönrock for the same journal, gave only a small glimpse of reality. Even so, the seriousness of the situation was obvious to any careful *Börsenblatt* reader. In 1934 the number of new titles dropped by 749 titles or 3.5 percent to 20,852, after a very slight recovery in 1933 (21,601 titles compared to 21,452 in 1932).[105] That result was worse than any seen during the Weimar Republic. The average retail price of books continued to fall as well: from 5.08 RM in 1932, to 4.23 RM in 1933, to 3.97 RM in 1934. The decline in the total retail price reveals the negative trend even more clearly: from 103,451.25 RM in 1932 to 86,625.45 RM in 1933, to 79,003.75 RM in 1934.[106] Book exports declined sharply, from 36,517,000 RM in 1932, to 30,022,000 RM in 1933, to 25,113,000 RM in 1934; and there was a corresponding fall in the number of new German-language titles published abroad, from 3,404 in 1933 to 3,090 in 1934.[107] Finally, the value of book imports into Germany also fell, from 10,525,000 RM (1932), to 7,731,000 RM (1933), then 6,790,000 RM (1934).

There were still 2.5 million people out of work in 1936, and both wages and pensions were lower than they had been in 1928,[108] leaving the German book sector hard pressed to recover from the Depression. In 1937 total book production, at 25,361 titles, was lower than that of 1930, and remained far below its previous peak, 28,182 titles in 1913.[109] In search of more gratifying statistics, at Wilhelm Baur's suggestion fifty of the larger and high-selling publishing companies, including Eher Verlag, were now asked to contribute to Menz's survey for the first time.[110] Yet even for 1938 the economic reports showed no radical improvement. Although publishers' turnover had risen since 1933/34, higher manufacturing costs—in combination with state-fixed retail prices and the compulsory payment of dues to the Chamber of Literature—kept

---

[105] On the following, see Ludwig Schönrock, "Der deutsche Büchermarkt im Jahre 1933 [Part I]," *Bbl.* no. 86, 14 April 1934, 325–9, and "Der deutsche Büchermarkt 1934 [Part I]," *Bbl.* no. 162, 16 July 1935, 579–81.

[106] Schönrock, "Der deutsche Büchermarkt im Jahre 1933 [Part II]," *Bbl.* no. 88, 17 April 1934, 334–7, and "Der deutsche Büchermarkt 1934 [Part II]," *Bbl.* no. 164, 18 July 1935, 587–9.

[107] On these points and on book imports, see Schönrock, "Der deutsche Büchermarkt im Jahre 1933 [Part III]," *Bbl.* no. 94, 24 April 1934, 377–82, and "Der deutsche Büchermarkt 1934 [Part III]," *Bbl.* no. 166, 20 July 1935, 596–600.

[108] Aly, *Hitler's Beneficiaries*, 36.

[109] Figures in Langenbucher, *Die Welt des Buches*, 146.

[110] See Baur to Börsenverein office, 7 January 1937, and to Menz, 5 March 1937, including the list of fifty publishers, StAL BV/643.

overall profits at a modest level. The contrast between these sobering portraits of the sector and the publicly broadcast success was striking, leading Börsenverein president Baur to criticize Menz in a 1938 letter: "I am enough of an optimist to believe that all these reports are not worth a damn in practice."[111] To achieve better-looking results, he again insisted that more of the larger companies be forced to participate in the survey. If this proved unsuccessful, wrote Baur, in future he would "drop the whole thing." He would still have the "Reich Chamber of Literature's statistics on turnover," which "in fact probably speak more eloquently of the economic upturn."

The recovery in the book trade that began in 1938 was the consequence of a broader economic upswing, favored by vigorous construction activity and the Nazi state's immense expenditure on arms. This led to more or less full employment, and thus to a noticeable growth in the public's purchasing power at a time when prices were stagnating. State subsidies for the German book sector amounting to millions of reichsmarks—whether through the book export compensation procedure or large-scale propaganda for book-buying—now started to take effect. In the period between 1940 and 1943, book sales rose rapidly. Although the number of new titles began to decline in 1941 (with 20,615 first editions in 1941 as compared to 22,289 in 1940),[112] the total number of copies printed rose that year to nearly 342 million, as against just over 242 million copies in 1940. The temporary slump in bookselling after the invasion of Poland in September 1939 was quickly overcome, and pre-Christmas sales that year heralded a book market boom that would continue unbroken until 1943.

It was initially fostered by the general resource shortage that accompanied the war and the public's fear of inflation. As Minister of Economics Funk wrote to Goebbels in September 1941, the resulting "surplus purchasing power" could now not be satisfied by the market, and resulted in a "flight to tangible assets."[113] This trend benefited the book trade as a whole because books, unlike all other

---

[111] Börsenverein president Baur to Börsenverein manager, 13 December 1938, StAL BV/644.
[112] "Bücherproduktions-Statistik 1941," Bbl. no. 196/197, 3 September 1942, 178–9.
[113] Goebbels, Tagebücher, Part II, vol. 1, 475 (23 September 1941). See also Meldungen aus dem Reich, vol. 9, no. 260, 16 February 1942, 3317.

everyday goods, could be purchased without ration coupons, and from 1940 on bookstores were more or less stripped bare by eager buyers. The greatest demand was for easily consumed works of quality fiction and entertainment, contemporary political and military nonfiction, biographies, and children's or young adult literature. In fall 1940, the Chamber and the Börsenverein succeeded in protecting the growing revenue of the businesses they represented against the Reich Commissioner for Price Control, who had alleged inflated profits after examining the accounts of 300 publishing companies.[114] Just as in 1937, the Price Commissioner and his agency, which reported to the Four-Year Plan Commission, again failed to abolish the fixed book price and reduce book prices more generally.

However, the drawbacks of an overheated economy soon made themselves felt. Publishers were finding it almost impossible to produce enough new books, hamstrung by the loss of personnel to the Wehrmacht, overstretched graphics and printing businesses, time-consuming paper allocation procedures, and the effects of aerial bombardment. In August 1941, the Chamber's Karl Heinrich Bischoff had to admit to a worried Party comrade, publisher Gustav Langenscheidt, that the paper question had now "become somewhat tricky after all," and that the literary authorities felt "like a woman whose shirt is too small: there isn't enough to go round whichever way you look."[115]

The growing discrepancy between constantly rising demand and dramatically falling supply created considerable resentment. Conflicts arose on many counts: between publishers and retail booksellers, who did not receive the required quantities for the orders they placed or else believed they were being fobbed off with unsalable remainders; between publishers and book wholesalers, who felt sidelined by the increase in direct ordering from retailers to publishers; between booksellers and their customers, who, after panic-buying their favorites, found themselves facing empty shelves and often attributed this privation to their local bookseller's incompetence or even actual ill will. Allied bombing inflicted serious

---

[114] For details, see Triebel, "Kultur und Kalkül."
[115] Bischoff to Langenscheidt (stationed in Brussels), 12 August 1941, BArch BDC/RK 2110/G. Langenscheidt Verlag.

losses in the great publishing locations of Berlin, Hamburg, Munich, and Stuttgart, and the heart of the German book trade, Leipzig, was largely destroyed in December 1943. By 1944, books had long since joined the list of goods in short supply.

But wartime conditions also engendered a shadow economy that contributed to a significant rise in turnover between 1939 and 1943. Numerous publishers, the large book wholesalers, and some retailers gained access to the lucrative commissions awarded from fall 1939 by the Zentrale der Frontbuchhandlungen, the OKW, the army, navy, and Luftwaffe, the SS, Organisation Todt, and the Armaments Ministry. This new book market was exploited chiefly by large companies and a few medium-sized ones: C. Bertelsmann with a total of 19 million copies supplied to the Wehrmacht, Eher (14 million copies), W. Kohlhammer and Bibliographisches Institut (10 million copies each), Verlag Deutsche Volksbücher, which was taken over in 1940 by Georg von Holtzbrinck and Wilhelm Schlösser (5 million copies), C. Gerber/Münchner Buchverlag (4 million copies), Insel and Reclam (1.9 million copies each), Eugen Diederichs (1.72 million copies), Gauverlag Bayerische Ostmark (1.2 million copies), and Langen-Müller Verlag (1.1 million copies).[116] The production of military or "field post" editions alone, more than 35 million copies of which were printed between 1940 and 1944, involved seventy-one publishers. Houses steeped in tradition such as Hermann Böhlau, F. A. Brockhaus, Droste, Engelhorns Nachfolger, Gräfe und Unzer, Ferdinand Hirt, Theodor Knaur, Paul List, E. S. Mittler & Sohn, Paul Neff, Rütten & Loening, and Ludwig Voggenreiter, and new publishers such as H. Goverts, Wilhelm Heyne, and Reinhard Piper also depended on mass sales to the Wehrmacht.[117] This closed market ultimately worked like a kind of giant book club: publishers produced a limited selection of book titles for its members—in this case the frontline soldiers—in high print runs and at special prices, distributing them through the network of branches built up by the Zentrale der Frontbuchhandlungen.[118]

---

[116] Figures in Friedländer et al., *Bertelsmann im Dritten Reich*, 423. See also Garke-Rothbart, *Georg von Holtzbrinck*, 137–74, esp. 156.
[117] Bühler and Bühler, *Der Frontbuchhandel*, 119–24. See also Keiderling, *F.A. Brockhaus*, 186–7; Wallrath-Janssen, *Der Verlag H. Goverts*, 339–50; Ziegler, *100 Jahre Piper*, 126–7.
[118] See Lokatis, "Hanseatische Verlagsanstalt," 147.

For publishers specializing in natural sciences and humanities, as well as for a large number of mid-sized and smaller publishers with no chance of winning commissions for the frontline book trade, the increasingly restrictive rationing of paper and binding materials was a threat to their very existence. Compared to the daily and periodical press, publishers and retail bookstores felt "shabbily treated in the whole matter of paper rationing," as *Meldungen aus dem Reich* reported in January 1943.[119] In a letter of 4 March 1943, Elwert'sche Universitäts- und Verlagsbuchhandlung complained to the Börsenverein that there could hardly be a genuine "general paper shortage," given "how much paper is still being frittered away in other quarters."[120] Evidently, the company observed, paper rationing was intended to open up the "path toward monopoly publishers." This was a trend that must be resisted, "since National Socialism from the very beginning challenged the excesses of what was once Jewish big business, so one may surely assume that nowadays the new big business must not be allowed, in turn, to destroy smaller companies."

By September 1944, even Bischoff had realized that the closure of publishers ordered by his organization, the Chamber of Literature, was leading to "a kind of nationalization of the book trade."[121] This development, which had resulted in the closure of his own publishing company in Vienna, ran "counter to the original idea of National Socialism"—but had now, he believed, become irreversible.

A Politicized Profession: Librarians

After the Nazi dictatorship, few librarians who had worked in Germany's public or research libraries between 1933 and 1945 looked back on the period in public—perhaps unsurprisingly, for in 1933 the librarians' associations had rushed to support the Nazi rulers. Far from being coerced, the profession as a whole proved a willing accessory, though this was partly because librarians were considerably more dependent on the regime than were writers, publishers,

---

[119] *Meldungen aus dem Reich*, vol. 12, no. 349, 11 January 1943, 4659–60.
[120] StAL BV/644.
[121] Bischoff to RSK manager Gentz, 8 September 1944, BArch R 56 V/152 fol. 63.

and booksellers: senior library personnel were appointed by the Reich Education Ministry, and the libraries were funded by the state. Librarian Hermann Stresau did publish his diaries after the war, and they provide striking insights into the extensive "self-alignment" of the public librarians. Stresau joined the town library in Berlin's Spandau district as a research assistant in 1929.[122] On 25 March 1933 this library's director, Max Wieser, publicly threatened all his colleagues with dismissal if they "sowed doubts about the great work of true German renewal" that had begun with the arrival of "the people's chancellor, Adolf Hitler."[123] Having expressed precisely such doubts to his proselytizing superior, on 6 April 1933 Stresau was given three months' notice to quit.[124] Despite the damning accusation of "Marxist activity," he found a teaching post at the new school of librarianship that opened in Berlin on 2 May. As he wrote in his journal on 8 September, during classes on German literature and "knowledge of the *Volk*" Stresau tried to teach the young librarians, force-fed with empty slogans, something "substantial"—knowing very well that this constantly brought him into the "political danger zone," or "at least the zone of heresy." Severe shortages of qualified teaching staff meant that from January 1934 Stresau was also allowed to hold guest lectures at the school of librarianship in Stettin (Szczecin), enabling him to observe at first hand the developments in German public librarianship during the early days of the Nazi dictatorship. In spring 1934, however, he was "quietly dropped" by Wilhelm Schuster, a powerful functionary in the professional association and the director of the Hamburg public library from 1930 until May 1934, when he succeeded the pensioned-off Gottlieb Fritz as director of Berlin's municipal library and school of librarianship.[125]

After attending the public librarians' conference in Hannover, a report of which was published in the first issue of the new journal *Die Bücherei*, Stresau remarked on 23 September 1933 that "a cold wind" was blowing in public librarianship, further whipped up by

---

[122] Curriculum vitae, 1937, BArch BDC/RSK/Stresau, H. F.
[123] Declaration published in *Bücherei und Bildungspflege* 13, no. 2 (1933), 98–9. On the following discussion of the political behavior of key German librarians, see also Stieg, *Public Libraries in Nazi Germany*, 32–55, 172–93.
[124] On this and the following, see Stresau, *Von Jahr zu Jahr*, 7–90.
[125] See Holzhausen, "Gottlieb Fritz."

Schuster's speech on "the public library and National Socialism." Schuster, he commented, "evidently for 'political' even more than for personal reasons, is making himself out to be more papist than the Pope."[126] Yet the man who was now placing himself "200 percent" in the service of the new state had told Stresau in late 1932 that "he would under no circumstances accept a book like Rosenberg's *Myth* for any library."

The librarian Wolfgang Herrmann had denigrated Hitler's *Mein Kampf* in similar terms. Even in early 1933, his annotated selection of titles for public libraries on "The new National Socialism and its literature" described *Mein Kampf* as containing "no scientifically original or 'theoretically' considered ideas."[127] Herrmann, with his colleagues Wieser and Engelhardt, nevertheless carried out the "new formation" of Berlin's public libraries in spring 1933 and, in preparation for the book burnings, drew up the first blacklists to be used right across the Reich. This turned out to be a wise career move for Herrmann, especially as he joined the NSDAP in February 1932 and had been active since then in the Pomeranian *Gau* leadership. In May 1933 he was promoted to department head in the Central Office for Popular Libraries, and in April 1934 became director of the municipal library in Königsberg.

Reading the latest issue of *Die Bücherei*, Stresau wondered on 20 November 1933 why, instead of remaining businesslike, Wilhelm Schuster was so eagerly propagating Nazi ideology: "Why does he make such a clamor, who is asking that of him? No one." Perhaps, Stresau speculated, his thinking was pragmatic: "To save whatever can be saved, I'll camouflage myself, so that the institutions of public education do not fall into completely incompetent hands and we can still retain some influence." But Stresau prophesied that such naive political amateurs among the public librarians, the fair-weather or "Sunday riders," would "slide backwards off their horse as soon as it begins to gallop, and then they'll be saying: That wasn't what we wanted!"

---

[126] Schuster's speech was published as "Bücherei und Nationalsozialismus," *Die Bücherei* 1, no. 1 (1934), 1–9.
[127] In Herrmann's 20 May 1933 statement regarding the "denunciation brought against me by the 'Großdeutscher Pressedienst,'" BArch BDC/RSK/Herrmann, W. The following points ibid.

This observant outsider recorded not only public librarians' considerable willingness to adapt, but also the different currents of opinion among them. After a sociable evening spent with Schuster, Herrmann, and various other colleagues, Stresau noted in his diary on 8 March 1934: "The way they talk to each other is intricately hedged, and that is how they act as well. Only in the official organ, our professional journal, are they all 100 to 200 percent of a single mind. And in the hands of such people lies something originally beautiful: public education. Yet what lies in their hands is now not education but just an apparatus, and education will go to the devil because there is no idea, no belief behind it." As Schuster himself confessed to Stresau, during a personal conversation about his dismissal from the school of librarianship, "such a lack of character" had taken hold in the profession "that decent people are urgently needed."[128] At the same time, however, he pressed the politically disgraced librarian to join the SA, the SS, or "some such club," so as to be able to return to his profession. Schuster had joined the NSDAP on 1 May 1933.[129] Because Stresau refused to consider doing the same, he was "thrown out" of librarianship with no real hope of return.

Stresau became a freelance writer, and translated the US authors Stephen Crane, William Faulkner, Frank Norris, and Webb Miller into German. He kept up his association with the Spandau municipal library, now as a reader, but on 28 August 1937 discovered that Max Wieser had removed Balzac, Flaubert, Zola, and certain other foreign authors from the shelves even though their works had not been banned. To fill the gaps, Wieser had acquired huge quantities of Nazi literature, which, as the lending staff openly told their former colleague, "absolutely nobody reads," so that use of the library had "declined to an extraordinary extent." Wieser's ideologically compliant acquisitions policy had, "whether on instructions from above or on his own initiative, quite devastated one of the best public libraries we have known." Stresau was similarly horrified at the appointment of a former colleague to manage the newly established Horst-Wessel-Bücherei—"the Reich capital's first Nazi public

---

[128] On this and the following, see Stresau, *Von Jahr zu Jahr*, 89 (28 August 1933).
[129] BArch BDC/RSK/Schuster, W.

library."[130] This librarian, who had been a "firm Catholic" before 1933, evidently owed his career leap to having joined the NSDAP and the SS.

What was the situation outside the capital? After working as an editor at Schünemann Verlag and editing the arts pages of Bremen local newspapers, in 1931 Friedo Lampe trained as a public librarian with Erwin Ackerknecht at the Stettin municipal library.[131] From 1932 to 1937, he worked for Wilhelm Schuster and his successor Albert Krebs at the Hamburg public library, as director of a branch library and a specialist assisting the development of collections across the city's library system. In 1933 Lampe not only joined the NSDAP (on 1 May), but also managed to get the administration of his home town, Bremen, to consider him for the post of director of its public libraries and reading rooms. These libraries' previous director, Arthur Heidenhain, having been dismissed for "racial" reasons, they were managed by Hinrich Knittermeyer alongside his other role as director of the state library in Bremen. On 30 September, Lampe asked Wolfgang Herrmann, whom he knew personally from their Stettin days, to put in a good word for him in Bremen.[132] Naively misjudging the political climate, Lampe's letter also mentioned a mutual colleague from Stettin, dismissed for being Jewish "even though her father had fought on the front and her brother was among the fallen. Very harsh. I'm sorry." Lampe himself was unlucky enough to have written a novel, *Am Rande der Nacht* ("At the edge of the night") that not only displeased Herrmann, but was publicly attacked at a Berlin book fair in early December 1933—primarily because of its publisher, Ernst Rowohlt—and banned shortly afterwards. In spring 1936, the directorship of the Bremen public libraries went to Kurd Schulz.[133] Unlike Lampe, Schulz had thoroughly commended himself for the post with his political stance: through his studies of

---

[130] Stresau is presumably referring to the Dietrich-Eckart-Bücherei, a library established in 1935 in Berlin's newly renamed "Horst Wessel" district (Friedrichshain). See *Die Bücherei* 2 (1935), 235–6; Anderhub, "Zwischen Umbruch und Tradition," 252–4.
[131] On this and the following, see Lampe's curriculum vitae, April 1941, BArch BDC/RSK/Lampe, F.
[132] Lampe to Herrmann, 30 September, and Herrmann to Lampe, 4 October 1933, ibid. On the following, see Herrmann to Lampe, 13 December 1933, ibid.
[133] Dähnhardt, Reich Education Ministry, to Undersecretary Stier, Thuringian Ministry of Public Instruction, 25 April 1936, StA Weimar Thüring. Min. f. Volksbildung/C 706.

the peasant novel and its significance for librarianship (1929/1933), as a literary expert in Rosenberg's Kampfbund für deutsche Kultur and the provincial section head of the Reichsstelle, and through his exemplary "cleansing" of the Thuringian public libraries while head of the province's Office for Public Libraries in Gera (from 1934 in Jena).[134] Lampe left the Hamburg public library in late May 1937, and returned to his old profession as an editor at Rowohlt.

In Leipzig, since 1913 Walter Hofmann had been making the municipal library and the Institut für Leser- und Schrifttumskunde, a research institute on reading and literature that he founded in 1926, into model institutions unmatched on the national stage.[135] In 1933, he tried to save his life's work by making numerous concessions when the library's collections were to be "cleansed" and restocked with regime-approved literature. Looking for ways to resist the political pressure from local Party agencies and his antagonist Schuster in Berlin, Hofmann sought to establish cooperation between his institute and Rosenberg's Reichsstelle. His efforts were ultimately in vain; when Carl Goerdeler was dismissed as Mayor of Leipzig in March 1937, Hofmann too lost his job.

His ideas remained influential, however. After Austrian *Anschluss*, on 1 January 1939 his pupil Hans Ruppe—hitherto the Leipzig municipal library's deputy director—moved to the top of the Viennese public library network, a post that included management of the State Public Libraries Office.[136] In his new realm, Ruppe applied the radical measures Hofmann had piloted in Leipzig, and halved the Viennese collections by 1940. His purges were by no means limited to the bans that now covered Austria as well, but also removed those outdated books, and ones he judged irrelevant or trivial in content, that had already been eliminated in the *Altreich*. Even Karl May, the hugely popular author of cowboy-and-Indian adventures, was banned

---

[134] See Thuringian provincial library Gera to the Thuringian Ministry of Public Instruction, 3 November 1933, StA Weimar Thüring. Min. f. Volksbildung/C 629 Thüringisches Büchereiwesen. Allgemeines, vol. 2, 1933–49 fol. 44; Die "Schwarze Liste" und die Säuberung der Büchereien 1933–1943, ibid. C 619; Berichte über die "Säuberung" der Büchereien, ibid. C 702.
[135] On the following, see Boese, "Die Säuberung der Leipziger Bücherhallen" and "Walter Hofmanns Institut"; Röska, "Walter Hofmann und der Nationalsozialismus."
[136] On this and the following, see Pfoser, "Die Wiener Städtischen Büchereien" and "Die Leipziger Radikalkur in Wien."

from Viennese municipal libraries in 1941. In terms of fiction, Ruppe instead promoted historical and war novels, novels about the border areas and the colonies, and regional or *Heimatliteratur*, to which he made his very own contribution in 1942 with a collection of stories entitled *Lachendes Wien* ("Vienna laughs").

In Essen, Eugen Sulz, a librarian whose expertise compared with Hofmann's, lost his post as director of the municipal library very early: on the basis of the "Law for the Restoration of the Professional Civil Service," he was dismissed on 10 May 1933 due to his SPD membership.[137] Sulz's replacement, Richard Euringer, knew nothing of libraries, but was a loyal Party author who acted fast to "cleanse" and reshape the city's collections. Within a few weeks, more than 18,000 books had been screened out. Euringer, also took the initiative to stage book burnings in Essen on 21 June 1933, imitating the events in Berlin and other cities. The holes he tore in the library holdings were filled with standard works by Nazi leaders, publications on race, and *völkisch* or nationalist fiction. Author readings were now held in branch libraries in cooperation with the local NSDAP groups. In October 1936, Euringer in turn was ousted; he had personally antagonized the city's mayor, who was also increasingly exasperated at the decline in usage of the municipal library. His successor, Heinrich Dicke, had once been a member of the Catholic Center Party, and now took care to show especially assiduous loyalty. In 1937 he set up a "library for the young squad" on the fourth floor of the Essen central library, supplying literature for Hitler Youth and League of German Girls activists. Dicke also organized a series of exhibitions promoting the policies of the Nazi state, and numerous readings of books by approved authors. Little of substance changed in the library's political orientation when Carl Jansen became its director in 1938.

The municipal library of Duisburg had been directed by Viktor Sallentien since 1916. Sallentien joined the NSDAP on 1 July 1932—"the day after membership was opened to civil servants," as he pointed out—and on his sudden death in October 1935 he left behind a library collection that conformed absolutely to the state's

---

[137] On this and the following, see Brenner and Wisotzky, *Der Schlüssel zur Welt*, 58–75; Wisotzky, "Essen"; Klotzbücher, "Städtische Bibliotheken im Ruhrgebiet."

requirements.[138] The post remained empty for a while, until Robert Hohlbaum was appointed on 1 June 1937. Hohlbaum's support for the NSDAP had made his position in Austria, as state librarian at the University of Vienna library, untenable after 1933, and Heinz Kindermann helped him into his new post in Duisburg.[139] At this time, he was teaching German literature at the University of Münster, and his Duisburg position enabled him to make a very particular contribution to the dissemination of his preferred, *völkisch* and nationalist literature. In October 1942 Hohlbaum, who earned more than twice as much from his literary writing as from his role as library director,[140] left the Ruhr area to direct the prestigious Thuringian State Library in Weimar.

At the 1936 annual conference of public librarians in Würzburg, the director of Düsseldorf's municipal library gave a keynote speech demanding that "the professional work and the political stance of a public library's personnel be unified, and the personnel join to form a single organism."[141] "As a general principle," Gerd Wunder continued, all members of the public libraries' staff should "work in formation," and no new appointment should be made unless the candidate could demonstrate "a vigorous connection with National Socialism." But even where these preconditions for public librarianship in the National Socialist spirit were satisfied, it must be assumed that "the degree of coverage differs and training within the associations is uneven." As a result, it was the duty of library directors to fill any gaps in professional and political training during their day-to-day work. Wunder's own career success was due exclusively to his early commitment to the NSDAP (he joined in 1930). Alongside his

---

[138] See the questionnaire he completed on 23 June 1933 as part of the implementation of the Law for the Restoration of the Professional Civil Service of 7 April 1933, StA Duisburg Personalakte Sallentien.

[139] See Kindermann to Mayor of Duisburg, 6 December 1936, and to the town council's head of culture Rouenhoff, 14 January 1937, StA Duisburg Personalakte Robert Hohlbaum fol. 113–15.

[140] See his declaration of his 1939 income before tax, 2 March 1940, BArch BDC/RSK/ Hohlbaum, R.

[141] Gerd Wunder, "Die fachliche und politische Weiterbildung der im Beruf stehenden Volksbibliothekare. Referat auf dem Würzburger Volksbüchereitag am 26.9.1936," *Die Bücherei* 4 (1937), 95–100. The following quotations ibid. For further information on Wunder, see StA Düsseldorf V 24910/Personalakte Dr. Gerhard Wunder (1908–88).

main job, he continued to run the Westphalian office of Rosenberg's Reichsstelle. In 1939 he moved to the "department for Jewish and Freemasonry questions" at Amt Rosenberg, and he was part of the taskforce Einsatzstab Reichsleiter Rosenberg from 1940.

Further accomplices of the Party and the Nazi state were Franz Schriewer, director of the Frankfurt an der Oder municipal library (1934–5, 1937–45) and first head of the Reich Office for Popular Libraries (1935–7), and Fritz Heiligenstaedt, who in 1933 joined not only the NSDAP but also the SS; he was director of the public libraries advisory office in the Hannover region and head of the Reich Office from 1937 to 1945. Joseph Caspar Witsch, too, can to some extent be counted as part of this circle, even though he was denounced in 1933 and dismissed from the technical library in Cologne. After a brief spell at the municipal library in the coastal town of Stralsund, in 1936 he made a comeback as director of the Ernst-Abbe-Bücherei in Jena and, succeeding Kurd Schulz, as director of the Thuringian Office for Popular Libraries, which influenced the development of public libraries in the Nazi state far beyond the boundaries of Thuringia itself.[142] From 1942, Witsch was also in charge of the central professional journal *Die Bücherei*.

If librarians later tried to defend their colleagues' conduct by citing political naiveté, ignorance of what was really happening, deliberate camouflage, or pure professionalism (as Adolf von Morzé did in 1987, recalling his training and teaching in Berlin between 1939 and 1944 and his superior there, Wilhelm Schuster[143]), they are missing a vital point. German public librarians themselves were instrumental in bringing about the "loss of the realm of education" lamented by von Morzé, a realm that can only flourish in a democratically pluralist and outward-looking society. Engelbrecht Boese's meticulous analysis reveals an inextricable tangle of "all sorts of different and overlapping professional attitudes, driven by the general insecurity toward the new regime and given individual accents by the personal

---

[142] For details, see Hexelschneider, "Joseph Caspar Witsch"; also the documents on the Thuringian public, school, and young people's libraries, StA Weimar Thüring. Min. f. Volksbildung/C 700, 703, 706–8.
[143] Von Morzé, "Erinnerung an Wilhelm Schuster" and "Verlust des Bildungsreiches." See also the critique by Jütte, "Volksbibliothekare im Nationalsozialismus."

qualities of each actor, by fear, opportunism, nationality."[144] Very few librarians consciously defied these constraints by changing their job, emigrating, evading or tacitly opposing political demands, or active resistance; the latter has only been demonstrated for Ernst Adler, Gottlieb Branz, Lotte Schleif, Arthur Werner, and Philipp Schaeffer.[145]

After the war, most public librarians were unwilling to acknowledge, either to themselves or to the public, the problematic role they had played in the Nazi state. One of the exceptions is Rudolf Joerden, who directed Wiesbaden's municipal library from 1933 to 1938, then the Hamburg public library. When he retired in August 1966, he remembered indifference to the loss of Jewish colleagues, acceptance of the "Aryan certificate" as a precondition for working as a librarian, and submissiveness "in executing state orders by following the zigzag path of so-called National Socialist literary policy."[146] Whatever the motives behind librarians' actions, noted Joerden, neither he nor his colleagues could in conscience be absolved of participation in a world "the full extent of whose crimes were not suspected, but whose destructive violence, invading even one's personal life, was obvious to everyone in the domain of libraries just as everywhere else."

The state, university, and provincial libraries displayed a similar degree of political conformism and willingness to place their professional expertise in the service of the Nazi state. When Rudolf Kummer took on responsibility for all state and university library-related matters within the Reich Education Ministry in 1935, he owed his senior position to his political commitment, not to his professional experience as a librarian in the cataloguing and operational department of the Bavarian State Library.[147] Kummer had already joined the NSDAP during the Weimar Republic, taking part in the failed putsch of 1923. In 1931 he rejoined the Party, and Himmler accepted him into the SS intelligence service. Upon the Party's rise to power, he and Achim Gercke, the "expert on race questions" in

---

[144] Boese, "Das Öffentliche Bibliothekswesen im Dritten Reich," 94.
[145] See Marks, "Dem Andenken deutscher antifaschistischer Bibliothekare," 810–11.
[146] Joerden, "Dreimal Bibliothekar," 137. The following quotation ibid.
[147] On the following, see Kummer's undated curriculum vitae [1935], BArch BDC/Research/Kummer, R., and the personnel report by the SD Main Office, n.d. [c. 1938], BArch BDC/SS/Kummer, R.

the NSDAP national leadership in Munich, published a "guide to writings on race lore" entitled *Die Rasse im Schrifttum* ("Race in literature"). This register made it possible for the regime to identify and persecute Jewish writers, journalists, and scholars. Alongside his work in the Ministry, from March 1935 Kummer headed the libraries section in Rosenberg's literature office. He also worked with the Deputy Führer's staff, the PPK, and the SD's "ideological evaluation" (Weltanschauliche Auswertung) department. By 1945, Kummer had become an *Obersturmbannführer* in the SS.

Joachim Kirchner only joined the NSDAP on 1 March 1933, but he made up for his late start with particularly vigorous efforts for the Nazi cause.[148] Kirchner worked for the Prussian State Library until 1928, when he became director of the Rothschild Library in Frankfurt am Main (renamed "municipal library for modern languages and music" in 1933). With the beginning of Nazi rule, he became the northwest regional "director of culture" for Rosenberg's Kampfbund, later the *Gau* literature commissioner for the Reichsstelle. He also provided literary expertise for the Frankfurt police. In return for his political services, on 25 September 1940 a personal "Führer decree" made Kirchner the director of the Munich University library, succeeding Adolf Hilsenbeck.

Fritz Prinzhorn presents a similar picture of political zeal.[149] He, too, began his career in librarianship at the Prussian State Library. In 1927 he was delegated to the provisional library administration of the Technical University Berlin, and in 1929 was appointed library director at the Technical University of Danzig (Gdańsk). In May 1934, in what was then still the "Free City of Danzig," Prinzhorn organized the thirtieth annual meeting of the research librarians' association VDB, making it a forum for Nazi library policy. He pledged himself to a "German *Volk* state that is pure in terms of morality, race, ethics, and character" and to the research libraries' political mission, namely "to make every German a National Socialist."[150] On behalf of his fellow librarians, Prinzhorn vowed allegiance—"like every German

[148] On the following, see BArch BDC/Partei-Kanzlei-Correspondence/Kirchner, J.

[149] See Richards, "Deutschlands wissenschaftliche Verbindungen," 131; Simon et al., *Buchfieber*, 147–78, 245–7.

[150] Prinzhorn, *Die Aufgaben der Bibliotheken*, 5, 9. The following quotation ibid. 25.

Volksgenosse"—"wholeheartedly to Adolf Hitler, the Führer, the *Volk*'s savior from deepest adversity, the warrior and ardent idealist for a unified German nation." From 1935, Prinzhorn was part of the Prussian (from 1936 Reich) Advisory Board for Library Affairs along with Kummer. In 1939 he moved to the library of Leipzig University, where, in May 1941, he founded the German Society for Documentation (Deutsche Gesellschaft für Dokumentation) and became its president. The Society evaluated literature from enemy countries, especially scientific and scholarly works, with a view to their usefulness for military, technical, and economic purposes; it published its results in centralized lists up to 1943. This institution of librarianship was clearly complicit in the Nazi state's management of research in basic science and armaments technology.

The jurist Hans Peter des Coudres joined the NSDAP in 1930. In September 1933 he took charge of the youth literature section of Rosenberg's Reichsstelle, which cooperated with both the Reich Youth Leadership and the national leadership of the National Socialist Teachers' League. After two years' practical training at the Deutsche Bücherei in Leipzig, in April 1935 des Coudres passed the state examinations for senior research librarianship.[151] The very same month he was admitted to the SS and made chief librarian for Himmler's proposed SS college at Wewelsburg. In spring 1939, des Coudres became director of the Hesse State Library in Kassel. His plans for comprehensive reorganization were halted on 9 September 1941 by the library's destruction, as one of the first research libraries in Germany to fall victim to Allied bombing raids.

A senior librarian with a much higher political profile was Rudolf Buttmann.[152] Trained at the Bavarian State Library, in 1910 he joined the library of the Bavarian state parliament and became its director in 1920. His NSDAP card bore the membership number 4, and in 1924 he was elected to the state parliament, leading the NSDAP group there. Buttmann's hopes of a ministerial role after 1933 were not fulfilled; he was only offered the cultural policy division in the Prussian Ministry of the Interior. With the support of his Party

---

[151] On this and the following, see Weber, "Landesbibliothek Kassel 1938"; Simon et al., *Buchfieber*, 207–10.

[152] On the following, see Dressler, "Die Bayerische Staatsbibliothek."

comrade Hitler, he moved back to librarianship in October 1935, now as director general of the Bavarian State Library.

At an NSDAP press conference in Munich on 19 February 1936, Buttmann set out the Nazi state's understanding of the tasks of research libraries:[153] it was up to librarians to "eliminate products endangering the foundations of *Volk* and state from general use in the library, following the instructions of the agencies appointed for this purpose." The "acquisition and safekeeping" of the writings of Marxism, pacifism, "world Jewry," and Freemasonry must, though, be maintained, because "the control of a disease" depended on "knowledge of its manifestations." Buttmann did note with regret that research libraries did "not always enjoy the respect in the new state that one would wish for them." In order to eradicate the state's "mistrust" and the "appearance of being remote from the *Volk* and detached from real life," he recommended using exhibitions on library premises "to draw the attention of large segments of our nation to the objects which are to be foregrounded or highlighted in each case."

When Buttmann moved to the Bavarian State Library, it was to fill a post that had been vacant since the previous director general, Georg Reismüller, was denounced in March 1935, arrested by the Political Police, and sent into compulsory retirement by Hitler on 1 July after his release from prison. Reismüller's experience highlights the political duress to which the Nazi dictatorship could subject librarians, like their compatriots, at will and which created a breeding-ground for compliance and collaboration.

Heinrich Uhlendahl, director general of the Deutsche Bücherei since 1924, was also arbitrarily arrested by the Gestapo.[154] At the prompting of the NSDAP district leadership, on 20 June 1933 the local *Leipziger Tageszeitung* reported—under the headline "One of the most dangerous Weimar bigwigs seized!"—that Uhlendahl had been arrested for "murky political machinations." The charge arose

---

[153] The lecture was published, in a version revised by Maier-Hartmann, as "Nationalsozialistische Bibliothekspolitik," *Bbl.* no. 49, 27 February 1936, 181–3.
[154] On the following, see Stummvoll, *Dira necessitas*, 4–6, and "IFLATION," 260–1. Also the file note on Bernhard Payr by Anneliese Brettschneider, who directed the "cultural policy archives" in Rosenberg's office from 1934 to 1939, re: visit by the Leipzig publisher Elert Seemann on 4 October 1935, BArch NS 15/137 fol. 19.

from a denunciation by Bernhard Payr, who had obtained a post at the Deutsche Bücherei thanks to his father's status as a renowned Leipzig surgeon. When Uhlendahl was away on business, Payr took the opportunity to rifle his superior's private files, and found two letters from Jews. Because this did not suffice as evidence of political opposition to the regime, Uhlendahl was released after one day of "preventive detention," but the local NSDAP leadership nonetheless announced in the *Leipziger Tageszeitung* of 4 July: "We continue to reject him as unreliable in the spirit of the National Socialist revolution, and will work steadfastly to ensure that the cultural treasures of the German *Volk* deposited in the Deutsche Bücherei are put untainted into the revolution's sole care." Uhlendahl was nationalist-conservative in his views and never joined the NSDAP. The fact that he continued to head the Deutsche Bücherei despite enormous pressures, not only during the dictatorship but right up to his death in December 1954, testifies to his unassailable professional expertise and authority—but also to a dexterity in adapting to changing political circumstances that appears to have been widespread in both periods.

In the years after 1933, Uhlendahl succeeded in making the Deutsche Bücherei the "complete archive of German-language writing" required by its 1912 founders, and Germany's leading library. This success came at a high political price. Goebbels, responsible for the Deutsche Bücherei since 1933, paid the building an official visit in March 1936, and in May 1938 turned its twenty-fifth anniversary celebrations into a propaganda extravaganza for Nazi library policy.[155] In 1940 the last remnants of the library's independence were lost: on 31 March it became a public-law institution and was subsequently fully funded by the Reich.[156]

In this context, many scholars have given credit to Uhlendahl and his assistant Albert Paust for their dogged insistence on fulfilling the Deutsche Bücherei's collecting mission, which secured a complete

---

[155] "Besuch des Reichsministers Dr. Goebbels in der Deutschen Bücherei," *Bbl.* no. 55, 5 March 1936, 206, "Bericht zum 25-jährigen Bestehen mit der Wiedergabe der Reden auf der Kundgebung des deutschen Buchhandels im Neuen Theater in Leipzig," *Bbl.* no. 118, 17 May 1938, 395–7.
[156] "Gesetz über die Deutsche Bücherei in Leipzig vom 18.4.1940," *RGBL*/Part I, no. 71, 22 April 1940, 657–8.

array of writing in German for the years 1933 through 1945. The cataloguing of banned literature (including books in German published in exile), prohibited by the Propaganda Ministry in October 1936 but in practice recommenced with the "List of publications kept locked up in the Deutsche Bücherei" (Liste der in der Deutschen Bücherei unter Verschluss gestellten Druckschriften) that was issued every month from January 1939 and published in 1949, is also regarded as a concession wrested from the Nazi rulers and a triumph of the institution. But this captures only part of the truth. Valuable though the achievements of the Deutsche Bücherei certainly were for postwar Germany, during the dictatorship they benefited not library users, but exclusively the agencies of state and Party literary policy, the Gestapo, and the SD. The thorough and professional work of the Leipzig librarians provided these bodies with very precise information about the output of publishers in the German Reich and in the adoptive countries of the German exiles, enabling the bans to be constantly updated. The same point can be made regarding the "Bibliography of Jewish authors writing in German 1901–1940." It was drawn up between 1941 and 1944 by Deutsche Bücherei staff on the instructions of the Propaganda Ministry, but on the responsibility of Uhlendahl and his colleague Hans Ruppert with the support of government and Party offices. The objective was a complete and definitive identification of texts by Jewish authors, so that they could be systematically deleted from the catalogues of all libraries in the Nazi state.

The growing political and legal status of the Deutsche Bücherei, which in 1931 had begun publishing the German National Bibliography and fifteen other bibliographies including the annual index of theses and dissertations,[157] inevitably led to rivalry with the Prussian State Library. Not until 11 December 1935 did Reich Education Minister Rust issue a decree effectively delimiting the two libraries' respective tasks and responsibilities. From then on, the Deutsche Bücherei in Leipzig was "charged with centrally cataloguing publications

---

[157] E. Rückert, "Die Deutsche Bücherei als bibliographische Auskunftszentrale," *Bbl.* Cantate Meeting supplement 1933, 7–8, and "Die Deutsche Bücherei und ihre Auskunftsstelle," *Jahrbuch des Großdeutschen Leihbuchhandels* 1941, 212–18; H. Uhlendahl, "Die Sonderstellung der Deutschen Bücherei unter den deutschen Bibliotheken," *Bbl.* Cantate Meeting supplement 1938, 7–12.

in German," whereas the Prussian State Library in Berlin was to catalogue foreign-language publications on behalf of all the German research libraries.[158] We may assume that Hugo Andres Krüss, director general of the Prussian State Library since 1925 and a former civil servant in the Prussian ministry of education and culture, did not count this as a great victory.[159] Even so, he grew to be a key figure in the library policy of the Nazi state. With his wealth of contacts abroad, Krüss served the regime in the area of international networking between libraries until 1939, and played an important role in research library legislation, personnel policy, and training, as chair of the Prussian (later Reich) Advisory Board for Library Affairs attached to the Reich Education Ministry.

The Prussian State Library's hand was also strengthened when, in 1934, it took over responsibility from the Emergency Association of German Science for the national exchange center, the Central Procurement Office for German Libraries, and the foreign book exchange center. Headed by Adolf Jürgens, the three new divisions subsequently supplied the Prussian State Library and many other research libraries across the Reich not only with purchased or exchanged items, but also with books from the confiscated property of Jewish communities and individuals, political opponents of the regime, and Masonic lodges. During World War II, books looted from German-occupied areas were added to these stocks; in summer 1940, Rust appointed Krüss "Reich commissioner for the safeguarding of libraries and supervision of book material in the occupied western areas." In November the same year Josef Becker, a Prussian State Library director since 1935, was made German commissioner for the national, university, and technical university libraries in Prague. Looking back in the 1950s, Axel von Harnack, a bibliographical expert at the State Library from 1929 to 1944, recalled the creeping Nazi "infiltration" of responses to individual and official bibliographical

---

[158] Education Ministry decree referred to in W. Frels, "Zwei Jahre deutsche Zettel-drucke," *Bbl.* vol. 106, no. 186, 12 August 1939, 597–8, quotation on 597.
[159] On the following, see Happel, *Das wissenschaftliche Bibliothekswesen,* 56–60; Greguletz, "Die Preußische Staatsbibliothek"; Schochow, "Hugo Andres Krüß und die Preußische Staatsbibliothek"; Bödeke and Bötte, *NS-Raubgut, Reichstauschstelle und Preußische Staatsbibliothek.*

enquiries and of the final examinations for new librarians,[160] a process of politicization that certainly extended to other areas of the renowned institution as well.

As well as Becker and Kirchner, two further examples serve to illustrate the strong presence of the Prussian State Library in the top echelons of Nazi-era research librarianship. Gustav Abb joined the board of the State Library in 1923, and headed the reader services division from 1928. In 1935 he became director of the Berlin University library, a dramatic career jump certainly facilitated by his NSDAP and SS membership. At the thirty-third conference of German librarians, in Cologne in 1937, Abb was elected president of the VDB after Georg Leyh's enforced "resignation." The unconditional subservience to the Nazi state that Abb practiced up to his death in April 1945 is obvious in his welcome address to the "first Greater German librarians' conference," held in late May and early June 1939 in the Austrian city of Graz.[161] There Abb conceded that libraries and librarians were not "by nature fervent vanguardists." Instead, they were "representatives of staunch, diligent German cultural work. Our profession is to collect, order, make ready a spiritual armory!" Abb's assessment of the regime's respect for the profession differed from Buttmann's more skeptical view; he proudly claimed that "just as a book, the Führer's *Mein Kampf*, prefigured the radiant fundamental idea of our Movement, so in all the world's history there has been no radical change, no spiritual revolution that more strongly recognizes the power of the book and of libraries than National Socialism, none that has taken libraries more thoroughly into its service." For Abb personally, from summer 1940 that service included heading the central administration of libraries in the General Government, based in Kraków. All the research libraries in occupied Poland and the Kraków state library, opened in April 1941, were under his control.[162] Finally, on 23 June 1941, the day after the Soviet Union was attacked, the Reich Education Minister also appointed

---

[160] Harnack, "Bibliothekar im 'Dritten Reich,'" 127.
[161] Text of the address in *ZfB* 56 (1939), 514–16. The following quotations ibid. 515.
[162] On this and the following, see Pirożyński and Ruszajowa, "Die nationalsozialis-tische Bibliothekspolitik in Polen"; Komorowski, "Deutsche Bibliothekspolitik in der Sowjetunion."

him "Reich commissioner for the safeguarding of libraries and super-vision of book material in the eastern operational area." Just a few days after Austrian *Anschluss*, on 16 March 1938, the Gestapo arrested another leading librarian, Josef Bick.[163] Director general of the Austrian National Library since 1923, Bick was respected nationally and internationally. On 1 April 1938, together with other prominent Austrian victims of the Nazi regime, he was taken to Dachau concentration camp and from there to Sachsenhausen. In late August he was released, after being "retired" from his post in June. The Reich Education Ministry replaced Bick with Paul Heigl, who had gone to Vienna on 12 March at the invitation of the new Austrian Chancellor, Arthur Seyss-Inquart. Heigl and Seyss-Inquart had met when Heigl was imprisoned in Austria for his NSDAP activism (he was sentenced to six months in August 1934) and dismissed from his position in the Institute for Austrian Historical Research in Vienna in February 1935. With Seyss-Inquart's help, he was able to enter the German Reich in July 1935 as a "political refugee." Kummer got him a job at the Greifswald University library in September and almost immediately afterwards in the Prussian State Library in Berlin. There he was responsible for periodicals and the politically important area of literature on Freemasonry. While in Berlin, Heigl, who had joined the NSDAP in May 1933 and the SS in 1934, made contacts in the SD Main Office and in Walter Frank's Reich Institute for the History of the New Germany with its affiliated Institute for Research into the Jewish Question, founded in 1936. When Heigl left the Prussian State Library for Vienna, Krüss forgot his previous close collaboration with the now-disgraced Bick on plans for a German union catalogue. He lost no time in sending Heigl a telegram of congratulation and had him appointed to the Reich Advisory Board for Library Affairs.[164]

Following the Prussian State Library's lead, in Austria the books plundered from expropriated Jewish publishing houses and bookstores, political opponents, and the dissolved lodges of the Freemasons were either absorbed into the National Library collection or distributed, via the "book utilization office" in Vienna, to research

---

[163] On this on the following, see Hall and Köstner, "... *allerlei für die Nationalbibliothek zu ergattern* ...," esp. 39–62.
[164] Schochow, *Die Preußische Staatsbibliothek*, 39.

libraries, archives, and the libraries of NSDAP agencies across the Reich. As he had in Berlin, in Vienna Heigl set up a special "office for National Socialist literature" within the Library. In April 1941, he too was appointed a "Reich commissioner," this time for the research libraries in occupied Yugoslavia.

Not all librarians felt obliged to curry favor with the Nazi regime. It was quite possible for them to exploit the niches left open by the system and thus avoid betraying their values, as is exemplified by the case of Hermann Reuter (1880–1970). Reuter, a Ph.D. in German literature, was appointed deputy director of the Düsseldorf state and municipal library in April 1907 and promoted to director on 1 April 1928, when Constantin Nörrenberg retired.[165] During the Weimar Republic, Reuter began to build up a Heinrich Heine collection as an intellectual memorial in the Jewish poet's home town,[166] efforts to set a public statue having been thwarted by antisemitic resistance over many years. With the help of private donations, Reuter assembled a "rich treasure of Heine manuscripts," Heine's Paris library, around 3,000 print volumes "almost completely" covering all first editions and reissues of his works and secondary literature, a cast of his death mask, and a "beautiful collection of drawings, etchings, engravings, lithographs on the iconography of Heine and those close to him." He opened the collection to the public in the library's Grabbeplatz building and the Heine House on Bolkerstrasse.[167]

With the beginning of Nazi rule, this jewel was threatened by antisemitic "cleansing" campaigns, but Reuter managed to shield the collection and keep open the door to continuing scholarly engagement with Heine's work in Germany and abroad. In September 1936, when a doctoral student in Paris asked whether the French press was correct in reporting that "the Heine library has been burned down," he told her: "In no German research library has any book whatsoever been destroyed since National Socialism came to power

---

[165] On the following, see StA Düsseldorf V 37371/Personalakte Dr. Hermann Reuter. I am grateful to Walter H. Pehle for drawing my attention to this remarkable person, largely forgotten today.

[166] Reuter to Izor Halmos, 17 July 1929, Heinrich-Heine-Archiv Düsseldorf Sammlung Hermann Reuter.

[167] Reuter to Gertrud Engel, 20 October 1947, ibid.

... We look forward to your visit to use the library."[168] And when the Berlin antiquarian bookstore F. A. Stargardt, prompted by a foreign customer's interest in buying up the Heine library, suggested in June 1938 that the Düsseldorf state and municipal library "presumably will no longer have any interest in ownership of these books," Reuter answered with a single sentence: "Please tell your foreign customer that there can be no question of disposing of any items belonging to a German research library."[169] In fall 1943, finally, Reuter accomplished the feat of packing the entire Heine collection in forty boxes and moving it to Schloss Wittgenstein, 120 km away, thus preserving it from destruction by bombing.[170] All this was achieved by a library director who never joined the NSDAP. His position was certainly strengthened by his "supporting membership" of the SS—forced on him by the Mayor of Düsseldorf in May 1933 but never paid for with concessions on matters of substance.[171] Classified as an "exonerated person" at an August 1947 denazification hearing, Reuter continued to direct the Düsseldorf state and municipal library until 1950, and in 1957 received an Order of Merit for his services to the Heine collection.[172]

These few examples are far from giving a comprehensive overview of state, university, and provincial librarians in the period.[173] Of the thirty-four directors of university libraries between 1933 and 1945, only twelve were NSDAP members; although this does not amount to resistance, it does express a certain reticence toward the blatant

---

[168] Andrée Delebarre to Reuter, 1 September 1936, and Reuter to Delebarre, 9 September, ibid.

[169] Bookstore proprietor F. A. Stargardt to Reuter, 17 June 1938, and Reuter's response, 18 June, ibid.

[170] See the report by Dutch writer Gerard J. M. van het Reve on his visit to the Düsseldorf state and municipal library (published on 17 September 1949 in *Vrij Nederland* as "Mathilde's papegaai...gevlogen! Op zoek naar herinneringen aan Heinrich Heine in Düsseldorf") along with a German translation, ibid.

[171] See the questionnaire issued by the Military Government of Germany, 6 July 1945, and Reuter's attached statement regarding his activities as a supporting member of the SS, StA Düsseldorf V 37371/Personalakte Dr. Hermann Reuter. Reuter's "clearance certificate" dated 18 August 1947, ibid.

[172] See the obituary "Der Retter der Heine-Sammlung. Dr. Hermann Reuter verstorben," 13 January 1970, ibid.

[173] See Komorowski, "Die Auseinandersetzung mit dem nationalsozialistischen Erbe"; Happel, *Das wissenschaftliche Bibliothekswesen*.

political co-optation of their institutions. At the same time, Manfred Komorowski is right to note that Party membership alone does not tell the full story: each individual can be judged only by his or her behavior and actions.[174] Moreover, research librarians' everyday work was marked not only by political challenges, but also by very practical ones. Like the public libraries, the research libraries had difficulty in recruiting new librarians during the war.[175] This was due in part to the steady expansion of the German research library system since the late 1930s, both within the *Altreich* and in the annexed and occupied countries. More seriously, promotion opportunities for mid-level civil servants in the research libraries were scanty compared to those in other public bodies, dissuading many young people from seeking a future in librarianship.[176] Another obstacle was the low social prestige attached by the profession to the mid-ranking positions that were open to non-college graduates. For all the talk of "folk community," the research libraries' senior personnel—even those who were dedicated Nazis—were still anxious to ward off claims by mid-level civil servants to more participation in the development of the library system.[177]

During the war, with Interior Ministry support and at the urgent request of the NSDAP Party Chancellery, former clergymen were taken on as librarians—partly to ease staff shortages in the research and public libraries, but partly as a politically calculated attempt to integrate people forsaking the Church infrastructure by offering them a future in public institutions attached to the Nazi state.[178] Research

---

[174] Komorowski, "Die Auseinandersetzung mit dem nationalsozialistischen Erbe," 279.
[175] See Reichsbeirat für Bibliotheksangelegenheiten to REM, 7 September 1943, pointing out the substantially increased need for qualified librarians since 1940. BArch R 21/10 634 fol. 56.
[176] Richard Hoffmann, "Die Nachwuchsfrage für den gehobenen Dienst an den Universitäts-Bibliotheken," *ZfB* 59 (1942), 268–9, here 269. On the following, see also Elli Hofmann, "Nochmals das geistige Berufsanliegen des mittleren gehobenen Dienstes," *ZfB* 60 (1944), 65–9; Helmut Deckert, "Das geistige Berufsanliegen des mittleren Dienstes," *ZfB* 59 (1942), 52–6.
[177] See, for example, Joachim Kirchner, "Zu den Berufsanliegen des mittleren Dienstes," *ZfB* 59 (1942), 265–8. Georg Leyh made fundamentally the same argument in a somewhat more sophisticated form, "Zu den Grenzfragen des wissenschaftlichen und des mittleren Dienstes," *ZfB* 60 (1944), 69–87.
[178] See Kummer's note for Dähnhardt, 6 February 1942, BArch R 21/10 633 fol. 74, and the processing of individual cases, ibid. fol. 69–70, 107, 157, 168, 177, 198–9.

libraries as a resocialization facility—the regime's contempt for these institutions of scholarship and public education could hardly have been expressed with more cynicism.

Public Propaganda and Individual Needs: Readers

The literature that appeared in Germany between 1933 and 1945 was dominated by the agencies of state and Party literary policy, which forced authors and their publishers to exercise self-censorship on new manuscripts and reprints. At the same time, literature was also saturated by the era's Nazi and *völkisch*-nationalist themes and values. Looking back after the war, Werner Bergengruen recollected this state of "monomania": "Just as back then there was barely a conversation that did not address the current situation, so almost nobody could write anything that was not deeply imprinted by the times."[179] Yet running alongside and in between those works were others that transported values—humanism, enlightenment, and pure aesthetics—far from conforming to the norms of the Nazi state. These authors and their readers understood each other very well. As Hans Carossa noted in a 1935 journal entry, "with every new book, you soon realize what kind of reader the author is addressing."[180]

Carossa's insight from the heart of the maelstrom was what Joachim Maass (based in the United States from spring 1939) tried to explain to a reluctant and disbelieving Thomas Mann in exile. On 20 June 1940, he countered Mann's acerbic criticism of the literature being published under the Nazis as follows: "If you had the knowledge of circumstances inside Germany that I gained from my personal experience in the country up to about a year ago, then you would take into account that at least certain strata of a nation react to such pressure on their conscience by becoming subtle and sensitive listeners; people are accustomed to speaking in symbols and under-standing symbols as such. And this circuitous way of speaking and

---

[179] Bergengruen, *Schreibtischerinnerungen*, 176.
[180] Carossa, *Tagebücher*, 335 (21 July 1935).

writing against power is not cowardly and ignominious, but the only true option for the mind against power: that is attested not only by justice and reason, but also by great and eternally honorable names in intellectual history such as Tacitus."[181]

A surprising range of authors could still be read in Germany until the outbreak of war. Although fourteen Erich Kästner titles had been banned in 1933, there were no restrictions that year on selling his new children's novel *Das fliegende Klassenzimmer* (*The Flying Classroom*, 1934). During December 1933, several of Kästner's letters to his mother mentioned its successful sales; he had found no fewer than seventeen copies of the novel in the window of one Berlin bookstore.[182] However, in fall 1934 the Propaganda Ministry literature department ruled that Kästner's books must only be published and sold outside German borders, as the author had not been granted membership of the Chamber of Literature. It is symptomatic of what Kästner himself often called a "hopeless muddle" in the literary apparatus[183] that the novels published after 1933 were still able to enter the German book market. Although the Propaganda Ministry complained to Kästner's Swiss publisher in early 1935 regarding the presence of *Drei Männer im Schnee* (*Three Men in the Snow*, 1935) in Berlin bookstore displays,[184] in November that year Kästner reported that the agent Jacob Picard had acquired more than a thousand advance orders for the sequel to his famous *Emil and the Detectives*, *Emil und die drei Zwillinge* (*Emil and the Three Twins*, 1935), in northern German bookstores alone.[185] In mid-December, the proprietor of a small bookstore in Berlin informed Kästner that he had sold five copies of the novel in one day and had immediately ordered another twenty.[186] By Christmas, more than 7,000 copies had been sold.[187] It was only in fall 1935, when a blanket ban on his

---

[181] DLA NL Joachim Maass.

[182] Letter of 11 December 1934, in *Mein liebes, gutes Muttchen, Du!*, 195; also 8 December 1934, ibid. 194.

[183] Letter to his mother, 22 October 1934, ibid. 200. On 4 October he described the Ministry's and Chamber's policy toward him as a "sweet confusion," ibid. 197.

[184] Letter to his mother, 11 February 1935, ibid. 205.

[185] Letter to his mother, 8 November 1935, ibid. 220.

[186] Letter to his mother, 14 December 1935, ibid. 222.

[187] Letter to his mother, 15 January 1936, ibid. 224.

writing appeared in List 1 of Harmful and Undesirable Literature, that Kästner was lost to his readers within Germany. All of Thomas Mann's works continued to be sold through S. Fischer after his emigration, and they were only indexed when Mann was deprived of his citizenship in December 1936.[188] The books of Ernst Wiechert, published by Langen-Müller, remained available in stores even in 1938, when the author was imprisoned in a concentration camp, and despite the Rosenberg office's attacks on him, which continued even after the 1939 appearance of his acclaimed *Das einfache Leben* (*The Simple Life*, 1954).[189] Berlin booksellers Marianne d'Hooghe of the Karl Buchholz store and Hans Benecke of Amelang both remember numerous banned and "undesirable" authors whose books were still kept in stock up to 1936 or 1937 and sold or lent to carefully selected customers.[190]

The correspondence and journals of writers themselves also confirm that a diversity of reading experiences survived in the period. Hans Carossa still took an interest in books by his colleagues Thomas Mann, Alfred Mombert, Franz Werfel, and Stefan Zweig. He discovered Marcel Proust and Thomas Wolfe, and found relevance to the Nazi present in Sophocles' *Antigone*.[191] Hermann Stresau turned to the Low German dialect writer Fritz Reuter and his 1862 novel *Ut mine Stromtid* (*An Old Story of My Farming Days*, 1878) as an "escape from the present day to a man who spoke straight out, not crookedly."[192] He praised Oskar Maria Graf's *Einer gegen alle* of 1932 (*The Wolf*, 1934) for the author's courage in "looking at life without the help of colored spectacles." Graf was "an honest man," he said, unable to sink to "the depths of a Steguweit or the other proud recipients of a Wartburg Poetry Rose." Reading Shakespeare's history plays, Stresau was surprised to note that "such conditions used to

---

[188] RSK to Gestapa, 4 December 1936, BArch BDC/RSK/Mann, Thomas.

[189] "Wichtige Hinweise," *Lektoren-Brief* 1, no. 1 (1938), 5; "Über Ernst Wiechert," *Lektoren-Brief* 2, no. 3 (1939), 7–8; model report on *Das einfache Leben*, *Lektoren-Brief* 2, no. 6 (1939), 8–10. See also Chatellier, "Ernst Wiechert im Urteil der deutschen Zeitschriftenpresse," and Reiner, *Ernst Wiechert im Dritten Reich*.

[190] D'Hooghe, *Mitbetroffen*, 74–102, and Benecke, *Eine Buchhandlung in Berlin*, 85–176.

[191] See Carossa, *Briefe II* and *Briefe III*.

[192] Stresau, *Von Jahr zu Jahr*, 68 (2 November 1933). The following quotations ibid. 73 (16 November 1933), 73–4 (20 November 1933), 86 (5 April 1934).

be considered the long-lost past, just because the political methods are different"—yet the "human type" that applied those methods had not changed since Shakespeare's day. "Only now do we realize the childishness of thinking that kind of thing no longer exists just because one is now more 'civilized.'" Aldous Huxley's *Brave New World* showed him how "nightmarishly close we have come to this ironic utopia."

At the suggestion of Ernst Rowohlt and Heinrich Maria Ledig, Hans Fallada read the Rowohlt authors Faulkner, Hemingway, Wolfe, Louis-Ferdinand Céline, and Jules Romains.[193] He was also fascinated by Kenneth Roberts's historical epic *Arundel*, the works of Dostoevsky, R. L. Stevenson, Jack London, and Voltaire, and the detective fiction of Edgar Wallace. In 1936 and 1938 he translated two humorous works by the best-selling US author Clarence Day for Rowohlt. As for the reading habits of Fallada's contemporaries, and especially the younger generation, the unexpected failures of his own publications persuaded him "that the ability to read somewhat more complex books is now dying out completely."[194] Trying to explain the discrepancy between excellent reviews and low sales of Dolf Sternberger's 1938 *Panorama oder Ansichten vom 19. Jahrhundert*, publisher Eugen Claassen likewise told his author that "books like yours now appeal to a dwindling elite."[195]

That this readership still survived is indicated by an enthusiastic letter from Annemarie Suhrkamp to Ina Seidel on 19 September 1937 about a writer "who has captured my attention indescribably—day and night, so to speak; there are such fortunate moments when one finds things coming together in just the right combination."[196] Suhrkamp was referring to Ernst Jünger's *Das abenteuerliche Herz. Aufzeichnungen bei Tag und Nacht* ("The adventurous heart. Notes by day and night"), the first version of which had appeared with Frundsberg Verlag of Berlin in 1929. On 4 January 1940 she referred to Jünger again, this time "rather obsessed" by his 1939 novella *Auf den Marmorklippen*,

---

[193] On this and the following, see Fallada, *Ewig auf der Rutschbahn*.
[194] Letter to Ernst Rowohlt, 23 January 1937, ibid. 223–4.
[195] Letter to Sternberger, 9 July 1938, in Claassen, *In Büchern denken*, 479–80. See also Wallrath-Janssen, *Der Verlag H. Goverts*, 199–201.
[196] On this and the following, see DLA NL Ina Seidel/Briefe an sie von Annemarie Suhrkamp, folders 2 and 3.

published by Hanseatische Verlagsanstalt (translated in 1947 as *On the Marble Cliffs*). For Jünger, she reasoned, the book must have been "an extraordinary process of detoxification, from a poison that is threatening to destroy many people." She came back to the book on 31 August 1940, as Berlin's destruction by British bombs began: "It is a strange feeling of 'sleep paralysis' when one sees in corporeal form what has previously always appeared in visions, and you can read about that in the *Marble Cliffs* book, with its masterly description of how 'the profundity of decay becomes evident in towering flames.'"[197] Suhrkamp's courageous formulation shows how the attentive reader could interpret Jünger's work in terms of contemporary events.

Despite the book bans and an obligation to disclose the acquisition of all rights from foreign publishers, introduced by the Chamber in 1935, until the war German booksellers could offer numerous translations of French, British, and American literature, as well as original editions in English published by Tauchnitz or The Albatross Modern Continental Library.[198] During the war, author Horst Lange read translations of Proust, of John Steinbeck's *The Grapes of Wrath*, Joyce's *Ulysses*, Tolstoy's stories and Romain Rolland's Tolstoy biography, Jean Giraudoux's play *Ondine*, Conrad's *The Arrow of Gold*, and Julien Green's *Léviathan*.[199] S. Fischer published the French writers Jean Giono and Paul Valéry; its Irish, British, and US authors included W. B. Yeats, Joseph Conrad, D. H. Lawrence, George Bernard Shaw, Frank Norris (with *The Octopus*), and twenty young American writers presented in a 1937 anthology.[200] Rowohlt Verlag translated novels by Sinclair Lewis, Joseph Hergesheimer, William Faulkner, and Thomas Wolfe, as well as seven volumes of Jules Romains's cycle *Les hommes de bonne volonté* translated in 1935–8 by Franz Hessel,

---

[197] Suhrkamp quotes from the novel's description of the inferno destroying the corrupt Marina; the published translation runs "the extent of the destruction could be read in towering flames." Jünger, *On the Marble Cliffs*, 109.
[198] See Fritz Thoma, "Die englische und amerikanische Literatur im Spiegel der Tauchnitz-Edition," *Das deutsche Wort. Der Literarischen Welt Neue Folge* 11, no. 15 (1935), 6–8; on The Albatross see Troy, "Books, Swords, and Readers"; on translated literature in the period see Leitel, "Die Aufnahme der amerikanischen Literatur," esp. 18–34, and Sturge, *"The Alien Within."*
[199] See Lange, *Tagebücher*.
[200] *Neu-Amerika. Zwanzig Erzähler der Gegenwart.* Ed. with an introduction by Kurt Ullrich. Berlin: S. Fischer, 1937.

who had worked with Walter Benjamin in the 1920s on a translation of Proust's *À la recherche du temps perdu*. H. Goverts published various British authors including Howard Spring with *O Absalom!* (a best-seller in German as *Geliebte Söhne*, 1938), Margaret Mitchell's *Gone with the Wind* (as *Vom Winde verweht*, 1937; by 1941 the translation had sold 276,900 copies in sixteen editions), and in 1938 *Billy Budd* by Hermann Melville—in 1940, the Goverts house even began planning a first complete works of Melville in German.[201] Insel Verlag found few readers for its translations of Paul Valéry and D. H. Lawrence, but Duff Cooper's biography *Talleyrand*, translated in 1935, was a surprise hit, with 48,000 copies sold by 1938.[202]

Apart from these companies, others publishing middle- and highbrow American fiction in German translation up to 1941 were C. H. Beck, Deutsche Verlags-Anstalt, Esche Verlag, F. A. Herbigs Verlagsbuchhandlung, Holle & Co., Paul List, Paul Neff, Universitas Verlag, Deutsche Verlags-Expedition (with a 1938 "USA" issue in its popular series Bibliothek der Unterhaltung und des Wissens), and Vorwerk Verlag.[203]

The authors and books mentioned so far made up only part, and a mainly middle-class part, of the literature read in the Nazi state. There was also a new "National Socialist mass book market," supplied primarily by the publishing and distribution companies associated with the German Labor Front (DAF).[204] The needs of the NSDAP's many organizations were filled by a "leisure literature" that reached from manuals on organizing company roll calls, festivities, labor service camps, or social gatherings, to anthologies excerpting the works of famous authors for public readings, to resources for amateur dramatics and singing. The series Kraft-durch-Freude-Buch ("Strength Through Joy books"), responding to the mass tourism run by the DAF, sold millions of copies of its travel and adventure novels.[205]

---

[201] Wallrath-Janssen, *Der Verlag H. Goverts*, 192–5, 336–9, 447.
[202] Sarkowski and Jeske, *Der Insel Verlag*, 368–9.
[203] See Barbian, "Die doppelte Indizierung," 271–82.
[204] Lokatis, "Hanseatische Verlagsanstalt," 75–89.
[205] W. Heudtlaß, "Das Buch bei 'Kraft durch Freude,'" *Buch und Volk* 15 (1938), 5, and "Das gute Buch auf dem KdF-Schiff. Die erste Gästebücherei an Bord der 'Wilhelm-Gustloff,'" *Bbl.* no. 80, 5 April 1938, 282–3. On the background, see Maase, *Grenzenloses Vergnügen*, 196–234.

It was not only the DAF publishers that exploited changing leisure habits and the tourism boom. In the period up to the war, large quantities of travel nonfiction appeared, going beyond the old favorites of Austria, Switzerland, and Italy to introduce readers to Spain, Madeira, Malta and Greece, Scandinavia, the Americas, Africa, and East Asia.[206] Travel fiction was popular and a special focus for the younger generation of authors, and travel journalism flourished in daily newspapers and periodicals. Devotees of sailing, canoeing, hiking, mountain climbing, or skiing could buy helpful books on their hobby, and vacation reading was provided for with large numbers of recommended entertainment titles. The "Aryanized" company Grieben and Verlag Karl Baedeker, saved from bankruptcy in 1934 by an interest-free state loan of 120,000 RM,[207] continued to publish their popular guidebooks for trips within Germany and abroad. The books now included practical hints to help "automobilists" find their way in unfamiliar surroundings. Anyone wanting to explore the occupied areas during the war had a choice of several different travel guides to France, Belgium, or Norway published between 1940 and 1943 by Verlag der DAF, Verlag Odé, and other companies commissioned by the Wehrmacht.[208] Or they could pick up the 1943 guide *Baedekers Generalgouvernement*, with an introduction by Governor General Hans Frank, three maps, and six city plans. It provided detailed information on the history and politics of Germany's new "adjunct" or *Nebenland* and the beauties of its towns and landscapes, tips on culture, hotels, and gastronomy—everything but, of course, the terror and mass murder raging there.[209]

Book clubs continued to play an important role in the development of reading habits during the Nazi period. Membership of the Deutsche Hausbücherei club, established in 1916 by the nationalist sales clerks' association DHV, declined at the start of the new regime but soon recovered under DAF ownership, growing from 140,353 in

---

[206] On this on the following, see Graf, *"Die notwendige Reise."*
[207] Baumgarten and Baumgarten, *Baedeker*, 53–5. The loan was paid out through the Reich Committee on Tourism (Reichsausschuss für Fremdenverkehr) and was funded by the Propaganda Ministry, the German railways, the national airline Lufthansa, and Strength Through Joy.
[208] See Bühler and Bühler, "Die Wehrmacht als Verleger."
[209] See Schreeb, "Baedekers Reisehandbuch."

1939 to 173,912 in 1941.[210] Each member agreed to buy at least eight books a year. In 1938, 75 percent of the DAF-owned Hanseatische Verlagsanstalt's book production (50 percent even in 1940) was sold via the club—over 1 million copies a year. Deutsche Hausbücherei's selections were far from being limited to the Nazi fiction of Blunck, Euringer, Hans Fuchs, Theodor Jakobs, Herybert Menzel, Ferdinand Oppenberg, Jakob Schaffner, or Heinz Steguweit; more important were books by nationalist-conservative authors such as Hermann Claudius, Eugen Diesel, Rudolf Fischer, Friedrich Griese, Friedrich Georg Jünger, Gustav Steinbömer (aka Gustav Hillard), Ludwig Tügel, Josef Magnus Wehner, or August Winnig, and even novels by Werner Bergengruen and Ernst Jünger that could be read as critical of the regime.

Whereas the Deutsche Hausbücherei club captured the loyalty of a middle-class readership, Büchergilde Gutenberg targeted the working class. The Büchergilde, too, experienced a considerable drop in membership in 1933, in this case due to the crushing of the free trade unions.[211] Once it entered DAF hands, membership rose again thanks to vigorous promotion in factories, lucrative rewards for attracting new members, and prices significantly lower than those in the retail book trade. By 1939 the club had 330,000 members, and they bought more than 1 million books every year up to the start of the war. The Büchergilde selection included classics by Goethe, Grabbe, Keller, and Meyer, the "worker poets" Max Barthel, Karl Bröger, and Heinrich Lersch, and Nazi-promoted authors such as Hermann Eris Busse, Paul Ernst, Euringer, Kurt Faber, Trygve Gulbranssen, Knut Hamsun, Grimm, Hohlbaum, Jelusich, Johst, Knittel, Mungenast, Wilhelm Pleyer, Peter Rosegger, Colin Ross, Schmückle, Tügel, Hans Watzlik, or Erwin Wittstock, but also less conformist books by Stefan Andres, Edgar Maass, August Scholtis, Benjamin Traven, and the twelve volumes of the "only popular edition of the works of Jack London to be licensed by the original German publisher."

---

[210] On this and the following, see Lokatis, "Hanseatische Verlagsanstalt," 125–30.
[211] Report on Büchergilde Gutenberg by the head of the RSK Book Trade Group's book clubs section, 24 June 1938, BArch BDC/RSK/Heffe, E. On the following, see ibid. and *Die wirtschaftlichen Unternehmungen der DAF*, 104–5.

The profile of the third big book club, Deutsche Buch-Gemeinschaft, no longer differed much from that of its competitors after it was forced to eliminate the highbrow figures of the Weimar Republic—including several celebrated Jewish authors, such as Bruno Frank, Leo Perutz, Jakob Wassermann, and Stefan Zweig—from its catalogue. Alongside classics, the works of Ludwig Ganghofer, and the inevitable translations of Scandinavian literature, Deutsche Buch-Gemeinschaft's approximately 200,000, mainly middle-class and conservatively minded members had a wide choice of books by authors acceptable to the regime. Like Büchergilde Gutenberg and Deutsche Hausbücherei, which kept their members up to date with the monthly magazines *Die Büchergilde* and *Herdfeuer* ("The hearth") respectively, Deutsche Buch-Gemeinschaft sent out more than 3 million copies of *Die Lesestunde* ("The reading hour") to members every year.

From 1937, Holtzbrinck published a monthly subscription book series, Bibliothek der Unterhaltung und des Wissens ("Library of entertainment and knowledge"), that increasingly went beyond pure entertainment to focus on the politically popular topics of the day. This club, too, showed its readers the world from the Nazi state's perspective, with themed issues like "Our Ostmark" in 1938, "Liberated Sudetenland" and "The campaign in Poland" in 1939, "Strength and beauty in life and art," "Women at work," "Beyond the forests" (on the Transylvanian Saxons), "Bunker stories," and "Alsace-Lorraine. Ancient German land" in 1940, or, in 1941–4, "In the realm of the mountains," "Spain: Tradition and present day," "South West African stories" by Hans Grimm, and novels by Beumelburg, Bonsels, Faber, Hamsun, Hedin, Johst, Lagerlöf, Löns, Schmückle, and Seidel.[212]

Alongside these regime-compliant selections, popular fiction continued to be offered on the book market and consumed in enormous quantities. Karl May remained the most popular author of young adult fiction,[213] and his books, marketed by the Radebeul-based company Karl-May-Verlag since 1913, were also highly

[212] See Garke-Rothbart, *Georg von Holtzbrinck*, 81–136, 215–25.
[213] Franz Heinrich Pohl, "Der Lieblingsschriftsteller unserer Jungen. Zu Karl May's 100. Geburtstag am 25. Februar 1942," *Der deutsche Schriftsteller* 7 (1942), 16–17.

sought-after by adults, especially Wehrmacht soldiers. From 1938, Party literary agencies noted with disapproval a "rise in the reading of trash" among young people,[214] and the popularity of such "trivial literature" increased even further after the outbreak of war.[215] The Reich Security Main Office even claimed to have identified a link between the reading of adventure or detective novels and juvenile delinquency. In 1941, SD and Gestapo officials across the Reich were instructed, when hearing of "abuses, crimes, etc., that can be attributed to young people," to "ascertain to what degree the cause may be found in the reading of particular types of publications."[216] Goebbels requested the state literary bureaucracy to stem the tide of mainly Anglophile popular literature.[217] In addition, bans were imposed on whole series of magazine-format pulp fiction in order to free up paper for political, literary, scientific, and technical books.[218] The dilemma remained that the book trade was becoming ever less capable of satisfying the population's—and especially young people's—growing demand for diversion with higher-quality entertainment fiction, making it almost impossible to prevent readers from turning to cheap novels that were easy to read and printed in mass editions.

For both youngsters and adults, reading preferences were developing in a way very different from that intended by the state and Party literary agencies with their elaborate propaganda campaigns

---

[214] NSLB youth literature section, instructing the *Gau* youth literature departments to monitor this increase with special vigilance, 7 June 1938, BArch NS 12/48. The Thuringian *Gau* department responded with a compilation of reports from Thuringian towns and communities, BArch NS 12/1292.

[215] Head of the Thuringian State Public Libraries Office to Thuringian Minister of Public Instruction, 11 November 1940, HStA Weimar Thüring. Min. f. Volksbildung/C 629 fol. 277.

[216] RSHA/Dept. III C 4 circular to all SD, criminal police, and Stapo divisions and to Security Police and SD inspectors, 21 October 1941, re: impact of inferior literature, HStA Düsseldorf RW 36/30 fol. 70.

[217] See reference ibid. Also *Meldungen aus dem Reich*, vol. 3, no. 30, 18 December 1939, 583–4.

[218] This was the tenor of Haegert's speech before the Börsenverein Cantate Sunday meeting in Leipzig in 1940, printed in *Bbl.* no. 94, 23 April 1940, 150. See also Stapoleitstelle Düsseldorf circular, 29 May 1941, re: seizure and confiscation of fourteen pulp series, the continued sale of which had been banned by the Propaganda Ministry on 25 April 1941 "on paper-saving grounds." HStA Düsseldorf RW 18/31 fol. 27.

and the unrelenting rhetoric of their literary comment. Writers of light fiction well-loved since Wilhelmine times—Felix Dahn, Warwick Deeping, Ludwig Ganghofer, Gustav Renker, Felicitas Rose, Ernst Zahn—continued to be bought in large numbers in the Nazi state. The best-seller list for 1933 through 1945 compiled by Tobias Schneider, with forty titles that sold between 300,000 and 920,000 copies, includes twelve authors who can be counted as part of the officially prescribed literary canon: Blunck, Josefa Berens-Totenohl, Bodenreuth, Dwinger (with two titles), Ettighoffer (two titles), Grimm, Werner Jansen, Kluge, Karl Aloys Schenzinger (three titles), Seidel, Kuni Tremel-Eggert, and Zöberlein.[219] But a breakdown into the periods 1933–5, 1936–8, and 1939–45 reveals a clear decline in sales of such conformist literature and a corresponding steady rise in light entertainment. With five best-sellers, including the cheerful *Die Feuerzangenbowle* ("The punch bowl") of 1934, made into a film still widely known today, Heinrich Spoerl was the most-sold and probably also the most-read author of the Nazi dictatorship.

When public cultural life, even in big cities, became increasingly restricted due to Allied bombing, books took on a very particular importance. As publisher Karl Heinrich Bischoff put it in 1944: "When night falls again, and most people cannot go out to the movies, they simply need something that really distracts them and gives them strength, something that is always at hand."[220] Readers anxious to escape the depressing reality of everyday wartime life, or waiting for the sirens in their air-raid shelters, were unlikely to choose a stodgy blood-and-soil or military novel, let alone a propaganda tract. They needed literature to give them "entertainment, distraction, and a sense of distance."[221]

---

[219] On this and the following, see Schneider, "Bestseller im Dritten Reich"; also Adam, *Lesen unter Hitler*; Stieg, *Public Libraries in Nazi Germany*, 145–71.
[220] Bischoff to RSK manager, 8 September 1944, R 56 V/152 fol. 64.
[221] D'Hooghe, *Mitbetroffen*, 150.

6

A Failed Experiment?
Books in the Nazi
Media Dictatorship

From today's perspective, the Nazi dictatorship may be seen as a gigantic squandering of resources—with respect to people, institutions, and assets both tangible and intangible. Even in 1940, Sebastian Haffner, a lawyer and journalist who had emigrated in 1938, noted that the much-propagated "Nazi efficiency" was an illusion: "What the Nazis intend at the moment is carried out on a 'gigantic,' 'colossal,' hitherto unheard-of scale, and each time on completion it is observed to be hydrocephalous. But it imposes on the Germans."[1] Looking behind the scenes of power, Haffner saw only the "cynical nihilism" of corrupt "fortune-hunters and careerists":[2] "These men are innocent of religion, morals, and aesthetics. They lack even a social norm; 'humanity' in their vocabulary is known as 'the human whirligig.'" Never before had "rulers so flauntingly treated the ruled as mere ciphers ... while insisting that they expend themselves wholly in such an existence."[3] Because the Nazis lacked "talent for life" and the "very elements" of life such as "love, responsibility, and joie de vivre,"[4] they needed "continual, and continually more vigorous sensations and adventures to escape boredom."[5] Propaganda—

---

[1] Haffner, *Germany: Jekyll and Hyde*, 30.
[2] Ibid. 32, 23.
[3] Ibid. 32–3, 35.
[4] Ibid. 53–4.
[5] Ibid. 56.

directed at both the "loyal" part of the population and inward at the Nazis themselves—was able to create "imaginary pictures and mental associations that supplant reality" or, as in the case of the concentration camps, "make reality vanish."[6] The "peculiar quality" of Nazi propaganda was that "it is not believed, yet it works." For Haffner, all such "well-contrived" propaganda "provides indications as to the mentality of those for whom it is intended."[7] He regarded his compatriots as leading a "double life like Dr Jekyll and Mr Hyde": the Germans were always standing "with one leg in this world" and the other "in the world of fantasy" supplied by the propaganda of the Nazi state.[8]

In 1944 Franz Neumann pointed out that as the new rulers attempted to build a Nazi social order, their strategy consisted in fragmenting the middle and working classes by destroying the institutions that mediated between these groups and the state, and constructing a bureaucracy that intervened in every area of life.[9] Free culture, hitherto constitutionally protected, was increasingly transformed into "propaganda and salable commodities,"[10] and the domain of literature and the book market did not escape the devastating consequences of that change. The first year of Nazi rule was marked by an ambivalent combination of construction and destruction, with a rather meager tally of new achievements. The Prussian Academy of Arts literature section, the German PEN Club, and the League of German Writers (SDS) were aligned with the regime in a matter of weeks and without significant resistance. But only the SDS (or rather its successor, the RDS) continued to play any important role over the twelve years to come—and then only as the nucleus of the newly established Reich Chamber of Literature, which absorbed it completely in October 1935. The case was little different for the Börsenverein, the public librarians' association VDV, or the association of research librarians VDB, all of which allied themselves with the new rulers of their own accord. These bodies, too, quickly lost their status as independent representatives of their professional

---

[6] Ibid. 72.
[7] Ibid. 71.
[8] Ibid. 70, 73–4.
[9] Neumann, *Behemoth*, 366.
[10] Ibid. 367.

groups, and eventually became mere executive organs of the Nazi state. The book burnings, as a symbolic expression of what Georg Bollenbeck has called the "self-Nazification of the educated," inaugurated the process of destroying literary modernism in Germany,[11] though it would take many more years to create a unified practice of censorship capable of completing that destruction.

On the construction side of the balance sheet, the literary bureaucracy's pioneer fervor and its public self-presentation masked a less impressive reality. Both the Reich Ministry of Popular Enlightenment and Propaganda and the Reich Chamber of Culture were institutional success stories only to the extent that they secured political control of "cultural workers," managed the dissemination of information, and intervened in the media. Their claims were sweeping, but proved difficult to realize from the very start. In the domain of literary policy, Goebbels had to fight long and hard for his responsibilities, defending them again and again—whether against long-established national agencies and provincial particularism or against new competition in the shape of the Reich Education Ministry, against Ley's German Labor Front, Amann's constantly growing media trust, the Party literature offices of Rosenberg and Bouhler, or the attempted omnipotence of Himmler and the Party Chancellery under Bormann. In these battles neither the Propaganda Ministry's literature department, set up in 1934, nor the Chamber of Literature were effective weapons. Both were weakened by frequent changes in their senior personnel and difficulties in establishing a sound organizational structure, and at times they pursued their own, diverging objectives in coalition with partners outside the Ministry. Goebbels's strong points did not include personnel management, administrative efficiency, or responsible budgeting, even if his diaries tried to suggest the opposite; his political capital and substantive influence on Hitler and the Nazi leadership also fluctuated considerably over the dictatorship's twelve years.

The apparently weaker Bernhard Rust soon gained ground over the Propaganda Minister, who had to cede control of the Prussian ministry of education and culture in 1933 and then, after a personal decision by Hitler, of schools, universities, scientific institutes, and

---

[11] See Bollenbeck, *Tradition, Avantgarde, Reaktion*, 290–7.

public and research libraries in 1934. If Goebbels gleefully quoted the allegedly popular quip that the Reich Education Ministry's emblem was "two decrees crossed,"[12] his indecisive rival Rust nevertheless succeeded—with a relatively small ministerial staff, but energetic support from librarians on the ground—in reorganizing the public, municipal, and school libraries and the national, provincial, and university research library system in line with the Nazi state's requirements. Cultural policy abroad remained the domain of another competitor, Ribbentrop, and it was closed to Goebbels except where specific interministerial agreements had been reached.

Goebbels differed from the Party-based Ley and Amann in arguing that the German Reich should "not burden itself so much with economic acquisition," as this would impede "political leadership."[13] Indeed, the two Reich Leaders never managed to build a unified system that could be tailored to their political purposes, despite their co-optation, plunder, "Aryanization," purchase, and new establishment of publishing companies, retail and wholesale booksellers, and book clubs. But Ley and Amann were clearly far more interested in profit and the creation of capitalist monopolies than in ideological rigor (though Goebbels did not lag behind other Nazi leaders when it came to personal enrichment[14]). After the experiment of closer cooperation between the Propaganda Ministry literature department and the PPK collapsed in fall 1938, Bouhler pursued a largely autonomous literary policy with the help of his manager Hederich, and had his right to censor expressly reconfirmed by Hitler.

Whereas Rosenberg, Himmler, and Bormann with their Party offices aimed to set the whole of German cultural life on a strictly Nazi course, the Propaganda Minister also tolerated writers, journalists, and publishers whose stance toward the regime was unresponsive or even critical. As Haffner remarked in retrospect, "in the Third Reich books continued to be written by Antis who circumvented official controls by writing romantic trifles, adventure stories, and similar confections. Their readers knew that these authors wished to distance themselves from the Nazis." Yet they too were caught up

---

[12] Goebbels, *Tagebücher*, Part II, vol. 6, 411 (8 December 1942).
[13] Goebbels, *Tagebücher*, Part I, vol. 5, 379–80 (14 July 1938).
[14] See Stephan, *Joseph Goebbels*, 73–82.

in the Minister's careful calculations: "Everyone who worked under Goebbels, regardless of any self-bestowed anti-Nazi credentials, played an instrument in Goebbels' orchestra. All those romances, those old-fashioned tales, everything that was part of so-called normal life, without directly challenging the Third Reich, was part of the grand scheme."[15] This was a strategy that Goebbels had to assert against the fundamentalists in the state and Party leadership, attracting harsh criticism from his opponents in the process.

On the other hand, when deviation, unspoken defiance, or overt opposition went too far, Goebbels like his fellow Nazi leaders did not hesitate to employ the more aggressive resources of intimidation and threatened or actual violence. Celebrity was no protection, as is shown by the cases of Keyserling, Wiechert, and Grimm. When the Minister took a dislike to the manuscript of Ernst Jünger's latest war novel in November 1941, he resolved "to get hold of that literary hermit … at the next opportunity and show him clearly what my standpoint is."[16] In the game of "cat and mouse," Goebbels made sure it was always perfectly obvious who had the final say.[17] And on one point he never differed from the other Nazi leaders: the "doctrine that it is permitted and even commanded to rob, torment, and kill Jews."[18] In that domain, the Propaganda Minister was by no means a man impelled, as his former employee Werner Stephan claimed in 1949, but himself an impelling force.[19]

The elimination of "non-Aryans" from German cultural life was carried out in stages from 1933 on. It affected first the so-called "full Jews," then, when the Nuremberg Laws came into effect, also "half" and "quarter Jews" and the "Jewish by marriage,"[20] but this was not the only distinction. Whereas all Jewish writers, sales representatives, and book-trade employees were banned from working by 1935, it took longer to remove the proprietors, managing directors, and authorized signatories of publishers and bookstores. By 1937/38,

---

[15] Haffner, *Germany's Self-Destruction*, 211.
[16] Goebbels, *Tagebücher*, Part II, vol. 2, 315–16 (19 November 1941).
[17] This may relativize Denkler's study "Katz und Maus," which, though incisive on the texts, tends to underestimate the political context.
[18] Haffner, *Germany: Jekyll and Hyde*, 33.
[19] Stephan, *Joseph Goebbels*, 181.
[20] See Essner, *Die "Nürnberger Gesetze."*

however, they too had been thrown out of their companies or forced to sell or liquidate their businesses in a complicated process of "Aryanization" that proceeded along many different lines, "contractually, illegally, and by statute."[21] Its actors were not only the Propaganda Ministry and the Chamber of Literature, but also the Ministry of Economics, the Reichsführer SS and Chief of the German Police in the Ministry of the Interior, Max Winkler's trust company Cautio, Eher Publishing, and from 1938 the "Reich Commissioner for the Reunion of Austria with the Reich"—quite apart from the multitude of private individuals who profited from the "Aryanization" of Jewish bookstores, secondhand dealerships, lending libraries, and department stores. The fate of authors, publishers, and booksellers classified as "Jewish by marriage" depended on "special permission" granted by the Propaganda Minister and revocable at any time.

The loss of Jewish Germans as producers, sellers, recipients, and disseminators of German literature had a more lasting impact on the book market than the Nazi rulers had anticipated. Although the Party- and state-promoted books by nationalist-conservative and Nazi authors sold well within Germany, in February 1940 the Chamber official (and later owner of Zsolnay Verlag) Karl Heinrich Bischoff reluctantly admitted that "after the removal of the Jewish scum, the number of translations from German fell more and more, even in those countries that used to translate large quantities of German work." He proposed mitigating the situation by establishing a state-promoted translation agency, discreetly hidden behind companies that were politically suspect at home but respected abroad, such as Rowohlt or Deutsche Verlags-Anstalt.[22] Even before the war, it was only through enormous subsidies from the Nazi state that the export of German writing stayed afloat, for if the German Reich was expanding across Europe in territorial terms, in intellectual and cultural terms it had long since forfeited its leading role. The failure of the "European Union of Writers" project underlines this point. Goebbels refuted the International PEN Club's right "to speak on

---

21 Neumann, *Behemoth*, 116–20, here 116.
22 Bischoff, proposal for the establishment of a translation agency, 1 February 1940, for the attention of RSK president Johst, pp. 1, 4, BArch BDC/RSK/Bischoff, K. H.

behalf of intellectual Europe,"[23] but its new rival organization proved to be little more than a brief propaganda episode. After Stalingrad, the ESV sank into oblivion just as its predecessor, the Union of Nationalist Writers founded by Johst in 1934, had before it.

Despite these failures, Goebbels's political thinking and action was certainly far more realistic and pragmatic than that of the theoretician Rosenberg. "There are still ideologues among us," wrote the Propaganda Minister in his diary on 27 February 1942,

> who believe that the submariner, emerging from the engine room dirty and oil-spattered, longs to open a copy of [Rosenberg's] *Myth of the Twentieth Century*. Of course, that is pure nonsense. This man sees things differently and he is in no mood to accept ideological lectures. He is living out our ideology, and doesn't need to be instructed about it. He wants to relax, and we must give him the opportunity for relaxation through literature of the lighter sort, through light radio music, and so on. I pursue this tendency in the leadership of radio and film as well as of literature.[24]

Goebbels found it "psychologically quite understandable" that, in the fourth year of the war, "interest in war books and political books has declined steeply" not only among soldiers, but also in the population at large: "The nation flees from the hardship and pressures of everyday life into mental spaces that have nothing to do with the war."[25] A regular reader of the SD's *Meldungen* on morale in the Reich, the Propaganda Minister did not tire of emphasizing that "mental recuperation" and "entertainment" were "a matter of state importance, or even decisive for our military success."[26]

However, in 1942 such diary entries, dictated for posterity, no longer reflected the reality of life outside the Ministry. Severe paper shortages were increasingly limiting the public's supply of books, and the "lack of entertainment literature" had become pressing.[27]

---

[23] Goebbels, *Tagebücher*, Part II, vol. 2, 190 (27 October 1941).
[24] Ibid. vol. 3, 382 (27 February 1942).
[25] Ibid. vol. 6, 332 (25 November 1942).
[26] Ibid. vol. 3, 274 (8 February 1942). See also the entries for 26 February 1942, ibid. 376, and 27 February 1942, ibid. 382–3.
[27] Goebbels, *Tagebücher*, Part II, vol. 5, 184 (25 July 1942).

Goebbels noted on 26 February that "in bookstores, everything there is to sell continues to be sold out immediately. The situation on the book market is turning into a disaster. People want to get rid of their surplus money. It's a shame they are seizing on the book market to do so. There is hardly a single book left for a decent person to buy. When the occasion arises, I will take appropriate measures to deal with this matter."[28] But the "appropriate measures" thought up by his ministerial bureaucracy and the Chamber of Literature did not resolve the underlying problems—especially as by now the Labor Front with its publishing operations and the Zentrale der Frontbuchhandlungen, the OKW and the individual forces, the Ministry of Armaments and War Production, and the SS had all begun to develop and supply a book market of their own.

According to *Meldungen aus dem Reich* in January 1943, book retailers were experiencing "what they call 'indiscriminate plundering,' 'buying frenzy,' and 'irrational hoarding.'"[29] The trade believed that the immense profits made during "the boom in the first war years" would turn out to have been a fleeting phenomenon. The German book retailing sector, which had a "cultural status of international proportions" to defend, would emerge from the war with a "loss of substance that will be very difficult to remedy": with empty shelves and, thanks to the high taxes levied on profits from "sold-out" books, lacking the money to buy new stock. Publishers complained of the unequal distribution of paper reserves between press and book publishing. The result was that "in a war being fought especially for the preservation of culture," the "great works of German intellectual history and literature" were now "almost impossible to obtain." Some publishers even voiced the accusation "that despite all the Propaganda Ministry's support, other parts of the leadership do not consider books important"; Leipzig, the heart of the German book trade, was thought to be particularly badly affected by this disregard, for the conscription of personnel from all areas of production had "reached dimensions that endanger the international status of this city of books in the long term." On the matter

---

[28] Ibid. vol. 3, 376 (26 February 1942).
[29] *Meldungen aus dem Reich*, vol. 12, no. 349, 11 January 1943, 4656–63. The following quotations ibid.

of print permits from the Propaganda Ministry and the Economic Office of the German Book Trade, "local-level agencies often seem to believe that if a company produces novels, for example, then this itself is evidence of having labor to spare." Such attitudes resulted in publishers, printers, and bookbinders scrambling for Wehrmacht commissions in the hope of "protecting themselves from further personnel losses." Snapshots like these, passed on by the SD's informants, demonstrate the failure of state literary policy, the rapidly widening discrepancy between its propaganda and the everyday realities of writers, publishers, booksellers, librarians, and readers. At the same time, their remarkably frank expression of hopelessness and fear for the future hints at the gradual dissolution of the Nazi state as a whole.

On the Propaganda Ministry agenda in March 1944 was a book that had appeared two years earlier with Oxford University Press in New York and then again, in an expanded edition, in 1944.[30] Its author was Franz Neumann, during the Weimar Republic a partner in Ernst Fraenkel's law firm who handled employment law for the SPD and the free trade unions. After emigrating, he worked first at the London School of Economics and Political Science, then from 1936 at the émigré Institute for Social Research in New York. In his analysis of Germany's politics, law, economy, military, and society, Neumann presented the Nazi dictatorship as a "behemoth." Thomas Hobbes had cited this monster from Jewish eschatology in his 1668 interpretation of the violent excesses and chaos of the English civil wars; for Neumann, it countered the concept of the "dual state" that Fraenkel had used in 1941 to describe the Nazi juxtaposition of "normative law" and "prerogative" or individual measures.[31] Denying that the Nazi system had a realm of law at all, Neumann showed that it possessed "no political theory of its own" and that "the ideologies it uses or discards" were nothing more than "techniques of domination," not taken seriously by the political leadership but deployed for purely propagandistic purposes.[32]

---

[30] Reference to collecting foreign books ordered in *Nachrichtenblatt des Reichsministeriums für Volksaufklärung und Propaganda* 12, no. 10, 28 March 1944, 32, BArch R 55/441.
[31] Fraenkel, *The Dual State*.
[32] Neumann, *Behemoth*, 467–8.

The same can be said of Nazi literary policy, where—except in its destructive measures against books and people—extensive and hectic activity revealed neither coherent planning nor a unified objective. But Neumann argued that there was no longer even a state in Germany, because "the monopolists in dealing with non-monopolists rely on individual measures and in their relations with the state and with competitors, on compromises which are determined by expedience and not by law." He saw a trend toward replacing the state with a new "form of society in which the ruling groups control the rest of the population directly, without the mediation of that rational though coercive apparatus hitherto known as the state."[33] No limits, in other words, were now set on particularist interests, egotism, profit maximization, corruption, caprice, exploitation, and terror.

The "Lackas affair" supports this interpretation. Lackas, a bookseller who made his fortune in paper dealing, and his allies from the publishing industry and Wehrmacht were charged with "repeated bribery, repeated war economy offenses, embezzlement, fraud, corrosion of Germany's military strength, deception and crimes against the Price Ordinance [*Preisstrafverordnung*], attempted blackmail, repeated foreign currency offenses, and repeated handling of the profits of tax evasion."[34] The trial was held *in camera* at a Berlin court in March and April 1944, and was not mentioned in the press; its details would have exposed the gap between propaganda and reality in Hitler's "*Volk* state." Myriad regulations, and the emergence of an unwieldy bureaucratic procedure for managing paper and binding materials during World War II, had resulted in an absurdly self-perpetuating momentum: in order to access scarce paper resources, publishers produced more and more Wehrmacht editions, in higher and higher print runs, for the closed book market of the Zentrale der Frontbuchhandlungen and the individual segments of the military. As Lackas and his associates worked the system, a situation arose whereby "during the military collapse in the deserts of Africa, German soldiers were reading romances that a Protestant

---

[33] Ibid. 468–70.
[34] For a detailed account, see Bühler and Simons, *Die blendenden Geschäfte*, 119–43, here 136.

company had published in the Westphalian provinces, printed in Italy or the Netherlands on paper that had to be delivered by freight train from Finland in the midst of infrastructural disintegration."[35]

This portrait of Lackas's partnership with Bertelsmann Verlag, his chief client, is echoed in other companies and other parts of the front as well, where print runs in the millions, using paper rations acquired through the military book market, assured huge profits often driven by corruption. This was a capitalist planned economy benefiting a few large companies—something that had not been intended as such by the state agencies, but in practice was funded from tax revenues and tacitly accepted because it sustained an illusion of normality and efficiency in the chaos of war. The small and medium-sized businesses that made up the bulk of German publishing and bookselling were left largely empty-handed. They were abandoned to their problems, and during 1943/44 also faced the threat of officially decreed closures. At the same time, the remaining paper stocks and the tried-and-tested mechanisms of the Nazi mass book market laid the material foundations for certain publishers—Heinrich and Reinhard Mohn of Bertelsmann, Georg von Holtzbrinck, and others—to rise like the proverbial phoenix from the ashes when the war was over.

Non-materially, in contrast, the end of the dictatorship confronted the educated middle class (to which publishers, along with writers, booksellers, and librarians, belonged) with the prospect of total ruin. Nazism had not burst into their world "like an alien force"; rather, the majority of them abetted it through "their desire for a purification of German art and for an authoritarian political order."[36] The Nazi state fulfilled these aspirations by repudiating the avant-garde, ending the Weimar Republic's modernist experiments, eliminating the creative influence of Jews on cultural life, redirecting attention to nationalist cultural products, and preserving the semblance of a high culture dominated by the bourgeoisie. But an exorbitant price was paid for its services. Art was robbed of autonomy and turned to the purposes of political rule. Public discourse—already crippled by the suppression and exile of the political Left—was rendered completely powerless,

---

[35] Ibid. 172.
[36] Bollenbeck, *Tradition, Avantgarde, Reaktion*, 297. On the following, see ibid. 298–346.

so that even those representatives of nationalist-conservative, liberal, and Christian cultural values who had remained in Germany no longer had a voice. Furthermore, Goebbels (among others) promoted the expansion of the mass media radio, film, and early television, and thus of a popular leisure and entertainment culture that would permanently turn everything the German *Bildungsbürgertum*, shaped by the traditions of the nineteenth century, had rejected into everyday reality for millions of people.

After 1945, writers, publishers, booksellers, and librarians preferred to forget the complicity they had entered into with the Nazi state. In a heated debate with Thomas Mann, protagonists of "inner emigration" led by Frank Thiess and Walter von Molo now presented themselves as victims of the dictatorship or even as having silently aided the resistance.[37] This tactic was by no means restricted to the *éminences grises* of German literature; key members of the new generation also asserted that their "response to the totalitarian state was total introversion."[38] Yet most of them, Erhard Schütz writes, had been made "guiltlessly guilty" by the era in which they emerged, "and what that era was does not simply adhere to them, but permeates their inner being," however much they tried to overcome it and claimed to have opposed it.[39] This is quite apart from figures such as Blunck, Brehm, Grimm, Johst, Kolbenheyer, or Vesper, who carried on writing as if nothing had happened.

Ina Seidel was one of the very few to admit she had been among the "idiots" who believed in Germany's "inner purification." Compromised by her willing participation in the Nazi state, but also chastened by the attacks on her son-in-law Ernst Schulte Strathaus and brother-in-law Peter Suhrkamp, she drew bitter conclusions in a 1945 diary entry: "We did not underestimate the power of evil, we underestimated its *reality*. May the consequences be an indelible lesson for all that lies before us. ... In our case it was probably a lack of self-awareness if we ... did not want to believe that 'something

---

[37] See Grosser, *Die große Kontroverse*; Hermand and Lange, *"Wollt ihr Thomas Mann wiederhaben?"*; Hermand, Peitsch, and Scherpe, *Nachkriegsliteratur in Westdeutschland*.

[38] Andersch, *The Cherries of Freedom*, 36. See also Reinhardt, *Alfred Andersch*, 52–104; Tuchel, "Alfred Andersch im Nationalsozialismus."

[39] Schütz, "'Ein Geruch von Blut und Schande...,'" 154.

like that,' the monstrous crimes in the concentration camps, 'could happen here': a lack of awareness of the possibilities inherent in our own human nature."[40] Hermann Stresau went a step further. After visiting the movies to watch the wartime newsreel from a comfortable plush seat, he asked himself and his contemporaries: "Do people now live only with the outermost surface of their organs? Can they now only see, hear—without understanding in the least? It seems that things can only be 'brought home' to them through a camera lens, and reality does not penetrate further than the retina, the eardrum, while deeper inside they remain dumb and deaf and blind."[41]

Stresau's comment was made on 14 August 1942, but it points forward to the unsettling reality of our present-day media world. Today, two lessons of the Nazi dictatorship—the moral responsibility of each individual for a society's political acts, and the obligation to deal with the complexities of lived reality in a critical, independent, and reflective way—are still as urgent as ever before.

---

[40] Seidel, *Aus den schwarzen Wachstuchheften*, 97.
[41] Stresau, *Von Jahr zu Jahr*, 305.

Sources and Bibliography

Archival Sources 1933–45

Archives of the Academy of Arts Berlin: Archiv der Akademie der Künste Berlin (AdK)
NL Erik Reger

Federal Archives: Bundesarchiv Berlin-Lichterfelde (BArch)
Reichsfinanzministerium (R 2); Reichsministerium des Innern (R 18); Reichsministerium für Wissenschaft, Erziehung und Volksbildung (R 21 alt/R 4901 neu); Reichsministerium der Justiz (R 22); Reichskanzlei (R 43 II); Reichsministerium für Volksaufklärung und Propaganda (R 55); Reichskulturkammer-Zentrale (R 56 I); Reichsschrifttumskammer (R 56 V); Reichssicherheitshauptamt (R 58); Partei-Kanzlei der NSDAP (NS 6); Kanzlei Rosenberg (NS 8); Parteiamtliche Prüfungskommission zum Schutze des nationalsozialistischen Schrifttums (NS 11); Hauptamt für Erzieher/ Reichswaltung des nationalsozialistischen Lehrerbundes (NS 12); Der Beauftragte des Führers für die Überwachung der gesamten geistigen und weltanschaulichen Schulung und Erziehung der NSDAP (NS 15); Reichspropagandaleitung der NSDAP (NS 18); Sammlung Schumacher. Printed materials: RD 39/1–1 bis 1–10: *Deutsche Wissenschaft, Erziehung und Volksbildung*. Amtsblatt des Reichsministeriums für Wissenschaft, Erziehung und Volksbildung und der Unterrichtsverwaltungen der Länder, Berlin 1/1935–10/1944; NSD 2/9–14: Parteiamtliche Prüfungskommission zum Schutze des NS-Schrifttums; NSD 3: Partei-Kanzlei der NSDAP; NSD 16: Der Beauftragte des Führers für die Überwachung der gesamten geistigen und weltanschaulichen Schulung und Erziehung der NSDAP; NSD 124: *Das Schwarze Korps*. Zeitung der Schutzstaffeln der NSDAP. Organ der Reichsführung SS, Berlin 1/1935–11/1945. Collections of the former GDR Central State Archives: Reichskanzlei (07.01); Reichsministerium des Innern (15.01); Reichsministerium für Wissenschaft, Erziehung und Volksbildung (49.01); Reichsministerium für Volksaufklärung und Propaganda (50.01); Reichskulturkammer (50.05). Collections of the former Berlin Document Center: personnel and

thematic files of the Reichskulturkammer/ Reichsschrifttumskammer, Reichsministerium für Volksaufklärung und Propaganda, Reichsministerium für Wissenschaft, Erziehung und Volksbildung; Masterfile (NSDAP-Mitgliederkartei); Partei-Kanzlei-Correspondence; SS; SA; Research

Political Archives of the Federal Foreign Office: Politisches Archiv des Auswärtigen Amtes, Berlin (PA AA)
Kulturabteilung/Kulturpolitische Abteilung; Referat Partei; Handakten Luther; Deutsche Botschaft Rom (Qu.); Propaganda—Verbreitung politischer, wirtschaftlicher und wissenschaftlicher Literatur pp. im Ausland und sonstige politische Propaganda

Berlin State Archive: Landesarchiv Berlin (LA)
Rep. 243, Acc. 1814: Landesleitung Berlin der Reichsschrifttumskammer

Central state archives for North Rhine-Westphalia: Nordrhein-Westfälisches Hauptstaatsarchiv Düsseldorf (HStA)
Außendienststellen der Stapoleitstelle Düsseldorf (RW 18); Stapostelle Köln und nachgeordnete Dienststellen (RW 34); Stapostelle Aachen und nachgeordnete Dienststellen (RW 35); Stapo(leit)stelle Düsseldorf (RW 36); Gestapo/Stapo(leit)stelle Düsseldorf (RW 58)

Düsseldorf city archives: Stadtarchiv Düsseldorf (StA)
NL Dr. Oskar Mücke: Kreisdienststelle Düsseldorf der Reichsstelle zur Förderung des deutschen Schrifttums; NL Ebel/142; personnel files Dr. Hermann Reuter (V 37371), Dr. Gerhard Wunder (V 24910)

Heinrich Heine archives: Heinrich-Heine-Archiv der Stadt Düsseldorf
Sammlung Hermann Reuter, Landes- und Stadtbibliothek Düsseldorf

Duisburg city archives: Stadtarchiv Duisburg (StA)
Personnel files Dr. Robert Hohlbaum, Dr. Viktor Sallentien, Dr. Wilhelm Schmitz-Veltin

State archives Karlsruhe: Generallandesarchiv Karlsruhe (GLA)
465d: NSDAP Gau Baden

Saxon state archives: Sächsisches Staatsarchiv Leipzig (StAL)
Börsenverein der Deutschen Buchhändler (BV) I; Börsenverein der Deutschen Buchhändler (BV) II; Firmenakten des Börsenvereins (F); Koehler & Volckmar

Archives of the Deutsche Bücherei: Archiv der Deutschen Bücherei, Leipzig (DB-Archiv)

Geschäftsführung, Erlasse und Anweisungen der Aufsichtsbehörden. Erlasse des Reichsministeriums für Volksaufklärung und Propaganda; Bibliographische Tätigkeit. Sammeltätigkeit. Sammlung der Verlagswerke; Bibliographische Tätigkeit. Listen des schädlichen und unerwünschten Schrifttums. Liste der in der Deutschen Bücherei unter Verschluss gestellten Druckschriften. Liste der für Jugendliche ungeeigneten Schriften (1941–5); Bibliographische Tätigkeit. Bibliographie des nationalsozialistischen Schrifttums. Bibliographie des jüdischen Schrifttums in deutscher Sprache. Bibliographie der wichtigsten vom 1.9.1939–30.6.1942 erschienenen reichsdeutschen Bücher

Archives of German Literature: Deutsches Literaturarchiv Marbach a.N. (DLA)
Gottfried Benn; Hans Grimm; Erich Kästner; Anton Kippenberg; Jochen Klepper; Langen-Müller Verlag; Wilhelm Lehmann; Joachim Maass; Agnes Miegel; Gustav Pezold; Kurt Pinthus; Ina Seidel; Will Vesper

Central Thuringian archives: Thüringisches Hauptstaatsarchiv Weimar (HStA)
Thüringisches Ministerium des Innern: Abteilungen A, G, P; Thüringisches Ministerium für Volksbildung, Abteilung C

State archives Würzburg: Staatsarchiv Würzburg (StA)
Reichsstudentenführung (RSF): I*21 C 14/1–4 (now BArch Berlin-Lichterfelde NS 38/2415–2418); Gestapostelle Würzburg; SD-Hauptaußenstelle Würzburg

Printed Sources and Literature 1933–45

Akten zur deutschen Auswärtigen Politik 1918–1945. 1971–81. Series C: 1933–37, vols. I.2–VI.2. Göttingen: Vandenhoeck und Ruprecht.
Akten zur deutschen Auswärtigen Politik 1918–1945. 1969–79. Series E: 1941–45, vols. I–VIII. Göttingen: Vandenhoeck und Ruprecht.
Boelcke, Willi A. 1966. *Kriegspropaganda 1939–1941. Geheime Ministerkonferenzen im Reichspropagandaministerium.* Stuttgart: Deutsche Verlags-Anstalt.
Boelcke, Willi A. 1969. *"Wollt Ihr den totalen Krieg?" Die geheimen Goebbels-Konferenzen 1939–1943.* Munich: Deutsche Verlags-Anstalt.

Das Buch ein Schwert des Geistes. Erste Grundliste für den Deutschen Leihbuchhandel. 1940. Compiled by RMVP/Abteilung Schrifttum. Leipzig: Börsenverein der Deutschen Buchhändler.

Das Buch ein Schwert des Geistes. Grundliste für den Deutschen Leihbuchhandel. 1941. Compiled by RMVP/Abteilung Schrifttum. 2nd edn. Leipzig: Börsenverein der Deutschen Buchhändler.

Das Buch ein Schwert des Geistes. Grundliste für den Deutschen Leihbuchhandel. 1943. Compiled by RMVP/Abteilung Schrifttum. 3rd edn. Leipzig: Börsenverein der Deutschen Buchhändler.

Der deutsche Buchhandel in Zahlen. 1937. Leipzig: Börsenverein der Deutschen Buchhändler.

Deutscher Fichte-Bund e.V., ed. 1936. *Deutsches Kulturrecht.* Hamburg: Falken-Verlag.

Deutschland-Berichte der Sozialdemokratischen Partei Deutschlands (Sopade) 1934–1940. 1980. Ed. Klaus Behnken. Frankfurt/Main: Zweitausendeins.

Dichter und Krieger. Weimarer Reden 1942. 1943. Hamburg: Hanseatische Verlagsanstalt.

Die Dichtung im Kampf des Reiches. Weimarer Reden 1940. 1941. Hamburg: Hanseatische Verlagsanstalt.

Die Dichtung im kommenden Europa. Weimarer Reden 1941. 1942. Hamburg: Hanseatische Verlagsanstalt.

Fraenkel, Ernst. 1941. *The Dual State.* New York: Oxford University Press.

Gentz, Günther, ed. 1936. *Das Recht der Reichsschrifttumskammer.* Leipzig: Börsenverein der Deutschen Buchhändler.

Goebbels, Joseph. 1934. *Kampf um Berlin. Der Anfang.* 6th edn. Munich: Eher.

Goebbels, Joseph. 1971–2. *Goebbels-Reden.* Ed. Helmut Heiber. 2 vols. Düsseldorf: Droste.

Goebbels, Joseph. 1993–2008. *Die Tagebücher von Joseph Goebbels.* Ed. Elke Fröhlich. 3 parts, 29 vols and index. Munich: Saur.

Haffner, Sebastian. 1940/2005. *Germany: Jekyll and Hyde.* Trans. Wilfrid David. London: Secker and Warburg.

Haffner, Sebastian. 2004. *Das Leben der Fußgänger. Feuilletons 1933–1938.* Ed. Jürgen Peter Schmied. Munich: Hanser.

Hasper, E. 1934. Über die notwendigen Maßnahmen auf dem Gebiete des Leihbüchereigewerbes. In *Das Kulturprogramm und die Gliederung der deutschen Leihbücherei. Überblick. Reden zur Fachschaftstagung 1934*, ed. L. Hürter, 27–32. Berlin: Achterberg.

Haupt, Gunther. 1934. *Was erwarten wir von der kommenden Dichtung?* Tübingen: Wunderlich.

Hederich, Karl-Heinz. 1937. *Nationalsozialismus und Buch.* Mainz: H. Marxen.

Hederich, Karl-Heinz. 1937. *Die Parteiamtliche Prüfungskommission zum Schutze des NS-Schrifttums, ihre Aufgaben und ihre Stellung in Partei und Staat.* Breslau: F. Hirt.

Heuduck, C. von. 1934. Die Organisation der Fachschaft. In *Das Kulturprogramm und die Gliederung der deutschen Leihbücherei. Überblick. Reden zur Fachschaftstagung 1934,* ed. L. Hürter, 23–6. Berlin: Achterberg.

Hinkel, Hans, ed. 1937. *Handbuch der Reichskulturkammer.* Berlin: Deutscher Verlag für Politik und Wirtschaft.

Hövel, Paul. 1942. *Wesen und Aufbau der Schrifttumsarbeit in Deutschland.* Essen: Essener Verlagsanstalt.

Hürter, L. 1934. Kulturpolitik in und durch die Leihbüchereien. In *Das Kulturprogramm und die Gliederung der deutschen Leihbücherei. Überblick. Reden zur Fachschaftstagung 1934,* ed. L. Hürter, 14–22. Berlin: Achterberg.

Ihde, Wilhelm, ed. 1942. *Handbuch der Reichsschrifttumskammer.* Leipzig: Verlag des Börsenvereins.

Jahresliste 1942 des schädlichen und unerwünschten Schrifttums. [1942]. Leipzig: Verlag des Börsenvereins.

Jahresliste 1943 des schädlichen und unerwünschten Schrifttums. [1943]. Leipzig: Verlag des Börsenvereins.

Jünger, Ernst. 1947. *On the Marble Cliffs.* Trans. Stuart Hood. London: New Directions.

Kirchner, Joachim. 1933. *Das Schrifttum und die wissenschaftlichen Bibliotheken im nationalsozialistischen Deutschland. Vortrag, gehalten auf der 29. Versammlung des Vereins Deutscher Bibliothekare in Darmstadt.* Leipzig: Harrassowitz.

Langenbucher, Hellmuth. 1935. *Nationalsozialistische Dichtung. Einführung und Übersicht.* Berlin: Junker und Dünnhaupt.

Langenbucher, Hellmuth, ed. 1938. *Die Welt des Buches. Eine Kunde vom Buch.* Ebenhausen: Langewiesche-Brandt.

Liste 1 des schädlichen und unerwünschten Schrifttums. [October 1935] Gemäß § 1 der Anordnung des Präsidenten der Reichsschrifttumskammer vom 25. April 1935 bearbeitet und herausgegeben von der Reichsschrifttumskammer. Berlin: Reichsdruckerei.

Liste 1 des schädlichen und unerwünschten Schrifttums: Nachträge I–III. [10 June 1936]. Berlin: Gestapa.

Liste des schädlichen und unerwünschten Schrifttums. Stand vom 31. Dezember 1938 und Jahreslisten 1939–1941. 1979. Facsimile reprint of the annual lists published in Leipzig 1938–41. Vaduz, Liechtenstein: Topos.

Liste der für Jugendliche und Büchereien ungeeigneten Druckschriften. 1940/43. Issued by RMVP/Abteilung Schrifttum, October 1940;

2nd, rev. edn. 1943. Leipzig: Börsenverein der Deutschen Buch-händler.

Mau, Johannes. 1934. Die Entwicklung und der gegenwärtige Stand der Leihbüchereibewegung. In *Das Kulturprogramm und die Gliederung der deutschen Leihbücherei. Überblick. Reden zur Fachschaftstagung 1934*, ed. L. Hürter, 8–13. Berlin: Achterberg.

Meldungen aus dem Reich 1938–1945. Die geheimen Lageberichte des Sicherheitsdienstes der SS. 1984. Ed. Heinz Boberach. 17 vols. Hersching: Pawlak.

Menz, Gerhard. 1938. *Der Aufbau des Kulturstandes. Die Reichs-kulturkammergesetzgebung, ihre Grundlagen und ihre Erfolge*. Munich: C. H. Beck.

Menz, Gerhard. 1942. *Der deutsche Buchhandel*. 2nd, rev. edn. Gotha: J. Perthes.

Metzner, Kurt O. Friedrich. 1935. *Geordnete Buchbesprechung. Ein Handbuch für Presse und Verlag*. Leipzig: Verlag des Börsenvereins.

Müller, Georg Wilhelm. 1940. *Das Reichsministerium für Volksauf-klärung und Propaganda*. Berlin: Junker und Dünnhaupt.

Nachrichtendienst "Buch-Feldpostsendung." 1940. Berlin: Werbe- und Beratungsamt für das deutsche Schrifttum beim Reichsministerium für Volksaufklärung und Propaganda.

Nachrichtendienst "Herbstveranstaltungen für das deutsche Schrifttum." 1940. Berlin: Werbe- und Beratungsamt für das deutsche Schrifttum beim Reichsministerium für Volksaufklärung und Propaganda.

Nachrichtendienst "Jugend und Buch." 1939. Berlin: Werbe- und Beratungsamt für das deutsche Schrifttum beim Reichsministerium für Volksaufklärung und Propaganda.

Neumann, Franz. 1944/1963. *Behemoth. The Structure and Practice of National Socialism, 1933–1944*. New York: Octagon.

Payr, Bernhard. 1941. *Das Amt Schrifttumspflege. Seine Entwicklungs-geschichte und seine Organisation*. Berlin: Junker und Dünnhaupt.

Prinzhorn, Fritz. 1934. *Die Aufgaben der Bibliotheken im national-sozialistischen Deutschland. Vortrag, gehalten am 25. Mai 1934 auf einer öffentlichen Kundgebung des Vereins deutscher Bibliothekare in Danzig*. Leipzig: Eichblatt.

Rantzau, Otto Graf zu. 1939. *Das Reichsministerium für Wissenschaft, Erziehung und Volksbildung*. Berlin: Junker und Dünnhaupt.

Reichsgesetzblatt. 1933–45. Issued by Reichsministerium des Innern. 2 parts. Berlin: Reichsverlagsamt.

Reichsliste für Dorfbüchereien. 1936. Zusammengestellt im Auftrage des Reichs- und Preußischen Ministeriums für Wissenschaft, Erziehung und Volksbildung von der Reichsstelle für volkstümliches Büchereiwesen. 2nd edn. 1938. Leipzig: Einkaufshaus für Büchereien.

Reichsliste für kleinere städtische Büchereien. 1936. Zusammengestellt im Auftrage des Reichs- und Preußischen Ministeriums für Wissenschaft, Erziehung und Volksbildung von der Reichsstelle für volkstümliches Büchereiwesen. 2nd edn. 1939. Leipzig: Einkaufshaus für Büchereien.

Reichsstelle zur Förderung des deutschen Schrifttums. [1933]. [Leipzig:] Reichsstelle zur Förderung des deutschen Schrifttums.

Rühle, Gerd. 1934–9. *Das Dritte Reich. Dokumentarische Darstellung des Aufbaus der Nation.* 6 vols. Berlin: Hummel.

Schlegel, Werner. 1934. *Dichter auf dem Scheiterhaufen.* Berlin: Verlag für Kulturpolitik.

Schmidt-Leonhardt, Hans. 1935. Einheit von nationaler Staatsführung und nationaler Geistesführung. *Deutsche Presse* 25: 654–5.

Schmidt-Leonhardt, Hans. 1935. Kultur und Staat des neuen Reiches. *Deutsches Recht* 5: 338–43.

Schramm, Percy Ernst, ed. 1982. *Kriegstagebuch des Oberkommandos der Wehrmacht (Wehrmachtführungsstab) 1940–1945. Geführt von Helmuth Greiner und Percy Ernst Schramm (Studienausgabe).* 4 vols. Herrsching: Pawlak.

Schrieber, Karl-Friedrich, ed. 1934. *Die Reichskulturkammer. Organisation und Ziele der deutschen Kulturpolitik.* Berlin: Junker & Dünnhaupt.

Schrieber, Karl-Friedrich, ed. 1935–7. *Das Recht der Reichskulturkammer. Sammlung der für den Kulturstand geltenden Gesetze und Verordnungen, der amtlichen Anordnungen und Bekanntmachungen der Reichskulturkammer und ihrer Einzelkammern. Unter Mitarbeit der Kammern.* 5 vols. Berlin: de Gruyter.

Schrieber, Karl-Friedrich, Alfred Metten, and Herbert Collatz, eds. 1943. *Das Recht der Reichskulturkammer. Sammlung der für den Kulturstand geltenden Gesetze und Verordnungen, der amtlichen Anordnungen und Bekanntmachungen der Reichskulturkammer und ihrer Einzelkammern.* 2 vols. Berlin: de Gruyter.

Schriewer, Franz. 1937. *Das ländliche Volksbüchereiwesen. Einführung in Grundfragen und Praxis der Dorf- und Kleinstadtbüchereien.* Jena: Diederichs.

Schriewer, Franz. 1938. *Die Staatlichen Volksbüchereistellen im Aufbau des deutschen Volksbüchereiwesens.* Leipzig: Einkaufshaus für Büchereien.

Schriewer, Franz. 1939. *Die deutsche Volksbücherei.* Jena: Diederichs.

Schriftsteller-Verzeichnis. 1942. Issued by the Reichsschrifttums-kammer (Berlin-Charlottenburg). Leipzig: RSK.

Sington, Derrick, and Arthur Weidenfeld. 1942. *The Goebbels Experiment. A Study of the Nazi Propaganda Machine.* London: John Murray.

Soenke, Jürgen. 1941. *Studien über zeitgenössische Zensursysteme.* Frankfurt/Main: Diesterweg.

Der Verlag Herder im Ausland. Pionierarbeit für das deutsche Buch. 1937. MS. Freiburg im Breisgau: Herder.

Verlagsveränderungen im deutschen Buchhandel 1933–1937. 1937. Leipzig: Börsenverein der Deutschen Buchhändler.

Verlagsveränderungen im deutschen Buchhandel 1937–1943. 1943. Leipzig: Börsenverein der Deutschen Buchhändler.

Vertrauliche Mitteilungen der [from 1938: *für die] Fachschaft Handel im Bund Reichsdeutscher Buchhändler* [from no. 3, 20 February 1937: *der Gruppe Buchhandel in der Reichsschrifttumskammer*]: *Fachgruppe Sortiment.* MS. Nos. 1, 20 July 1936–266, 12 February 1945.

Vertrauliche Mitteilungen der [from 1938: *für die] Fachschaft Verlag im Bund Reichsdeutscher Buchhändler* [from no. 17, 17 November 1936: *der Gruppe Buchhandel in der Reichsschrifttumskammer*]. MS. Nos. 1, 31 May 1935–533, 20 February 1945.

Verzeichnis der polizeilich beschlagnahmten und eingezogenen, sowie der für Leihbüchereien verbotenen Druckschriften. [1934]. Munich: Bayerische Politische Polizei.

Verzeichnis englischer und nordamerikanischer Schriftsteller. 1942. Issued by RMVP/Abteilung Schrifttum. Leipzig: Verlag des Börsenvereins.

Verzeichnis jüdischer Autoren. Vorläufige Zusammenstellung der Reichsstelle zur Förderung des deutschen Schrifttums [from Part 3: *des Amtes Schrifttumspflege bei dem Beauftragten des Führers zur Überwachung der gesamten geistigen und weltanschaulichen Schulung und Erziehung der NSDAP*]. 1938–9. 7 parts (A–Z). Berlin: Reichsstelle zur Förderung des deutschen Schrifttums.

Das Volk lebt im Buch. Ein Führer durch die Schau der "Woche des deutschen Buches 1936." 1936. Potsdam: Reichsschrifttumsstelle.

Vorschlagsliste für Dichterlesungen 1937/38. 1937. Berlin: Reichs-schrifttumsstelle beim Reichsministerium für Volksaufklärung und Propaganda, Vortragsamt.

Vorschlagsliste für Dichterlesungen 1940/41. 1940. Berlin: Werbe- und Beratungsamt für das deutsche Schrifttum beim Reichsministerium für Volksaufklärung und Propaganda.

Vorschlagsliste für Dichterlesungen 1941/42. 1941. Berlin: Werbe- und Beratungsamt für das deutsche Schrifttum beim Reichsministerium für Volksaufklärung und Propaganda.

Vorschlagsliste für Dichterlesungen und Schriftstellervorträge 1938: Soldatischer Vortragsdienst. 1937. Berlin: Reichsschrifttumsstelle beim Reichsministerium für Volksaufklärung und Propaganda, Vortragsamt.

Weimarer Reden des Großdeutschen Dichtertreffens 1938. 1939.
Hamburg: Hanseatische Verlags-Anstalt.
Die wirtschaftlichen Unternehmungen der Deutschen Arbeitsfront.
1939. Berlin: DAF, Zentralstelle für die Finanzwirtschaft.
*Die Zeit lebt im Buch. Führer durch die "Jahresschau des deutschen
Schrifttums" anläßlich der Woche des Deutschen Buches 1937.*
1937. Issued by Reichsschrifttumsstelle beim Reichsministerium für
Volksaufklärung und Propaganda. Berlin: Poeschel & Trepte.

Periodicals 1927–45

Das Archiv. Nachschlagewerk für Politik, Wirtschaft, Kultur. Ed. Alfred-
Ingemar Berndt. Berlin: Stollberg. Vols. 1 (1934/35)–11 (1944/45);
supplement I January–May 1933, supplement II June–October 1933,
supplement III November 1933–March 1934.
Börsenblatt für den Deutschen Buchhandel. Ausgabe A. Leipzig:
Börsenverein der Deutschen Buchhändler. Nos. 100 (1933)–112 (1945).
*Buch und Volk. Buchberatungszeitschrift der Reichsstelle zur Förderung
des deutschen Schrifttums.* Leipzig. Vols. 10 (1933)–20 (1943).
*Bücherei und Bildungspflege. Zeitschrift für die gesamten
außerschulmäßigen Bildungsmittel.* Stettin: Verlag Bücherei und
Bildungspflege. Vol. 13 (1933).
Die Bücherei. Zeitschrift für deutsche Schrifttumspflege. Leipzig:
Einkaufshaus für Büchereien. Vols. 1 (1934)–11 (1944), March.
*Bücherkunde der Reichsstelle zur Förderung des deutschen
Schrifttums.* Bayreuth: Gauverlag Bayerische Ostmark. Vols. 1
(1934)–11 (1944), September/October.
Der Buchhändler im neuen Reich. Berlin. Vols. 1 (1936)–6 (1941).
Deutsche Kultur-Wacht. Blätter des Kampfbundes für deutsche Kultur.
Ed. Hans Hinkel. Berlin. Nos. 1–2 (1933).
*Der deutsche Schriftsteller. Zeitschrift für die Schriftsteller in der
Reichsschrifttumskammer.* Ed. Kurt O. Friedrich Metzner. Berlin.
Vols. 1 (1936)–9 (1944), July.
Großdeutsches Leihbüchereiblatt [from 5/1943: *Deutsches
Büchereiblatt*]. *Mitteilungsblatt der Reichsschrifttumskammer für
den Deutschen Leihbuchhandel.* Leipzig: Verlag des Börsenvereins
der Deutschen Buchhändler. Vols. 1 (1939)–6 (1944), September.
Jahrbuch des Großdeutschen Leihbuchhandels. Leipzig. Vols. 1941,
1942–3.
Mitteilungen des Kampfbundes für deutsche Kultur. Munich:
Kampfbund. Vols. 1 (1929)–3 (1931).
Nationalsozialistische Bibliographie. Monatshefte der Parteiamtlichen

Prüfungskommission zum Schutze des NS-Schrifttums. Ed. Philipp
Bouhler. Berlin: Zentralverlag der NSDAP. Vols. 1 (1936)–9 (1944).
Nationalsozialistisches Jahrbuch. Ed. with the NSDAP Reichsleitung
by Philipp Bouhler (from 13/1939 Robert Ley). Munich: Eher. Vols. 1
(1927)–18 (1944).
Die Neue Literatur. Ed. Will Vesper. Leipzig: Avenarius. Vols. 34
(1933)–44 (1943).
*Die Reichskulturkammer. Amtliches Mitteilungsblatt der Reichskultur-
kammer.* Ed. Hans Hinkel. Berlin: Reichskulturkammer. Vols. 1
(1943)–3 (1945), February.
*Der Schriftsteller. Zeitschrift des Schutzverbandes Deutscher
Schriftsteller* [from 1933, no. 8, *des Reichsverbandes Deutscher
Schriftsteller*]. Berlin. 1933–1935.
*Unseren Kameraden bei der Wehrmacht diese Mitteilungen der
Reichsschrifttumskammer.* Leipzig: Reichsschrifttumskammer.
October/November 1944.
Die Weltliteratur: Berichte, Leseproben und Wertung. Dortmund:
Schwerter-Verlag. Vols. 15 (1940)–19 (1944).
Zentralblatt für Bibliothekswesen. Leipzig: Bibliographisches Institut.
Vols. 50 (1933)–61 (1947).

Memoirs, Diaries, and Correspondence of Writers, Publishers, and Booksellers

Andersch, Alfred. 2004. *The Cherries of Freedom. A Report.* Trans.
Michael Hulse. New Milford, CT: The Toby Press.
Baur, Karl. 1968/1985. *Wenn ich so zurückdenke … Ein Leben als
Verleger in bewegter Zeit.* Munich: dtv.
Becker, Heinrich. 1972. *Zwischen Wahn und Wahrheit. Autobiographie.*
Berlin: Verlag der Nation.
Benecke, Hans. 1995. *Eine Buchhandlung in Berlin. Erinnerung an eine
schwere Zeit.* Frankfurt/Main: Fischer.
Benn, Gottfried. 1977. *Briefe an F.W. Oelze 1932–1945.* Ed. Harald
Steinhagen and Jürgen Schröder. Wiesbaden: Limes.
Benn, Gottfried. 1986. *Briefe an Tilly Wedekind 1930–1955.* Ed.
Marguerite Valerie Schlüter. Stuttgart: Klett-Cotta.
Benn, Gottfried. 1992. *Briefe an Elinor Büller 1930–1937.* Ed.
Marguerite Valerie Schlüter. Stuttgart: Klett-Cotta.
Bergengruen, Werner. 1961. *Schreibtischerinnerungen.* Munich:
Nymphenburger.
Bermann Fischer, Gottfried. 1967. *Bedroht—Bewahrt. Der Weg eines
Verlegers.* Frankfurt/Main: Fischer.

Blunck, Hans Friedrich. 1952. *Unwegsame Zeiten. Lebensbericht 2.*
Mannheim: Kessler.
Carossa, Hans. 1951. *Ungleiche Welten.* Wiesbaden: Insel.
Carossa, Hans. 1978. *Hans Carossa. Briefe II 1919–1936.* Ed. Eva
Kampmann-Carossa. Frankfurt/Main: Insel.
Carossa, Hans. 1981. *Hans Carossa. Briefe III 1937–1956.* Ed. Eva
Kampmann-Carossa. Frankfurt/Main: Insel.
Carossa, Hans. 1993. *Tagebücher 1925–1935.* Ed. Eva Kampmann-
Carossa. Frankfurt/Main: Insel.
Claassen, Eugen. 1970. *In Büchern denken. Briefwechsel mit*
Autoren und Übersetzern. Ed. Hilde Claassen. Hamburg:
Claassen.
d'Hooghe, Marianne. 1969. *"Mitbetroffen."* Darmstadt: Darmstädter
Bücherstube.
Ebermayer, Erich. 1959. *Denn heute gehört uns Deutschland ...*
Persönliches und politisches Tagebuch. Von der Machtergreifung bis
zum 31. Dezember 1935. Hamburg: Zsolnay.
Ebermayer, Erich. 1966. *"... und morgen die ganze Welt." Erinnerungen*
an Deutschlands dunkle Zeit. Bayreuth: Hestia.
Eggebrecht, Axel. 1975. *Der halbe Weg. Zwischenbilanz einer Epoche.*
Reinbek: Rowohlt.
Fallada, Hans. 2008. *Ewig auf der Rutschbahn. Briefwechsel mit dem*
Rowohlt Verlag. Ed. Michael Töteberg and Sabine Buck. Reinbek:
Rowohlt.
Fallada, Hans. 2009. *In meinem fremden Land. Gefängnistagebuch*
1944. Ed. Jenny Williams and Sabine Lange. Berlin: Aufbau.
Fulda, Ludwig. 1988. *Briefwechsel 1882–1939. Zeugnisse des*
literarischen Lebens in Deutschland. Ed. Bernhard Gajek and
Wolfgang von Ungern-Sternberg. 2 vols. Frankfurt/Main: Lang.
Goldmann, Wilhelm [Verlag]. 1962. *Wilhelm Goldmann Verlag 1922–*
1962. Munich: Goldmann.
Gonski, Heinrich. 1977. *50 Jahre Buchhandlung Gonski Köln, 1.3.1927–*
28.2.1977. Cologne: Gonski.
Haecker, Theodor. 1950. *Journal in the Night.* Trans. Alexander Dru.
New York: Pantheon.
Haffner, Sebastian. 2003. *Defying Hitler: A Memoir.* Trans. Oliver
Pretzel. London: Phoenix.
Harnack, Axel von. 1956–7. Bibliothekar im "Dritten Reich." Kulturpo-
litische Erinnerungen an die Berliner Staatsbibliothek. *Neue*
Deutsche Hefte 3: 123–32.
Hausenstein, Wilhelm. 1967. *Licht unter dem Horizont. Tagebücher von*
1942 bis 1946. Munich: Bruckmann.
Hinze, Friedrich. 1999. *Frontbuchhandlung Paris: Erinnerungen eines*
Beteiligten. Friedrichsdorf: Hardt und Wörner.

Joerden, Rudolf. 1967. Dreimal Bibliothekar. Eine Abschiedsrede. *Bücherei und Bildung* 19: 135–9.

Kästner, Erich. 1981. *Mein liebes, gutes Muttchen, Du! Dein oller Junge. Briefe und Postkarten aus 30 Jahren.* Ed. Luiselotte Enderle. Hamburg: Knaus.

Kästner, Erich. 1998. Notabene 45. Ein Tagebuch. In *Splitter und Balken. Publizistik*, ed. Hans Sarkowicz and Franz Josef Görz, 301–480. Munich: Carl Hanser.

Kästner, Erich. 2007. *Das Blaue Buch. Kriegstagebuch und Roman-Notizen.* Ed. Ulrich von Bülow and Silke Becker. 2nd, rev. edn. Marbach: Deutsche Schillergesellschaft.

Klepper, Jochen. 1956. *Unter dem Schatten deiner Flügel. Aus den Tagebüchern 1932–1942.* Ed. Hildegard Klepper and Benno Mascher. Stuttgart: Deutsche Verlags-Anstalt.

Korn, Karl. 1975. *Lange Lehrzeit. Ein deutsches Leben.* Frankfurt/Main: Societäts-Verlag.

Kraft, Werner. 1973. *Spiegelung der Jugend.* Frankfurt/Main: Suhrkamp.

Lampe, Friedo. 1956. Briefe [1932–1945]. *Neue deutsche Hefte* 3: 108–22.

Landshoff, Fritz H. 1991. *Amsterdam, Keizersgracht 333, Querido Verlag. Erinnerungen eines Verlegers.* 2nd edn. Berlin: Aufbau.

Lange, Horst. 1979. *Tagebücher aus dem Zweiten Weltkrieg.* Ed. Hans Dieter Schäfer. Mainz: Hase & Koehler.

Loerke, Oskar. 1956. *Tagebücher 1903–1939.* Hermann Kasack. 2nd edn. Heidelberg: L. Schneider.

Mann, Thomas. 1977. *Tagebücher 1933–1934.* Ed. Peter de Mendelssohn. Frankfurt/Main: Fischer.

Niekisch, Ernst. 1958. *Gewagtes Leben. Begegnungen und Begebnisse.* Cologne: Kiepenheuer & Witsch.

Pechel, Rudolf. 1948. *Zwischen den Zeilen: Der Kampf einer Zeitschrift für Freiheit u. Recht. 1932–1942. Aufsätze.* Wiesentheid: Droemer.

Reck-Malleczewen, Friedrich. 1970. *Diary of a Man in Despair.* Trans. Paul Rubens. London: Macmillan.

Salomon, Ernst von. 1961. *Der Fragebogen.* Reinbek: Rowohlt.

Schaefer, Oda. 1970. *Auch wenn Du träumst, gehen die Uhren. Lebenserinnerungen.* Munich: Piper.

Seidel, Ina. 1980. *Aus den schwarzen Wachstuchheften. Monologe, Notizen, Fragmente.* Ed. Christian Ferber. Stuttgart: Deutsche Verlags-Anstalt.

Stresau, Hermann. 1948. *Von Jahr zu Jahr.* Berlin: Minerva.

Thiess, Frank. 1972. *Jahre des Unheils. Fragmente erlebter Geschichte.* Vienna: Zsolnay.

Wiechert, Ernst. [1945–6]. *Der Totenwald. Ein Bericht.* Munich: Desch.

Wiechert, Ernst. 1959. *Jahre und Zeiten.* Munich: Desch.

Winkler, Eugen Gottlob. 1949. *Briefe 1932–1936*. Ed. Walter Warnach. Bad Salzig: Rauch.

Post–1945 Works

Abele, Bernd. 1990. 1933–1938: Der Verlag Bruno Cassirer im Nationalsozialismus. *Buchhandelsgeschichte* 1990, no. 1: B1–B18.
Adam, Christian. 2010. *Lesen unter Hitler. Autoren, Bestseller, Leser im Dritten Reich*. Berlin: Galiani.
Adorno, Theodor W. 1977. Jene zwanziger Jahre. In *Gesammelte Schriften*, ed. Rolf Tiedemann, vol. 10/2, 499–506. Frankfurt/Main: Suhrkamp.
Adorno, Theodor W. 2002. "Marginalia on Mahler," in *Essays on Music*, ed. Richard Leppert. Berkeley: University of California Press, p. 612
Aigner, Dietrich. 1971. *Die Indizierung "schädlichen und unerwünschten Schrifttums" im Dritten Reich*. Frankfurt/Main: Buchhändler-Vereinigung.
Alker, Stefan, Christina Köstner, and Markus Stumpf, eds. 2008. *Bibliotheken in der NS-Zeit. Provenienzforschung und Bibliotheksgeschichte*. Göttingen: V&R unipress.
Aly, Götz. 2008. *Hitler's Beneficiaries: Plunder, Racial War, and the Nazi Welfare State*. Trans. Jefferson Chase. New York: Henry Holt.
Amann, Klaus. 1996. *Zahltag. Der Anschluß österreichischer Schriftsteller an das Dritte Reich*. 2nd, rev. edn. Bodenheim: Philo.
Amann, Klaus. 2007. *Robert Musil—Literatur und Politik. Mit einer Neuedition ausgewählter politischer Schriften aus dem Nachlass*. Reinbek: Rowohlt.
Anderhub, Andreas. 1989. Zwischen Umbruch und Tradition—Die Berliner Volksbüchereien während der Zeit des Nationalsozialismus. In *Bibliotheken während des Nationalsozialismus*, ed. Peter Vodosek and Manfred Komorowski, vol. I, 235–56. Wiesbaden: Harrassowitz.
Andrae, Friedrich, ed. 1970. *Volksbücherei und Nationalsozialismus. Materialien zur Theorie und Politik des öffentlichen Büchereiwesens in Deutschland 1933–1945*. Wiesbaden: Harrassowitz.
Aspetsberger, Friedbert. 1995. *Arnolt Bronnen. Biographie*. Vienna: Böhlau.
Barbian, Jan-Pieter. 1992. "Kulturwerte im Zeitkampf." Die Kulturabkommen des "Dritten Reiches" als Instrumente nationalsozialistischer Außenpolitik. *Archiv für Kulturgeschichte* 74, no. 2: 415–59.

Barbian, Jan-Pieter. 2000. Der Börsenverein der Deutschen Buchhändler 1933–1945. In *Der Börsenverein des Deutschen Buchhandels 1825–2000. Ein geschichtlicher Aufriß*, ed. Stephan Füssel, Georg Jäger, and Hermann Staub with Monika Estermann, 91–117. Frankfurt/Main: Buchhändler-Vereinigung.

Barbian, Jan-Pieter. 2008. *Die vollendete Ohnmacht? Schriftsteller, Verleger und Buchhändler im NS-Staat. Ausgewählte Aufsätze.* Essen: Klartext.

Barbian, Jan-Pieter. 2010. Die doppelte Indizierung. Verbote US-amerikanischer Literatur zwischen 1933 und 1941. In *Verfemt und verboten. Vorgeschichte und Folgen der Bücherverbrennungen 1933*, ed. Julius H. Schoeps and Werner Treß, 259–90. Hildesheim: Olms.

Bäre, Ralf. 1997. Hellmuth Langenbucher (1905–1980). Beschreibung einer literaturpolitischen Karriere. *Archiv für Geschichte des Buchwesens* 47: 249–308.

Barkai, Avraham. 1989. *From boycott to annihilation. The economic struggle of German Jews, 1933–1943.* Trans. William Templer. Hanover, NH: University Press of New England.

Baumgarten, Peter, and Monika I. Baumgarten, eds. 1998. *Baedeker— ein Name wird zur Weltmarke. Die Geschichte des Verlages.* Ostfildern: Baedeker.

Baur, Uwe, Karin Gradwohl-Schlacher, and Sabine Fuchs, eds. 1998. *Macht Literatur Krieg. Österreichische Literatur im National- sozialismus.* Vienna: Böhlau.

Beiknüfer, Uta, and Hania Siebenpfeiffer, eds. 2000. *Zwischen den Zeiten. Junge Literatur in Deutschland von 1933 bis 1945.* Hamburg: Libri.

Benner, Ernst Karl. 1954. Deutsche Literatur im Urteil des "Völkischen Beobachters" 1920–1933. Ein Beitrag zur publizistischen Vorge- schichte des 10.Mai 1933. Ph.D. dissertation, Ludwig-Maximilian- Universität Munich.

Berglund, Gisela. 1980. *Der Kampf um den Leser im Dritten Reich. Die Literaturpolitik der "Neuen Literatur" (Will Vesper) und der "Nationalsozialistischen Monatshefte."* Worms: Heintz.

Blasius, Dirk. 2005. *Weimars Ende. Bürgerkrieg und Politik 1930–1933.* Göttingen: Vandenhoeck und Ruprecht.

Bode, Dietrich. 2003. *Reclam. Daten, Bilder und Dokumente zur Verlagsgeschichte 1828–2003.* Stuttgart: Reclam.

Bödeker, Hans Erich, and Gerd-Josef Bötte, eds. 2008. *NS-Raubgut, Reichstauschstelle und Preußische Staatsbibliothek. Vorträge des Berliner Symposiums am 3. und 4. Mai 2007.* Munich: Saur.

Bodsch, Ingrid. 2008. Bonn. 10. Mai 1933 auf dem Marktplatz. In *Bücherverbrennungen in Deutschland 1933*, ed. Julius H. Schoeps and Werner Treß, 149–63. Hildesheim: Olms.

Boelcke, Willi A. 1983. *Die deutsche Wirtschaft 1930–1945. Interna des Reichswirtschaftsministeriums.* Düsseldorf: Droste.

Boese, Engelbrecht. 1981. Walter Hofmanns Institut für Leser- und Schrifttumskunde 1926–37. *Bibliothek* 5: 3–23.

Boese, Engelbrecht. 1983. Die Bestandspolitik der Öffentlichen Büchereien im Dritten Reich. *Bibliotheksdienst* 17: 263–82.

Boese, Engelbrecht. 1983. Die Säuberung der Leipziger Bücherhallen 1933–36. *Buch und Bibliothek* 35: 283–96.

Boese, Engelbrecht. 1987. *Das Öffentliche Bibliothekswesen im Dritten Reich.* Bad Honnef: Bock und Herchen.

Boese, Engelbrecht. 1989. Das Öffentliche Bibliothekswesen im Dritten Reich. In *Bibliotheken während des Nationalsozialismus,* ed. Peter Vodosek and Manfred Komorowski, vol. I, 91–111. Wiesbaden: Harrassowitz.

Bollenbeck, Georg. 1999. *Tradition, Avantgarde, Reaktion. Deutsche Kontroversen um die kulturelle Moderne 1880–1945.* Frankfurt/Main: Fischer.

Bollmus, Reinhard. 1970. *Das Amt Rosenberg und seine Gegner. Studien zum Machtkampf im nationalsozialistischen Herrschaftssystem.* Stuttgart: Deutsche Verlags-Anstalt.

Bramsted, Ernest K. 1965. *Goebbels and National Socialist Propaganda, 1925–1945.* East Lansing: Michigan State University Press.

Braun, Michael. 1997. *Stefan Andres. Leben und Werk.* Bonn: Bouvier.

Brenner, Hildegard. 1963. *Die Kunstpolitik des Nationalsozialismus.* Reinbek: Rowohlt.

Brenner, Hildegard. 1972. *Ende einer bürgerlichen Kunst-Institution. Die politische Formierung der Preußischen Akademie der Künste ab 1933.* Stuttgart: Deutsche Verlags-Anstalt.

Brenner, Reinhard, and Klaus Wisotzky, eds. 2002. *Der Schlüssel zur Welt. 100 Jahre Stadtbibliothek Essen.* Essen: Klartext.

Broszat, Martin. 1981. *The Hitler State. The Foundation and Development of the Internal Structure of the Third Reich.* Trans. John W. Hiden. London: Longman.

Browning, Christopher. 2004. *The Origins of the Final Solution. The Evolution of Nazi Jewish policy, September 1939–March 1942.* London: Heinemann.

Buchheim, Hans. 1968. The SS—Instrument of Domination. Trans. Richard Barry. In *Anatomy of the SS State,* Helmut Krausnick, Hans Buchheim, Martin Broszat, and Hans-Adolf Jacobsen, 127–301. London: Collins.

Buchholz, Godula. 2005. *Karl Buchholz. Buch- und Kunsthändler im 20. Jahrhundert. Sein Leben und seine Buchhandlungen und Galerien Berlin, New York, Bukarest, Lissabon, Madrid, Bogotá.* Cologne: DuMont.

Bühler, Edelgard, and Hans-Eugen Bühler. Die Wehrmacht als
Verleger. Annäherungsweisen an die Kultur der besetzten Länder.
Buchhandelsgeschichte 2002, no. 3: B74–B83.

Bühler, Hans-Eugen, with Edelgard Bühler. 2002. *Der Frontbuchhandel
1939–1945*. Frankfurt/Main: de Gruyter Saur.

Bühler, Hans-Eugen, and Klaus Kirbach. 1998. Die Wehrmachtsausgaben deutscher Verlage von 1939–1945, Teil 1: Feldpostausgaben
zwischen 1939 und 1945 und die Sonderaktion Feldpost 1942.
Archiv für Geschichte des Buchwesens 50: 251–94.

Bühler, Hans-Eugen, and Olaf Simons. 2004. *Die blendenden Geschäfte
des Matthias Lackas. Korruptionsermittlungen in der Verlagswelt des
Dritten Reichs*. Cologne: Pierre Marteau.

Burgess, Gordon, and Hans-Gerd Winter, eds. 1996. *"Pack das Leben
bei den Haaren." Wolfgang Borchert in neuer Sicht*. Hamburg: Dölling
und Galitz.

Burleigh, Michael. 2000. *The Third Reich. A New History*. London:
Macmillan.

Bussemer, Thymian. 2000. *Propaganda und Populärkultur. Konstruierte
Erlebniswelten im Nationalsozialismus*. Wiesbaden: Deutscher
Universitäts-Verlag.

Bussemer, Thymian. 2005. "Über Propaganda zu diskutieren, hat
wenig Zweck". Zur Medien- und Propagandapolitik von Joseph
Goebbels. In *Das Goebbels-Experiment. Propaganda und Politik*,
ed. Lutz Hachmeister and Michael Kloft, 49–63. Munich: Deutsche
Verlags-Anstalt.

Caemmerer, Christiane, and Walter Delabar, eds. 1996. *Dichtung im
Dritten Reich? Zur Literatur in Deutschland 1933–1945*. Opladen:
Westdeutscher Verlag.

Chatellier, Hildegard. 1973. Ernst Wiechert im Urteil der deutschen
Zeitschriftenpresse 1933–1945. Ein Beitrag zur national-sozialistischen
Literatur- und Pressepolitik. *Recherches Germaniques* 3: 153–95.

Conze, Eckart, Norbert Frei, Peter Hayes, and Moshe Zimmermann.
2010. *Das Amt und die Vergangenheit. Deutsche Diplomaten im
Dritten Reich und in der Bundesrepublik*. Munich: Blessing.

Corino, Karl. 2003. *Robert Musil. Eine Biographie*. Reinbek: Rowohlt.

Cuomo, Glenn R. 1986. Purging an "Art-Bolshevist": The Persecution of
Gottfried Benn in the Years 1933–1938. *German Studies Review* 9:
85–105.

Cuomo, Glenn R. 1989. *Career at the Cost of Compromise: Günter
Eich's Life and Work in the Years 1933–1945*. Amsterdam: Rodopi.

Cuomo, Glenn R., ed. 1995. *National Socialist Cultural Policy*. New York:
Palgrave Macmillan.

Dahm, Volker. 1986. Anfänge und Ideologie der Reichskulturkammer.
Die "Berufsgemeinschaft" als Instrument kulturpolitischer

Steuerung und sozialer Reglementierung. *Vierteljahreshefte für Zeitgeschichte* 34: 53–84.

Dahm, Volker. 1988. Kulturelles und geistiges Leben. In *Die Juden in Deutschland 1933–1945. Leben unter nationalsozialistischer Herrschaft*, ed. Wolfgang Benz, 75–267. Munich: Beck.

Dahm, Volker. 1993. *Das jüdische Buch im Dritten Reich*. 2nd, rev. edn. Munich: Beck.

Dahm, Volker. 1995. Nationale Einheit und partikulare Vielfalt. Zur Frage der kulturpolitischen Gleichschaltung im Dritten Reich. *Vierteljahreshefte für Zeitgeschichte* 43: 221–65.

Dahm, Volker. 1997. Ein Kampf um Familienerbe und Lebenswerk. Otto Wilhelm Klemm und die Reichsschrifttumskammer, 1937–1939. *Buchhandelsgeschichte* 1997, no. 3: B152–B159.

Dahm, Volker. 2000. Systemische Grundlagen und Lenkungsinstrumente der Kulturpolitik des Dritten Reiches. In *Im Dschungel der Macht. Intellektuelle Professionen unter Stalin und Hitler*, ed. Dietrich Beyrau, 244–59. Göttingen: Vandenhoeck und Ruprecht.

Delabar, Walter, Horst Denkler, and Erhard Schütz, eds. 1999. *Banalität mit Stil. Zur Widersprüchlichkeit der Literaturproduktion im Nationalsozialismus*. Berne: Lang.

Denk, Friedrich. 1995. *Die Zensur der Nachgeborenen. Zur regimekritischen Literatur im Dritten Reich*. Weilheim: Denk.

Denkler, Horst. 1999. Was war und was bleibt? Versuch einer Bestandsaufnahme der erzählenden Literatur aus dem "Dritten Reich." *Zeitschrift für Germanistik*, new series 9, no. 2: 279–93.

Denkler, Horst. 2002. Katz und Maus. Oppositionelle Schreibstrategien im "Dritten Reich." In *Geist und Macht. Schriftsteller und Staat im Mitteleuropa des "kurzen Jahrhunderts" 1914–1991*, ed. Marek Zybura, 27–38. Dresden: Thelem.

Denkler, Horst, and Karl Prümm, eds. 1976. *Die deutsche Literatur im Dritten Reich. Themen—Traditionen—Wirkungen*. Stuttgart: Reclam.

Denkler, Horst, and Eberhard Lämmert, eds. 1985. *"Das war ein Vorspiel nur ...." Berliner Colloquium zur Literaturpolitik im "Dritten Reich."* Berlin: Frölich und Kaufmann.

Deutsche Buch-Gemeinschaft, ed. 1974. *50 Jahre Deutsche Buch-Gemeinschaft 1924–1974*. Darmstadt: Deutsche Buch-Gemeinschaft.

Diederichs, Ulf. 1999–2000. Verleger im Schatten. Der Eugen Diederichs Verlag 1929 bis 1948. *Buchhandelsgeschichte* 1999, no. 3: B90–B155; 1999, no. 4: B138–B163; 2000, no. 1: B2–B16.

Döring, Jörg. 2003. *"... ich stellte mich unter, ich machte mich klein ...." Wolfgang Koeppen 1933–1948*. Frankfurt/Main: Suhrkamp.

Döscher, Hans-Jürgen. 1987. *Das Auswärtige Amt im Dritten Reich. Diplomatie im Schatten der "Endlösung."* Berlin: Siedler.

Dressler, Fridolin. 1989. Die Bayerische Staatsbibliothek im Dritten Reich. Eine historische Skizze. In *Bibliotheken während des Nationalsozialismus*, ed. Peter Vodosek and Manfred Komorowski, vol. I, 49–89. Wiesbaden: Harrassowitz.

Dufay, François. 2000. *Le voyage d'automne: Octobre 1941, des écrivains français en Allemagne*. Paris: Plon (published in German as *Die Herbstreise*, 2001).

Düsterberg, Rolf. 2004. *Hanns Johst: "Der Barde der SS." Karrieren eines deutschen Dichters*. Paderborn: Schöningh.

Düsterberg, Rolf, ed. 2009. *Dichter für das "Dritte Reich." Biografische Studien zum Verhältnis von Literatur und Ideologie. 10 Autorenporträts*. Bielefeld: Aisthesis Verlag.

Düsterberg, Rolf, ed. 2011. *Dichter für das "Dritte Reich." Band 2. Biografische Studien zum Verhältnis von Literatur und Ideologie. 9 Autorenporträts*. Bielefeld: Aisthesis Verlag.

Dyck, Joachim. 2006. *Der Zeitzeuge. Gottfried Benn 1929–1949*. Göttingen: Wallstein.

Echternkamp, Jörg, ed. 2004–5. *Die deutsche Kriegsgesellschaft 1939 bis 1945*. Vols. 9/1 and 9/2 of *Das Deutsche Reich und der Zweite Weltkrieg*. Munich: Deutsche Verlags-Anstalt.

Ehrke-Rotermund, Heidrun, and Erwin Rotermund, eds. 1999. *Zwischenreiche und Gegenwelten. Texte und Vorstudien zur "Verdeckten Schreibweise" im "Dritten Reich."* Munich: Fink.

Essner, Cornelia. 2002. *Die "Nürnberger Gesetze" oder Die Verwaltung des Rassenwahns 1933–1945*. Paderborn: Schöningh.

Evans, Richard J. 2005. *The Third Reich in Power 1933–1939*. London: Penguin.

Evans, Richard J. 2008. *The Third Reich at War 1939–1945*. London: Penguin.

Faust, Anselm. 1973. *Der Nationalsozialistische Deutsche Studentenbund*. 2 vols. Düsseldorf: Schwann.

Faustmann, Uwe Julius. 1995. *Die Reichskulturkammer. Aufbau, Funktion und rechtliche Grundlagen einer Körperschaft des öffentlichen Rechts im nationalsozialistischen Regime*. Aachen: Shaker.

Fest, Joachim C. 1970. *The Face of the Third Reich: Portraits of the Nazi Leadership*. Trans. Michael Bullock. London: Weidenfeld & Nicholson.

Fischer, Erica, and Simone Ladwig-Winters. 2004. *Die Wertheims. Geschichte einer Familie*. Berlin: Rowohlt.

Fischer, Ernst. 1980. Der "Schutzverband deutscher Schriftsteller" 1909–1933. *Archiv für Geschichte des Buchwesens* 21: cols. 1–666.

Fischer, Ernst. 2011. *Verleger, Buchhändler & Antiquare aus Deutschland und Österreich in der Emigration nach 1933. Ein biographisches Handbuch*. Elbingen: Verband deutscher Antiquare.

Flachowsky, Sören. 2000. *Die Bibliothek der Berliner Universität während der Zeit des Nationalsozialismus.* Berlin: Logos.

Frei, Norbert. 1993. *National Socialist Rule in Germany. The Führerstaat 1933–1945.* Trans. Simon B. Steyne. Oxford: Blackwell.

Friedländer, Saul. 1997–2007. *Nazi Germany and the Jews.* 2 vols. New York: HarperCollins.

Friedländer, Saul, Norbert Frei, Trutz Rendtorff, and Reinhard Wittmann. 2002. *Bertelsmann im Dritten Reich.* 2 vols. Munich: Bertelsmann.

Friedo-Lampe-Gesellschaft e.V., ed. 1999. *Ein Autor wird wiederentdeckt. Friedo Lampe 1899–1945.* Göttingen: Wallstein.

Friedrich, Jörg. 2006. *The Fire. The Bombing of Germany 1940–1945.* Trans. Allison Brown. New York: Columbia University Press.

Funke, Cornelia Caroline. 1999. *"Im Verleger verkörpert sich das Gesicht seiner Zeit." Unternehmensführung und Programmgestaltung im Gustav Kiepenheuer Verlag 1909 bis 1944.* Wiesbaden: Harrassowitz.

Gahlings, Ute. 2000. *"An mir haben die Nazis beinahe ganze Arbeit geleistet." Über den Umgang der Nationalsozialisten mit Hermann Graf Keyserling.* In *Deutsche Autoren des Ostens als Gegner und Opfer des Nationalsozialismus,* ed. Frank-Lothar Kroll, 47–74. Berlin: Duncker & Humblot.

Garke-Rothbarth, Thomas. 2008. *".. für unseren Betrieb lebensnotwendig ..." Georg von Holtzbrinck als Verlagsunternehmer im Dritten Reich.* Munich: Saur.

Genge, Hans-Joachim. 1992. Militärbibliotheken im Dritten Reich. In *Bibliotheken während des Nationalsozialismus,* ed. Peter Vodosek and Manfred Komorowski, vol. II, 169–87. Wiesbaden: Harrassowitz.

Gieselbusch, Hermann, Dirk Moldenhauer, Uwe Naumann, and Michael Töteberg. 2008. *100 Jahre Rowohlt. Eine illustrierte Chronik.* Reinbek: Rowohlt.

Gillessen, Günther. 1986. *Auf verlorenem Posten. Die Frankfurter Zeitung im Dritten Reich.* Berlin: Siedler.

Goebel, Klaus. 2009. Von der Gewalt und ihren Schergen. Rudolf Alexander Schröders Ablehnung des Nationalsozialismus. In *Religion braucht Bildung—Bildung braucht Religion,* ed. Lars Bednorz, Olaf Kühl-Freudenstein, and Magdalena Munzert, 123–34. Würzburg: Königshausen & Neumann.

Graeb-Könneker, Sebastian. 1996. *Autochthone Modernität. Eine Untersuchung der vom Nationalsozialismus geförderten Literatur.* Opladen: Westdeutscher Verlag.

Graeb-Könneker, Sebastian, ed. 2001. *Literatur im Dritten Reich. Dokumente und Texte.* Stuttgart: Reclam.

Graf, Christoph. 1983. *Politische Polizei zwischen Demokratie und Diktatur. Die Entwicklung der preußischen Politischen Polizei vom Staatsschutzorgan der Weimarer Republik zum Geheimen Staatspolizeiamt des Dritten Reiches.* Berlin: Colloquium.

Graf, Hans-Dieter. 1988. Die Verlags- und Sortimentsbuchhandlung Franz Borgmeyer in der Zeit des Nationalsozialismus. *Gutenberg-Jahrbuch* 63: 206–43.

Graf, Hans-Dieter. 1989. Der Trierer Buchdrucker Josef Herzig und das Schicksal seiner Druckerei im Dritten Reich. *Gutenberg-Jahrbuch* 64: 249–88.

Graf, Johannes. 1995. *"Die notwendige Reise". Reisen und Reiseliteratur junger Autoren während des Nationalsozialismus.* Stuttgart: M&P.

Graf, Johannes, ed. 2004. *Heimat, liebe Heimat. Exil und Innere Emigration (1933–1945). Das 3. Berliner Symposium.* Berlin: Bostelmann und Siebenhaar.

Greguletz, Alexander. 1992. Die Preußische Staatsbibliothek in den ersten Jahren des Nationalsozialismus (1933–1936). In *Bibliotheken während des Nationalsozialismus*, ed. Peter Vodosek and Manfred Komorowski, vol. II, 243–71. Wiesbaden: Harrassowitz.

Grosser, J. F. G., ed. 1963. *Die große Kontroverse. Ein Briefwechsel um Deutschland.* Hamburg: Nagel.

Haase, Yorck Alexander. 2000. Die Bibliothekartage in der Zeit des Nationalsozialismus. In *Verein Deutscher Bibliothekare 1900–2000. Festschrift*, ed. Engelbert Plassmann and Ludger Syré, 81–100. Wiesbaden: Harrassowitz.

Habermann, Alexandra, Rainer Klemmt, and Frauke Siefkes. 1985. *Lexikon deutscher wissenschaftlicher Bibliothekare 1925–1980.* Frankfurt/Main: Klostermann.

Hachmeister, Lutz. 1998. *Der Gegnerforscher. Die Karriere des SS-Führers Franz Alfred Six.* Munich: Beck.

Hachmeister, Lutz, and Michael Kloft, eds. 2005. *Das Goebbels-Experiment. Propaganda und Politik.* Munich: Deutsche Verlags-Anstalt.

Hachtmann, Rüdiger. 2012. *Das Wirtschaftsimperium der Deutschen Arbeitsfront 1933–1945.* Göttingen: Wallstein.

Haefs, Wilhelm, ed. 2009. *Nationalsozialismus und Exil 1933–1945.* Munich: Hanser.

Haefs, Wilhelm, and Walter Schmitz, eds. 2002. *Martin Raschke (1905–1943). Leben und Werk.* Dresden: Thelem.

Haffner, Sebastian. 1987. *Germany's Self-Destruction. Germany from Bismarck to Hitler.* Trans. Jean Steinberg. London: Simon & Schuster.

Hale, Oron J. 1964. *The Captive Press in the Third Reich.* Princeton, NJ: Princeton University Press.

Hall, Murray G. 1988. Jüdische Buchhändler und Verleger im Schicksalsjahr 1938 in Wien. *Anzeiger des österreichischen Buchhandels* 123, no. 5: 40–5.

Hall, Murray G. 1988. Verlagswesen in Österreich 1938 bis 1945. In *Kontinuität und Bruch 1938–1945–1955*. Beiträge zur österreichischen Kultur- und Wissenschaftsgeschichte, ed. Friedrich Stadler, 83–92. Vienna: Jugend und Volk.

Hall, Murray G. 1994. *Der Paul Zsolnay Verlag. Von der Gründung bis zur Rückkehr aus dem Exil*. Tübingen: Niemeyer.

Hall, Murray G., ed. 1994. *70 Jahre Paul Zsolnay Verlag 1924–1994*. Vienna: Zsolnay.

Hall, Murray G., and Christina Köstner. 2006. *"... allerlei für die Nationalbibliothek zu ergattern ..." Eine österreichische Institution in der NS-Zeit*. Vienna: Böhlau.

Hanuschek, Sven. 1999. *Keiner blickt dir hinter das Gesicht. Das Leben Erich Kästners*. Munich: Hanser.

Happel, Hans-Gerd. 1989. *Das wissenschaftliche Bibliothekswesen im Nationalsozialismus. Unter besonderer Berücksichtigung der Universitätsbibliotheken*. Munich: Saur.

Härtel, Christian. 2004. *Stromlinien. Wilfrid Bade—Eine Karriere im Dritten Reich*. Berlin: be.bra Wissenschaft.

Härtel, Christian. 2005. "Soldat unter Soldaten". Der Journalist Joseph Goebbels. In *Das Goebbels-Experiment. Propaganda und Politik*, ed. Lutz Hachmeister and Michael Kloft, 16–28. Munich: Deutsche Verlags-Anstalt.

Hausmann, Frank-Rutger. 2004. *"Dichte, Dichter, tage nicht!" Die Europäische Schriftsteller-Vereinigung in Weimar 1941–1948*. Frankfurt/Main: Klostermann.

Heiber, Helmut. 1962. *Joseph Goebbels*. Berlin: Colloquium.

Herder Verlag. 1976. *175 Jahre Herder: kleines Alphabet einer Verlagsarbeit*. Freiburg im Breisgau: Herder.

Hermand, Jost, and Wigand Lange. 1999. *"Wollt ihr Thomas Mann wiederhaben?" Deutschland und die Emigranten*. Hamburg: Europäische Verlags-Anstalt.

Hermand, Jost, Helmut Peitsch, and Klaus Rüdiger Scherpe, eds. 1982. *Nachkriegsliteratur in Westdeutschland 1945–49. Schreibweisen, Gattungen, Institutionen*. Berlin: Argument.

Heyde, Konrad. 1989. Die Staatlichen Volksbüchereistellen am Beispiel Freiburg im Breisgau. In *Bibliotheken während des Nationalsozialismus*, ed. Peter Vodosek and Manfred Komorowski, vol. I, 113–61. Wiesbaden: Harrassowitz.

Hexelschneider, Gerd. 1992. Joseph Caspar Witsch als Volksbibliothekar in den Jahren 1936 bis 1942. *Buch und Bibliothek* 44: 436–43.

Hillesheim, Jürgen, and Elisabeth Michael. 1993. *Lexikon nationalsozialistischer Dichter. Biographien—Analysen—Bibliographien*. Würzburg: Königshausen und Neumann.

Hoerle, W. Scott. 2003. *Hans Friedrich Blunck. Poet and Nazi Collaborator, 1888–1961*. Oxford: Lang.

Hoffmeister, Barbara. 2009. *S. Fischer, der Verleger. Eine Lebensbeschreibung*. Frankfurt/Main: Fischer.

Holzbach, Heidrun. 1981. *Das "System Hugenberg." Die Organisation bürgerlicher Sammlungspolitik vor dem Aufstieg der NSDAP*. Stuttgart: Deutsche Verlags-Anstalt.

Holzhausen, Hans-Dieter. 1989. Gottlieb Fritz und seine Entfernung aus dem Amt des Direktors der Berliner Stadtbibliothek 1933/34. In *Bibliotheken während des Nationalsozialismus*, ed. Peter Vodosek and Manfred Komorowski, vol. I, 261–71. Wiesbaden: Harrassowitz.

Holzner, Johann, and Karl Müller, eds. 1998. *Literatur der "inneren Emigration" aus Österreich*. Vienna: Döcker.

Hoser, Paul. 2012. Franz Eher Nachf. Verlag (Zentralverlag der NSDAP), www.historisches-lexikon-bayerns.de/artikel/artikel_44492 (14 December 2012).

Hövel, Paul. 1984. Die Wirtschaftsstelle des deutschen Buchhandels, Berlin 1935 bis 1945. Ein Augenzeugenbericht. *Buchhandelsgeschichte* 1984, no. 1: B1–B16.

Hübinger, Paul Egon. 1974. *Thomas Mann, die Universität Bonn und die Zeitgeschichte. Drei Kapitel deutscher Vergangenheit aus dem Leben des Dichters 1905–1955*. Munich: Oldenbourg.

Huder, Walter. 1986. Die sogenannte Reinigung. Die "Gleichschaltung" der Sektion für Dichtkunst der Preußischen Akademie der Künste 1933. *Exilforschung* 4: 144–59.

Humbach, Karl-Theo, ed. 2001. *Der Verlag Herder 1801–2001. Chronologischer Abriss seiner Geschichte mit Synchronopse zum Geistes- und Weltgeschehen*. Freiburg im Breisgau: Herder.

Hüttenberger, Peter. 1976. Nationalsozialistische Polykratie. *Geschichte und Gesellschaft* 2: 417–42 (abridged translation: National Socialist Polycracy. In *Nazism*, ed. Neil Gregor, 194–8. Oxford: Oxford University Press, 2000).

Jens, Inge. 1979. *Dichter zwischen rechts und links. Die Geschichte der Sektion für Dichtkunst an der Preußischen Akademie der Künste, dargestellt nach den Dokumenten*. Munich: Piper.

Jung, Otmar 2006. Der literarische Judenstern. Die Indizierung der "jüdischen" Rechtsliteratur im nationalsozialistischen Deutschland. *Vierteljahreshefte für Zeitgeschichte* 54: 25–59.

Jütte, Werner. 1987. Volksbibliothekare im Nationalsozialismus. Einige Anmerkungen zum Beitrag von Adolf von Morzé. *Buch und Bibliothek* 39: 345–8.

Kalbhenn, Rita. 1992. Werkbibliotheken im Dritten Reich. In *Bibliotheken während des Nationalsozialismus*, ed. Peter

Vodosek and Manfred Komorowski, vol. II, 27–51. Wiesbaden: Harrassowitz.

Kast, Raimund. 1991. Der deutsche Leihbuchhandel und seine Organisation im 20. Jahrhundert. *Archiv für Geschichte des Buchwesens* 36: 165–349.

Kater, Michael H. 1975. *Studentenschaft und Rechtsradikalismus in Deutschland 1918–1933*. Hamburg: Hoffmann und Campe.

Der Katholizismus in Deutschland und der Verlag Herder 1801–1951. 1951. Freiburg im Breisgau: Herder.

Keiderling, Thomas. 2005. *F. A. Brockhaus 1905–2005*. Leipzig: Brockhaus.

Keiderling, Thomas. 2008. *Unternehmer im Nationalsozialismus. Machtkampf um den Konzern Koehler & Volckmar AG & Co.* 2nd, rev. edn. Beucha: Sax.

Keiderling, Thomas. 2012. *Aufstieg und Niedergang der Buchstadt Leipzig*. Beucha: Sax.

Ketelsen, Uwe-Karsten. 1980. Kulturpolitik des III. Reiches und Ansätze zu ihrer Interpretation. *Text & Kontext* 8: 217–42.

Ketelsen, Uwe-Karsten. 1994. *Literatur und Drittes Reich*. 2nd, rev. edn. Greifswald: SH-Verlag.

Kettel, Andreas. 1981. *Volksbibliothekare und Nationalsozialismus. Zum Verhalten führender Berufsvertreter während der nationalsozialistischen Machtübernahme*. Cologne: Pahl-Rugenstein.

Kiaulehn, Walther. 1967. *Mein Freund, der Verleger. Ernst Rowohlt und seine Zeit*. Reinbek: Rowohlt.

Kilcher, Andreas B., ed. 2000. *Lexikon der deutsch-jüdischen Literatur. Jüdische Autorinnen und Autoren deutscher Sprache von der Aufklärung bis in die Gegenwart*. Stuttgart: Metzler.

Kirchner, Doris. 1993. *Doppelbödige Wirklichkeit. Magischer Realismus und nicht-faschistische Literatur*. Tübingen: Stauffenburg.

Klotzbücher, Alois. 1992. Städtische Bibliotheken im Ruhrgebiet während des Nationalsozialismus. In *Bibliotheken während des Nationalsozialismus*, ed. Peter Vodosek and Manfred Komorowski, vol. II, 53–89. Wiesbaden: Harrassowitz.

Knoche, Michael, and Wolfgang Schmitz, eds. 2011. *Wissenschaftliche Bibliothekare im Nationalsozialismus. Handlungsspielräume, Kontinuitäten, Deutungsmuster*. Wiesbaden: Harrassowitz.

Komorowski, Manfred. 1989. Deutsche Bibliothekspolitik in der Sowjetunion (1941–1944). In *Bibliotheken während des Nationalsozialismus*, ed. Peter Vodosek and Manfred Komorowski, vol. I, 475–84. Wiesbaden: Harrassowitz.

Komorowski, Manfred. 1989. Die wissenschaftlichen Bibliotheken während des Nationalsozialismus. In *Bibliotheken während des Nationalsozialismus*, ed. Peter Vodosek and Manfred Komorowski, vol. I, 1–23. Wiesbaden: Harrassowitz.

Komorowski, Manfred. 1992. Die Auseinandersetzung mit dem nationalsozialistischen Erbe im wissenschaftlichen Bibliothekswesen nach 1945. In *Bibliotheken während des Nationalsozialismus*, ed, Peter Vodosek and Manfred Komorowski, vol. II, 273–95. Wiesbaden: Harrassowitz.

Komorowski, Manfred. 1992. Die Tagungsprotokolle des Reichsbeirats für Bibliotheksangelegenheiten (1937–1943). *Bibliothek. Forschung und Praxis* 16: 66–90.

Krings, Stefan. 2005. Das Propagandaministerium. Joseph Goebbels und seine Spezialisten. In *Das Goebbels-Experiment. Propaganda und Politik*, ed. Lutz Hachmeister and Michael Kloft, 29–48. Munich: Deutsche Verlags-Anstalt.

Krohn, Claus-Dieter, Erwin Rotermund, Lutz Winckler, and Wulf Köpke, eds. 1994. *Aspekte der künstlerischen inneren Emigration 1933–1945*. Special issue, *Exilforschung: Ein internationales Jahrbuch* 12.

Kroll, Frank-Lothar, ed. 2003. *Die totalitäre Erfahrung. Deutsche Literatur und Drittes Reich*. Berlin: Duncker & Humblot.

Kroll, Frank-Lothar, and Rüdiger von Voss, eds. 2012. *Schriftsteller im Widerstand. Facetten und Probleme der "Inneren Emigration."* Göttingen: Wallstein.

Krosta, Frank. 2008. *Die Universitätsbibliothek Bonn in der Zeit des Nationalsozialismus. Personal, Erwerbung, Benutzung*. Munich: Meidenbauer.

Kugel, Wilfried. 1992. *Der Unverantwortliche. Das Leben des Hanns Heinz Ewers*. Düsseldorf: Grupello.

Kuttner, Sven, and Bernd Reifenberg, eds. 2004. *Das bibliothekarische Gedächtnis. Aspekte der Erinnerungskultur an braune Zeiten im deutschen Bibliothekswesen*. Marburg: Universitäts-Bibliothek.

Labach, Michael. 2000. Der VDB während des Nationalsozialismus. In *Verein Deutscher Bibliothekare 1900–2000. Festschrift*, ed. Engelbert Plassmann and Ludger Syré, 59–80. Wiesbaden: Harrassowitz.

Lämmert, Eberhard. 1975. Beherrschte Prosa. Poetische Lizenzen in Deutschland zwischen 1933 und 1945. *Neue Rundschau* 86: 404–21.

Lamp, Hannes. 2002. *Fallada unter Wölfen. Schreiben im Dritten Reich. Die Geschichte des Inflationsromans "Wolf unter Wölfen."* Friedland: Steffen.

Laqueur, Walter. 1974. *Weimar: A Cultural History 1918–33*. London: Weidenfeld & Nicholson.

Leitel, Erich. 1958. Die Aufnahme der amerikanischen Literatur in Deutschland. Übersetzungen der Jahre 1914–1944. Mit einer Bibliographie. Ph.D. diss. Friedrich-Schiller-Universität Jena.

Lemberg, Margret, ed. 2001. *Verboten und nicht verbrannt*. 2 vols. Marburg: Universitäts-Bibliothek.

Leyh, Georg. 1947. *Die deutschen wissenschaftlichen Bibliotheken nach dem Krieg.* Tübingen: Mohr.

Linthout, Ine van. 2012. *Das Buch in der nationalsozialistischen Propagandapolitik.* Berlin: de Gruyter.

Lokatis, Siegfried. 1992. Hanseatische Verlagsanstalt. Politisches Buch-marketing im "Dritten Reich." *Archiv für Geschichte des Buchwesens* 38: 1–189.

Lokatis, Siegfried, and Ingrid Sonntag, eds. 2011. *100 Jahre Kiepenheuer Verlage.* Berlin: Links.

Longerich, Peter. 1992. *Hitlers Stellvertreter. Führung der Partei und Kontrolle des Staatsapparates durch den Stab Heß und die Partei-Kanzlei Bormann.* Munich: Saur.

Longerich, Peter. 1998. *Politik der Vernichtung. Eine Gesamtdarstellung der nationalsozialistischen Judenverfolgung.* Munich: Piper.

Longerich, Peter. 2008. *Heinrich Himmler. Eine Biographie.* Munich: Siedler.

Longerich, Peter. 2010. *Joseph Goebbels. Biographie.* Munich: Siedler.

Loewy, Ernst. 1967. *Literatur unterm Hakenkreuz. Das Dritte Reich und seine Dichtung. Eine Dokumentation.* Frankfurt/Main: Europäische Verlagsanstalt.

Maase, Kaspar. 1997. *Grenzenloses Vergnügen. Der Aufstieg der Massenkultur 1850–1970.* Frankfurt/Main: Fischer.

Mallmann, Klaus-Michael, and Gerhard Paul. 1993. Resistenz oder loyale Widerwilligkeit? Anmerkungen zu einem umstrittenen Begriff. *Zeitschrift für Geschichtswissenschaft* 41, no. 2: 96–116.

Mallmann, Klaus-Michael, and Gerhard Paul, eds. 2004. *Karrieren der Gewalt. Nationalsozialistische Täterbiographien.* Darmstadt: WBG.

Mallmann, Marion. 1978. *"Das Innere Reich." Analyse einer konservativen Kulturzeitschrift im Dritten Reich.* Bonn: Bouvier.

Mank, Dieter. 1981. *Erich Kästner im nationalsozialistischen Deutschland 1933–1945: Zeit ohne Werk?* Frankfurt/Main: Lang.

Marks, Erwin. 1975. Dem Andenken deutscher antifaschistischer Bibliothekare (with a response by Rudolf Joerden: Bemerkungen zum Aufsatz von Erwin Marks). *Buch und Bibliothek* 27: 807–16.

Meyer, Andreas. 1989. Die Verlagsfusion Langen-Müller. Zur Buchmarkt- und Kulturpolitik des Deutschnationalen Handlungsgehilfen-Verbands (DHV) in der Endphase der Weimarer Republik. *Archiv für Geschichte des Buchwesens* 32: cols. 1–271.

Meyer, Jochen, ed. 1985. *Berlin-Provinz. Literarische Kontroversen um 1930.* Marbach: Deutsche Schillergesellschaft.

Mirbt, Karl-Wolfgang. 1964. Theorie und Technik der Camouflage. Die "Deutsche Rundschau" im Dritten Reich als Beispiel publizistischer Opposition unter totalitärer Gewalt. *Publizistik* 9: 3–16.

Mittenzwei, Werner. 1992. *Der Untergang einer Akademie oder Die Mentalität des ewigen Deutschen. Der Einfluß nationalkonservativer Dichter an der Preußischen Akademie der Künste 1918 bis 1947.* Berlin: Aufbau.

Möller, Horst. 1984. *Exodus der Kultur. Schriftsteller, Wissenschaftler und Künstler in der Emigration nach 1933.* Munich: Beck.

Mommsen, Hans. 1966. *Beamtentum im Dritten Reich. Mit ausgewählten Quellen zur nationalsozialistischen Beamtenpolitik.* Stuttgart: Deutsche Verlags-Anstalt.

Mommsen, Hans. 1991. *Der Nationalsozialismus und die deutsche Gesellschaft. Ausgewählte Aufsätze.* Ed. Lutz Niethammer and Bernd Weisbrod. Reinbek: Rowohlt.

Morzé, Adolf von. 1971. Erinnerung an Wilhelm Schuster (10.6.1888–15.3.1971). *Buch und Bibliothek* 23: 733–7.

Morzé, Adolf von. 1987. Verlust des Bildungsreiches. Volksbibliothekare im Nationalsozialismus. *Buch und Bibliothek* 39: 106–26.

Müller-Jerina, Alwin. 1992. Zwischen Ausgrenzung und Vernichtung. Jüdische Bibliothekare im Dritten Reich. In *Bibliotheken während des Nationalsozialismus*, ed. Peter Vodosek and Manfred Komorowski, vol. II, 227–42. Wiesbaden: Harrassowitz.

Nagel, Anne C. 2012. *Hitlers Bildungsreformer. Das Reichsministerium für Wissenschaft, Erziehung und Volksbildung 1934–1945.* Frankfurt/Main: Fischer.

Oelze, Klaus-Dieter. 1990. *Das Feuilleton der Kölnischen Zeitung im Dritten Reich.* Frankfurt/Main: Lang.

Orlowski, Hubert. 1985. "Krakauer Zeitung" 1939–1945. Nichtnationalsozialistische Literatur im Generalgouvernement? In *"Das war ein Vorspiel nur ...." Berliner Colloquium zur Literaturpolitik im "Dritten Reich,"* ed. Horst Denkler and Eberhard Lämmert, 136–62. Berlin: Frölich und Kaufmann.

Paul, Gerhard. 1990. *Aufstand der Bilder. Die NS-Propaganda vor 1933.* Bonn: Dietz.

Paul, Gerhard, and Klaus-Michael Mallmann, eds. 1995. *Die Gestapo—Mythos und Realität.* Darmstadt: Wissenschaftliche Buchgesellschaft.

Peukert, Detlev J.K. 1987. *Die Weimarer Republik. Krisenjahre der Klassischen Moderne.* Frankfurt/Main: Suhrkamp.

Pfäfflin, Friedrich, and Ingrid Kussmaul, eds. 1986. *S. Fischer, Verlag. Von der Gründung bis zur Rückkehr aus dem Exil. Eine Ausstellung des Deutschen Literaturarchivs im Schiller-Nationalmuseum Marbach am Neckar.* 2nd, rev. edn. Marbach: Deutsches Literatur-Archiv.

Pfoser, Alfred. 1989. Die Wiener Städtischen Büchereien im Nationalsozialismus. In *Bibliotheken während des Nationalsozialismus,* ed.

Peter Vodosek and Manfred Komorowski, vol. I, 273–93. Wiesbaden: Harrassowitz.

Pfoser, Alfred. 1992. Die Leipziger Radikalkur in Wien. In *Bibliotheken während des Nationalsozialismus*, ed. Peter Vodosek and Manfred Komorowski, vol. II, 91–110. Wiesbaden: Harrassowitz.

Piper, Ernst. 2005. *Alfred Rosenberg. Hitlers Chefideologe*. Munich: Blessing.

Pirożyński, Jan, and Krystyna Ruszajowa. 1989. Die national-sozialistische Bibliothekspolitik in Polen während des Zweiten Weltkrieges. In *Bibliotheken während des Nationalsozialismus*, ed. Peter Vodosek and Manfred Komorowski, vol. I, 199–232. Wiesbaden: Harrassowitz.

Plassmann, Engelbert, and Ludger Syré, eds. 2000. *Verein Deutscher Bibliothekare 1900–2000. Festschrift*. Wiesbaden: Harrassowitz.

Plessner, Helmuth. 1982. Die Legende von den zwanziger Jahren. In *Gesammelte Schriften*, ed. Günter Dux, Odo Marquard, and Elisabeth Ströker, vol. VI, 263–79. Frankfurt/Main: Suhrkamp.

Plöckinger, Othmar. 2006. *Geschichte eines Buches: Adolf Hitlers "Mein Kampf" 1922–1945*. Munich: Oldenbourg.

Prinz, Michael, and Rainer Zitelmann, eds. 1991. *Nationalsozialismus und Modernisierung*. Darmstadt: Wissenschaftliche Buchgesellschaft.

Rathkolb, Oliver. 1991. *Führertreu und gottbegnadet. Künstlereliten im Dritten Reich*. Vienna: ÖBV.

Rebentisch, Dieter. 1989. *Führerstaat und Verwaltung im Zweiten Weltkrieg. Verfassungsentwicklung und Verwaltungspolitik 1939–1945*. Stuttgart: Steiner.

Reichel, Peter. 1991. *Der schöne Schein des Dritten Reiches. Faszination und Gewalt des Faschismus*. Munich: Hanser.

Reiner, Guido. 1974. *Ernst Wiechert im Dritten Reich. Eine Dokumentation. Mit einem Verzeichnis der Ernst-Wiechert-Manuskripte im Haus Königsberg*. Paris: G. Reiner.

Reinhardt, Stephan. 1990. *Alfred Andersch. Eine Biographie*. Zurich: Diogenes.

Renner, Gerhard. 1986. Österreichische Schriftsteller und der Nationalsozialismus (1933–1945). Der "Bund der deutschen Schriftsteller Österreichs" und der Aufbau der Reichsschrifttumskammer in der "Ostmark." *Archiv für Geschichte des Buchwesens* 27: 195–314.

Renner, Gerhard. 1990. Frank Thiess: Ein "freier Schriftsteller" im Nationalsozialismus. *Buchhandelsgeschichte* 1990, no. 2: B41–B50.

Richards, Pamela Spence. 1985. German Libraries and Scientific and Technical Information in Nazi Germany. *The Library Quarterly* 55: 151–73.

Richards, Pamela Spence. 1992. Deutschlands wissenschaftliche Verbindungen mit dem Ausland 1933–1945. In *Bibliotheken während des Nationalsozialismus*, ed. Peter Vodosek and Manfred Komorowski, vol. II, 111–32. Wiesbaden: Harrassowitz.

Riemschneider, Ernst G. 1975. *Der Fall Klepper. Eine Dokumentation*. Stuttgart: Deutsche Verlags-Anstalt.

Rischer, Walter. 1972. *Die nationalsozialistische Kulturpolitik in Düsseldorf 1933–1945*. Düsseldorf: Triltsch.

Robenek, Brigitte. 1983. *Geschichte der Stadtbücherei Köln von den Anfängen im Jahre 1890 bis zum Ende des Zweiten Weltkrieges*. Cologne: Greven.

Rosenkranz, Jutta. 2007. *Mascha Kaléko. Biografie*. Munich: dtv.

Röska, Günther. 2000. Walter Hofmann und der Nationalsozialismus. Auseinandersetzung um das Leipziger Volksbüchereiwesen. *Buchhandelsgeschichte* 2000, no. 4: B172–B175.

Rothe, Wolfgang, ed. 1974. *Die deutsche Literatur in der Weimarer Republik*. Stuttgart: Reclam.

Röttig, Sabine. 2004. "'... bleiben Sie wie bisher getrost in Dichters Landen und nähren sich redlich'." Der Gustav Kiepenheuer Verlag 1933–1949. *Archiv für Geschichte des Buchwesens* 58: 1–139.

Ruppelt, Georg. 1989. Die Herzog August Bibliothek zwischen 1933 und 1945. In *Bibliotheken während des Nationalsozialismus*, ed. Peter Vodosek and Manfred Komorowski, vol. I, 377–88. Wiesbaden: Harrassowitz.

Rüther, Günther, ed. 1997. *Literatur in der Diktatur. Schreiben im Nationalsozialismus und DDR-Sozialismus*. Paderborn: Schöningh.

Sánchez de Murillo, José. 2011. *Luise Rinser. Ein Leben in Widersprüchen*. Frankfurt/Main: Fischer.

Sarkowicz, Hans, ed. 2004. *Hitlers Künstler. Die Kultur im Dienst des Nationalsozialismus*. Frankfurt/Main: Insel.

Sarkowicz, Hans, and Alf Mentzer. 2011. *Schriftsteller im Nationalsozialismus. Ein Lexikon*. Berlin: Insel.

Sarkowski, Heinz. 1976. *Das Bibliographische Institut. Verlagsgeschichte und Bibliographie 1826–1976*. Mannheim: Bibliographisches Institut.

Sarkowski, Heinz. 1996. *Springer Verlag. History of a Scientific Publishing House. Part I: 1842–1945. Foundation, Maturation, Adversity*. Trans. Gerald Graham. Berlin: Springer.

Sarkowski, Heinz. 2002. Die Insel-Bücherei unter dem Hakenkreuz. *Insel-Bücherei. Mitteilungen für Freunde* 22: 7–63.

Sarkowski, Heinz, with Wolfgang Jeske. 1999. *Der Insel Verlag 1899–1999. Die Geschichte des Verlags*. Frankfurt/Main: Insel.

Sartorius, Joachim. 2011. *The Princes' Islands*. Trans. Stephen Brown. London: Haus.

Sasse, Heinz Günther, and Ekkehard Eickhoff, eds. 1970. *100 Jahre Auswärtiges Amt 1870–1970*. Bonn: Auswärtiges Amt.

Sauder, Gerhard. 1983. Akademischer "Frühlingssturm". Germanisten als Redner bei der Bücherverbrennung. In *10. Mai 1933. Bücherverbrennung in Deutschland und die Folgen*, ed. Ulrich Walberer, 140–59. Frankfurt/Main: Fischer.

Sauder, Gerhard, ed. 1983. *Die Bücherverbrennung. Zum 10. Mai 1933*. Munich: Hanser.

Sauder, Gerhard. 1985. Der Germanist Goebbels als Redner bei der Berliner Bücherverbrennung. In *"Das war ein Vorspiel nur …" Berliner Colloquium zur Literaturpolitik im "Dritten Reich,"* ed. Horst Denkler and Eberhard Lämmert, 56–88. Berlin: Frölich und Kaufmann.

Saur, Klaus G., ed. 2013. *Verlage im "Dritten Reich."* Frankfurt/Main: Vittorio Klostermann.

Schäfer, Hans Dieter. 1979. Horst Langes Tagebücher 1939–1945. In Horst Lange, *Tagebücher aus dem Zweiten Weltkrieg*, ed. Hans Dieter Schäfer, 293–322. Mainz: Hase & Koehler.

Schäfer, Hans Dieter. 2009. *Das gespaltene Bewusstsein. Vom Dritten Reich bis zu den langen Fünfziger Jahren*. Rev. ed. Göttingen: Wallstein.

Schenker, Anatol. 2003. *Der Jüdische Verlag 1902–1938. Zwischen Aufbruch, Blüte und Vernichtung*. Tübingen: Niemeyer.

Schneider, Tobias. 2004. Bestseller im Dritten Reich. Ermittlung und Analyse der meistverkauften Romane in Deutschland 1933–1944. *Vierteljahreshefte für Zeitgeschichte* 52: 77–97.

Schnell, Ralf. 1998. *Dichtung in finsteren Zeiten. Deutsche Literatur und Faschismus*. Reinbek: Rowohlt.

Schochow, Werner. 1989. *Die Preußische Staatsbibliothek 1918–1945. Ein geschichtlicher Überblick. Mit einem Quellenteil*. Cologne: Böhlau.

Schochow, Werner. 1995. Hugo Andres Krüß und die Preußische Staatsbibliothek. *Bibliothek. Forschung und Praxis* 19: 7–19.

Schoenbaum, David. 1966. *Hitler's Social Revolution. Class and Status in Nazi Germany 1933–1939*. New York: Doubleday.

Schoeps, Julius H., and Werner Treß, eds. 2008. *Orte der Bücherverbrennungen in Deutschland 1933*. Hildesheim: Olms.

Schoeps, Karl-Heinz Joachim. 2000. *Literatur im Dritten Reich (1933–1945)*. 2nd, rev. edn. Berlin: Weidler.

Scholdt, Günter. 1993. *Autoren über Hitler. Deutschsprachige Schriftsteller 1919–1945 und ihr Bild vom "Führer."* Bonn: Bouvier.

Scholz, Kai-Uwe. 1999. Chamäleon oder Die vielen Gesichter des Hans Friedrich Blunck. Anpassungsstrategien eines prominenten NS-Kulturfunktionärs vor und nach 1945. In *Studien zur literarischen*

Kultur in Hamburg 1945–1950, ed. Ludwig Fischer, Klaas Jarchow, Horst Ohde, and Hans-Gerd Winter, 131–67. Hamburg: Dölling und Galitz.

Schreeb, Hans Dieter. 2003. Baedekers Reisehandbuch "Das Generalgouvernement." *Aus dem Antiquariat*, new series 1, no. 5: 342–7.

Schreuder, Saskia, and Claude Weber, eds. 1994. *Der Schocken Verlag/Berlin. Jüdische Selbstbehauptung in Deutschland 1931–1938. Essayband zur Ausstellung "Dem suchenden Leser unserer Tage" der Nationalbibliothek Luxemburg.* Berlin: Akademie.

Schroeder, Werner. 2009. Die "Arisierung" jüdischer Antiquariate zwischen 1933 und 1942. *Aus dem Antiquariat* new series 7, no. 5: 295–320, no. 6: 359–86.

Schütz, Erhard. 1993. "Jene blassgrauen Bänder." Die Reichsautobahn in Literatur und anderen Medien des "Dritten Reiches." *Internationales Archiv für Sozialgeschichte der deutschen Literatur* 18, no. 2: 76–120.

Schütz, Erhard. 1995. Das "Dritte Reich" als Mediendiktatur: Medienpolitik und Modernisierung in Deutschland 1933 bis 1945. *Monatshefte* 87, no. 2: 129–50.

Schütz, Erhard. 1996. "Ein Geruch von Blut und Schande ..." Literarhistorischer Versuch zum Roman im "Dritten Reich." *Juni. Magazin für Literatur & Politik* 24: 139–55.

Schwarz, Falk. 1972. *Literarisches Zeitgespräch im Dritten Reich, dargestellt an der Zeitschrift "Neue Rundschau."* Frankfurt/Main: Buchhändler-Vereinigung.

Seier, Hellmut. 1959. Kollaborative und oppositionelle Momente der inneren Emigration Jochen Kleppers. *Jahrbuch für die Geschichte Mittel- und Ostdeutschlands* 8: 319–47.

Seifert, Otto. 2000. *Die große Säuberung des Schrifttums. Der Börsenverein der Deutschen Buchhändler zu Leipzig 1933 bis 1945.* Schkeuditz: GNN.

Simon, Gerd, et al. 2006. *Buchfieber. Zur Geschichte des Buches im 3. Reich.* Tübingen: GIFT.

Smelser, Ronald. 1988. *Robert Ley. Hitler's Labor Front Leader.* Oxford: Berg.

Sösemann, Bernd. 1993. "Ein tieferer geschichtlicher Sinn aus dem Wahnsinn." Die Goebbels-Tagebuchaufzeichnungen als Quelle für das Verständnis des nationalsozialistischen Herrschaftssystems. In *Weltbürgerkrieg der Ideologien. Antworten an Ernst Nolte. Festschrift zum 70. Geburtstag*, ed. Thomas Nipperdey, Anselm Doering-Manteuffel, and Hans-Ulrich Thamer, 135–74. Berlin: Propyläen.

Sösemann, Bernd. ed. 2002. *Der Nationalsozialismus und die deutsche Gesellschaft. Einführung und Überblick.* Stuttgart: Deutsche Verlags-Anstalt.

Sösemann, Bernd, ed. 2008. Alles nur Goebbels-Propaganda? Untersuchungen zur revidierten Ausgabe der sogenannten Goebbels-Tagebücher des Münchner Instituts für Zeitgeschichte. *Jahrbuch für Kommunikationsgeschichte* 10: 52–76.

Sprengel, Peter. 2009. *Der Dichter stand auf hoher Küste. Gerhart Hauptmann im Dritten Reich.* Berlin: Propyläen.

Steinweis, Alan E. 1993. *Art, Ideology, and Economics in Nazi Germany. The Reich Chambers of Music, Theater, and the Visual Arts.* Chapel Hill: University of North Carolina Press.

Stephan, Werner. 1949. *Joseph Goebbels. Dämon einer Diktatur.* Stuttgart: Union.

Stieg, Margaret F. 1992. The Impact of National Socialism on Librarians. In *Bibliotheken während des Nationalsozialismus,* ed. Peter Vodosek and Manfred Komorowski, vol. II, 11–26. Wiesbaden: Harrassowitz.

Stieg, Margaret F. 1992. *Public Libraries in Nazi Germany.* Tuscaloosa: The University of Alabama Press.

Strenge, Irene. 2002. *Machtübernahme 1933—Alles auf legalem Weg?* Berlin: Duncker & Humblot.

Stummvoll, Josef. 1968. *Dira necessitas: Der Fall Leyh–Uhlendahl mit Bemerkungen über Nationalbibliotheken und Nationalbibliographien.* Vienna: Österreichische Nationalbibliothek.

Stummvoll, Josef. 1977. IFLATION: Erinnerungen an die IFLA und an markante Bibliothekare seit 1929. *Biblos* 26: 257–75.

Sturge, Kate. 2004. *"The Alien Within." Translation into German during the Nazi Regime.* Munich: iudicium.

Sywottek, Jutta. 1983. Die Gleichschaltung der deutschen Volksbüchereien 1933 bis 1937. *Archiv für Geschichte des Buchwesens* 24: cols. 385–536.

Tavernaro, Thomas. 2004. *Der Verlag Hitlers und der NSDAP. Die Franz Eher Nachfolger GmbH.* Vienna: Praesens.

Tgahrt, Reinhard, ed. 1981. *Eugen Claassen. Von der Arbeit eines Verlegers. Mit einer Bibliographie der Verlage H. Goverts, Claassen & Goverts, Claassen 1935–1966.* Marbach: Deutsche Schillergesellschaft.

Thamer, Hans-Ulrich. 1986. *Verführung und Gewalt. Deutschland 1933–1945.* Berlin: Siedler.

Thunecke, Jörg, ed. 1987. *Leid der Worte. Panorama des literarischen Nationalsozialismus.* Bonn: Bouvier.

Tooze, Adam. 2006. *The Wages of Destruction. The Making and Breaking of the Nazi Economy.* London: Allen Lane.

Toussaint, Ingo. 1984. *Die Universitätsbibliothek Freiburg im Dritten Reich*. 2nd, rev. edn. Munich: Saur.

Toussaint, Ingo, ed. 1989. *Die Universitätsbibliotheken Heidelberg, Jena und Köln unter dem Nationalsozialismus*. Munich: Saur.

Treß, Werner. 2003. *"Wider den undeutschen Geist." Bücherverbrennung 1933*. Berlin: Parthas.

Treß, Werner. 2008. Berlin. In *Orte der Bücherverbrennungen in Deutschland 1933*, ed. Julius H. Schoeps and Werner Treß, 47–142. Hildesheim: Olms.

Treß, Werner. 2008. Phasen und Akteure der Bücherverbrennungen. In *Orte der Bücherverbrennungen in Deutschland 1933*, ed. Julius H. Schoeps and Werner Treß, 9–28. Hildesheim: Olms.

Triebel, Florian. 2000. Kultur und Kalkül. Kampf um die Buchpreisbindung im Herbst 1940. *Buchhandelsgeschichte* 2000, no. 1: B2–B9.

Triebel, Florian. 2004. Die "Meldungen aus dem Reich" als buchhandelsgeschichtliche Quellen in der NS-Zeit. *Archiv für Geschichte des Buchwesens* 58: 197–209.

Troy, Michele K. 2010. Books, Swords, and Readers. The Albatross Press and the Third Reich. In *Moveable Type, Mobile Nations: Interactions in Transnational Book History*, ed. Simon Frost and Robert W. Rix, 55–72. Copenhagen: Museum Tusculanum Press.

Tuchel, Johannes. 2008. Alfred Andersch im Nationalsozialismus. In *Sansibar ist überall. Alfred Andersch. Seine Welt—in Texten, Bildern, Dokumenten*, ed. Marcel Korolnik and Annette Korolnik-Andersch, 30–41. Munich: Text + Kritik.

Ulbricht, Justus H. 1990. "Die Quellen des Lebens rauschen in leicht zugänglicher Fassung ...." Zur Literaturpolitik völkischer Verlage in der Weimarer Republik. In *Von Göschen bis Rowohlt. Beiträge zur Geschichte des deutschen Verlagswesens*, ed. Monika Estermann and Michael Knoche, 177–97. Wiesbaden: Harrassowitz.

Ulbricht, Justus H., and Meike G. Werner, eds. 1999. *Romantik, Revolution und Reform. Der Eugen Diederichs Verlag im Epochenkontext 1900–1949*. Göttingen: Wallstein.

Vieregg, Axel. 1993. *Der eigenen Fehlbarkeit begegnet. Günter Eichs Realitäten 1933–1945*. Eggingen: Isele.

Vodosek, Peter, and Manfred Komorowski, eds. 1989–92. *Bibliotheken während des Nationalsozialismus*. 2 vols. Wiesbaden: Harrassowitz.

Volke, Werner, ed. 1983. *Das "Innere Reich" 1934–1944. Eine "Zeitschrift für Dichtung, Kunst und deutsches Leben."* Marbach: Deutsche Schillergesellschaft.

Walberer, Ulrich, ed. 1983. *10. Mai 1933. Bücherverbrennung in Deutschland und die Folgen*. Frankfurt/Main: Fischer.

Wallrath-Janssen, Anne M. 2007. *Der Verlag H. Goverts im Dritten Reich*. Munich: Saur.

Walter, Hans-Albert. 2003. *Deutsche Exilliteratur 1933–1950*, vol. 1.1. Stuttgart: Metzler.

Warketin, Erwin J. 1997. *Unpublishable Works. Wolfgang Borchert's Literary Production in Nazi Germany*. Columbia, SC: Camden House.

Weber, Hans-Oskar. 1989. Landesbibliothek Kassel 1938. In *Bibliotheken während des Nationalsozialismus*, ed. Peter Vodosek and Manfred Komorowski, vol. I, 369–75. Wiesbaden: Harrassowitz.

Wehler, Hans-Ulrich. 2003. *Vom Beginn des Ersten Weltkriegs bis zur Gründung der beiden deutschen Staaten 1914–1949*. Vol. IV of *Deutsche Gesellschaftsgeschichte*. Munich: Beck.

Wernecke, Klaus, and Peter Heller. 1982. *Der vergessene Führer. Alfred Hugenberg. Pressemacht und Nationalsozialismus*. Hamburg: VSA.

Westhoff, Adelheid, ed. 1983. *Das "Innere Reich" 1934–1944. Eine "Zeitschrift für Dichtung, Kunst und deutsches Leben". Verzeichnis der Beiträge*. Marbach: Deutsche Schillergesellschaft.

Wildt, Michael. 2002. *Generation des Unbedingten. Das Führungskorps des Reichssicherheitshauptamtes*. Hamburg: Hamburger Edition.

Wildt, Michael, ed. 2003. *Nachrichtendienst, politische Elite und Mordeinheit. Der Sicherheitsdienst des Reichsführers SS*. Hamburg: Hamburger Edition.

Wildt, Michael. 2005. Goebbels in Berlin. Eindrücke und Urteile von Zeitgenossen aus den Jahren 1926 bis 1932. In *Das Goebbels-Experiment. Propaganda und Politik*, ed. Lutz Hachmeister and Michael Kloft, 73–84. Munich: Deutsche Verlags-Anstalt.

Wisotzky, Klaus. 2008. Essen. In *Orte der Bücherverbrennungen in Deutschland 1933*, ed. Julius H. Schoeps and Werner Treß, 322–7. Hildesheim: Olms.

Wittmann, Reinhard. 2008. *Wissen für die Zukunft. 150 Jahre Oldenbourg Verlag*. Munich: Oldenbourg.

Woltmann, Johanna, ed. 1993. *Gertrud Kolmar 1894–1943*. Marbach: Deutsche Schillergesellschaft.

Wulf, Joseph. 1963. *Literatur und Dichtung im Dritten Reich. Eine Dokumentation*. Gütersloh: Mohn.

Zeck, Mario. 2002. *Das Schwarze Korps. Geschichte und Gestalt des Organs der Reichsführung SS*. Tübingen: Niemeyer.

Zeller, Bernhard, ed. 1983. *Klassiker in finsteren Zeiten 1933–1945. Eine Ausstellung des Literaturarchivs im Schiller-Nationalmuseum Marbach am Neckar. Katalog*. 2 vols. 2nd, rev. edn. Marbach: Deutsche Schillergesellschaft.

Ziegler, Edda. 2004. *100 Jahre Piper. Die Geschichte eines Verlags*. Munich: Piper.

Index

The letter t following a page number denotes a table